W9-BGR-225

ALL STAR COMICS
ARCHIVES ▾ VOLUME 5

ARCHIVE EDITIONS

DC COMICS

JENETTE KAHN
PRESIDENT & EDITOR-IN-CHIEF

PAUL LEVITZ
EXECUTIVE VICE PRESIDENT
& PUBLISHER

MIKE CARLIN
EXECUTIVE EDITOR

DALE CRAIN
EDITOR

MICHAEL WRIGHT
ASSISTANT EDITOR

GEORG BREWER
DESIGN DIRECTOR

ROBBIN BROSTERMAN
ART DIRECTOR

RICHARD BRUNING
VP-CREATIVE DIRECTOR

PATRICK CALDON
VP-FINANCE & OPERATIONS

DOROTHY CROUCH
VP-LICENSED PUBLISHING

TERRI CUNNINGHAM
VP-MANAGING EDITOR

JOEL EHRLICH
SENIOR VP-ADVERTISING
& PROMOTIONS

ALISON GILL
EXEC. DIRECTOR-
MANUFACTURING

LILLIAN LASERSON
VP & GENERAL COUNSEL

JIM LEE
EDITORIAL DIRECTOR-
WILDSTORM

JOHN NEE
VP & GENERAL MANAGER-
WILDSTORM

BOB WAYNE
VP-DIRECT SALES

ALL STAR COMICS ARCHIVES
VOLUME 5

ISBN 1-56389-497-1

PUBLISHED BY DC COMICS
COVER, INTRODUCTION AND COMPILATION
COPYRIGHT ©1999 DC COMICS.

ORIGINALLY PUBLISHED IN SINGLE MAGAZINE
FORM IN ALL STAR COMICS 19-23.
COPYRIGHT 1943, 1944 DC COMICS.
ALL RIGHTS RESERVED.

ALL STAR COMICS, THE JUSTICE SOCIETY OF
AMERICA AND ALL RELATED CHARACTERS,
THE DISTINCTIVE LIKENESSES THEREOF, AND
ALL RELATED INDICIA ARE TRADEMARKS OF
DC COMICS. THE STORIES, CHARACTERS,
AND INCIDENTS FEATURED IN THIS
PUBLICATION ARE ENTIRELY FICTIONAL.

DC COMICS
1700 BROADWAY
NEW YORK, NY 10019

A DIVISION OF WARNER BROS. -
A TIME WARNER ENTERTAINMENT COMPANY
PRINTED AND BOUND IN CANADA.
FIRST PRINTING.

THE DC ARCHIVE EDITIONS

COVER ILLUSTRATION BY
PETE POPLASKI.

COVER COLOR BY
LEE LOUGHRIDGE.

SERIES DESIGN BY ALEX JAY/STUDIO J

PUBLICATION DESIGN BY JASON LYONS

BLACK-AND-WHITE RECONSTRUCTION
BY RICK KEENE.

COLOR RECONSTRUCTION BY
DIGITAL CHAMELEON.

TABLE OF CONTENTS

TABLE OF CONTENTS

FOREWORD

By R. C. Harvey

We don't know, exactly, whose idea it was – this teaming up of several super-heroes. Writer Gardner Fox and editor Sheldon Mayer always worked together concocting the stories for the Justice Society of America. But neither claimed the credit for having the idea that resulted in the first super-hero team. Dr. Jerry Bails, the medium's most assiduous historian and one of the JSA's most fervent fans, talked to both Fox and Mayer at various times. Recently, he told me: "Fox never claimed credit for originating the idea despite many opportunities to do so; therefore, I suspect he was given the idea by Mayer but wasn't sure if that's where it originated. Mayer never claimed to originate it in a letter where the opportunity was there. . . . I'd say the chances are very good that the idea came to Mayer when editing the first two anthology issues; it would be a natural progression with super-heroes being hot."

Bails allows that publisher Max Gaines might have suggested the team idea, but whoever hatched the notion, Mayer and Fox fleshed it out. They devised a way to put eight super-heroes into a single adventure story by dividing the story into chapters, one for each of the super-heroes to star in, a maneuver that yielded a bonus: each distinct stand alone chapter permitted the artists most closely associated with that chapter's character to draw the chapter.

Teaming super-heroes was an extraordinary concept. I wasn't reading comic books (or anything else) at the time of the first JSA meeting, but when I chanced upon their comic book later, an unspoken and even uncomprehended fantasy was fulfilled. Somehow once these characters started speaking to one another, they became more real: in conversing, they validated each other's existence, proclaiming their actualities. Until they actually met and worked together, you could imagine that their individual adventures took place in some sort of make-believe world; but once they'd encountered one another – in person, so to speak – their world became real. They could not meet each other except in a real world. Or so it seemed to my young mind.

The real world of super-heroes in the volume at hand includes such minor masterpieces as "The Man Who Relived His Life" in No. 21. Quite apart from the intriguing time-travel logic of Fox's tale, we get a short course in twentieth century American history. The research evident here in the opening captions of each chapter, while not vast or comprehensive, is accurate. And it is impressive that a writer of comic books would take the trouble to assemble so meticulously such authentic detail to serve simply as background information for an adventure story.

Fox's interest in history is again displayed in "The Test of Time" in No. 22, a story which reminds us that these books were being published during World War II when patriotism ran rampant. This propagandizing fable, Bails says, was written in response to a request from the Office of War Information and the Writers' War Board (which included Paul Gallico, Rex Stout, and Clifton Fadiman among others).

We also have herein more than the usual allotment of nifty pictures – the very *raison d'être* for comic books. By 1944, the year most of the issues at hand were first published, the artistic skills of those who drew comic books had improved considerably since their often clumsy attempts in the medium's infancy. Anatomy was now rendered competently, and the linework itself was clear and sharp.

This collection includes noteworthy examples of the work of a couple of rarely remarked-on artists. Stan Aschmeier (a.k.a. Stan Josephs), for instance, whose career in comics was defined pretty much by his work on Dr. Mid-Nite, Johnny Thunder, and Dr. Fate, is represented here in the stories on the first two of these and Starman, all done in an impressive manner evocative of Alex Raymond but scarcely slavish in imitation. Joe Gallagher turns in another impressive performance.

His boldly brushed linework gives his pictures a nimbus of simplicity, but his compositions and storytelling are expertly done, and his use of solid black and shadow is equally adept (as is his wholesale swipe of the Blue Fairy from Disney's 1940 *Pinocchio* in visualizing "The Conscience of Man" in No. 22). Also noteworthy is Joe Kubert's first solo flight at DC on Dr. Fate in No. 21 – "obviously under the influence of Mort Meskin," as Bails notes, but carried off with extraordinary aplomb, employing a delicacy and fluidity of line worthy of the master himself.

The master is Jack Kirby, whose Sandman story conveniently supplies us with the means of assessing, one more time, Kirby's surpassing storytelling skill in this visual medium. In addition to his superior drawing ability – his lively line, deftly modeling with flexing widths and spotted blacks and only minimum feathering, his rendering of figures in violent motion from virtually any angle, and the sheer variety of his compositions – he deployed the visual resources of the medium to enhance the drama of the action with greater effect than most of his colleagues. Kirby's page layout at this stage of his career is a straightforward grid, but the panels are deftly composed: they include the visual information necessary to the narrative and do it in varying ways for interesting imagery. Kirby leaves no inexplicable visual voids of the sort we see with Aschmeier (page 95, first panel; why all that space under the arch?) whose figures are sometimes too far from the camera or who leaves nonfunctional space in the pictures. None of Kirby's panels contain any superfluous visual information – for instance, like Aschmeier's last panel on page 40, which seems to be telling us something about the ceiling machinery but it isn't anything we need to know.

And Kirby knew how to depict motion in the most dramatic ways. He knew that showing a figure running in simple profile (as Aschmeier does with Dr. Mid-Nite in the fifth panel on page 39) is not the best way to convey a sense of vigorous activity. Instead, Kirby twists bodies (second panel, page 33) or shifts the camera angle (page 35 when Sandman and Sandy charge into the room at the bottom of the page).

An even more dramatic display of Kirby's skill is evident in his handling of fight scenes. If we compare the action in the bottom tier of page 35 and the top tier of page 36 (the fourth and fifth pages of the Sandman chapter) to, say, Aschmeier's depiction of the action on page 13 (the second page of his Starman tale), Kirby's superior understanding of action imagery is vividly revealed. Even the seeming energy displayed with Dr. Mid-Nite in the action on page 128 by Aschmeier pales in comparison to the final two pages of Kirby's effort. It is this sort of visual excitement that puts Kirby's work above that of so many of his fellows, and we're lucky in this volume to have so persuasive a demonstration of that energy.

Alert perusers of the pages that follow will notice that the cover of No. 21 is missing two of the heroes who appear on the following splash page, which otherwise duplicates the cover. This mystery was solved years ago by the good Doctor Bails. The cover of No. 21 was drawn before the splash, and it was drawn to reflect a decision to reduce JSA membership by two heroes in order to get chapters for all the members into the smaller 52-page magazine that was inaugurated with No. 20. The decision actually started to take effect in that issue, which (if you're counting) includes only six chapters, not the customary eight, leaving out Sandman and Dr. Fate, the two scheduled to be dropped from the rolls. At the last minute, however, it was decided to keep these two aboard for one more issue; and to that purpose, they are mentioned in No. 20's introduction (page 63) so they would still be on hand for No. 21. To make room for their swan songs in No. 21, the Atom and the Spectre sit out that issue. (The Sandman story in No. 21 is actually the Atom's story with the art reworked and patched to change the identity of the hero.) The decision to delay discharging Sandman and Dr. Fate for an issue may have resulted, Bails speculates, from a desire to try to sell a few more Junior Justice Society of America kits, which included both Sandman and Dr. Fate. In any case, by No. 22, the new roster had settled in.

But now, enough Foreword. Onward.

R. C. Harvey has been writing about cartooning for a quarter of a century, beginning with a column in the Menomonee Falls Gazette (a weekly newspaper of adventure comic strips) in the fall of 1973 and continuing with regular appearances in Cartoonist PROfiles, The Comics Journal, and The Comics Buyer's Guide. A one-time freelance cartoonist (of the "bush league" variety, he says), Harvey has published work in nearly all the cartooning modes – comic strips, editorial cartoons, comic books, and magazine cartoons. Under the guise of Robert C., he is the author of several books about comics, including The Art of the Comic Book, an analytical history of the medium (1996, University Press of Mississippi), and, most recently, Children of the Yellow Kid: The Evolution of the Newspaper Comic Strip (1998, Washington University Press).

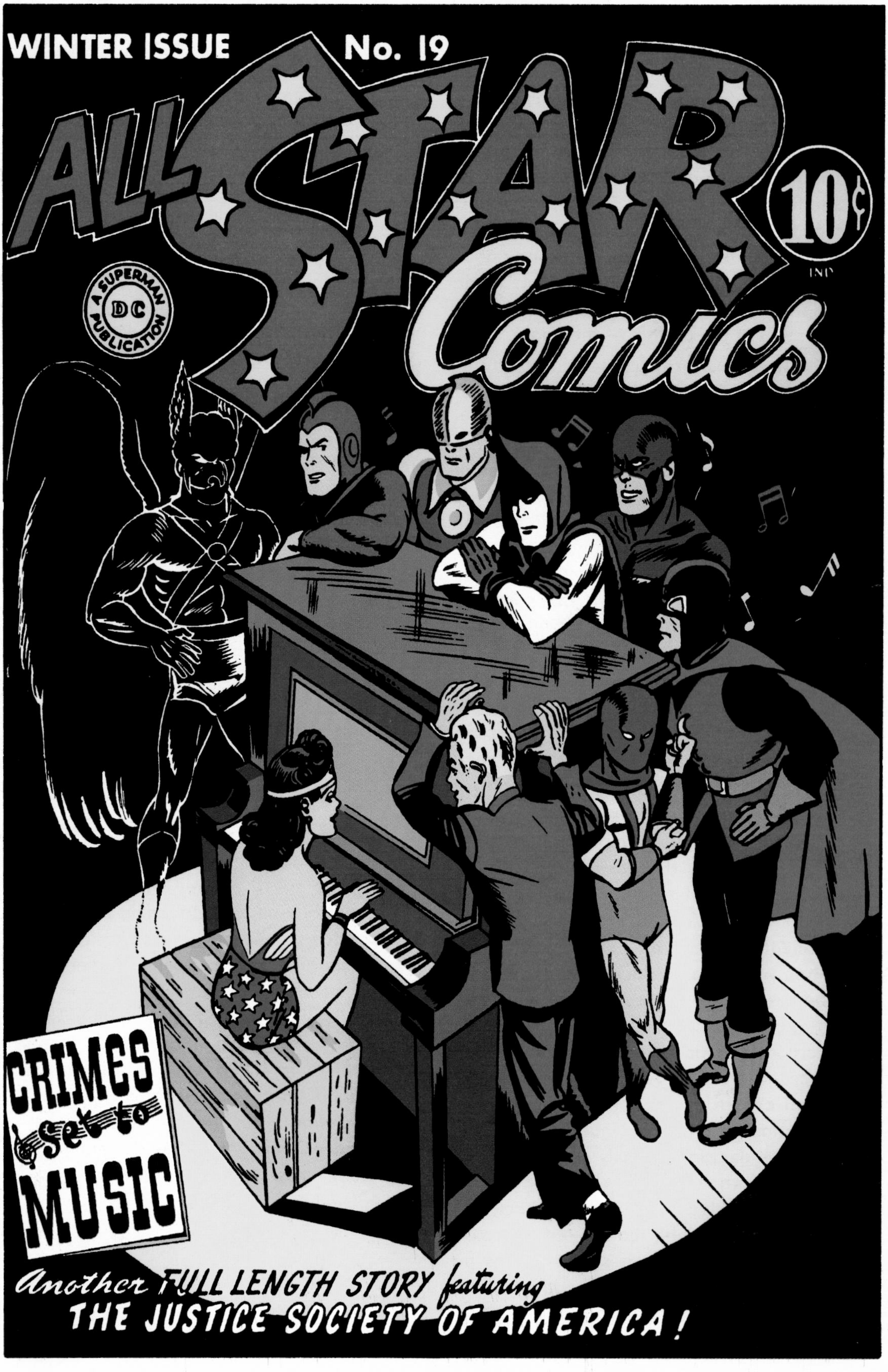
WINTER ISSUE
No. 19
ALL STAR Comics
10¢
A SUPERMAN DC PUBLICATION
CRIMES set to MUSIC
Another FULL LENGTH STORY featuring
THE JUSTICE SOCIETY OF AMERICA!

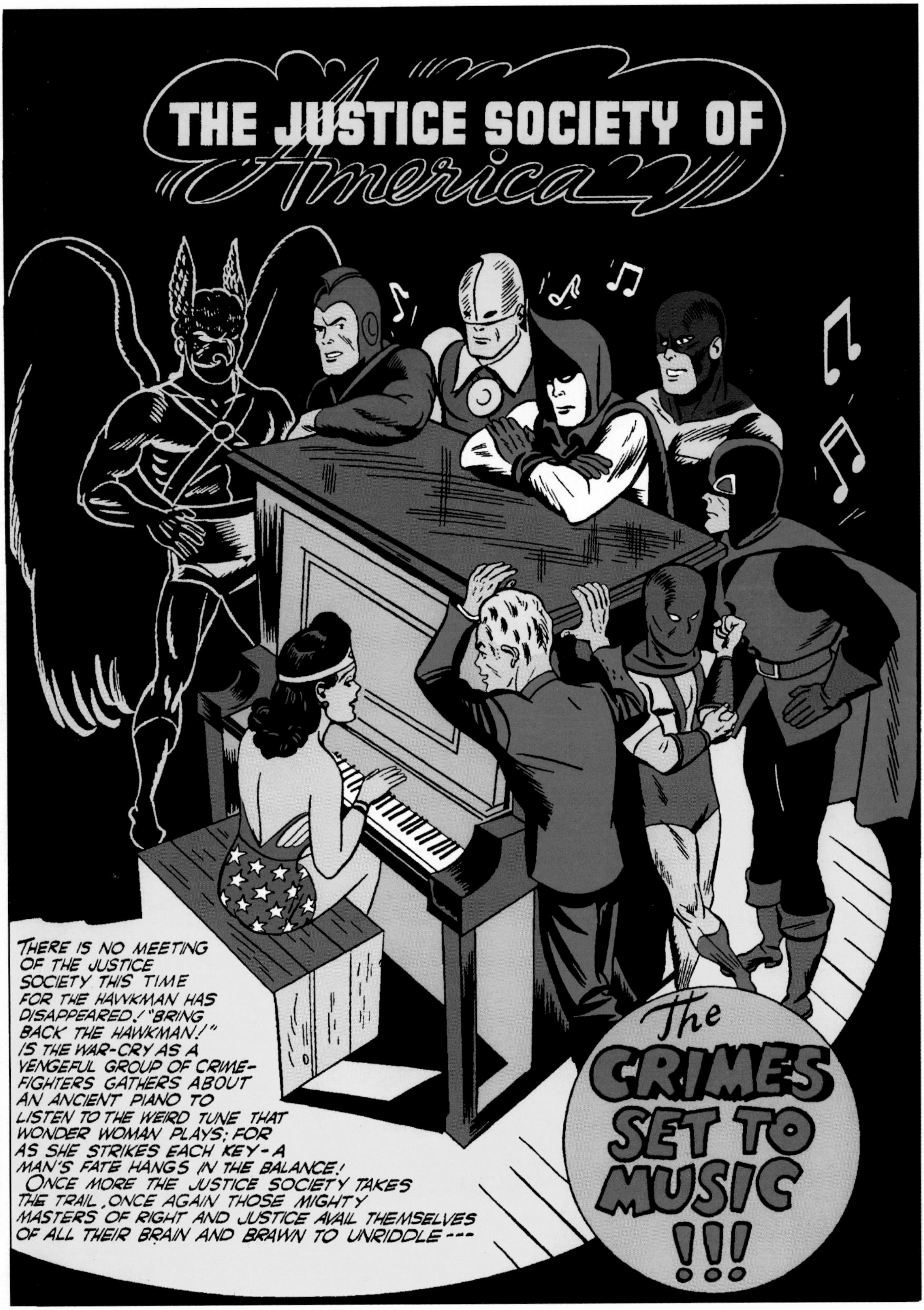
THE JUSTICE SOCIETY OF America
THERE IS NO MEETING OF THE JUSTICE SOCIETY THIS TIME FOR THE HAWKMAN HAS DISAPPEARED! "BRING BACK THE HAWKMAN!" IS THE WAR-CRY AS A VENGEFUL GROUP OF CRIME-FIGHTERS GATHERS ABOUT AN ANCIENT PIANO TO LISTEN TO THE WEIRD TUNE THAT WONDER WOMAN PLAYS; FOR AS SHE STRIKES EACH KEY- A MAN'S FATE HANGS IN THE BALANCE! ONCE MORE THE JUSTICE SOCIETY TAKES THE TRAIL, ONCE AGAIN THOSE MIGHTY MASTERS OF RIGHT AND JUSTICE AVAIL THEMSELVES OF ALL THEIR BRAIN AND BRAWN TO UNRIDDLE---
The CRIMES SET TO MUSIC !!!

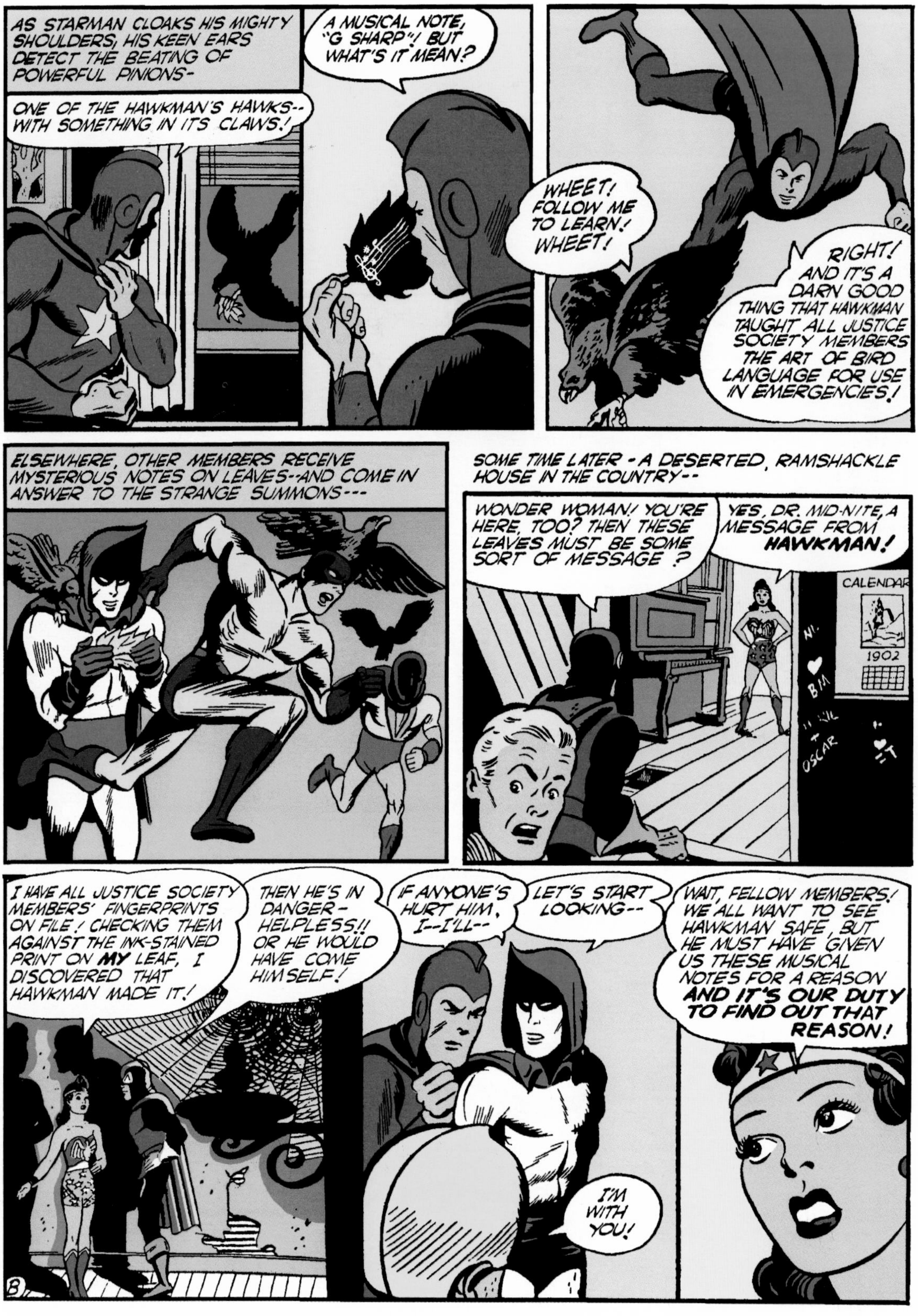
AS STARMAN CLOAKS HIS MIGHTY SHOULDERS, HIS KEEN EARS DETECT THE BEATING OF POWERFUL PINIONS-
ONE OF THE HAWKMAN'S HAWKS-- WITH SOMETHING IN ITS CLAWS!
A MUSICAL NOTE, "G SHARP"! BUT WHAT'S IT MEAN?
WHEET! FOLLOW ME TO LEARN! WHEET!
RIGHT! AND IT'S A DARN GOOD THING THAT HAWKMAN TAUGHT ALL JUSTICE SOCIETY MEMBERS THE ART OF BIRD LANGUAGE FOR USE IN EMERGENCIES!
ELSEWHERE, OTHER MEMBERS RECEIVE MYSTERIOUS NOTES ON LEAVES--AND COME IN ANSWER TO THE STRANGE SUMMONS---
SOME TIME LATER - A DESERTED, RAMSHACKLE HOUSE IN THE COUNTRY--
WONDER WOMAN! YOU'RE HERE, TOO? THEN THESE LEAVES MUST BE SOME SORT OF MESSAGE ?
YES, DR. MID-NITE, A MESSAGE FROM HAWKMAN!
CALENDAR
1902
OSCAR
I HAVE ALL JUSTICE SOCIETY MEMBERS' FINGERPRINTS ON FILE! CHECKING THEM AGAINST THE INK-STAINED PRINT ON MY LEAF, I DISCOVERED THAT HAWKMAN MADE IT!
THEN HE'S IN DANGER- HELPLESS!! OR HE WOULD HAVE COME HIMSELF!
IF ANYONE'S HURT HIM, I--I'LL--
LET'S START LOOKING--
WAIT, FELLOW MEMBERS! WE ALL WANT TO SEE HAWKMAN SAFE, BUT HE MUST HAVE GIVEN US THESE MUSICAL NOTES FOR A REASON AND IT'S OUR DUTY TO FIND OUT THAT REASON!
I'M WITH YOU!
8

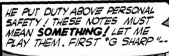

HE PUT DUTY ABOVE PERSONAL SAFETY! THESE NOTES MUST MEAN **SOMETHING!** LET ME PLAY THEM. FIRST "G SHARP"--

SOAP

AS WONDER WOMAN'S FINGER STRIKES THE NOTE, A CONCEALED PANEL IN THE FRONT OF THE PIANO SLIDES OPEN AND--

A NAME AND ADDRESS ON IT-- MARK NELSON, 243 GARAND DRIVE AND A CRYPTIC NOTATION: "FIDDLE, FIDDLE, ON THE WALL YOU ARE RIDING FOR A FALL."

WHAT COULD **THAT** MEAN?

THE PECULIAR WORDING MIGHT DENOTE A CRIME ABOUT TO BE COMMITTED--**I HAVE IT!** HAWKMAN SENT US THESE **AS ASSIGNMENTS!**

SO'S WE CAN BUST UP THOSE CRIMES BEFORE THEY HAPPEN, HUH?

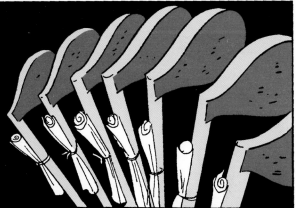

ONE AFTER THE OTHER, SEVEN NOTES ARE STRUCK, AND EACH OF THE JUSTICE SOCIETY MEMBERS RECEIVES A NAME, AN ADDRESS, WITH QUEER CRYPTIC WORDS ATTACHED--

WELL, NOW THAT WE ALL KNOW WHERE TO GO, PERHAPS SOME RATS WILL SOON BE DANCING TO THE TUNES **WE** SET!

I HEAR YOU TALKING !

BAAM

GOOD LUCK, BOYS! I HOPE YOU SOLVE THOSE RIDDLES-- AND GET TO HAWKMAN, TOO-- BEFORE IT'S TOO **LATE!**

THE MEMBERS DEPART, AND THE ROOM IS SILENT AS THE GRAVE, EXCEPT FOR WONDER WOMAN'S SOFT WHISPERED PRAYER---

FLASHING COMET-LIKE THROUGH SPACE,
STARMAN
ZOOMS DOWN TOWARD THE HOME OF MARK NELSON, AS TWO SKULKING FORMS LURK AMONG THE SHADOWY CLUMPS OF FOLIAGE.....
MARK NELSON 243 GARAND DRIVE
FIDDLE, FIDDLE, ON THE WALL... YOU ARE RIDING FOR A FALL!
AS VIOLINIST MARK NELSON LEAVES HIS HOME, A WINDOW IS JIMMIED OPEN.... THEN—
DE SAFE'S SOMEPLACE IN DE WALL— LEMME SEE NOW....
HERE IT IS!
—AN' DERE'S DE VIOLIN, SAFE AN' SOUND!
DIS FIDDLE IS PLAYIN' IT'S LAST TUNE!
THEN START SINGING AN ACCOMPANIMENT, RATS!

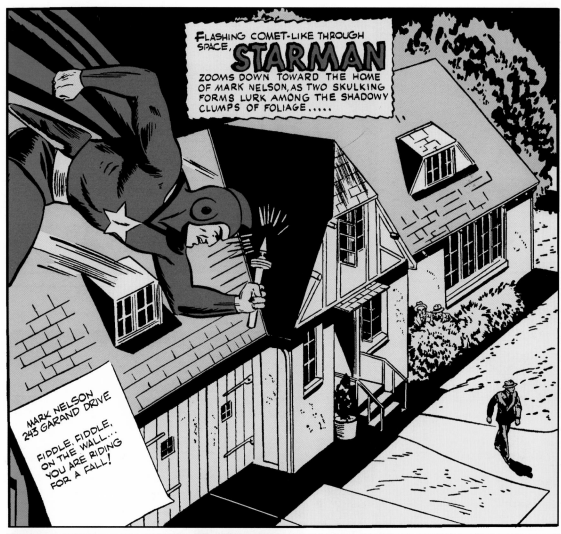

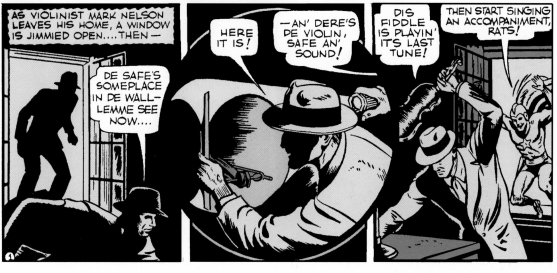

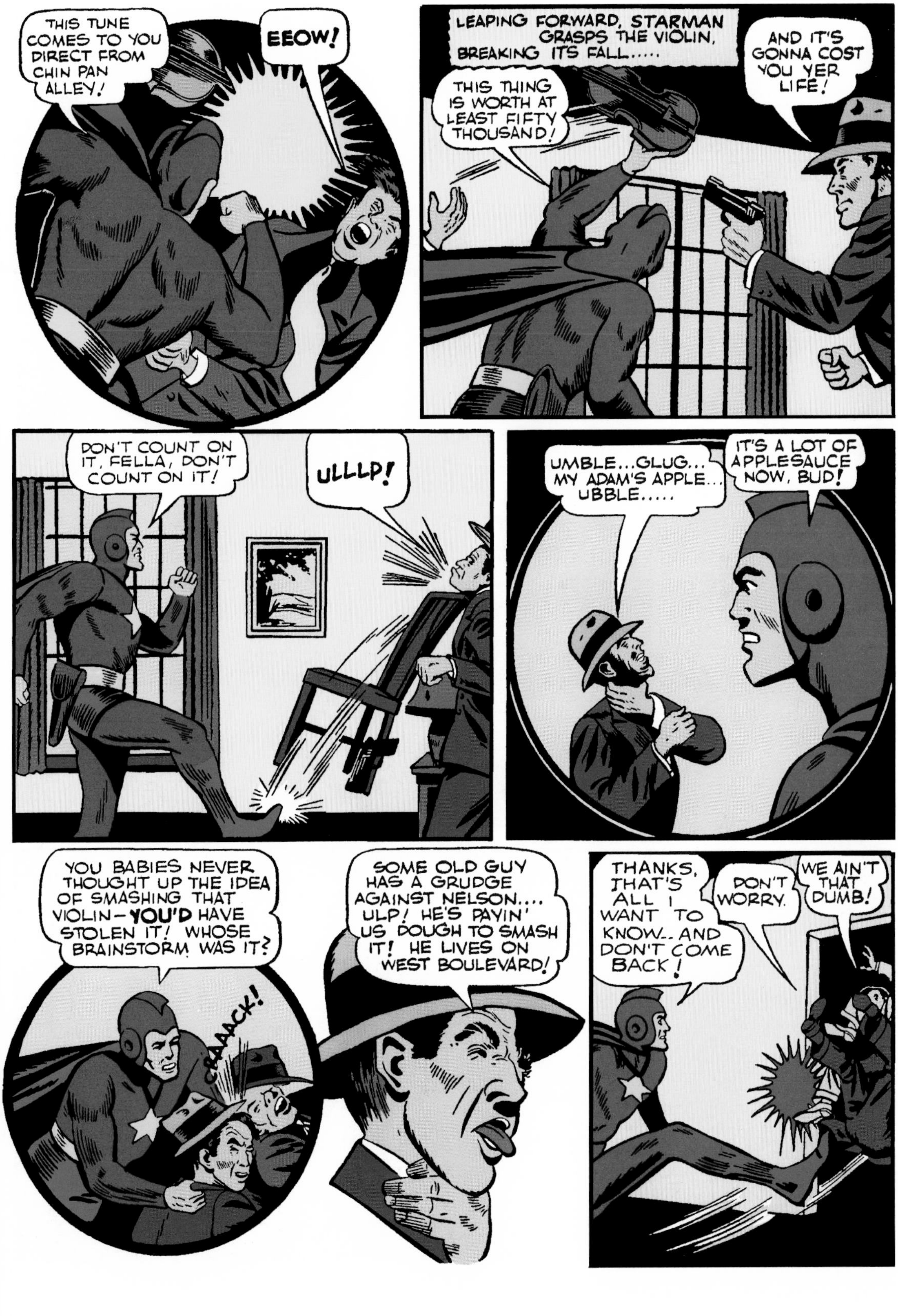
THIS TUNE COMES TO YOU DIRECT FROM CHIN PAN ALLEY!
EEOW!
LEAPING FORWARD, STARMAN GRASPS THE VIOLIN, BREAKING ITS FALL.....
THIS THING IS WORTH AT LEAST FIFTY THOUSAND!
AND IT'S GONNA COST YOU YER LIFE!
DON'T COUNT ON IT, FELLA, DON'T COUNT ON IT!
ULLLP!
UMBLE...GLUG... MY ADAM'S APPLE... UBBLE.....
IT'S A LOT OF APPLESAUCE NOW, BUD!
YOU BABIES NEVER THOUGHT UP THE IDEA OF SMASHING THAT VIOLIN—YOU'D HAVE STOLEN IT! WHOSE BRAINSTORM WAS IT?
GRAAACK!
SOME OLD GUY HAS A GRUDGE AGAINST NELSON.... ULP! HE'S PAYIN' US DOUGH TO SMASH IT! HE LIVES ON WEST BOULEVARD!
THANKS, THAT'S ALL I WANT TO KNOW.. AND DON'T COME BACK!
DON'T WORRY.
WE AIN'T THAT DUMB!

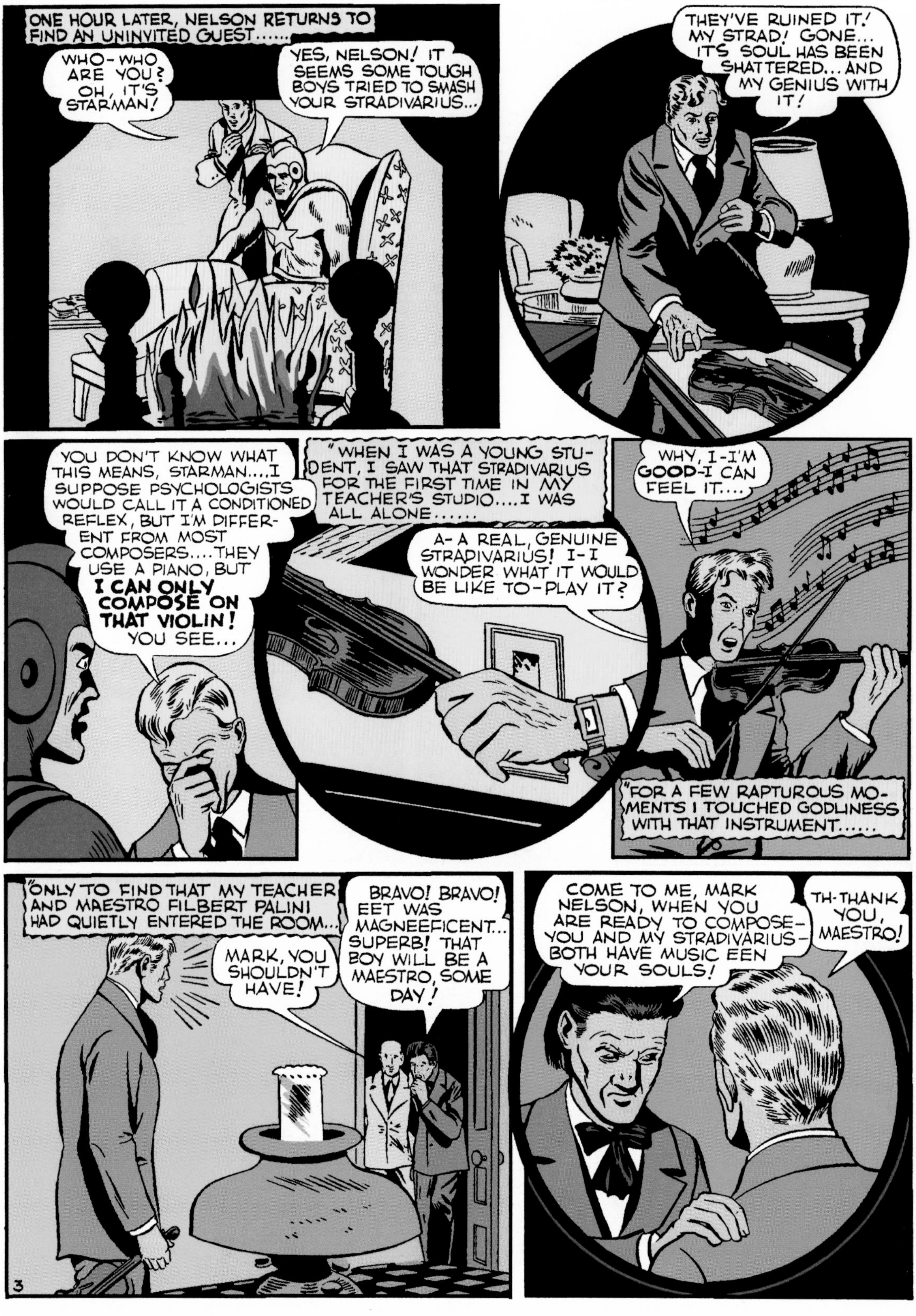
ONE HOUR LATER, NELSON RETURNS TO FIND AN UNINVITED GUEST......
WHO-WHO ARE YOU? OH, IT'S STARMAN!
YES, NELSON! IT SEEMS SOME TOUGH BOYS TRIED TO SMASH YOUR STRADIVARIUS...
THEY'VE RUINED IT! MY STRAD! GONE... ITS SOUL HAS BEEN SHATTERED... AND MY GENIUS WITH IT!
YOU DON'T KNOW WHAT THIS MEANS, STARMAN....I SUPPOSE PSYCHOLOGISTS WOULD CALL IT A CONDITIONED REFLEX, BUT I'M DIFFERENT FROM MOST COMPOSERS....THEY USE A PIANO, BUT I CAN ONLY COMPOSE ON THAT VIOLIN! YOU SEE...
"WHEN I WAS A YOUNG STUDENT, I SAW THAT STRADIVARIUS FOR THE FIRST TIME IN MY TEACHER'S STUDIO....I WAS ALL ALONE......
A-A REAL, GENUINE STRADIVARIUS! I-I WONDER WHAT IT WOULD BE LIKE TO-PLAY IT?
WHY, I-I'M GOOD-I CAN FEEL IT....
"FOR A FEW RAPTUROUS MOMENTS I TOUCHED GODLINESS WITH THAT INSTRUMENT......
"ONLY TO FIND THAT MY TEACHER AND MAESTRO FILBERT PALINI HAD QUIETLY ENTERED THE ROOM...
MARK, YOU SHOULDN'T HAVE!
BRAVO! BRAVO! EET WAS MAGNEEFICENT... SUPERB! THAT BOY WILL BE A MAESTRO, SOME DAY!
3
COME TO ME, MARK NELSON, WHEN YOU ARE READY TO COMPOSE-YOU AND MY STRADIVARIUS-BOTH HAVE MUSIC EEN YOUR SOULS!
TH-THANK YOU, MAESTRO!

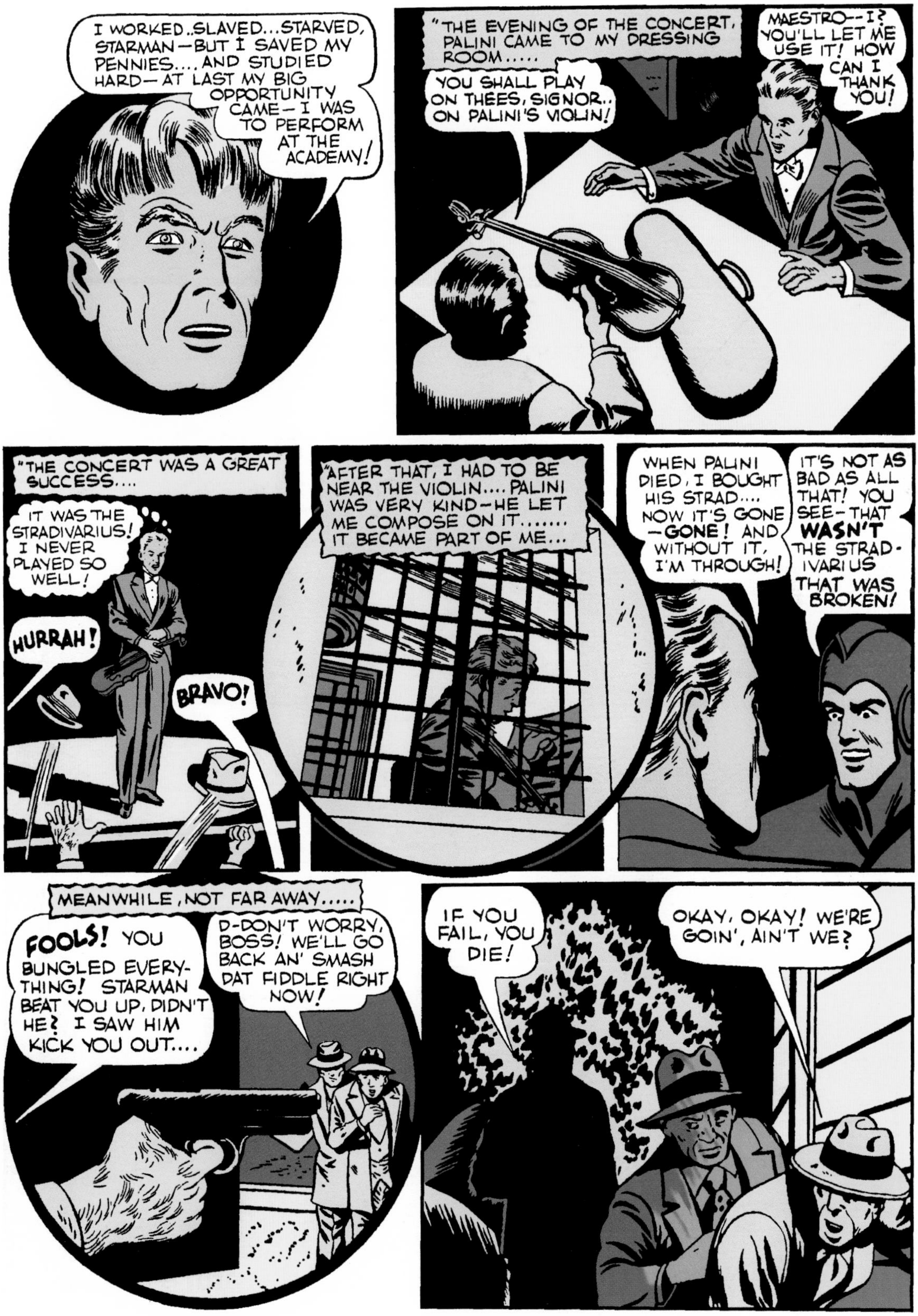
I WORKED..SLAVED...STARVED, STARMAN—BUT I SAVED MY PENNIES.... AND STUDIED HARD—AT LAST MY BIG OPPORTUNITY CAME—I WAS TO PERFORM AT THE ACADEMY!
"THE EVENING OF THE CONCERT, PALINI CAME TO MY DRESSING ROOM.....
YOU SHALL PLAY ON THEES, SIGNOR.. ON PALINI'S VIOLIN!
MAESTRO--I? YOU'LL LET ME USE IT! HOW CAN I THANK YOU!
"THE CONCERT WAS A GREAT SUCCESS....
IT WAS THE STRADIVARIUS! I NEVER PLAYED SO WELL!
HURRAH!
BRAVO!
"AFTER THAT, I HAD TO BE NEAR THE VIOLIN.... PALINI WAS VERY KIND—HE LET ME COMPOSE ON IT....... IT BECAME PART OF ME...
WHEN PALINI DIED, I BOUGHT HIS STRAD.... NOW IT'S GONE —GONE! AND WITHOUT IT, I'M THROUGH!
IT'S NOT AS BAD AS ALL THAT! YOU SEE—THAT WASN'T THE STRADIVARIUS THAT WAS BROKEN!
MEANWHILE, NOT FAR AWAY.....
FOOLS! YOU BUNGLED EVERYTHING! STARMAN BEAT YOU UP, DIDN'T HE? I SAW HIM KICK YOU OUT....
D-DON'T WORRY, BOSS! WE'LL GO BACK AN' SMASH DAT FIDDLE RIGHT NOW!
IF YOU FAIL, YOU DIE!
OKAY, OKAY! WE'RE GOIN', AIN'T WE?

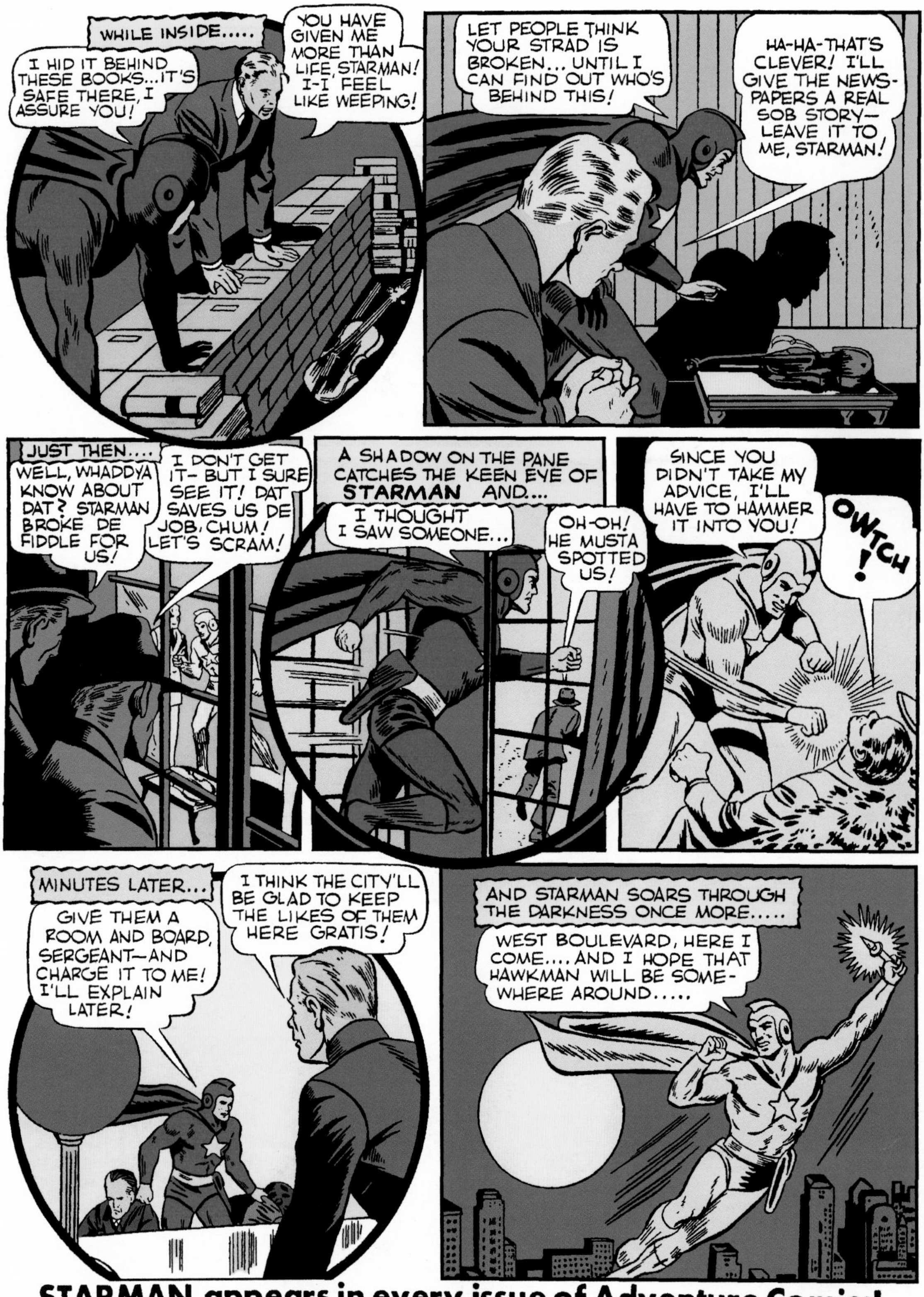
WHILE INSIDE.....
I HID IT BEHIND THESE BOOKS...IT'S SAFE THERE, I ASSURE YOU!
YOU HAVE GIVEN ME MORE THAN LIFE, STARMAN! I-I FEEL LIKE WEEPING!
LET PEOPLE THINK YOUR STRAD IS BROKEN... UNTIL I CAN FIND OUT WHO'S BEHIND THIS!
HA-HA-THAT'S CLEVER! I'LL GIVE THE NEWSPAPERS A REAL SOB STORY—LEAVE IT TO ME, STARMAN!
JUST THEN....
WELL, WHADDYA KNOW ABOUT DAT? STARMAN BROKE DE FIDDLE FOR US!
I DON'T GET IT- BUT I SURE SEE IT! DAT SAVES US DE JOB, CHUM! LET'S SCRAM!
A SHADOW ON THE PANE CATCHES THE KEEN EYE OF STARMAN AND....
I THOUGHT I SAW SOMEONE...
OH-OH! HE MUSTA SPOTTED US!
SINCE YOU DIDN'T TAKE MY ADVICE, I'LL HAVE TO HAMMER IT INTO YOU!
OWTCH!
MINUTES LATER...
GIVE THEM A ROOM AND BOARD, SERGEANT—AND CHARGE IT TO ME! I'LL EXPLAIN LATER!
I THINK THE CITY'LL BE GLAD TO KEEP THE LIKES OF THEM HERE GRATIS!
AND STARMAN SOARS THROUGH THE DARKNESS ONCE MORE.....
WEST BOULEVARD, HERE I COME.... AND I HOPE THAT HAWKMAN WILL BE SOMEWHERE AROUND.....

STARMAN appears in every issue of Adventure Comics!

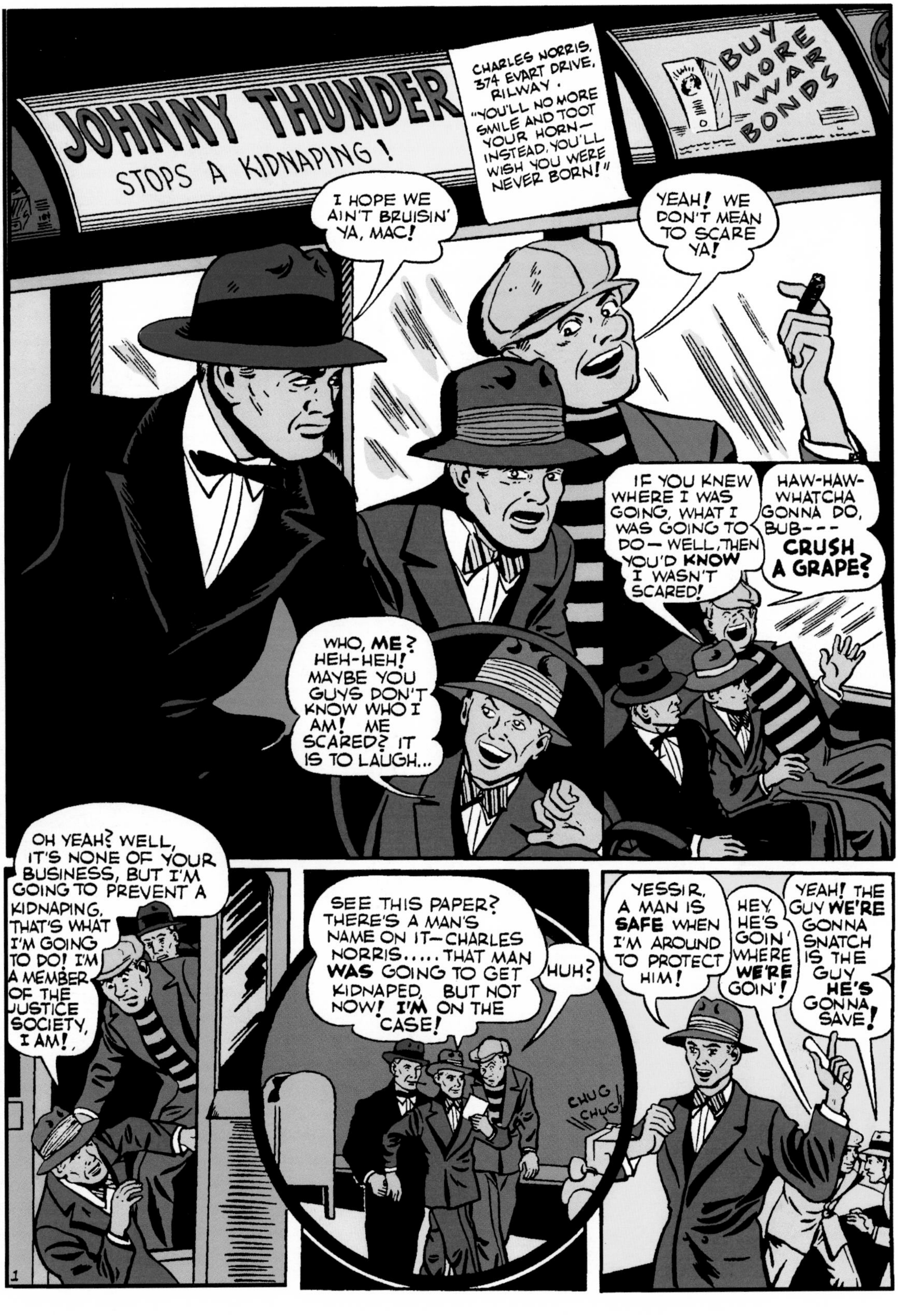
JOHNNY THUNDER
STOPS A KIDNAPING!
CHARLES NORRIS, 374 EVART DRIVE, RILWAY. "YOU'LL NO MORE SMILE AND TOOT YOUR HORN— INSTEAD, YOU'LL WISH YOU WERE NEVER BORN!"
BUY MORE WAR BONDS
I HOPE WE AIN'T BRUISIN' YA, MAC!
YEAH! WE DON'T MEAN TO SCARE YA!
IF YOU KNEW WHERE I WAS GOING, WHAT I WAS GOING TO DO— WELL, THEN YOU'D KNOW I WASN'T SCARED!
HAW-HAW- WHATCHA GONNA DO, BUB--- CRUSH A GRAPE?
WHO, ME? HEH-HEH! MAYBE YOU GUYS DON'T KNOW WHO I AM! ME SCARED? IT IS TO LAUGH...
1
OH YEAH? WELL, IT'S NONE OF YOUR BUSINESS, BUT I'M GOING TO PREVENT A KIDNAPING, THAT'S WHAT I'M GOING TO DO! I'M A MEMBER OF THE JUSTICE SOCIETY, I AM!
SEE THIS PAPER? THERE'S A MAN'S NAME ON IT—CHARLES NORRIS..... THAT MAN WAS GOING TO GET KIDNAPED, BUT NOT NOW! I'M ON THE CASE!
HUH?
CHUG CHUG
YESSIR, A MAN IS SAFE WHEN I'M AROUND TO PROTECT HIM!
HEY, HE'S GOIN' WHERE WE'RE GOIN'!
YEAH! THE GUY WE'RE GONNA SNATCH IS THE GUY HE'S GONNA SAVE!

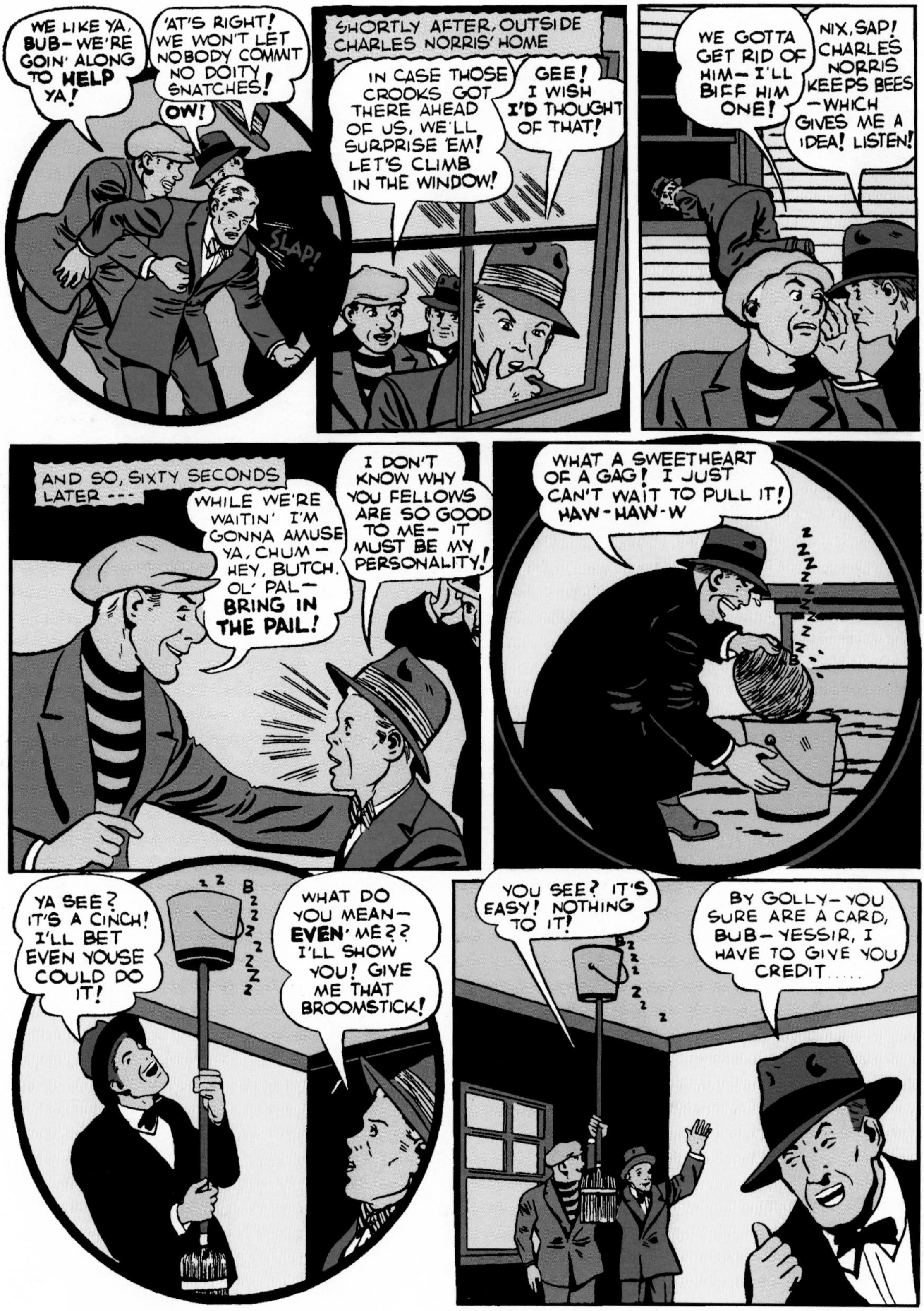
WE LIKE YA, BUB—WE'RE GOIN' ALONG TO HELP YA!
'AT'S RIGHT! WE WON'T LET NOBODY COMMIT NO DOITY SNATCHES!
OW!
SLAP!
SHORTLY AFTER, OUTSIDE CHARLES NORRIS' HOME
IN CASE THOSE CROOKS GOT THERE AHEAD OF US, WE'LL SURPRISE 'EM! LET'S CLIMB IN THE WINDOW!
GEE! I WISH I'D THOUGHT OF THAT!
WE GOTTA GET RID OF HIM—I'LL BIFF HIM ONE!
NIX, SAP! CHARLES NORRIS KEEPS BEES —WHICH GIVES ME A IDEA! LISTEN!
AND SO, SIXTY SECONDS LATER---
WHILE WE'RE WAITIN' I'M GONNA AMUSE YA, CHUM—HEY, BUTCH, OL' PAL—BRING IN THE PAIL!
I DON'T KNOW WHY YOU FELLOWS ARE SO GOOD TO ME—IT MUST BE MY PERSONALITY!
WHAT A SWEETHEART OF A GAG! I JUST CAN'T WAIT TO PULL IT! HAW-HAW-W
YA SEE? IT'S A CINCH! I'LL BET EVEN YOUSE COULD DO IT!
WHAT DO YOU MEAN—EVEN ME?? I'LL SHOW YOU! GIVE ME THAT BROOMSTICK!
YOU SEE? IT'S EASY! NOTHING TO IT!
BY GOLLY—YOU SURE ARE A CARD, BUB—YESSIR, I HAVE TO GIVE YOU CREDIT.....

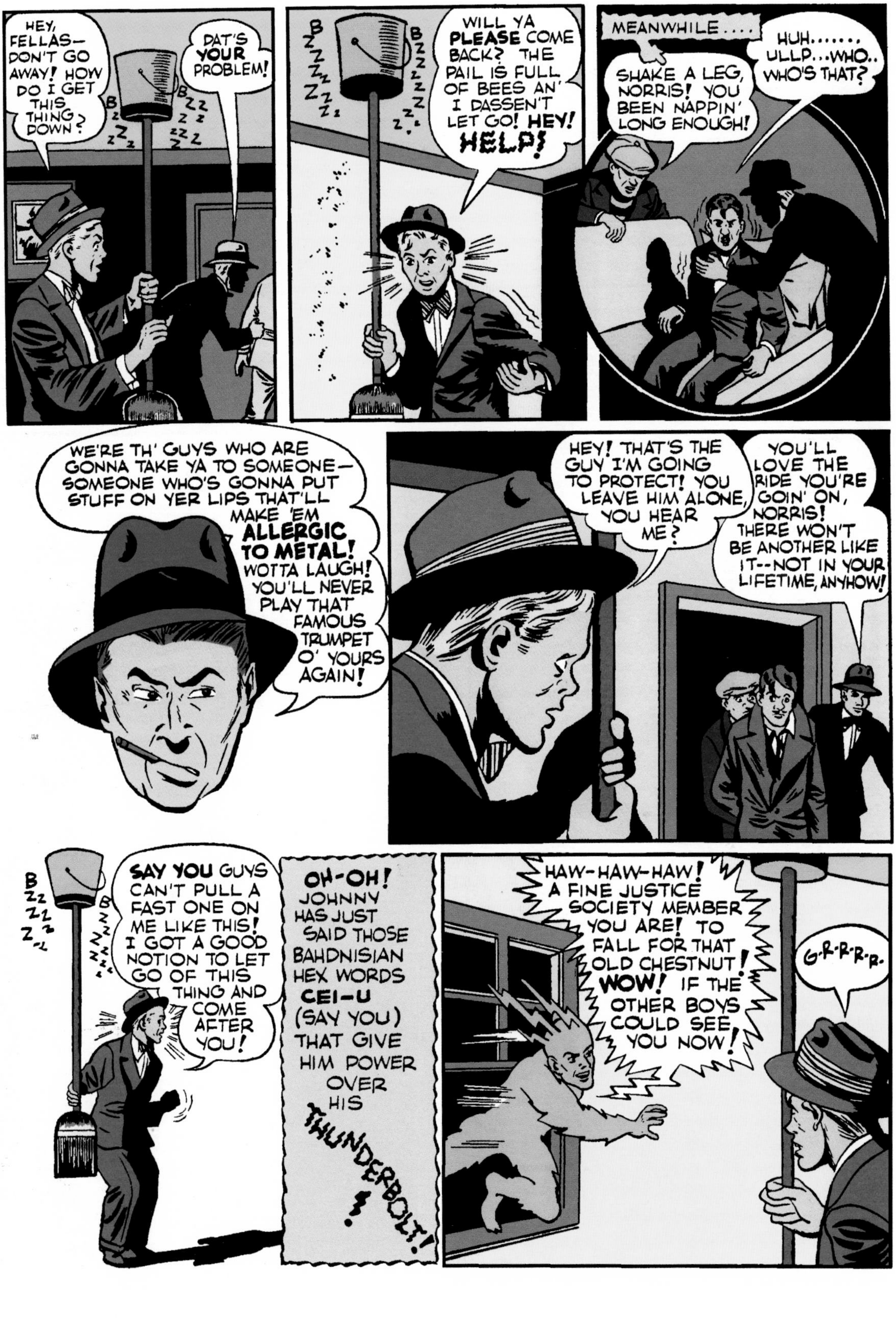
HEY, FELLAS— DON'T GO AWAY! HOW DO I GET THIS THING DOWN?
DAT'S YOUR PROBLEM!
BZZZ
WILL YA PLEASE COME BACK? THE PAIL IS FULL OF BEES AN' I DASSEN'T LET GO! HEY! HELP!
MEANWHILE....
SHAKE A LEG, NORRIS! YOU BEEN NAPPIN' LONG ENOUGH!
HUH....... ULLP...WHO.. WHO'S THAT?
WE'RE TH' GUYS WHO ARE GONNA TAKE YA TO SOMEONE— SOMEONE WHO'S GONNA PUT STUFF ON YER LIPS THAT'LL MAKE 'EM ALLERGIC TO METAL! WOTTA LAUGH! YOU'LL NEVER PLAY THAT FAMOUS TRUMPET O' YOURS AGAIN!
HEY! THAT'S THE GUY I'M GOING TO PROTECT! YOU LEAVE HIM ALONE, YOU HEAR ME?
YOU'LL LOVE THE RIDE YOU'RE GOIN' ON, NORRIS! THERE WON'T BE ANOTHER LIKE IT--NOT IN YOUR LIFETIME, ANYHOW!
SAY YOU GUYS CAN'T PULL A FAST ONE ON ME LIKE THIS! I GOT A GOOD NOTION TO LET GO OF THIS THING AND COME AFTER YOU!
OH-OH! JOHNNY HAS JUST SAID THOSE BAHDNISIAN HEX WORDS CEI-U (SAY YOU) THAT GIVE HIM POWER OVER HIS THUNDERBOLT!
HAW-HAW-HAW! A FINE JUSTICE SOCIETY MEMBER YOU ARE! TO FALL FOR THAT OLD CHESTNUT! WOW! IF THE OTHER BOYS COULD SEE YOU NOW!
G-R-R-R-R.

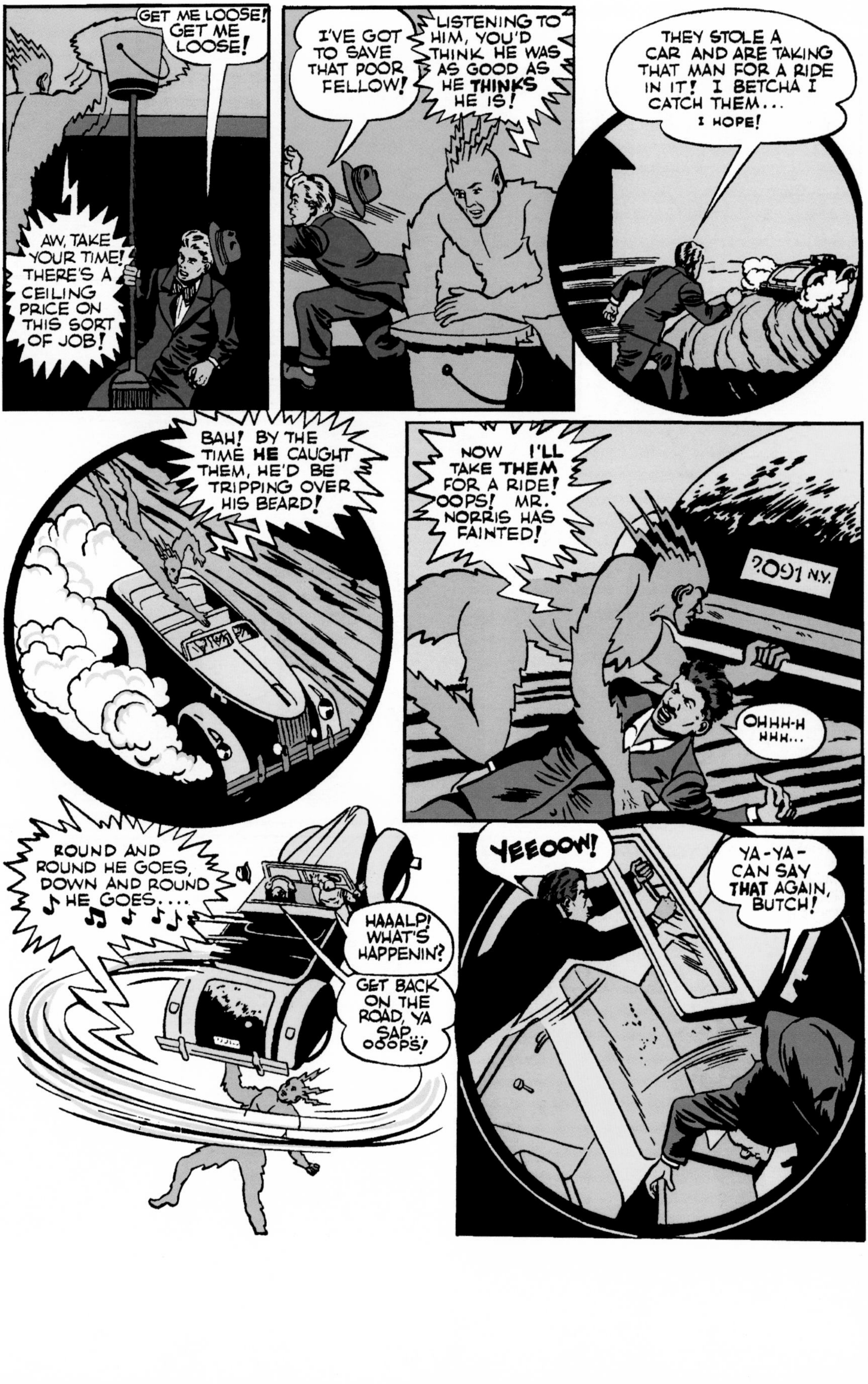
GET ME LOOSE! GET ME LOOSE!
AW, TAKE YOUR TIME! THERE'S A CEILING PRICE ON THIS SORT OF JOB!
I'VE GOT TO SAVE THAT POOR FELLOW!
LISTENING TO HIM, YOU'D THINK HE WAS AS GOOD AS HE THINKS HE IS!
THEY STOLE A CAR AND ARE TAKING THAT MAN FOR A RIDE IN IT! I BETCHA I CATCH THEM... I HOPE!
BAH! BY THE TIME HE CAUGHT THEM, HE'D BE TRIPPING OVER HIS BEARD!
NOW I'LL TAKE THEM FOR A RIDE! OOPS! MR. NORRIS HAS FAINTED!
?091 N.Y.
OHHH-H HHH...
ROUND AND ROUND HE GOES, DOWN AND ROUND HE GOES....
HAAALP! WHAT'S HAPPENIN'?
GET BACK ON THE ROAD, YA SAP... OOOPS!
YEEOOW!
YA-YA- CAN SAY THAT AGAIN, BUTCH!

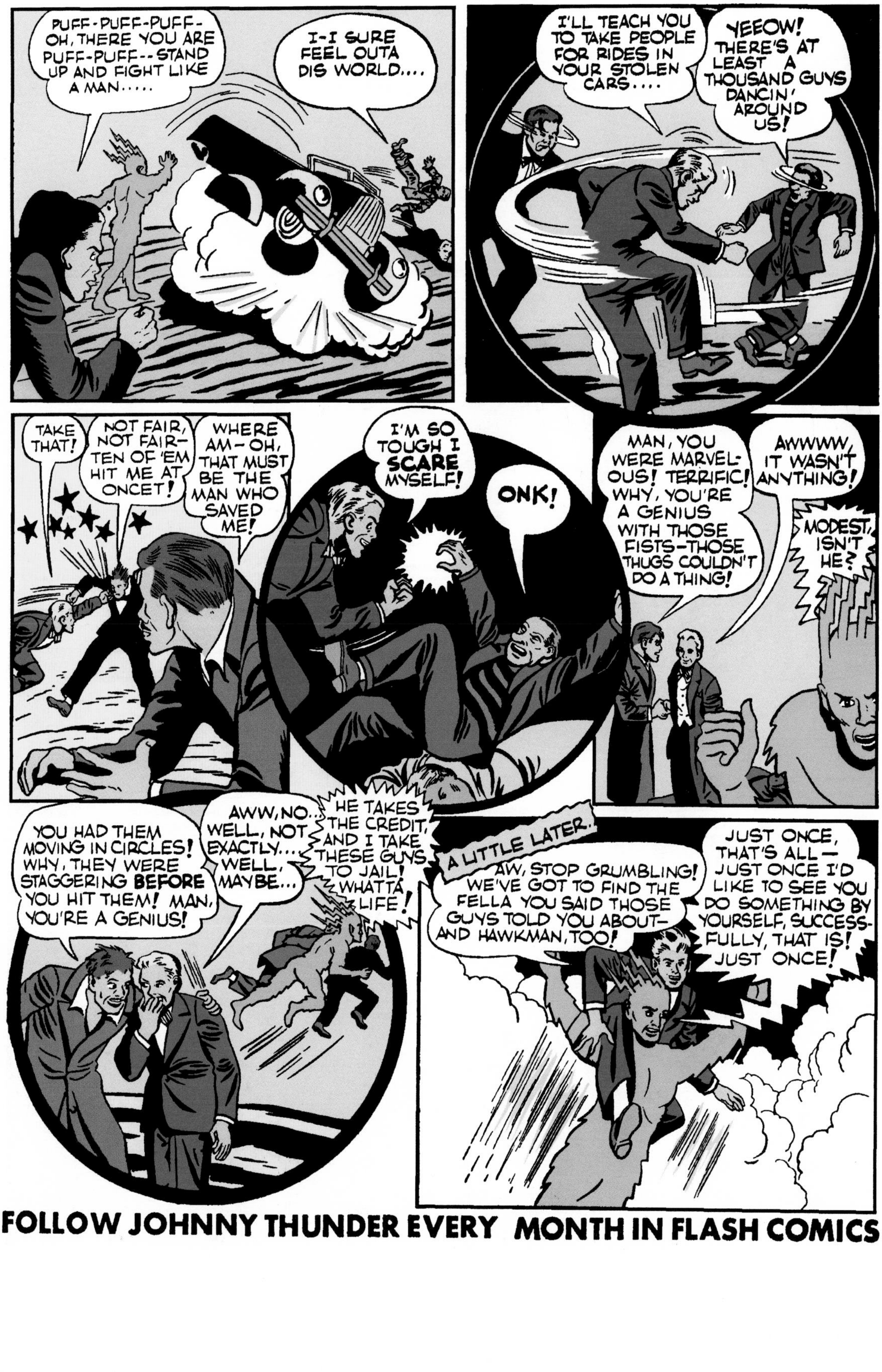
PUFF-PUFF-PUFF-OH, THERE YOU ARE PUFF-PUFF--STAND UP AND FIGHT LIKE A MAN.....
I-I SURE FEEL OUTA DIS WORLD....
I'LL TEACH YOU TO TAKE PEOPLE FOR RIDES IN YOUR STOLEN CARS....
YEEOW! THERE'S AT LEAST A THOUSAND GUYS DANCIN' AROUND US!
TAKE THAT!
NOT FAIR, NOT FAIR-TEN OF 'EM HIT ME AT ONCET!
WHERE AM-OH, THAT MUST BE THE MAN WHO SAVED ME!
I'M SO TOUGH I SCARE MYSELF!
ONK!
MAN, YOU WERE MARVEL-OUS! TERRIFIC! WHY, YOU'RE A GENIUS WITH THOSE FISTS-THOSE THUGS COULDN'T DO A THING!
AWWWW, IT WASN'T ANYTHING!
MODEST, ISN'T HE?
YOU HAD THEM MOVING IN CIRCLES! WHY, THEY WERE STAGGERING BEFORE YOU HIT THEM! MAN, YOU'RE A GENIUS!
AWW, NO... WELL, NOT EXACTLY... WELL, MAYBE...
HE TAKES THE CREDIT, AND I TAKE THESE GUYS TO JAIL! WHATTA LIFE!
A LITTLE LATER..
AW, STOP GRUMBLING! WE'VE GOT TO FIND THE FELLA YOU SAID THOSE GUYS TOLD YOU ABOUT-AND HAWKMAN, TOO!
JUST ONCE, THAT'S ALL-JUST ONCE I'D LIKE TO SEE YOU DO SOMETHING BY YOURSELF, SUCCESS-FULLY, THAT IS! JUST ONCE!

FOLLOW JOHNNY THUNDER EVERY MONTH IN FLASH COMICS

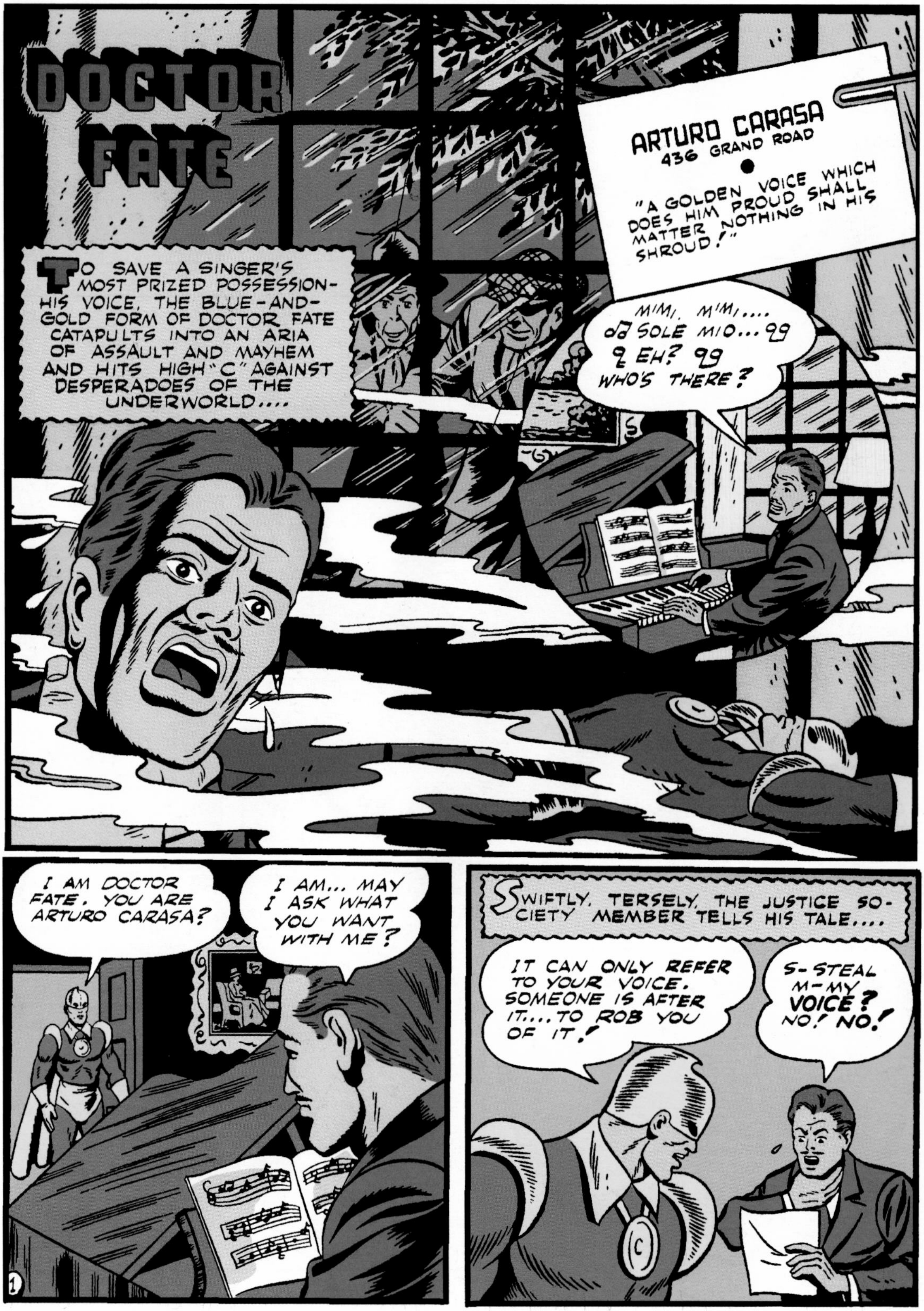
DOCTOR FATE
ARTURO CARASA
436 GRAND ROAD
"A GOLDEN VOICE WHICH DOES HIM PROUD SHALL MATTER NOTHING IN HIS SHROUD!"
TO SAVE A SINGER'S MOST PRIZED POSSESSION- HIS VOICE, THE BLUE-AND-GOLD FORM OF DOCTOR FATE CATAPULTS INTO AN ARIA OF ASSAULT AND MAYHEM AND HITS HIGH "C" AGAINST DESPERADOES OF THE UNDERWORLD....
M'MI, M'MI.... SOLE MIO... EH? WHO'S THERE?
I AM DOCTOR FATE. YOU ARE ARTURO CARASA?
I AM... MAY I ASK WHAT YOU WANT WITH ME?
1
SWIFTLY, TERSELY, THE JUSTICE SOCIETY MEMBER TELLS HIS TALE....
IT CAN ONLY REFER TO YOUR VOICE. SOMEONE IS AFTER IT.... TO ROB YOU OF IT!
S-STEAL M-MY VOICE? NO! NO!

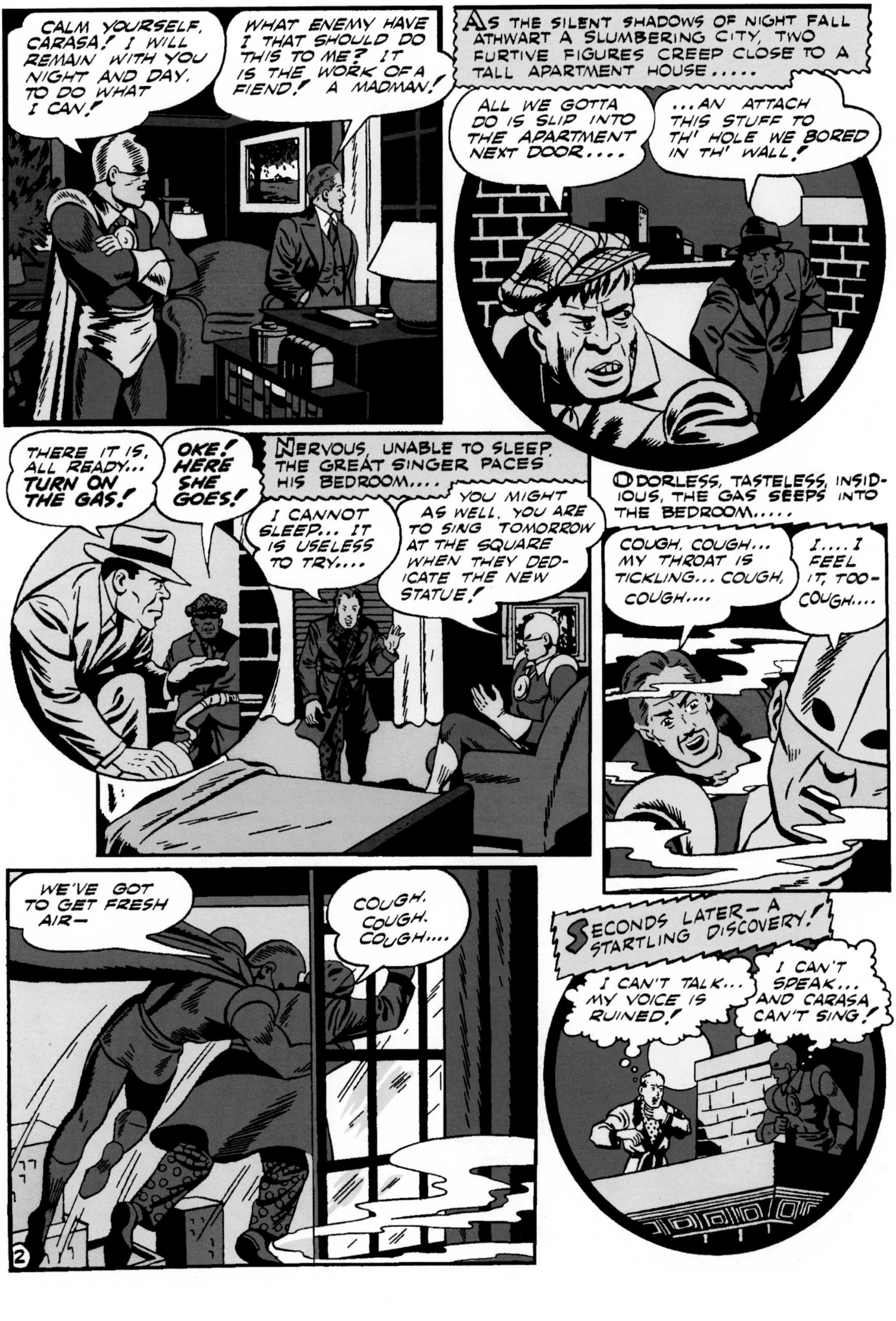
CALM YOURSELF, CARASA! I WILL REMAIN WITH YOU NIGHT AND DAY. TO DO WHAT I CAN!
WHAT ENEMY HAVE I THAT SHOULD DO THIS TO ME? IT IS THE WORK OF A FIEND! A MADMAN!
AS THE SILENT SHADOWS OF NIGHT FALL ATHWART A SLUMBERING CITY, TWO FURTIVE FIGURES CREEP CLOSE TO A TALL APARTMENT HOUSE.....
ALL WE GOTTA DO IS SLIP INTO THE APARTMENT NEXT DOOR....
...AN ATTACH THIS STUFF TO TH' HOLE WE BORED IN TH' WALL!
THERE IT IS, ALL READY... TURN ON THE GAS!
OKE! HERE SHE GOES!
NERVOUS, UNABLE TO SLEEP, THE GREAT SINGER PACES HIS BEDROOM....
I CANNOT SLEEP... IT IS USELESS TO TRY....
YOU MIGHT AS WELL. YOU ARE TO SING TOMORROW AT THE SQUARE WHEN THEY DEDICATE THE NEW STATUE!
ODORLESS, TASTELESS, INSIDIOUS, THE GAS SEEPS INTO THE BEDROOM.....
COUGH, COUGH... MY THROAT IS TICKLING... COUGH, COUGH....
I....I FEEL IT, TOO-COUGH....
WE'VE GOT TO GET FRESH AIR-
COUGH. COUGH. COUGH....
2
SECONDS LATER- A STARTLING DISCOVERY!
I CAN'T TALK... MY VOICE IS RUINED!
I CAN'T SPEAK... AND CARASA CAN'T SING!

THE FOLLOWING MORNING....

NO VOICE! FINE, FINE! OH, THIS IS SPLENDID! YOU ARE TO SING AT NOON, AND YOU HAVE NO VOICE! RUINED! WE ARE RUINED!

UNABLE TO SPEAK, I MUST WRITE WHAT I WISH....

CARASA MUST SING. I WILL ARRANGE IT. TAKE HIM TO THE SQUARE. WE MUST NOT LET THE ONES WHO DID THIS TO KNOW IT WAS A SUCCESS...

HE IS TO SING WHEN HE CANNOT EVEN TALK! NONSENSE! WHAT A MANAGER HAS TO PUT UP WITH! MA FOI!

AT THE SQUARE....

AND NOW IT IS MY PRIVILEGE TO PRESENT THE GREAT ARTURO CARASA!

WHAT AM I TO DO? I CANNOT SING....

BUT AS THE SINGER OPENS HIS LIPS A FLOOD OF MELLOW GOLDEN NOTES POURS FORTH..... RICH, VIBRANT!

OH, SAY, CAN YOU SEE.... ♪♫

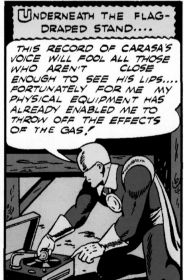

UNDERNEATH THE FLAG-DRAPED STAND....

THIS RECORD OF CARASA'S VOICE WILL FOOL ALL THOSE WHO AREN'T CLOSE ENOUGH TO SEE HIS LIPS.... FORTUNATELY FOR ME MY PHYSICAL EQUIPMENT HAS ALREADY ENABLED ME TO THROW OFF THE EFFECTS OF THE GAS!

THINKING THEY FAILED, THE RATS WHO PULLED THE JOB WILL PROBABLY RETURN TONIGHT— BUT THIS TIME I'LL BE READY FOR THEM!

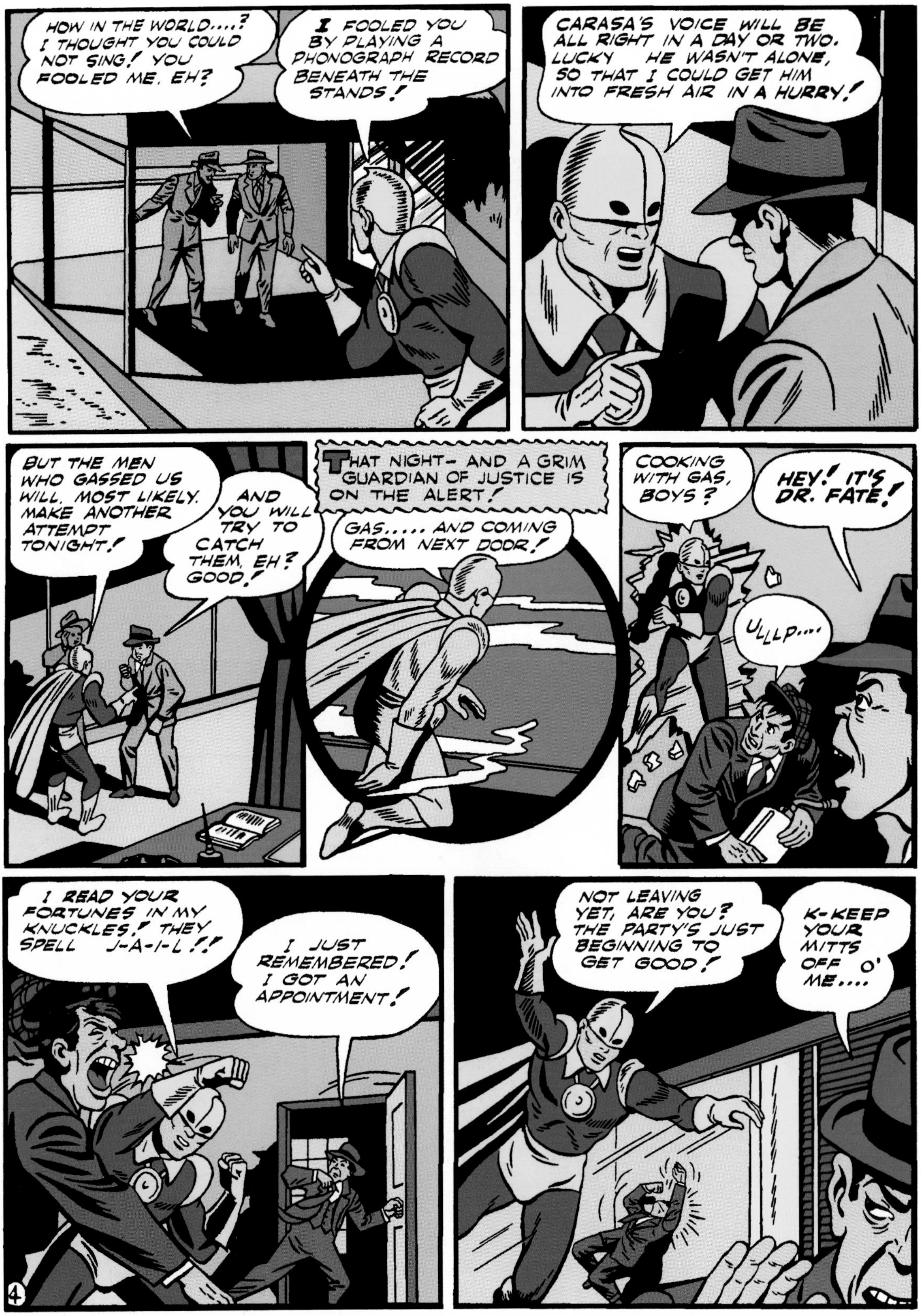
HOW IN THE WORLD....? I THOUGHT YOU COULD NOT SING! YOU FOOLED ME, EH?
I FOOLED YOU BY PLAYING A PHONOGRAPH RECORD BENEATH THE STANDS!
CARASA'S VOICE WILL BE ALL RIGHT IN A DAY OR TWO. LUCKY HE WASN'T ALONE, SO THAT I COULD GET HIM INTO FRESH AIR IN A HURRY!
BUT THE MEN WHO GASSED US WILL, MOST LIKELY, MAKE ANOTHER ATTEMPT TONIGHT!
AND YOU WILL TRY TO CATCH THEM, EH? GOOD!
THAT NIGHT– AND A GRIM GUARDIAN OF JUSTICE IS ON THE ALERT!
GAS..... AND COMING FROM NEXT DOOR!
COOKING WITH GAS, BOYS?
HEY! IT'S DR. FATE!
ULLLP....
I READ YOUR FORTUNES IN MY KNUCKLES! THEY SPELL J-A-I-L!!
I JUST REMEMBERED! I GOT AN APPOINTMENT!
4
NOT LEAVING YET, ARE YOU? THE PARTY'S JUST BEGINNING TO GET GOOD!
K-KEEP YOUR MITTS OFF O' ME....

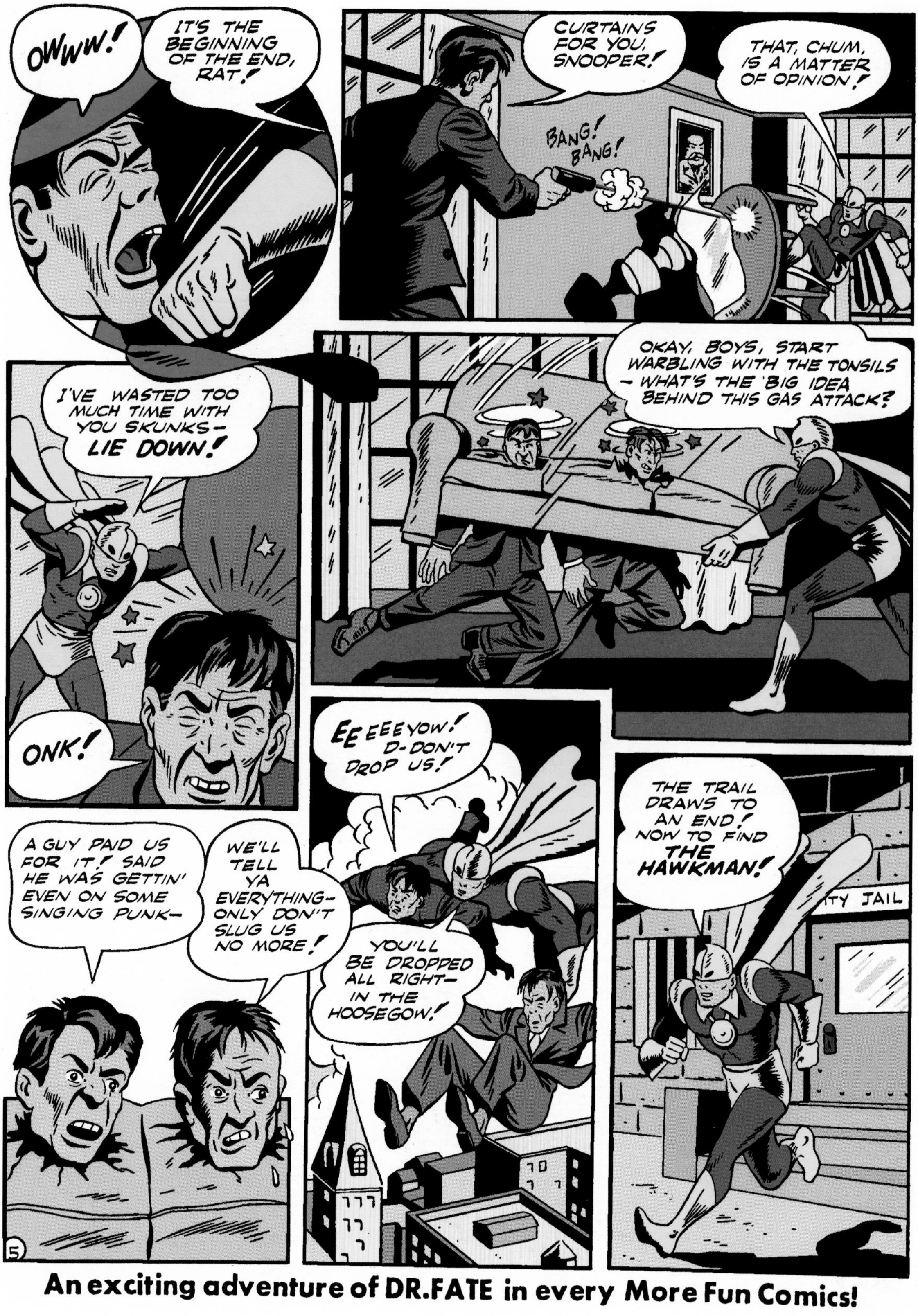
OWWW!
IT'S THE BEGINNING OF THE END, RAT!
CURTAINS FOR YOU, SNOOPER!
BANG! BANG!
THAT, CHUM, IS A MATTER OF OPINION!
I'VE WASTED TOO MUCH TIME WITH YOU SKUNKS- LIE DOWN!
ONK!
OKAY, BOYS, START WARBLING WITH THE TONSILS - WHAT'S THE BIG IDEA BEHIND THIS GAS ATTACK?
A GUY PAID US FOR IT! SAID HE WAS GETTIN' EVEN ON SOME SINGING PUNK-
WE'LL TELL YA EVERYTHING- ONLY DON'T SLUG US NO MORE!
EEEEEYOW! D-DON'T DROP US!
YOU'LL BE DROPPED ALL RIGHT- IN THE HOOSEGOW!
THE TRAIL DRAWS TO AN END! NOW TO FIND THE HAWKMAN!
ITY JAIL
5

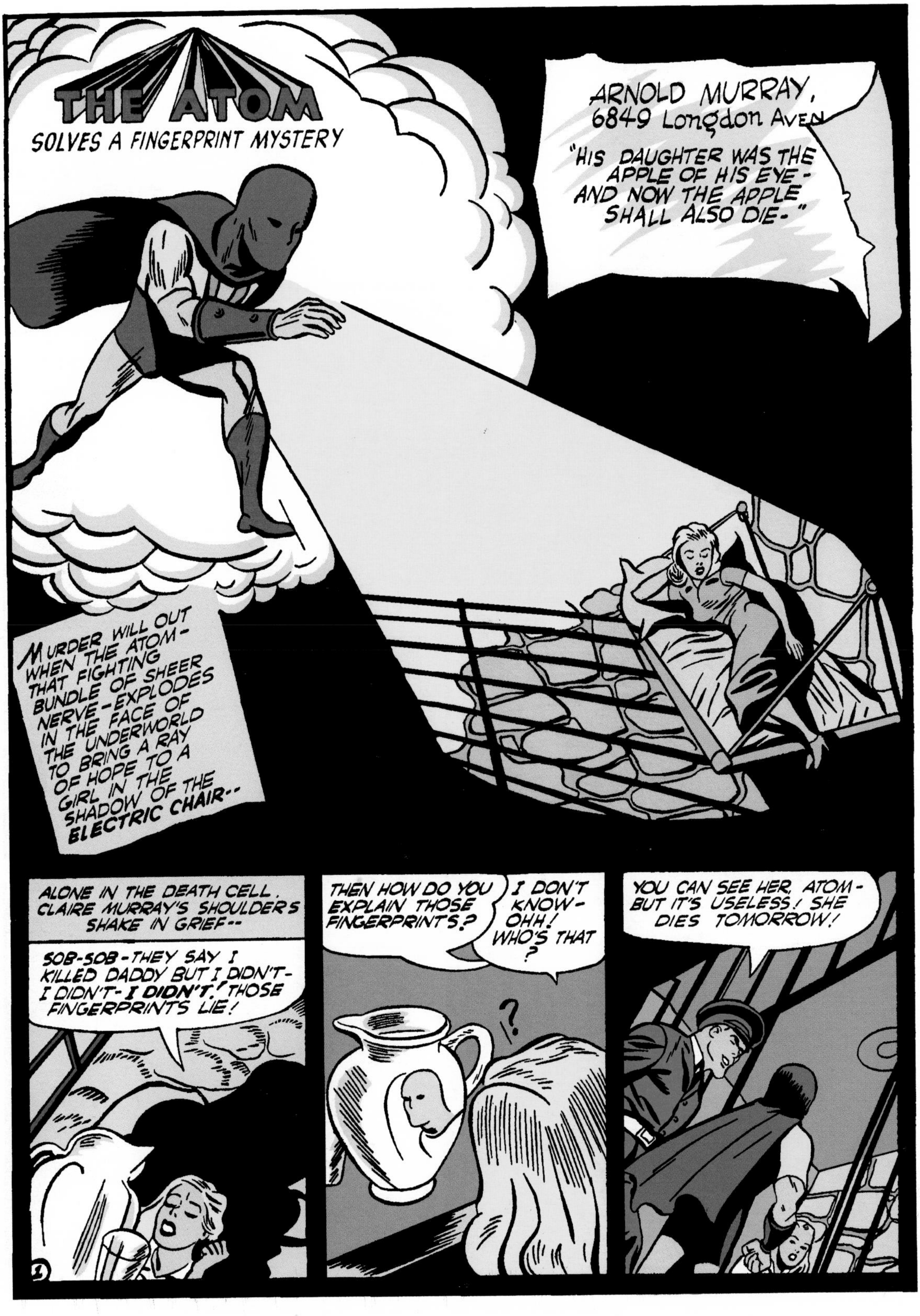
THE ATOM
SOLVES A FINGERPRINT MYSTERY
ARNOLD MURRAY, 6849 Longdon AVEN
"HIS DAUGHTER WAS THE APPLE OF HIS EYE - AND NOW THE APPLE SHALL ALSO DIE-"
MURDER WILL OUT WHEN THE ATOM - THAT FIGHTING BUNDLE OF SHEER NERVE - EXPLODES IN THE FACE OF THE UNDERWORLD TO BRING A RAY OF HOPE TO A GIRL IN THE SHADOW OF THE ELECTRIC CHAIR..
ALONE IN THE DEATH CELL, CLAIRE MURRAY'S SHOULDERS SHAKE IN GRIEF--
SOB-SOB - THEY SAY I KILLED DADDY BUT I DIDN'T - I DIDN'T - I DIDN'T! THOSE FINGERPRINTS LIE!
1
THEN HOW DO YOU EXPLAIN THOSE FINGERPRINTS?
I DON'T KNOW - OHH! WHO'S THAT?
?
YOU CAN SEE HER, ATOM - BUT IT'S USELESS! SHE DIES TOMORROW!

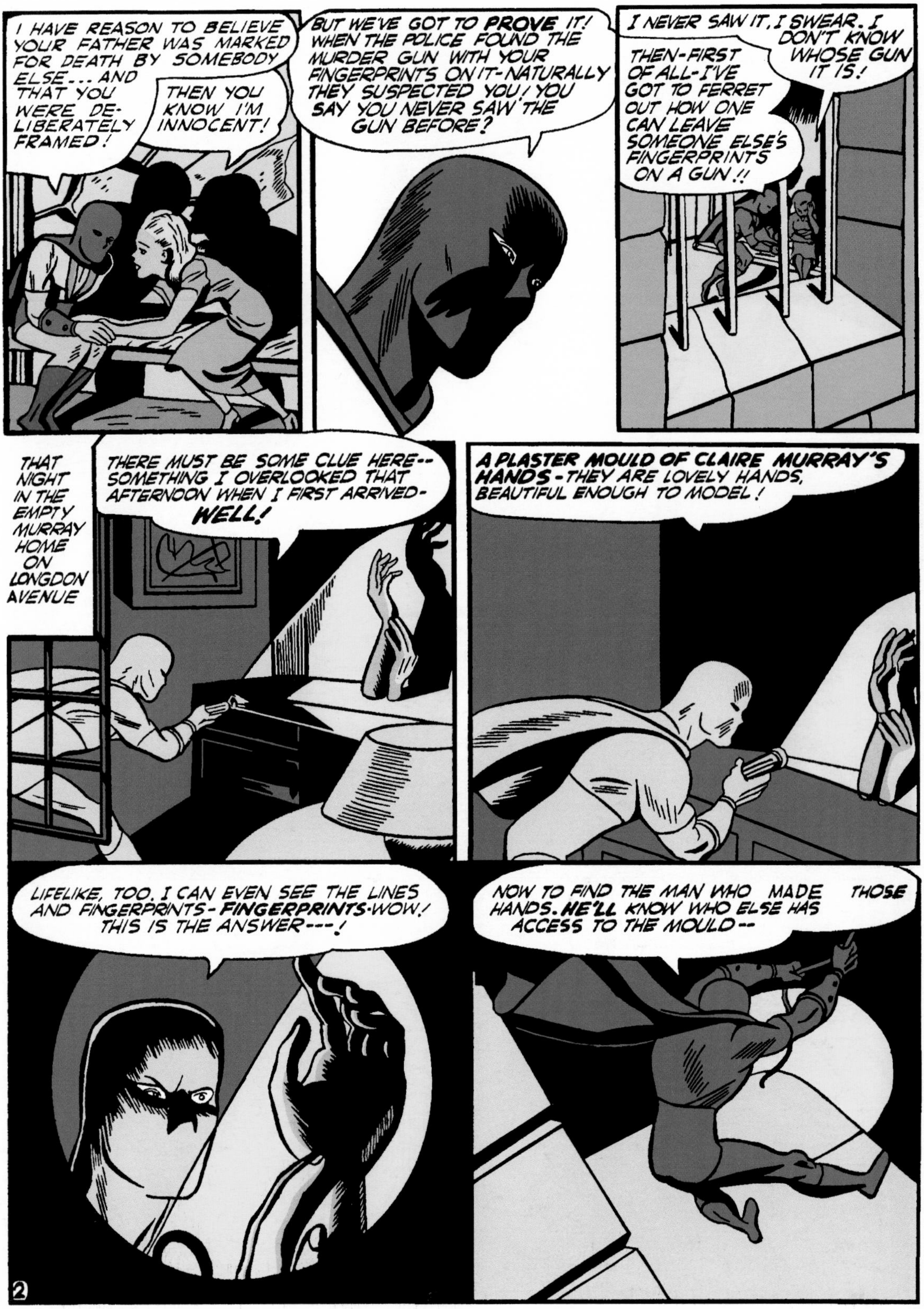
I HAVE REASON TO BELIEVE YOUR FATHER WAS MARKED FOR DEATH BY SOMEBODY ELSE... AND THAT YOU WERE DE-LIBERATELY FRAMED!
THEN YOU KNOW I'M INNOCENT!
BUT WE'VE GOT TO PROVE IT! WHEN THE POLICE FOUND THE MURDER GUN WITH YOUR FINGERPRINTS ON IT-NATURALLY THEY SUSPECTED YOU! YOU SAY YOU NEVER SAW THE GUN BEFORE?
I NEVER SAW IT, I SWEAR. I DON'T KNOW WHOSE GUN IT IS!
THEN-FIRST OF ALL-I'VE GOT TO FERRET OUT HOW ONE CAN LEAVE SOMEONE ELSE'S FINGERPRINTS ON A GUN!!
THAT NIGHT IN THE EMPTY MURRAY HOME ON LONGDON AVENUE
THERE MUST BE SOME CLUE HERE-- SOMETHING I OVERLOOKED THAT AFTERNOON WHEN I FIRST ARRIVED- WELL!
A PLASTER MOULD OF CLAIRE MURRAY'S HANDS-THEY ARE LOVELY HANDS, BEAUTIFUL ENOUGH TO MODEL!
LIFELIKE, TOO. I CAN EVEN SEE THE LINES AND FINGERPRINTS-FINGERPRINTS-WOW! THIS IS THE ANSWER---!
NOW TO FIND THE MAN WHO MADE THOSE HANDS. HE'LL KNOW WHO ELSE HAS ACCESS TO THE MOULD--
2

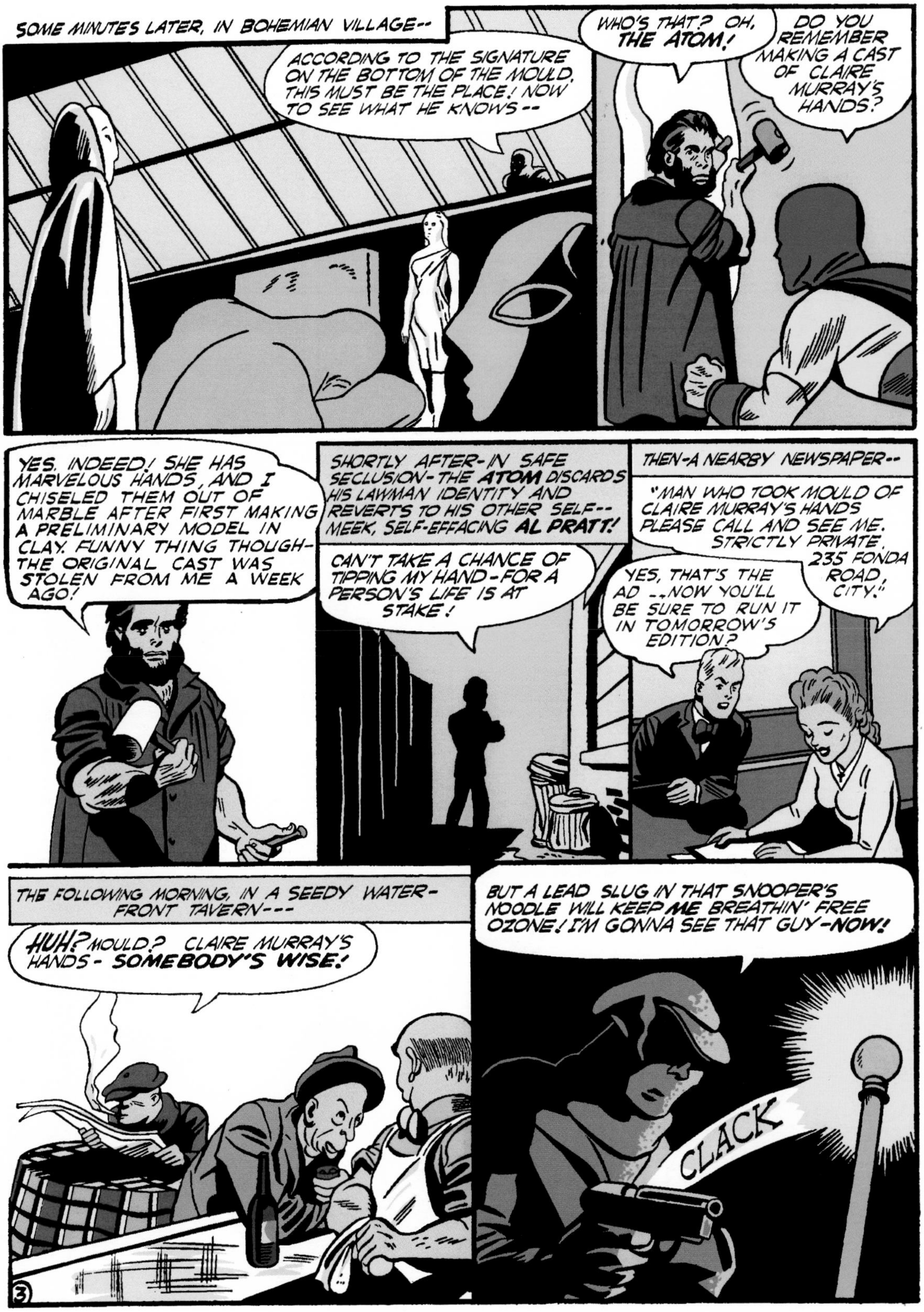
SOME MINUTES LATER, IN BOHEMIAN VILLAGE--
ACCORDING TO THE SIGNATURE ON THE BOTTOM OF THE MOULD, THIS MUST BE THE PLACE! NOW TO SEE WHAT HE KNOWS--
WHO'S THAT? OH, THE ATOM!
DO YOU REMEMBER MAKING A CAST OF CLAIRE MURRAY'S HANDS?
YES, INDEED! SHE HAS MARVELOUS HANDS, AND I CHISELED THEM OUT OF MARBLE AFTER FIRST MAKING A PRELIMINARY MODEL IN CLAY. FUNNY THING THOUGH-THE ORIGINAL CAST WAS STOLEN FROM ME A WEEK AGO!
SHORTLY AFTER-IN SAFE SECLUSION-THE ATOM DISCARDS HIS LAWMAN IDENTITY AND REVERTS TO HIS OTHER SELF--MEEK, SELF-EFFACING AL PRATT!
CAN'T TAKE A CHANCE OF TIPPING MY HAND-FOR A PERSON'S LIFE IS AT STAKE!
THEN-A NEARBY NEWSPAPER--
"MAN WHO TOOK MOULD OF CLAIRE MURRAY'S HANDS PLEASE CALL AND SEE ME. STRICTLY PRIVATE. 235 FONDA ROAD, CITY."
YES, THAT'S THE AD--NOW YOU'LL BE SURE TO RUN IT IN TOMORROW'S EDITION?
THE FOLLOWING MORNING, IN A SEEDY WATER-FRONT TAVERN---
HUH? MOULD? CLAIRE MURRAY'S HANDS- SOMEBODY'S WISE!
3
BUT A LEAD SLUG IN THAT SNOOPER'S NOODLE WILL KEEP ME BREATHIN' FREE OZONE! I'M GONNA SEE THAT GUY-NOW!
CLACK

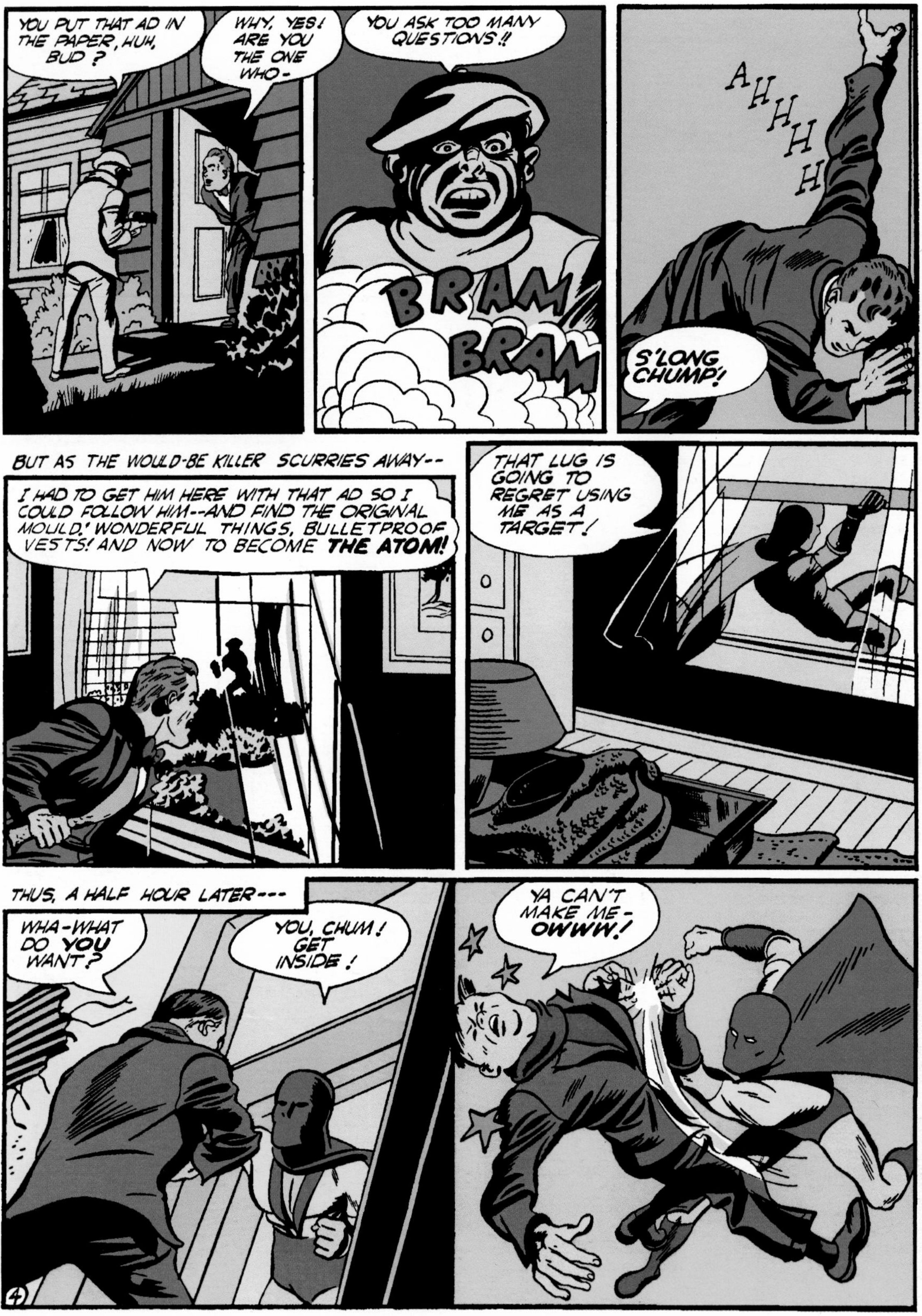
YOU PUT THAT AD IN THE PAPER, HUH, BUD ?
WHY, YES! ARE YOU THE ONE WHO-
YOU ASK TOO MANY QUESTIONS!!
BRAM BRAM
AHHHH
S'LONG CHUMP!
BUT AS THE WOULD-BE KILLER SCURRIES AWAY--
I HAD TO GET HIM HERE WITH THAT AD SO I COULD FOLLOW HIM--AND FIND THE ORIGINAL MOULD! WONDERFUL THINGS, BULLETPROOF VESTS! AND NOW TO BECOME THE ATOM!
THAT LUG IS GOING TO REGRET USING ME AS A TARGET!
THUS, A HALF HOUR LATER---
WHA-WHAT DO YOU WANT?
YOU, CHUM! GET INSIDE!
YA CAN'T MAKE ME- OWWW!
4

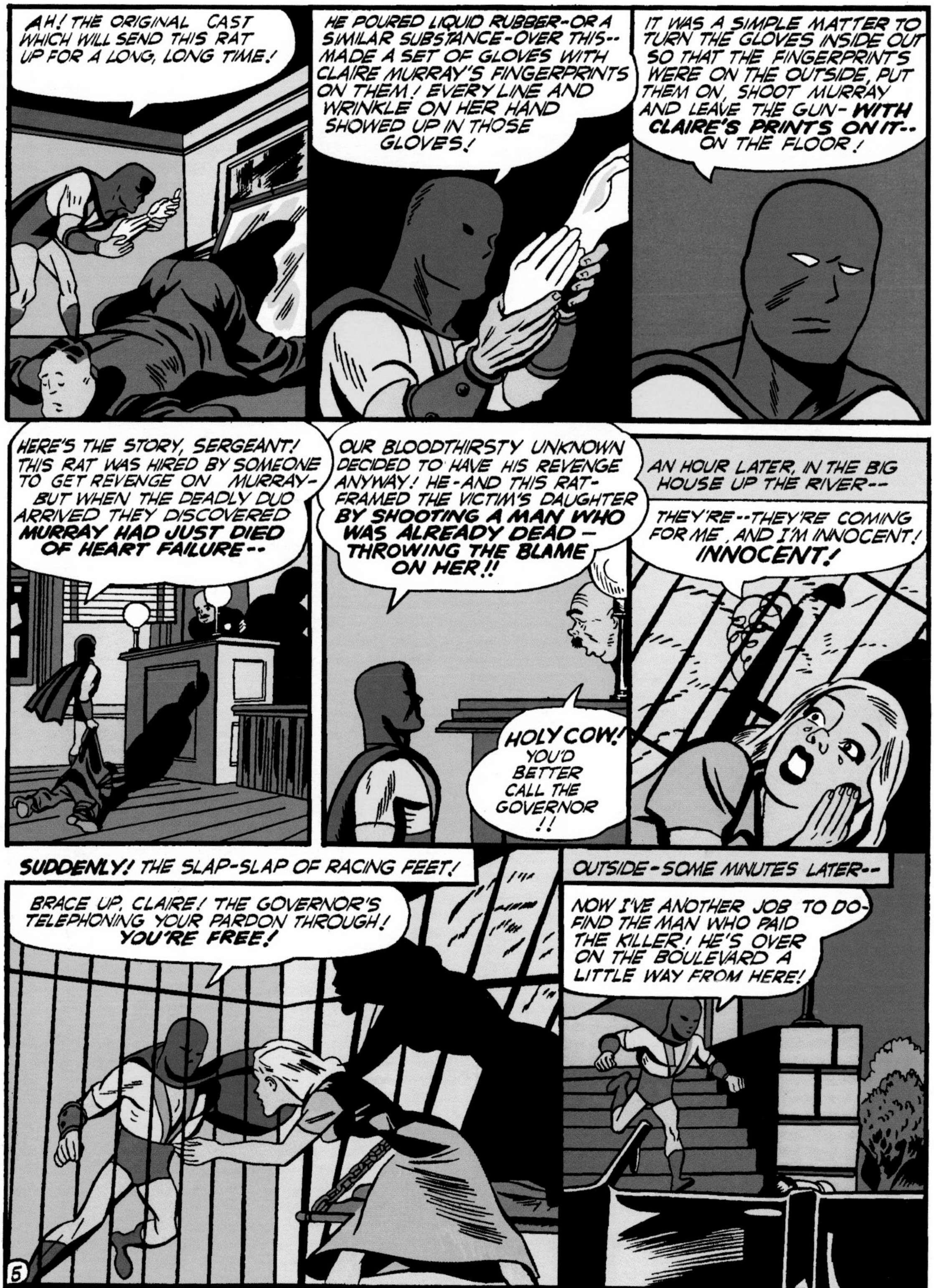
AH! THE ORIGINAL CAST WHICH WILL SEND THIS RAT UP FOR A LONG, LONG TIME!
HE POURED LIQUID RUBBER-OR A SIMILAR SUBSTANCE-OVER THIS--MADE A SET OF GLOVES WITH CLAIRE MURRAY'S FINGERPRINTS ON THEM! EVERY LINE AND WRINKLE ON HER HAND SHOWED UP IN THOSE GLOVES!
IT WAS A SIMPLE MATTER TO TURN THE GLOVES INSIDE OUT SO THAT THE FINGERPRINTS WERE ON THE OUTSIDE, PUT THEM ON, SHOOT MURRAY AND LEAVE THE GUN- WITH CLAIRE'S PRINTS ON IT-- ON THE FLOOR!
HERE'S THE STORY, SERGEANT! THIS RAT WAS HIRED BY SOMEONE TO GET REVENGE ON MURRAY- BUT WHEN THE DEADLY DUO ARRIVED THEY DISCOVERED MURRAY HAD JUST DIED OF HEART FAILURE--
OUR BLOODTHIRSTY UNKNOWN DECIDED TO HAVE HIS REVENGE ANYWAY! HE-AND THIS RAT-FRAMED THE VICTIM'S DAUGHTER BY SHOOTING A MAN WHO WAS ALREADY DEAD - THROWING THE BLAME ON HER!!
HOLY COW! YOU'D BETTER CALL THE GOVERNOR !!
AN HOUR LATER, IN THE BIG HOUSE UP THE RIVER--
THEY'RE--THEY'RE COMING FOR ME, AND I'M INNOCENT! INNOCENT!
SUDDENLY! THE SLAP-SLAP OF RACING FEET!
BRACE UP, CLAIRE! THE GOVERNOR'S TELEPHONING YOUR PARDON THROUGH! YOU'RE FREE!
OUTSIDE-SOME MINUTES LATER--
NOW I'VE ANOTHER JOB TO DO-FIND THE MAN WHO PAID THE KILLER! HE'S OVER ON THE BOULEVARD A LITTLE WAY FROM HERE!
6

Follow the adventures of The ATOM *in every issue of* All-American Comics!

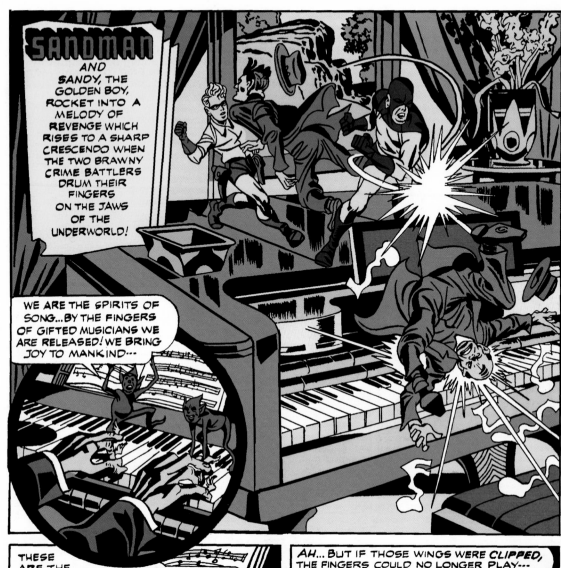

SANDMAN

AND SANDY, THE GOLDEN BOY, ROCKET INTO A MELODY OF REVENGE WHICH RISES TO A SHARP CRESCENDO WHEN THE TWO BRAWNY CRIME BATTLERS DRUM THEIR FINGERS ON THE JAWS OF THE UNDERWORLD!

WE ARE THE SPIRITS OF SONG...BY THE FINGERS OF GIFTED MUSICIANS WE ARE RELEASED! WE BRING JOY TO MANKIND...

THESE ARE THE FINGERS OF *THEODOR KOROWSKI*... GREATEST LIVING PIANIST! THEY BEAR THE TALENT OF A PADEREWSKI... THEY ARE WINGED, ETHEREAL!

AH... BUT IF THOSE WINGS WERE *CLIPPED*, THE FINGERS COULD NO LONGER PLAY... NOR MAKE MAGIC MELODIES TO HAUNT AND THRILL!

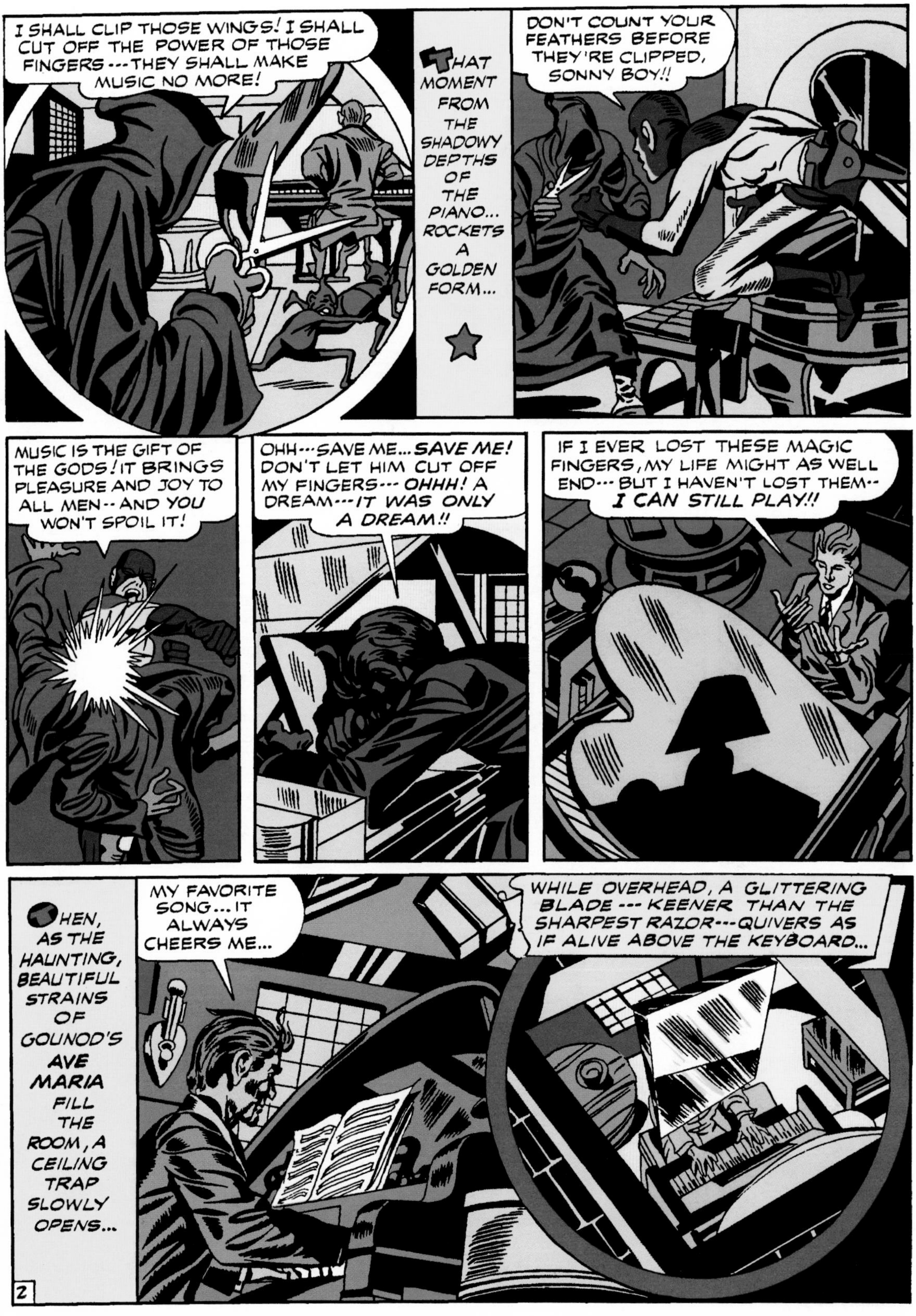
I SHALL CLIP THOSE WINGS! I SHALL CUT OFF THE POWER OF THOSE FINGERS---THEY SHALL MAKE MUSIC NO MORE!
THAT MOMENT FROM THE SHADOWY DEPTHS OF THE PIANO... ROCKETS A GOLDEN FORM...
DON'T COUNT YOUR FEATHERS BEFORE THEY'RE CLIPPED, SONNY BOY!!
MUSIC IS THE GIFT OF THE GODS! IT BRINGS PLEASURE AND JOY TO ALL MEN--AND YOU WON'T SPOIL IT!
OHH---SAVE ME...SAVE ME! DON'T LET HIM CUT OFF MY FINGERS---OHHH! A DREAM---IT WAS ONLY A DREAM!!
IF I EVER LOST THESE MAGIC FINGERS, MY LIFE MIGHT AS WELL END---BUT I HAVEN'T LOST THEM--I CAN STILL PLAY!!
THEN, AS THE HAUNTING, BEAUTIFUL STRAINS OF GOUNOD'S AVE MARIA FILL THE ROOM, A CEILING TRAP SLOWLY OPENS...
MY FAVORITE SONG... IT ALWAYS CHEERS ME...
WHILE OVERHEAD, A GLITTERING BLADE---KEENER THAN THE SHARPEST RAZOR---QUIVERS AS IF ALIVE ABOVE THE KEYBOARD...
2

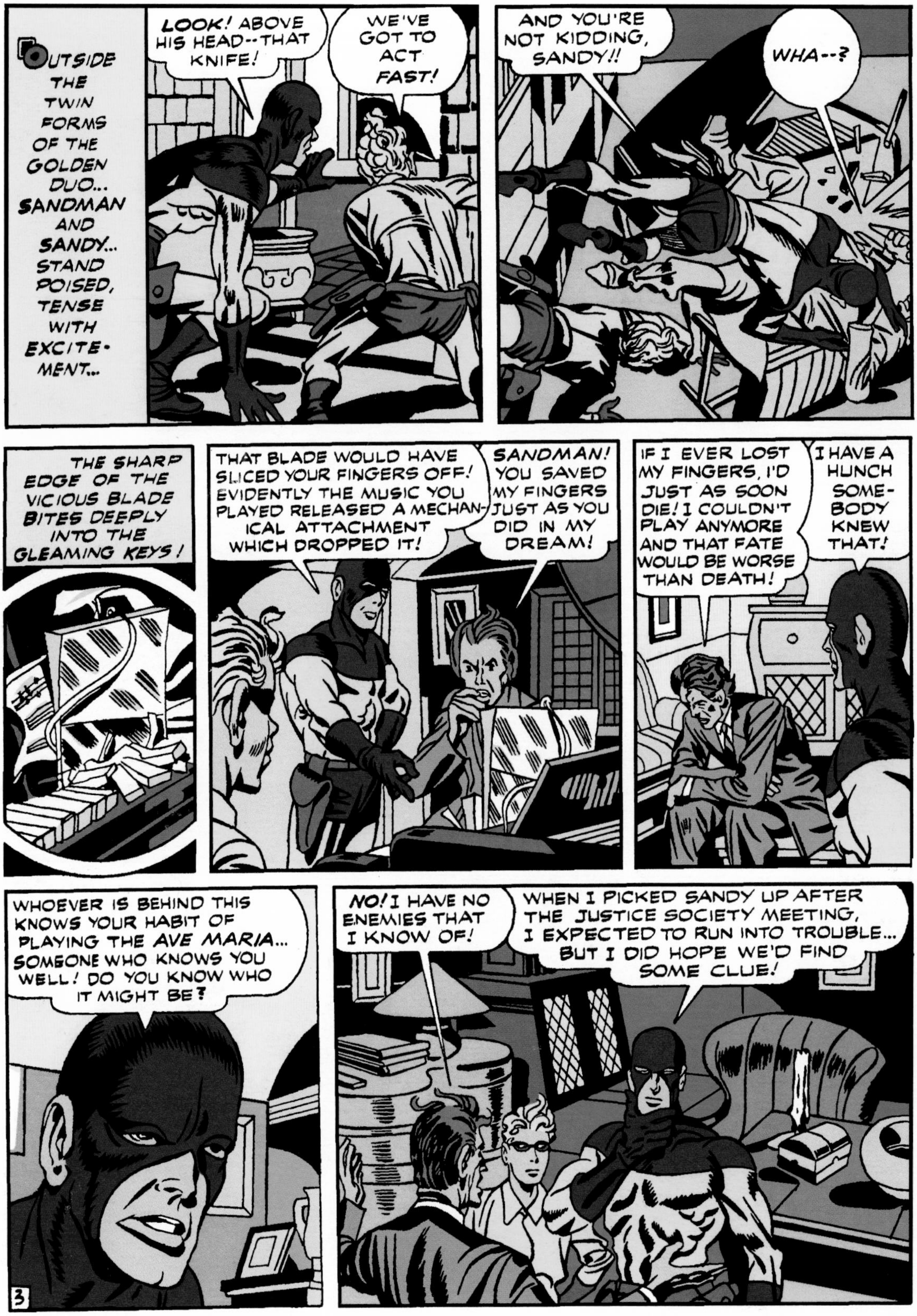
OUTSIDE THE TWIN FORMS OF THE GOLDEN DUO... SANDMAN AND SANDY... STAND POISED, TENSE WITH EXCITEMENT...
LOOK! ABOVE HIS HEAD--THAT KNIFE!
WE'VE GOT TO ACT FAST!
AND YOU'RE NOT KIDDING, SANDY!!
WHA--?
THE SHARP EDGE OF THE VICIOUS BLADE BITES DEEPLY INTO THE GLEAMING KEYS!
THAT BLADE WOULD HAVE SLICED YOUR FINGERS OFF! EVIDENTLY THE MUSIC YOU PLAYED RELEASED A MECHANICAL ATTACHMENT WHICH DROPPED IT!
SANDMAN! YOU SAVED MY FINGERS JUST AS YOU DID IN MY DREAM!
IF I EVER LOST MY FINGERS, I'D JUST AS SOON DIE! I COULDN'T PLAY ANYMORE AND THAT FATE WOULD BE WORSE THAN DEATH!
I HAVE A HUNCH SOMEBODY KNEW THAT!
WHOEVER IS BEHIND THIS KNOWS YOUR HABIT OF PLAYING THE AVE MARIA... SOMEONE WHO KNOWS YOU WELL! DO YOU KNOW WHO IT MIGHT BE?
NO! I HAVE NO ENEMIES THAT I KNOW OF!
WHEN I PICKED SANDY UP AFTER THE JUSTICE SOCIETY MEETING, I EXPECTED TO RUN INTO TROUBLE... BUT I DID HOPE WE'D FIND SOME CLUE!
3

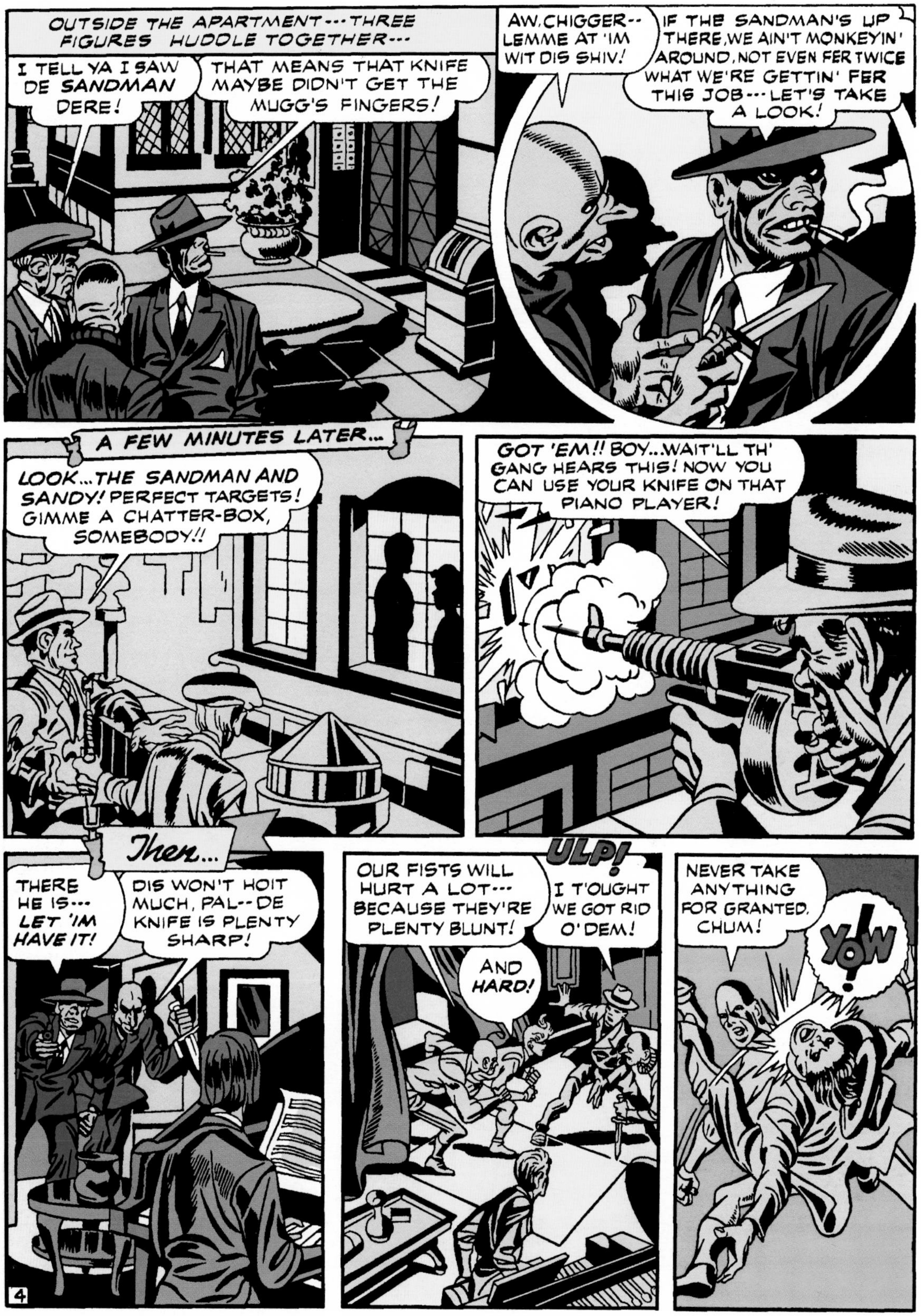
OUTSIDE THE APARTMENT--- THREE FIGURES HUDDLE TOGETHER---
I TELL YA I SAW DE SANDMAN DERE!
THAT MEANS THAT KNIFE MAYBE DIDN'T GET THE MUGG'S FINGERS!
AW, CHIGGER-- LEMME AT 'IM WIT DIS SHIV!
IF THE SANDMAN'S UP THERE, WE AIN'T MONKEYIN' AROUND, NOT EVEN FER TWICE WHAT WE'RE GETTIN' FER THIS JOB--- LET'S TAKE A LOOK!
A FEW MINUTES LATER...
LOOK...THE SANDMAN AND SANDY! PERFECT TARGETS! GIMME A CHATTER-BOX, SOMEBODY!!
GOT 'EM!! BOY...WAIT'LL TH' GANG HEARS THIS! NOW YOU CAN USE YOUR KNIFE ON THAT PIANO PLAYER!
Then...
THERE HE IS--- LET 'IM HAVE IT!
DIS WON'T HOIT MUCH, PAL-- DE KNIFE IS PLENTY SHARP!
4
ULP!
OUR FISTS WILL HURT A LOT--- BECAUSE THEY'RE PLENTY BLUNT!
I T'OUGHT WE GOT RID O' DEM!
AND HARD!
NEVER TAKE ANYTHING FOR GRANTED, CHUM!
YOW!

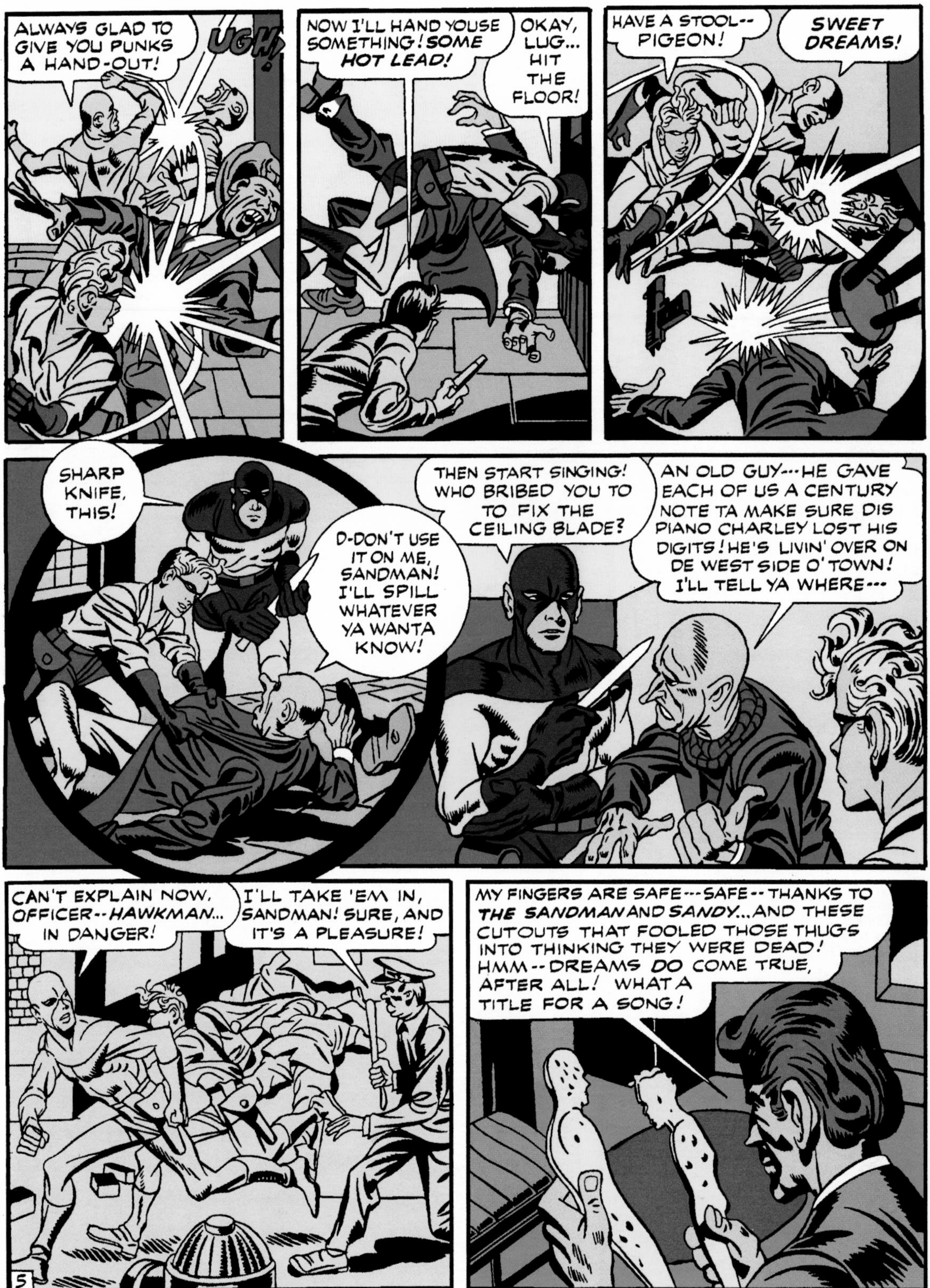
ALWAYS GLAD TO GIVE YOU PUNKS A HAND-OUT!
UGH!
NOW I'LL HAND YOUSE SOMETHING! SOME HOT LEAD!
OKAY, LUG... HIT THE FLOOR!
HAVE A STOOL-- PIGEON!
SWEET DREAMS!
SHARP KNIFE, THIS!
D-DON'T USE IT ON ME, SANDMAN! I'LL SPILL WHATEVER YA WANTA KNOW!
THEN START SINGING! WHO BRIBED YOU TO TO FIX THE CEILING BLADE?
AN OLD GUY--- HE GAVE EACH OF US A CENTURY NOTE TA MAKE SURE DIS PIANO CHARLEY LOST HIS DIGITS! HE'S LIVIN' OVER ON DE WEST SIDE O' TOWN! I'LL TELL YA WHERE---
CAN'T EXPLAIN NOW, OFFICER-- HAWKMAN... IN DANGER!
I'LL TAKE 'EM IN, SANDMAN! SURE, AND IT'S A PLEASURE!
5
MY FINGERS ARE SAFE---SAFE-- THANKS TO THE SANDMAN AND SANDY... AND THESE CUTOUTS THAT FOOLED THOSE THUGS INTO THINKING THEY WERE DEAD! HMM-- DREAMS DO COME TRUE, AFTER ALL! WHAT A TITLE FOR A SONG!

The SANDMAN appears in every issue of Adventure Comics!

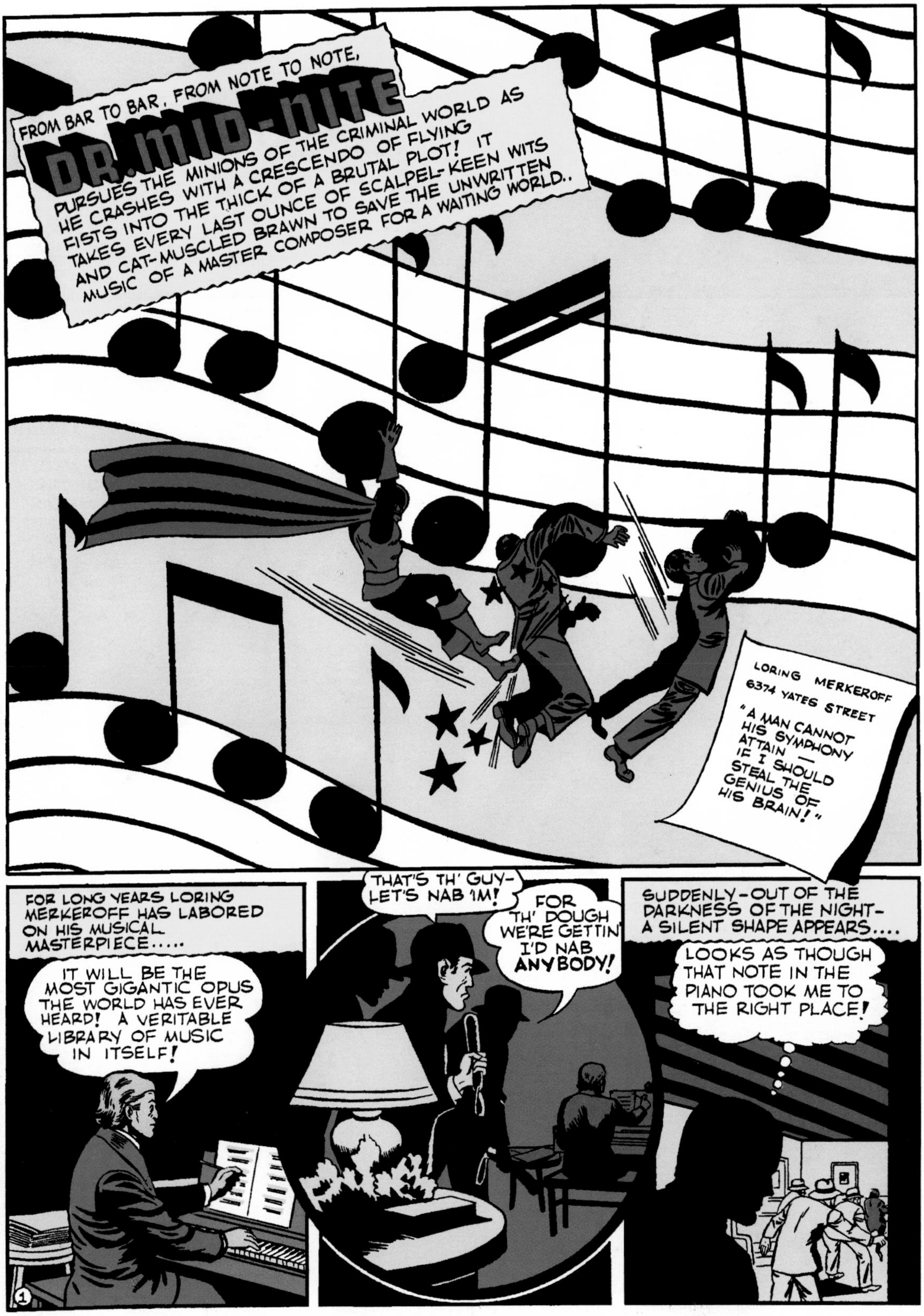
FROM BAR TO BAR, FROM NOTE TO NOTE,
DR. MID-NITE
PURSUES THE MINIONS OF THE CRIMINAL WORLD AS HE CRASHES WITH A CRESCENDO OF FLYING FISTS INTO THE THICK OF A BRUTAL PLOT! IT TAKES EVERY LAST OUNCE OF SCALPEL-KEEN WITS AND CAT-MUSCLED BRAWN TO SAVE THE UNWRITTEN MUSIC OF A MASTER COMPOSER FOR A WAITING WORLD..
LORING MERKEROFF
6374 YATES STREET
"A MAN CANNOT HIS SYMPHONY ATTAIN — IF I SHOULD STEAL THE GENIUS OF HIS BRAIN!"
FOR LONG YEARS LORING MERKEROFF HAS LABORED ON HIS MUSICAL MASTERPIECE.....
IT WILL BE THE MOST GIGANTIC OPUS THE WORLD HAS EVER HEARD! A VERITABLE LIBRARY OF MUSIC IN ITSELF!
1
THAT'S TH' GUY-LET'S NAB 'IM!
FOR TH' DOUGH WE'RE GETTIN' I'D NAB ANYBODY!
SUDDENLY-OUT OF THE DARKNESS OF THE NIGHT-A SILENT SHAPE APPEARS....
LOOKS AS THOUGH THAT NOTE IN THE PIANO TOOK ME TO THE RIGHT PLACE!

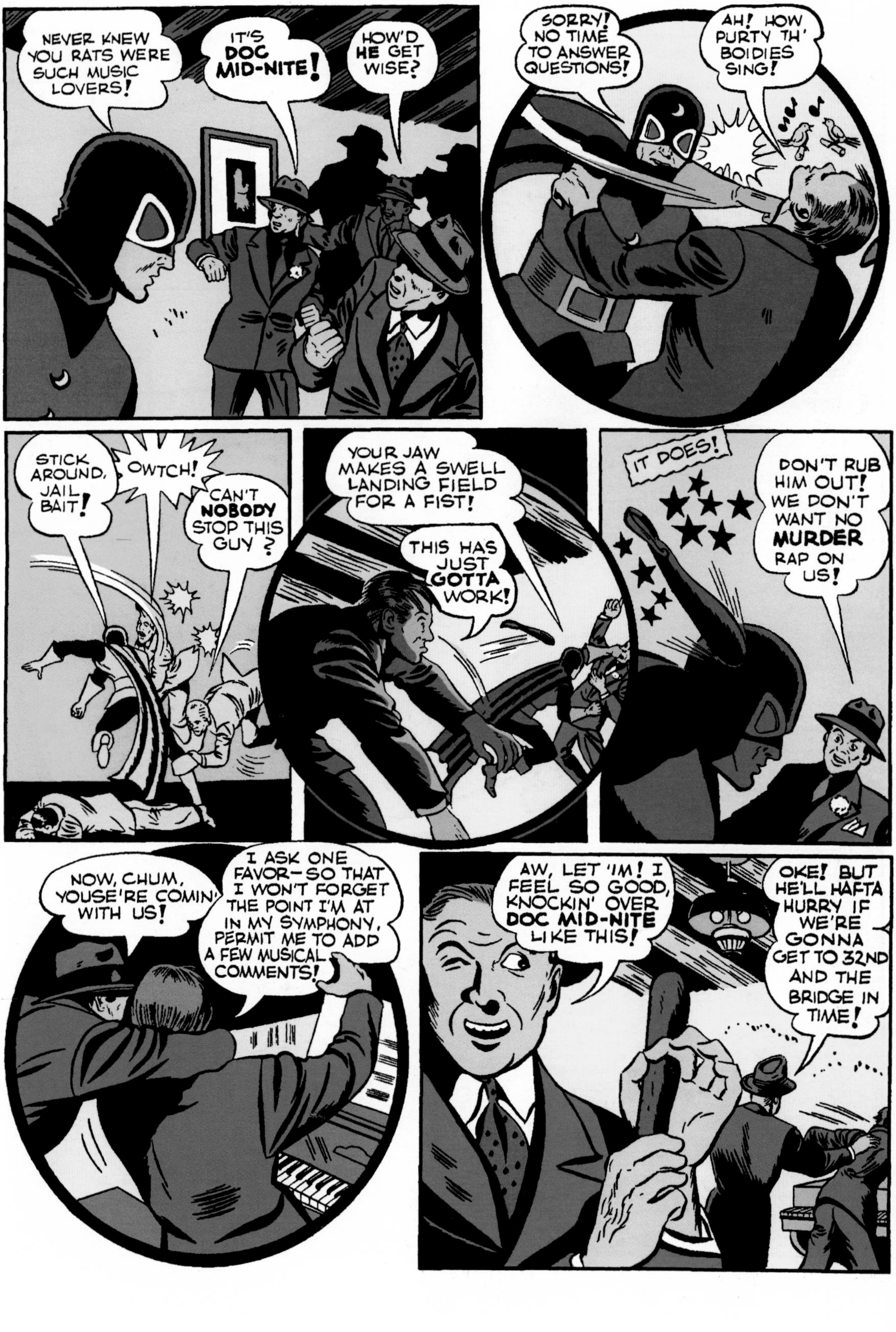
NEVER KNEW YOU RATS WERE SUCH MUSIC LOVERS!
IT'S DOC MID-NITE!
HOW'D HE GET WISE?
SORRY! NO TIME TO ANSWER QUESTIONS!
AH! HOW PURTY TH' BOIDIES SING!
STICK AROUND, JAIL BAIT!
OWTCH!
CAN'T NOBODY STOP THIS GUY ?
YOUR JAW MAKES A SWELL LANDING FIELD FOR A FIST!
THIS HAS JUST GOTTA WORK!
IT DOES!
DON'T RUB HIM OUT! WE DON'T WANT NO MURDER RAP ON US!
NOW, CHUM, YOUSE'RE COMIN' WITH US!
I ASK ONE FAVOR—SO THAT I WON'T FORGET THE POINT I'M AT IN MY SYMPHONY, PERMIT ME TO ADD A FEW MUSICAL COMMENTS!
AW, LET 'IM! I FEEL SO GOOD, KNOCKIN' OVER DOC MID-NITE LIKE THIS!
OKE! BUT HE'LL HAFTA HURRY IF WE'RE GONNA GET TO 32ND AND THE BRIDGE IN TIME!

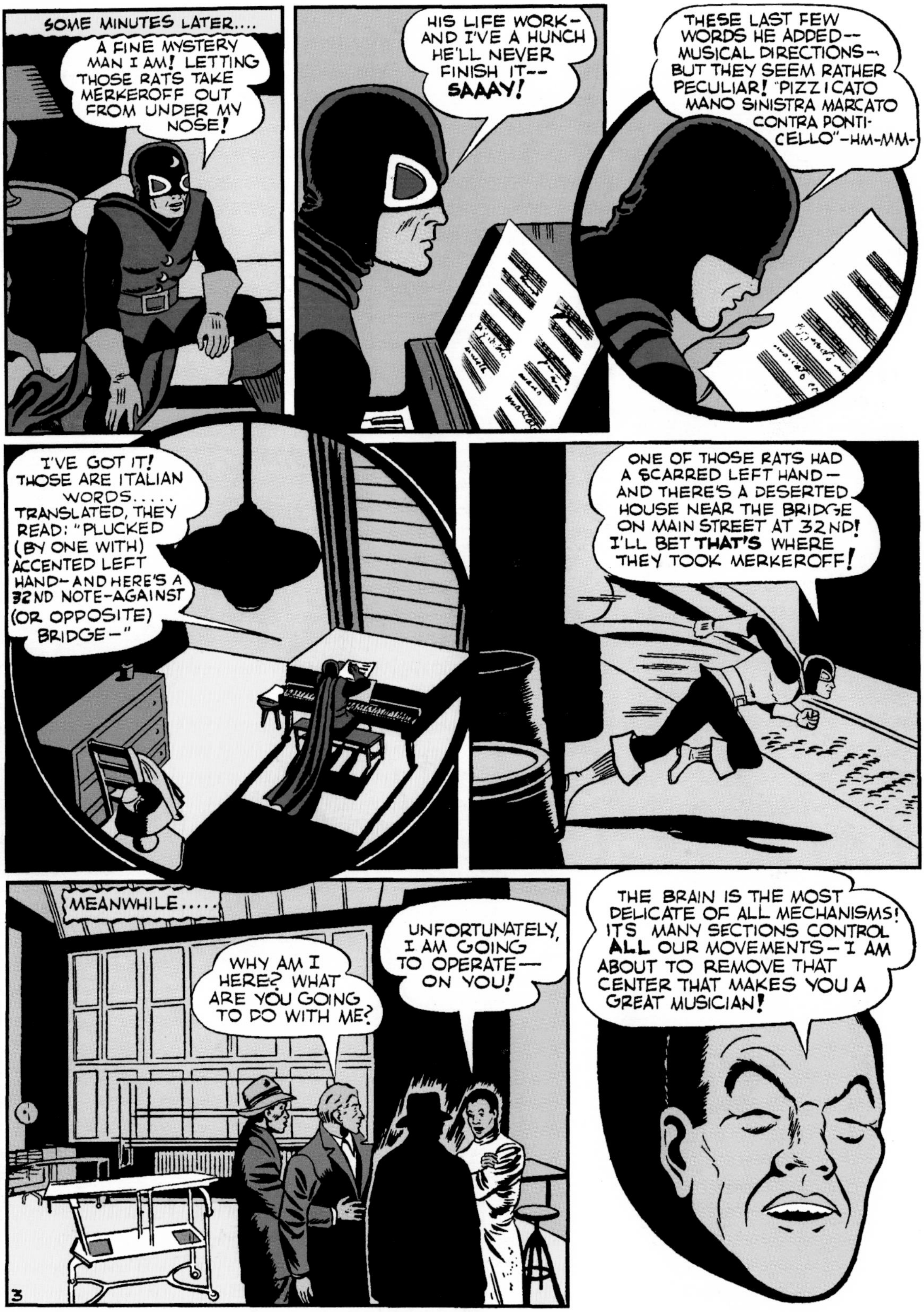
SOME MINUTES LATER....
A FINE MYSTERY MAN I AM! LETTING THOSE RATS TAKE MERKEROFF OUT FROM UNDER MY NOSE!
HIS LIFE WORK-AND I'VE A HUNCH HE'LL NEVER FINISH IT-- SAAAY!
THESE LAST FEW WORDS HE ADDED--MUSICAL DIRECTIONS--BUT THEY SEEM RATHER PECULIAR! "PIZZICATO MANO SINISTRA MARCATO CONTRA PONTI-CELLO"-HM-MM-
I'VE GOT IT! THOSE ARE ITALIAN WORDS..... TRANSLATED, THEY READ: "PLUCKED (BY ONE WITH) ACCENTED LEFT HAND-AND HERE'S A 32ND NOTE-AGAINST (OR OPPOSITE) BRIDGE-"
ONE OF THOSE RATS HAD A SCARRED LEFT HAND-AND THERE'S A DESERTED HOUSE NEAR THE BRIDGE ON MAIN STREET AT 32ND! I'LL BET THAT'S WHERE THEY TOOK MERKEROFF!
MEANWHILE.....
WHY AM I HERE? WHAT ARE YOU GOING TO DO WITH ME?
UNFORTUNATELY, I AM GOING TO OPERATE--ON YOU!
3
THE BRAIN IS THE MOST DELICATE OF ALL MECHANISMS! ITS MANY SECTIONS CONTROL ALL OUR MOVEMENTS-I AM ABOUT TO REMOVE THAT CENTER THAT MAKES YOU A GREAT MUSICIAN!

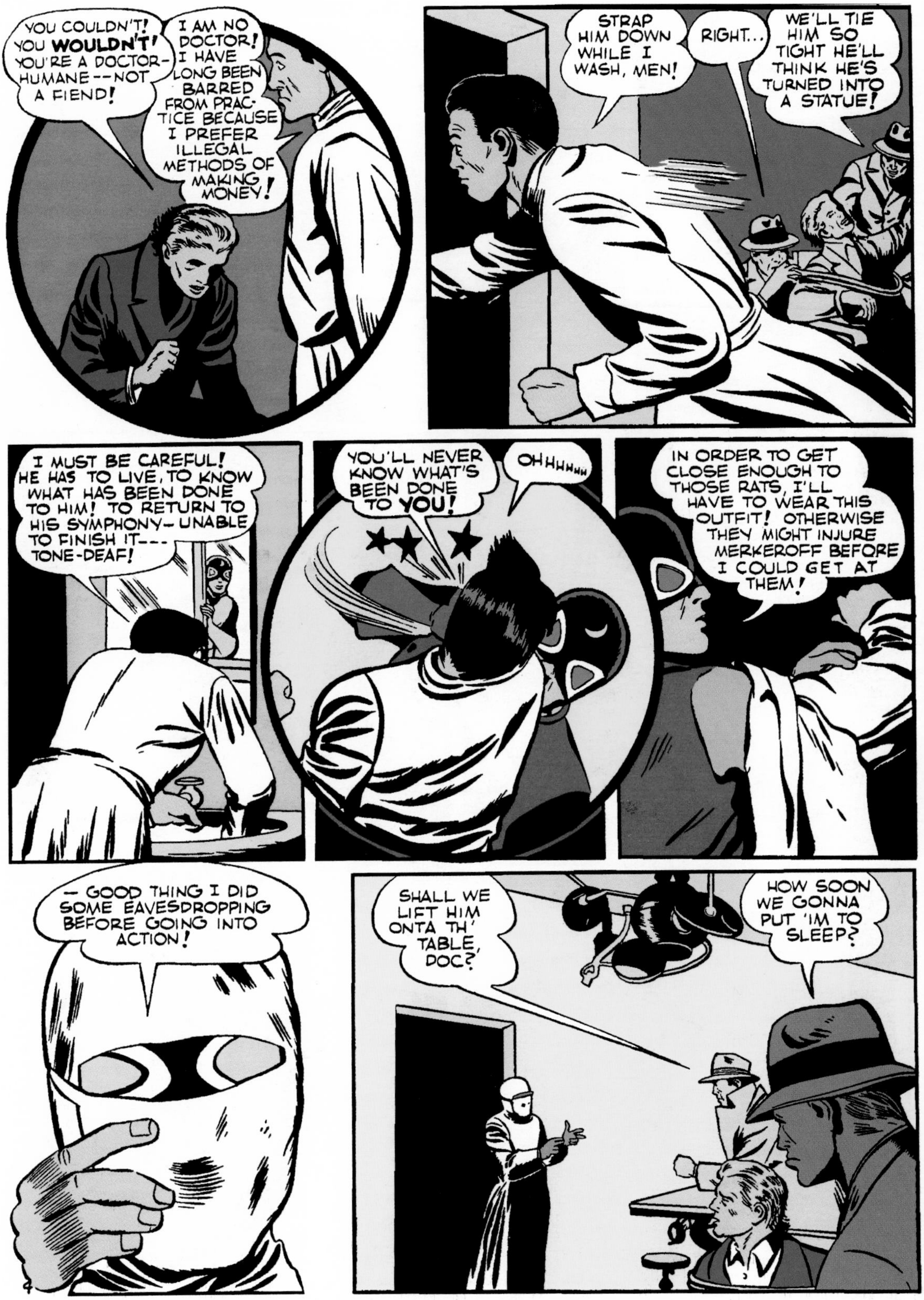
YOU COULDN'T! YOU WOULDN'T! YOU'RE A DOCTOR-HUMANE--NOT A FIEND!
I AM NO DOCTOR! I HAVE LONG BEEN BARRED FROM PRACTICE BECAUSE I PREFER ILLEGAL METHODS OF MAKING MONEY!
STRAP HIM DOWN WHILE I WASH, MEN!
RIGHT...
WE'LL TIE HIM SO TIGHT HE'LL THINK HE'S TURNED INTO A STATUE!
I MUST BE CAREFUL! HE HAS TO LIVE, TO KNOW WHAT HAS BEEN DONE TO HIM! TO RETURN TO HIS SYMPHONY- UNABLE TO FINISH IT--- TONE-DEAF!
YOU'LL NEVER KNOW WHAT'S BEEN DONE TO YOU!
OHHHHHH
IN ORDER TO GET CLOSE ENOUGH TO THOSE RATS, I'LL HAVE TO WEAR THIS OUTFIT! OTHERWISE THEY MIGHT INJURE MERKEROFF BEFORE I COULD GET AT THEM!
-GOOD THING I DID SOME EAVESDROPPING BEFORE GOING INTO ACTION!
SHALL WE LIFT HIM ONTA TH' TABLE, DOC?
HOW SOON WE GONNA PUT 'IM TO SLEEP?

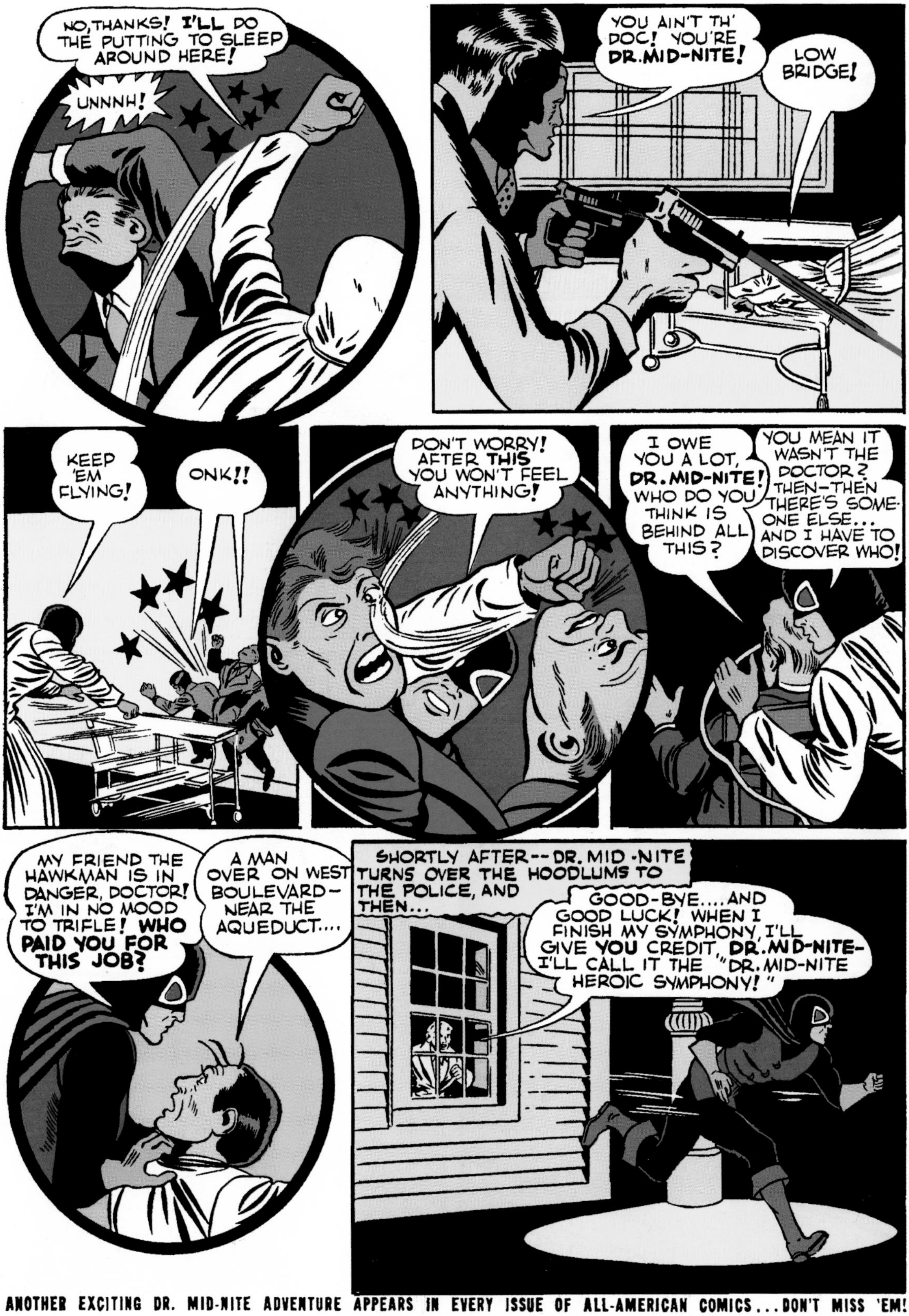
NO, THANKS! I'LL DO THE PUTTING TO SLEEP AROUND HERE!
UNNNH!
YOU AIN'T TH' DOC! YOU'RE DR. MID-NITE!
LOW BRIDGE!
KEEP 'EM FLYING!
ONK!!
DON'T WORRY! AFTER THIS YOU WON'T FEEL ANYTHING!
I OWE YOU A LOT, DR. MID-NITE! WHO DO YOU THINK IS BEHIND ALL THIS?
YOU MEAN IT WASN'T THE DOCTOR? THEN—THEN THERE'S SOME-ONE ELSE... AND I HAVE TO DISCOVER WHO!
MY FRIEND THE HAWKMAN IS IN DANGER, DOCTOR! I'M IN NO MOOD TO TRIFLE! WHO PAID YOU FOR THIS JOB?
A MAN OVER ON WEST BOULEVARD— NEAR THE AQUEDUCT....
SHORTLY AFTER-- DR. MID-NITE TURNS OVER THE HOODLUMS TO THE POLICE, AND THEN...
GOOD-BYE....AND GOOD LUCK! WHEN I FINISH MY SYMPHONY, I'LL GIVE YOU CREDIT, DR. MID-NITE- I'LL CALL IT THE "DR. MID-NITE HEROIC SYMPHONY!"

ANOTHER EXCITING DR. MID-NITE ADVENTURE APPEARS IN EVERY ISSUE OF ALL-AMERICAN COMICS...DON'T MISS 'EM!

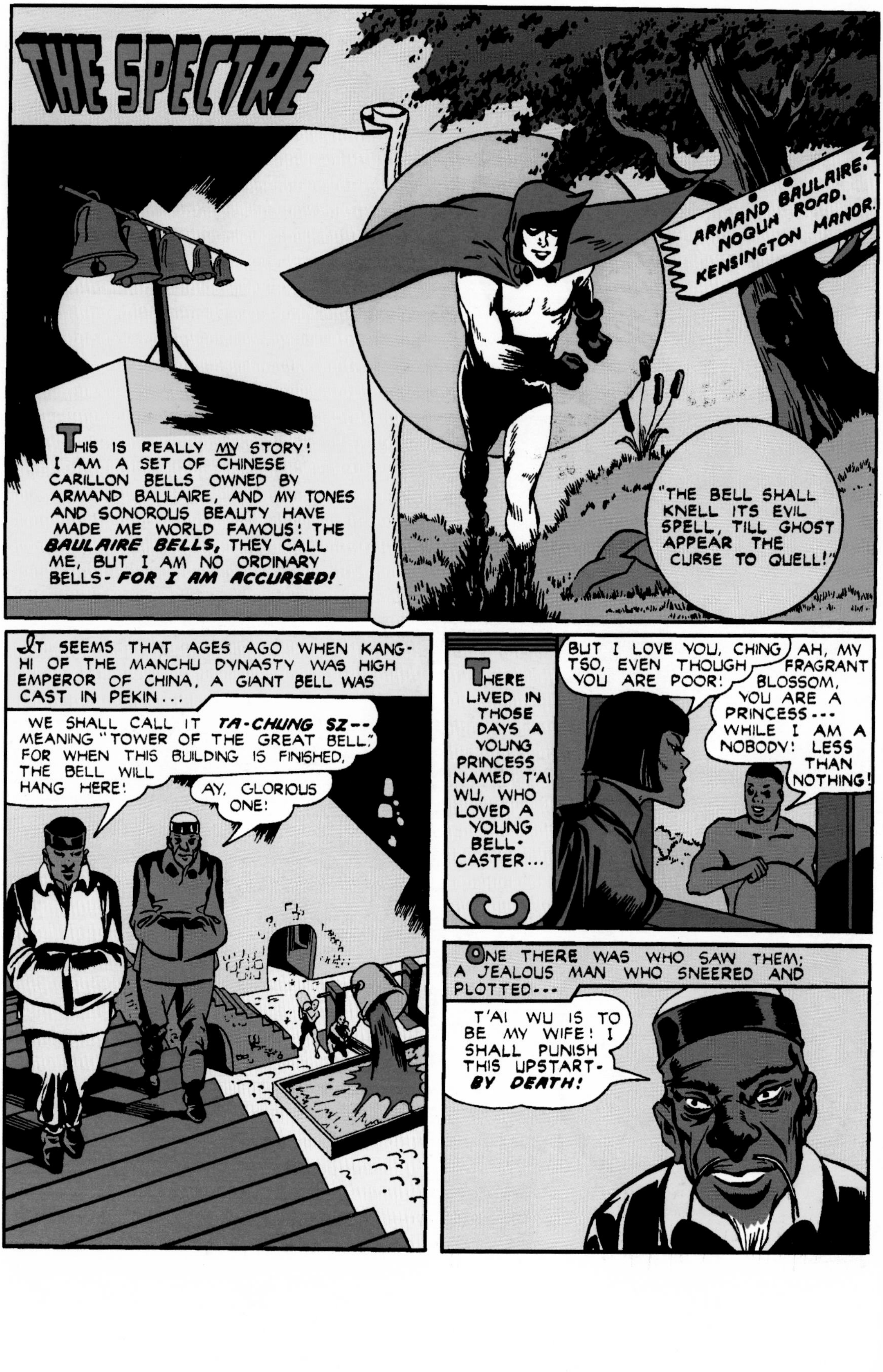
THE SPECTRE
ARMAND BAULAIRE, NOGUH ROAD, KENSINGTON MANOR.
THIS IS REALLY MY STORY! I AM A SET OF CHINESE CARILLON BELLS OWNED BY ARMAND BAULAIRE, AND MY TONES AND SONOROUS BEAUTY HAVE MADE ME WORLD FAMOUS: THE BAULAIRE BELLS, THEY CALL ME, BUT I AM NO ORDINARY BELLS- FOR I AM ACCURSED!
"THE BELL SHALL KNELL ITS EVIL SPELL, TILL GHOST APPEAR THE CURSE TO QUELL!"
IT SEEMS THAT AGES AGO WHEN KANG-HI OF THE MANCHU DYNASTY WAS HIGH EMPEROR OF CHINA, A GIANT BELL WAS CAST IN PEKIN...
WE SHALL CALL IT TA-CHUNG SZ-- MEANING "TOWER OF THE GREAT BELL." FOR WHEN THIS BUILDING IS FINISHED, THE BELL WILL HANG HERE!
AY, GLORIOUS ONE!
THERE LIVED IN THOSE DAYS A YOUNG PRINCESS NAMED T'AI WU, WHO LOVED A YOUNG BELL-CASTER...
BUT I LOVE YOU, CHING TSO, EVEN THOUGH YOU ARE POOR!
AH, MY FRAGRANT BLOSSOM, YOU ARE A PRINCESS--- WHILE I AM A NOBODY! LESS THAN NOTHING!
ONE THERE WAS WHO SAW THEM: A JEALOUS MAN WHO SNEERED AND PLOTTED---
T'AI WU IS TO BE MY WIFE! I SHALL PUNISH THIS UPSTART- BY DEATH!

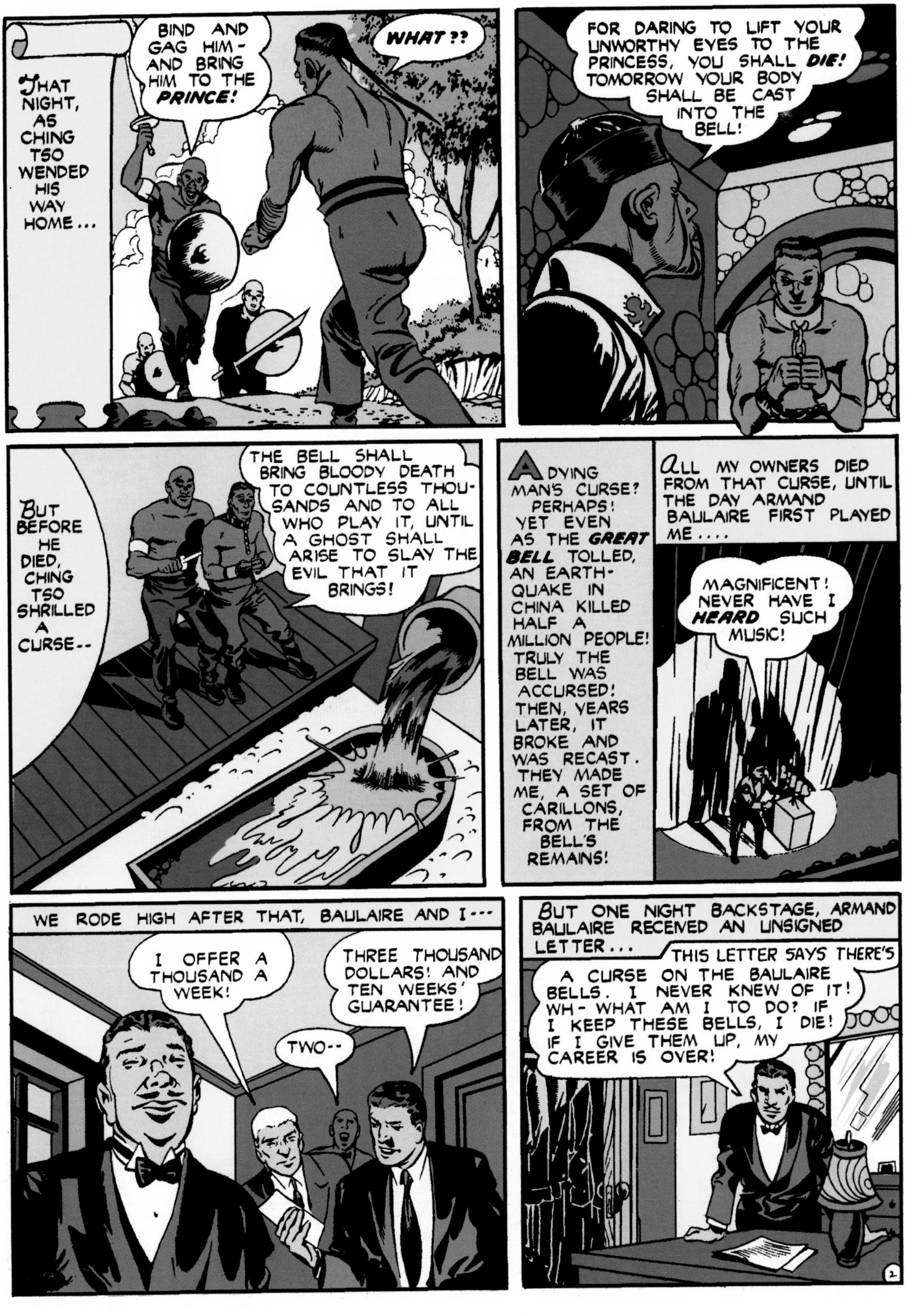
THAT NIGHT, AS CHING TSO WENDED HIS WAY HOME...
BIND AND GAG HIM - AND BRING HIM TO THE PRINCE!
WHAT??
FOR DARING TO LIFT YOUR UNWORTHY EYES TO THE PRINCESS, YOU SHALL DIE! TOMORROW YOUR BODY SHALL BE CAST INTO THE BELL!
BUT BEFORE HE DIED, CHING TSO SHRILLED A CURSE--
THE BELL SHALL BRING BLOODY DEATH TO COUNTLESS THOUSANDS AND TO ALL WHO PLAY IT, UNTIL A GHOST SHALL ARISE TO SLAY THE EVIL THAT IT BRINGS!
A DYING MAN'S CURSE? PERHAPS! YET EVEN AS THE GREAT BELL TOLLED, AN EARTHQUAKE IN CHINA KILLED HALF A MILLION PEOPLE! TRULY THE BELL WAS ACCURSED! THEN, YEARS LATER, IT BROKE AND WAS RECAST. THEY MADE ME, A SET OF CARILLONS, FROM THE BELL'S REMAINS!
ALL MY OWNERS DIED FROM THAT CURSE, UNTIL THE DAY ARMAND BAULAIRE FIRST PLAYED ME....
MAGNIFICENT! NEVER HAVE I HEARD SUCH MUSIC!
WE RODE HIGH AFTER THAT, BAULAIRE AND I---
I OFFER A THOUSAND A WEEK!
TWO--
THREE THOUSAND DOLLARS! AND TEN WEEKS' GUARANTEE!
BUT ONE NIGHT BACKSTAGE, ARMAND BAULAIRE RECEIVED AN UNSIGNED LETTER...
THIS LETTER SAYS THERE'S A CURSE ON THE BAULAIRE BELLS. I NEVER KNEW OF IT! WH- WHAT AM I TO DO? IF I KEEP THESE BELLS, I DIE! IF I GIVE THEM UP, MY CAREER IS OVER!
2

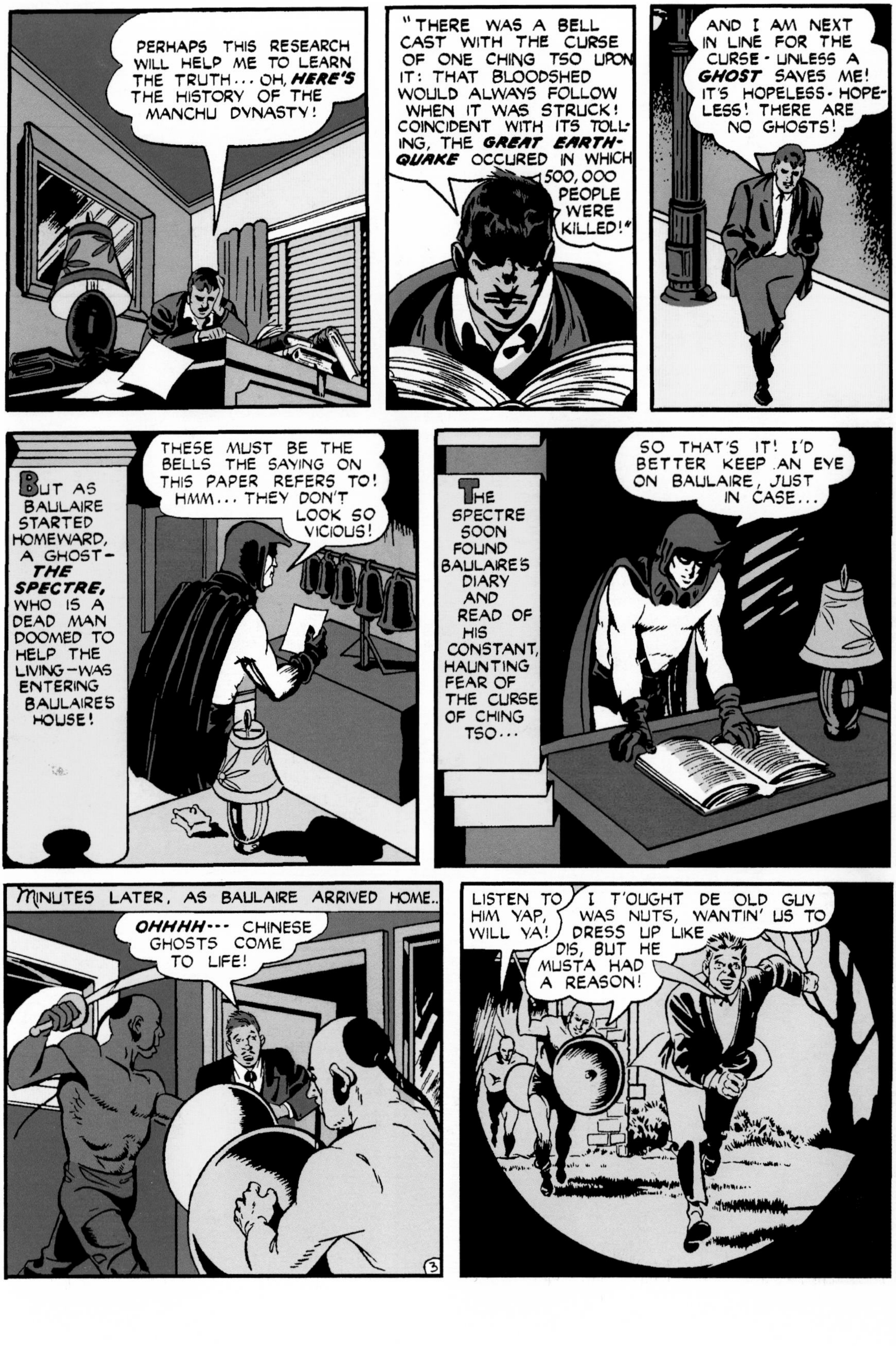
PERHAPS THIS RESEARCH WILL HELP ME TO LEARN THE TRUTH... OH, **HERE'S** THE HISTORY OF THE MANCHU DYNASTY!
"THERE WAS A BELL CAST WITH THE CURSE OF ONE CHING TSO UPON IT: THAT BLOODSHED WOULD ALWAYS FOLLOW WHEN IT WAS STRUCK! COINCIDENT WITH ITS TOLLING, THE **GREAT EARTHQUAKE** OCCURED IN WHICH 500,000 PEOPLE WERE KILLED!"
AND I AM NEXT IN LINE FOR THE CURSE - UNLESS A **GHOST** SAVES ME! IT'S HOPELESS- HOPELESS! THERE ARE NO GHOSTS!
BUT AS BAULAIRE STARTED HOMEWARD, A GHOST- **THE SPECTRE,** WHO IS A DEAD MAN DOOMED TO HELP THE LIVING-WAS ENTERING BAULAIRE'S HOUSE!
THESE MUST BE THE BELLS THE SAYING ON THIS PAPER REFERS TO! HMM... THEY DON'T LOOK SO VICIOUS!
THE SPECTRE SOON FOUND BAULAIRE'S DIARY AND READ OF HIS CONSTANT, HAUNTING FEAR OF THE CURSE OF CHING TSO...
SO THAT'S IT! I'D BETTER KEEP AN EYE ON BAULAIRE, JUST IN CASE...
MINUTES LATER, AS BAULAIRE ARRIVED HOME..
OHHHH--- CHINESE GHOSTS COME TO LIFE!
3
LISTEN TO HIM YAP, WILL YA!
I T'OUGHT DE OLD GUY WAS NUTS, WANTIN' US TO DRESS UP LIKE DIS, BUT HE MUSTA HAD A REASON!

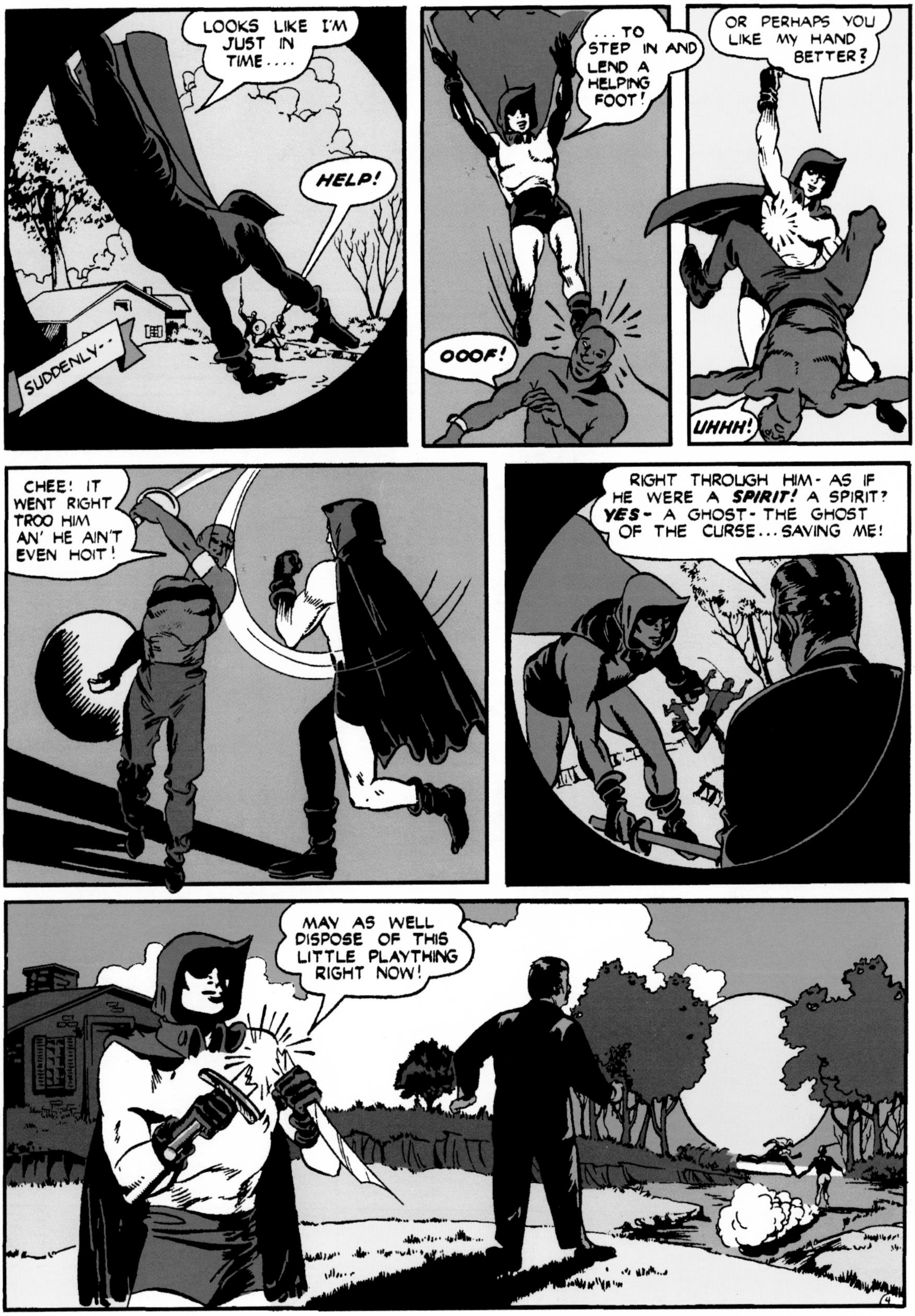
LOOKS LIKE I'M JUST IN TIME....
HELP!
SUDDENLY--
...TO STEP IN AND LEND A HELPING FOOT!
OOOF!
OR PERHAPS YOU LIKE MY HAND BETTER?
UHHH!
CHEE! IT WENT RIGHT TROO HIM AN' HE AIN'T EVEN HOIT!
RIGHT THROUGH HIM- AS IF HE WERE A SPIRIT! A SPIRIT? YES- A GHOST- THE GHOST OF THE CURSE... SAVING ME!
MAY AS WELL DISPOSE OF THIS LITTLE PLAYTHING RIGHT NOW!

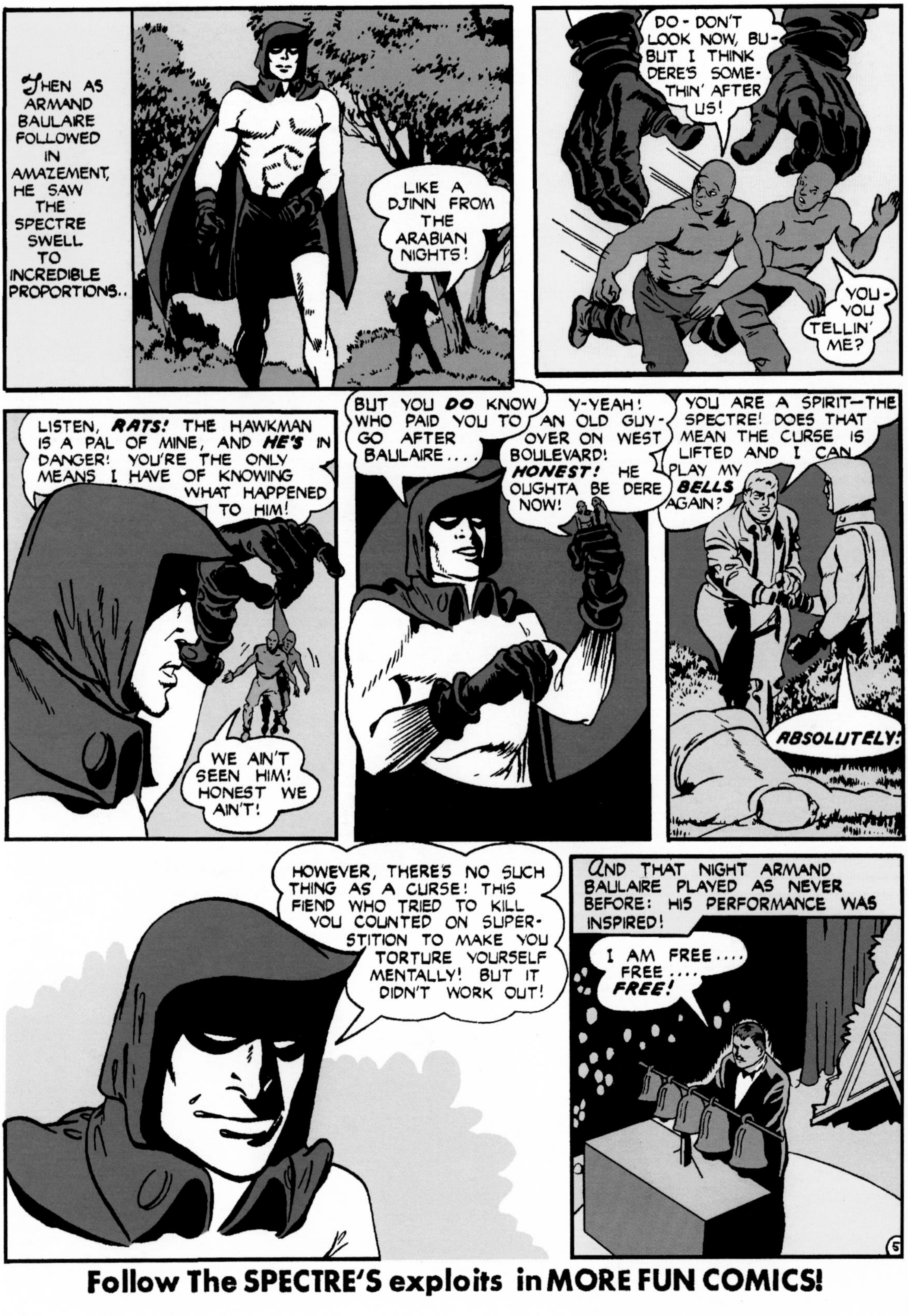
THEN AS ARMAND BAULAIRE FOLLOWED IN AMAZEMENT, HE SAW THE SPECTRE SWELL TO INCREDIBLE PROPORTIONS..
LIKE A DJINN FROM THE ARABIAN NIGHTS!
DO - DON'T LOOK NOW, BU- BUT I THINK DERE'S SOME- THIN' AFTER US!
YOU- YOU TELLIN' ME?
LISTEN, RATS! THE HAWKMAN IS A PAL OF MINE, AND HE'S IN DANGER! YOU'RE THE ONLY MEANS I HAVE OF KNOWING WHAT HAPPENED TO HIM!
WE AIN'T SEEN HIM! HONEST WE AIN'T!
BUT YOU DO KNOW WHO PAID YOU TO GO AFTER BAULAIRE....
Y-YEAH! AN OLD GUY- OVER ON WEST BOULEVARD! HONEST! HE OUGHTA BE DERE NOW!
YOU ARE A SPIRIT—THE SPECTRE! DOES THAT MEAN THE CURSE IS LIFTED AND I CAN PLAY MY BELLS AGAIN?
ABSOLUTELY!
HOWEVER, THERE'S NO SUCH THING AS A CURSE! THIS FIEND WHO TRIED TO KILL YOU COUNTED ON SUPER- STITION TO MAKE YOU TORTURE YOURSELF MENTALLY! BUT IT DIDN'T WORK OUT!
AND THAT NIGHT ARMAND BAULAIRE PLAYED AS NEVER BEFORE: HIS PERFORMANCE WAS INSPIRED!
I AM FREE.... FREE.... FREE!
5

Follow The SPECTRE'S exploits in MORE FUN COMICS!

HOP HARRIGAN over TORRES STRAIT

JON L. BLUMMER'S
HOP HARRIGAN STORIES
APPEAR IN
EVERY ISSUE OF
ALL-AMERICAN COMICS

COLONEL BRYSON looked up from his desk in the small shack that was field headquarters.

"Job for you, Harrigan," he said, tersely. "A hospital ship left the Cape a couple of days ago, to pick up wounded at Port Moresby. It hasn't shown up—and neither has any information as to its whereabouts.

"It's just possible that it was hit and is limping around somewhere in the Torres Strait. Or it may have received an S.O.S. and gone off course to pick up survivors. We don't know. That's your job—to find out.

"A B-25 is warming up on the field. The rest of the crew have been told to report. That's all, Harrigan—and good luck!"

Hop gripped the Colonel's hand, saluted, and went out. He met the rest of the crew on the tarmac. Tank Tinker, his flying mate, was bombardier and gunner on this trip. Hop and Tank sprinted into the ship. Hastings, navigator and radio operator, and tail-gunner Powers climbed after.

In the fast Mitchell, they were all set for trouble—not only to take it, but to dish it out!

Hop nosed the ship up to a thousand. He banked, then headed for Cape York, Australia. From that point, the mercy ship had started out for Port Moresby. The most sensible course, Hop decided, was to fly across the Torres Strait, along the same route the Red Cross ship should have taken.

Cruising along at ten thousand, a glance in the rear-view mirror snapped Hop to alertness. Three Zeros were tearing after the bomber, in pitchfork formation.

Hop rapped into the intercom, "Get those peashooters warmed up, Tank! Trouble's right on our tail!"

"Let 'em come!" Tank's voice boomed from the nose. "I got a royal welcome for 'em!"

"My typewriter's all set, too!" called Powers, in the tail, as he cut loose with the m.g.'s.

A tracer stitched across one wing of the leading Zero. But the Jap was fast. He nosed his plane down right under the Mitchell and angled for a belly attack. At the same time, the two other Zeros whipped overhead.

"Hey, they're crowding us!" Hop yelled. "Pour it on 'em, boys! Send 'em running!"

The Japs were obviously counting on their maneuver confusing the Yank pilot. Hop, ignoring the two Zeros above, looped down swiftly and came up *below* the lowest Zero! Then the Jap was taking an underside burst instead of giving! The dazed look stayed on the Nip's face as his plane coughed flame and fell away.

Between a withering crossfire, Hop climbed the Mitchell. Lead flung at the ship made it jerk and buckle, as Hop shot her into the sun. Then, in a swift turn, he met the second surprised Jap head-on, and Tank Tinker poured lead.

Hop had no time to watch the crash. The third Jap's slugs were whining uncomfortably close about his head.

Hop kicked right rudder and the ship rocked into a new position. A stream of American bullets hit the enemy's gas tank. The Zero blew up in midair. Pieces of wreckage hurtled down, disappeared in the altocumulus below. Hop watched, feeling strange.

"That fluffy stuff down there looks like cotton," he muttered, watching the clouds. "You'd almost think it could hold up those falling pieces of plane—"

"Hey, you're talking crazy—" Tank began. Then he saw Hop's arm. "You're hit!"

"I'm okay!" Hop said, harshly. "How about the others? Anyone hit?"

"Hastings got it in the head. Powers fixed up a bandage, and he'll be okay when we get back to base. No one else hit—but you. What now, Hop?"

Hop said, "That dogfight took us off our course!" He looked at the instrument board for the compass. There was no compass! It had been shot away!

"Hastings, we're off course!" Harrigan called into the intercom. "Get working on that radio. Get us a bearing."

No answer came, so Hop observed, "He must have passed out. I'll get the bearing myself. Take over, Tank."

Tank sat down at the wheel, took the plane down through the fluffy cloud formation to normal cruising range of ten thousand. When he came out of the cloud, he whooped for joy. There it was—the hospital ship!

"Hop!" he boomed, "forget about finding our course! We're here! Thar she blows—the hospital ship—and she's right as rain! Sailing along nice as you please!"

Hop came out of the cabin saying, "I'll take over, Tank."

He dove the Mitchell until she was barely skimming the water, just a hundred feet up. Then he opened machine gun fire at the Red Cross ship! Tank stared, slack-jawed.

HEAR HOP HARRIGAN ON YOUR RADIO—MONDAYS THROUGH FRIDAYS—

"My best pal—daft!" he bleated. "Hop, y-you must be d-delirious!"

He lunged at Hop, but Hop's good arm streaked out and flung the redhead against the cabin wall. Gritting his teeth, Tank inched toward Hop, huddled over the wheel. He hated to do this, but—

The plane wobbled crazily. It had been struck by shellfire! Then Tank saw, and understood. Belching up at them from the decks of the Red Cross ship were anti-aircraft guns!

"I was right!" breathed Hop, painfully. "Get down in your nest! Do your stuff!"

Tank didn't need to be told twice. He moved faster than Hop had ever seen! As Hop zoomed the Mitchell to twelve-hundred, Tank aimed the ship in his bombsight and sent a five-hundred-pounder hurtling down.

"Bull's-eye!" yelled Tank.

The ship was in two pieces, capsizing before their eyes! Hop circled, watching with grim satisfaction, then lifted the plane and winged back toward base.

"You were right, all right!" gasped Tank. "The ship was manned by Japs! But heck, Hop, how did you *know* it?"

"R a d i o," explained Hop, briefly. "When I turned it on to get our bearings, I heard Jap voices jabbering. Then, the second we hove into sight from those clouds, the voices stopped! That made me think they were coming from the hospital ship, and that we'd been spotted by the Nips!

"I couldn't afford to make a mistake! I machine-gunned the ship, *deliberately missing*, to see what would happen. When the big guns opened up, I knew that the hospital ship had been captured by the Japs! Imagine, Tank, we might have *escorted* t h a t Trojan Horse right into Port Moresby!

"As it was, we bagged three Zeros and a whole boatload of Nips! That makes up a little —for *one* of the Americans they killed!"

THE END

on the BLUE NETWORK

On Silver Wings

★ ★ ★ ★ ★

The true story of Sergeant George Philip Corl, U. S. Army Air Forces, whose parents received the second Hop Harrigan Award for Flying Heroism

CURLY dashed out of the pay office at the coal mine in Rock Springs, Wyo., just as the morning shift of miners climbed off the little flatcars.

It was a cold day, that 7th of December, 1941, but Curly hadn't stopped to put on his coat or hat.

"Hey, fellers," he shouted excitedly. "Wait a minute! Don't go 'way! Listen!"

Big Butch shouted back, "It can wait till tomorrow! We're tired. We wanna go home now."

"No, no!" Curly had caught up to the miners. "It's war! The Japs just bombed Pearl Harbor! I heard it on the radio!"

The miners stopped walking, then, and it was quiet for a few seconds as the news sank in. Then through their rising voices cut the clear tones of George Philip Corl:

"You, Curly! Gimme my pay, now! I gotta go fight. I got to join up, get in the Army! Why, I got a couple o' kid brothers— no Jap's gonna get a chance to boss *them* around! Come on, Curly, move—gimme my pay!"

And so 21-year-old George went to the recruiting office at Denver and was accepted for the U. S. Army Air Corps.

To Texas, to Florida, he went for training; soon rose to the rank of Sergeant.

Then came another morning, when orders took George across the sea to North Africa. At a bomber base there, he became aerial gunner in the crew of a B-26 Martin Marauder.

The invasion of Sicily was in progress. In the ready room at the base, George was planning a letter home when the loud-speaker called his crew for immediate takeoff.

Up zoomed the squadron in battle formation, over the blue Mediterranean, close to Trapani. The flak came up heavy, scarred the pilot's face; but the B-26 kept to the appointed course, laid its eggs.

Suddenly a machine gun bullet whined close to the starboard gun nest—another, and another, blending with a scream of pain as George Philip Corl writhed on the floor.

"They got me—but not bad enough!" he gasped to Staff Sergeant Ed Bullian. "Help me up, Ed, there's nothin' wrong with my trigger finger . . . look, Ed, there's the Nazi dog. A Messerschmitt. Come on, you Mess— that's it, little more . . . aah! I got 'im, Ed, I got 'im! Look at 'im go down!"

Then George Philip Corl slumped again, and lapsed into a coma. He spoke a few words as the bomber taxied down to its North Africa base, but the three bullets in him had struck too well.

George Philip Corl met his Maker on silver wings on July 11, 1943. In Africa there is a little white cross; in Sicily, a crumpled Messerschmitt; in Denver, a golden star on a service flag that two kid brothers worship. . . .

*   *   *

In the Corl home in Denver, too, there is a $1000.00 War Bond—the second Hop Harrigan Quarterly Award for Flying Heroism, presented to the Sergeant's parents, Mr. and Mrs. Frank Corl, on the nationwide broadcast of the Hop Harrigan radio program over the Blue Network, Sept. 15, 1943.

THE STORY OF SERGEANT GEORGE PHILIP CORL IS TOLD IN FULL COLOR PICTURES IN COMIC CAVALCADE No. 5, NOW ON SALE.

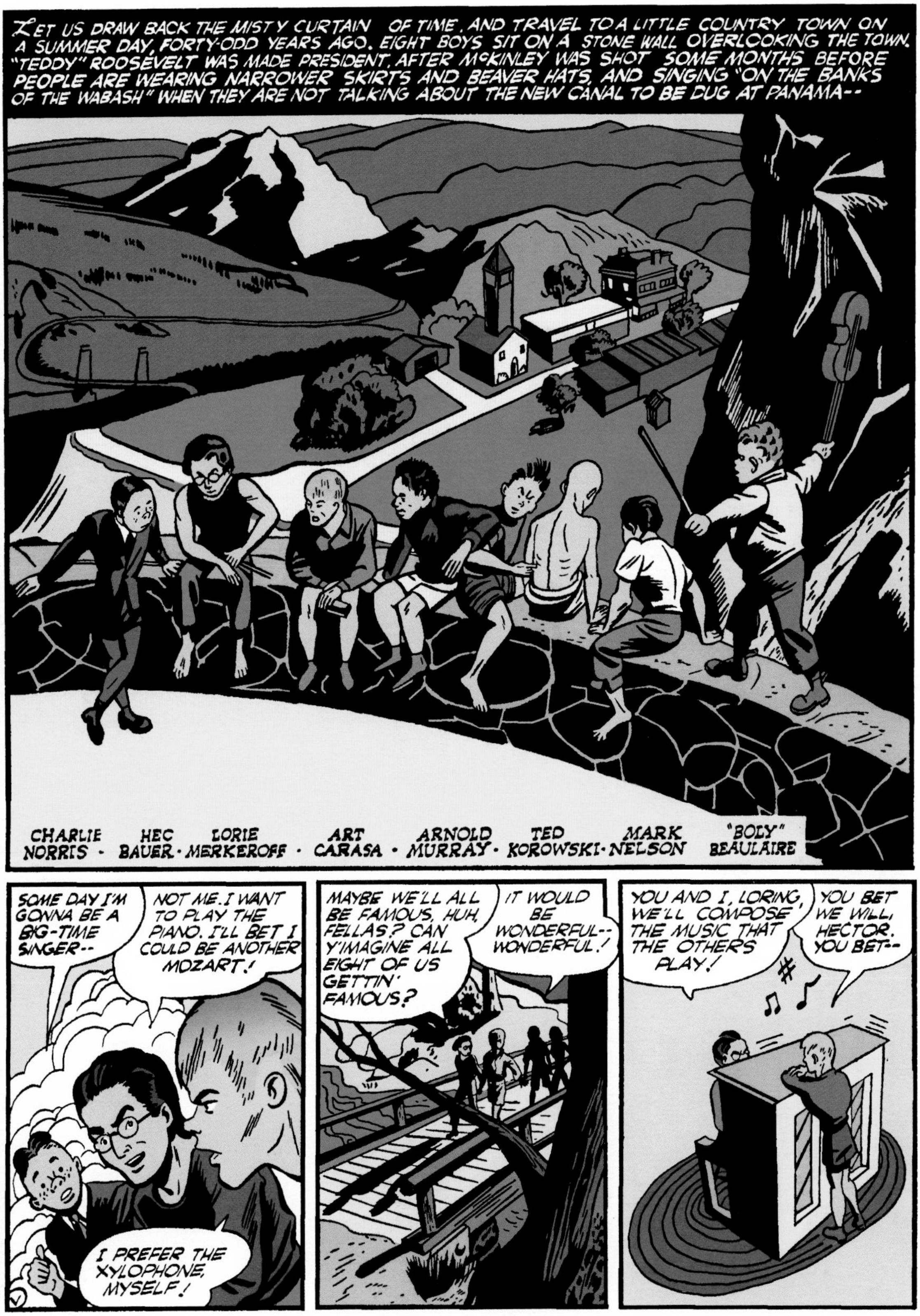
LET US DRAW BACK THE MISTY CURTAIN OF TIME, AND TRAVEL TO A LITTLE COUNTRY TOWN ON A SUMMER DAY, FORTY-ODD YEARS AGO. EIGHT BOYS SIT ON A STONE WALL OVERLOOKING THE TOWN. "TEDDY" ROOSEVELT WAS MADE PRESIDENT, AFTER McKINLEY WAS SHOT SOME MONTHS BEFORE PEOPLE ARE WEARING NARROWER SKIRTS AND BEAVER HATS, AND SINGING "ON THE BANKS OF THE WABASH" WHEN THEY ARE NOT TALKING ABOUT THE NEW CANAL TO BE DUG AT PANAMA--
CHARLIE NORRIS · HEC BAUER · LORIE MERKEROFF · ART CARASA · ARNOLD MURRAY · TED KOROWSKI · MARK NELSON "BOLY" BEAULAIRE
SOME DAY I'M GONNA BE A BIG-TIME SINGER--
NOT ME. I WANT TO PLAY THE PIANO. I'LL BET I COULD BE ANOTHER MOZART!
I PREFER THE XYLOPHONE, MYSELF!
MAYBE WE'LL ALL BE FAMOUS, HUH, FELLAS? CAN Y'IMAGINE ALL EIGHT OF US GETTIN' FAMOUS?
IT WOULD BE WONDERFUL-- WONDERFUL!
YOU AND I, LORING, WE'LL COMPOSE THE MUSIC THAT THE OTHERS PLAY!
YOU BET WE WILL, HECTOR. YOU BET--

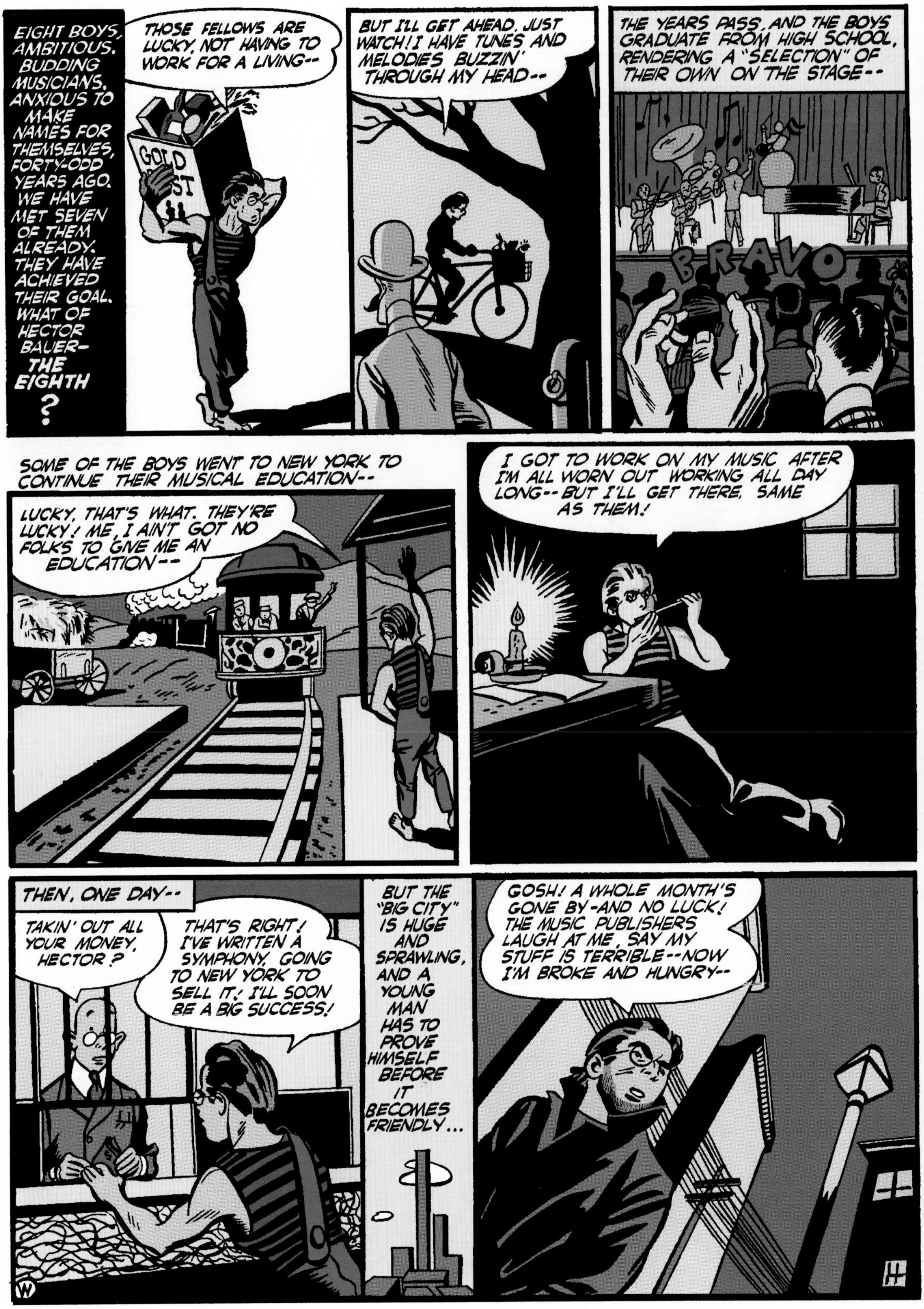

EIGHT BOYS, AMBITIOUS, BUDDING MUSICIANS, ANXIOUS TO MAKE NAMES FOR THEMSELVES, FORTY-ODD YEARS AGO. WE HAVE MET SEVEN OF THEM ALREADY. THEY HAVE ACHIEVED THEIR GOAL. WHAT OF HECTOR BAUER– THE EIGHTH ?
THOSE FELLOWS ARE LUCKY, NOT HAVING TO WORK FOR A LIVING--
BUT I'LL GET AHEAD, JUST WATCH! I HAVE TUNES AND MELODIES BUZZIN' THROUGH MY HEAD--
THE YEARS PASS, AND THE BOYS GRADUATE FROM HIGH SCHOOL, RENDERING A "SELECTION" OF THEIR OWN ON THE STAGE--
BRAVO
SOME OF THE BOYS WENT TO NEW YORK TO CONTINUE THEIR MUSICAL EDUCATION--
LUCKY, THAT'S WHAT. THEY'RE LUCKY! ME, I AIN'T GOT NO FOLKS TO GIVE ME AN EDUCATION--
I GOT TO WORK ON MY MUSIC AFTER I'M ALL WORN OUT WORKING ALL DAY LONG--BUT I'LL GET THERE, SAME AS THEM!
THEN, ONE DAY--
TAKIN' OUT ALL YOUR MONEY, HECTOR?
THAT'S RIGHT! I'VE WRITTEN A SYMPHONY, GOING TO NEW YORK TO SELL IT! I'LL SOON BE A BIG SUCCESS!
BUT THE "BIG CITY" IS HUGE AND SPRAWLING, AND A YOUNG MAN HAS TO PROVE HIMSELF BEFORE IT BECOMES FRIENDLY...
GOSH! A WHOLE MONTH'S GONE BY-AND NO LUCK! THE MUSIC PUBLISHERS LAUGH AT ME, SAY MY STUFF IS TERRIBLE--NOW I'M BROKE AND HUNGRY--

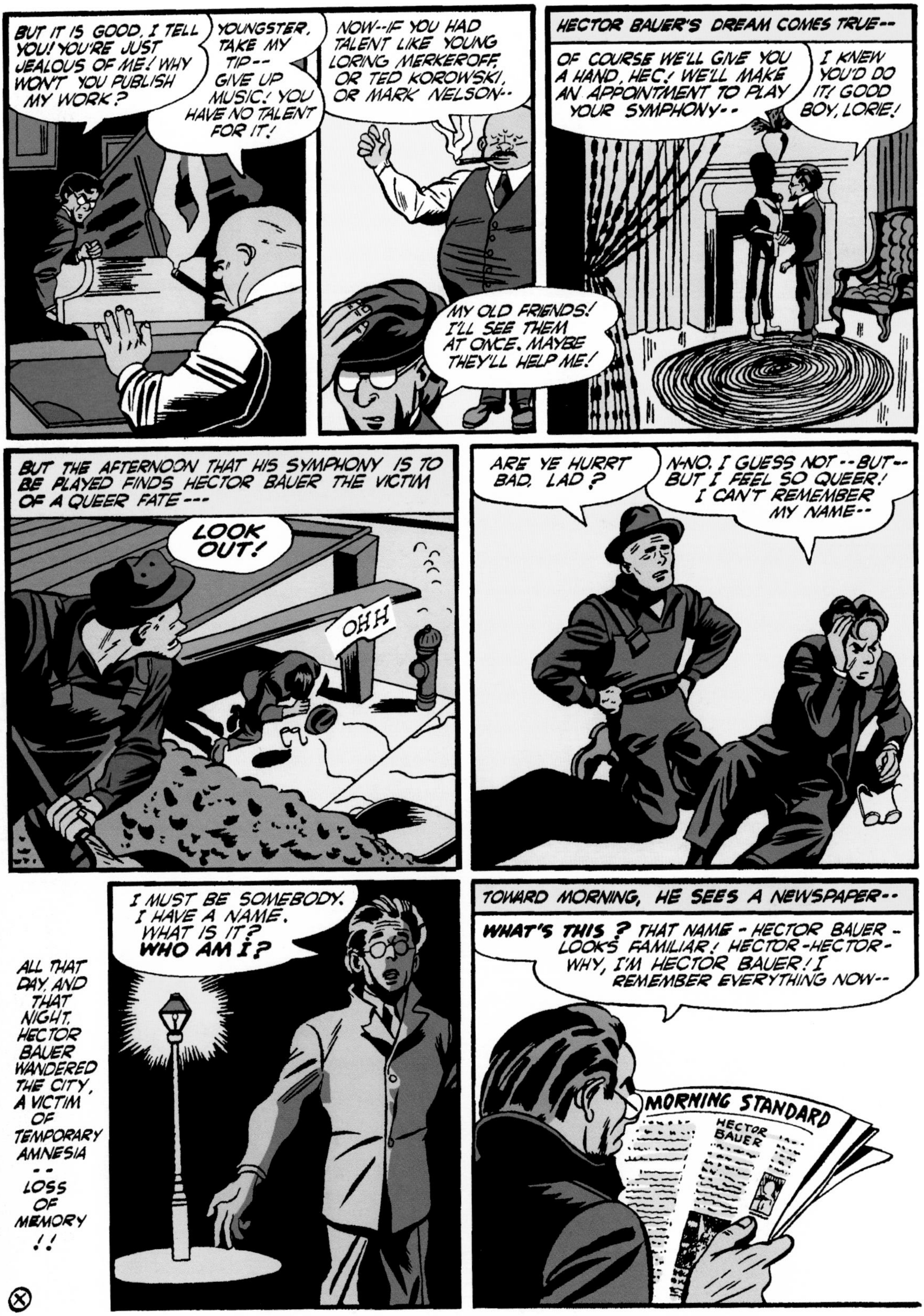
BUT IT IS GOOD, I TELL YOU! YOU'RE JUST JEALOUS OF ME! WHY WON'T YOU PUBLISH MY WORK?
YOUNGSTER, TAKE MY TIP-- GIVE UP MUSIC! YOU HAVE NO TALENT FOR IT!
NOW--IF YOU HAD TALENT LIKE YOUNG LORING MERKEROFF, OR TED KOROWSKI, OR MARK NELSON--
MY OLD FRIENDS! I'LL SEE THEM AT ONCE. MAYBE THEY'LL HELP ME!
HECTOR BAUER'S DREAM COMES TRUE--
OF COURSE WE'LL GIVE YOU A HAND, HEC! WE'LL MAKE AN APPOINTMENT TO PLAY YOUR SYMPHONY--
I KNEW YOU'D DO IT! GOOD BOY, LORIE!
BUT THE AFTERNOON THAT HIS SYMPHONY IS TO BE PLAYED FINDS HECTOR BAUER THE VICTIM OF A QUEER FATE---
LOOK OUT!
OHH
ARE YE HURRT BAD, LAD?
N-NO, I GUESS NOT--BUT--BUT I FEEL SO QUEER! I CAN'T REMEMBER MY NAME--
ALL THAT DAY AND THAT NIGHT, HECTOR BAUER WANDERED THE CITY, A VICTIM OF TEMPORARY AMNESIA -- LOSS OF MEMORY !!
I MUST BE SOMEBODY. I HAVE A NAME. WHAT IS IT? WHO AM I?
TOWARD MORNING, HE SEES A NEWSPAPER--
WHAT'S THIS? THAT NAME - HECTOR BAUER - LOOKS FAMILIAR! HECTOR-HECTOR- WHY, I'M HECTOR BAUER! I REMEMBER EVERYTHING NOW--
MORNING STANDARD
HECTOR BAUER

"MY SYMPHONY--A FAILURE! "LUDICROUS, JARRING, FLAUNTS ALL MUSICAL RULES!" IF THAT'S WHAT THEY'RE SAYING, IT'S BECAUSE THOSE SO-CALLED FRIENDS DELIBERATELY MIS-PLAYED MY SYMPHONY!

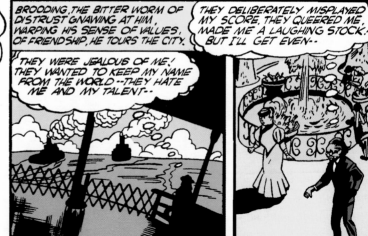

BROODING, THE BITTER WORM OF DISTRUST GNAWING AT HIM, WARPING HIS SENSE OF VALUES, OF FRIENDSHIP, HE TOURS THE CITY.

THEY WERE JEALOUS OF ME! THEY WANTED TO KEEP MY NAME FROM THE WORLD--THEY HATE ME AND MY TALENT--

THEY DELIBERATELY MISPLAYED MY SCORE, THEY QUEERED ME, MADE ME A LAUGHING STOCK! BUT I'LL GET EVEN--

I'LL GET A JOB HERE, AND FIGURE OUT A WAY TO GET EVEN WITH THOSE CHISELING RATS--

PIANO FACTORY

MEN WANTED CHEAP

AT THAT MOMENT--

A CHANCE, THAT'S ALL. MAYBE WE BUNGLED THE SCORE OR SOMETHING-- JUST GIVE HIM A CHANCE!

BOYS, YOU PLAYED THAT SCORE PERFECT-LY--BUT IT'S NO USE! BAUER HAS NO TALENT! NONE WHAT-SOEVER! HE'S IMAGINED HE'S A MUSICIAN--BUT HE ISN'T!

THROUGH THE YEARS HECTOR BAUER TOILED AT PIANO MAKING AND BROODED CONSTANTLY

I'LL GET THEM SOME DAY! IT WON'T BE A SIMPLE REVENGE - BUT A REVENGE THAT WILL BE RELENTLESS-- IMPLACABLE! SOME DAY IT WILL COME, SOME DAY---

AND NOW--MANY YEARS LATER, IN 1943...

YOU NOW KNOW EVERYTHING - BUT ARE POWERLESS TO STOP MY VENGEANCE! BY NOW, ALL THOSE FIENDS WILL BE DEPRIVED OF WHAT THEY VALUE MOST IN LIFE--EH? WHAT'S THAT?

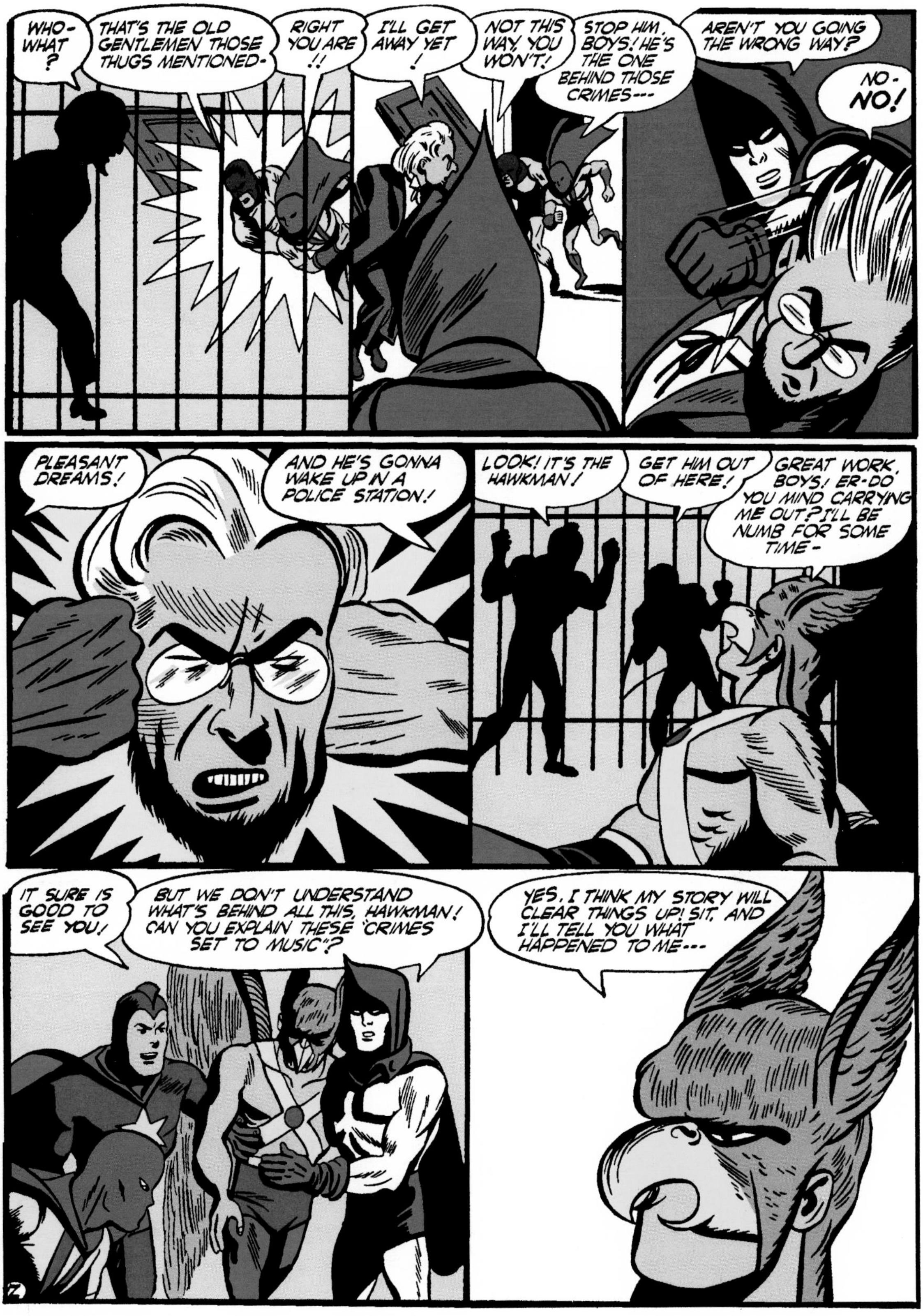
WHO-WHAT?
THAT'S THE OLD GENTLEMEN THOSE THUGS MENTIONED-
RIGHT YOU ARE!!
I'LL GET AWAY YET!
NOT THIS WAY, YOU WON'T!
STOP HIM, BOYS! HE'S THE ONE BEHIND THOSE CRIMES---
AREN'T YOU GOING THE WRONG WAY?
NO-NO!
PLEASANT DREAMS!
AND HE'S GONNA WAKE UP IN A POLICE STATION!
LOOK! IT'S THE HAWKMAN!
GET HIM OUT OF HERE!
GREAT WORK, BOYS! ER-DO YOU MIND CARRYING ME OUT? I'LL BE NUMB FOR SOME TIME-
IT SURE IS GOOD TO SEE YOU!
BUT WE DON'T UNDERSTAND WHAT'S BEHIND ALL THIS, HAWKMAN! CAN YOU EXPLAIN THESE "CRIMES SET TO MUSIC"?
YES. I THINK MY STORY WILL CLEAR THINGS UP! SIT, AND I'LL TELL YOU WHAT HAPPENED TO ME---
7

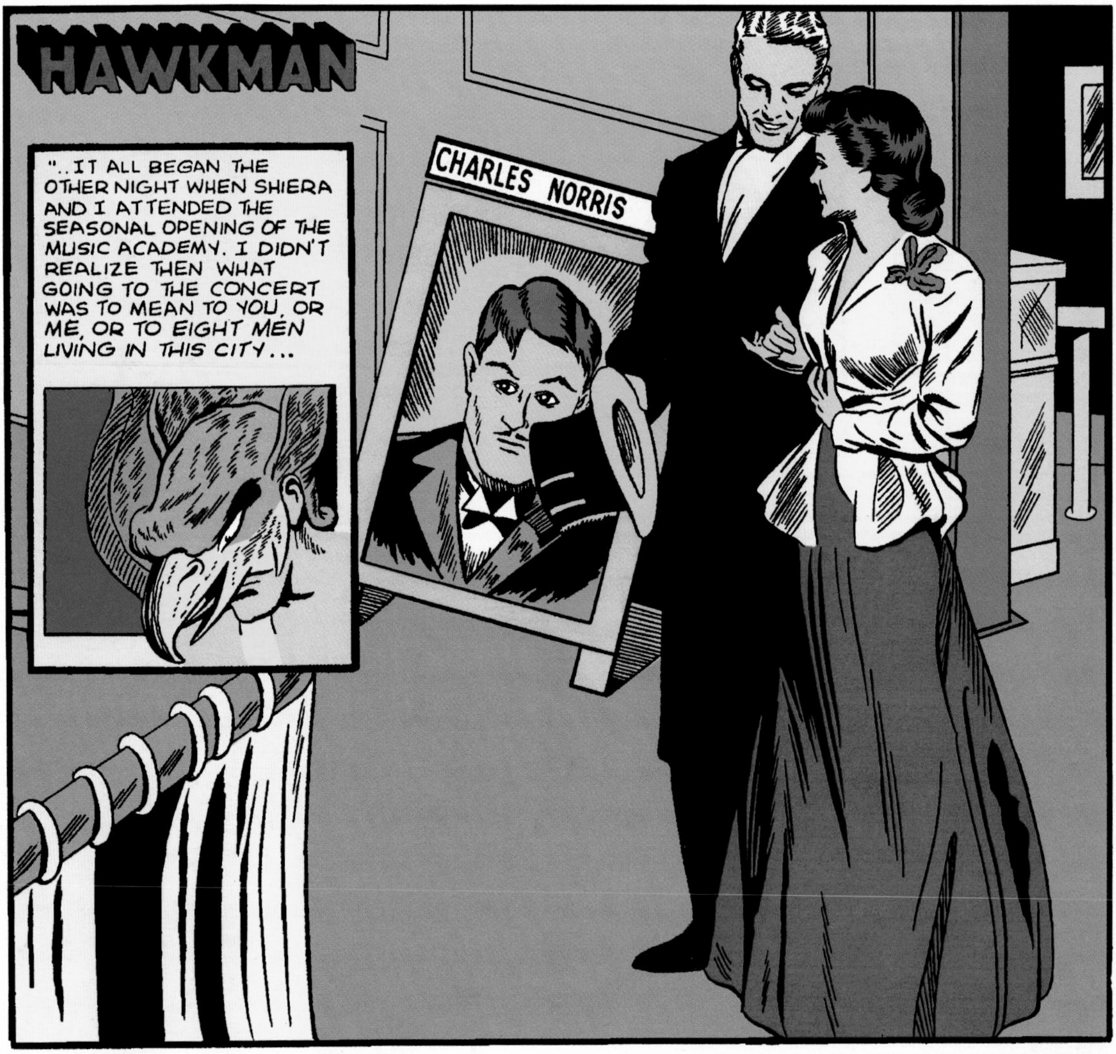
HAWKMAN
"..IT ALL BEGAN THE OTHER NIGHT WHEN SHIERA AND I ATTENDED THE SEASONAL OPENING OF THE MUSIC ACADEMY. I DIDN'T REALIZE THEN WHAT GOING TO THE CONCERT WAS TO MEAN TO YOU, OR ME, OR TO EIGHT MEN LIVING IN THIS CITY...
CHARLES NORRIS

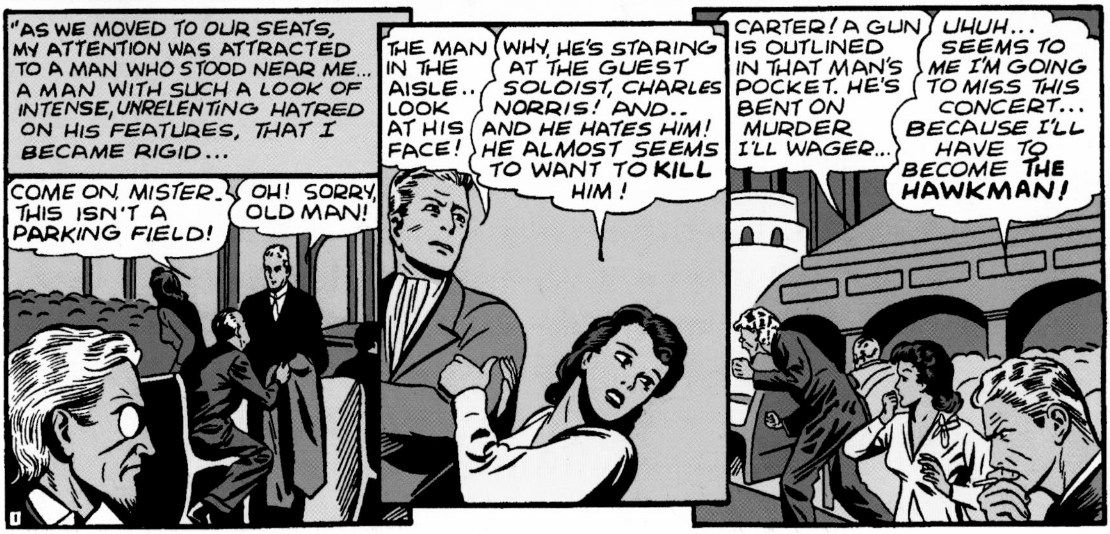
"AS WE MOVED TO OUR SEATS, MY ATTENTION WAS ATTRACTED TO A MAN WHO STOOD NEAR ME... A MAN WITH SUCH A LOOK OF INTENSE, UNRELENTING HATRED ON HIS FEATURES, THAT I BECAME RIGID...
COME ON, MISTER-- THIS ISN'T A PARKING FIELD!
OH! SORRY, OLD MAN!
THE MAN IN THE AISLE.. LOOK AT HIS FACE!
WHY, HE'S STARING AT THE GUEST SOLOIST, CHARLES NORRIS! AND.. AND HE HATES HIM! HE ALMOST SEEMS TO WANT TO KILL HIM!
CARTER! A GUN IS OUTLINED IN THAT MAN'S POCKET. HE'S BENT ON MURDER I'LL WAGER...
UHUH... SEEMS TO ME I'M GOING TO MISS THIS CONCERT... BECAUSE I'LL HAVE TO BECOME THE HAWKMAN!

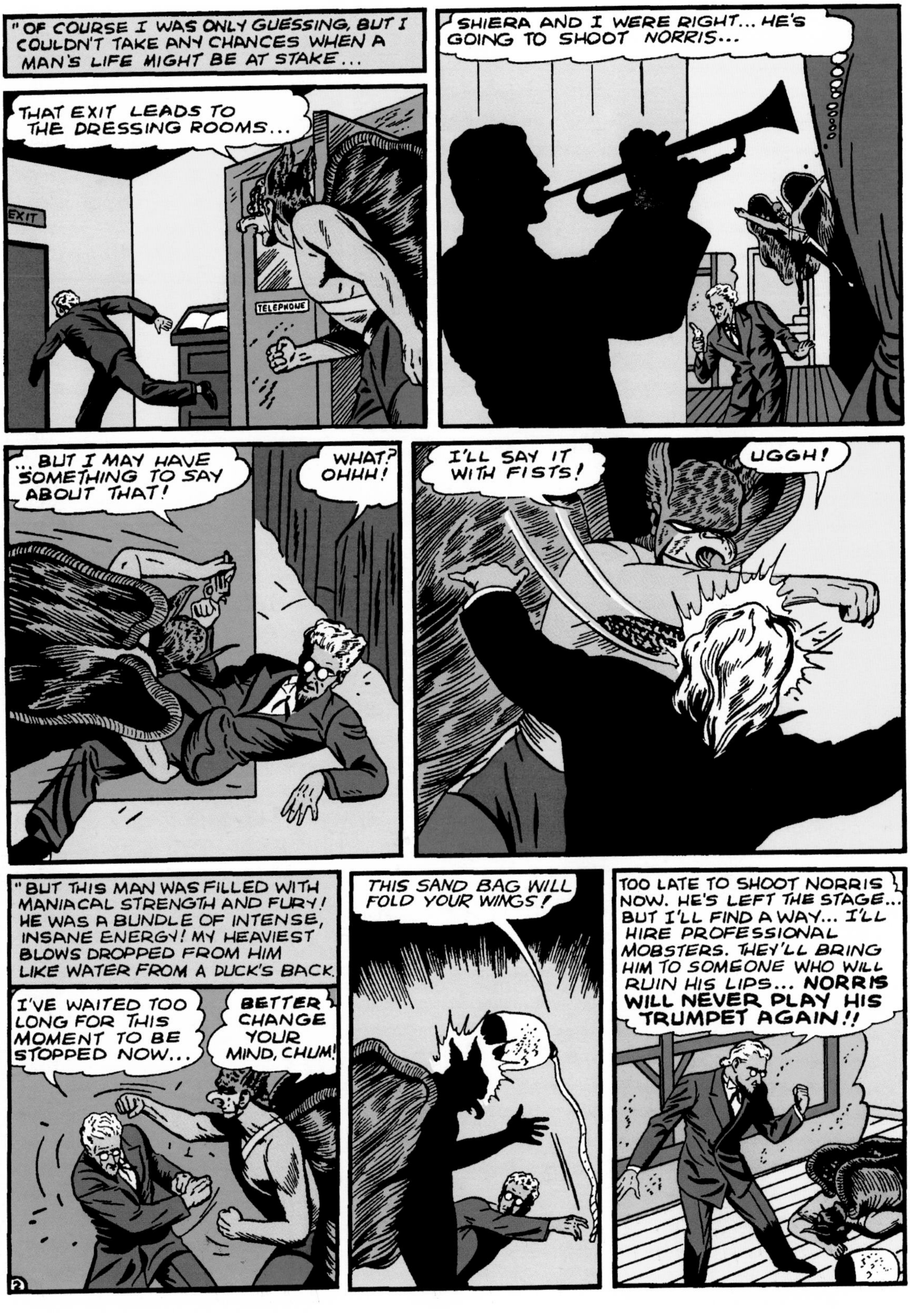
"OF COURSE I WAS ONLY GUESSING, BUT I COULDN'T TAKE ANY CHANCES WHEN A MAN'S LIFE MIGHT BE AT STAKE...
THAT EXIT LEADS TO THE DRESSING ROOMS...
EXIT
TELEPHONE
SHIERA AND I WERE RIGHT... HE'S GOING TO SHOOT NORRIS...
... BUT I MAY HAVE SOMETHING TO SAY ABOUT THAT!
WHAT? OHHH!
I'LL SAY IT WITH FISTS!
UGGH!
"BUT THIS MAN WAS FILLED WITH MANIACAL STRENGTH AND FURY! HE WAS A BUNDLE OF INTENSE, INSANE ENERGY! MY HEAVIEST BLOWS DROPPED FROM HIM LIKE WATER FROM A DUCK'S BACK.
I'VE WAITED TOO LONG FOR THIS MOMENT TO BE STOPPED NOW...
BETTER CHANGE YOUR MIND, CHUM!
THIS SAND BAG WILL FOLD YOUR WINGS!
TOO LATE TO SHOOT NORRIS NOW. HE'S LEFT THE STAGE... BUT I'LL FIND A WAY... I'LL HIRE PROFESSIONAL MOBSTERS. THEY'LL BRING HIM TO SOMEONE WHO WILL RUIN HIS LIPS... NORRIS WILL NEVER PLAY HIS TRUMPET AGAIN!!

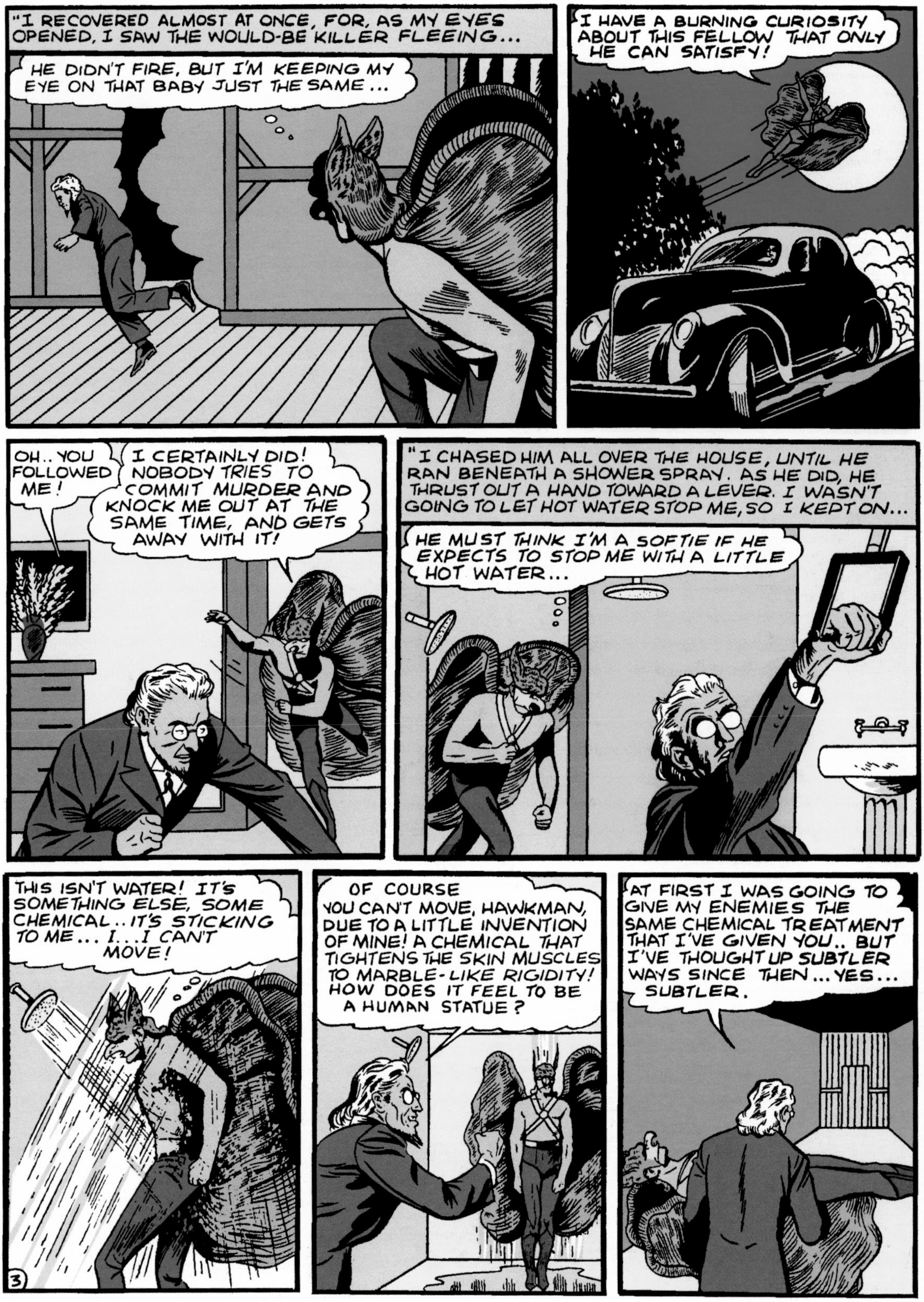
"I RECOVERED ALMOST AT ONCE, FOR, AS MY EYES OPENED, I SAW THE WOULD-BE KILLER FLEEING...
HE DIDN'T FIRE, BUT I'M KEEPING MY EYE ON THAT BABY JUST THE SAME...
I HAVE A BURNING CURIOSITY ABOUT THIS FELLOW THAT ONLY HE CAN SATISFY!
OH.. YOU FOLLOWED ME!
I CERTAINLY DID! NOBODY TRIES TO COMMIT MURDER AND KNOCK ME OUT AT THE SAME TIME, AND GETS AWAY WITH IT!
"I CHASED HIM ALL OVER THE HOUSE, UNTIL HE RAN BENEATH A SHOWER SPRAY. AS HE DID, HE THRUST OUT A HAND TOWARD A LEVER. I WASN'T GOING TO LET HOT WATER STOP ME, SO I KEPT ON...
HE MUST THINK I'M A SOFTIE IF HE EXPECTS TO STOP ME WITH A LITTLE HOT WATER...
THIS ISN'T WATER! IT'S SOMETHING ELSE, SOME CHEMICAL.. IT'S STICKING TO ME... I...I CAN'T MOVE!
3
OF COURSE YOU CAN'T MOVE, HAWKMAN, DUE TO A LITTLE INVENTION OF MINE! A CHEMICAL THAT TIGHTENS THE SKIN MUSCLES TO MARBLE-LIKE RIGIDITY! HOW DOES IT FEEL TO BE A HUMAN STATUE?
AT FIRST I WAS GOING TO GIVE MY ENEMIES THE SAME CHEMICAL TREATMENT THAT I'VE GIVEN YOU.. BUT I'VE THOUGHT UP SUBTLER WAYS SINCE THEN... YES... SUBTLER.

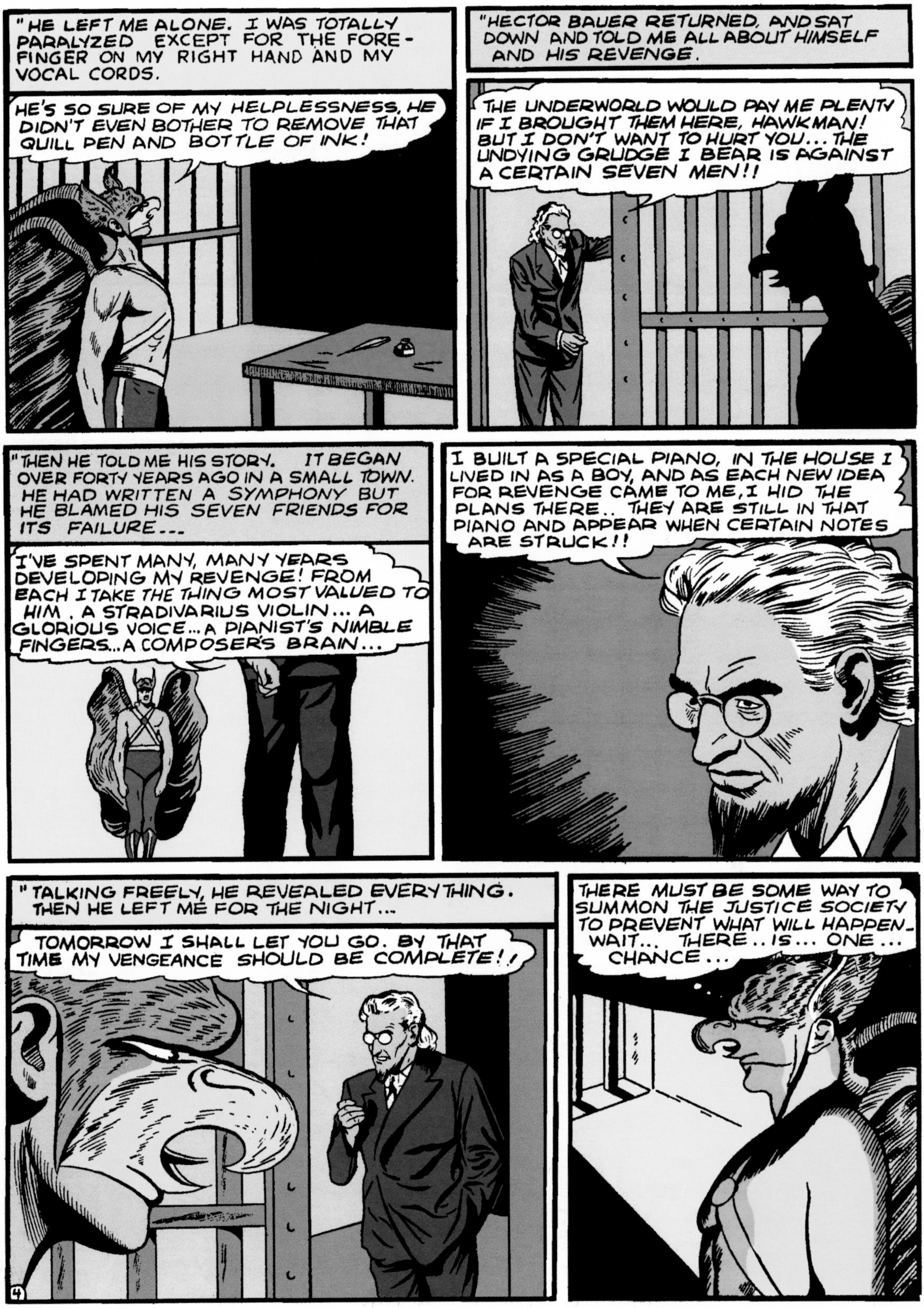
"HE LEFT ME ALONE. I WAS TOTALLY PARALYZED EXCEPT FOR THE FORE-FINGER ON MY RIGHT HAND AND MY VOCAL CORDS.
HE'S SO SURE OF MY HELPLESSNESS, HE DIDN'T EVEN BOTHER TO REMOVE THAT QUILL PEN AND BOTTLE OF INK!
"HECTOR BAUER RETURNED, AND SAT DOWN AND TOLD ME ALL ABOUT HIMSELF AND HIS REVENGE.
THE UNDERWORLD WOULD PAY ME PLENTY IF I BROUGHT THEM HERE, HAWKMAN! BUT I DON'T WANT TO HURT YOU... THE UNDYING GRUDGE I BEAR IS AGAINST A CERTAIN SEVEN MEN!!
"THEN HE TOLD ME HIS STORY. IT BEGAN OVER FORTY YEARS AGO IN A SMALL TOWN. HE HAD WRITTEN A SYMPHONY BUT HE BLAMED HIS SEVEN FRIENDS FOR ITS FAILURE...
I'VE SPENT MANY, MANY YEARS DEVELOPING MY REVENGE! FROM EACH I TAKE THE THING MOST VALUED TO HIM. A STRADIVARIUS VIOLIN... A GLORIOUS VOICE... A PIANIST'S NIMBLE FINGERS... A COMPOSER'S BRAIN...
I BUILT A SPECIAL PIANO, IN THE HOUSE I LIVED IN AS A BOY, AND AS EACH NEW IDEA FOR REVENGE CAME TO ME, I HID THE PLANS THERE.. THEY ARE STILL IN THAT PIANO AND APPEAR WHEN CERTAIN NOTES ARE STRUCK!!
"TALKING FREELY, HE REVEALED EVERYTHING. THEN HE LEFT ME FOR THE NIGHT...
TOMORROW I SHALL LET YOU GO. BY THAT TIME MY VENGEANCE SHOULD BE COMPLETE!!
4
THERE MUST BE SOME WAY TO SUMMON THE JUSTICE SOCIETY TO PREVENT WHAT WILL HAPPEN. WAIT... THERE.. IS... ONE... CHANCE...

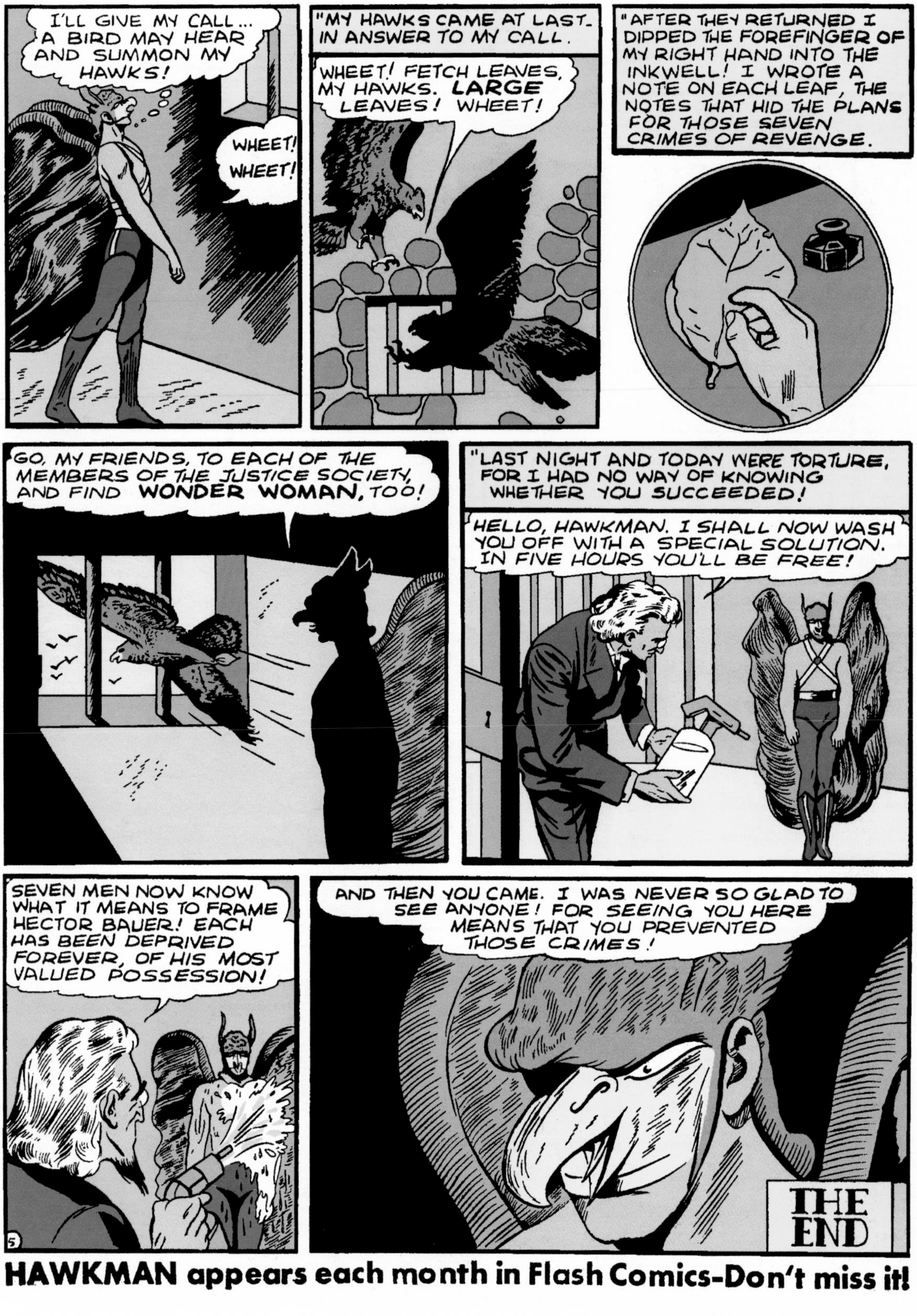
I'LL GIVE MY CALL... A BIRD MAY HEAR AND SUMMON MY HAWKS!
WHEET! WHEET!
"MY HAWKS CAME AT LAST- IN ANSWER TO MY CALL.
WHEET! FETCH LEAVES, MY HAWKS. LARGE LEAVES! WHEET!
"AFTER THEY RETURNED I DIPPED THE FOREFINGER OF MY RIGHT HAND INTO THE INKWELL! I WROTE A NOTE ON EACH LEAF, THE NOTES THAT HID THE PLANS FOR THOSE SEVEN CRIMES OF REVENGE.
GO, MY FRIENDS, TO EACH OF THE MEMBERS OF THE JUSTICE SOCIETY, AND FIND WONDER WOMAN, TOO!
"LAST NIGHT AND TODAY WERE TORTURE, FOR I HAD NO WAY OF KNOWING WHETHER YOU SUCCEEDED!
HELLO, HAWKMAN. I SHALL NOW WASH YOU OFF WITH A SPECIAL SOLUTION. IN FIVE HOURS YOU'LL BE FREE!
SEVEN MEN NOW KNOW WHAT IT MEANS TO FRAME HECTOR BAUER! EACH HAS BEEN DEPRIVED FOREVER, OF HIS MOST VALUED POSSESSION!
AND THEN YOU CAME. I WAS NEVER SO GLAD TO SEE ANYONE! FOR SEEING YOU HERE MEANS THAT YOU PREVENTED THOSE CRIMES!
THE END

HAWKMAN appears each month in Flash Comics-Don't miss it!

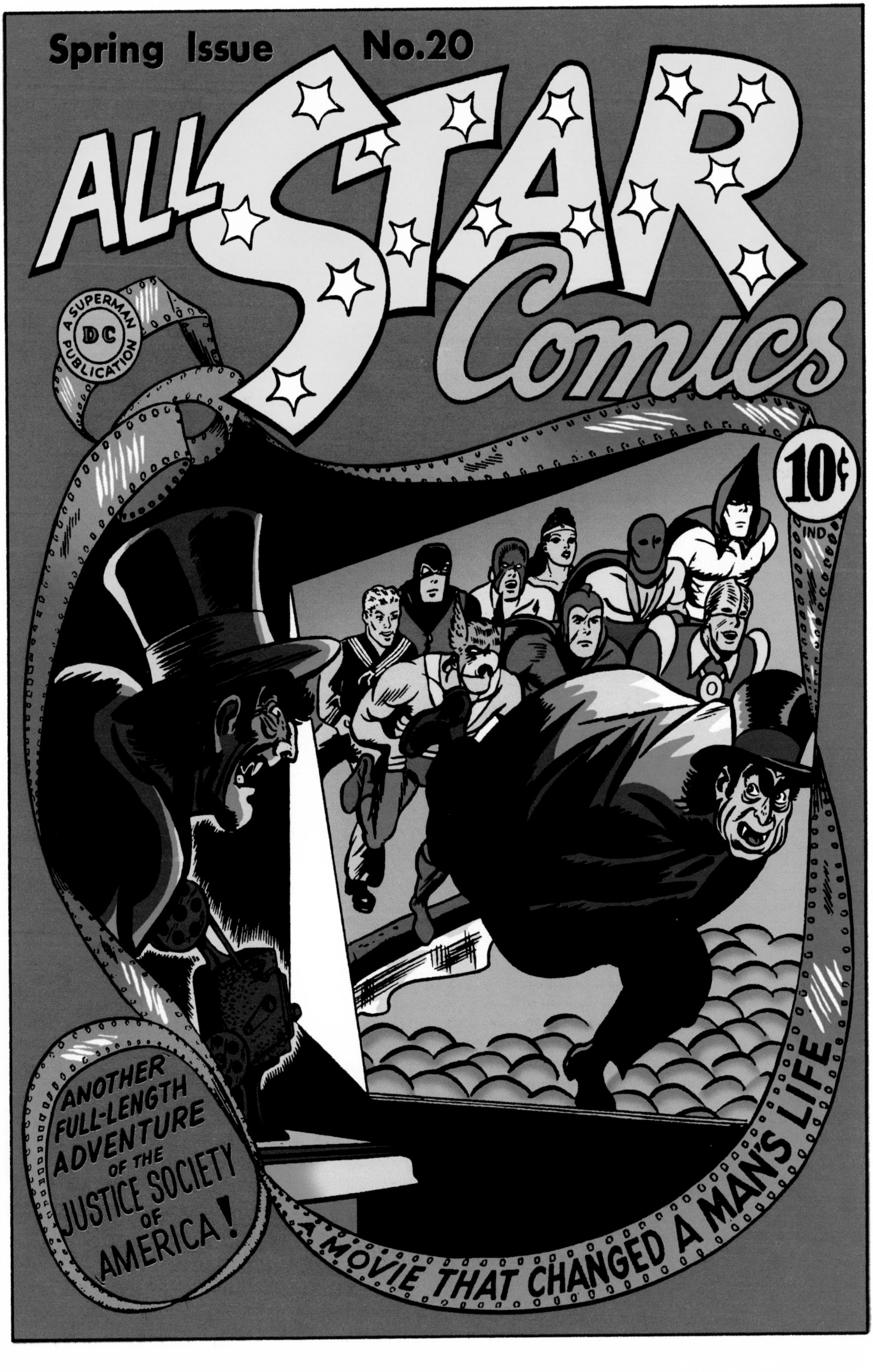
Spring Issue No.20
ALL STAR Comics
A SUPERMAN DC PUBLICATION
10¢
IND
ANOTHER FULL-LENGTH ADVENTURE OF THE JUSTICE SOCIETY OF AMERICA!
A MOVIE THAT CHANGED A MAN'S LIFE

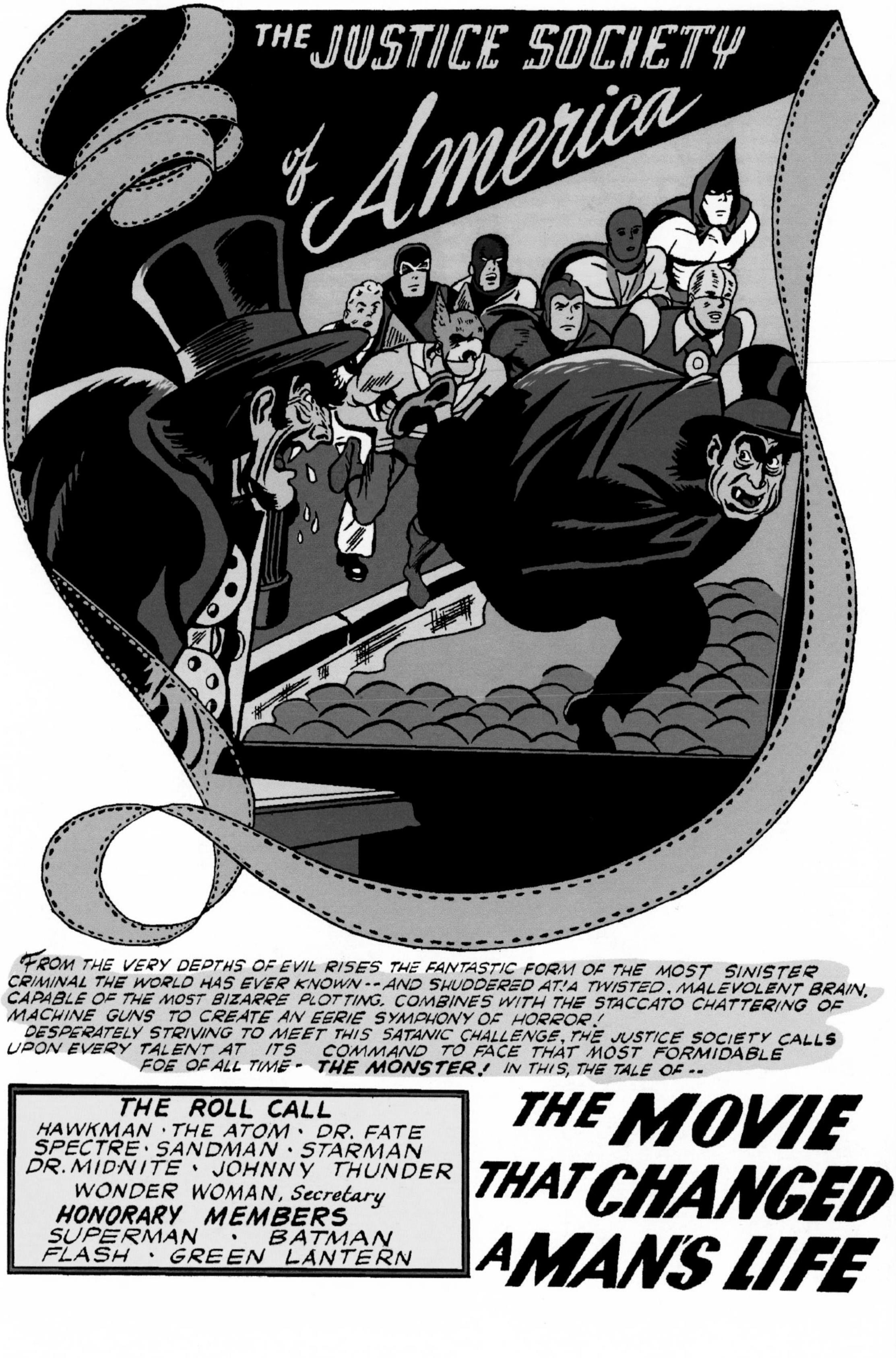
THE JUSTICE SOCIETY of America
FROM THE VERY DEPTHS OF EVIL RISES THE FANTASTIC FORM OF THE MOST SINISTER CRIMINAL THE WORLD HAS EVER KNOWN -- AND SHUDDERED AT!A TWISTED, MALEVOLENT BRAIN, CAPABLE OF THE MOST BIZARRE PLOTTING, COMBINES WITH THE STACCATO CHATTERING OF MACHINE GUNS TO CREATE AN EERIE SYMPHONY OF HORROR!
DESPERATELY STRIVING TO MEET THIS SATANIC CHALLENGE, THE JUSTICE SOCIETY CALLS UPON EVERY TALENT AT ITS COMMAND TO FACE THAT MOST FORMIDABLE FOE OF ALL TIME - THE MONSTER! IN THIS, THE TALE OF --
THE ROLL CALL
HAWKMAN · THE ATOM · DR. FATE
SPECTRE · SANDMAN · STARMAN
DR. MIDNITE · JOHNNY THUNDER
WONDER WOMAN, Secretary
HONORARY MEMBERS
SUPERMAN · BATMAN
FLASH · GREEN LANTERN
THE MOVIE THAT CHANGED A MAN'S LIFE

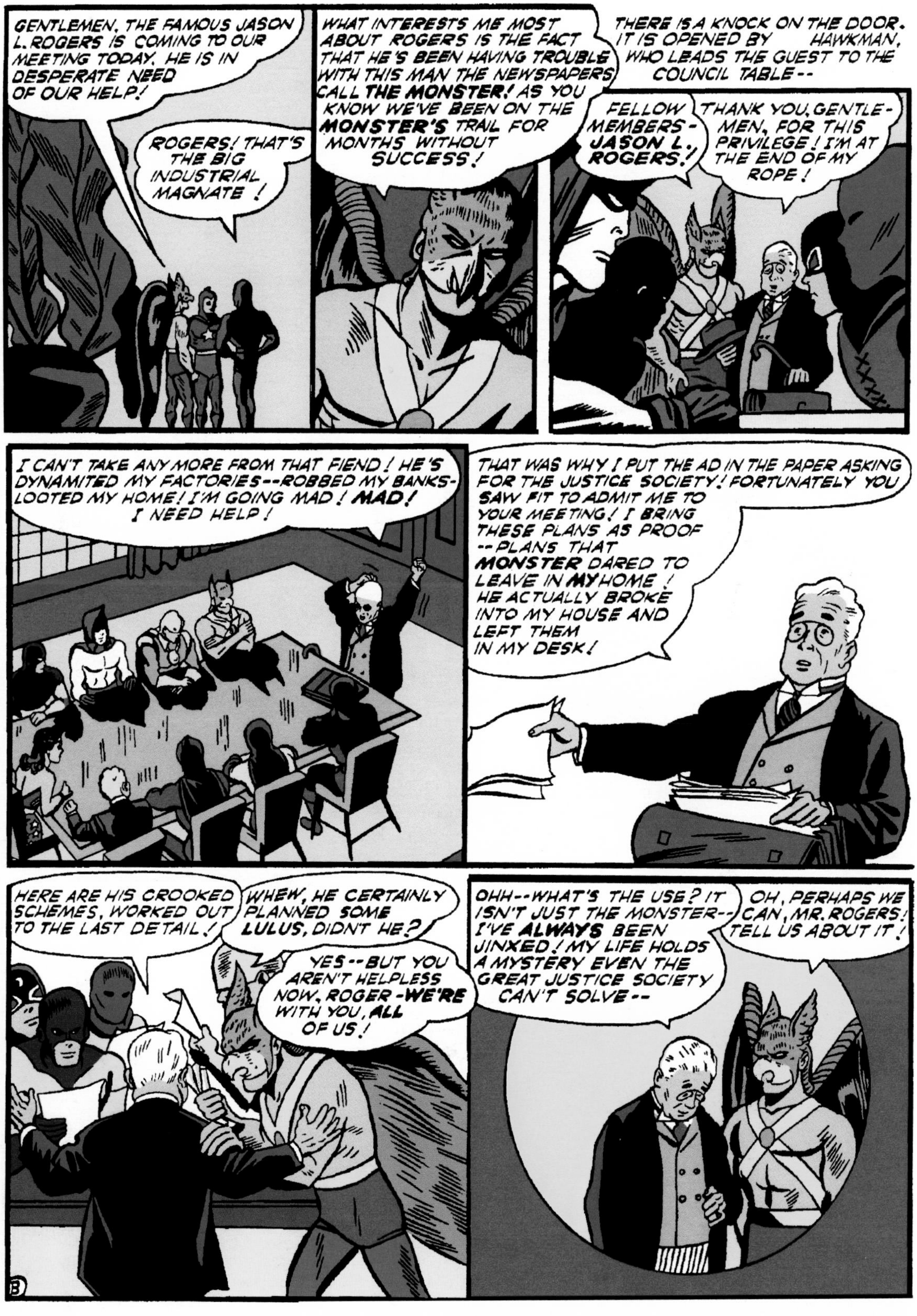
GENTLEMEN, THE FAMOUS JASON L. ROGERS IS COMING TO OUR MEETING TODAY. HE IS IN DESPERATE NEED OF OUR HELP!
ROGERS! THAT'S THE BIG INDUSTRIAL MAGNATE!
WHAT INTERESTS ME MOST ABOUT ROGERS IS THE FACT THAT HE'S BEEN HAVING TROUBLE WITH THIS MAN THE NEWSPAPERS CALL THE MONSTER! AS YOU KNOW WE'VE BEEN ON THE MONSTER'S TRAIL FOR MONTHS WITHOUT SUCCESS!
THERE IS A KNOCK ON THE DOOR. IT IS OPENED BY HAWKMAN, WHO LEADS THE GUEST TO THE COUNCIL TABLE--
FELLOW MEMBERS- JASON L. ROGERS!
THANK YOU, GENTLEMEN, FOR THIS PRIVILEGE! I'M AT THE END OF MY ROPE!
I CAN'T TAKE ANY MORE FROM THAT FIEND! HE'S DYNAMITED MY FACTORIES--ROBBED MY BANKS-LOOTED MY HOME! I'M GOING MAD! MAD! I NEED HELP!
THAT WAS WHY I PUT THE AD IN THE PAPER ASKING FOR THE JUSTICE SOCIETY! FORTUNATELY YOU SAW FIT TO ADMIT ME TO YOUR MEETING! I BRING THESE PLANS AS PROOF --PLANS THAT MONSTER DARED TO LEAVE IN MY HOME! HE ACTUALLY BROKE INTO MY HOUSE AND LEFT THEM IN MY DESK!
HERE ARE HIS CROOKED SCHEMES, WORKED OUT TO THE LAST DETAIL!
WHEW, HE CERTAINLY PLANNED SOME LULUS, DIDN'T HE?
YES--BUT YOU AREN'T HELPLESS NOW, ROGER-WE'RE WITH YOU, ALL OF US!
OHH--WHAT'S THE USE? IT ISN'T JUST THE MONSTER--I'VE ALWAYS BEEN JINXED! MY LIFE HOLDS A MYSTERY EVEN THE GREAT JUSTICE SOCIETY CAN'T SOLVE--
OH, PERHAPS WE CAN, MR. ROGERS! TELL US ABOUT IT!
B

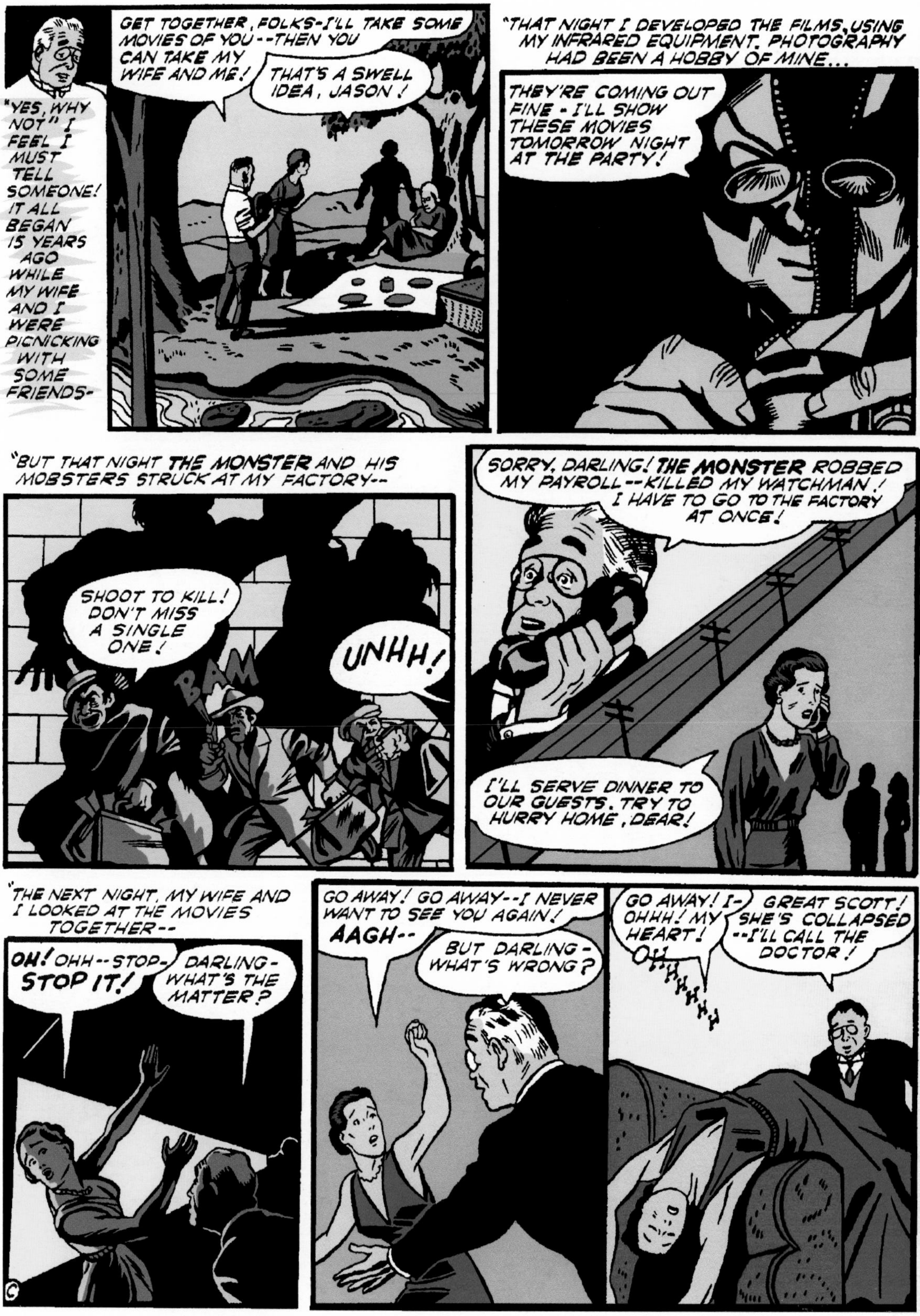
"YES, WHY NOT" I FEEL I MUST TELL SOMEONE! IT ALL BEGAN 15 YEARS AGO WHILE MY WIFE AND I WERE PICNICKING WITH SOME FRIENDS-
GET TOGETHER, FOLKS-I'LL TAKE SOME MOVIES OF YOU--THEN YOU CAN TAKE MY WIFE AND ME!
THAT'S A SWELL IDEA, JASON!
"THAT NIGHT I DEVELOPED THE FILMS, USING MY INFRARED EQUIPMENT. PHOTOGRAPHY HAD BEEN A HOBBY OF MINE...
THEY'RE COMING OUT FINE - I'LL SHOW THESE MOVIES TOMORROW NIGHT AT THE PARTY!
"BUT THAT NIGHT THE MONSTER AND HIS MOBSTERS STRUCK AT MY FACTORY--
SHOOT TO KILL! DON'T MISS A SINGLE ONE!
BAM
UNHH!
SORRY, DARLING! THE MONSTER ROBBED MY PAYROLL--KILLED MY WATCHMAN! I HAVE TO GO TO THE FACTORY AT ONCE!
I'LL SERVE DINNER TO OUR GUESTS. TRY TO HURRY HOME, DEAR!
"THE NEXT NIGHT, MY WIFE AND I LOOKED AT THE MOVIES TOGETHER--
OH! OHH--STOP-STOP IT!
DARLING-WHAT'S THE MATTER?
GO AWAY! GO AWAY--I NEVER WANT TO SEE YOU AGAIN! AAGH--
BUT DARLING-WHAT'S WRONG?
GO AWAY! I-OHHH! MY HEART!
OHHHHHH
GREAT SCOTT! SHE'S COLLAPSED--I'LL CALL THE DOCTOR!

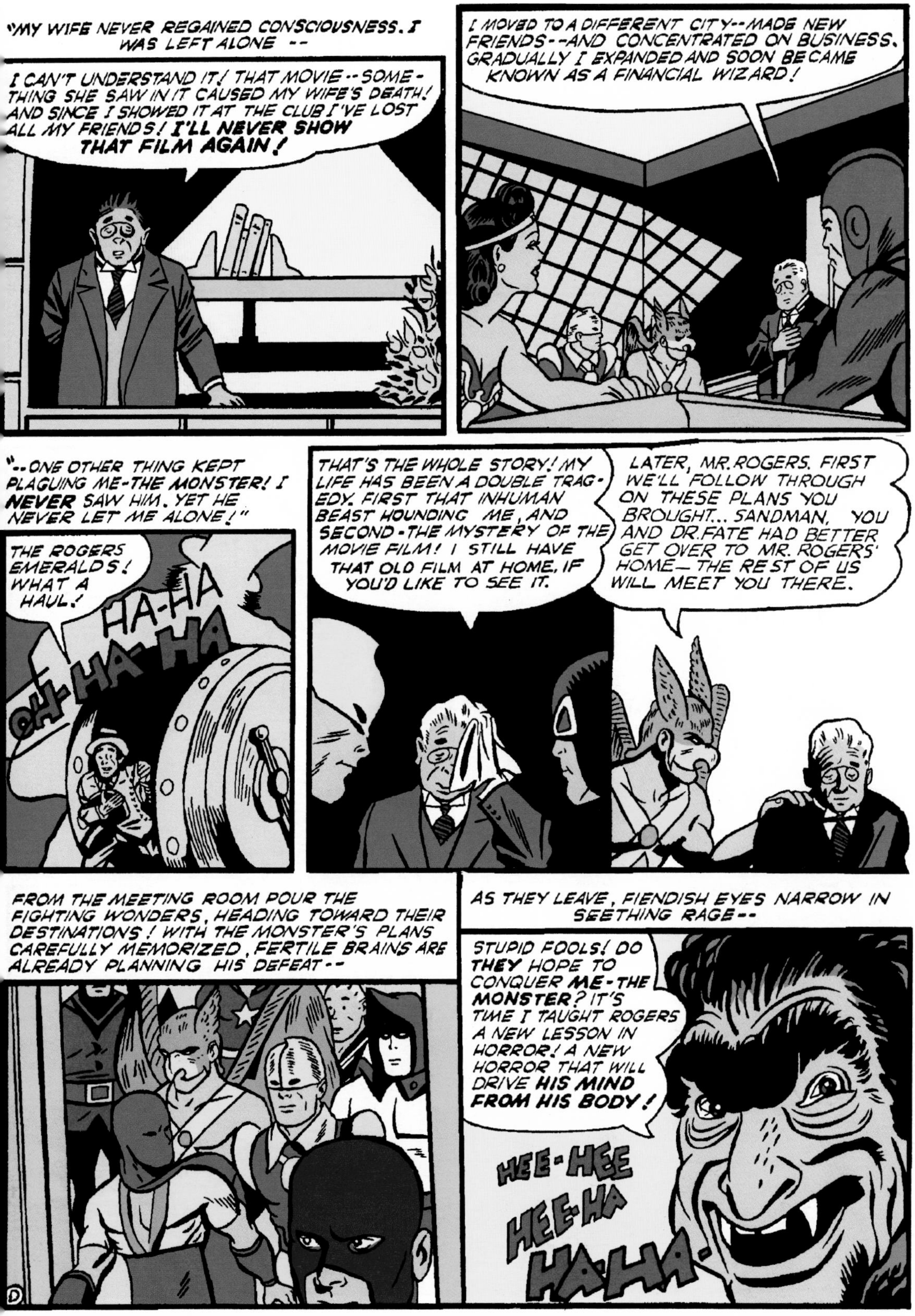
"MY WIFE NEVER REGAINED CONSCIOUSNESS. I WAS LEFT ALONE --
I CAN'T UNDERSTAND IT! THAT MOVIE -- SOMETHING SHE SAW IN IT CAUSED MY WIFE'S DEATH! AND SINCE I SHOWED IT AT THE CLUB I'VE LOST ALL MY FRIENDS! I'LL NEVER SHOW THAT FILM AGAIN!
I MOVED TO A DIFFERENT CITY--MADE NEW FRIENDS--AND CONCENTRATED ON BUSINESS. GRADUALLY I EXPANDED AND SOON BECAME KNOWN AS A FINANCIAL WIZARD!
"--ONE OTHER THING KEPT PLAGUING ME-THE MONSTER! I NEVER SAW HIM. YET HE NEVER LET ME ALONE!"
THE ROGERS EMERALDS! WHAT A HAUL!
HA-HA
OH-HA-HA-HA
THAT'S THE WHOLE STORY! MY LIFE HAS BEEN A DOUBLE TRAGEDY. FIRST THAT INHUMAN BEAST HOUNDING ME, AND SECOND-THE MYSTERY OF THE MOVIE FILM! I STILL HAVE THAT OLD FILM AT HOME, IF YOU'D LIKE TO SEE IT.
LATER, MR. ROGERS. FIRST WE'LL FOLLOW THROUGH ON THESE PLANS YOU BROUGHT... SANDMAN, YOU AND DR. FATE HAD BETTER GET OVER TO MR. ROGERS' HOME— THE REST OF US WILL MEET YOU THERE.
FROM THE MEETING ROOM POUR THE FIGHTING WONDERS, HEADING TOWARD THEIR DESTINATIONS! WITH THE MONSTER'S PLANS CAREFULLY MEMORIZED, FERTILE BRAINS ARE ALREADY PLANNING HIS DEFEAT--
D
AS THEY LEAVE, FIENDISH EYES NARROW IN SEETHING RAGE--
STUPID FOOLS! DO THEY HOPE TO CONQUER ME-THE MONSTER? IT'S TIME I TAUGHT ROGERS A NEW LESSON IN HORROR! A NEW HORROR THAT WILL DRIVE HIS MIND FROM HIS BODY!
HEE-HEE
HEE-HA
HA-HA-

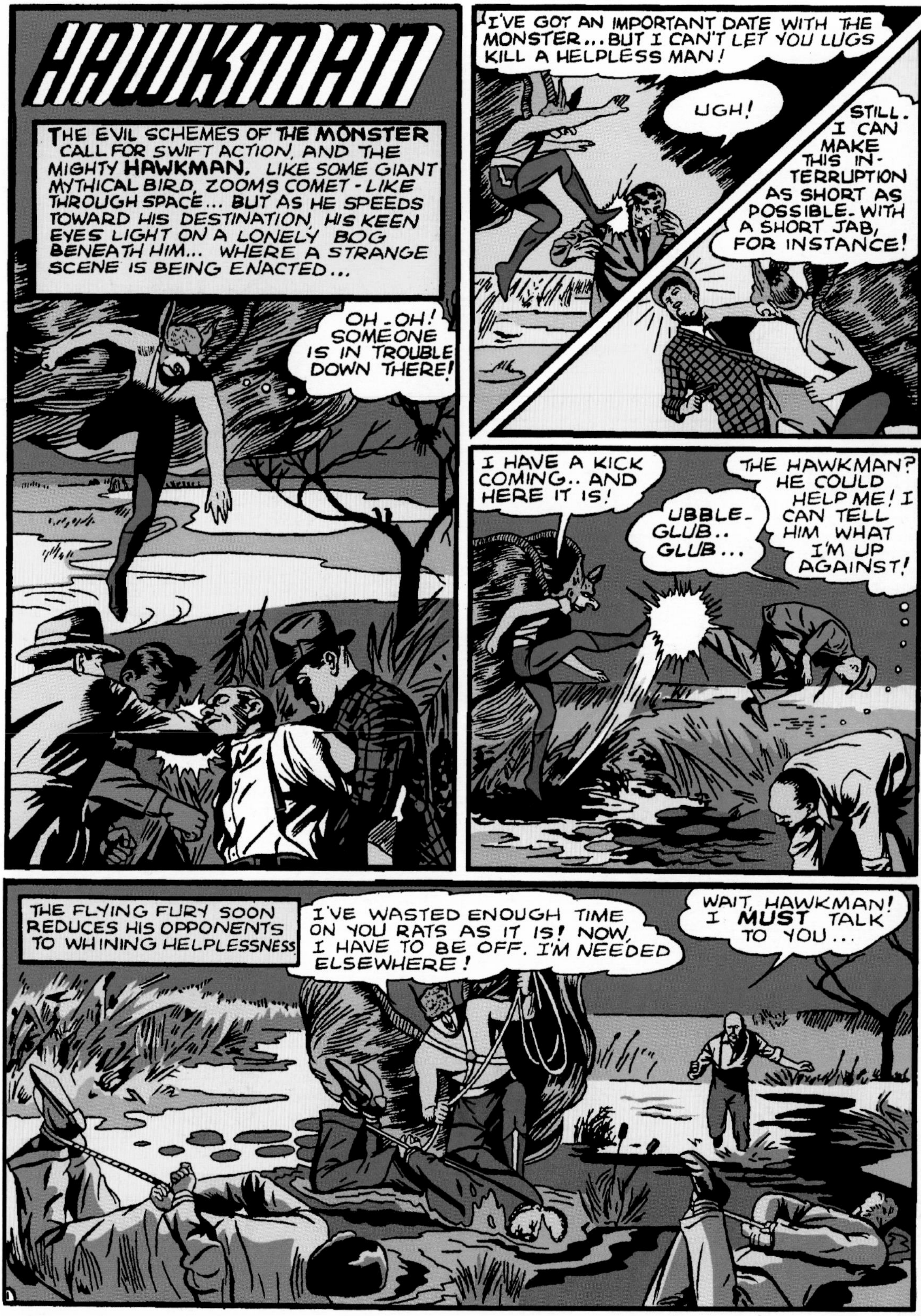
HAWKMAN
THE EVIL SCHEMES OF THE MONSTER CALL FOR SWIFT ACTION, AND THE MIGHTY HAWKMAN, LIKE SOME GIANT MYTHICAL BIRD, ZOOMS COMET-LIKE THROUGH SPACE... BUT AS HE SPEEDS TOWARD HIS DESTINATION, HIS KEEN EYES LIGHT ON A LONELY BOG BENEATH HIM... WHERE A STRANGE SCENE IS BEING ENACTED...
OH-OH! SOMEONE IS IN TROUBLE DOWN THERE!
I'VE GOT AN IMPORTANT DATE WITH THE MONSTER... BUT I CAN'T LET YOU LUGS KILL A HELPLESS MAN!
UGH!
STILL, I CAN MAKE THIS INTERRUPTION AS SHORT AS POSSIBLE- WITH A SHORT JAB, FOR INSTANCE!
I HAVE A KICK COMING.. AND HERE IT IS!
UBBLE-GLUB.. GLUB...
THE HAWKMAN? HE COULD HELP ME! I CAN TELL HIM WHAT I'M UP AGAINST!
THE FLYING FURY SOON REDUCES HIS OPPONENTS TO WHINING HELPLESSNESS
I'VE WASTED ENOUGH TIME ON YOU RATS AS IT IS! NOW, I HAVE TO BE OFF. I'M NEEDED ELSEWHERE!
WAIT, HAWKMAN! I MUST TALK TO YOU...

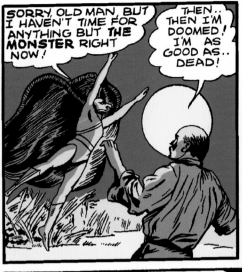

SORRY, OLD MAN, BUT I HAVEN'T TIME FOR ANYTHING BUT *THE MONSTER* RIGHT NOW!

THEN.. THEN I'M DOOMED! I'M AS GOOD AS.. DEAD!

WHILE AT THE HOME OF HARLAN WALSH, STEEL BARON.

HAWKMAN WILL SOON BE HERE! TELL HIM HE'S NOT WANTED! AND DON'T WEAKEN. REMEMBER, THE ARM OF THE MONSTER REACHES FAR AND STRIKES HARD!

I - I'LL REMEMBER.

HERE HE COMES NOW. I'M GOING! I LEAVE YOU TO HANDLE HIM...

YES. YES! I'LL TELL HIM!

YOU! HOW DID YOU GET HERE BEFORE ME? ARE YOU HARLAN WALSH?

YES! BUT WHAT DO YOU WANT?

HMM.. A FEW MOMENTS AGO YOU WERE MIGHTY ANXIOUS TO TELL ME YOUR TROUBLES! BUT NO MATTER - I CAME HERE TO WARN YOU OF THE MONSTER. HE'S PLANNING TO ROB YOU OF YOUR STEEL INDUSTRIES!

ONCE HE GETS CONTROL OF YOUR BUSINESS, YOU'LL BE AT HIS MERCY! HE'LL STRIP YOU OF YOUR WEALTH, YOUR HOUSES, YOUR...

SO WHAT? I CAN TAKE CARE OF MYSELF!

NOW - GET OUT! I WANT NOTHING FROM YOU OR YOUR KIND! I'LL HANDLE MY OWN AFFAIRS! GET OUT!

CERTAINLY! SORRY TO HAVE INTRUDED!

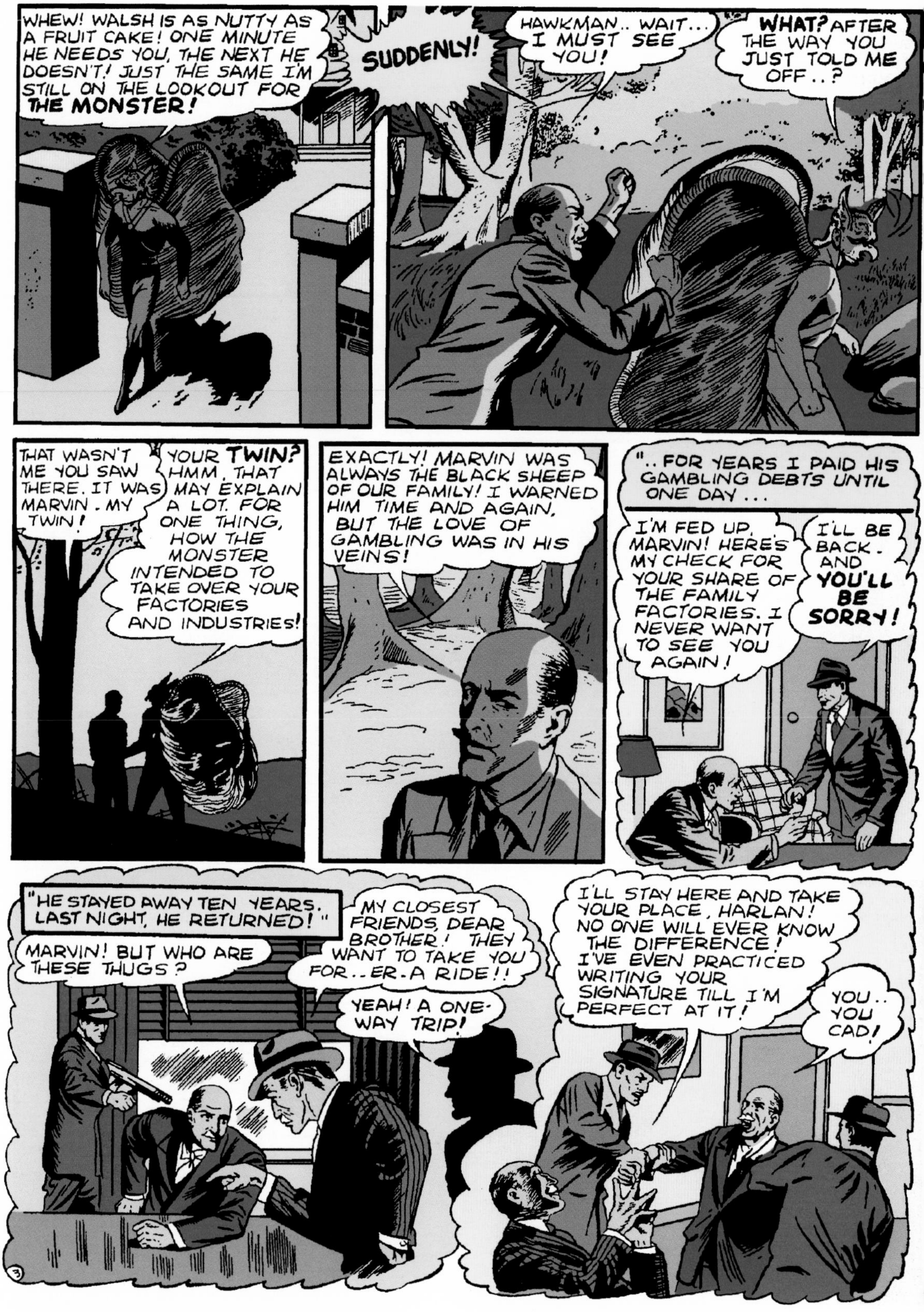
WHEW! WALSH IS AS NUTTY AS A FRUIT CAKE! ONE MINUTE HE NEEDS YOU, THE NEXT HE DOESN'T! JUST THE SAME I'M STILL ON THE LOOKOUT FOR THE MONSTER!
SUDDENLY!
HAWKMAN.. WAIT... I MUST SEE YOU!
WHAT? AFTER THE WAY YOU JUST TOLD ME OFF..?
THAT WASN'T ME YOU SAW THERE. IT WAS MARVIN. MY TWIN!
YOUR TWIN? HMM, THAT MAY EXPLAIN A LOT. FOR ONE THING, HOW THE MONSTER INTENDED TO TAKE OVER YOUR FACTORIES AND INDUSTRIES!
EXACTLY! MARVIN WAS ALWAYS THE BLACK SHEEP OF OUR FAMILY! I WARNED HIM TIME AND AGAIN, BUT THE LOVE OF GAMBLING WAS IN HIS VEINS!
"..FOR YEARS I PAID HIS GAMBLING DEBTS UNTIL ONE DAY...
I'M FED UP, MARVIN! HERE'S MY CHECK FOR YOUR SHARE OF THE FAMILY FACTORIES. I NEVER WANT TO SEE YOU AGAIN!
I'LL BE BACK - AND YOU'LL BE SORRY!
"HE STAYED AWAY TEN YEARS. LAST NIGHT, HE RETURNED!"
MARVIN! BUT WHO ARE THESE THUGS?
MY CLOSEST FRIENDS, DEAR BROTHER! THEY WANT TO TAKE YOU FOR..ER-A RIDE!!
YEAH! A ONE-WAY TRIP!
I'LL STAY HERE AND TAKE YOUR PLACE, HARLAN! NO ONE WILL EVER KNOW THE DIFFERENCE! I'VE EVEN PRACTICED WRITING YOUR SIGNATURE TILL I'M PERFECT AT IT!
YOU.. YOU CAD!
3

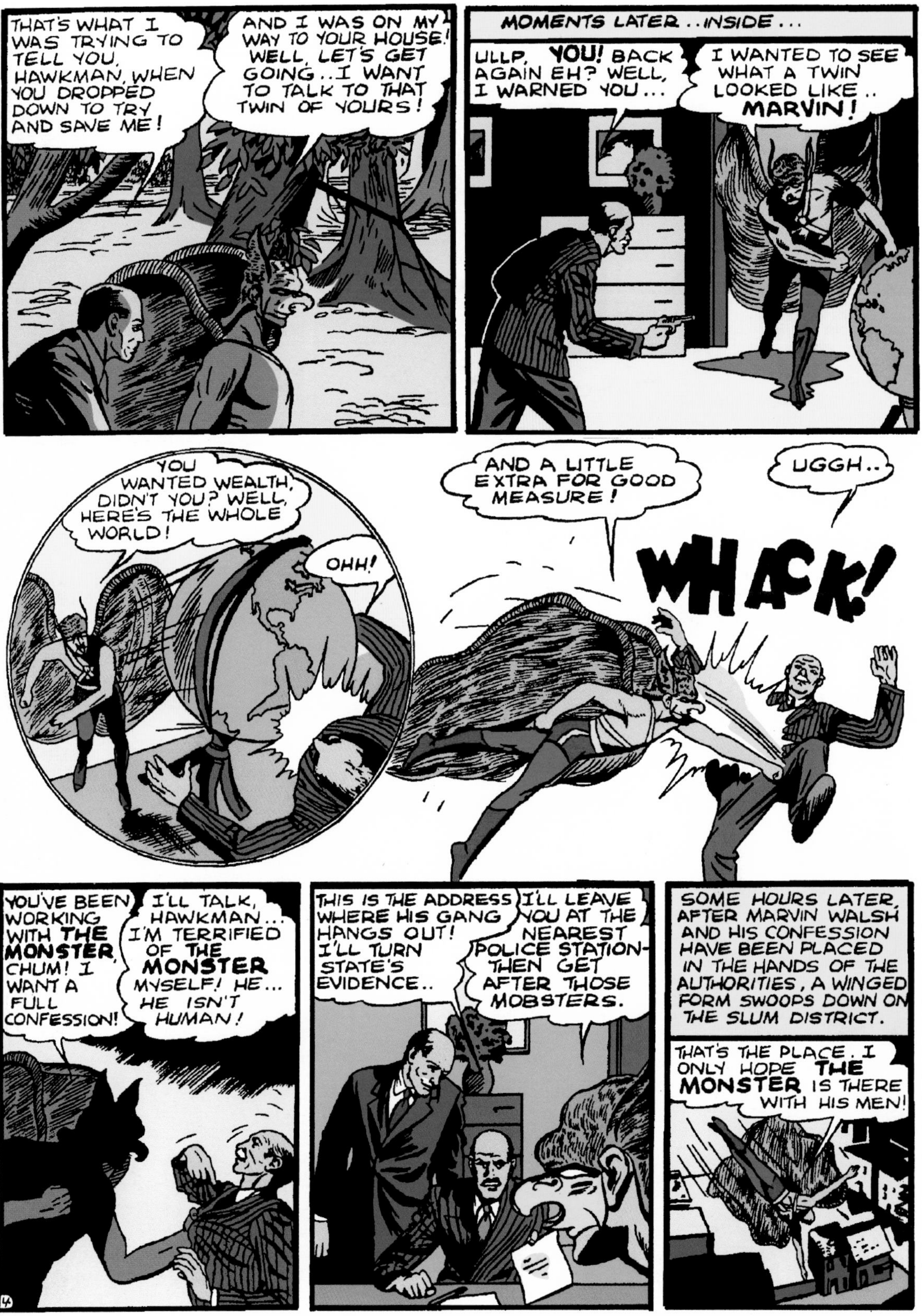
THAT'S WHAT I WAS TRYING TO TELL YOU, HAWKMAN, WHEN YOU DROPPED DOWN TO TRY AND SAVE ME!
AND I WAS ON MY WAY TO YOUR HOUSE! WELL, LET'S GET GOING.. I WANT TO TALK TO THAT TWIN OF YOURS!
MOMENTS LATER.. INSIDE...
ULLP, YOU! BACK AGAIN EH? WELL, I WARNED YOU...
I WANTED TO SEE WHAT A TWIN LOOKED LIKE.. MARVIN!
YOU WANTED WEALTH, DIDN'T YOU? WELL, HERE'S THE WHOLE WORLD!
OHH!
AND A LITTLE EXTRA FOR GOOD MEASURE!
UGGH..
WHACK!
YOU'VE BEEN WORKING WITH THE MONSTER, CHUM! I WANT A FULL CONFESSION!
I'LL TALK, HAWKMAN... I'M TERRIFIED OF THE MONSTER MYSELF! HE... HE ISN'T HUMAN!
THIS IS THE ADDRESS WHERE HIS GANG HANGS OUT! I'LL TURN STATE'S EVIDENCE..
I'LL LEAVE YOU AT THE NEAREST POLICE STATION- THEN GET AFTER THOSE MOBSTERS.
SOME HOURS LATER, AFTER MARVIN WALSH AND HIS CONFESSION HAVE BEEN PLACED IN THE HANDS OF THE AUTHORITIES, A WINGED FORM SWOOPS DOWN ON THE SLUM DISTRICT.
THAT'S THE PLACE. I ONLY HOPE THE MONSTER IS THERE WITH HIS MEN!
4

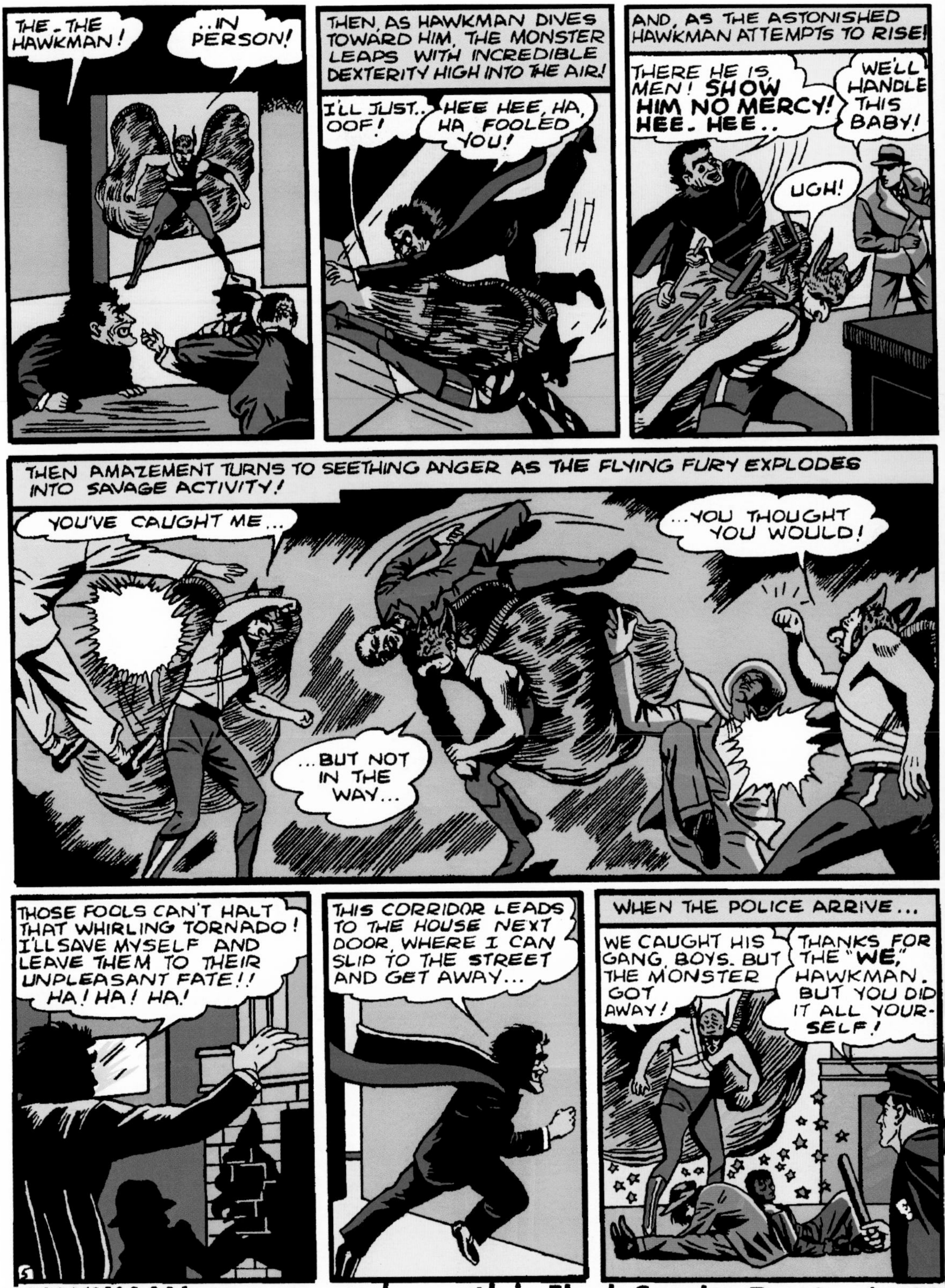
THE - THE HAWKMAN!
..IN PERSON!
THEN, AS HAWKMAN DIVES TOWARD HIM, THE MONSTER LEAPS WITH INCREDIBLE DEXTERITY HIGH INTO THE AIR!
I'LL JUST.. OOF!
HEE HEE, HA, HA FOOLED YOU!
AND, AS THE ASTONISHED HAWKMAN ATTEMPTS TO RISE!
THERE HE IS, MEN! SHOW HIM NO MERCY! HEE - HEE..
WE'LL HANDLE THIS BABY!
UGH!
THEN AMAZEMENT TURNS TO SEETHING ANGER AS THE FLYING FURY EXPLODES INTO SAVAGE ACTIVITY!
YOU'VE CAUGHT ME...
...BUT NOT IN THE WAY...
...YOU THOUGHT YOU WOULD!
THOSE FOOLS CAN'T HALT THAT WHIRLING TORNADO! I'LL SAVE MYSELF AND LEAVE THEM TO THEIR UNPLEASANT FATE!! HA! HA! HA!
5
THIS CORRIDOR LEADS TO THE HOUSE NEXT DOOR, WHERE I CAN SLIP TO THE STREET AND GET AWAY...
WHEN THE POLICE ARRIVE...
WE CAUGHT HIS GANG, BOYS. BUT THE MONSTER GOT AWAY!
THANKS FOR THE "WE," HAWKMAN. BUT YOU DID IT ALL YOURSELF!

HAWKMAN appears each month in Flash Comics-Don't miss it!

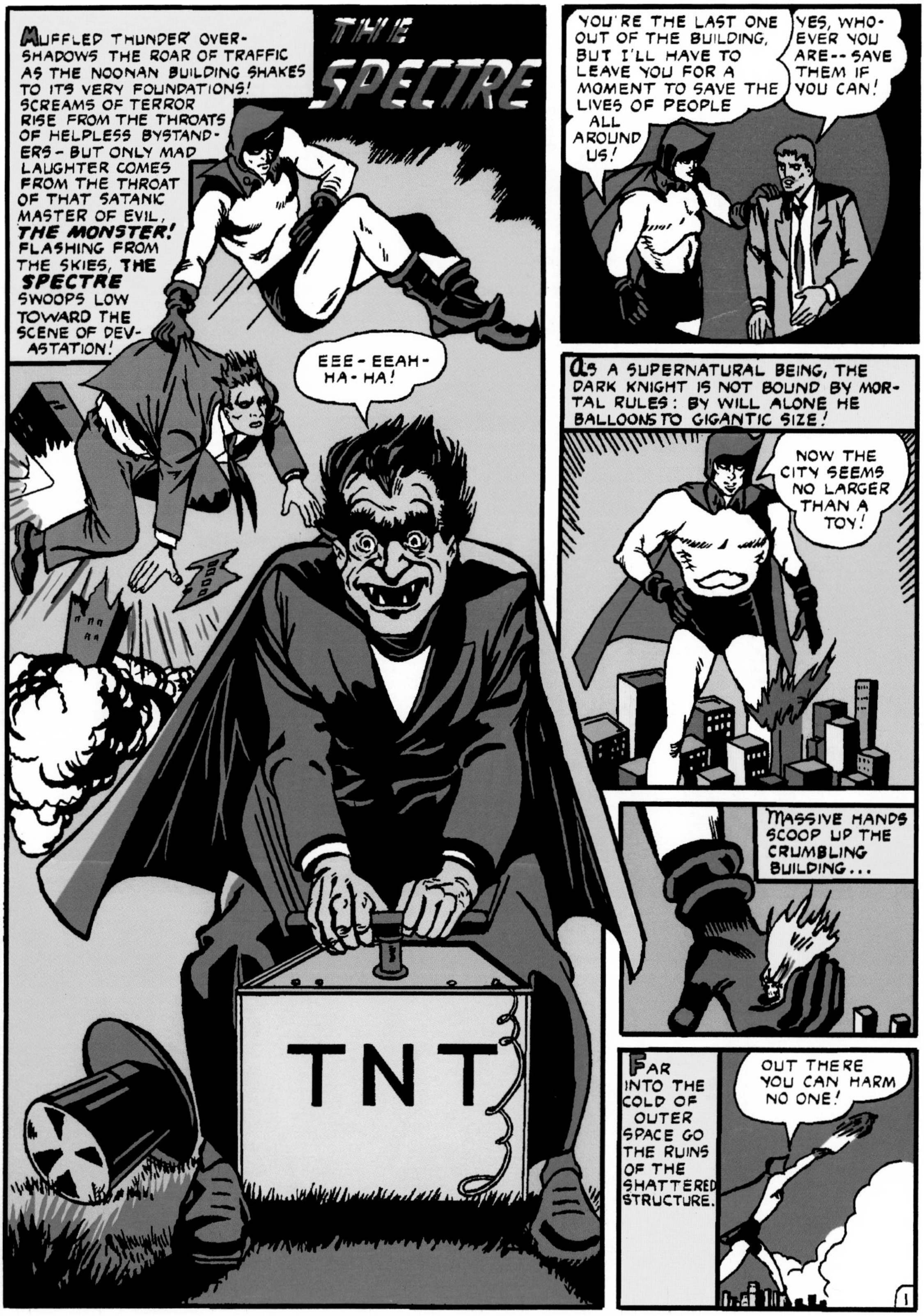
THE SPECTRE
MUFFLED THUNDER OVER-SHADOWS THE ROAR OF TRAFFIC AS THE NOONAN BUILDING SHAKES TO ITS VERY FOUNDATIONS! SCREAMS OF TERROR RISE FROM THE THROATS OF HELPLESS BYSTANDERS - BUT ONLY MAD LAUGHTER COMES FROM THE THROAT OF THAT SATANIC MASTER OF EVIL, THE MONSTER! FLASHING FROM THE SKIES, THE SPECTRE SWOOPS LOW TOWARD THE SCENE OF DEVASTATION!
EEE-EEAH-HA-HA!
TNT
YOU'RE THE LAST ONE OUT OF THE BUILDING, BUT I'LL HAVE TO LEAVE YOU FOR A MOMENT TO SAVE THE LIVES OF PEOPLE ALL AROUND US!
YES, WHO-EVER YOU ARE--SAVE THEM IF YOU CAN!
AS A SUPERNATURAL BEING, THE DARK KNIGHT IS NOT BOUND BY MORTAL RULES: BY WILL ALONE HE BALLOONS TO GIGANTIC SIZE!
NOW THE CITY SEEMS NO LARGER THAN A TOY!
MASSIVE HANDS SCOOP UP THE CRUMBLING BUILDING...
FAR INTO THE COLD OF OUTER SPACE GO THE RUINS OF THE SHATTERED STRUCTURE.
OUT THERE YOU CAN HARM NO ONE!
1

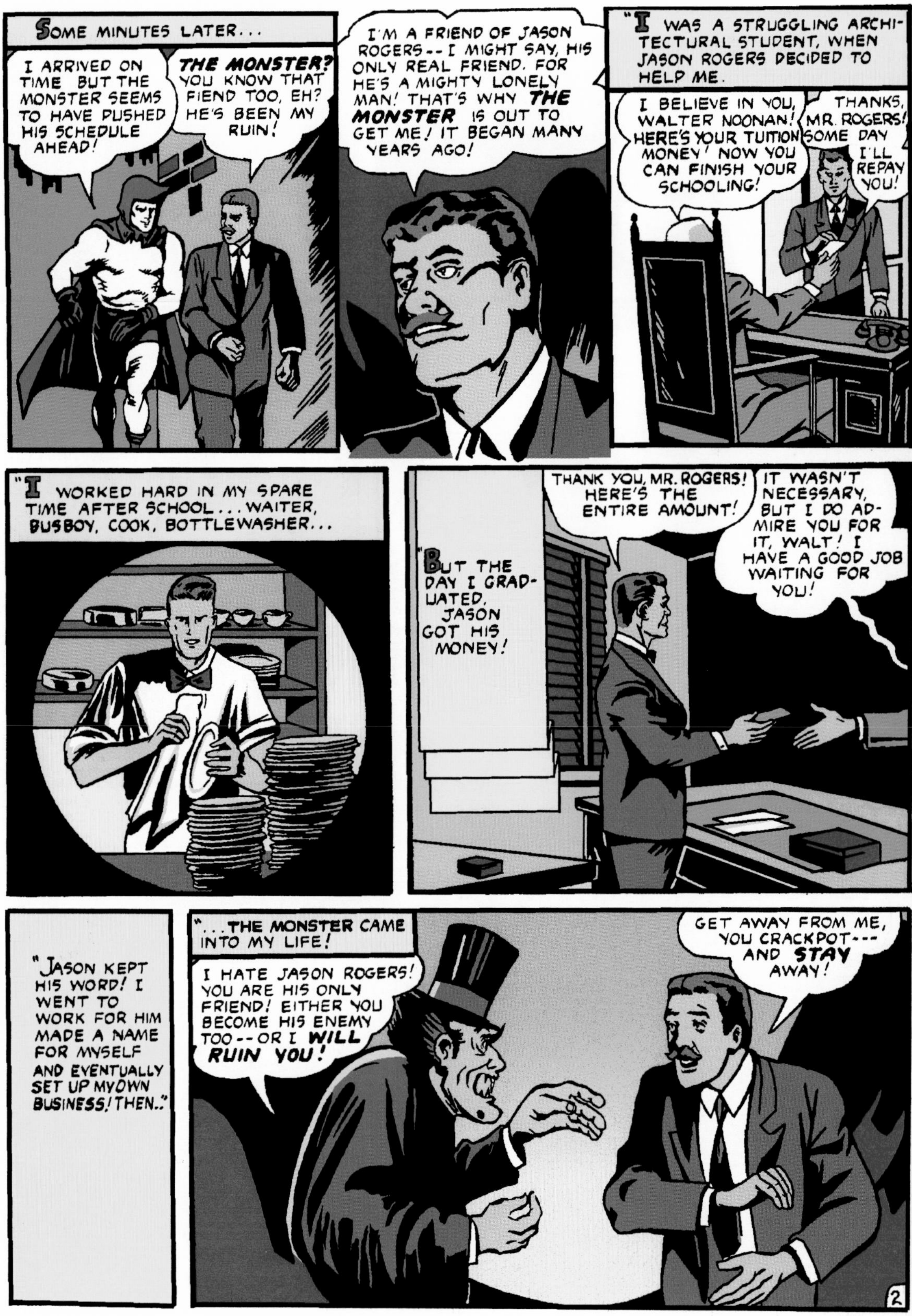

SOME MINUTES LATER...
I ARRIVED ON TIME BUT THE MONSTER SEEMS TO HAVE PUSHED HIS SCHEDULE AHEAD!
THE MONSTER? YOU KNOW THAT FIEND TOO, EH? HE'S BEEN MY RUIN!
I'M A FRIEND OF JASON ROGERS-- I MIGHT SAY, HIS ONLY REAL FRIEND. FOR HE'S A MIGHTY LONELY MAN! THAT'S WHY THE MONSTER IS OUT TO GET ME! IT BEGAN MANY YEARS AGO!
"I WAS A STRUGGLING ARCHITECTURAL STUDENT, WHEN JASON ROGERS DECIDED TO HELP ME.
I BELIEVE IN YOU, WALTER NOONAN! HERE'S YOUR TUITION MONEY! NOW YOU CAN FINISH YOUR SCHOOLING!
THANKS, MR. ROGERS! SOME DAY I'LL REPAY YOU!
"I WORKED HARD IN MY SPARE TIME AFTER SCHOOL... WAITER, BUSBOY, COOK, BOTTLEWASHER...
"BUT THE DAY I GRADUATED, JASON GOT HIS MONEY!
THANK YOU, MR. ROGERS! HERE'S THE ENTIRE AMOUNT!
IT WASN'T NECESSARY, BUT I DO ADMIRE YOU FOR IT, WALT! I HAVE A GOOD JOB WAITING FOR YOU!
"JASON KEPT HIS WORD! I WENT TO WORK FOR HIM MADE A NAME FOR MYSELF AND EVENTUALLY SET UP MY OWN BUSINESS! THEN.."
"...THE MONSTER CAME INTO MY LIFE!
I HATE JASON ROGERS! YOU ARE HIS ONLY FRIEND! EITHER YOU BECOME HIS ENEMY TOO--OR I WILL RUIN YOU!
GET AWAY FROM ME, YOU CRACKPOT--- AND STAY AWAY!
2

"ROGERS WAS AFRAID FOR ME... WANTED TO STOP OUR FRIENDSHIP, BUT I WAS STUBBORN!

HMM... THE MONSTER WANTS FIFTY THOUSAND DOLLARS FROM ME OR HE'LL DYNAMITE THE NEW DAM! HE'S JUST BLUFFING!

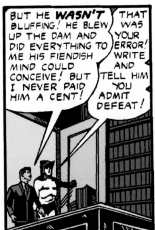

BUT HE *WASN'T* BLUFFING! HE BLEW UP THE DAM AND DID EVERYTHING TO ME HIS FIENDISH MIND COULD CONCEIVE! BUT I NEVER PAID HIM A CENT!

THAT WAS YOUR ERROR! WRITE AND TELL HIM YOU ADMIT DEFEAT!

NEVER! I'D RATHER DIE! I'M SURPRISED THAT YOU EVEN MAKE THAT SUGGESTION, SPECTRE!

I MUST LOCATE THE MONSTER IN ORDER TO DEFEAT HIM! IF YOU WERE TO TELL HIM TO MEET YOU HERE ...I COULD...

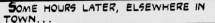

SOME HOURS LATER, ELSEWHERE IN TOWN...

HEEHEEHEEHAHAHA! NOONAN IS WILLING TO PAY ME OFF, EH? *VERY* INTERESTING, ESPECIALLY SINCE *THE SPECTRE* HAS HAD AMPLE TIME TO VISIT HIM!

DAT'S SMART, BOSS! HE'S SETTIN' A TRAP, AN' WE WOULD O' WALKED RIGHT INTO IT!

THE FOOL! TRYING TO TRICK ME LIKE THAT! I'LL SHOW HIM!

I'LL WALK INTO HIS TRAP! AND YOU MEN WILL WALK INTO THE TRAP WITH ME! THEN IF HE WANTS TO CAPTURE ME -- *LET HIM TRY!* EEE-EEA-HA-HA!

THE CLOCK IN THE NOONAN LIBRARY TOLLS THE HOUR OF MIDNIGHT, AS A HIDEOUS FORM APPEARS IN THE DOORWAY...

I HAVE COME FOR YOUR TRIBUTE, WALTER NOONAN!

I HAVE IT READY FOR YOU! HERE IT IS!

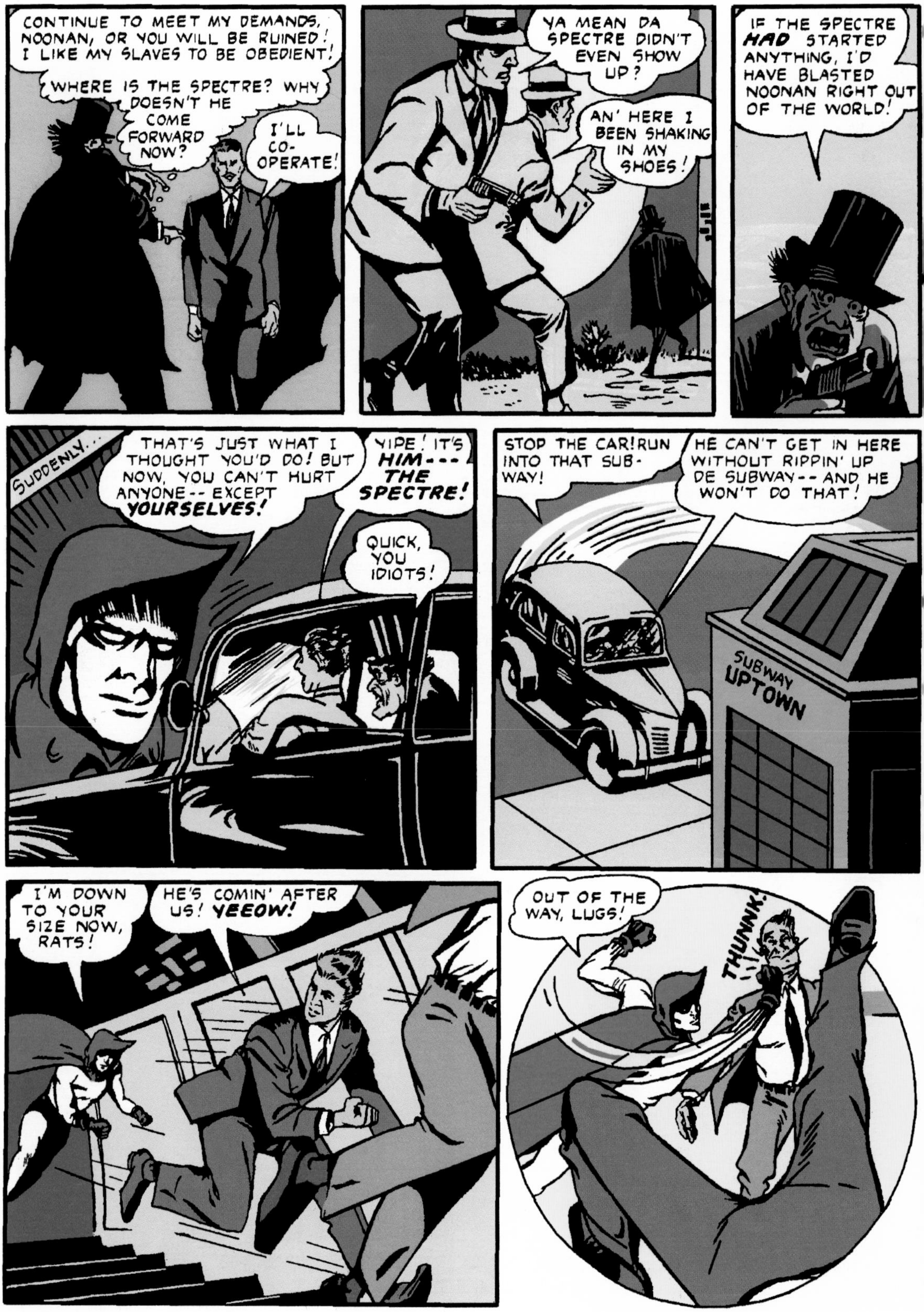
CONTINUE TO MEET MY DEMANDS, NOONAN, OR YOU WILL BE RUINED! I LIKE MY SLAVES TO BE OBEDIENT!
WHERE IS THE SPECTRE? WHY DOESN'T HE COME FORWARD NOW?
I'LL CO-OPERATE!
YA MEAN DA SPECTRE DIDN'T EVEN SHOW UP?
AN' HERE I BEEN SHAKING IN MY SHOES!
IF THE SPECTRE HAD STARTED ANYTHING, I'D HAVE BLASTED NOONAN RIGHT OUT OF THE WORLD!
SUDDENLY...
THAT'S JUST WHAT I THOUGHT YOU'D DO! BUT NOW, YOU CAN'T HURT ANYONE -- EXCEPT YOURSELVES!
YIPE! IT'S HIM--- THE SPECTRE!
QUICK, YOU IDIOTS!
STOP THE CAR! RUN INTO THAT SUB-WAY!
HE CAN'T GET IN HERE WITHOUT RIPPIN' UP DE SUBWAY-- AND HE WON'T DO THAT!
SUBWAY UPTOWN
I'M DOWN TO YOUR SIZE NOW, RATS!
HE'S COMIN' AFTER US! YEEOW!
OUT OF THE WAY, LUGS!
THUNNK!

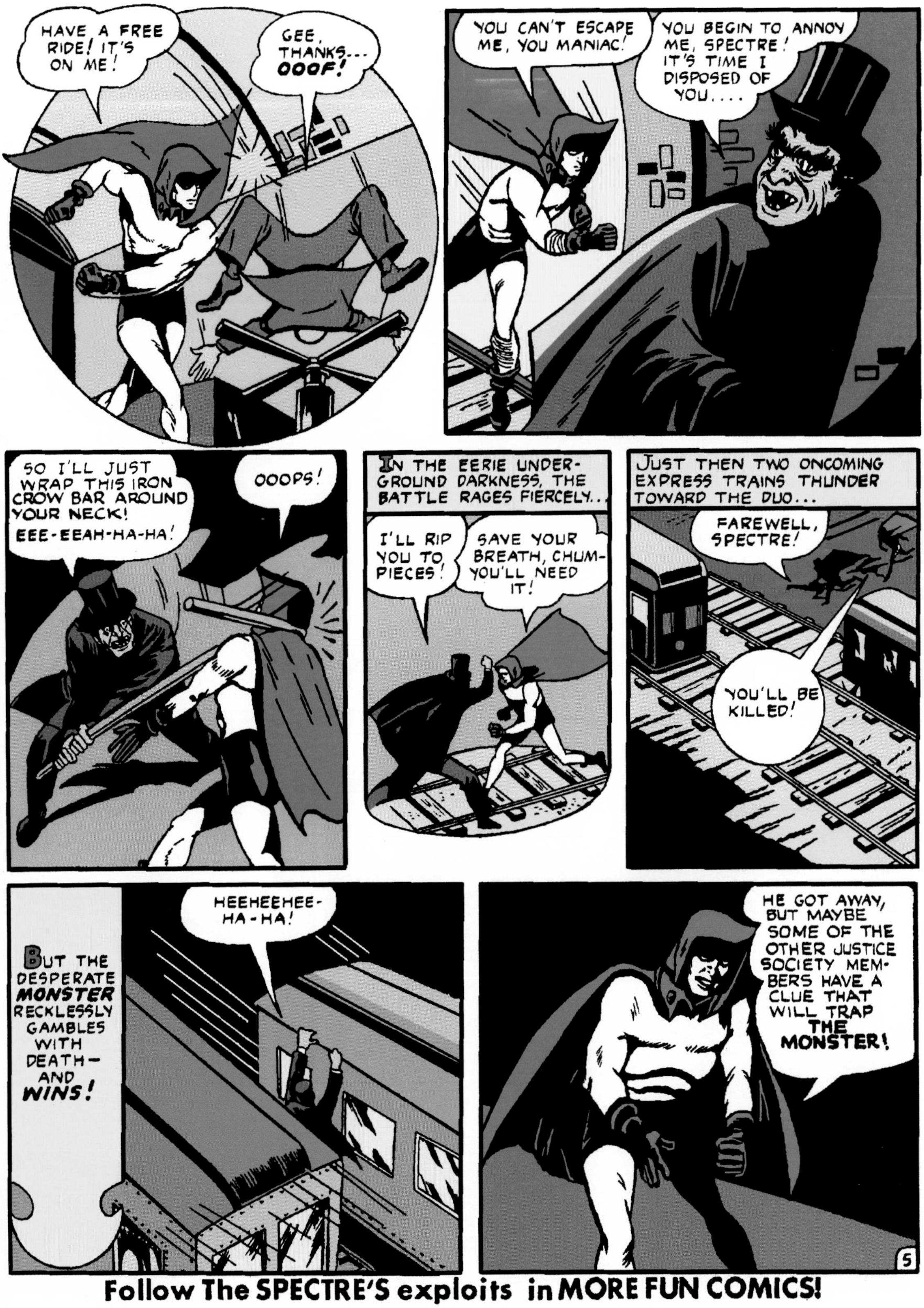
HAVE A FREE RIDE! IT'S ON ME!
GEE, THANKS... OOOF!
YOU CAN'T ESCAPE ME, YOU MANIAC!
YOU BEGIN TO ANNOY ME, SPECTRE! IT'S TIME I DISPOSED OF YOU....
SO I'LL JUST WRAP THIS IRON CROW BAR AROUND YOUR NECK! EEE-EEAH-HA-HA!
OOOPS!
IN THE EERIE UNDER-GROUND DARKNESS, THE BATTLE RAGES FIERCELY...
I'LL RIP YOU TO PIECES!
SAVE YOUR BREATH, CHUM-YOU'LL NEED IT!
JUST THEN TWO ONCOMING EXPRESS TRAINS THUNDER TOWARD THE DUO...
FAREWELL, SPECTRE!
YOU'LL BE KILLED!
BUT THE DESPERATE MONSTER RECKLESSLY GAMBLES WITH DEATH- AND WINS!
HEEHEEHEE-HA-HA!
HE GOT AWAY, BUT MAYBE SOME OF THE OTHER JUSTICE SOCIETY MEM-BERS HAVE A CLUE THAT WILL TRAP THE MONSTER!
5

Follow The SPECTRE'S exploits in MORE FUN COMICS!

LEAVING THE JUSTICE SOCIETY MEETING, **THE ATOM** HEADS STRAIGHT FOR THE SCENE OF **THE MONSTER'S** INTENDED CRIME! STANDING LIKE A WALL BETWEEN THE GRIM MACHINATIONS OF **THE MONSTER** AND THE VICTIMS OF HIS TYRANNY, THE MIGHTY MIDGET WAITS EXPECTANTLY FOR THE FIRST SIGN OF TROUBLE--

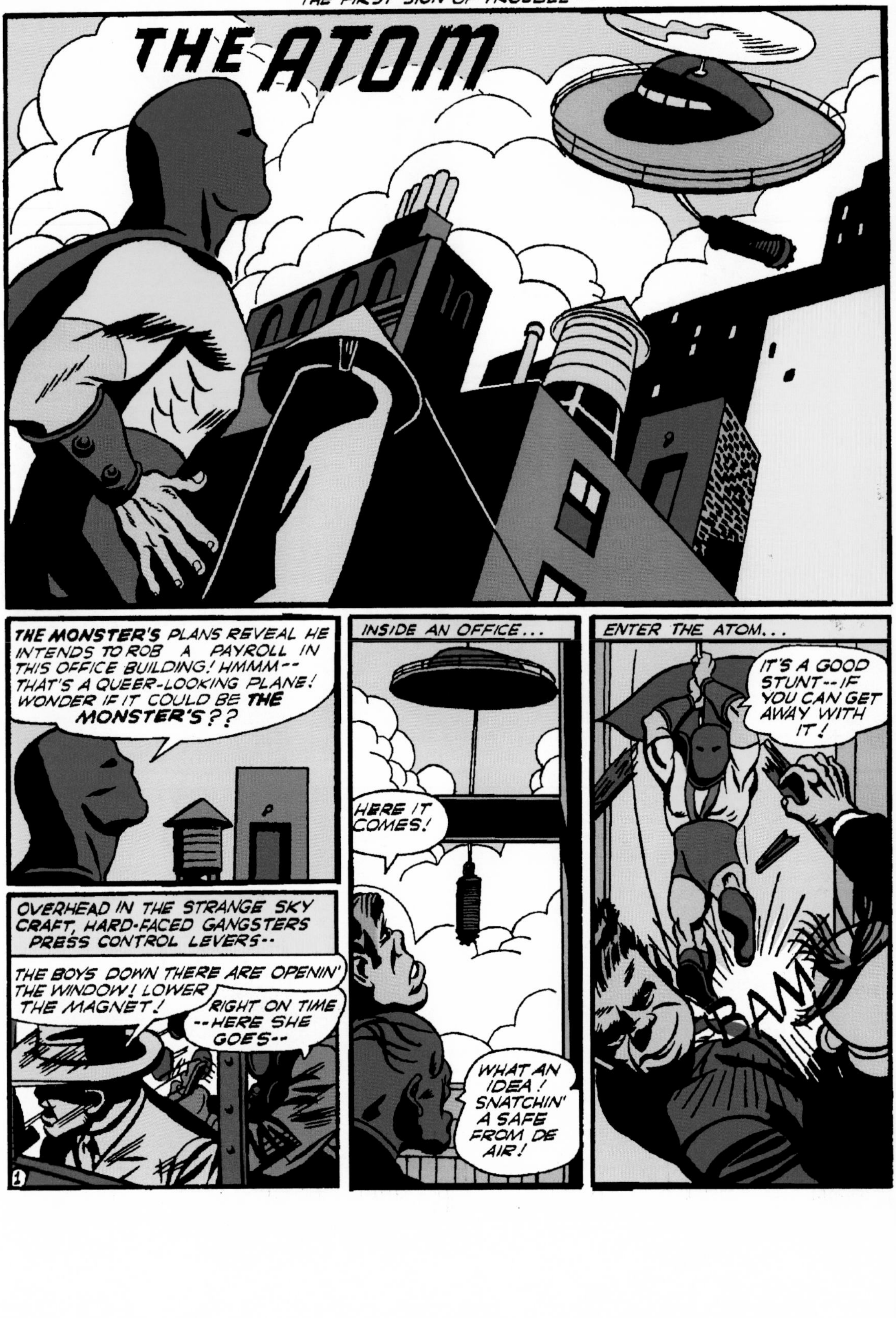
THE ATOM
THE MONSTER'S PLANS REVEAL HE INTENDS TO ROB A PAYROLL IN THIS OFFICE BUILDING! HMMM-- THAT'S A QUEER-LOOKING PLANE! WONDER IF IT COULD BE THE MONSTER'S??
OVERHEAD IN THE STRANGE SKY CRAFT, HARD-FACED GANGSTERS PRESS CONTROL LEVERS--
THE BOYS DOWN THERE ARE OPENIN' THE WINDOW! LOWER THE MAGNET!
RIGHT ON TIME --HERE SHE GOES--
1
INSIDE AN OFFICE...
HERE IT COMES!
WHAT AN IDEA! SNATCHIN' A SAFE FROM DE AIR!
ENTER THE ATOM...
IT'S A GOOD STUNT--IF YOU CAN GET AWAY WITH IT!
BAM

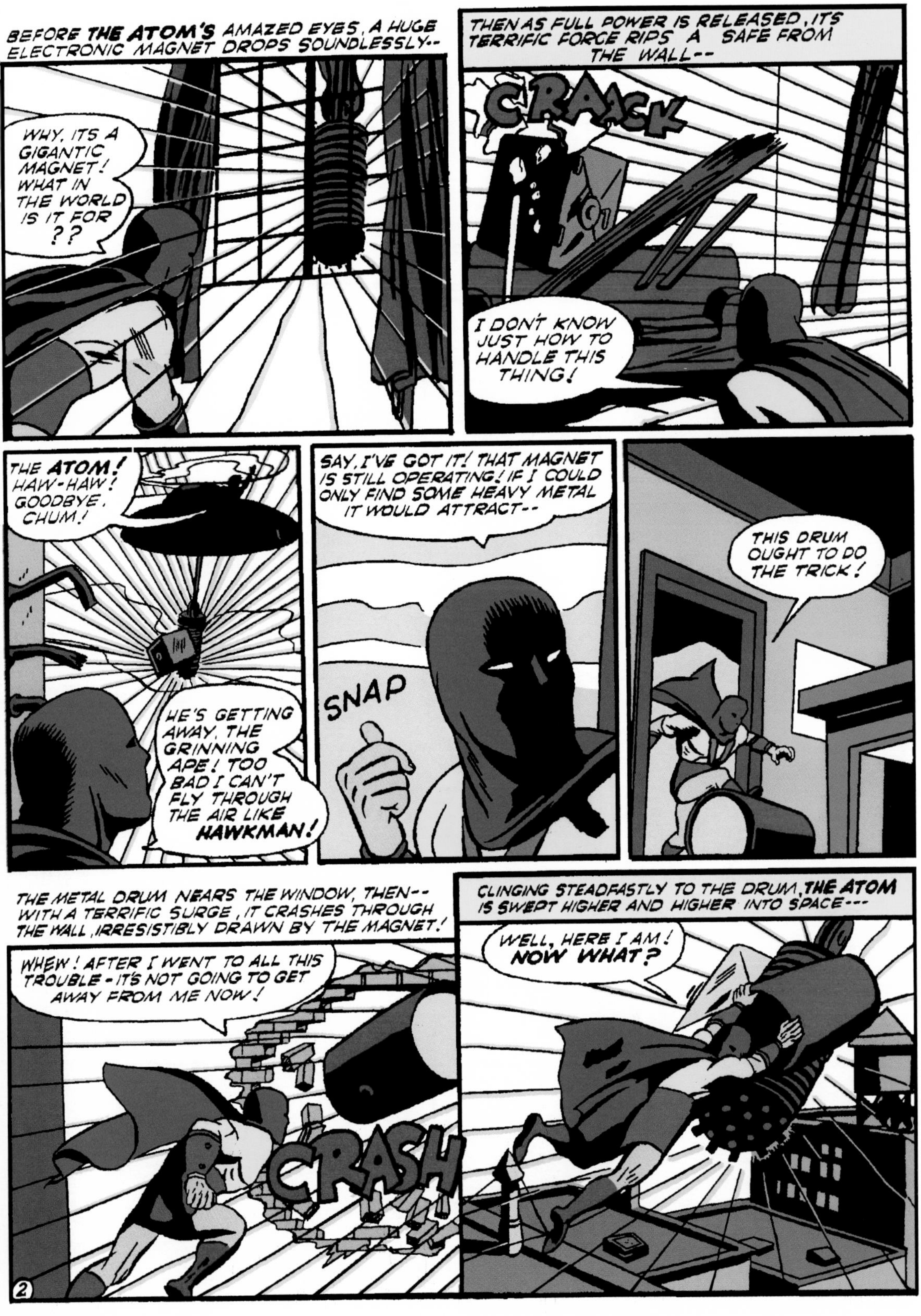
BEFORE THE ATOM'S AMAZED EYES, A HUGE ELECTRONIC MAGNET DROPS SOUNDLESSLY--
WHY, ITS A GIGANTIC MAGNET! WHAT IN THE WORLD IS IT FOR ??
THEN AS FULL POWER IS RELEASED, ITS TERRIFIC FORCE RIPS A SAFE FROM THE WALL--
CRAACK
I DON'T KNOW JUST HOW TO HANDLE THIS THING!
THE ATOM! HAW-HAW! GOODBYE, CHUM!
HE'S GETTING AWAY, THE GRINNING APE! TOO BAD I CAN'T FLY THROUGH THE AIR LIKE HAWKMAN!
SAY, I'VE GOT IT! THAT MAGNET IS STILL OPERATING! IF I COULD ONLY FIND SOME HEAVY METAL IT WOULD ATTRACT--
SNAP
THIS DRUM OUGHT TO DO THE TRICK!
THE METAL DRUM NEARS THE WINDOW, THEN-- WITH A TERRIFIC SURGE, IT CRASHES THROUGH THE WALL, IRRESISTIBLY DRAWN BY THE MAGNET!
WHEW! AFTER I WENT TO ALL THIS TROUBLE - IT'S NOT GOING TO GET AWAY FROM ME NOW!
CRASH
2
CLINGING STEADFASTLY TO THE DRUM, THE ATOM IS SWEPT HIGHER AND HIGHER INTO SPACE---
WELL, HERE I AM! NOW WHAT?

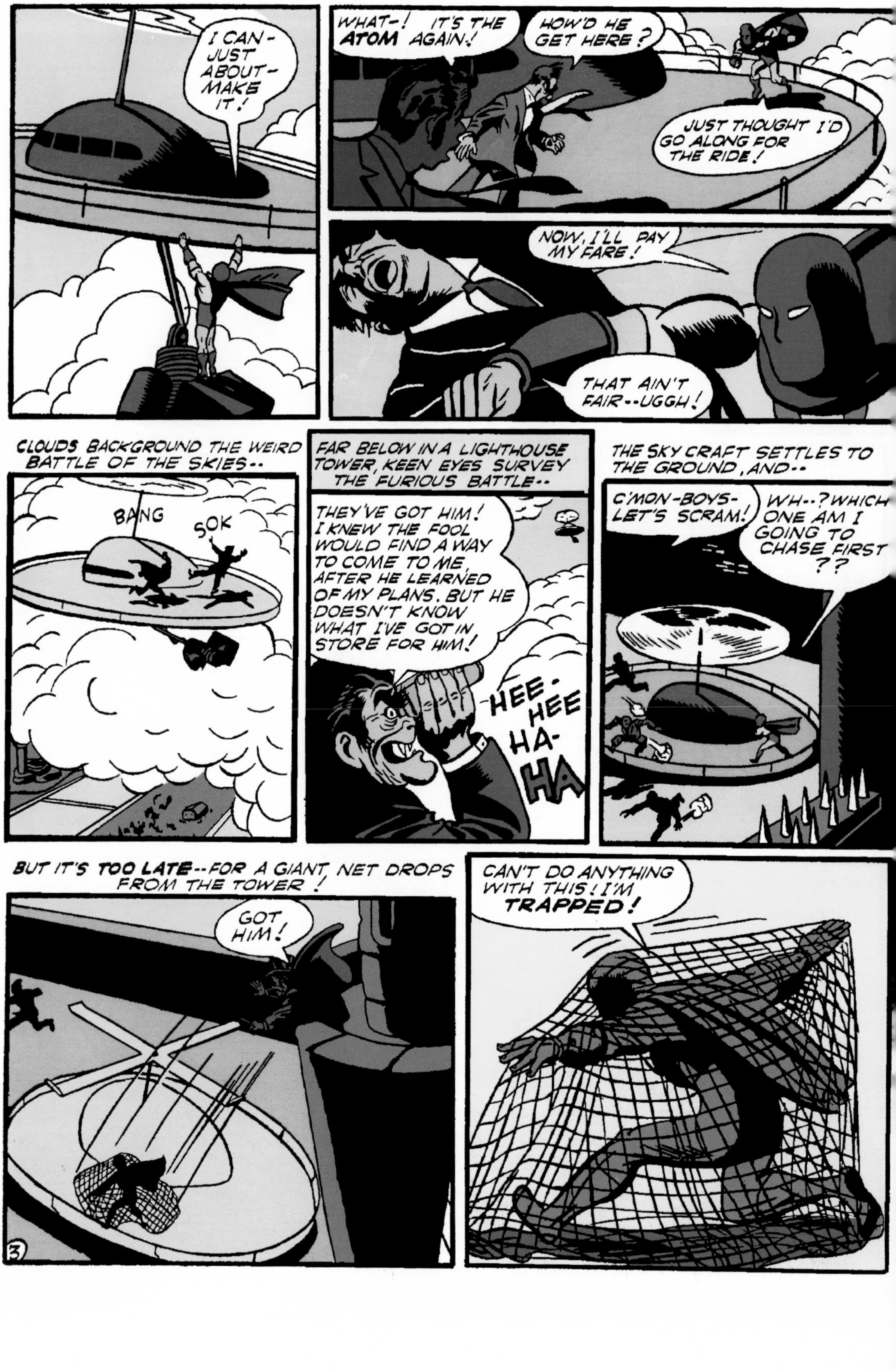
I CAN-JUST ABOUT-MAKE IT!
WHAT-! IT'S THE ATOM AGAIN!
HOW'D HE GET HERE?
JUST THOUGHT I'D GO ALONG FOR THE RIDE!
NOW, I'LL PAY MY FARE!
THAT AIN'T FAIR--UGGH!
CLOUDS BACKGROUND THE WEIRD BATTLE OF THE SKIES--
BANG
SOK
FAR BELOW IN A LIGHTHOUSE TOWER, KEEN EYES SURVEY THE FURIOUS BATTLE--
THEY'VE GOT HIM! I KNEW THE FOOL WOULD FIND A WAY TO COME TO ME, AFTER HE LEARNED OF MY PLANS. BUT HE DOESN'T KNOW WHAT I'VE GOT IN STORE FOR HIM!
HEE-HEE HA-HA
THE SKY CRAFT SETTLES TO THE GROUND, AND--
C'MON-BOYS-LET'S SCRAM!
WH--? WHICH ONE AM I GOING TO CHASE FIRST??
BUT IT'S TOO LATE--FOR A GIANT NET DROPS FROM THE TOWER!
GOT HIM!
CAN'T DO ANYTHING WITH THIS! I'M TRAPPED!
3

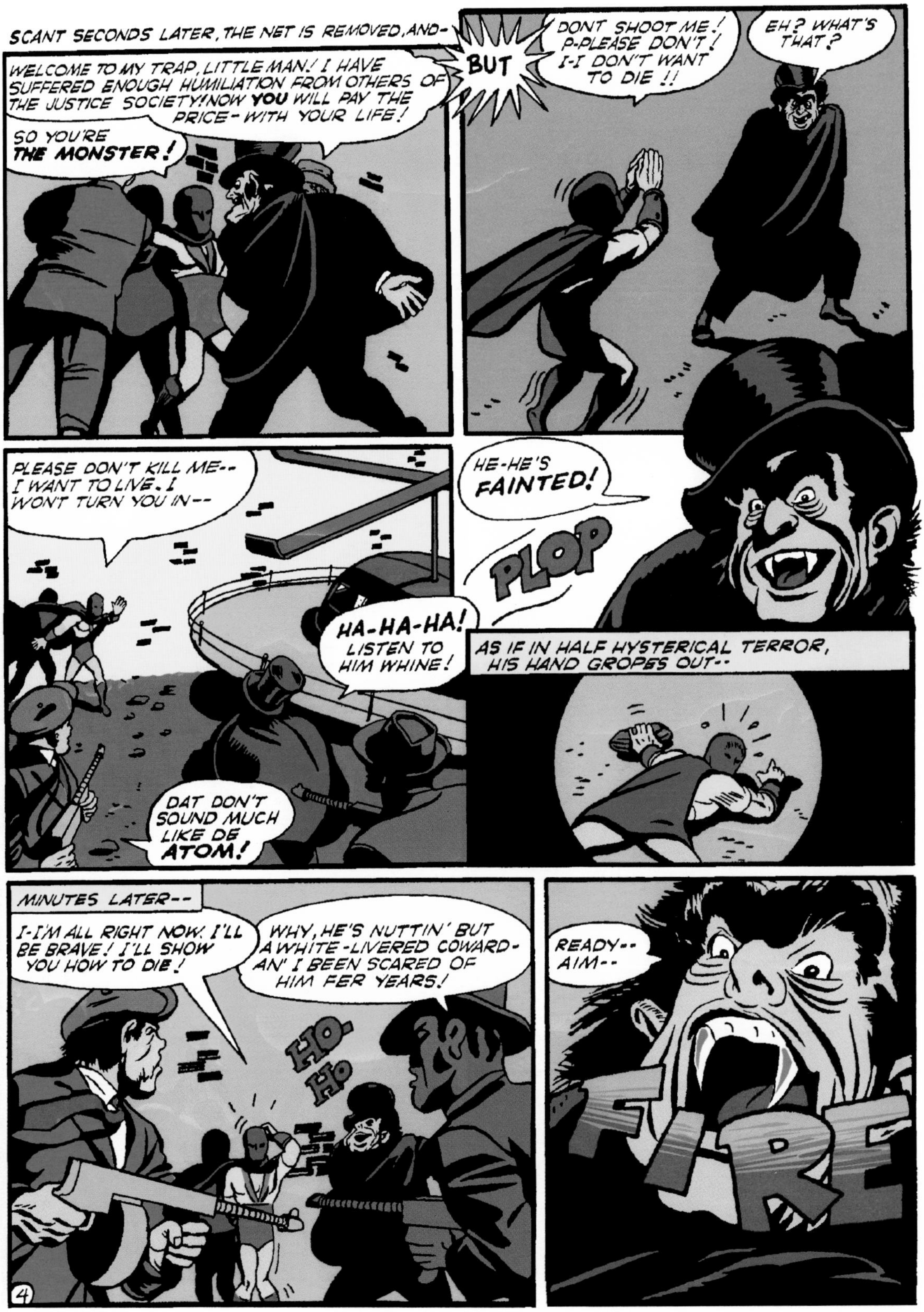
SCANT SECONDS LATER, THE NET IS REMOVED, AND-
WELCOME TO MY TRAP, LITTLE MAN! I HAVE SUFFERED ENOUGH HUMILIATION FROM OTHERS OF THE JUSTICE SOCIETY! NOW YOU WILL PAY THE PRICE- WITH YOUR LIFE!
SO YOU'RE THE MONSTER!
BUT
DONT SHOOT ME! P-PLEASE DON'T! I-I DON'T WANT TO DIE!!
EH? WHAT'S THAT?
PLEASE DON'T KILL ME-- I WANT TO LIVE. I WONT TURN YOU IN--
HA-HA-HA! LISTEN TO HIM WHINE!
DAT DON'T SOUND MUCH LIKE DE ATOM!
HE-HE'S FAINTED!
PLOP
AS IF IN HALF HYSTERICAL TERROR, HIS HAND GROPES OUT--
MINUTES LATER--
I-I'M ALL RIGHT NOW. I'LL BE BRAVE! I'LL SHOW YOU HOW TO DIE!
WHY, HE'S NUTTIN' BUT A WHITE-LIVERED COWARD- AN' I BEEN SCARED OF HIM FER YEARS!
HO-HO
4
READY-- AIM--
FIRE

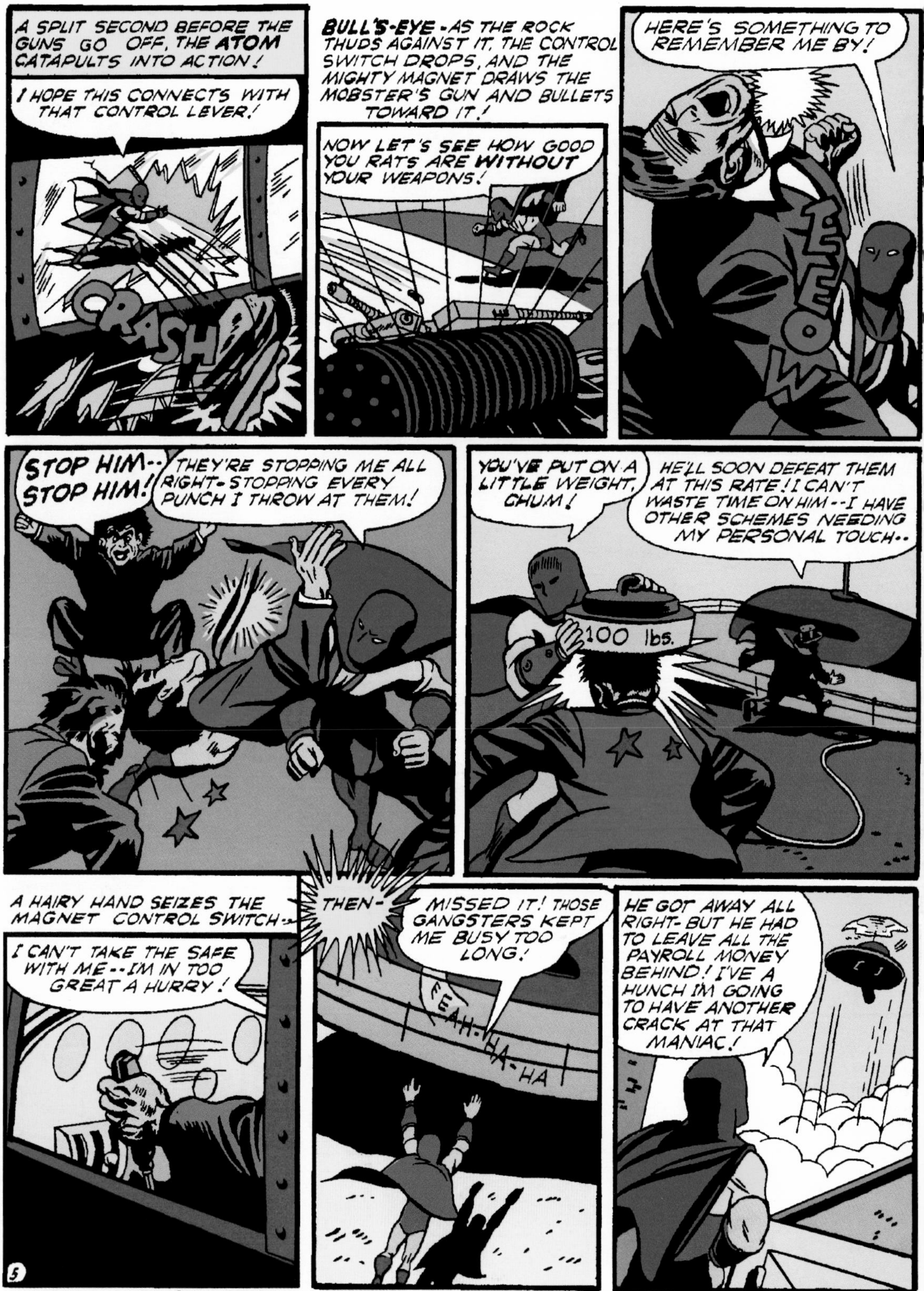
A SPLIT SECOND BEFORE THE GUNS GO OFF, THE ATOM CATAPULTS INTO ACTION!
I HOPE THIS CONNECTS WITH THAT CONTROL LEVER!
CRASH
BULL'S-EYE -AS THE ROCK THUDS AGAINST IT, THE CONTROL SWITCH DROPS, AND THE MIGHTY MAGNET DRAWS THE MOBSTER'S GUN AND BULLETS TOWARD IT!
NOW LET'S SEE HOW GOOD YOU RATS ARE WITHOUT YOUR WEAPONS!
HERE'S SOMETHING TO REMEMBER ME BY!
EEEOW
STOP HIM-- STOP HIM!
THEY'RE STOPPING ME ALL RIGHT- STOPPING EVERY PUNCH I THROW AT THEM!
YOU'VE PUT ON A LITTLE WEIGHT, CHUM!
100 lbs.
HE'LL SOON DEFEAT THEM AT THIS RATE! I CAN'T WASTE TIME ON HIM --I HAVE OTHER SCHEMES NEEDING MY PERSONAL TOUCH..
A HAIRY HAND SEIZES THE MAGNET CONTROL SWITCH--
I CAN'T TAKE THE SAFE WITH ME --I'M IN TOO GREAT A HURRY!
THEN-
MISSED IT! THOSE GANGSTERS KEPT ME BUSY TOO LONG!
HEAH-HA-HA
HE GOT AWAY ALL RIGHT- BUT HE HAD TO LEAVE ALL THE PAYROLL MONEY BEHIND! I'VE A HUNCH I'M GOING TO HAVE ANOTHER CRACK AT THAT MANIAC!
5

Follow the adventures of The ATOM *in every issue of* **All-American Comics!**

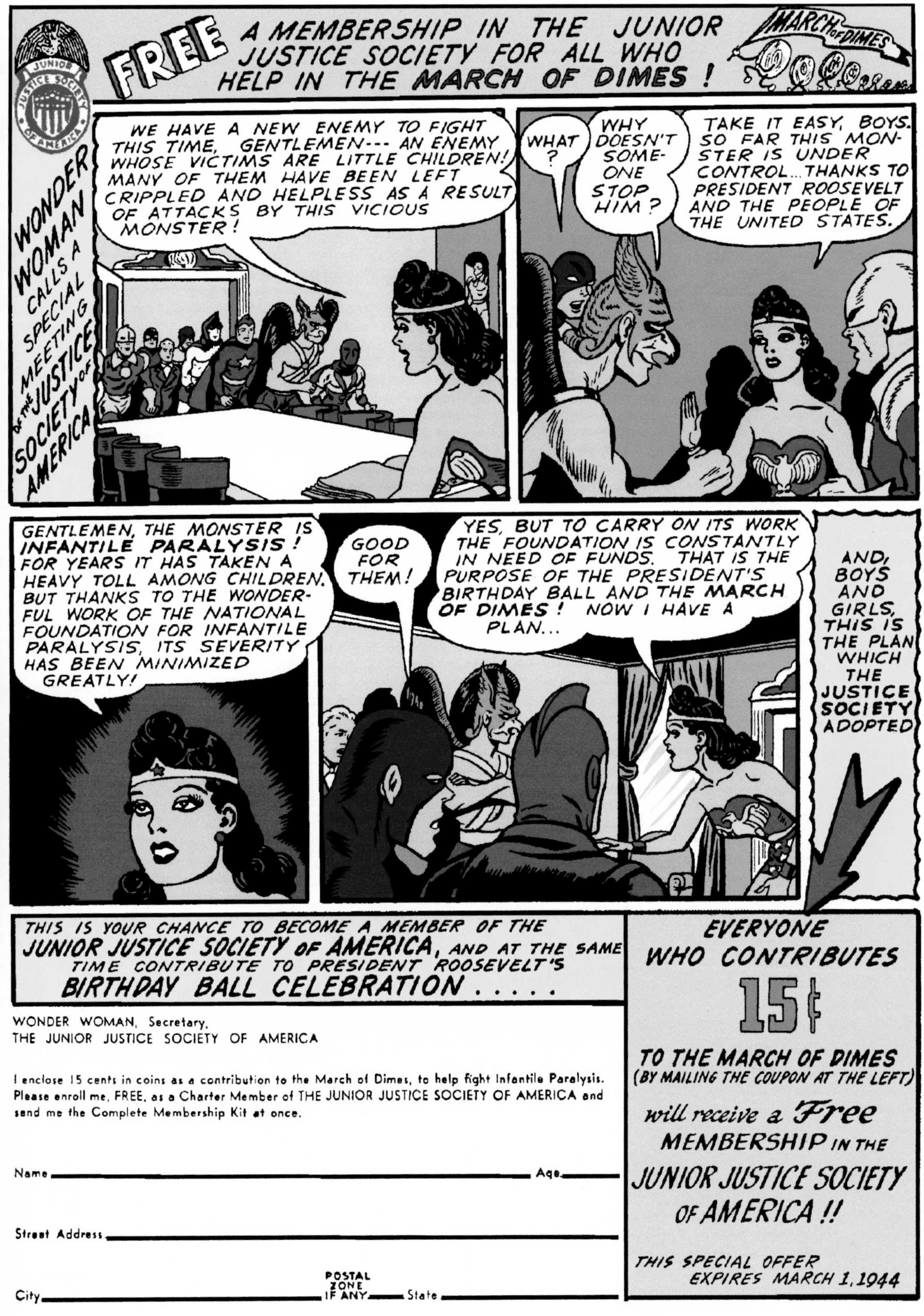
FREE
A MEMBERSHIP IN THE JUNIOR JUSTICE SOCIETY FOR ALL WHO HELP IN THE MARCH OF DIMES!
MARCH OF DIMES
JUNIOR JUSTICE SOCIETY OF AMERICA
WONDER WOMAN CALLS A SPECIAL MEETING OF THE JUSTICE SOCIETY OF AMERICA
WE HAVE A NEW ENEMY TO FIGHT THIS TIME, GENTLEMEN--- AN ENEMY WHOSE VICTIMS ARE LITTLE CHILDREN! MANY OF THEM HAVE BEEN LEFT CRIPPLED AND HELPLESS AS A RESULT OF ATTACKS BY THIS VICIOUS MONSTER!
WHAT?
WHY DOESN'T SOME-ONE STOP HIM?
TAKE IT EASY, BOYS. SO FAR THIS MON-STER IS UNDER CONTROL... THANKS TO PRESIDENT ROOSEVELT AND THE PEOPLE OF THE UNITED STATES.
GENTLEMEN, THE MONSTER IS INFANTILE PARALYSIS! FOR YEARS IT HAS TAKEN A HEAVY TOLL AMONG CHILDREN. BUT THANKS TO THE WONDER-FUL WORK OF THE NATIONAL FOUNDATION FOR INFANTILE PARALYSIS, ITS SEVERITY HAS BEEN MINIMIZED GREATLY!
GOOD FOR THEM!
YES, BUT TO CARRY ON ITS WORK THE FOUNDATION IS CONSTANTLY IN NEED OF FUNDS. THAT IS THE PURPOSE OF THE PRESIDENT'S BIRTHDAY BALL AND THE MARCH OF DIMES! NOW I HAVE A PLAN...
AND, BOYS AND GIRLS, THIS IS THE PLAN WHICH THE JUSTICE SOCIETY ADOPTED

THIS IS YOUR CHANCE TO BECOME A MEMBER OF THE **JUNIOR JUSTICE SOCIETY OF AMERICA**, AND AT THE SAME TIME CONTRIBUTE TO PRESIDENT ROOSEVELT'S **BIRTHDAY BALL CELEBRATION .....**

WONDER WOMAN, Secretary,
THE JUNIOR JUSTICE SOCIETY OF AMERICA

I enclose 15 cents in coins as a contribution to the March of Dimes, to help fight Infantile Paralysis. Please enroll me, FREE, as a Charter Member of THE JUNIOR JUSTICE SOCIETY OF AMERICA and send me the Complete Membership Kit at once.

Name ______________________ Age ______

Street Address ______________________

City ______________ POSTAL ZONE IF ANY ______ State ______________

EVERYONE WHO CONTRIBUTES

15¢

TO THE MARCH OF DIMES
(BY MAILING THE COUPON AT THE LEFT)

will receive a Free
MEMBERSHIP IN THE
JUNIOR JUSTICE SOCIETY OF AMERICA!!

THIS SPECIAL OFFER EXPIRES MARCH 1, 1944

BOMBS fell again without warning. Huge chunks of earth went flying through the air, leaving craters all around the landing field. Two Bostons, caught on the fringe of the field, would never fly again.

Parts of their fuselages whistled past the heads of Hop Harrigan and his flying partner, Tank Tinker, as they plowed through the mass of hurtling destruction onto the bomb-pocked field. They were going to have trouble getting their Lightnings into the air from the roughened tarmac, but no amount of trouble could have dissuaded the fighting duo from taking a crack at that *ghost plane!*

"You can't tell me a ghost did this job! The damage that blasted plane is doing is too darned real!" grunted Tinker.

"Plane? How do you know it's a plane?" retorted Hop, adjusting his helmet. "How does anyone know *what* it is? You never see it! You never hear it! You don't even see the bombs when they fall! That thing just flies over every night and lays its eggs, pretty as you please, and tears up half our airfield. When we scoot up after it—poof! It's gone! Nothing there!"

Hop shook his head disgustedly, climbed into the front office and signaled to the mechanic to kick away the chocks. Then his Lightning was tearing into the sky at a tremendous clip, winging up, up, to where that mystery bomber or ghost plane

or whatever it was, haunted the sky.

He couldn't understand how it was possible. Why couldn't they *see* this thing that kept raining death on them, night after night? Why couldn't they see the bombs? And worst of all, most crazy of all, why couldn't they *hear* anything?

Silent bombing! It was enough to drive a guy nuts! Even the electronic plane detectors could not pick up a sound. They had no warning whatever—just sudden death raining down on them. And by the time they got their interceptors into the air, the thing, whatever it was, was gone.

Ghost plane!

Hop smiled grimly as he wheeled his Lightning at 10,000 feet and climbed for altitude in great, sweeping circles. *Ghost Plane* was the nickname the men at the field had given the silent marauder of the skies. *You can't fight a ghost*, they had expostulated with Major Dunning, when called to account for not stopping the bomber.

"Nonsense!" Major Dunning had replied curtly. "He's probably just fast—too fast for you men. Gets away before you climb into the sky. If one of you doesn't knock him out of the sky next time he strikes, there's only one alternative. That is to have a constant patrol of interceptors in the air, day and night, watching for him.

"You men know what that means. It means that planes and men who should be out dealing blows to the enemy will have to stay here to guard the airport, on *defensive* maneuvers. Our efficiency as a fighting squadron will be cut in half.

"Now next time he strikes, go out and get him—and don't come back with any crazy tales about meeting a ghost—even a Jap ghost!"

Hop had asked a pointed question, then, which had made the Major nearly choke with rage, "If it's just an ordinary bomber, why don't we *hear* him?"

He was still wondering as he banked at 25,000 and searched the skies for signs of the enemy. He could not be hiding in a cloud, for the sky was as clear as a mirror. No planes were in the heavens, for as far as Harrigan could see, except the familiar twin-bodied Lockheeds.

Fury at being hoodwinked by the enemy tugged at Hop's heart as he wheeled the P-38 once more and headed toward northeast New Guinea. It was more likely that the *Ghost Plane* had headed that way, for the area there was Jap-held territory.

* * *

He didn't see it at once, because for the first few seconds he thought he was dreaming. Or maybe it was a mirage—an air mirage. He'd heard of them. About a mile ahead, a faint, shimmering outline of an airplane took shape.

Hop's eyes nearly started from his head. The plane looked so ghostlike, so unreal, that he could actually see through it! There was something in the place where the pilot should have been, but it didn't look like a human being—not even a Jap, Hop thought ironically.

Hop swallowed hard. For as suddenly as the shimmering vision had come into view, it disappeared. Although he revved his engines to the limit and streaked in the direction where he thought he had seen the

Ghost Plane, when he got there he was alone!

Abruptly, Hop took hold of himself. All this was crazy. He had been carried away by the ghostlike appearance of the plane. But he thought he knew now what it was. Yes, and he thought he knew how to stop it. . . .

*   *   *

Major Dunning's snicker, when Hop told him the story, was audible all over the ready room.

"So you say it wouldn't do any good to keep a patrol in the sky?" he rapped. "And why not?"

"Oh, I didn't say it wouldn't do good, sir," Hop hastened to add. "It would keep the *Ghost Plane* away, but,—well, you'll never capture her that way.

You see, the *Ghost Plane* is silent. Her pilot can hear our planes miles away, and pre-warned, won't attack us as long as our planes are in the sky. But we want to catch it, and if you'll try my way, I'm sure we will. Tank here is willing to play along and—"

"I'm not so sure I like it," muttered Tank under his breath, but Hop's elbow in his ribs changed his mind.

"Tank'll be glad to go up in the balloon and radio me when he sights the *Ghost Plane*. The balloon is silent, too. We'll simply be stealing some of the *Ghost Plane*'s thunder. He won't know anyone is around, watching. And, Tank, you'll have to keep a sharp lookout. He's not easy to see. All you get is a vague, ghostlike view—"

The big redhead listened quietly to the rest of Hop's instructions. He didn't relish the thought of staying in the same sky with a ghost, 15,000 feet in the air.

But after chow and a vacuum jug of steaming hot coffee was stowed into the basket of the balloon, the redhead brightened considerably. Tossing a couple of bags of ballast off to lighten her, Tank waved brightly to Hop. The men released the guy lines and the balloon started climbing slowly into the wind.

It was cold up there in the sky, and still no sign of the *Ghost Plane*. Tank stood waiting, tense, expecting it to pop out before his eyes any minute. He wiped his frosted goggles with a piece of cloth, suddenly started as he saw, just as Hop

had, the shimmering outline of a plane below and to the right of him. Jubilant, Tank yelled into the radio.

"Come and get her, Hop!" he shouted. "The *Ghost Plane* is spookin' right below me! Come and haunt 'er out of the sky, Hop, ol' boy!"

Tank realized with a start that that dull, plopping sound was tracer fire directed at his balloon. With startling suddenness, the gas-filled balloon collapsed and Tank was hurtling down, down, down in the basket. He tugged at his rip-cord frantically, at the same time aware that the *Ghost Plane* was swooping in for the kill. The enemy would puncture that parachute just as quickly, just as mercilessly, as he had punctured the balloon.

Nothing could have looked more beautiful to Tank, at that moment, than Hop's plane zooming up from below. The *Ghost Plane*'s pilot, warned by the throb of the motor, tried to hightail it. Too late!

"Oh, mama!" beamed Tank, now tranquilly floating earthward in his silk umbrella. "That was bee-yootiful, Hop!" Harrigan had gotten the strange craft's pilot right in his sights and pressed stick-trips smartly.

And now, before Tank's startled gaze, the ace of the airways was dropping a ladder from his P-38, climbing down it and hanging directly over the cockpit of the *Ghost Plane* which was still on an even keel although the pilot was dead at the controls. Hop hung perilously for a moment, 15,000 feet up, then dropped into the *Ghost Plane*'s cockpit, on top of a very dead Jap.

Hop brought her down to the bomb-torn airfield.

"Here's your *Ghost Plane*," he said, smiling grimly. "Nothing supernatural about it! It's simply the best camouflage job I've ever seen—transparent, with controls and bombs covered with an almost invisible paint and the pilot wearing clothes dyed the same color. And the reason we didn't *hear* it is that it ran on heated air, by jet propulsion, instead of using powerful engines like our own!"

Suddenly Major Dunning's face went white. He gripped Hop's arm and pointed an unsteady finger off toward the edge of the field. Something wrapped in a white coverall was approaching slowly.

"Don't let your nerves get the best of you, Major," laughed Hop. "That's just Tank Tinker entangled in his parachute!"

THE END

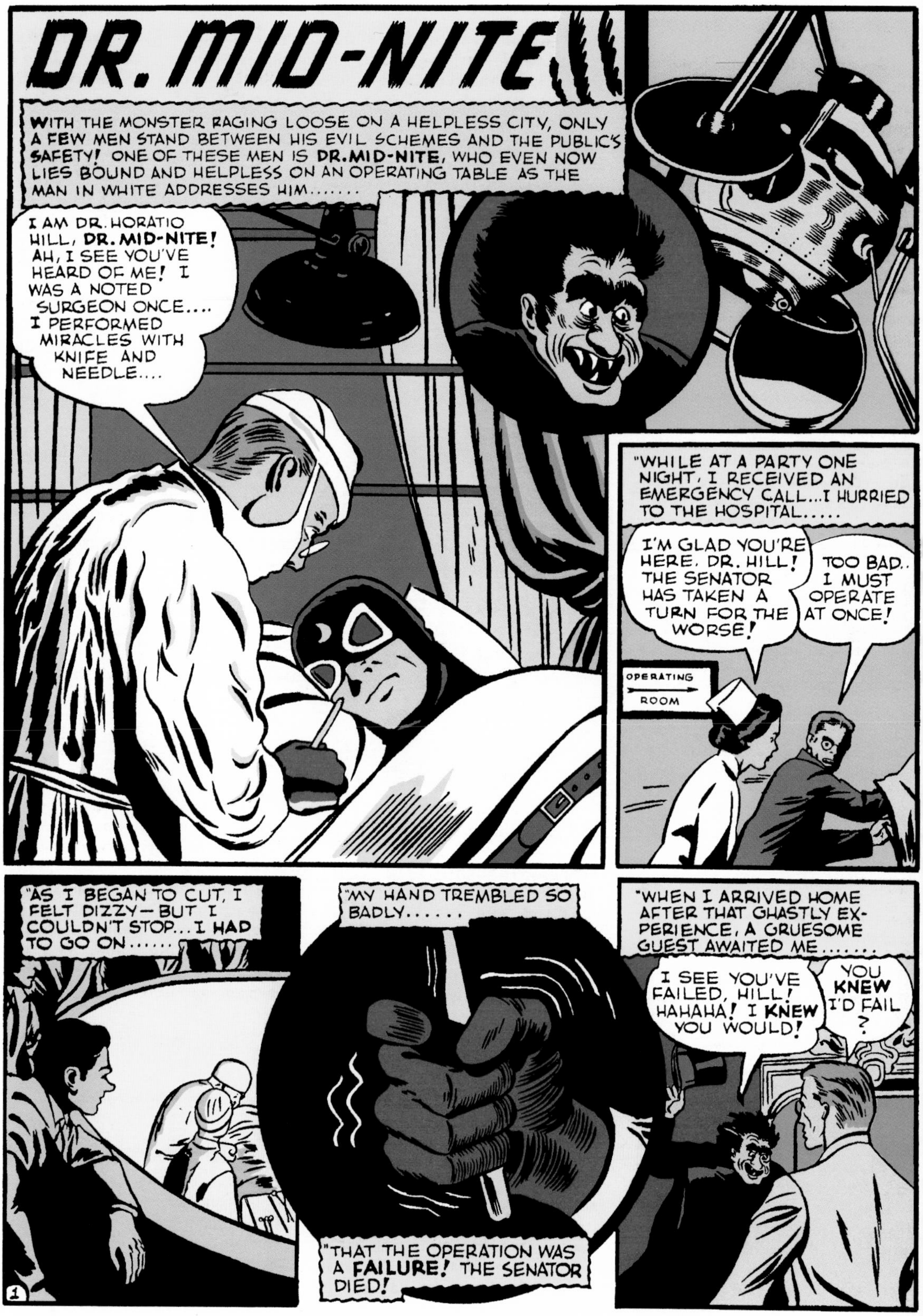
DR. MID-NITE
WITH THE MONSTER RAGING LOOSE ON A HELPLESS CITY, ONLY A FEW MEN STAND BETWEEN HIS EVIL SCHEMES AND THE PUBLIC'S SAFETY! ONE OF THESE MEN IS DR. MID-NITE, WHO EVEN NOW LIES BOUND AND HELPLESS ON AN OPERATING TABLE AS THE MAN IN WHITE ADDRESSES HIM.......
I AM DR. HORATIO HILL, DR. MID-NITE! AH, I SEE YOU'VE HEARD OF ME! I WAS A NOTED SURGEON ONCE.... I PERFORMED MIRACLES WITH KNIFE AND NEEDLE....
"WHILE AT A PARTY ONE NIGHT, I RECEIVED AN EMERGENCY CALL...I HURRIED TO THE HOSPITAL.....
I'M GLAD YOU'RE HERE, DR. HILL! THE SENATOR HAS TAKEN A TURN FOR THE WORSE!
TOO BAD.. I MUST OPERATE AT ONCE!
OPERATING ROOM
"AS I BEGAN TO CUT, I FELT DIZZY—BUT I COULDN'T STOP... I HAD TO GO ON......
"MY HAND TREMBLED SO BADLY......
"THAT THE OPERATION WAS A FAILURE! THE SENATOR DIED!
"WHEN I ARRIVED HOME AFTER THAT GHASTLY EXPERIENCE, A GRUESOME GUEST AWAITED ME.......
I SEE YOU'VE FAILED, HILL! HAHAHA! I KNEW YOU WOULD!
YOU KNEW I'D FAIL ?
1

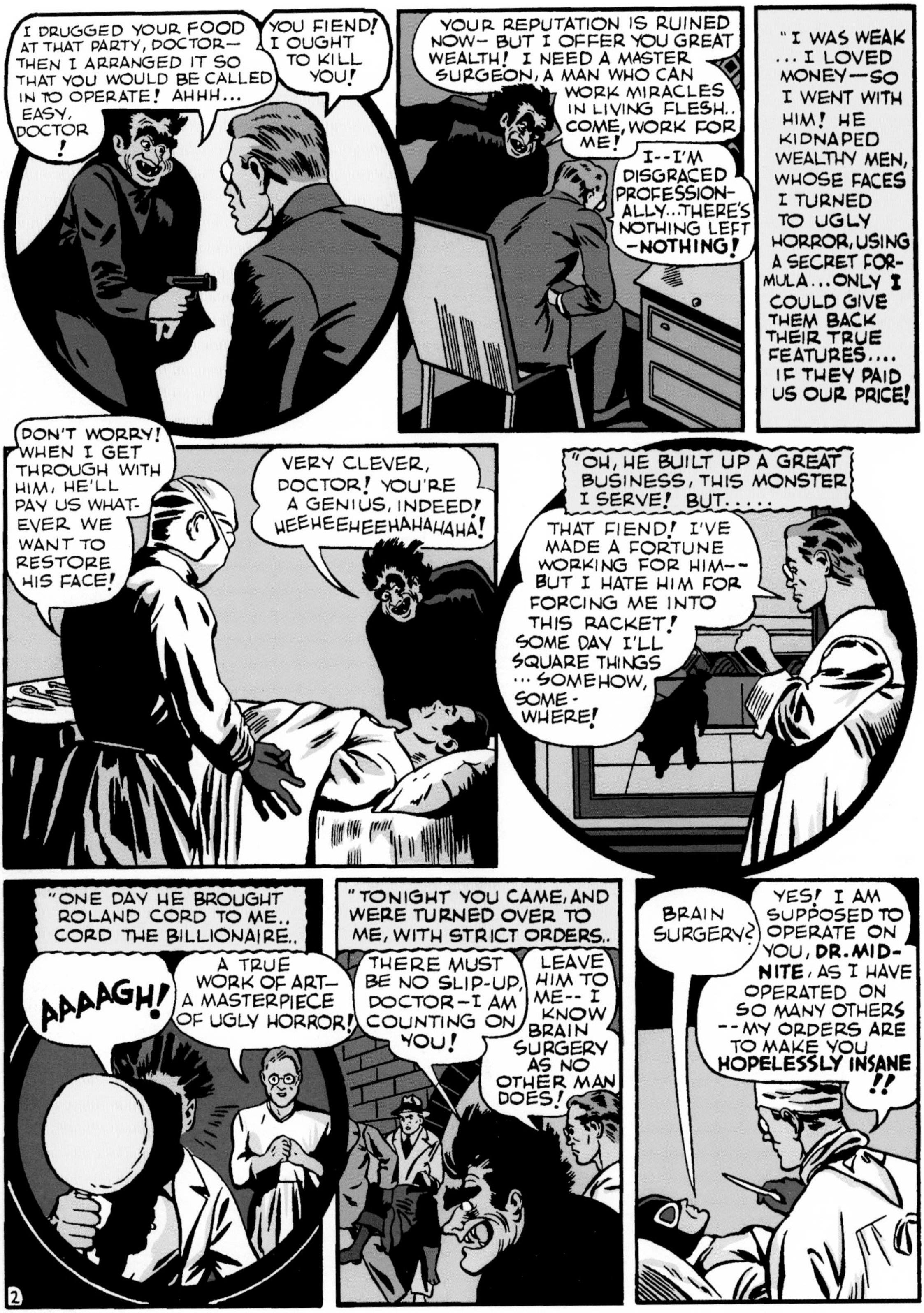
I DRUGGED YOUR FOOD AT THAT PARTY, DOCTOR— THEN I ARRANGED IT SO THAT YOU WOULD BE CALLED IN TO OPERATE! AHHH... EASY, DOCTOR!
YOU FIEND! I OUGHT TO KILL YOU!
YOUR REPUTATION IS RUINED NOW— BUT I OFFER YOU GREAT WEALTH! I NEED A MASTER SURGEON, A MAN WHO CAN WORK MIRACLES IN LIVING FLESH.. COME, WORK FOR ME!
I--I'M DISGRACED PROFESSION-ALLY..THERE'S NOTHING LEFT —NOTHING!
"I WAS WEAK ... I LOVED MONEY—SO I WENT WITH HIM! HE KIDNAPED WEALTHY MEN, WHOSE FACES I TURNED TO UGLY HORROR, USING A SECRET FOR-MULA...ONLY I COULD GIVE THEM BACK THEIR TRUE FEATURES.... IF THEY PAID US OUR PRICE!
DON'T WORRY! WHEN I GET THROUGH WITH HIM, HE'LL PAY US WHAT-EVER WE WANT TO RESTORE HIS FACE!
VERY CLEVER, DOCTOR! YOU'RE A GENIUS, INDEED! HEEHEEHEEHAHAHAHA!
"OH, HE BUILT UP A GREAT BUSINESS, THIS MONSTER I SERVE! BUT.....
THAT FIEND! I'VE MADE A FORTUNE WORKING FOR HIM-- BUT I HATE HIM FOR FORCING ME INTO THIS RACKET! SOME DAY I'LL SQUARE THINGS ... SOMEHOW, SOME-WHERE!
"ONE DAY HE BROUGHT ROLAND CORD TO ME.. CORD THE BILLIONAIRE..
AAAAGH!
A TRUE WORK OF ART— A MASTERPIECE OF UGLY HORROR!
2
"TONIGHT YOU CAME, AND WERE TURNED OVER TO ME, WITH STRICT ORDERS..
THERE MUST BE NO SLIP-UP, DOCTOR—I AM COUNTING ON YOU!
LEAVE HIM TO ME-- I KNOW BRAIN SURGERY AS NO OTHER MAN DOES!
BRAIN SURGERY?
YES! I AM SUPPOSED TO OPERATE ON YOU, DR. MID-NITE, AS I HAVE OPERATED ON SO MANY OTHERS --MY ORDERS ARE TO MAKE YOU HOPELESSLY INSANE!!

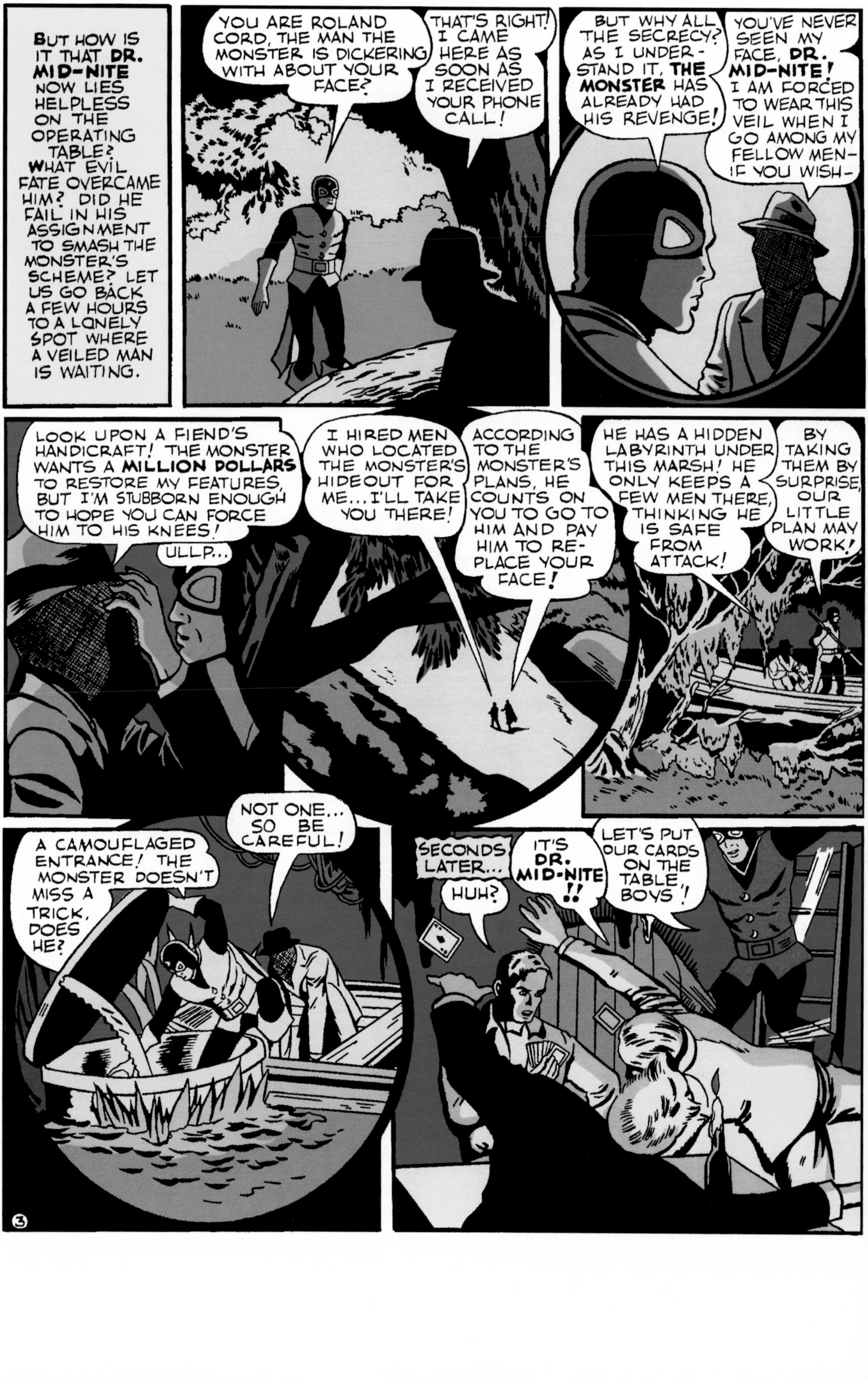
BUT HOW IS IT THAT DR. MID-NITE NOW LIES HELPLESS ON THE OPERATING TABLE? WHAT EVIL FATE OVERCAME HIM? DID HE FAIL IN HIS ASSIGNMENT TO SMASH THE MONSTER'S SCHEME? LET US GO BACK A FEW HOURS TO A LONELY SPOT WHERE A VEILED MAN IS WAITING.
YOU ARE ROLAND CORD, THE MAN THE MONSTER IS DICKERING WITH ABOUT YOUR FACE?
THAT'S RIGHT! I CAME HERE AS SOON AS I RECEIVED YOUR PHONE CALL!
BUT WHY ALL THE SECRECY? AS I UNDERSTAND IT, THE MONSTER HAS ALREADY HAD HIS REVENGE!
YOU'VE NEVER SEEN MY FACE, DR. MID-NITE! I AM FORCED TO WEAR THIS VEIL WHEN I GO AMONG MY FELLOW MEN- IF YOU WISH-
LOOK UPON A FIEND'S HANDICRAFT! THE MONSTER WANTS A MILLION DOLLARS TO RESTORE MY FEATURES, BUT I'M STUBBORN ENOUGH TO HOPE YOU CAN FORCE HIM TO HIS KNEES!
ULLP..
I HIRED MEN WHO LOCATED THE MONSTER'S HIDEOUT FOR ME... I'LL TAKE YOU THERE!
ACCORDING TO THE MONSTER'S PLANS, HE COUNTS ON YOU TO GO TO HIM AND PAY HIM TO REPLACE YOUR FACE!
HE HAS A HIDDEN LABYRINTH UNDER THIS MARSH! HE ONLY KEEPS A FEW MEN THERE, THINKING HE IS SAFE FROM ATTACK!
BY TAKING THEM BY SURPRISE, OUR LITTLE PLAN MAY WORK!
A CAMOUFLAGED ENTRANCE! THE MONSTER DOESN'T MISS A TRICK, DOES HE?
NOT ONE... SO BE CAREFUL!
SECONDS LATER...
HUH?
IT'S DR. MID-NITE!!
LET'S PUT OUR CARDS ON THE TABLE, BOYS!
3

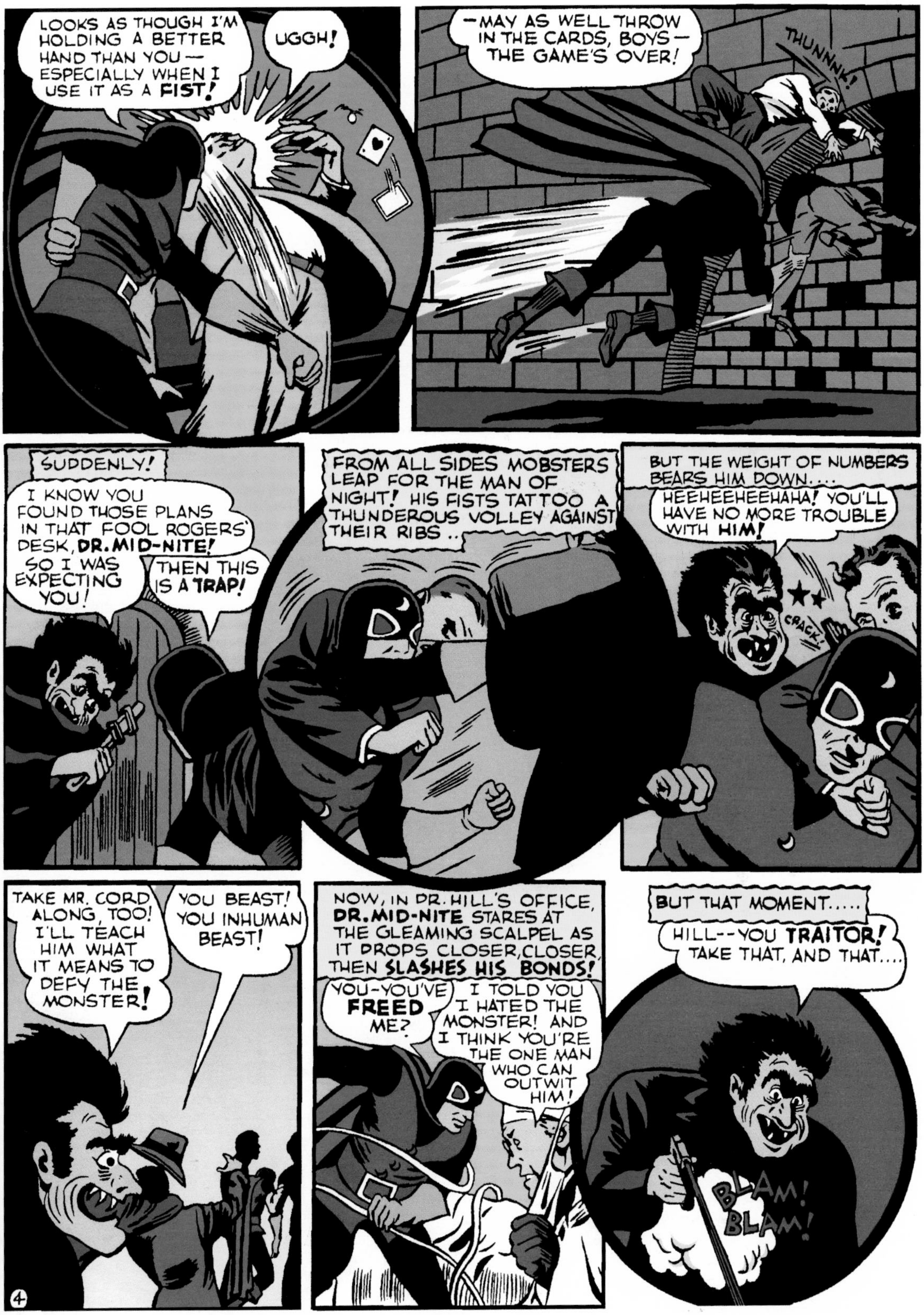

LOOKS AS THOUGH I'M HOLDING A BETTER HAND THAN YOU— ESPECIALLY WHEN I USE IT AS A FIST!
UGGH!
—MAY AS WELL THROW IN THE CARDS, BOYS— THE GAME'S OVER!
THUNNNK!
SUDDENLY!
I KNOW YOU FOUND THOSE PLANS IN THAT FOOL ROGERS' DESK, DR. MID-NITE! SO I WAS EXPECTING YOU!
THEN THIS IS A TRAP!
FROM ALL SIDES MOBSTERS LEAP FOR THE MAN OF NIGHT! HIS FISTS TATTOO A THUNDEROUS VOLLEY AGAINST THEIR RIBS..
BUT THE WEIGHT OF NUMBERS BEARS HIM DOWN....
HEEHEEHEEHAHA! YOU'LL HAVE NO MORE TROUBLE WITH HIM!
CRACK!
TAKE MR. CORD ALONG, TOO! I'LL TEACH HIM WHAT IT MEANS TO DEFY THE MONSTER!
YOU BEAST! YOU INHUMAN BEAST!
4
NOW, IN DR. HILL'S OFFICE, DR. MID-NITE STARES AT THE GLEAMING SCALPEL AS IT DROPS CLOSER, CLOSER, THEN SLASHES HIS BONDS!
YOU-YOU'VE FREED ME?
I TOLD YOU I HATED THE MONSTER! AND I THINK YOU'RE THE ONE MAN WHO CAN OUTWIT HIM!
BUT THAT MOMENT.....
HILL--YOU TRAITOR! TAKE THAT, AND THAT....
BLAM! BLAM!

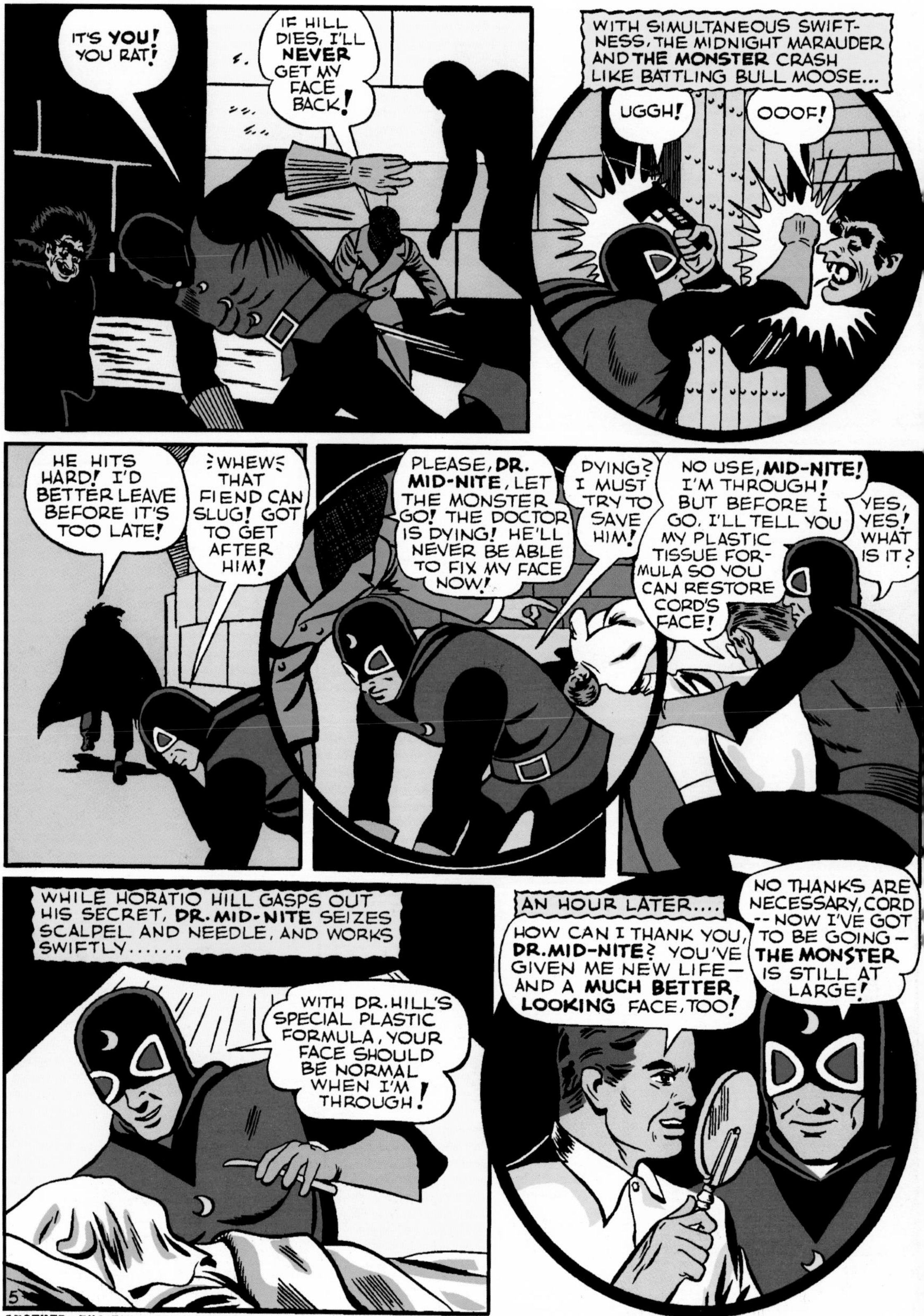
IT'S YOU! YOU RAT!
IF HILL DIES, I'LL NEVER GET MY FACE BACK!
WITH SIMULTANEOUS SWIFTNESS, THE MIDNIGHT MARAUDER AND THE MONSTER CRASH LIKE BATTLING BULL MOOSE...
UGGH!
OOOF!
HE HITS HARD! I'D BETTER LEAVE BEFORE IT'S TOO LATE!
WHEW THAT FIEND CAN SLUG! GOT TO GET AFTER HIM!
PLEASE, DR. MID-NITE, LET THE MONSTER GO! THE DOCTOR IS DYING! HE'LL NEVER BE ABLE TO FIX MY FACE NOW!
DYING? I MUST TRY TO SAVE HIM!
NO USE, MID-NITE! I'M THROUGH! BUT BEFORE I GO, I'LL TELL YOU MY PLASTIC TISSUE FORMULA SO YOU CAN RESTORE CORD'S FACE!
YES, YES! WHAT IS IT?
WHILE HORATIO HILL GASPS OUT HIS SECRET, DR. MID-NITE SEIZES SCALPEL AND NEEDLE, AND WORKS SWIFTLY.......
WITH DR. HILL'S SPECIAL PLASTIC FORMULA, YOUR FACE SHOULD BE NORMAL WHEN I'M THROUGH!
5
AN HOUR LATER....
HOW CAN I THANK YOU, DR. MID-NITE? YOU'VE GIVEN ME NEW LIFE—AND A MUCH BETTER LOOKING FACE, TOO!
NO THANKS ARE NECESSARY, CORD -- NOW I'VE GOT TO BE GOING—THE MONSTER IS STILL AT LARGE!

ANOTHER EXCITING DR. MID-NITE ADVENTURE APPEARS IN EVERY ISSUE OF ALL-AMERICAN COMICS... READ 'EM ALL!

DOIBY DICKLES GOES ON A CASE: PAPER SALVAGE!

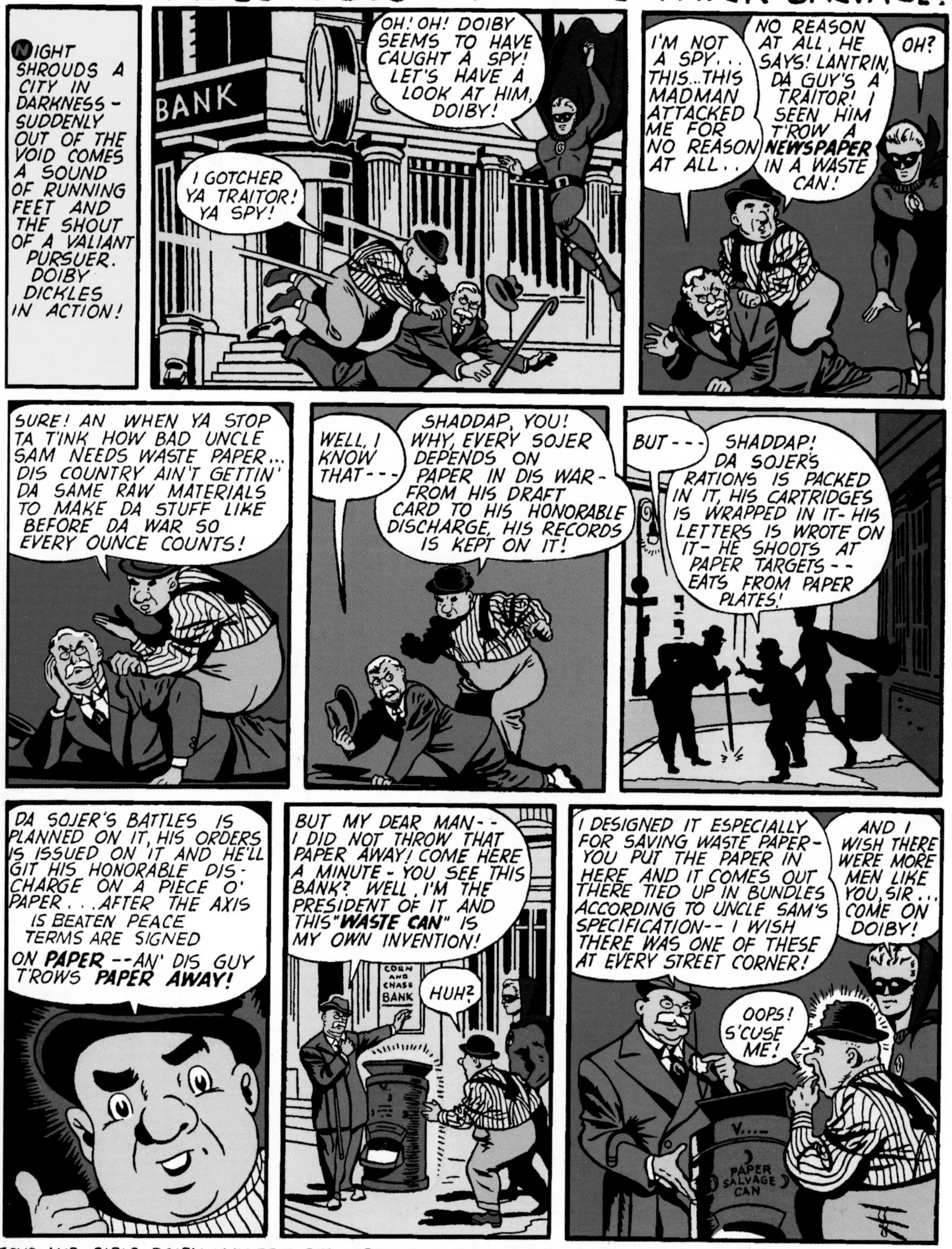
NIGHT SHROUDS A CITY IN DARKNESS - SUDDENLY OUT OF THE VOID COMES A SOUND OF RUNNING FEET AND THE SHOUT OF A VALIANT PURSUER. DOIBY DICKLES IN ACTION!
BANK
OH! OH! DOIBY SEEMS TO HAVE CAUGHT A SPY! LET'S HAVE A LOOK AT HIM, DOIBY!
I GOTCHER YA TRAITOR! YA SPY!
I'M NOT A SPY... THIS...THIS MADMAN ATTACKED ME FOR NO REASON AT ALL..
NO REASON AT ALL, HE SAYS! LANTRIN, DA GUY'S A TRAITOR! I SEEN HIM T'ROW A NEWSPAPER IN A WASTE CAN!
OH?
SURE! AN WHEN YA STOP TA T'INK HOW BAD UNCLE SAM NEEDS WASTE PAPER... DIS COUNTRY AIN'T GETTIN' DA SAME RAW MATERIALS TO MAKE DA STUFF LIKE BEFORE DA WAR SO EVERY OUNCE COUNTS!
WELL, I KNOW THAT---
SHADDAP, YOU! WHY, EVERY SOJER DEPENDS ON PAPER IN DIS WAR - FROM HIS DRAFT CARD TO HIS HONORABLE DISCHARGE, HIS RECORDS IS KEPT ON IT!
BUT---
SHADDAP! DA SOJER'S RATIONS IS PACKED IN IT, HIS CARTRIDGES IS WRAPPED IN IT - HIS LETTERS IS WROTE ON IT - HE SHOOTS AT PAPER TARGETS -- EATS FROM PAPER PLATES!
DA SOJER'S BATTLES IS PLANNED ON IT, HIS ORDERS IS ISSUED ON IT AND HE'LL GIT HIS HONORABLE DIS-CHARGE ON A PIECE O' PAPER... AFTER THE AXIS IS BEATEN PEACE TERMS ARE SIGNED ON PAPER -- AN' DIS GUY T'ROWS PAPER AWAY!
BUT MY DEAR MAN-- I DID NOT THROW THAT PAPER AWAY! COME HERE A MINUTE - YOU SEE THIS BANK? WELL, I'M THE PRESIDENT OF IT AND THIS "WASTE CAN" IS MY OWN INVENTION!
CORN AND CHASE BANK
HUH?
I DESIGNED IT ESPECIALLY FOR SAVING WASTE PAPER - YOU PUT THE PAPER IN HERE AND IT COMES OUT THERE TIED UP IN BUNDLES ACCORDING TO UNCLE SAM'S SPECIFICATION-- I WISH THERE WAS ONE OF THESE AT EVERY STREET CORNER!
AND I WISH THERE WERE MORE MEN LIKE YOU, SIR... COME ON DOIBY!
OOPS! S'CUSE ME!
PAPER SALVAGE CAN

BOYS AND GIRLS-DOIBY MAY BE A BIT IMPETUOUS--BUT NEVERTHELESS EVERYTHING HE SAID IS TRUE! ARE YOU HELPING TO SAVE PAPER? REMEMBER CARDBOARD AND CORRUGATED BOARD ARE NEEDED TOO- **EVERY OUNCE COUNTS!** ASK YOUR TEACHER TO TELL YOU HOW YOU CAN HELP!

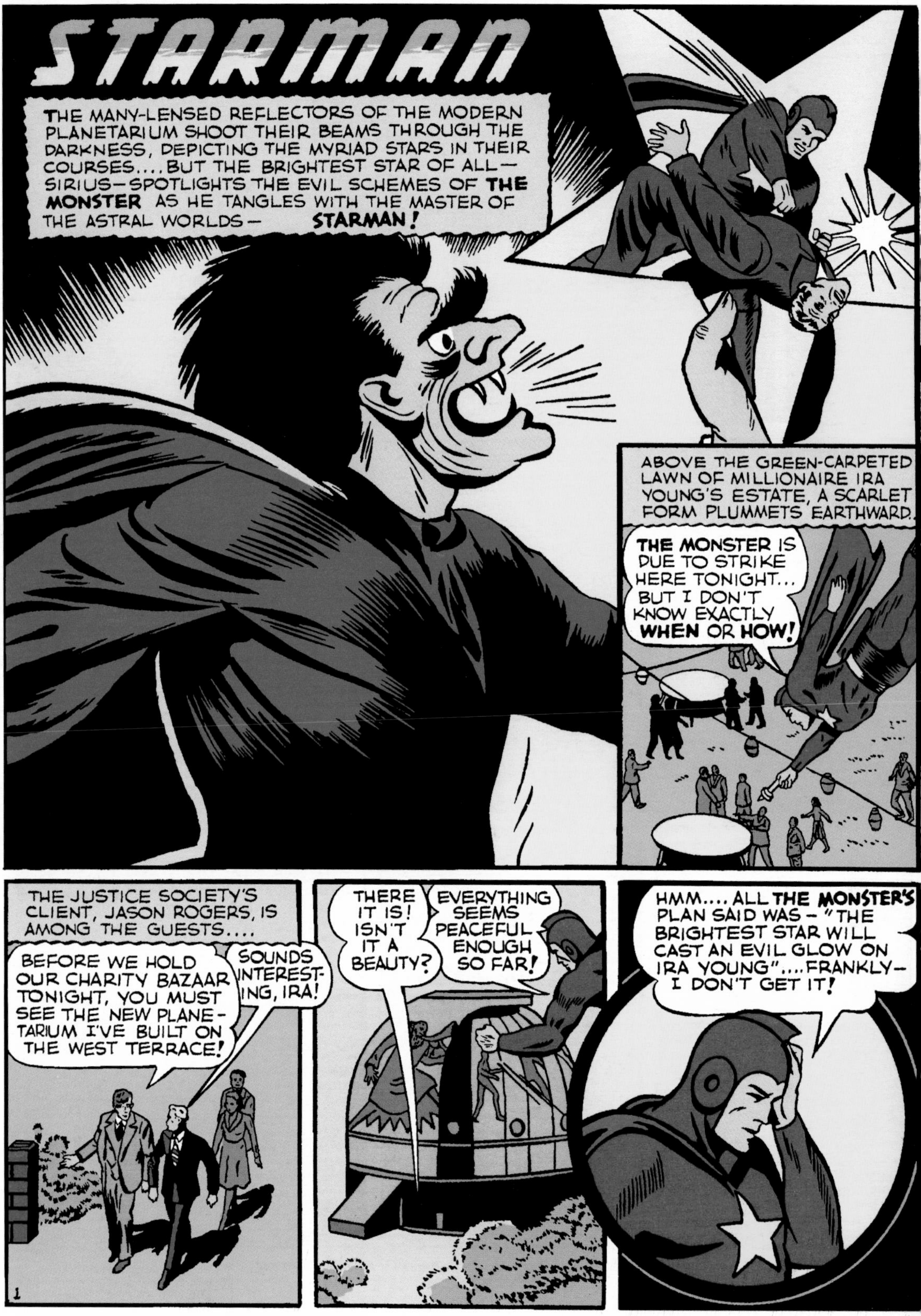
STARMAN
THE MANY-LENSED REFLECTORS OF THE MODERN PLANETARIUM SHOOT THEIR BEAMS THROUGH THE DARKNESS, DEPICTING THE MYRIAD STARS IN THEIR COURSES.... BUT THE BRIGHTEST STAR OF ALL— SIRIUS—SPOTLIGHTS THE EVIL SCHEMES OF THE MONSTER AS HE TANGLES WITH THE MASTER OF THE ASTRAL WORLDS— STARMAN!
ABOVE THE GREEN-CARPETED LAWN OF MILLIONAIRE IRA YOUNG'S ESTATE, A SCARLET FORM PLUMMETS EARTHWARD.
THE MONSTER IS DUE TO STRIKE HERE TONIGHT... BUT I DON'T KNOW EXACTLY WHEN OR HOW!
THE JUSTICE SOCIETY'S CLIENT, JASON ROGERS, IS AMONG THE GUESTS....
BEFORE WE HOLD OUR CHARITY BAZAAR TONIGHT, YOU MUST SEE THE NEW PLANE-TARIUM I'VE BUILT ON THE WEST TERRACE!
SOUNDS INTEREST-ING, IRA!
1
THERE IT IS! ISN'T IT A BEAUTY?
EVERYTHING SEEMS PEACEFUL ENOUGH SO FAR!
HMM.... ALL THE MONSTER'S PLAN SAID WAS—"THE BRIGHTEST STAR WILL CAST AN EVIL GLOW ON IRA YOUNG"....FRANKLY— I DON'T GET IT!

WITHIN THE ROUNDED BOWL OF THE PLANETARIUM, THE MILLIONAIRE AND HIS GUESTS SEAT THEMSELVES......

ALL RIGHT, HANK— LET 'ER GO!

YES, SIR!

QUITE A SHOW YOUNG'S PUTTING ON! DEPICTING THE STARS! OHOH! **THERE'S SOMETHING WRONG!**

STARMAN, WHO IS TED KNIGHT, AN AMATEUR ASTRONOMER, IN DAILY LIFE— IS AMAZED TO SEE ONLY A **BLANK SPACE** ON THE BLUE DOME OF THE PLANETARIUM WHERE THE BRIGHT STAR SIRIUS OF THE CONSTELLATION CANIS MAJOR OUGHT TO BE!

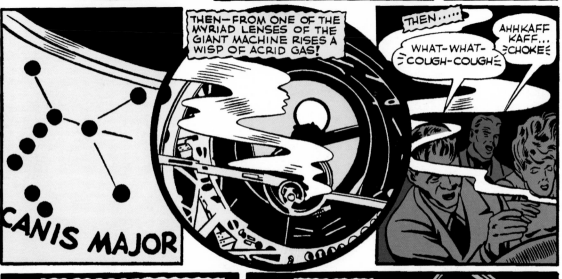

THEN—FROM ONE OF THE MYRIAD LENSES OF THE GIANT MACHINE RISES A WISP OF ACRID GAS!

CANIS MAJOR

THEN.....

WHAT—WHAT— COUGH-COUGH—

AHHKAFF KAFF... —CHOKE—

GRIM-FACED GUNMEN RACE IN THROUGH A DOOR!...

HAW-HAW! DEY'RE OUT LIKE A LIGHT!

DIS IS GONNA BE EASY PICKIN'S!

SUDDENLY!

STARMAN! UGHHH...

RIGHT THE FIRST TIME, CHUM!

2

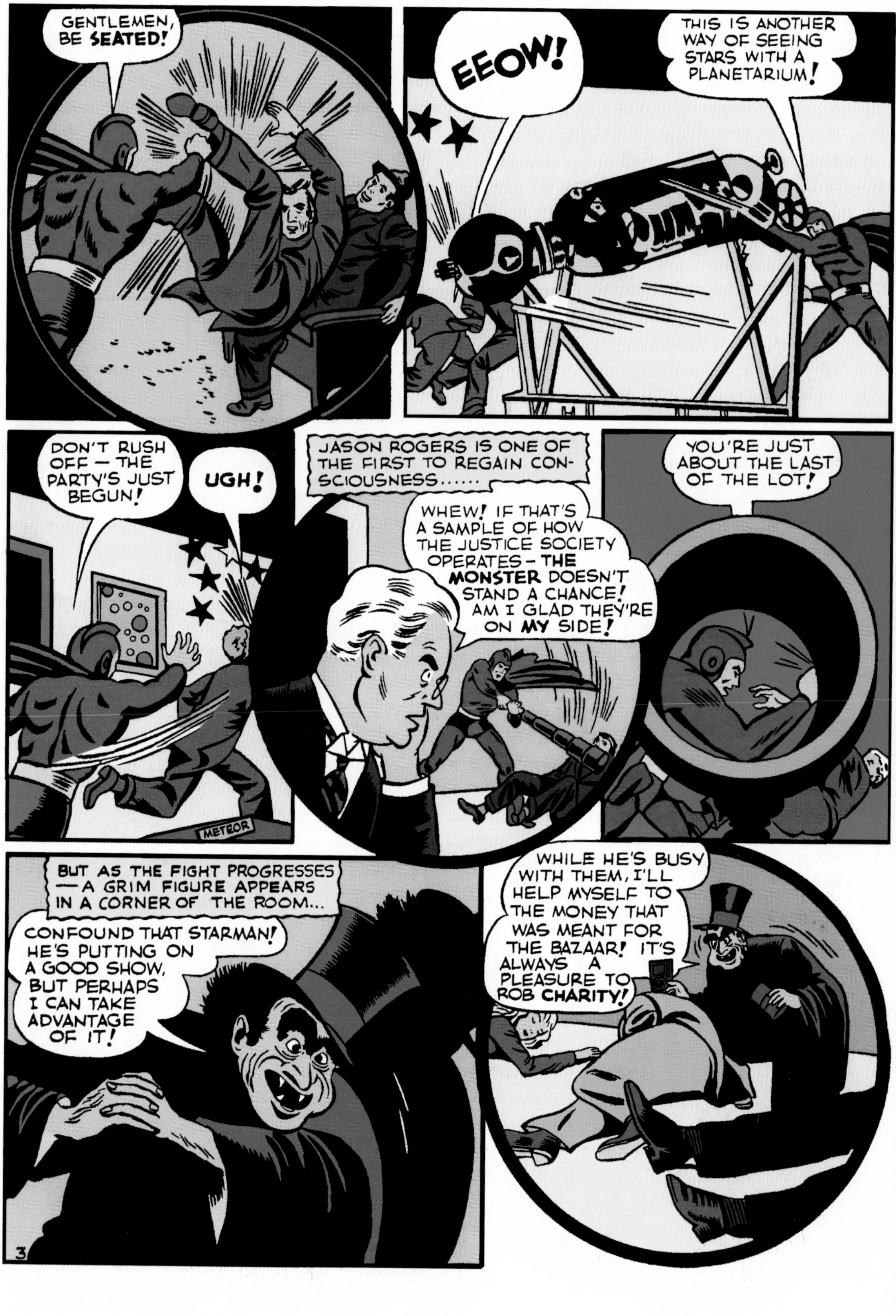
GENTLEMEN, BE SEATED!
EEOW!
THIS IS ANOTHER WAY OF SEEING STARS WITH A PLANETARIUM!
DON'T RUSH OFF — THE PARTY'S JUST BEGUN!
UGH!
METEOR
JASON ROGERS IS ONE OF THE FIRST TO REGAIN CONSCIOUSNESS......
WHEW! IF THAT'S A SAMPLE OF HOW THE JUSTICE SOCIETY OPERATES — THE MONSTER DOESN'T STAND A CHANCE! AM I GLAD THEY'RE ON MY SIDE!
YOU'RE JUST ABOUT THE LAST OF THE LOT!
BUT AS THE FIGHT PROGRESSES — A GRIM FIGURE APPEARS IN A CORNER OF THE ROOM...
CONFOUND THAT STARMAN! HE'S PUTTING ON A GOOD SHOW, BUT PERHAPS I CAN TAKE ADVANTAGE OF IT!
WHILE HE'S BUSY WITH THEM, I'LL HELP MYSELF TO THE MONEY THAT WAS MEANT FOR THE BAZAAR! IT'S ALWAYS A PLEASURE TO ROB CHARITY!
3

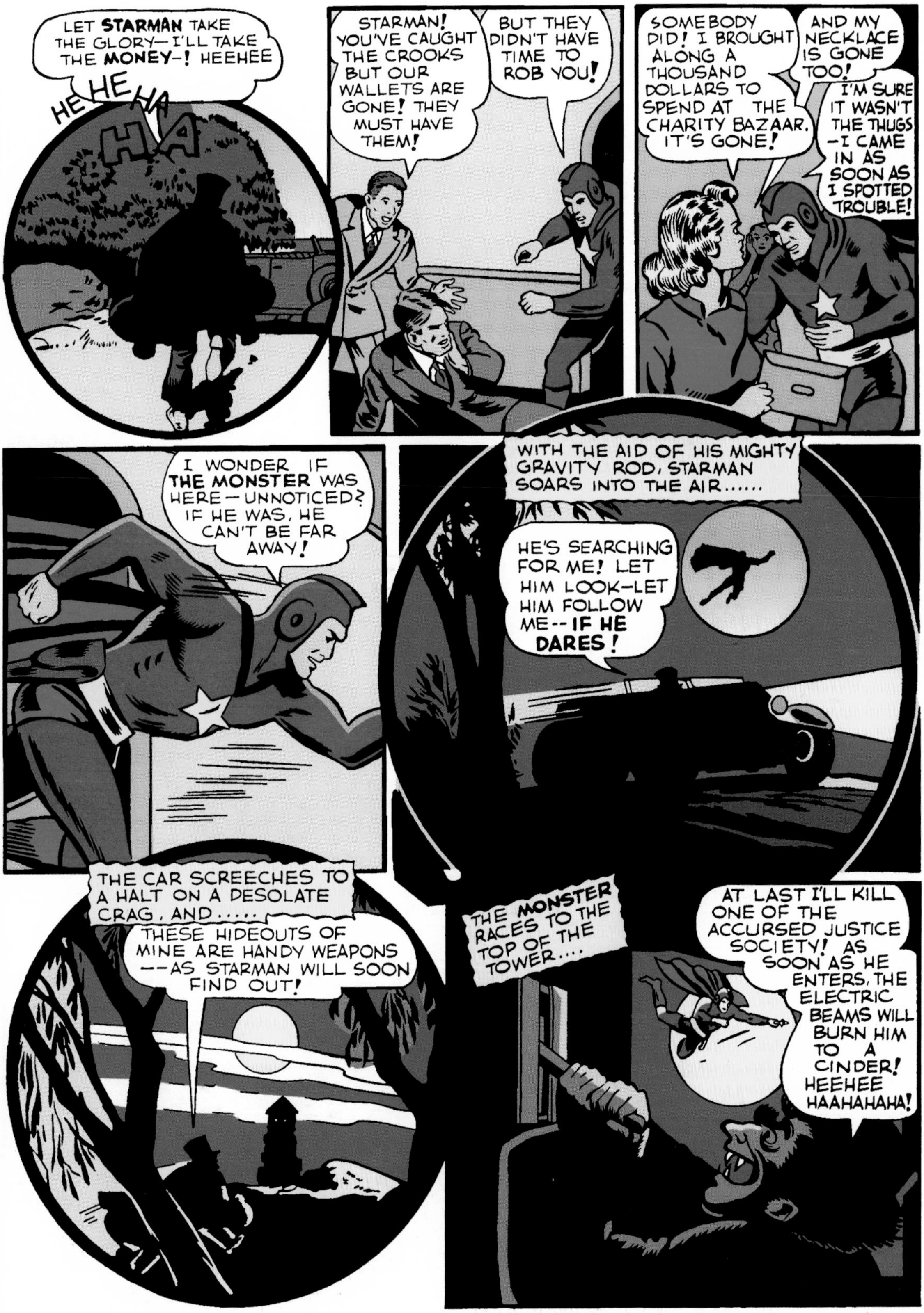
LET STARMAN TAKE THE GLORY—I'LL TAKE THE MONEY—! HEEHEE
HE HE HA HA
STARMAN! YOU'VE CAUGHT THE CROOKS BUT OUR WALLETS ARE GONE! THEY MUST HAVE THEM!
BUT THEY DIDN'T HAVE TIME TO ROB YOU!
SOMEBODY DID! I BROUGHT ALONG A THOUSAND DOLLARS TO SPEND AT THE CHARITY BAZAAR. IT'S GONE!
AND MY NECKLACE IS GONE TOO!
I'M SURE IT WASN'T THE THUGS —I CAME IN AS SOON AS I SPOTTED TROUBLE!
I WONDER IF THE MONSTER WAS HERE—UNNOTICED? IF HE WAS, HE CAN'T BE FAR AWAY!
WITH THE AID OF HIS MIGHTY GRAVITY ROD, STARMAN SOARS INTO THE AIR......
HE'S SEARCHING FOR ME! LET HIM LOOK—LET HIM FOLLOW ME--IF HE DARES!
THE CAR SCREECHES TO A HALT ON A DESOLATE CRAG, AND.....
THESE HIDEOUTS OF MINE ARE HANDY WEAPONS --AS STARMAN WILL SOON FIND OUT!
THE MONSTER RACES TO THE TOP OF THE TOWER....
AT LAST I'LL KILL ONE OF THE ACCURSED JUSTICE SOCIETY! AS SOON AS HE ENTERS, THE ELECTRIC BEAMS WILL BURN HIM TO A CINDER! HEEHEE HAAHAHAHA!

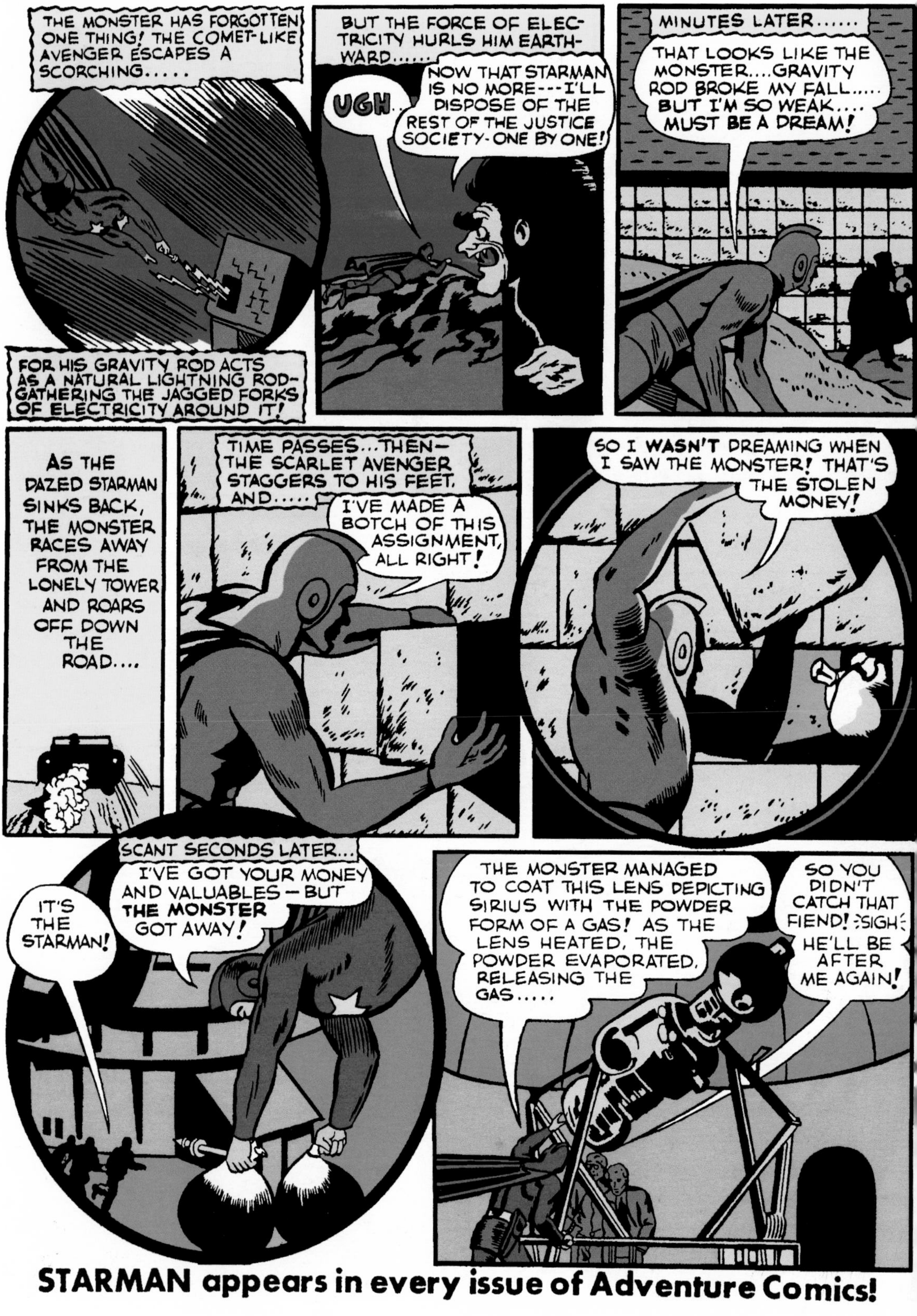
THE MONSTER HAS FORGOTTEN ONE THING! THE COMET-LIKE AVENGER ESCAPES A SCORCHING.....
FOR HIS GRAVITY ROD ACTS AS A NATURAL LIGHTNING ROD- GATHERING THE JAGGED FORKS OF ELECTRICITY AROUND IT!
BUT THE FORCE OF ELECTRICITY HURLS HIM EARTHWARD......
UGH..
NOW THAT STARMAN IS NO MORE---I'LL DISPOSE OF THE REST OF THE JUSTICE SOCIETY- ONE BY ONE!
MINUTES LATER......
THAT LOOKS LIKE THE MONSTER....GRAVITY ROD BROKE MY FALL..... BUT I'M SO WEAK.... MUST BE A DREAM!
AS THE DAZED STARMAN SINKS BACK, THE MONSTER RACES AWAY FROM THE LONELY TOWER AND ROARS OFF DOWN THE ROAD....
TIME PASSES...THEN- THE SCARLET AVENGER STAGGERS TO HIS FEET. AND.....
I'VE MADE A BOTCH OF THIS ASSIGNMENT, ALL RIGHT!
SO I WASN'T DREAMING WHEN I SAW THE MONSTER! THAT'S THE STOLEN MONEY!
SCANT SECONDS LATER...
IT'S THE STARMAN!
I'VE GOT YOUR MONEY AND VALUABLES - BUT THE MONSTER GOT AWAY!
THE MONSTER MANAGED TO COAT THIS LENS DEPICTING SIRIUS WITH THE POWDER FORM OF A GAS! AS THE LENS HEATED, THE POWDER EVAPORATED, RELEASING THE GAS.....
SO YOU DIDN'T CATCH THAT FIEND! SIGH HE'LL BE AFTER ME AGAIN!

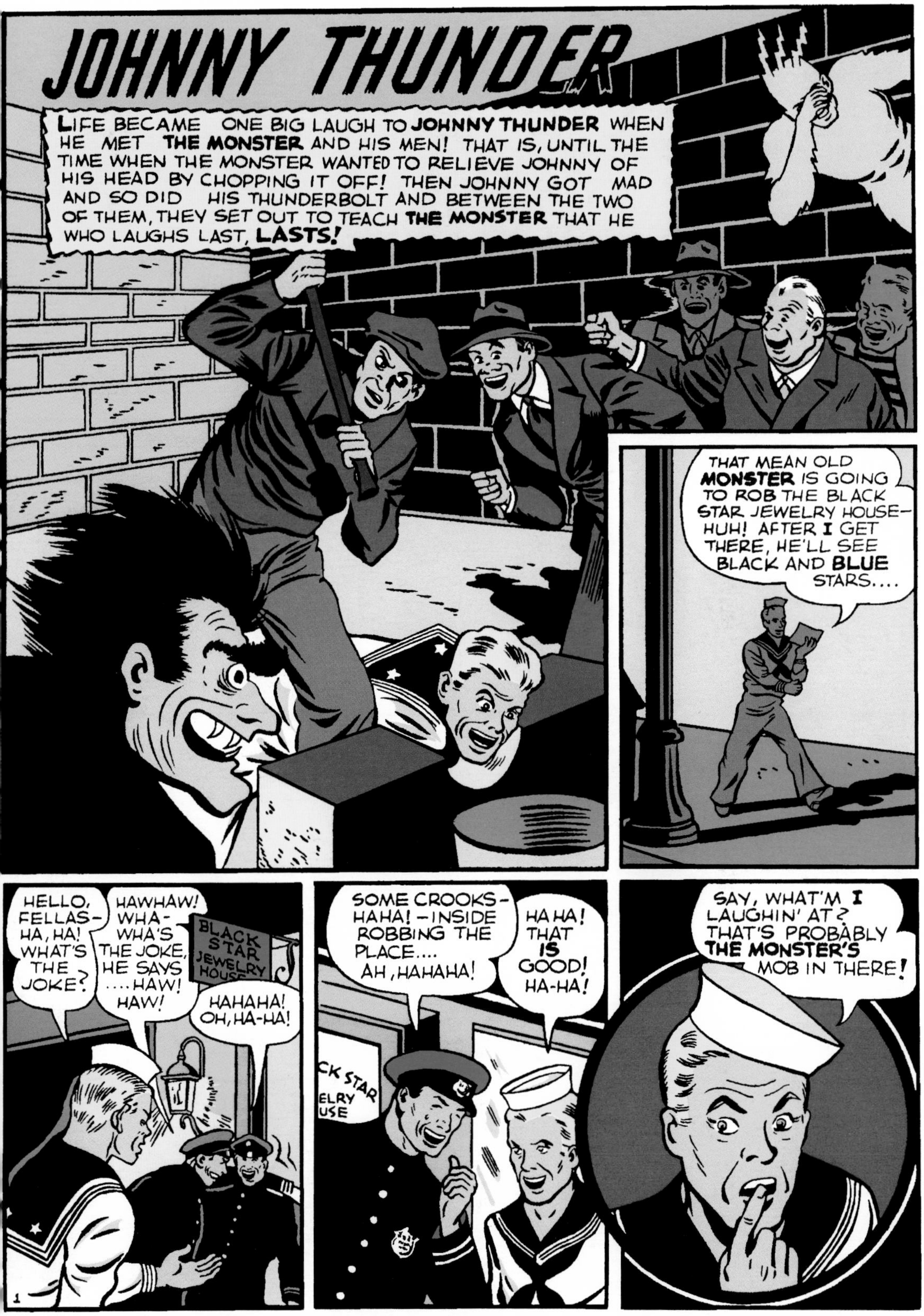
JOHNNY THUNDER
LIFE BECAME ONE BIG LAUGH TO JOHNNY THUNDER WHEN HE MET THE MONSTER AND HIS MEN! THAT IS, UNTIL THE TIME WHEN THE MONSTER WANTED TO RELIEVE JOHNNY OF HIS HEAD BY CHOPPING IT OFF! THEN JOHNNY GOT MAD AND SO DID HIS THUNDERBOLT AND BETWEEN THE TWO OF THEM, THEY SET OUT TO TEACH THE MONSTER THAT HE WHO LAUGHS LAST, LASTS!
THAT MEAN OLD MONSTER IS GOING TO ROB THE BLACK STAR JEWELRY HOUSE– HUH! AFTER I GET THERE, HE'LL SEE BLACK AND BLUE STARS....
HELLO, FELLAS– HA, HA! WHAT'S THE JOKE?
HAWHAW! WHA– WHA'S THE JOKE, HE SAYS ....HAW! HAW!
BLACK STAR JEWELRY HOUSE
HAHAHA! OH, HA-HA!
SOME CROOKS– HAHA! –INSIDE ROBBING THE PLACE.... AH, HAHAHA!
HA HA! THAT IS GOOD! HA-HA!
SAY, WHAT'M I LAUGHIN' AT? THAT'S PROBABLY THE MONSTER'S MOB IN THERE!

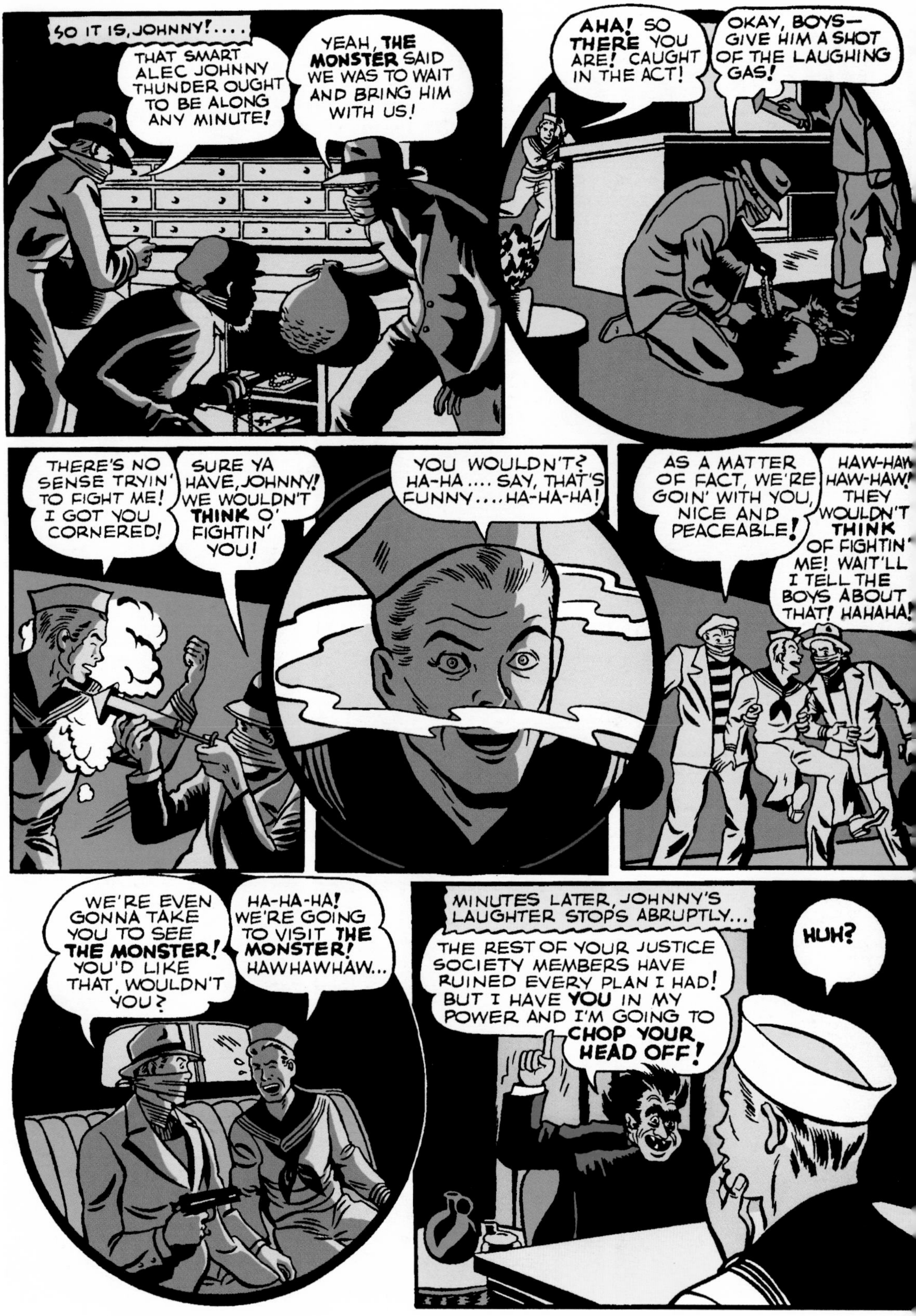
SO IT IS, JOHNNY!....
THAT SMART ALEC JOHNNY THUNDER OUGHT TO BE ALONG ANY MINUTE!
YEAH, THE MONSTER SAID WE WAS TO WAIT AND BRING HIM WITH US!
AHA! SO THERE YOU ARE! CAUGHT IN THE ACT!
OKAY, BOYS— GIVE HIM A SHOT OF THE LAUGHING GAS!
THERE'S NO SENSE TRYIN' TO FIGHT ME! I GOT YOU CORNERED!
SURE YA HAVE, JOHNNY! WE WOULDN'T THINK O' FIGHTIN' YOU!
YOU WOULDN'T? HA-HA.... SAY, THAT'S FUNNY....HA-HA-HA!
AS A MATTER OF FACT, WE'RE GOIN' WITH YOU, NICE AND PEACEABLE!
HAW-HAW HAW-HAW! THEY WOULDN'T THINK OF FIGHTIN' ME! WAIT'LL I TELL THE BOYS ABOUT THAT! HAHAHA!
WE'RE EVEN GONNA TAKE YOU TO SEE THE MONSTER! YOU'D LIKE THAT, WOULDN'T YOU?
HA-HA-HA! WE'RE GOING TO VISIT THE MONSTER! HAWHAWHAW...
MINUTES LATER, JOHNNY'S LAUGHTER STOPS ABRUPTLY...
THE REST OF YOUR JUSTICE SOCIETY MEMBERS HAVE RUINED EVERY PLAN I HAD! BUT I HAVE YOU IN MY POWER AND I'M GOING TO CHOP YOUR HEAD OFF!
HUH?

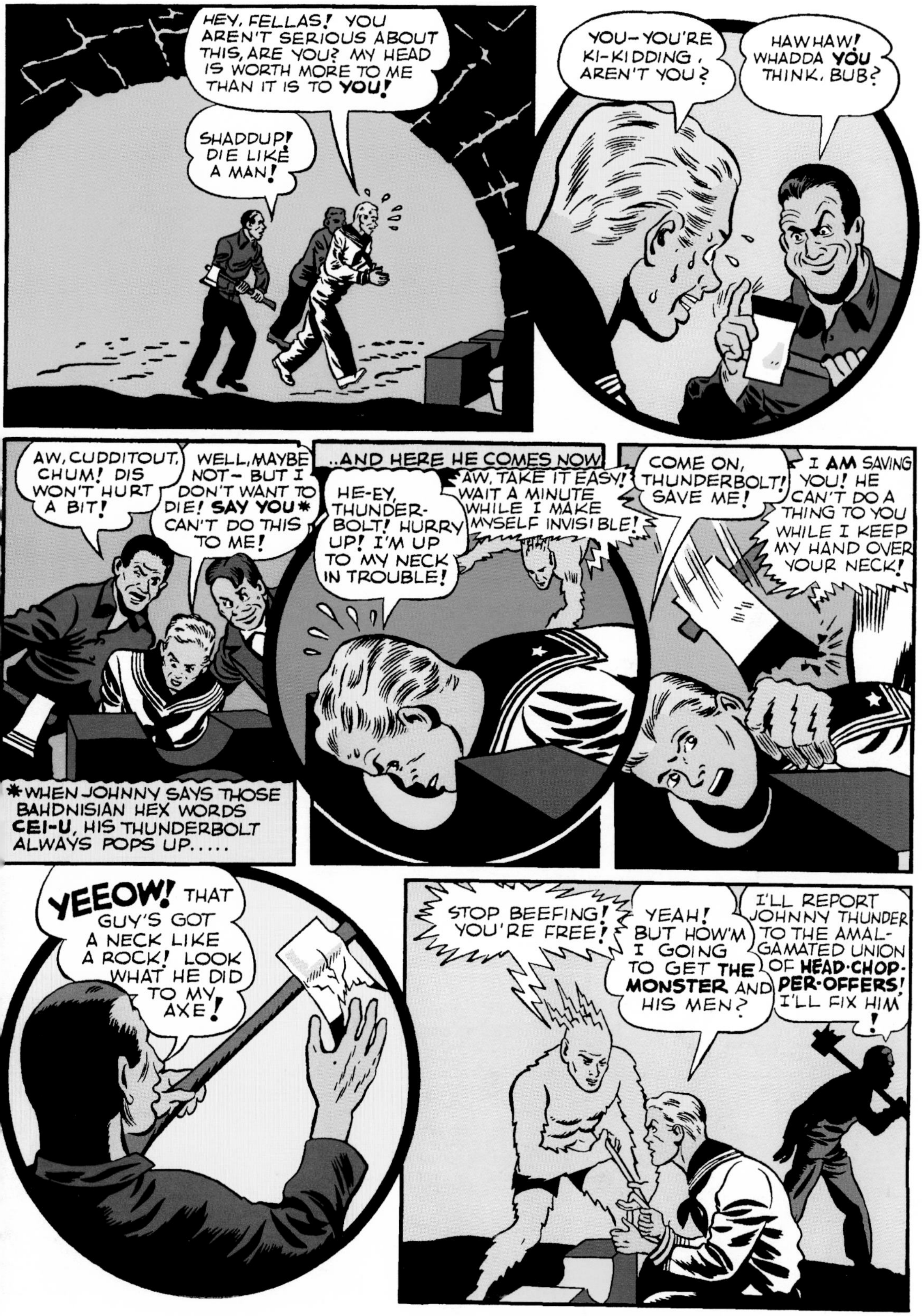
HEY, FELLAS! YOU AREN'T SERIOUS ABOUT THIS, ARE YOU? MY HEAD IS WORTH MORE TO ME THAN IT IS TO YOU!
SHADDUP! DIE LIKE A MAN!
YOU-YOU'RE KI-KIDDING, AREN'T YOU?
HAWHAW! WHADDA YOU THINK, BUB?
AW, CUDDITOUT, CHUM! DIS WON'T HURT A BIT!
WELL, MAYBE NOT- BUT I DON'T WANT TO DIE! SAY YOU* CAN'T DO THIS TO ME!
*WHEN JOHNNY SAYS THOSE BAHDNISIAN HEX WORDS CEI-U, HIS THUNDERBOLT ALWAYS POPS UP.....
..AND HERE HE COMES NOW
HE-EY, THUNDERBOLT! HURRY UP! I'M UP TO MY NECK IN TROUBLE!
AW, TAKE IT EASY! WAIT A MINUTE WHILE I MAKE MYSELF INVISIBLE!
COME ON, THUNDERBOLT! SAVE ME!
I AM SAVING YOU! HE CAN'T DO A THING TO YOU WHILE I KEEP MY HAND OVER YOUR NECK!
YEEOW! THAT GUY'S GOT A NECK LIKE A ROCK! LOOK WHAT HE DID TO MY AXE!
STOP BEEFING! YOU'RE FREE!
YEAH! BUT HOW'M I GOING TO GET THE MONSTER AND HIS MEN?
I'LL REPORT JOHNNY THUNDER TO THE AMALGAMATED UNION OF HEAD-CHOPPER-OFFERS! I'LL FIX HIM!

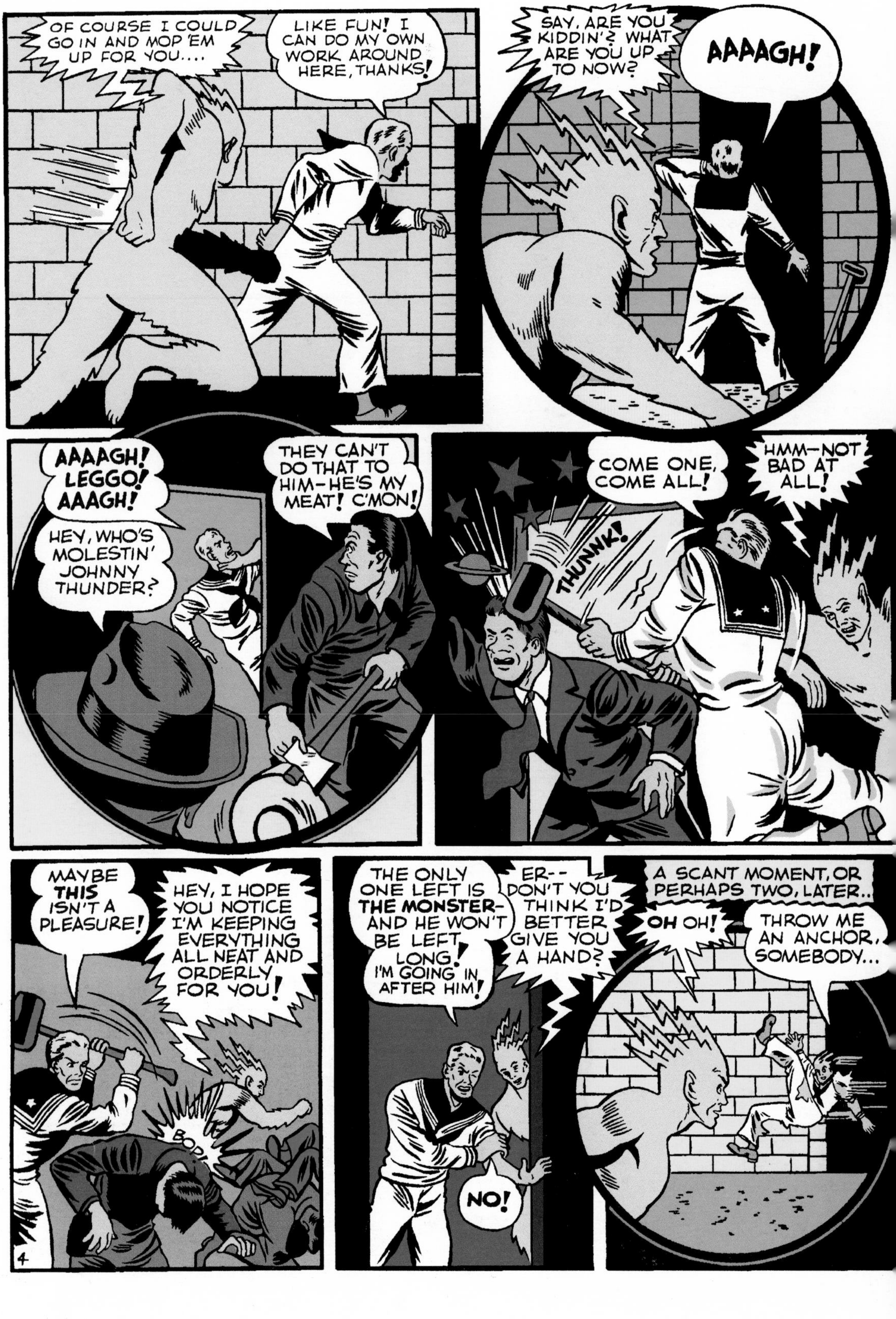
OF COURSE I COULD GO IN AND MOP 'EM UP FOR YOU....
LIKE FUN! I CAN DO MY OWN WORK AROUND HERE, THANKS!
SAY, ARE YOU KIDDIN'? WHAT ARE YOU UP TO NOW?
AAAAGH!
AAAAGH! LEGGO! AAAGH!
HEY, WHO'S MOLESTIN' JOHNNY THUNDER?
THEY CAN'T DO THAT TO HIM—HE'S MY MEAT! C'MON!
COME ONE, COME ALL!
HMM—NOT BAD AT ALL!
THUNNK!
MAYBE THIS ISN'T A PLEASURE!
HEY, I HOPE YOU NOTICE I'M KEEPING EVERYTHING ALL NEAT AND ORDERLY FOR YOU!
BOP!
4
THE ONLY ONE LEFT IS THE MONSTER— AND HE WON'T BE LEFT LONG! I'M GOING IN AFTER HIM!
ER-- DON'T YOU THINK I'D BETTER GIVE YOU A HAND?
NO!
A SCANT MOMENT, OR PERHAPS TWO, LATER..
OH OH!
THROW ME AN ANCHOR, SOMEBODY...

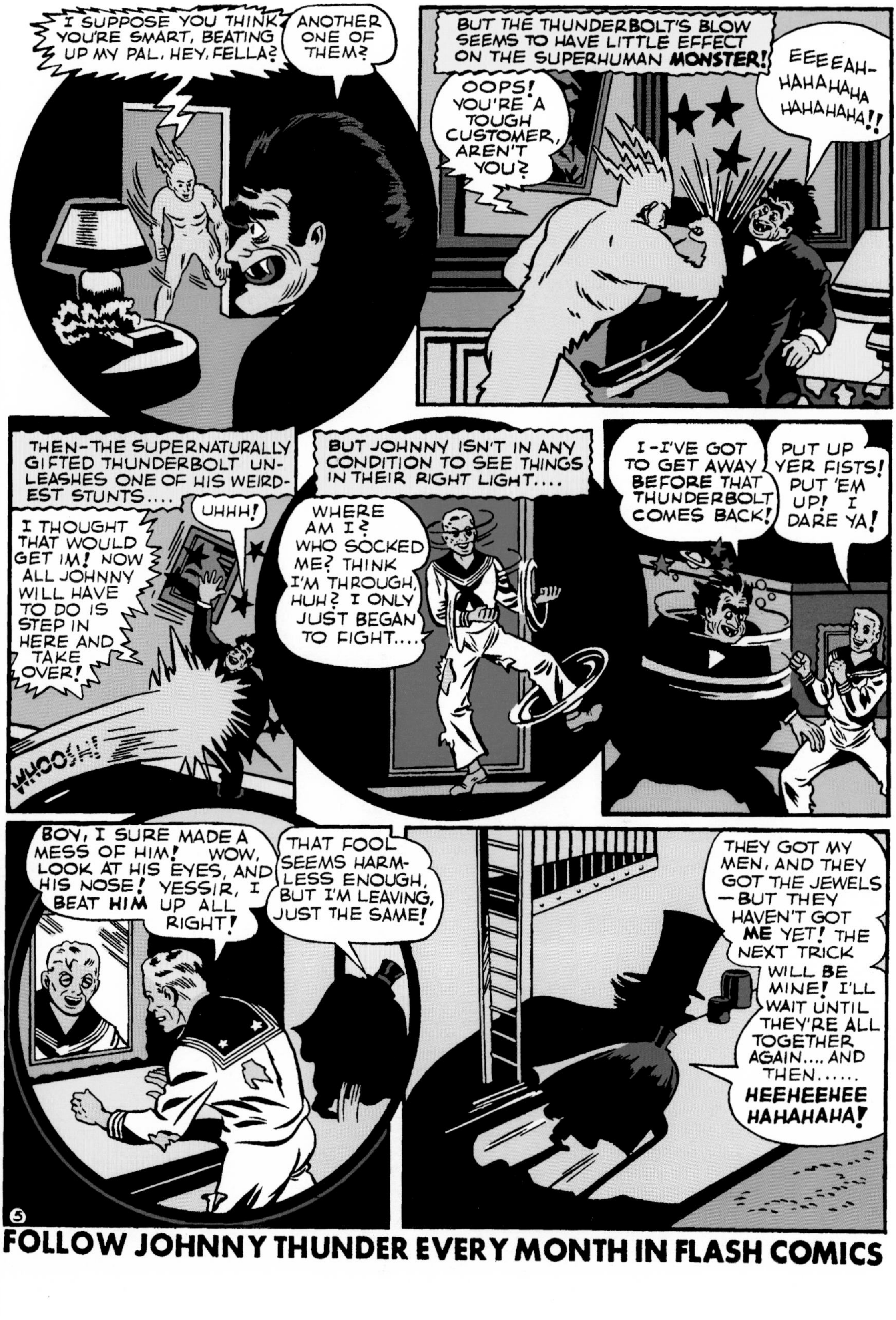
I SUPPOSE YOU THINK YOU'RE SMART, BEATING UP MY PAL, HEY, FELLA?
ANOTHER ONE OF THEM?
BUT THE THUNDERBOLT'S BLOW SEEMS TO HAVE LITTLE EFFECT ON THE SUPERHUMAN MONSTER!
OOPS! YOU'RE A TOUGH CUSTOMER, AREN'T YOU?
EEEEAH-HAHAHAHA HAHAHAHA!!
THEN—THE SUPERNATURALLY GIFTED THUNDERBOLT UNLEASHES ONE OF HIS WEIRDEST STUNTS....
UHHH!
I THOUGHT THAT WOULD GET IM! NOW ALL JOHNNY WILL HAVE TO DO IS STEP IN HERE AND TAKE OVER!
WHOOSH!
BUT JOHNNY ISN'T IN ANY CONDITION TO SEE THINGS IN THEIR RIGHT LIGHT....
WHERE AM I? WHO SOCKED ME? THINK I'M THROUGH, HUH? I ONLY JUST BEGAN TO FIGHT....
I-I'VE GOT TO GET AWAY BEFORE THAT THUNDERBOLT COMES BACK!
PUT UP YER FISTS! PUT 'EM UP! I DARE YA!
BOY, I SURE MADE A MESS OF HIM! WOW, LOOK AT HIS EYES, AND HIS NOSE! YESSIR, I BEAT HIM UP ALL RIGHT!
THAT FOOL SEEMS HARMLESS ENOUGH, BUT I'M LEAVING, JUST THE SAME!
THEY GOT MY MEN, AND THEY GOT THE JEWELS—BUT THEY HAVEN'T GOT ME YET! THE NEXT TRICK WILL BE MINE! I'LL WAIT UNTIL THEY'RE ALL TOGETHER AGAIN.... AND THEN...... HEEHEEHEE HAHAHAHA!
5
FOLLOW JOHNNY THUNDER EVERY MONTH IN FLASH COMICS

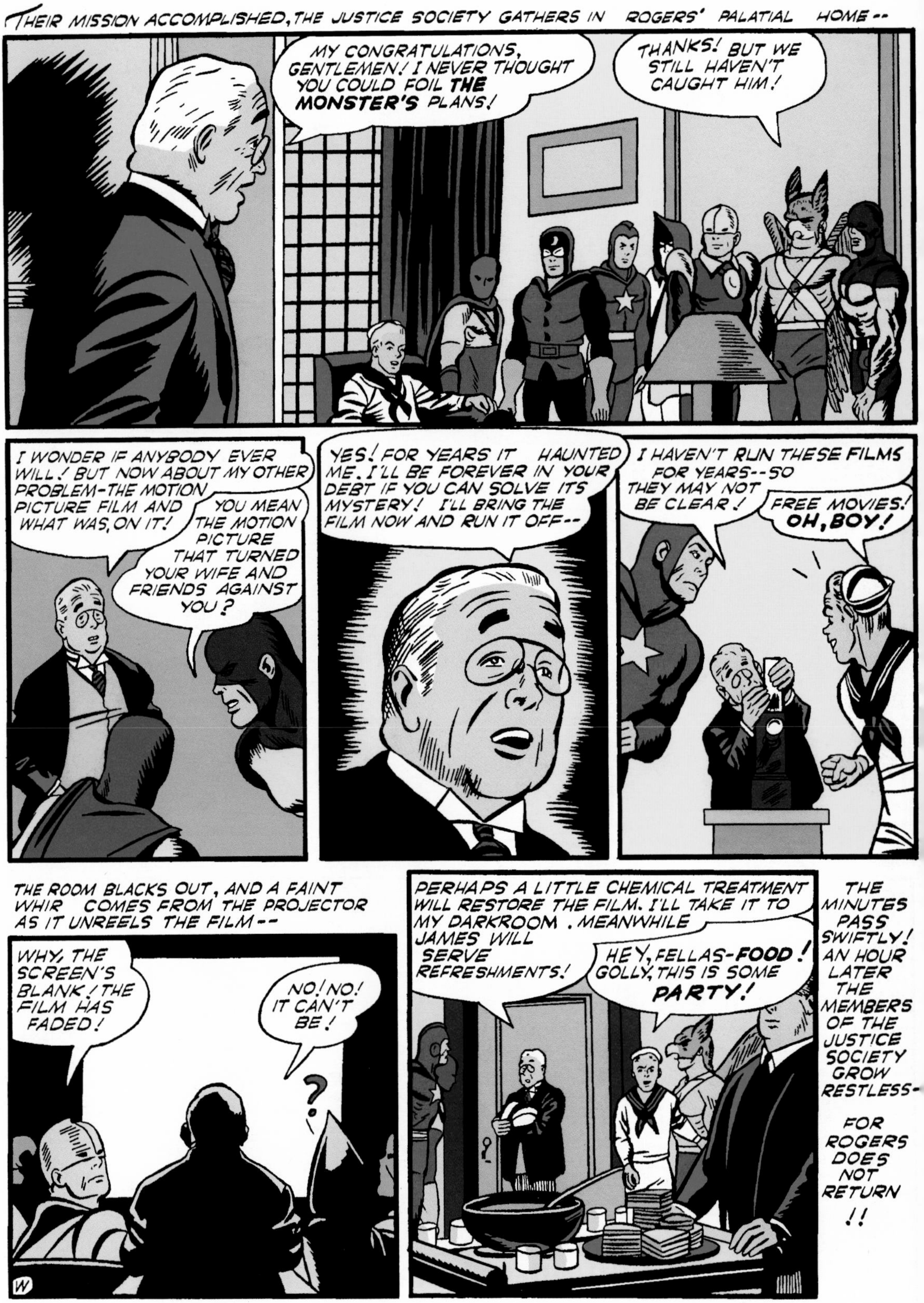
THEIR MISSION ACCOMPLISHED, THE JUSTICE SOCIETY GATHERS IN ROGERS' PALATIAL HOME--
MY CONGRATULATIONS, GENTLEMEN! I NEVER THOUGHT YOU COULD FOIL THE MONSTER'S PLANS!
THANKS! BUT WE STILL HAVEN'T CAUGHT HIM!
I WONDER IF ANYBODY EVER WILL! BUT NOW ABOUT MY OTHER PROBLEM-THE MOTION PICTURE FILM AND WHAT WAS ON IT!
YOU MEAN THE MOTION PICTURE THAT TURNED YOUR WIFE AND FRIENDS AGAINST YOU?
YES! FOR YEARS IT HAUNTED ME. I'LL BE FOREVER IN YOUR DEBT IF YOU CAN SOLVE ITS MYSTERY! I'LL BRING THE FILM NOW AND RUN IT OFF--
I HAVEN'T RUN THESE FILMS FOR YEARS--SO THEY MAY NOT BE CLEAR!
FREE MOVIES! OH, BOY!
THE ROOM BLACKS OUT, AND A FAINT WHIR COMES FROM THE PROJECTOR AS IT UNREELS THE FILM--
WHY, THE SCREEN'S BLANK! THE FILM HAS FADED!
NO! NO! IT CAN'T BE!
?
PERHAPS A LITTLE CHEMICAL TREATMENT WILL RESTORE THE FILM. I'LL TAKE IT TO MY DARKROOM. MEANWHILE JAMES WILL SERVE REFRESHMENTS!
HEY, FELLAS-FOOD! GOLLY, THIS IS SOME PARTY!
THE MINUTES PASS SWIFTLY! AN HOUR LATER THE MEMBERS OF THE JUSTICE SOCIETY GROW RESTLESS-
FOR ROGERS DOES NOT RETURN !!

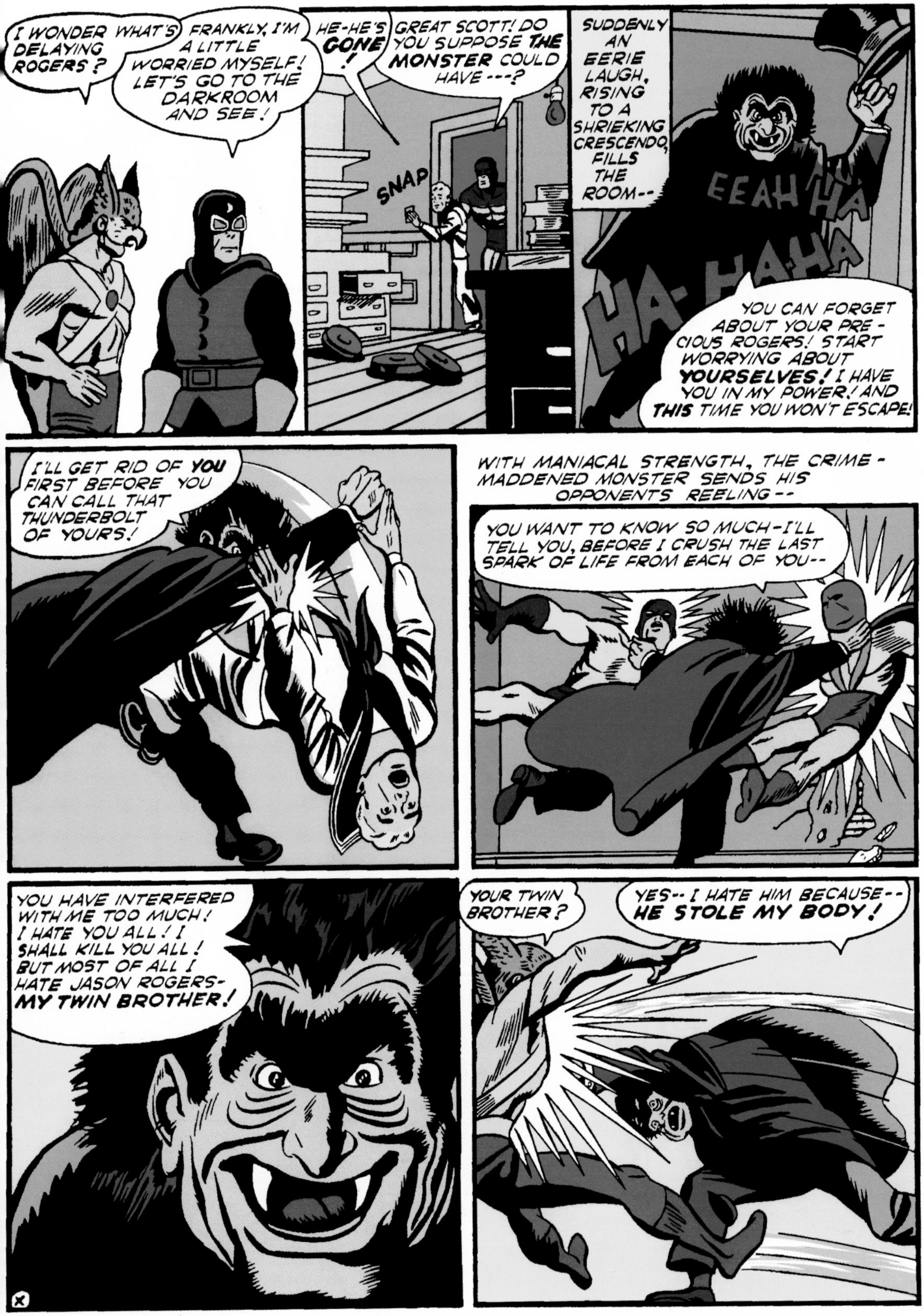
I WONDER WHAT'S DELAYING ROGERS?
FRANKLY, I'M A LITTLE WORRIED MYSELF! LET'S GO TO THE DARKROOM AND SEE!
HE-HE'S GONE!
GREAT SCOTT! DO YOU SUPPOSE THE MONSTER COULD HAVE ---?
SNAP
SUDDENLY AN EERIE LAUGH, RISING TO A SHRIEKING CRESCENDO, FILLS THE ROOM--
EEAH HA HA-HA-HA
YOU CAN FORGET ABOUT YOUR PRECIOUS ROGERS! START WORRYING ABOUT YOURSELVES! I HAVE YOU IN MY POWER! AND THIS TIME YOU WON'T ESCAPE!
I'LL GET RID OF YOU FIRST BEFORE YOU CAN CALL THAT THUNDERBOLT OF YOURS!
WITH MANIACAL STRENGTH, THE CRIME-MADDENED MONSTER SENDS HIS OPPONENTS REELING--
YOU WANT TO KNOW SO MUCH-I'LL TELL YOU, BEFORE I CRUSH THE LAST SPARK OF LIFE FROM EACH OF YOU--
YOU HAVE INTERFERED WITH ME TOO MUCH! I HATE YOU ALL! I SHALL KILL YOU ALL! BUT MOST OF ALL I HATE JASON ROGERS-MY TWIN BROTHER!
YOUR TWIN BROTHER?
YES-- I HATE HIM BECAUSE-- HE STOLE MY BODY!

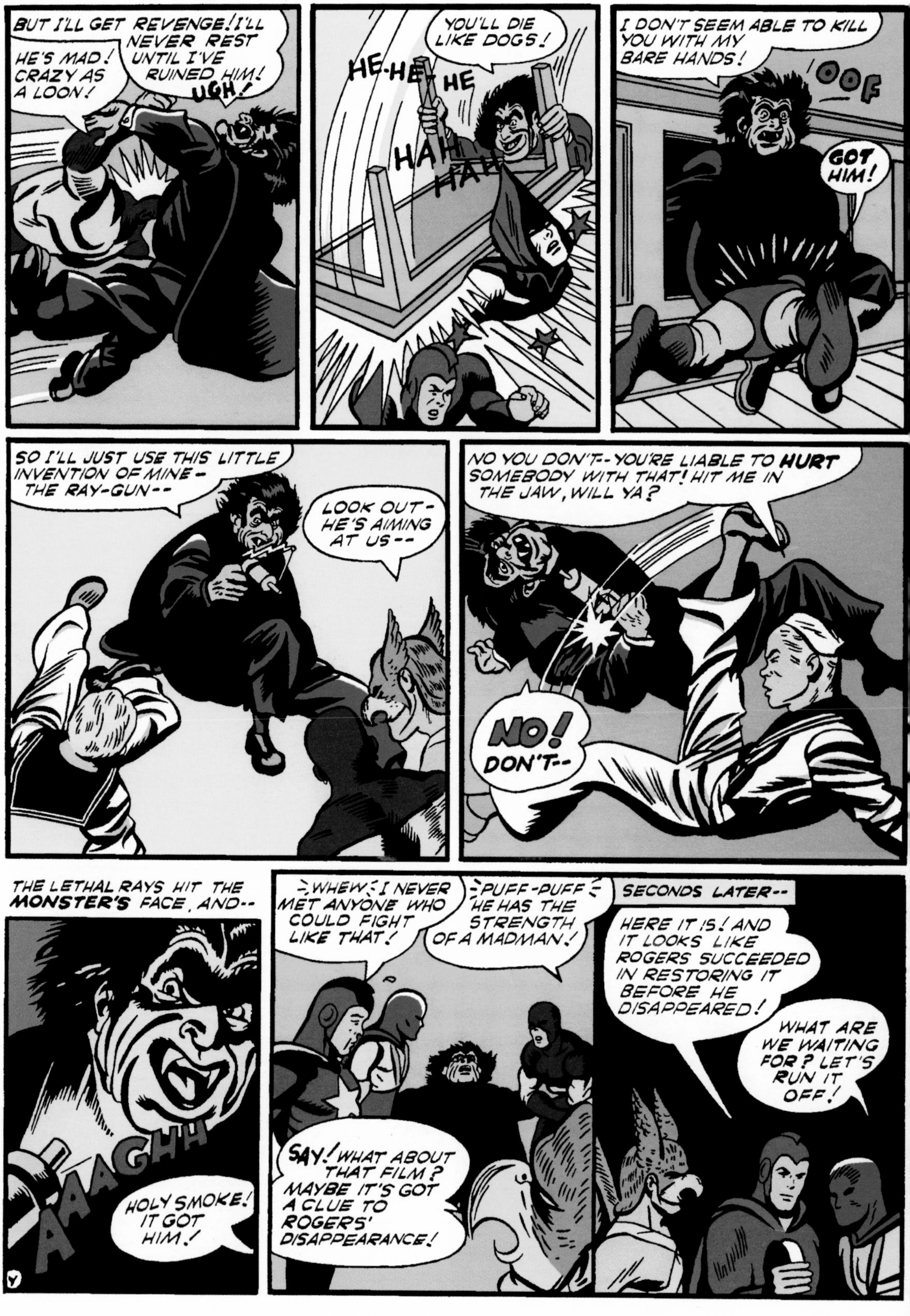
BUT I'LL GET REVENGE! I'LL NEVER REST UNTIL I'VE RUINED HIM!
HE'S MAD! CRAZY AS A LOON!
UGH!
YOU'LL DIE LIKE DOGS!
HE-HE-HE
HAH HAH
I DON'T SEEM ABLE TO KILL YOU WITH MY BARE HANDS!
OOF
GOT HIM!
SO I'LL JUST USE THIS LITTLE INVENTION OF MINE - THE RAY-GUN--
LOOK OUT- HE'S AIMING AT US--
NO YOU DON'T--YOU'RE LIABLE TO HURT SOMEBODY WITH THAT! HIT ME IN THE JAW, WILL YA?
NO! DON'T--
THE LETHAL RAYS HIT THE MONSTER'S FACE, AND--
AAAGHH
HOLY SMOKE! IT GOT HIM!
WHEW! I NEVER MET ANYONE WHO COULD FIGHT LIKE THAT!
PUFF-PUFF HE HAS THE STRENGTH OF A MADMAN!
SAY! WHAT ABOUT THAT FILM? MAYBE IT'S GOT A CLUE TO ROGERS' DISAPPEARANCE!
SECONDS LATER--
HERE IT IS! AND IT LOOKS LIKE ROGERS SUCCEEDED IN RESTORING IT BEFORE HE DISAPPEARED!
WHAT ARE WE WAITING FOR? LET'S RUN IT OFF!

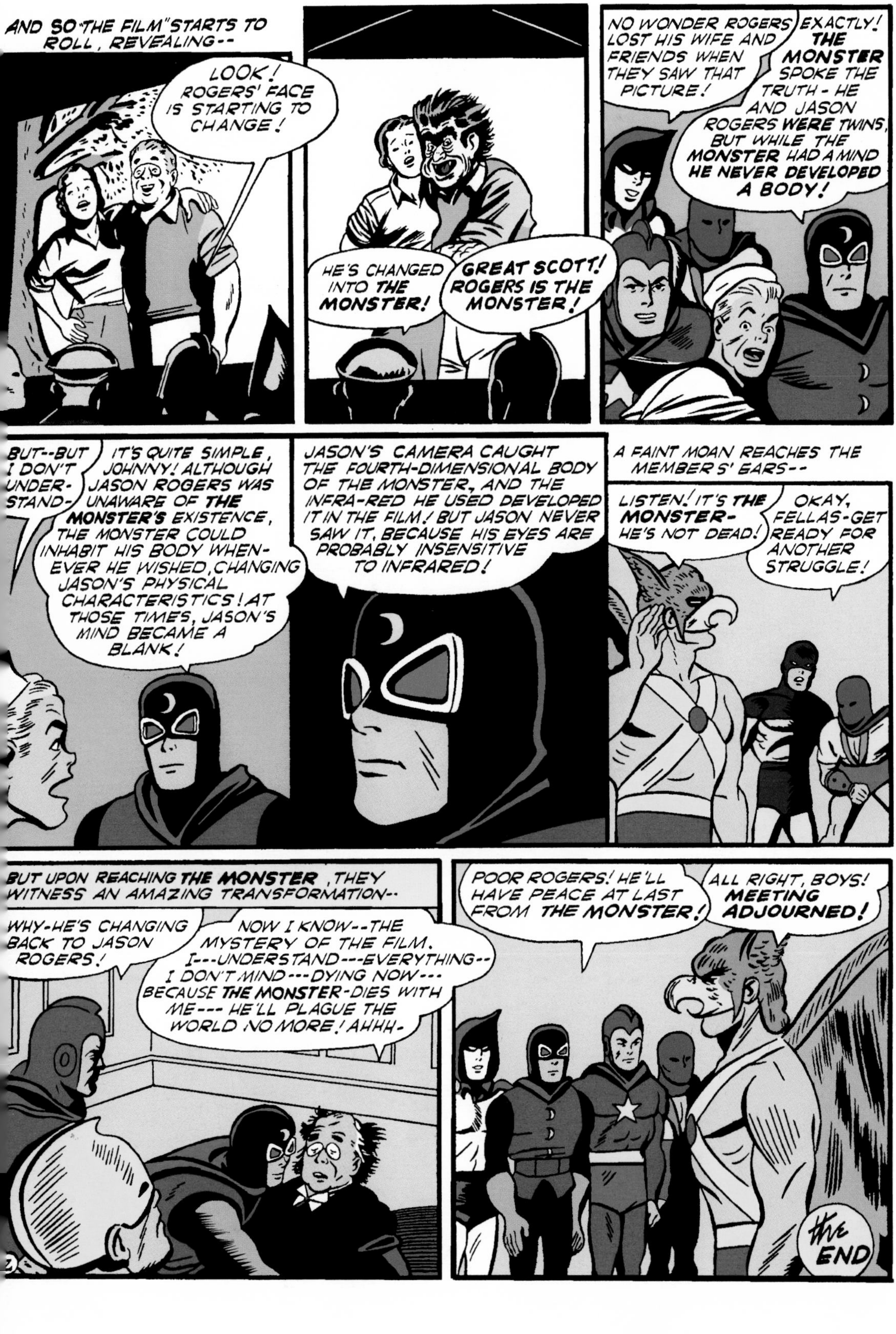
AND SO "THE FILM" STARTS TO ROLL, REVEALING--
LOOK! ROGERS' FACE IS STARTING TO CHANGE!
HE'S CHANGED INTO THE MONSTER!
GREAT SCOTT! ROGERS IS THE MONSTER!
NO WONDER ROGERS LOST HIS WIFE AND FRIENDS WHEN THEY SAW THAT PICTURE!
EXACTLY! THE MONSTER SPOKE THE TRUTH - HE AND JASON ROGERS WERE TWINS, BUT WHILE THE MONSTER HAD A MIND HE NEVER DEVELOPED A BODY!
BUT--BUT I DON'T UNDERSTAND-
IT'S QUITE SIMPLE, JOHNNY! ALTHOUGH JASON ROGERS WAS UNAWARE OF THE MONSTER'S EXISTENCE, THE MONSTER COULD INHABIT HIS BODY WHENEVER HE WISHED, CHANGING JASON'S PHYSICAL CHARACTERISTICS! AT THOSE TIMES, JASON'S MIND BECAME A BLANK!
JASON'S CAMERA CAUGHT THE FOURTH-DIMENSIONAL BODY OF THE MONSTER, AND THE INFRA-RED HE USED DEVELOPED IT IN THE FILM! BUT JASON NEVER SAW IT, BECAUSE HIS EYES ARE PROBABLY INSENSITIVE TO INFRARED!
A FAINT MOAN REACHES THE MEMBER'S' EARS--
LISTEN! IT'S THE MONSTER- HE'S NOT DEAD!
OKAY, FELLAS-GET READY FOR ANOTHER STRUGGLE!
BUT UPON REACHING THE MONSTER, THEY WITNESS AN AMAZING TRANSFORMATION--
WHY-HE'S CHANGING BACK TO JASON ROGERS!
NOW I KNOW--THE MYSTERY OF THE FILM. I---UNDERSTAND---EVERYTHING-- I DON'T MIND---DYING NOW--- BECAUSE THE MONSTER-DIES WITH ME--- HE'LL PLAGUE THE WORLD NO MORE! AHHH-
POOR ROGERS! HE'LL HAVE PEACE AT LAST FROM THE MONSTER!
ALL RIGHT, BOYS! MEETING ADJOURNED!
THE END

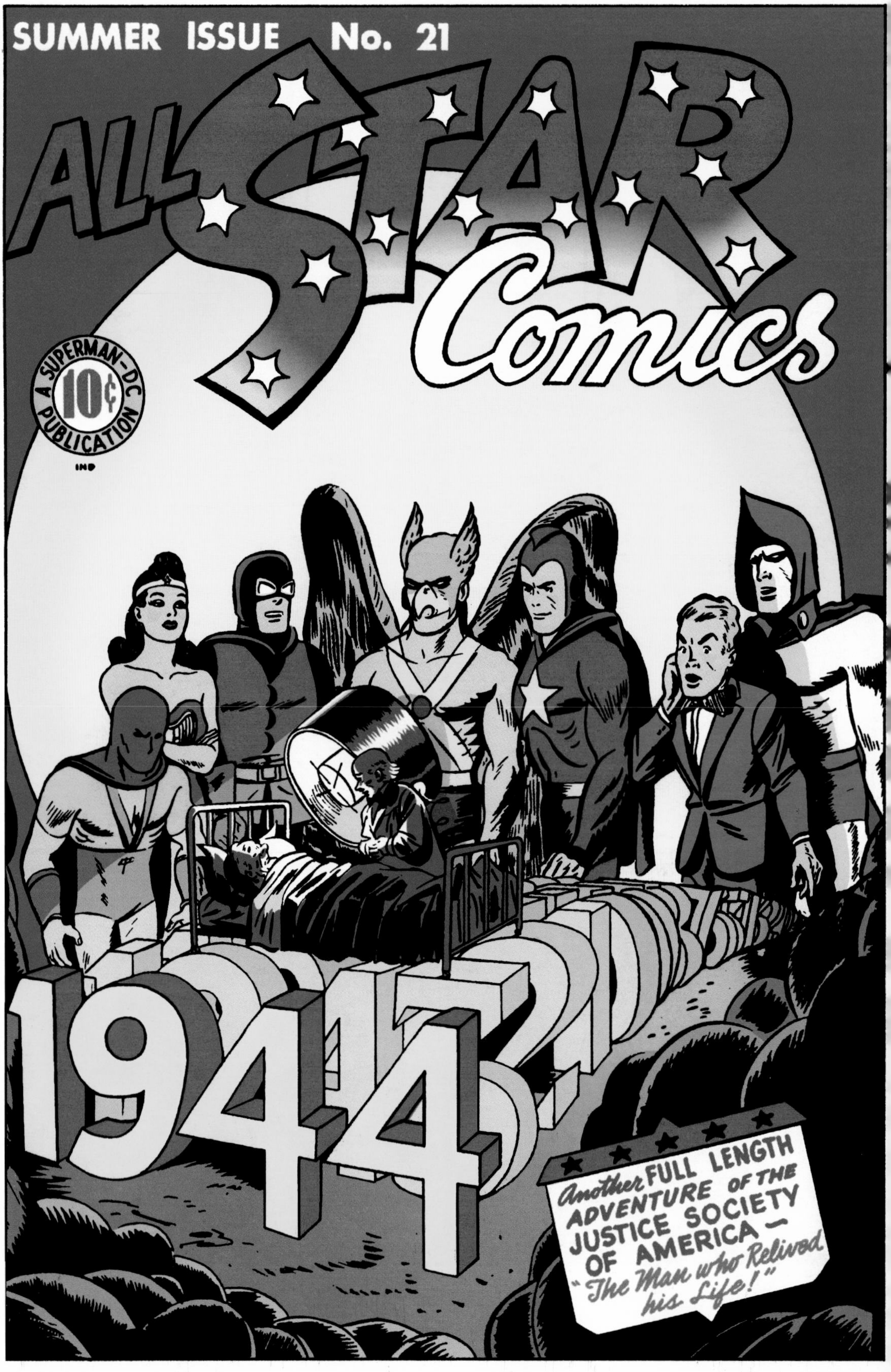
SUMMER ISSUE No. 21
ALL STAR Comics
A SUPERMAN-DC PUBLICATION 10¢
1944
Another FULL LENGTH ADVENTURE OF THE JUSTICE SOCIETY OF AMERICA —
"The Man who Relived his Life!"

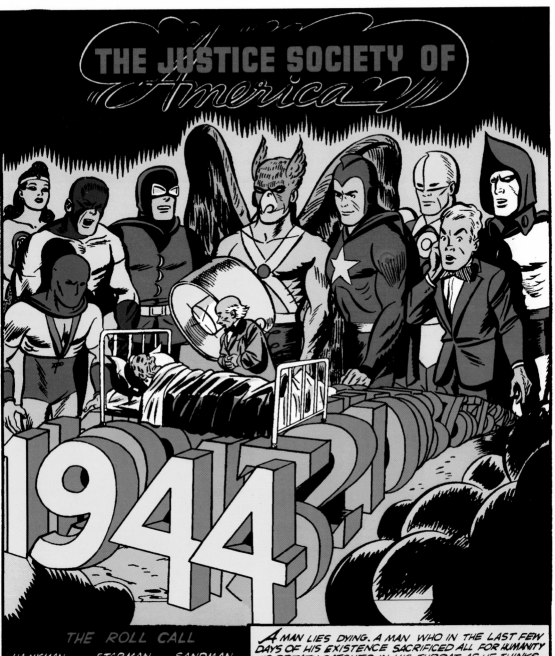

THE JUSTICE SOCIETY OF America

1944

THE ROLL CALL

HAWKMAN   STARMAN   SANDMAN
DOCTOR FATE   THE ATOM   DR. MIDNITE
THE SPECTRE   JOHNNY   WONDER
               THUNDER   WOMAN,
                              SECRETARY

PRESENTING THE JUSTICE SOCIETY
IN

"THE MAN WHO
RELIVED HIS LIFE"

A MAN LIES DYING. A MAN WHO IN THE LAST FEW DAYS OF HIS EXISTENCE SACRIFICED ALL FOR HUMANITY. HIS BREATH CATCHES IN HIS THROAT AS HE THINKS OF THE LIFE HE LIVED BEFORE THAT!-- OF THE STEPS THAT TOOK HIM SLOWLY BUT SURELY ALONG THE VICIOUS PATH TO CRIME AND DISGRACE! IF ONLY HE COULD FEEL THAT HE HADN'T DONE THOSE THINGS! IF ONLY HE COULD REMOLD HIS PAST SO HE COULD LEAVE THIS LIFE IN PEACE-- WITH A CLEAR CONSCIENCE!

BUT THAT IS IMPOSSIBLE--OR IS IT? TO HIS HELP COMES THE FORMIDABLE JUSTICE SOCIETY, TO WHOM TIME AND SPACE ARE NO BARRIERS WHEN A MAN'S HAPPINESS HANGS IN THE BALANCE!

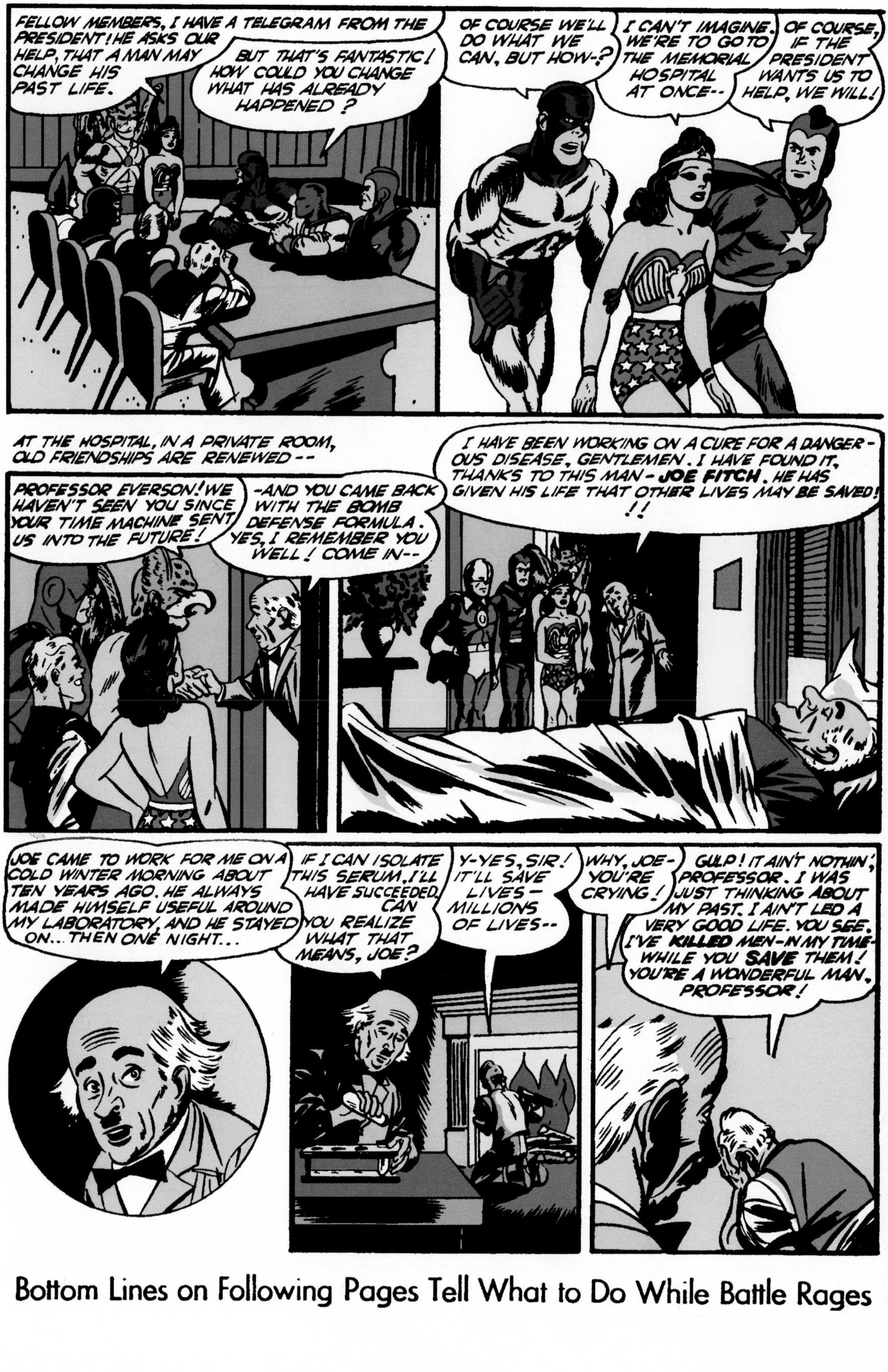
FELLOW MEMBERS, I HAVE A TELEGRAM FROM THE PRESIDENT! HE ASKS OUR HELP, THAT A MAN MAY CHANGE HIS PAST LIFE.
BUT THAT'S FANTASTIC! HOW COULD YOU CHANGE WHAT HAS ALREADY HAPPENED?
OF COURSE WE'LL DO WHAT WE CAN, BUT HOW-?
I CAN'T IMAGINE. WE'RE TO GO TO THE MEMORIAL HOSPITAL AT ONCE--
OF COURSE, IF THE PRESIDENT WANTS US TO HELP, WE WILL!
AT THE HOSPITAL, IN A PRIVATE ROOM, OLD FRIENDSHIPS ARE RENEWED--
PROFESSOR EVERSON! WE HAVEN'T SEEN YOU SINCE YOUR TIME MACHINE SENT US INTO THE FUTURE!
-AND YOU CAME BACK WITH THE BOMB DEFENSE FORMULA. YES, I REMEMBER YOU WELL! COME IN--
I HAVE BEEN WORKING ON A CURE FOR A DANGEROUS DISEASE, GENTLEMEN. I HAVE FOUND IT, THANKS TO THIS MAN - JOE FITCH. HE HAS GIVEN HIS LIFE THAT OTHER LIVES MAY BE SAVED!!!
JOE CAME TO WORK FOR ME ON A COLD WINTER MORNING ABOUT TEN YEARS AGO. HE ALWAYS MADE HIMSELF USEFUL AROUND MY LABORATORY, AND HE STAYED ON... THEN ONE NIGHT...
IF I CAN ISOLATE THIS SERUM, I'LL HAVE SUCCEEDED. CAN YOU REALIZE WHAT THAT MEANS, JOE?
Y-YES, SIR! IT'LL SAVE LIVES— MILLIONS OF LIVES--
WHY, JOE- YOU'RE CRYING!
GULP! IT AIN'T NOTHIN', PROFESSOR. I WAS JUST THINKING ABOUT MY PAST. I AIN'T LED A VERY GOOD LIFE. YOU SEE, I'VE KILLED MEN-IN MY TIME- WHILE YOU SAVE THEM! YOU'RE A WONDERFUL MAN, PROFESSOR!

Bottom Lines on Following Pages Tell What to Do While Battle Rages

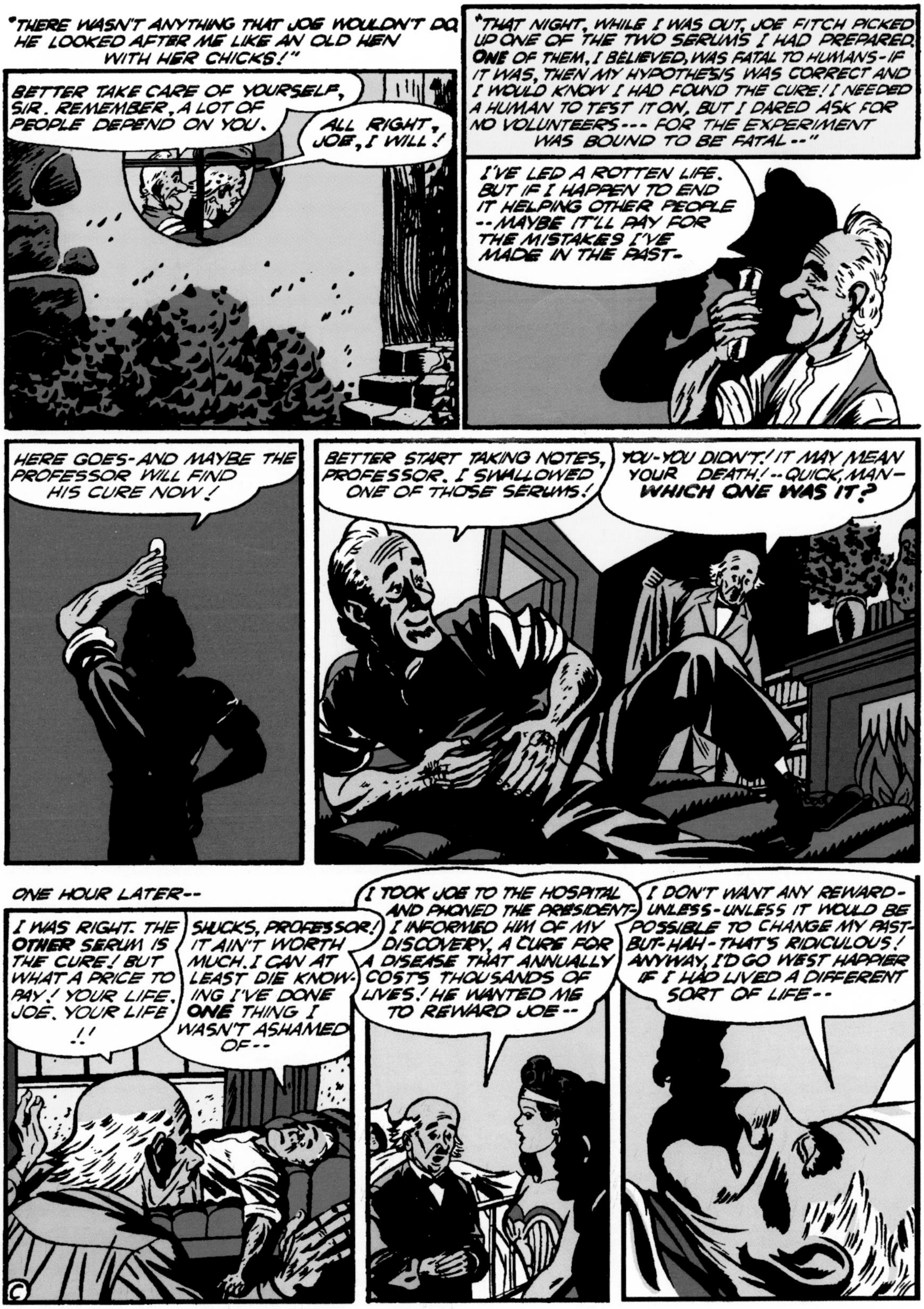
"THERE WASN'T ANYTHING THAT JOE WOULDN'T DO. HE LOOKED AFTER ME LIKE AN OLD HEN WITH HER CHICKS!"
BETTER TAKE CARE OF YOURSELF, SIR. REMEMBER, A LOT OF PEOPLE DEPEND ON YOU.
ALL RIGHT, JOE, I WILL!
"THAT NIGHT, WHILE I WAS OUT, JOE FITCH PICKED UP ONE OF THE TWO SERUMS I HAD PREPARED. ONE OF THEM, I BELIEVED, WAS FATAL TO HUMANS - IF IT WAS, THEN MY HYPOTHESIS WAS CORRECT AND I WOULD KNOW I HAD FOUND THE CURE! I NEEDED A HUMAN TO TEST IT ON, BUT I DARED ASK FOR NO VOLUNTEERS--- FOR THE EXPERIMENT WAS BOUND TO BE FATAL--"
I'VE LED A ROTTEN LIFE. BUT IF I HAPPEN TO END IT HELPING OTHER PEOPLE --MAYBE IT'LL PAY FOR THE MISTAKES I'VE MADE IN THE PAST-
HERE GOES- AND MAYBE THE PROFESSOR WILL FIND HIS CURE NOW!
BETTER START TAKING NOTES, PROFESSOR. I SWALLOWED ONE OF THOSE SERUMS!
YOU-YOU DIDN'T! IT MAY MEAN YOUR DEATH! --QUICK, MAN- WHICH ONE WAS IT?
ONE HOUR LATER--
I WAS RIGHT. THE OTHER SERUM IS THE CURE! BUT WHAT A PRICE TO PAY! YOUR LIFE, JOE. YOUR LIFE!!
SHUCKS, PROFESSOR! IT AIN'T WORTH MUCH. I CAN AT LEAST DIE KNOWING I'VE DONE ONE THING I WASN'T ASHAMED OF--
I TOOK JOE TO THE HOSPITAL AND PHONED THE PRESIDENT- I INFORMED HIM OF MY DISCOVERY, A CURE FOR A DISEASE THAT ANNUALLY COSTS THOUSANDS OF LIVES! HE WANTED ME TO REWARD JOE--
I DON'T WANT ANY REWARD- UNLESS- UNLESS IT WOULD BE POSSIBLE TO CHANGE MY PAST- BUT- HAH- THAT'S RIDICULOUS! ANYWAY, I'D GO WEST HAPPIER IF I HAD LIVED A DIFFERENT SORT OF LIFE--

Tin Cans in the Garbage Pile Are Just a Way of Saying "Heil!"

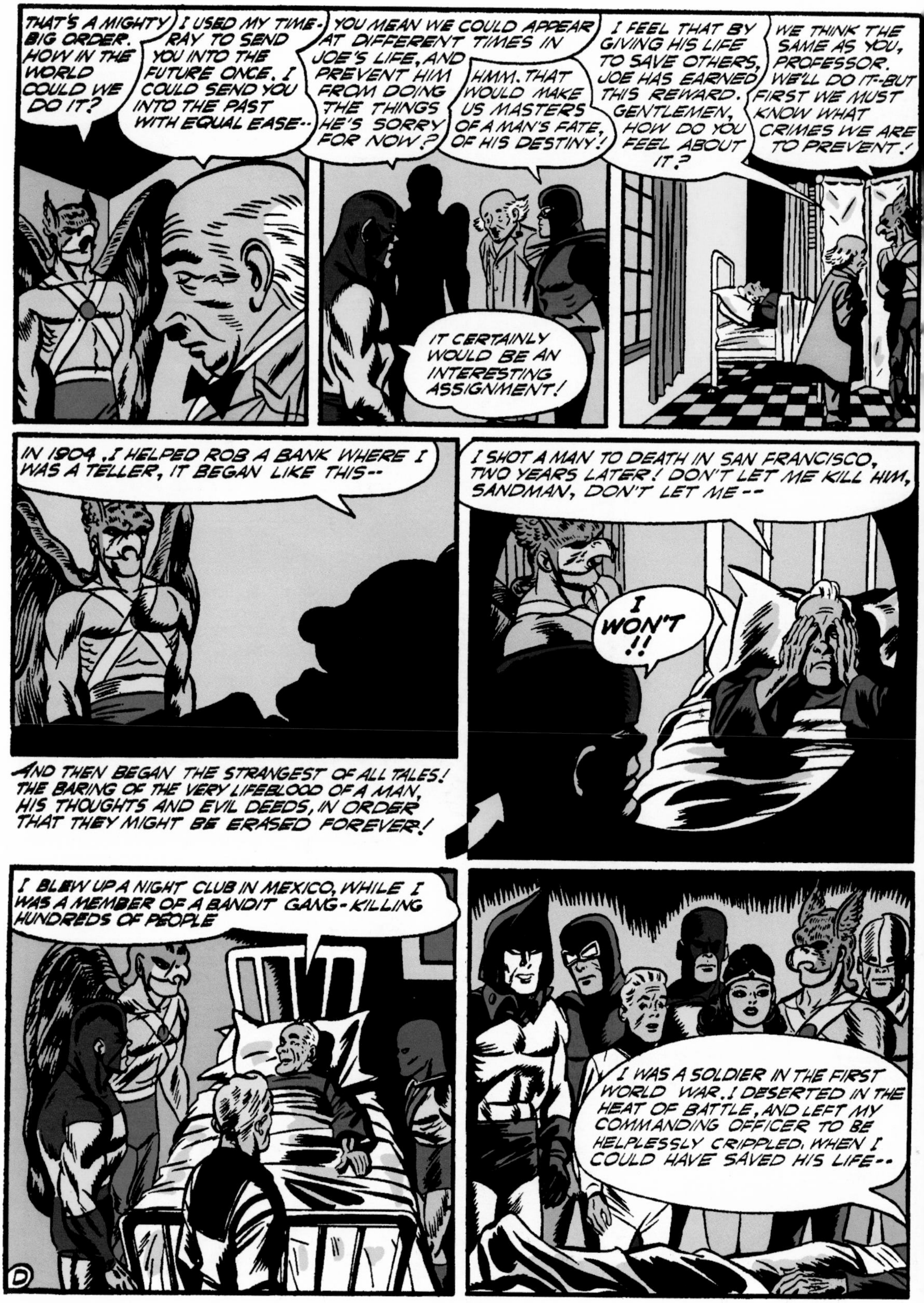
THAT'S A MIGHTY BIG ORDER. HOW IN THE WORLD COULD WE DO IT?
I USED MY TIME-RAY TO SEND YOU INTO THE FUTURE ONCE. I COULD SEND YOU INTO THE PAST WITH EQUAL EASE--
YOU MEAN WE COULD APPEAR AT DIFFERENT TIMES IN JOE'S LIFE, AND PREVENT HIM FROM DOING THE THINGS HE'S SORRY FOR NOW?
HMM. THAT WOULD MAKE US MASTERS OF A MAN'S FATE, OF HIS DESTINY!
IT CERTAINLY WOULD BE AN INTERESTING ASSIGNMENT!
I FEEL THAT BY GIVING HIS LIFE TO SAVE OTHERS, JOE HAS EARNED THIS REWARD. GENTLEMEN, HOW DO YOU FEEL ABOUT IT?
WE THINK THE SAME AS YOU, PROFESSOR. WE'LL DO IT-BUT FIRST WE MUST KNOW WHAT CRIMES WE ARE TO PREVENT!
IN 1904, I HELPED ROB A BANK WHERE I WAS A TELLER, IT BEGAN LIKE THIS--
AND THEN BEGAN THE STRANGEST OF ALL TALES! THE BARING OF THE VERY LIFEBLOOD OF A MAN, HIS THOUGHTS AND EVIL DEEDS, IN ORDER THAT THEY MIGHT BE ERASED FOREVER!
I SHOT A MAN TO DEATH IN SAN FRANCISCO, TWO YEARS LATER! DON'T LET ME KILL HIM, SANDMAN, DON'T LET ME--
I WON'T!!
I BLEW UP A NIGHT CLUB IN MEXICO, WHILE I WAS A MEMBER OF A BANDIT GANG-KILLING HUNDREDS OF PEOPLE
D
I WAS A SOLDIER IN THE FIRST WORLD WAR. I DESERTED IN THE HEAT OF BATTLE, AND LEFT MY COMMANDING OFFICER TO BE HELPLESSLY CRIPPLED, WHEN I COULD HAVE SAVED HIS LIFE--

Waste Fats in Good Condition Help to Make Fine Ammunition

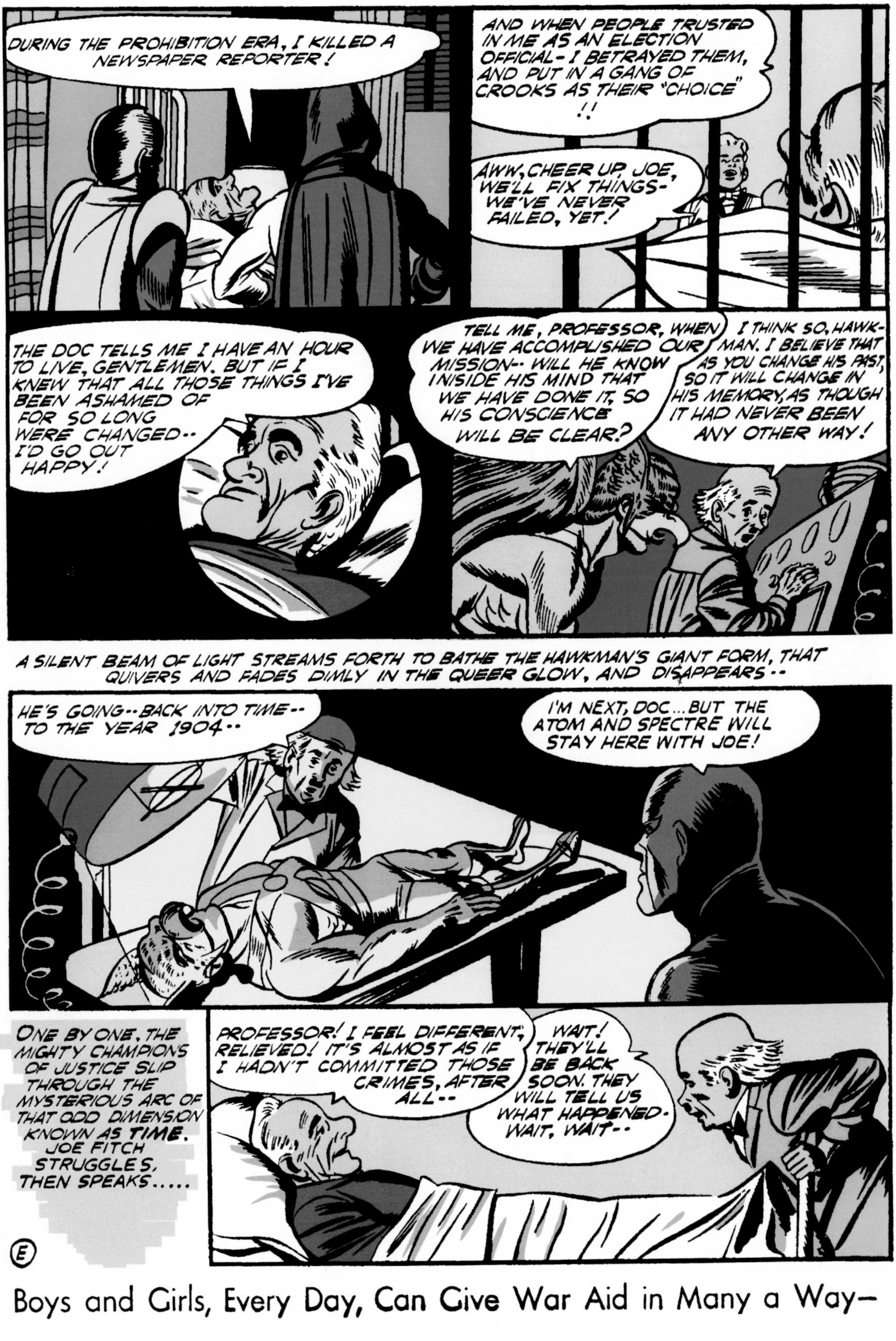
DURING THE PROHIBITION ERA, I KILLED A NEWSPAPER REPORTER!
AND WHEN PEOPLE TRUSTED IN ME AS AN ELECTION OFFICIAL- I BETRAYED THEM, AND PUT IN A GANG OF CROOKS AS THEIR "CHOICE" !!
AWW, CHEER UP, JOE, WE'LL FIX THINGS- WE'VE NEVER FAILED, YET!
THE DOC TELLS ME I HAVE AN HOUR TO LIVE, GENTLEMEN. BUT IF I KNEW THAT ALL THOSE THINGS I'VE BEEN ASHAMED OF FOR SO LONG WERE CHANGED.. I'D GO OUT HAPPY!
TELL ME, PROFESSOR, WHEN WE HAVE ACCOMPLISHED OUR MISSION-- WILL HE KNOW INSIDE HIS MIND THAT WE HAVE DONE IT, SO HIS CONSCIENCE WILL BE CLEAR?
I THINK SO, HAWKMAN. I BELIEVE THAT AS YOU CHANGE HIS PAST, SO IT WILL CHANGE IN HIS MEMORY, AS THOUGH IT HAD NEVER BEEN ANY OTHER WAY!
A SILENT BEAM OF LIGHT STREAMS FORTH TO BATHE THE HAWKMAN'S GIANT FORM, THAT QUIVERS AND FADES DIMLY IN THE QUEER GLOW, AND DISAPPEARS--
HE'S GOING--BACK INTO TIME-- TO THE YEAR 1904--
I'M NEXT, DOC...BUT THE ATOM AND SPECTRE WILL STAY HERE WITH JOE!
ONE BY ONE, THE MIGHTY CHAMPIONS OF JUSTICE SLIP THROUGH THE MYSTERIOUS ARC OF THAT ODD DIMENSION KNOWN AS TIME. JOE FITCH STRUGGLES, THEN SPEAKS.....
PROFESSOR! I FEEL DIFFERENT, RELIEVED! IT'S ALMOST AS IF I HADN'T COMMITTED THOSE CRIMES, AFTER ALL--
WAIT! THEY'LL BE BACK SOON. THEY WILL TELL US WHAT HAPPENED. WAIT, WAIT--
E

Boys and Girls, Every Day, Can Give War Aid in Many a Way—

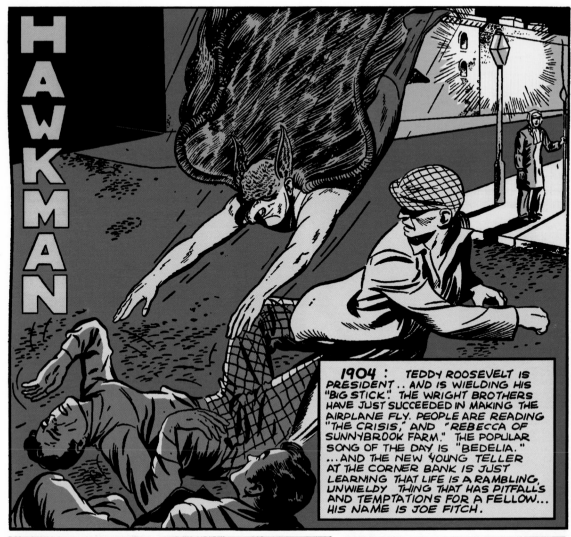

HAWKMAN

1904: TEDDY ROOSEVELT IS PRESIDENT .. AND IS WIELDING HIS "BIG STICK". THE WRIGHT BROTHERS HAVE JUST SUCCEEDED IN MAKING THE AIRPLANE FLY. PEOPLE ARE READING "THE CRISIS," AND "REBECCA OF SUNNYBROOK FARM." THE POPULAR SONG OF THE DAY IS "BEDELIA." ...AND THE NEW YOUNG TELLER AT THE CORNER BANK IS JUST LEARNING THAT LIFE IS A RAMBLING, UNWIELDY THING THAT HAS PITFALLS AND TEMPTATIONS FOR A FELLOW... HIS NAME IS JOE FITCH.

JOSEPH J. FITCH WAS BORN IN 1884, ON A FARM NEAR NEW YORK. TODAY, THAT FARMLAND IS PART OF THE BOROUGH OF BROOKLYN. HIS DAD WAS A FARMER AND WANTED JOE TO BE ONE, TOO. BUT THE GLAMOUR OF THE BIG "CITY" WAS TOO STRONG, SO JOE TOOK A FERRY ACROSS THE EAST RIVER AND BECAME A BANK TELLER...

! !

WHY NOT DROP AROUND TO MY PLACE SOME NIGHT, FITCH? HAVE SOME FUN! YOU'LL ENJOY YOURSELF...

THANKS, MR. SPEARS I WILL...

TELLER

BETTER STAY AWAY FROM THAT MAN, JOE. HE'S SAPPHIRE SLIM.. A GAMBLER.. RUNS A RED-HOT PLACE UPTOWN.

OH, IT WON'T HURT ME, SIR. I NEVER GAMBLE.

Every Time You Buy a Stamp, You Feed the Flame in Freedom's Lamp!

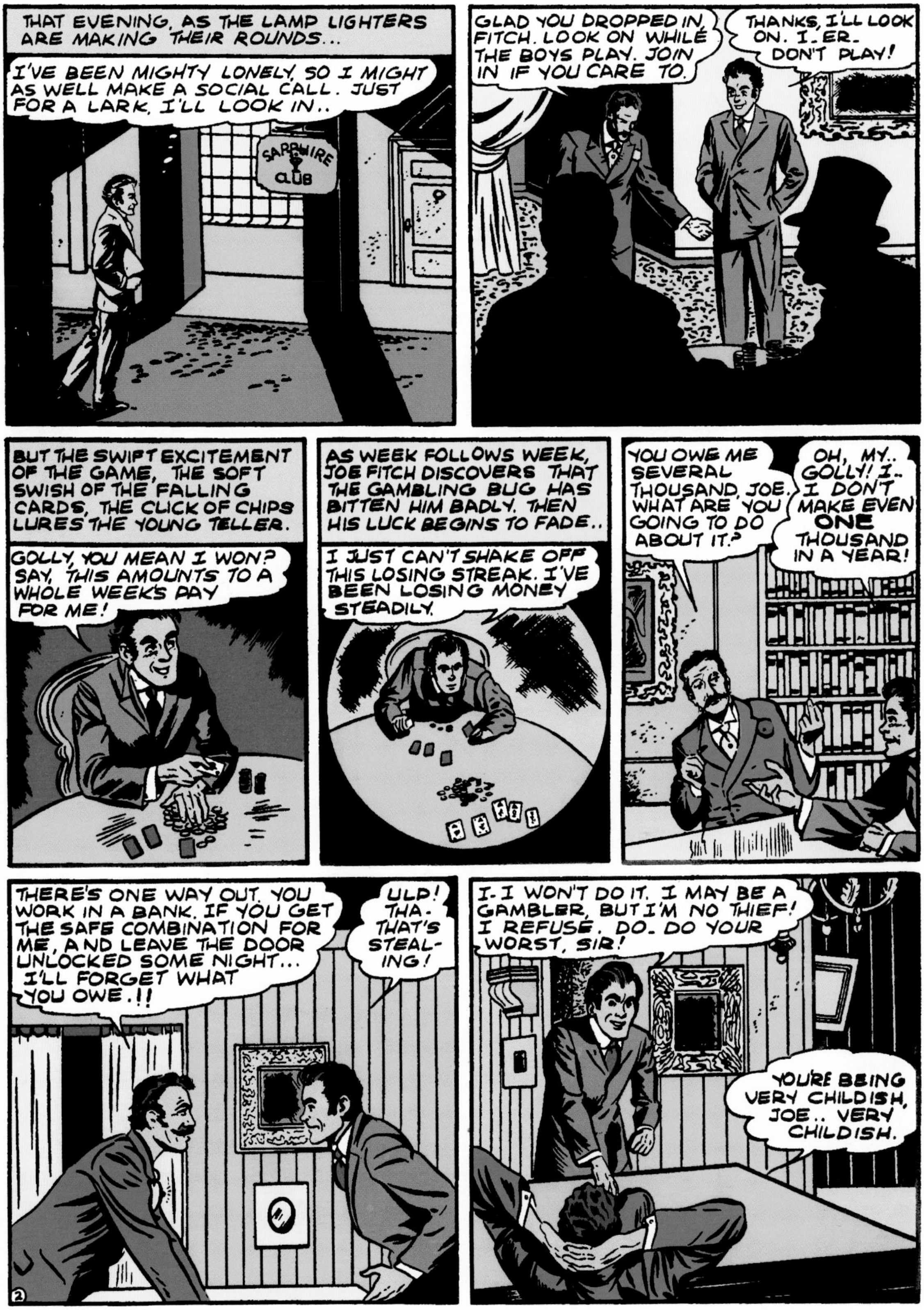
THAT EVENING, AS THE LAMP LIGHTERS ARE MAKING THEIR ROUNDS...
I'VE BEEN MIGHTY LONELY, SO I MIGHT AS WELL MAKE A SOCIAL CALL. JUST FOR A LARK, I'LL LOOK IN..
SAPPHIRE CLUB
GLAD YOU DROPPED IN, FITCH. LOOK ON WHILE THE BOYS PLAY. JOIN IN IF YOU CARE TO.
THANKS, I'LL LOOK ON. I-ER- DON'T PLAY!
BUT THE SWIFT EXCITEMENT OF THE GAME, THE SOFT SWISH OF THE FALLING CARDS, THE CLICK OF CHIPS LURES THE YOUNG TELLER.
GOLLY, YOU MEAN I WON? SAY, THIS AMOUNTS TO A WHOLE WEEK'S PAY FOR ME!
AS WEEK FOLLOWS WEEK, JOE FITCH DISCOVERS THAT THE GAMBLING BUG HAS BITTEN HIM BADLY. THEN HIS LUCK BEGINS TO FADE..
I JUST CAN'T SHAKE OFF THIS LOSING STREAK. I'VE BEEN LOSING MONEY STEADILY.
YOU OWE ME SEVERAL THOUSAND, JOE. WHAT ARE YOU GOING TO DO ABOUT IT?
OH, MY.. GOLLY! I.. I DON'T MAKE EVEN ONE THOUSAND IN A YEAR!
THERE'S ONE WAY OUT. YOU WORK IN A BANK. IF YOU GET THE SAFE COMBINATION FOR ME, AND LEAVE THE DOOR UNLOCKED SOME NIGHT... I'LL FORGET WHAT YOU OWE.!!
ULP! THA- THAT'S STEAL- ING!
I-I WON'T DO IT. I MAY BE A GAMBLER, BUT I'M NO THIEF! I REFUSE. DO-DO YOUR WORST, SIR!
YOU'RE BEING VERY CHILDISH, JOE.. VERY CHILDISH.
2

If You Have an Extra Quarter, Buy a Stamp to Make War Shorter

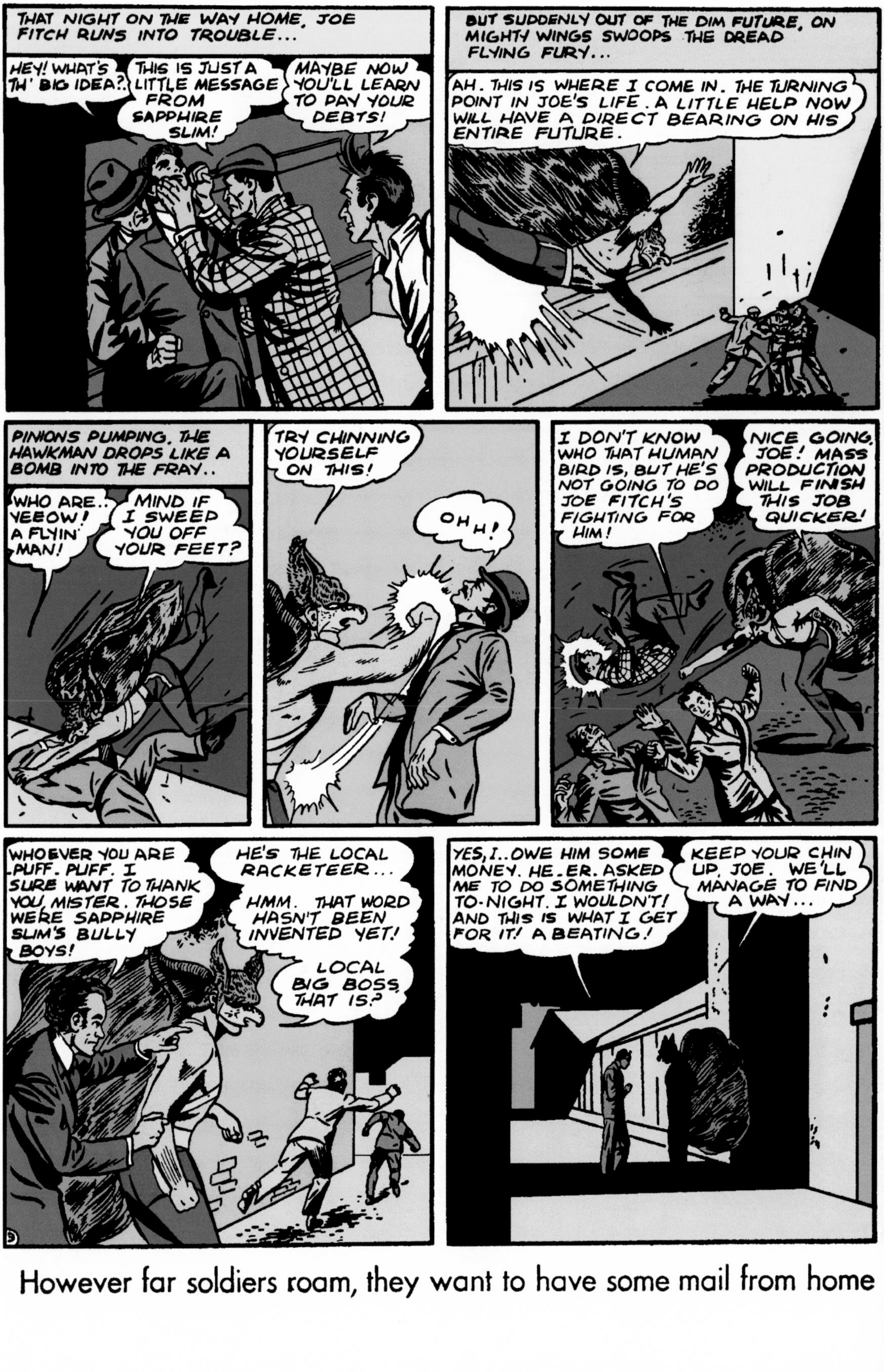
THAT NIGHT ON THE WAY HOME, JOE FITCH RUNS INTO TROUBLE...
HEY! WHAT'S TH' BIG IDEA?
THIS IS JUST A LITTLE MESSAGE FROM SAPPHIRE SLIM!
MAYBE NOW YOU'LL LEARN TO PAY YOUR DEBTS!
BUT SUDDENLY OUT OF THE DIM FUTURE, ON MIGHTY WINGS SWOOPS THE DREAD FLYING FURY...
AH. THIS IS WHERE I COME IN. THE TURNING POINT IN JOE'S LIFE. A LITTLE HELP NOW WILL HAVE A DIRECT BEARING ON HIS ENTIRE FUTURE.
PINIONS PUMPING, THE HAWKMAN DROPS LIKE A BOMB INTO THE FRAY..
WHO ARE.. YEEOW! A FLYIN' MAN!
MIND IF I SWEEP YOU OFF YOUR FEET?
TRY CHINNING YOURSELF ON THIS!
OHH!
I DON'T KNOW WHO THAT HUMAN BIRD IS, BUT HE'S NOT GOING TO DO JOE FITCH'S FIGHTING FOR HIM!
NICE GOING, JOE! MASS PRODUCTION WILL FINISH THIS JOB QUICKER!
WHOEVER YOU ARE .PUFF. PUFF. I SURE WANT TO THANK YOU, MISTER. THOSE WERE SAPPHIRE SLIM'S BULLY BOYS!
HE'S THE LOCAL RACKETEER...
HMM. THAT WORD HASN'T BEEN INVENTED YET!
LOCAL BIG BOSS THAT IS?
YES, I..OWE HIM SOME MONEY. HE..ER. ASKED ME TO DO SOMETHING TO-NIGHT. I WOULDN'T! AND THIS IS WHAT I GET FOR IT! A BEATING!
KEEP YOUR CHIN UP, JOE. WE'LL MANAGE TO FIND A WAY...

However far soldiers roam, they want to have some mail from home

ALONE IN HIS ROOM AN HOUR LATER...

IT'S OKAY TO KEEP MY CHIN UP, BUT I OWE MONEY TO A MIGHTY TOUGH MAN! SOONER OR LATER, HIS THUGS WILL GET ME AGAIN.. *ALONE!*

JOE IS RIGHT, FOR SAPPHIRE SLIM IS NOT A MAN WHO GIVES UP EASILY...

YOU WOULDN'T LIKE THE BANK OFFICIALS TO LEARN YOU'VE BEEN GAMBLING— WOULD YOU, JOE? YOU'D LOSE YOUR JOB, YOU KNOW!

YOU _GULP! MEAN YOU'D TELL THEM?

NO NEED FOR 'EM TO KNOW... IF YOU LISTEN TO REASON AND GET ME THAT SAFE COMBINATION, I MIGHT EVEN SEE THAT YOU GET A SLICE OF THE MELON!

ALL DAY LONG, JOE FITCH BROODS AND PONDERS, HIS HANDS TREMBLE WITH FRIGHT. THEN HIS LIPS TIGHTEN WITH DETERMINATION...

WHY SHOULDN'T I? I COULD GO AWAY SOME PLACE AND START LIFE ALL OVER WITH THE "SLICE" THAT SLIM'LL GIVE ME...

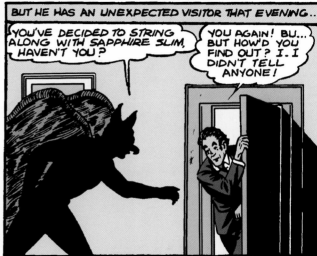

BUT HE HAS AN UNEXPECTED VISITOR THAT EVENING..

YOU'VE DECIDED TO STRING ALONG WITH SAPPHIRE SLIM, HAVEN'T YOU?

YOU AGAIN! BU... BUT HOW'D YOU FIND OUT? I..I DIDN'T TELL ANYONE!

I KNOW A LOT YOU DON'T SUSPECT I KNOW. THE TROUBLE WITH YOU IS YOU'RE WEAK, JOE. YOU AREN'T BAD BUT YOU ALWAYS TAKE THE EASY WAY OUT...

EASY WAY OUT, HUH! I SUPPOSE YOU'VE GOT A *BETTER* WAY!

I HAVE. NOW IF YOU'LL LET ME TELL IT TO YOU... PRETEND TO FALL IN WITH SPEARS...GIVE HIM THE COMBINATION. LEAVE THE DOOR UNLOCKED...

HUH? *THAT* ADVICE FROM YOU... BUT YOU SAID...

Collect Old Paper, Turn It In—Help Your Uncle Sam to Win

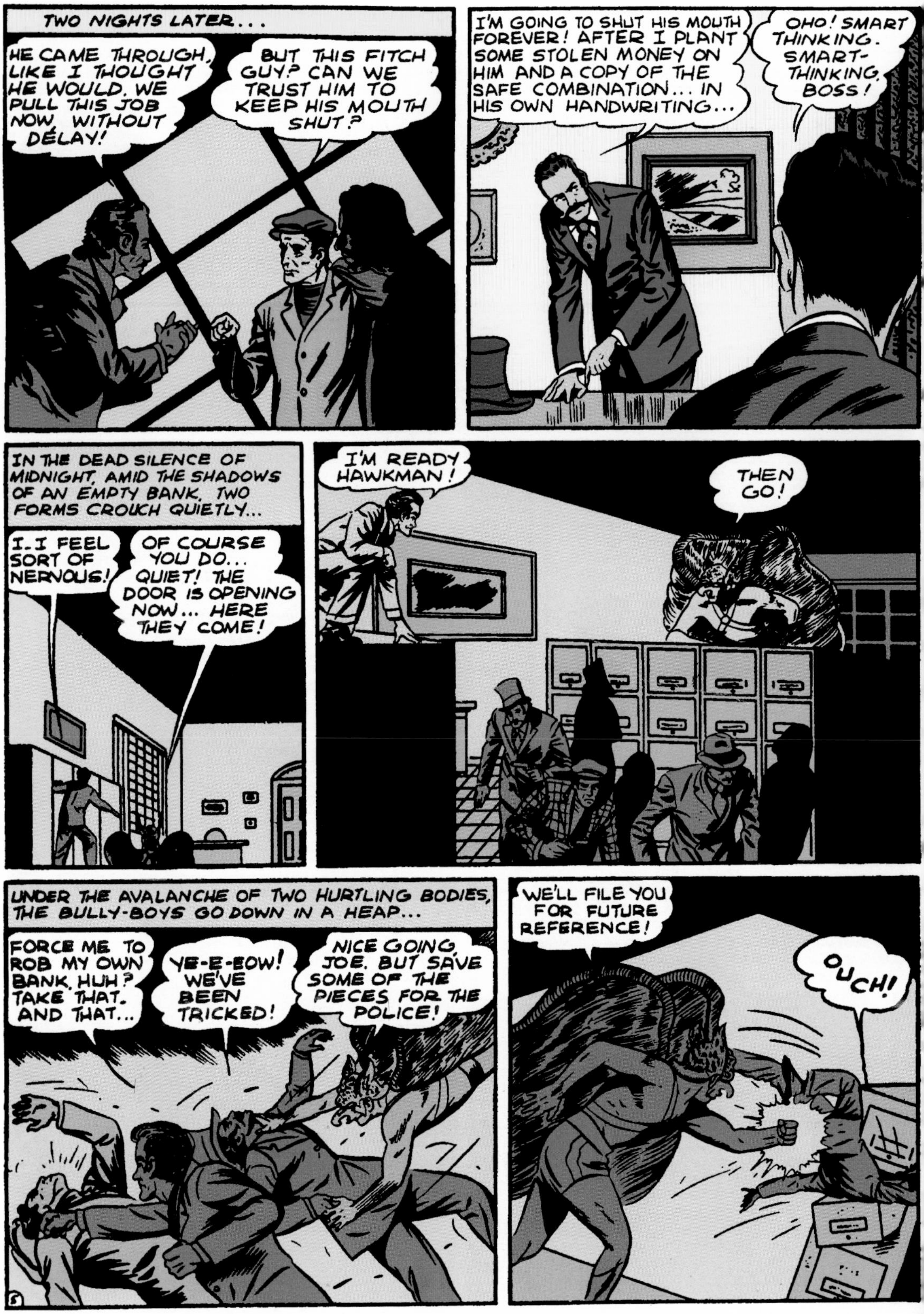
TWO NIGHTS LATER...
HE CAME THROUGH, LIKE I THOUGHT HE WOULD. WE PULL THIS JOB NOW, WITHOUT DELAY!
BUT THIS FITCH GUY? CAN WE TRUST HIM TO KEEP HIS MOUTH SHUT?
I'M GOING TO SHUT HIS MOUTH FOREVER! AFTER I PLANT SOME STOLEN MONEY ON HIM AND A COPY OF THE SAFE COMBINATION... IN HIS OWN HANDWRITING...
OHO! SMART THINKING. SMART-THINKING, BOSS!
IN THE DEAD SILENCE OF MIDNIGHT, AMID THE SHADOWS OF AN EMPTY BANK, TWO FORMS CROUCH QUIETLY...
I-I FEEL SORT OF NERVOUS!
OF COURSE YOU DO... QUIET! THE DOOR IS OPENING NOW... HERE THEY COME!
I'M READY HAWKMAN!
THEN GO!
UNDER THE AVALANCHE OF TWO HURTLING BODIES, THE BULLY-BOYS GO DOWN IN A HEAP...
FORCE ME TO ROB MY OWN BANK, HUH? TAKE THAT. AND THAT...
YE-E-EOW! WE'VE BEEN TRICKED!
NICE GOING, JOE. BUT SAVE SOME OF THE PIECES FOR THE POLICE!
WE'LL FILE YOU FOR FUTURE REFERENCE!
OUCH!

You Can Walk to School and Store! Saving Gas Helps Win the War!

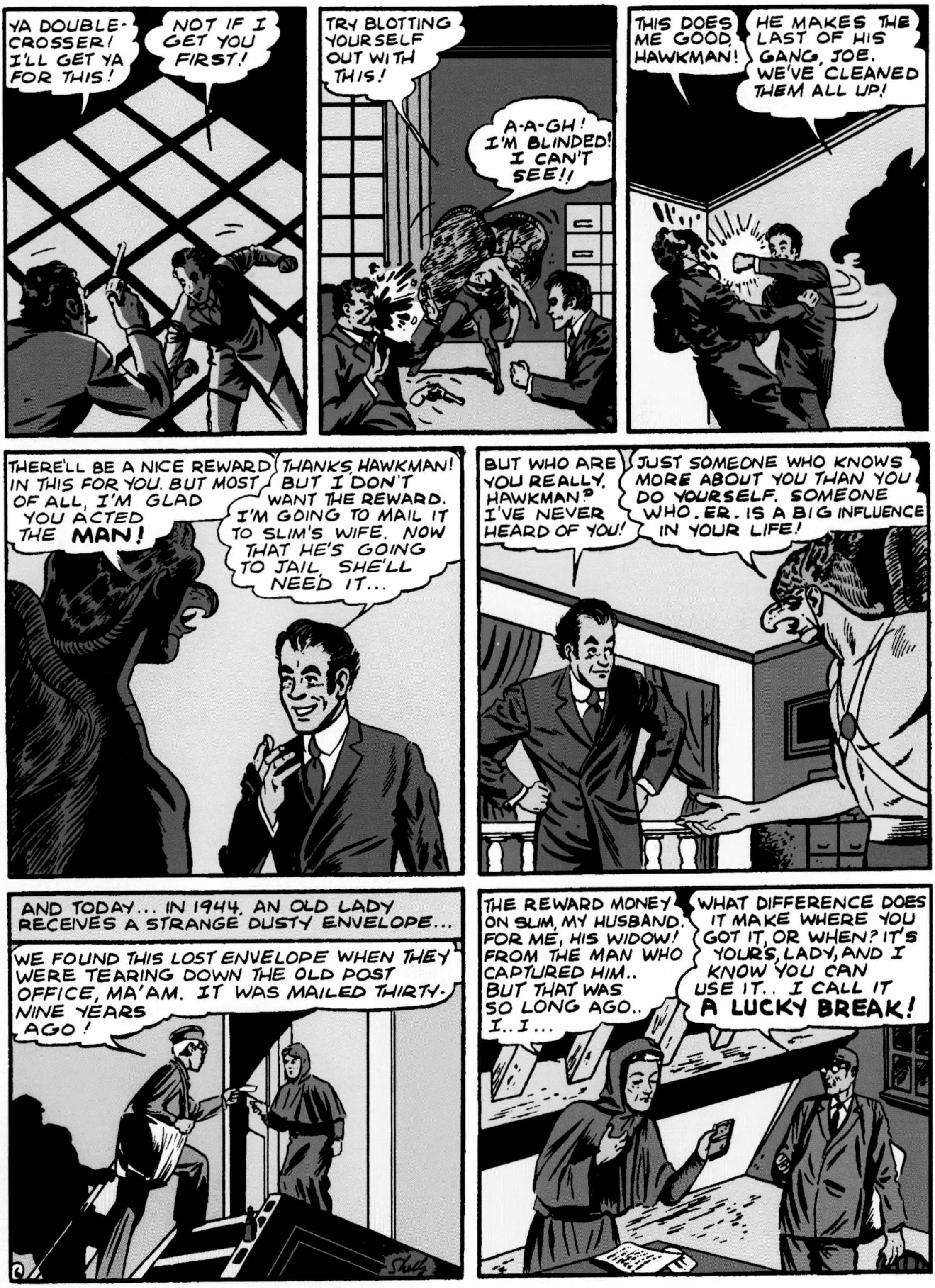

YA DOUBLE-CROSSER! I'LL GET YA FOR THIS!
NOT IF I GET YOU FIRST!
TRY BLOTTING YOURSELF OUT WITH THIS!
A-A-GH! I'M BLINDED! I CAN'T SEE!!
THIS DOES ME GOOD, HAWKMAN!
HE MAKES THE LAST OF HIS GANG, JOE. WE'VE CLEANED THEM ALL UP!
THERE'LL BE A NICE REWARD IN THIS FOR YOU. BUT MOST OF ALL, I'M GLAD YOU ACTED THE MAN!
THANKS, HAWKMAN! BUT I DON'T WANT THE REWARD. I'M GOING TO MAIL IT TO SLIM'S WIFE. NOW THAT HE'S GOING TO JAIL, SHE'LL NEED IT...
BUT WHO ARE YOU REALLY, HAWKMAN? I'VE NEVER HEARD OF YOU!
JUST SOMEONE WHO KNOWS MORE ABOUT YOU THAN YOU DO YOURSELF. SOMEONE WHO..ER.. IS A BIG INFLUENCE IN YOUR LIFE!
AND TODAY... IN 1944, AN OLD LADY RECEIVES A STRANGE DUSTY ENVELOPE...
WE FOUND THIS LOST ENVELOPE WHEN THEY WERE TEARING DOWN THE OLD POST OFFICE, MA'AM. IT WAS MAILED THIRTY-NINE YEARS AGO!
THE REWARD MONEY ON SLIM, MY HUSBAND, FOR ME, HIS WIDOW! FROM THE MAN WHO CAPTURED HIM.. BUT THAT WAS SO LONG AGO.. I.. I...
WHAT DIFFERENCE DOES IT MAKE WHERE YOU GOT IT, OR WHEN? IT'S YOURS, LADY, AND I KNOW YOU CAN USE IT.. I CALL IT A LUCKY BREAK!

HAWKMAN appears each month in Flash Comics-Don't miss it!

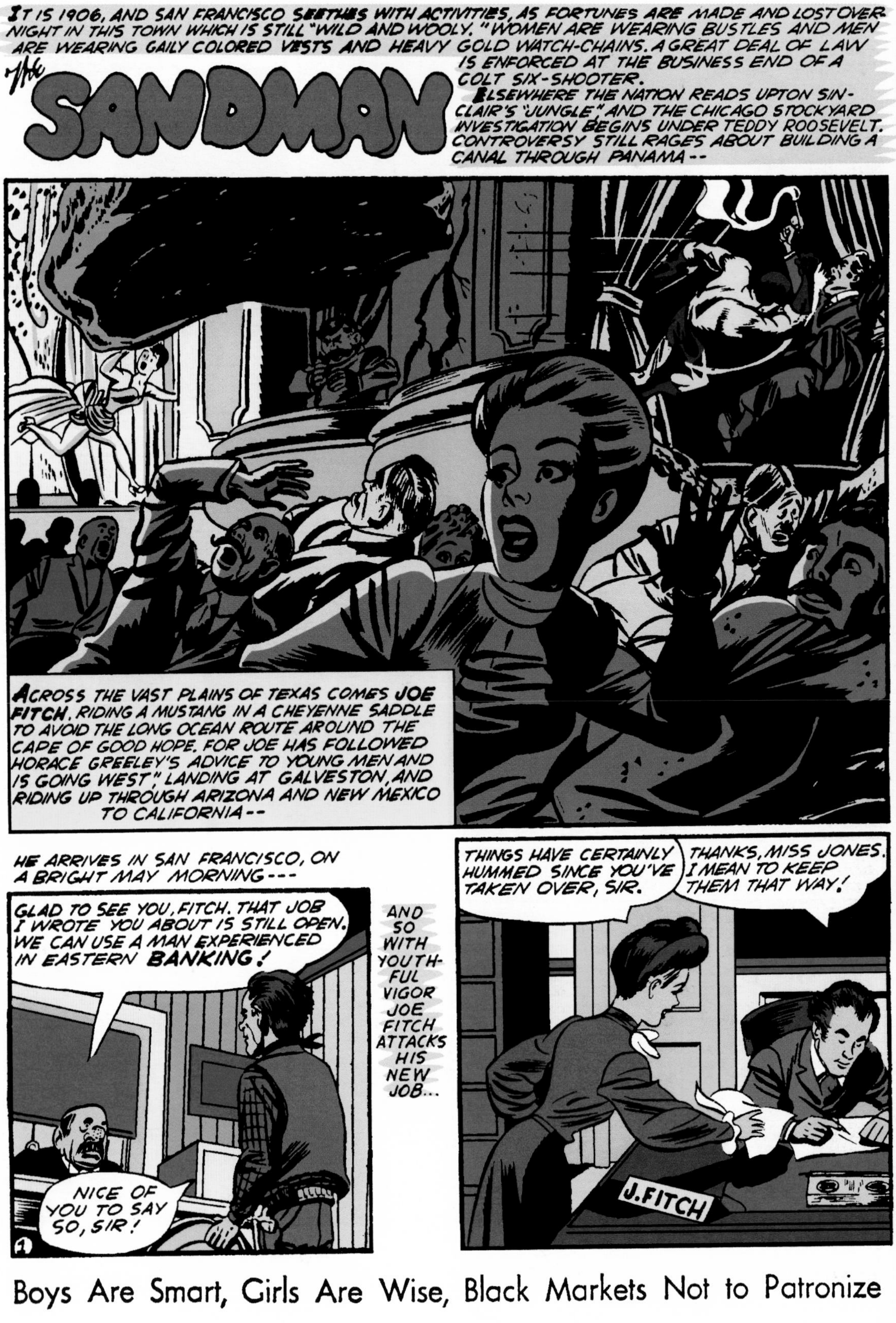
IT IS 1906, AND SAN FRANCISCO SEETHES WITH ACTIVITIES, AS FORTUNES ARE MADE AND LOST OVERNIGHT IN THIS TOWN WHICH IS STILL "WILD AND WOOLY." WOMEN ARE WEARING BUSTLES AND MEN ARE WEARING GAILY COLORED VESTS AND HEAVY GOLD WATCH-CHAINS. A GREAT DEAL OF LAW IS ENFORCED AT THE BUSINESS END OF A COLT SIX-SHOOTER.
The SANDMAN
ELSEWHERE THE NATION READS UPTON SINCLAIR'S "JUNGLE" AND THE CHICAGO STOCKYARD INVESTIGATION BEGINS UNDER TEDDY ROOSEVELT. CONTROVERSY STILL RAGES ABOUT BUILDING A CANAL THROUGH PANAMA--
ACROSS THE VAST PLAINS OF TEXAS COMES JOE FITCH, RIDING A MUSTANG IN A CHEYENNE SADDLE TO AVOID THE LONG OCEAN ROUTE AROUND THE CAPE OF GOOD HOPE. FOR JOE HAS FOLLOWED HORACE GREELEY'S ADVICE TO YOUNG MEN AND IS GOING WEST," LANDING AT GALVESTON, AND RIDING UP THROUGH ARIZONA AND NEW MEXICO TO CALIFORNIA--
HE ARRIVES IN SAN FRANCISCO, ON A BRIGHT MAY MORNING---
GLAD TO SEE YOU, FITCH. THAT JOB I WROTE YOU ABOUT IS STILL OPEN. WE CAN USE A MAN EXPERIENCED IN EASTERN BANKING!
NICE OF YOU TO SAY SO, SIR!
1
AND SO WITH YOUTHFUL VIGOR JOE FITCH ATTACKS HIS NEW JOB...
THINGS HAVE CERTAINLY HUMMED SINCE YOU'VE TAKEN OVER, SIR.
THANKS, MISS JONES. I MEAN TO KEEP THEM THAT WAY!
J. FITCH

Boys Are Smart, Girls Are Wise, Black Markets Not to Patronize

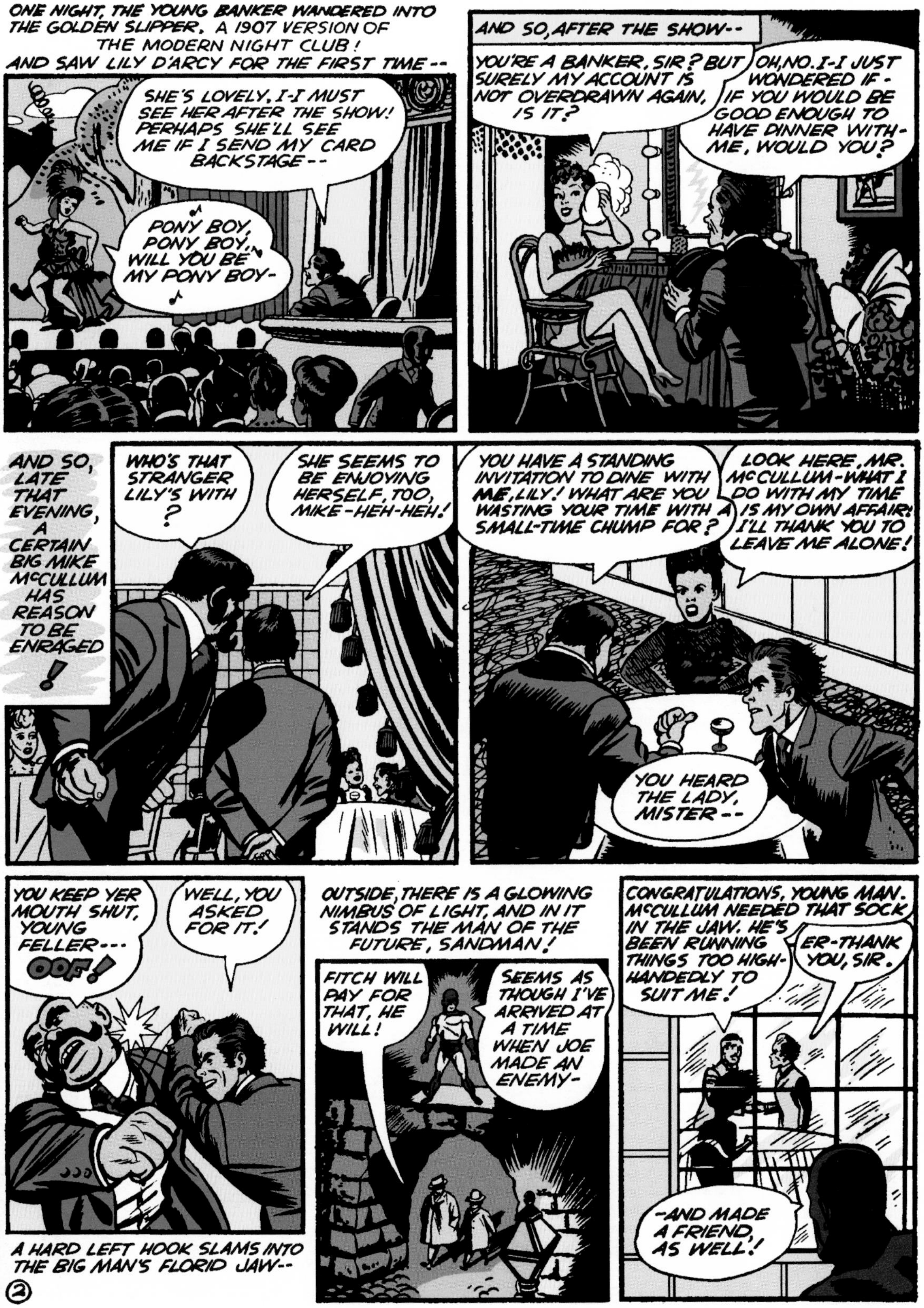

ONE NIGHT, THE YOUNG BANKER WANDERED INTO THE GOLDEN SLIPPER, A 1907 VERSION OF THE MODERN NIGHT CLUB! AND SAW LILY D'ARCY FOR THE FIRST TIME--
SHE'S LOVELY. I-I MUST SEE HER AFTER THE SHOW! PERHAPS SHE'LL SEE ME IF I SEND MY CARD BACKSTAGE--
PONY BOY, PONY BOY, WILL YOU BE MY PONY BOY-
AND SO, AFTER THE SHOW--
YOU'RE A BANKER, SIR? BUT SURELY MY ACCOUNT IS NOT OVERDRAWN AGAIN, IS IT?
OH, NO. I-I JUST WONDERED IF - IF YOU WOULD BE GOOD ENOUGH TO HAVE DINNER WITH ME, WOULD YOU?
AND SO, LATE THAT EVENING, A CERTAIN BIG MIKE McCULLUM HAS REASON TO BE ENRAGED!
WHO'S THAT STRANGER LILY'S WITH?
SHE SEEMS TO BE ENJOYING HERSELF, TOO, MIKE-HEH-HEH!
YOU HAVE A STANDING INVITATION TO DINE WITH ME, LILY! WHAT ARE YOU WASTING YOUR TIME WITH A SMALL-TIME CHUMP FOR?
LOOK HERE, MR. McCULLUM-WHAT I DO WITH MY TIME IS MY OWN AFFAIR! I'LL THANK YOU TO LEAVE ME ALONE!
YOU HEARD THE LADY, MISTER--
YOU KEEP YER MOUTH SHUT, YOUNG FELLER---
OOF!
WELL, YOU ASKED FOR IT!
A HARD LEFT HOOK SLAMS INTO THE BIG MAN'S FLORID JAW--
OUTSIDE, THERE IS A GLOWING NIMBUS OF LIGHT, AND IN IT STANDS THE MAN OF THE FUTURE, SANDMAN!
FITCH WILL PAY FOR THAT, HE WILL!
SEEMS AS THOUGH I'VE ARRIVED AT A TIME WHEN JOE MADE AN ENEMY-
CONGRATULATIONS, YOUNG MAN. McCULLUM NEEDED THAT SOCK IN THE JAW. HE'S BEEN RUNNING THINGS TOO HIGH-HANDEDLY TO SUIT ME!
ER-THANK YOU, SIR.
-AND MADE A FRIEND, AS WELL!
2

IF YOU STILL HAVE METAL SCRAP, TURN IT IN TO BEAT THE JAP

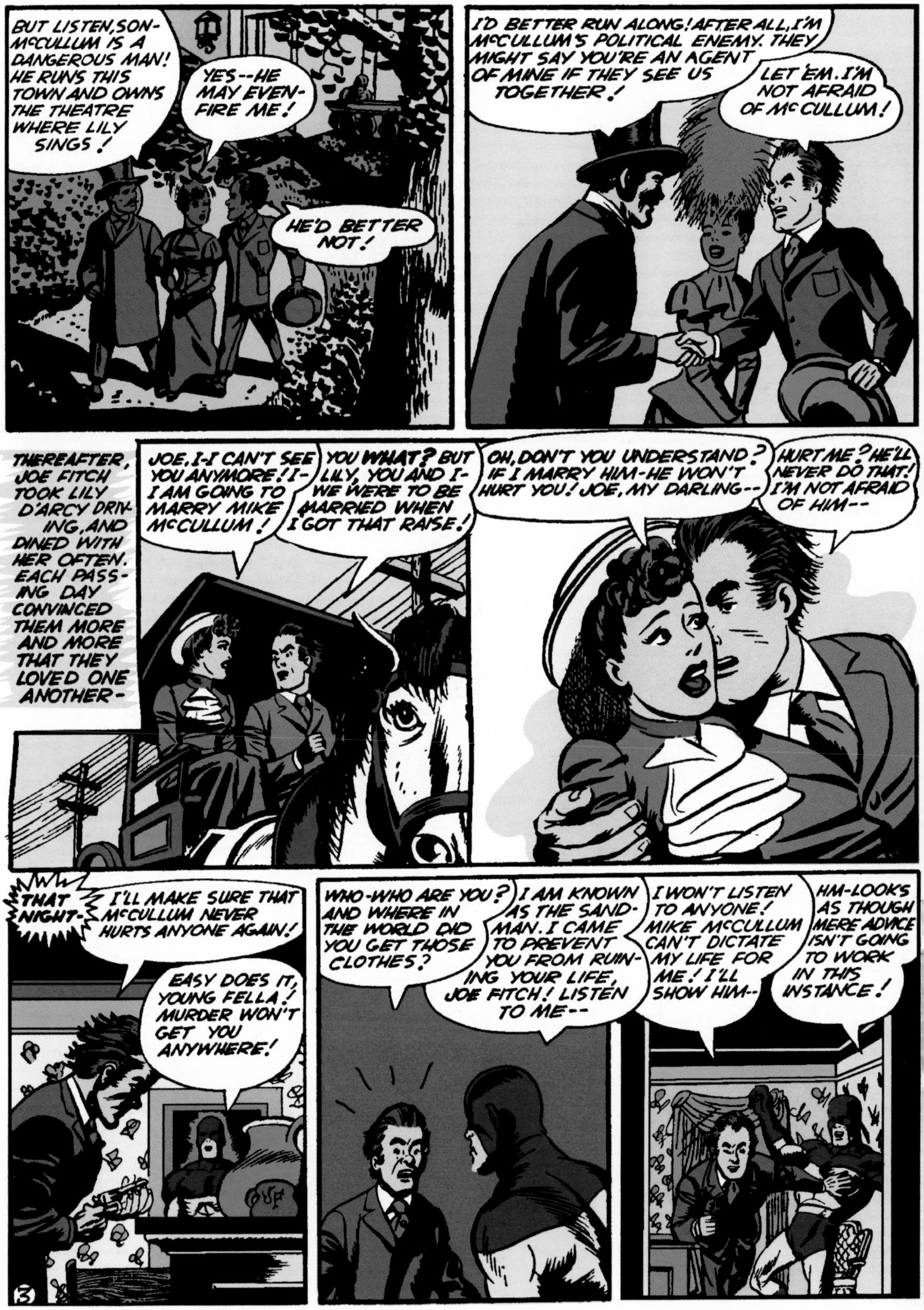
BUT LISTEN, SON- McCULLUM IS A DANGEROUS MAN! HE RUNS THIS TOWN AND OWNS THE THEATRE WHERE LILY SINGS!
YES--HE MAY EVEN FIRE ME!
HE'D BETTER NOT!
I'D BETTER RUN ALONG! AFTER ALL, I'M McCULLUM'S POLITICAL ENEMY. THEY MIGHT SAY YOU'RE AN AGENT OF MINE IF THEY SEE US TOGETHER!
LET 'EM. I'M NOT AFRAID OF McCULLUM!
THEREAFTER, JOE FITCH TOOK LILY D'ARCY DRIVING, AND DINED WITH HER OFTEN. EACH PASSING DAY CONVINCED THEM MORE AND MORE THAT THEY LOVED ONE ANOTHER-
JOE, I-I CAN'T SEE YOU ANYMORE! I-I AM GOING TO MARRY MIKE McCULLUM!
YOU WHAT? BUT LILY, YOU AND I- WE WERE TO BE MARRIED WHEN I GOT THAT RAISE!
OH, DON'T YOU UNDERSTAND? IF I MARRY HIM-HE WON'T HURT YOU! JOE, MY DARLING--
HURT ME? HE'LL NEVER DO THAT! I'M NOT AFRAID OF HIM--
THAT NIGHT-
I'LL MAKE SURE THAT McCULLUM NEVER HURTS ANYONE AGAIN!
EASY DOES IT, YOUNG FELLA! MURDER WON'T GET YOU ANYWHERE!
3
WHO-WHO ARE YOU? AND WHERE IN THE WORLD DID YOU GET THOSE CLOTHES?
I AM KNOWN AS THE SANDMAN. I CAME TO PREVENT YOU FROM RUINING YOUR LIFE, JOE FITCH! LISTEN TO ME--
I WON'T LISTEN TO ANYONE! MIKE McCULLUM CAN'T DICTATE MY LIFE FOR ME! I'LL SHOW HIM-
HM-LOOKS AS THOUGH MERE ADVICE ISN'T GOING TO WORK IN THIS INSTANCE!

Turn Out Lights Not in Use—War Production Needs the "Juice"

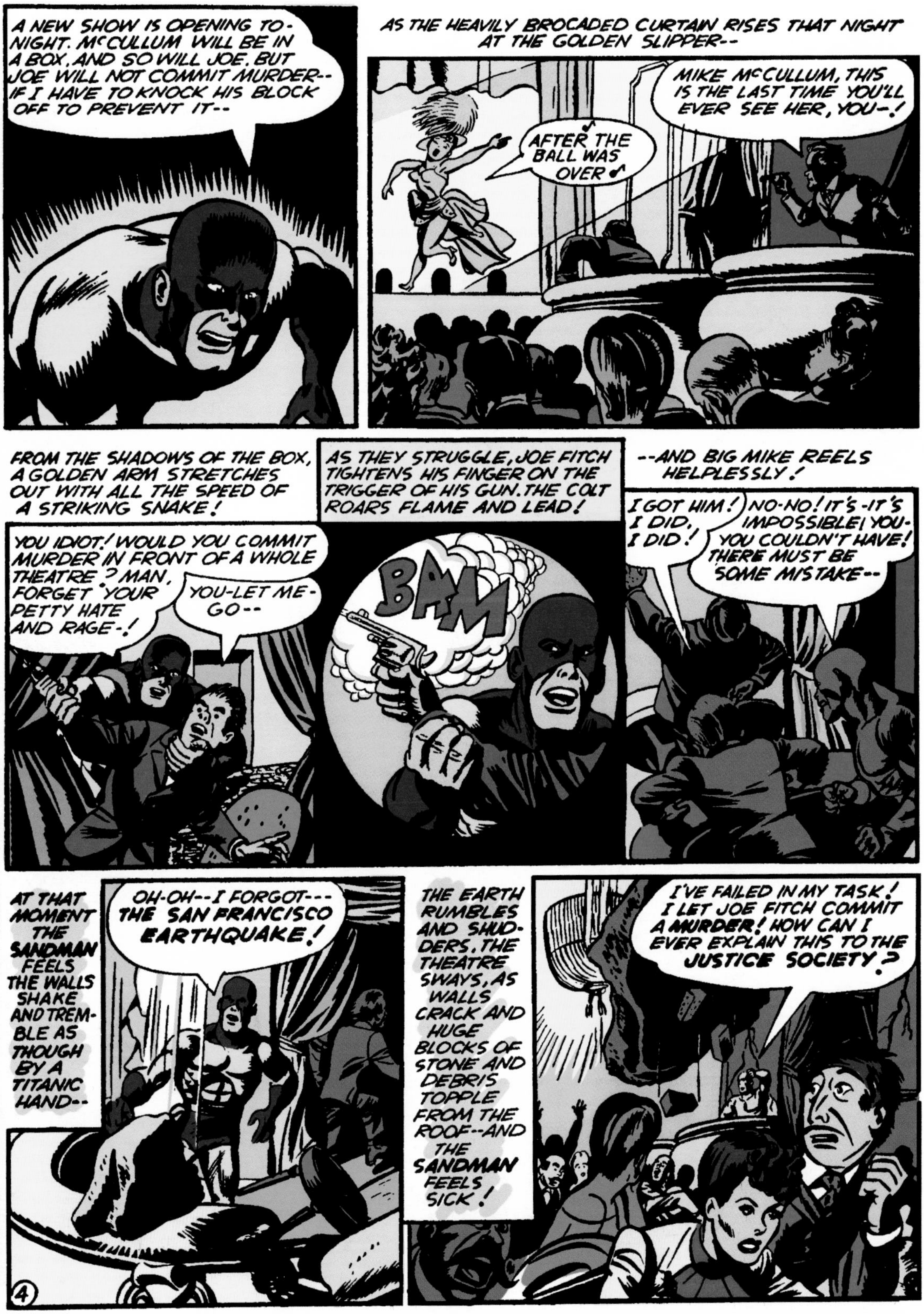
A NEW SHOW IS OPENING TO-NIGHT. McCULLUM WILL BE IN A BOX, AND SO WILL JOE. BUT JOE WILL NOT COMMIT MURDER--IF I HAVE TO KNOCK HIS BLOCK OFF TO PREVENT IT--
AS THE HEAVILY BROCADED CURTAIN RISES THAT NIGHT AT THE GOLDEN SLIPPER--
AFTER THE BALL WAS OVER
MIKE McCULLUM, THIS IS THE LAST TIME YOU'LL EVER SEE HER, YOU--!
FROM THE SHADOWS OF THE BOX, A GOLDEN ARM STRETCHES OUT WITH ALL THE SPEED OF A STRIKING SNAKE!
YOU IDIOT! WOULD YOU COMMIT MURDER IN FRONT OF A WHOLE THEATRE? MAN, FORGET YOUR PETTY HATE AND RAGE-!
YOU-LET ME-GO--
AS THEY STRUGGLE, JOE FITCH TIGHTENS HIS FINGER ON THE TRIGGER OF HIS GUN. THE COLT ROARS FLAME AND LEAD!
BAM
--AND BIG MIKE REELS HELPLESSLY!
I GOT HIM! I DID, I DID!
NO-NO! IT'S-IT'S IMPOSSIBLE! YOU-YOU COULDN'T HAVE! THERE MUST BE SOME MISTAKE--
AT THAT MOMENT THE SANDMAN FEELS THE WALLS SHAKE AND TREMBLE AS THOUGH BY A TITANIC HAND--
OH-OH--I FORGOT--- THE SAN FRANCISCO EARTHQUAKE!
4
THE EARTH RUMBLES AND SHUDDERS. THE THEATRE SWAYS, AS WALLS CRACK AND HUGE BLOCKS OF STONE AND DEBRIS TOPPLE FROM THE ROOF--AND THE SANDMAN FEELS SICK!
I'VE FAILED IN MY TASK! I LET JOE FITCH COMMIT A MURDER! HOW CAN I EVER EXPLAIN THIS TO THE JUSTICE SOCIETY?

Tin Cans in the Garbage Pile Are Just a Way of Saying "Heil!"

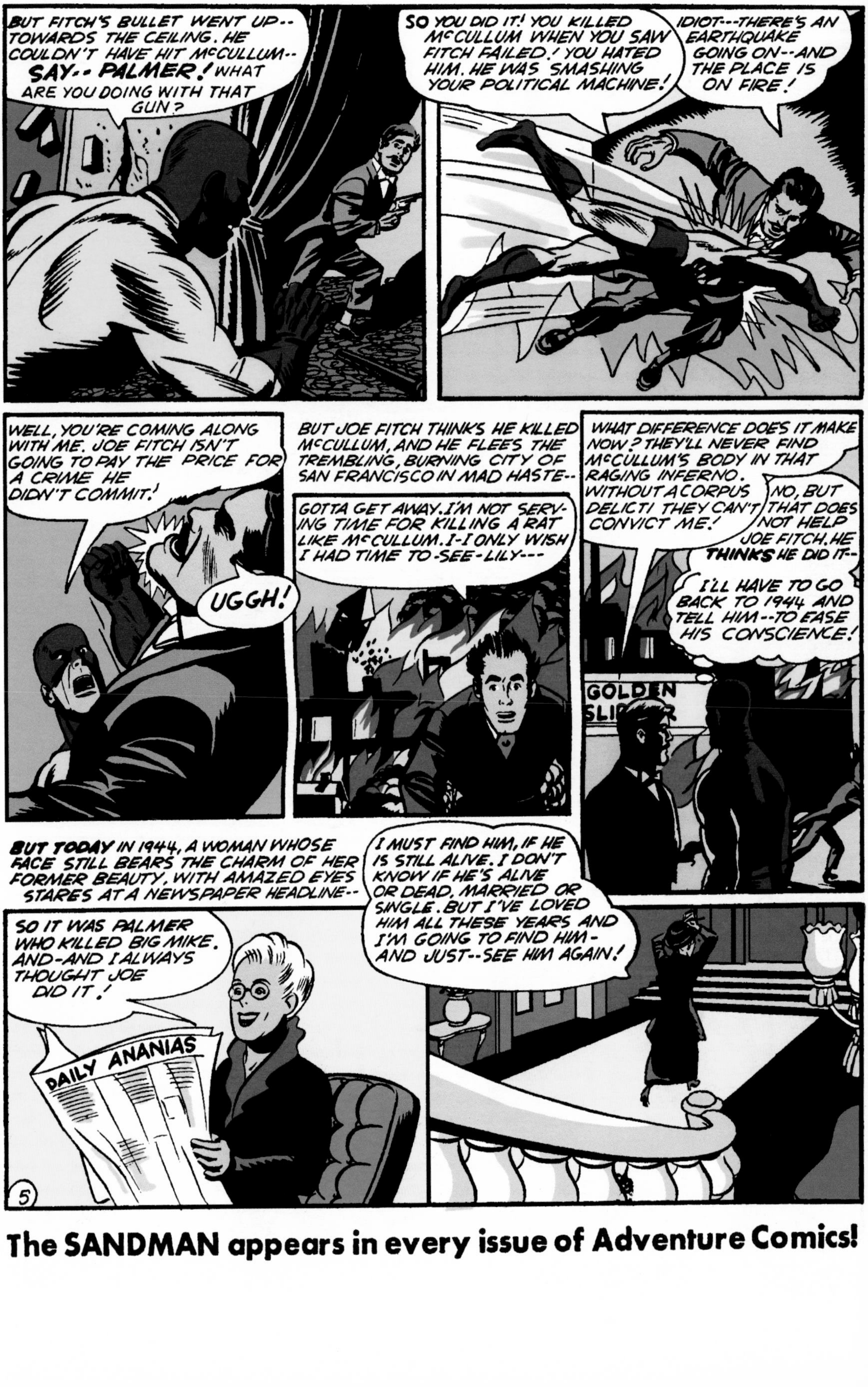

BUT FITCH'S BULLET WENT UP-- TOWARDS THE CEILING. HE COULDN'T HAVE HIT McCULLUM-- SAY-- PALMER! WHAT ARE YOU DOING WITH THAT GUN?
SO YOU DID IT! YOU KILLED McCULLUM WHEN YOU SAW FITCH FAILED! YOU HATED HIM. HE WAS SMASHING YOUR POLITICAL MACHINE!
IDIOT---THERE'S AN EARTHQUAKE GOING ON--AND THE PLACE IS ON FIRE!
WELL, YOU'RE COMING ALONG WITH ME. JOE FITCH ISN'T GOING TO PAY THE PRICE FOR A CRIME HE DIDN'T COMMIT!
UGGH!
BUT JOE FITCH THINKS HE KILLED McCULLUM, AND HE FLEES THE TREMBLING, BURNING CITY OF SAN FRANCISCO IN MAD HASTE--
GOTTA GET AWAY. I'M NOT SERVING TIME FOR KILLING A RAT LIKE McCULLUM. I-I ONLY WISH I HAD TIME TO-SEE-LILY---
WHAT DIFFERENCE DOES IT MAKE NOW? THEY'LL NEVER FIND McCULLUM'S BODY IN THAT RAGING INFERNO. WITHOUT A CORPUS DELICTI THEY CAN'T CONVICT ME!
NO, BUT THAT DOES NOT HELP JOE FITCH. HE THINKS HE DID IT--
I'LL HAVE TO GO BACK TO 1944 AND TELL HIM--TO EASE HIS CONSCIENCE!
GOLDEN SLIP
BUT TODAY IN 1944, A WOMAN WHOSE FACE STILL BEARS THE CHARM OF HER FORMER BEAUTY, WITH AMAZED EYES STARES AT A NEWSPAPER HEADLINE--
SO IT WAS PALMER WHO KILLED BIG MIKE. AND-AND I ALWAYS THOUGHT JOE DID IT!
DAILY ANANIAS
I MUST FIND HIM, IF HE IS STILL ALIVE. I DON'T KNOW IF HE'S ALIVE OR DEAD, MARRIED OR SINGLE. BUT I'VE LOVED HIM ALL THESE YEARS AND I'M GOING TO FIND HIM-AND JUST--SEE HIM AGAIN!
5

STARMAN

IT IS 1914—THE ENTIRE WORLD IS ABOUT TO PLUNGE INTO THE FIERY HOLOCAUST OF THE FIRST WORLD WAR....IN MEXICO, WARRING FACTIONS UNDER VILLA AND HUERTA WERE CAUSING TROUBLE WITH THE UNITED STATES....CONSTANT RAIDS OVER THE BORDER INTO TEXAS BY MEXICAN BANDITS WERE RAPIDLY ASSUMING AN INTERNATIONAL CHARACTER-- AMONG THOSE HARD-BITTEN VILLISTAS RODE ADVENTURER JOE FITCH.......

JOSEPH FITCH FLED FROM THE BURNING CITY OF SAN FRANCISCO TO MEXICO WHERE IN TIME HE PROVED HIS WORTH TO THE LAWLESS BANDITS..... AN EXPERT SHOT, CARELESS OF CONSEQUENCE, HE BECAME A VALUED ASSIST- ANT TO VILLA..

1

THEES MAN SMEETH, WHO OWNS THEE HORSESHOE SALOON IN RED GULCH MUST BE DISPOSED OF, SEÑOR-THEES EES A JOB FOR YOU! CAN DO?

SURE- I GUESS SO- I UNDERSTAND SMITH'S BEEN RUNNIN' A SPY RING FOR CARRANZA-

SMEETH EES PAID TO LEARN FROM OUR MEN WHAT OUR MOVE- MENTS ARE-SOME OF OUR MEN HE HAS EVEN KEELED! HE MUST PAY-HEEM AND HEES SALOON!

DYNAMITE, EH? OKAY, WHEN DO I LEAVE?

Waste Fats in Good Condition Help to Make Fine Ammunition

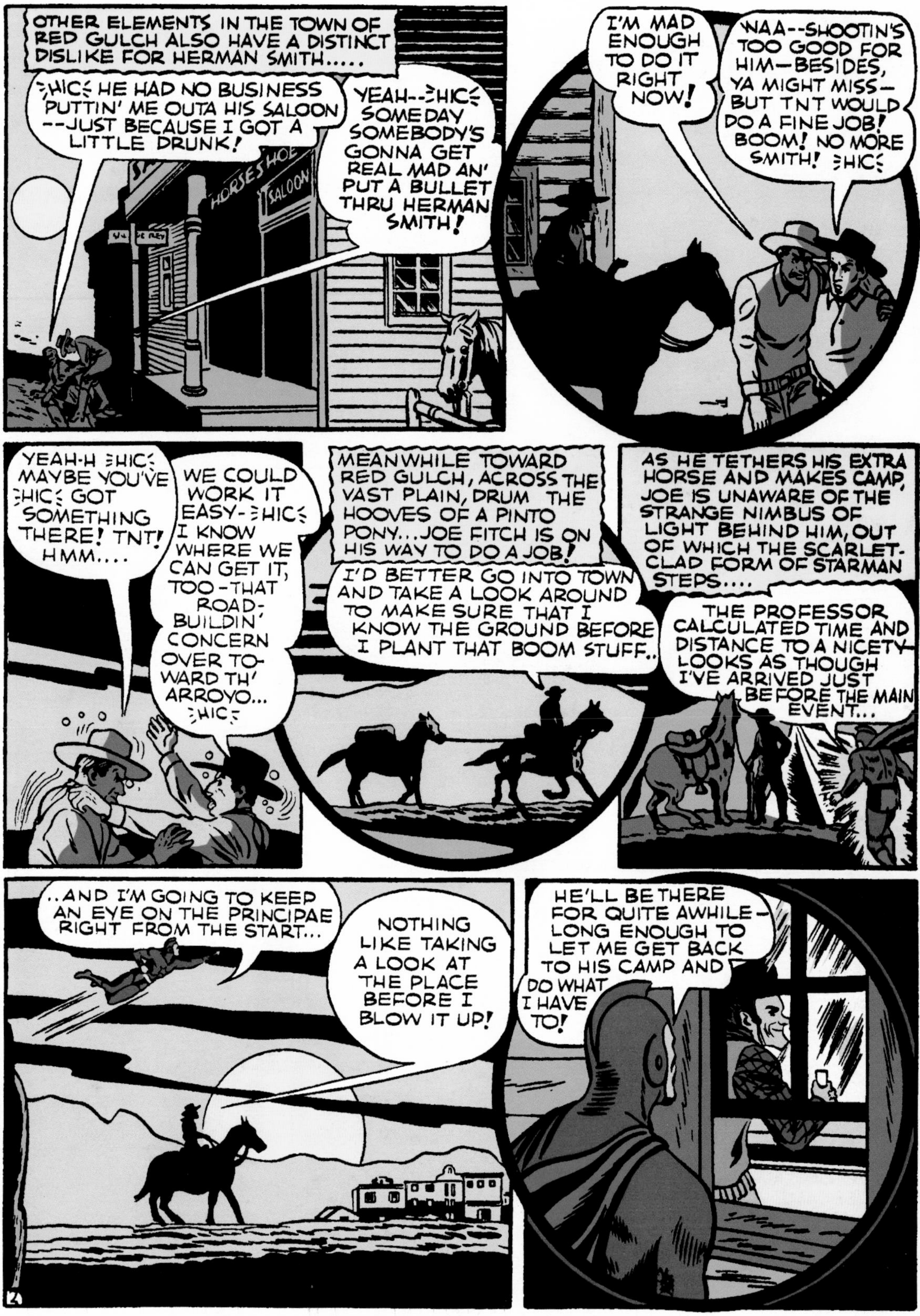
OTHER ELEMENTS IN THE TOWN OF RED GULCH ALSO HAVE A DISTINCT DISLIKE FOR HERMAN SMITH.....
HIC HE HAD NO BUSINESS PUTTIN' ME OUTA HIS SALOON --JUST BECAUSE I GOT A LITTLE DRUNK!
YEAH-- HIC SOMEDAY SOMEBODY'S GONNA GET REAL MAD AN' PUT A BULLET THRU HERMAN SMITH!
HORSESHOE
SALOON
I'M MAD ENOUGH TO DO IT RIGHT NOW!
WAA--SHOOTIN'S TOO GOOD FOR HIM—BESIDES, YA MIGHT MISS—BUT TNT WOULD DO A FINE JOB! BOOM! NO MORE SMITH! HIC
YEAH-H HIC MAYBE YOU'VE HIC GOT SOMETHING THERE! TNT! HMM....
WE COULD WORK IT EASY- HIC I KNOW WHERE WE CAN GET IT, TOO-THAT ROAD-BUILDIN' CONCERN OVER TO-WARD TH' ARROYO... HIC
MEANWHILE TOWARD RED GULCH, ACROSS THE VAST PLAIN, DRUM THE HOOVES OF A PINTO PONY...JOE FITCH IS ON HIS WAY TO DO A JOB!
I'D BETTER GO INTO TOWN AND TAKE A LOOK AROUND TO MAKE SURE THAT I KNOW THE GROUND BEFORE I PLANT THAT BOOM STUFF..
AS HE TETHERS HIS EXTRA HORSE AND MAKES CAMP, JOE IS UNAWARE OF THE STRANGE NIMBUS OF LIGHT BEHIND HIM, OUT OF WHICH THE SCARLET-CLAD FORM OF STARMAN STEPS....
THE PROFESSOR CALCULATED TIME AND DISTANCE TO A NICETY—LOOKS AS THOUGH I'VE ARRIVED JUST BEFORE THE MAIN EVENT...
..AND I'M GOING TO KEEP AN EYE ON THE PRINCIPAE RIGHT FROM THE START...
NOTHING LIKE TAKING A LOOK AT THE PLACE BEFORE I BLOW IT UP!
HE'LL BE THERE FOR QUITE AWHILE—LONG ENOUGH TO LET ME GET BACK TO HIS CAMP AND DO WHAT I HAVE TO!

Boys and Girls, Every Day, Can Give War Aid in Many a Way—

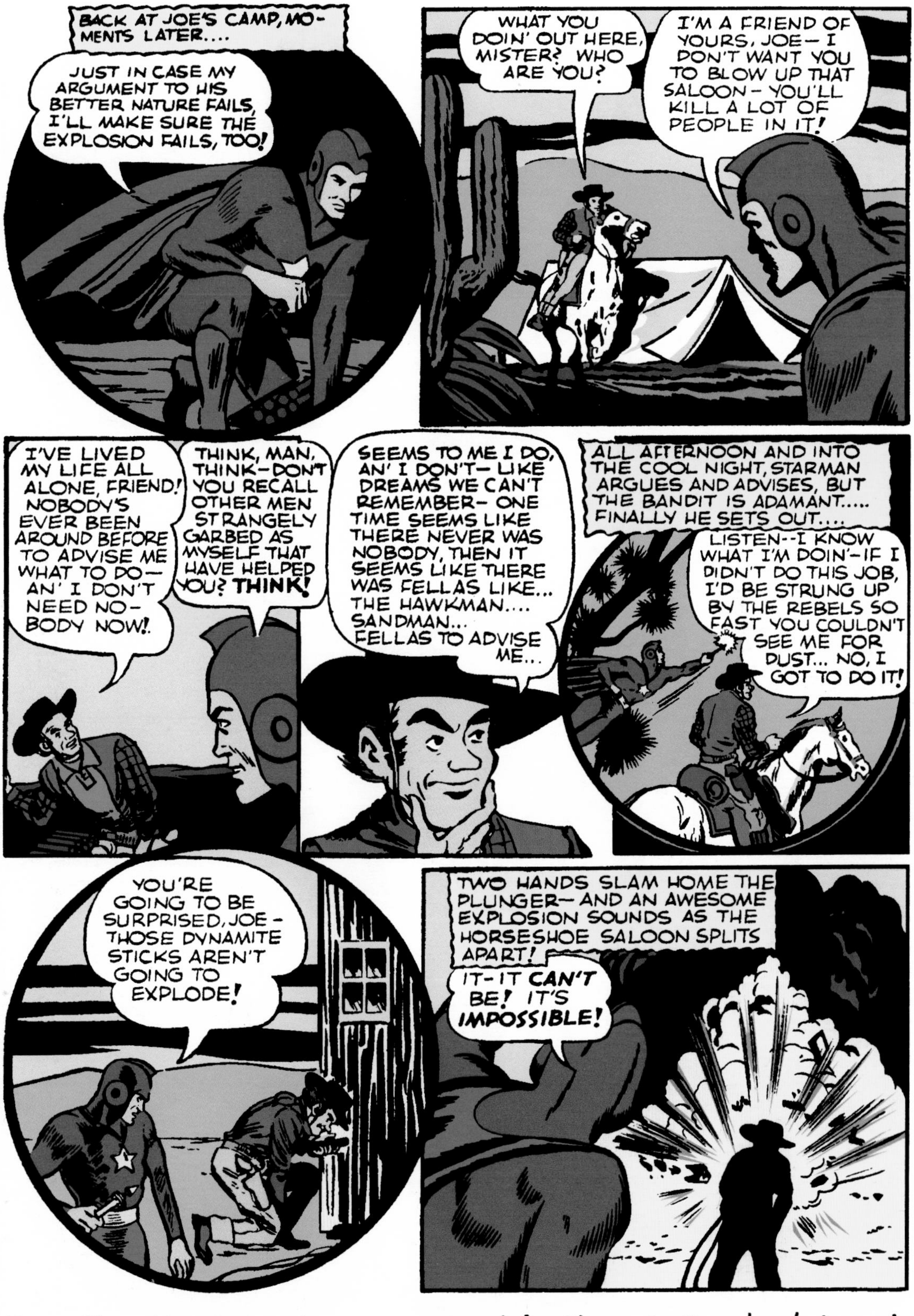
BACK AT JOE'S CAMP, MOMENTS LATER....
JUST IN CASE MY ARGUMENT TO HIS BETTER NATURE FAILS, I'LL MAKE SURE THE EXPLOSION FAILS, TOO!
WHAT YOU DOIN' OUT HERE, MISTER? WHO ARE YOU?
I'M A FRIEND OF YOURS, JOE— I DON'T WANT YOU TO BLOW UP THAT SALOON - YOU'LL KILL A LOT OF PEOPLE IN IT!
I'VE LIVED MY LIFE ALL ALONE, FRIEND! NOBODY'S EVER BEEN AROUND BEFORE TO ADVISE ME WHAT TO DO— AN' I DON'T NEED NOBODY NOW!
THINK, MAN, THINK—DON'T YOU RECALL OTHER MEN STRANGELY GARBED AS MYSELF THAT HAVE HELPED YOU? THINK!
SEEMS TO ME I DO, AN' I DON'T— LIKE DREAMS WE CAN'T REMEMBER— ONE TIME SEEMS LIKE THERE NEVER WAS NOBODY, THEN IT SEEMS LIKE THERE WAS FELLAS LIKE... THE HAWKMAN.... SANDMAN... FELLAS TO ADVISE ME...
ALL AFTERNOON AND INTO THE COOL NIGHT, STARMAN ARGUES AND ADVISES, BUT THE BANDIT IS ADAMANT..... FINALLY HE SETS OUT....
LISTEN--I KNOW WHAT I'M DOIN'-IF I DIDN'T DO THIS JOB, I'D BE STRUNG UP BY THE REBELS SO FAST YOU COULDN'T SEE ME FOR DUST... NO, I GOT TO DO IT!
YOU'RE GOING TO BE SURPRISED, JOE - THOSE DYNAMITE STICKS AREN'T GOING TO EXPLODE!
TWO HANDS SLAM HOME THE PLUNGER— AND AN AWESOME EXPLOSION SOUNDS AS THE HORSESHOE SALOON SPLITS APART!
IT-IT CAN'T BE! IT'S IMPOSSIBLE!

Every Time You Buy a Stamp, You Feed the Flame in Freedom's Lamp!

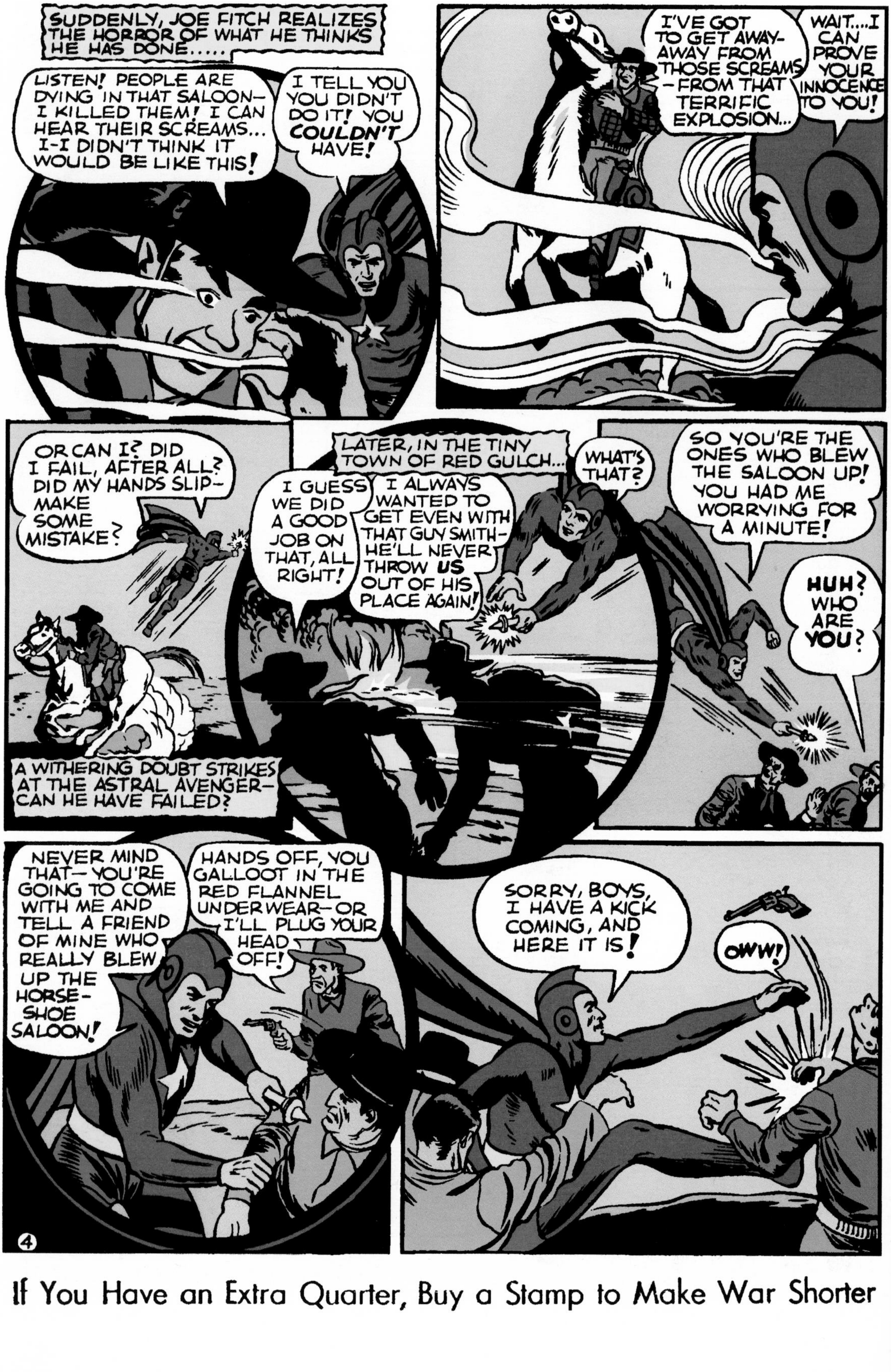
SUDDENLY, JOE FITCH REALIZES THE HORROR OF WHAT HE THINKS HE HAS DONE.....
LISTEN! PEOPLE ARE DYING IN THAT SALOON— I KILLED THEM! I CAN HEAR THEIR SCREAMS... I-I DIDN'T THINK IT WOULD BE LIKE THIS!
I TELL YOU YOU DIDN'T DO IT! YOU COULDN'T HAVE!
I'VE GOT TO GET AWAY— AWAY FROM THOSE SCREAMS —FROM THAT TERRIFIC EXPLOSION...
WAIT....I CAN PROVE YOUR INNOCENCE TO YOU!
OR CAN I? DID I FAIL, AFTER ALL? DID MY HANDS SLIP— MAKE SOME MISTAKE?
A WITHERING DOUBT STRIKES AT THE ASTRAL AVENGER— CAN HE HAVE FAILED?
LATER, IN THE TINY TOWN OF RED GULCH...
I GUESS WE DID A GOOD JOB ON THAT, ALL RIGHT!
I ALWAYS WANTED TO GET EVEN WITH THAT GUY SMITH— HE'LL NEVER THROW US OUT OF HIS PLACE AGAIN!
WHAT'S THAT?
SO YOU'RE THE ONES WHO BLEW THE SALOON UP! YOU HAD ME WORRYING FOR A MINUTE!
HUH? WHO ARE YOU?
NEVER MIND THAT— YOU'RE GOING TO COME WITH ME AND TELL A FRIEND OF MINE WHO REALLY BLEW UP THE HORSE-SHOE SALOON!
HANDS OFF, YOU GALLOOT IN THE RED FLANNEL UNDERWEAR— OR I'LL PLUG YOUR HEAD OFF!
SORRY, BOYS, I HAVE A KICK COMING, AND HERE IT IS!
OWW!
4

If You Have an Extra Quarter, Buy a Stamp to Make War Shorter

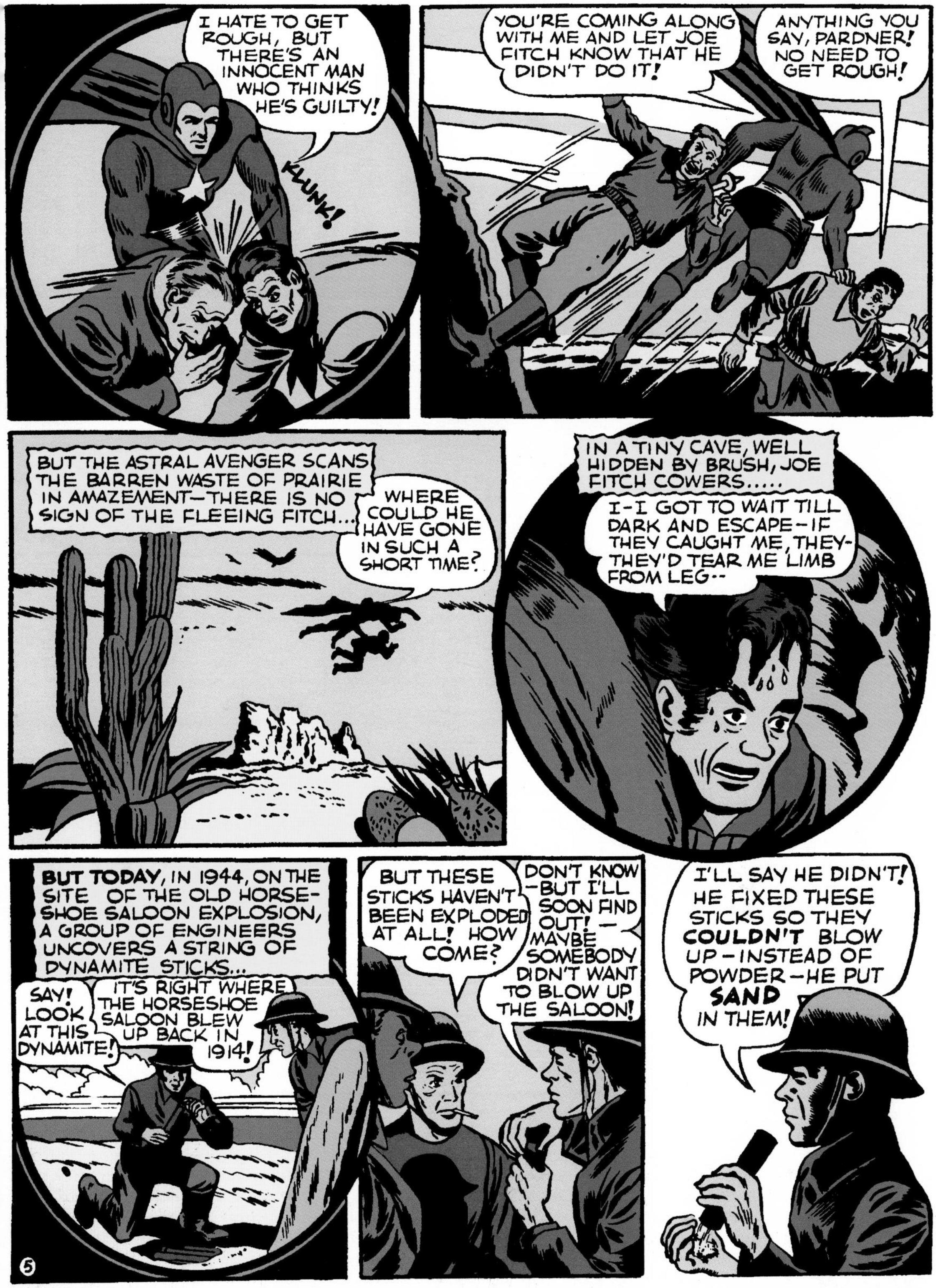
I HATE TO GET ROUGH, BUT THERE'S AN INNOCENT MAN WHO THINKS HE'S GUILTY!
KLUNK!
YOU'RE COMING ALONG WITH ME AND LET JOE FITCH KNOW THAT HE DIDN'T DO IT!
ANYTHING YOU SAY, PARDNER! NO NEED TO GET ROUGH!
BUT THE ASTRAL AVENGER SCANS THE BARREN WASTE OF PRAIRIE IN AMAZEMENT—THERE IS NO SIGN OF THE FLEEING FITCH...
WHERE COULD HE HAVE GONE IN SUCH A SHORT TIME?
IN A TINY CAVE, WELL HIDDEN BY BRUSH, JOE FITCH COWERS.....
I-I GOT TO WAIT TILL DARK AND ESCAPE—IF THEY CAUGHT ME, THEY-THEY'D TEAR ME LIMB FROM LEG--
BUT TODAY, IN 1944, ON THE SITE OF THE OLD HORSE-SHOE SALOON EXPLOSION, A GROUP OF ENGINEERS UNCOVERS A STRING OF DYNAMITE STICKS...
SAY! LOOK AT THIS DYNAMITE!
IT'S RIGHT WHERE THE HORSESHOE SALOON BLEW UP BACK IN 1914!
5
BUT THESE STICKS HAVEN'T BEEN EXPLODED AT ALL! HOW COME?
DON'T KNOW—BUT I'LL SOON FIND OUT!—MAYBE SOMEBODY DIDN'T WANT TO BLOW UP THE SALOON!
I'LL SAY HE DIDN'T! HE FIXED THESE STICKS SO THEY COULDN'T BLOW UP—INSTEAD OF POWDER—HE PUT SAND IN THEM!

The STARMAN appears in every issue of Adventure Comics!

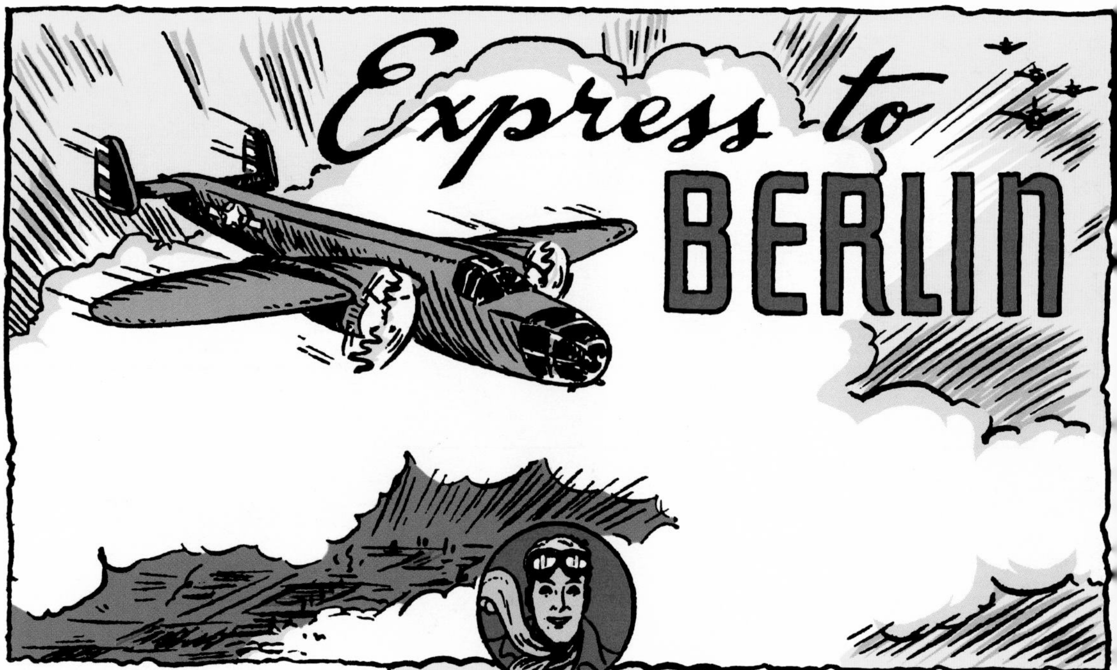
Express to
BERLIN

AS the B-25 roared into the wind over an English airdrome, a sigh escaped the pilot, Lieutenant Hop Harrigan of the AAF. Here he was, flying a ship built to haul over two tons of bombs—with her bomb bays *empty!*

"Not even a little hundred-pounder lashed to the wing!" grumbled Tank Tinker, Harrigan's redheaded flying mate, who was acting as co-pilot on this trip. "It'll just break my heart to pass over Lorient and not drop any calling cards!"

"Me, too," Hop nodded. "You know that old saying, 'Brighten the corner where you are'! Well, I'd sure love to brighten Berlin—with a couple of hundred fires!" A resigned look swept Harrigan's face. "But our job is to ferry this plane to Tunis in one piece!" he added. "They need all the bombers they can get—to mess up The Muss! So we might as well get set for a nice, quiet trip!"

"Say, Hop," Tank Tinker said, drowsily, between yawns, "wake me up when you get tired of steering this crate. Gonna get me some—shuteye—" Tinker's head flopped onto his chest. In a few minutes, his loud snores rivaled the rhythmic throb of the twin Wright Cyclones!

JON L. BLUMMER'S HOP HARRIGAN STORIES APPEAR IN EVERY ISSUE OF ALL-AMERICAN COMICS

Hop, at the controls, was left to meditate about the sealed glass tube, carefully crated, on the floor of the cockpit. During their furlough in London, the two airmen had not been idle. They had spent days in the laboratory of Arthur Stacey, a scientist friend—working out the potent gas contained in that tube.

Poison gas atrocities of the Japs against the Chinese had steeled Hop and Tank to the need of being prepared, so the two airmen had developed a powerful gas, efficient and painless. Ferrying the Mitchell to Tunis afforded a good chance to take a sample of it to Colonel Leigh, stationed there, who, the airmen knew, was an authority on poison gases.

The mid-wing ship was cruising along at 250 mph. The altimeter showed ten thousand. They had left The Ditch—the English Channel — far behind and were slicing through air over France. Hop had just shot out of a cloud bank when a flight of planes loomed into view about half a mile away and a little above them.

Hop squinted through goggles and made out the short, square wing-tips and deep nose of the swift Messerschmitt 109E! There were six of them, flying in a shallow V.

Hop gave a low whistle. Roughly, he shook Tank awake. The big redhead had sighted the Me's and was instantly alert, ready for trouble.

"Hang onto your hat!" breathed Hop. "Here's where we try to outclimb those babies!"

"Flap your wings, brother!" Tank murmured, watching the Nazi planes sweep closer. "Get us out of this, and I'll pin a medal on you!"

Hop shoved the throttles full on, and stood the mid-wing ship on her tail. The B-25 screamed upstairs, prop-clawing for altitude.

The six Me's came on, and for a minute Hop thought they would continue on their way without bothering to scrap with one Yank bomber. But Hop was wrong. One of the Me's tore away from its brothers, zoomed up under the Mitchell and angled for an underside attack. Hop streaked the plane along at top speed, and the Messerschmitt raced after, trying to get the Yank in his sights.

"Funny how tail-end Charlie left the rest of the flight to come up after us!" Tank said, frowning. "The others went right ahead as if they didn't even notice us!"

Hop got a glimpse of two more Nazis speeding toward them.

"Well, they're making up for it, now!" Hop breathed. "Here come two more of those swastika-sons!"

Hop rocked back on the stick, and the plane went into a sudden, sickening climb. He heard the rat-a-tat-tat of tracers on his tail. The Nazi was stubborn. He kept following right up. Then machine-gun chatter from two other Jerries joined the mad medley of sound. Red and green tracers whizzed through the air. The cr-rack of dural bounced against Hop's brain, and a shredded ship was plunging off at a crazy angle. It was a Messerschmitt.

Hop blinked his eyes. What had happened? Who had hit the Messerschmitt? He hadn't! He peered overside. The other two Nazis were scooting back to their flight! They rejoined formation, and the five Me's continued on their way, as cool as if they hadn't just shot down one of *their own planes!*

"What's it mean?" Tank demanded. "Since when do those goose-steppers shoot each other down for attacking American planes!"

"Ask me something easy!" Hop countered. "Like how long it would take me to swim the Mediterranean!"

"Perhaps," offered a soft voice behind them, "I can offer an explanation!"

Steel muzzles jabbed against their spines before either of the airmen could make a move. "The plane that attacked us was acting against orders. Probably its radio was out of commission and the flight leader couldn't inform the pilot not to attack. That's why he had to order the others to shoot him down!"

A shudder ran through Hop as he recognized that voice.

"Chambers, y o u rat!" he muttered. "How did you get on this ship?"

"I hid out in the bomb bays," the spy went on. "It was easy. No one suspected *me*—the mechanic assigned to check this plane. I'll admit it's not the most comfortable way to ride to Berlin—but one can't be too choosy!"

"B e r l i n!" exploded Hop. "Over our dead bodies!"

"I think not, my friend!" said Chambers, prodding the gun-muzzles closer. "You will do as I say! Der Fuehrer expects us. Just land where I direct you."

The spy's cool insolence made Hop tremble in anger. Yet he was trapped, and he knew it. Chambers wouldn't hesitate to shoot them both, if he had to. Hop wasn't s u r e Chambers could fly, but he knew enough to attempt a landing. Even if Hop and Tank gave up their lives rather than land an enemy spy in Berlin, Chambers would still get there—to carry out his scheme against the Allies, whatever it might be. Smoldering with r a g e, Hop forced himself to say coolly:

"What makes you think you have fooled the British? Even now, they've got planes coming after us. I picked the message up by radio, just this instant! So it won't do you any good, Chambers!"

The spy chuckled. "Bluffing won't do *you* any good, Harrigan," he said. "That's a smart trick to get me to lay down one of these guns and put on the radio headset, but it won't work!" He sneered. "Nothing will do the British any good, now! Do you know what I've got with me? A map showing the location of a l l t h e secret RAF airdromes dispersed throughout England! Next time the Luftwaffe comes over, it will be England's swan song— and then will come America's!"

A chill ran down Hop's spine —a chill not caused by the weapon in the Nazi's hands, but by his words. England's hope of survival against the Luftwaffe lay in keeping the location of its widely scattered RAF fields secret! If it became known to the Nazis, America's great ally

would be doomed. Hop groaned. He had to do *something*—but what?

"Hmmph! Once we land you in Berlin, we won't live to breathe this to a soul, eh, Chambers?" Tank snickered.

Hop was silent a long moment. Then he spoke in a rush: "I'll make a bargain with you, Chambers!" he said. "I don't want to die! There's a—secret invention—in that box. We were supposed to deliver it to Tunis. Take it—but use your influence to see that the Nazis don't kill us!"

Tank's voice cut in: "Hop, you wouldn't—"

"Quiet!" The Nazi's voice was like a whip. "Invention? How do I know it's not a trick?"

"I'm not lying!" Hop said.

The spy hesitated. "Y o u, Tinker, open that box!" he clipped. Tank picked it up. For agonizing seconds, he fumbled with the wrapping. Hop could feel Chambers' hot breath on his neck, as the Nazi's greedy eyes peered over his shoulder.

Then in a lightning move, Tank's hand plunged into the box and dropped the glass vial on the floor! It shattered. The spy stiffened, and plummeted back like a board. The guns rolled from his hands. Hop and Tank didn't wait a second more to jab on oxygen masks. Then, with a shock of relief, they emptied their lungs of stored-up air and g u l p e d fresh draughts of oxygen. As at a signal, they had both held their breaths from the moment Tank opened the box.

"Am I glad you caught my message!" grinned the big redhead, after they had shattered the plexiglass cowling to let the gas escape. Hop, holding up the map that was hidden in the dead spy's c l o t h e s, grinned back: "How could I miss!" he retorted. "You said to this ape, 'And we won't live to *breathe* it to a soul'!"

He climbed back to the controls, took over:

"We're a little off course," he said, swinging the B-25 away from Berlin and nosing her toward the south. "This crate is the express for *Tunis!*"

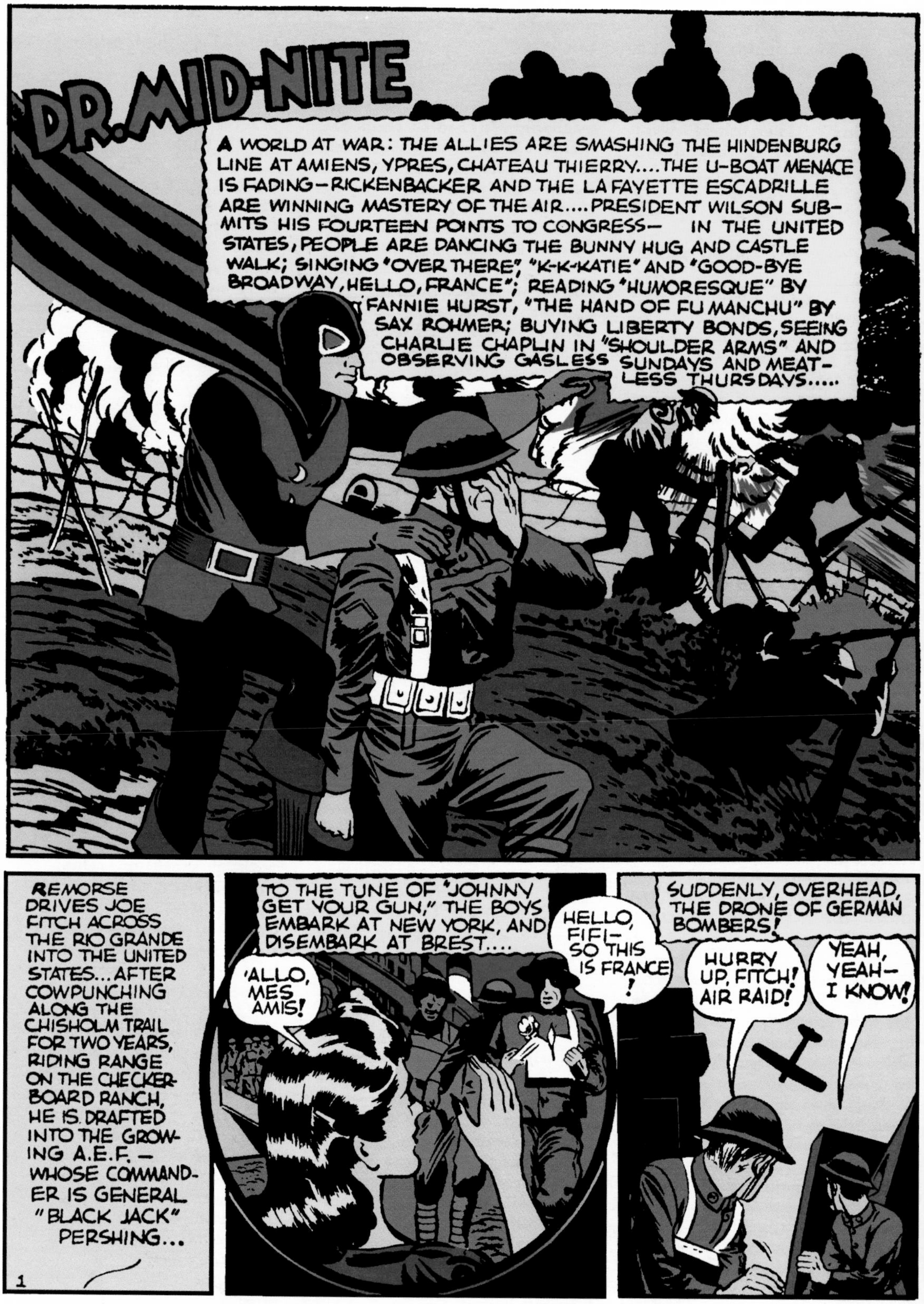
DR. MID-NITE
A WORLD AT WAR: THE ALLIES ARE SMASHING THE HINDENBURG LINE AT AMIENS, YPRES, CHATEAU THIERRY....THE U-BOAT MENACE IS FADING—RICKENBACKER AND THE LAFAYETTE ESCADRILLE ARE WINNING MASTERY OF THE AIR....PRESIDENT WILSON SUBMITS HIS FOURTEEN POINTS TO CONGRESS— IN THE UNITED STATES, PEOPLE ARE DANCING THE BUNNY HUG AND CASTLE WALK; SINGING "OVER THERE", "K-K-KATIE" AND "GOOD-BYE BROADWAY, HELLO, FRANCE"; READING "HUMORESQUE" BY FANNIE HURST, "THE HAND OF FU MANCHU" BY SAX ROHMER; BUYING LIBERTY BONDS, SEEING CHARLIE CHAPLIN IN "SHOULDER ARMS" AND OBSERVING GASLESS SUNDAYS AND MEATLESS THURSDAYS.....
REMORSE DRIVES JOE FITCH ACROSS THE RIO GRANDE INTO THE UNITED STATES...AFTER COWPUNCHING ALONG THE CHISHOLM TRAIL FOR TWO YEARS, RIDING RANGE ON THE CHECKERBOARD RANCH, HE IS DRAFTED INTO THE GROWING A.E.F. —WHOSE COMMANDER IS GENERAL "BLACK JACK" PERSHING...
1
TO THE TUNE OF "JOHNNY GET YOUR GUN," THE BOYS EMBARK AT NEW YORK, AND DISEMBARK AT BREST....
'ALLO, MES AMIS!
HELLO, FIFI— SO THIS IS FRANCE!
SUDDENLY, OVERHEAD, THE DRONE OF GERMAN BOMBERS!
HURRY UP, FITCH! AIR RAID!
YEAH, YEAH— I KNOW!

However far soldiers roam, they want to have some mail from home

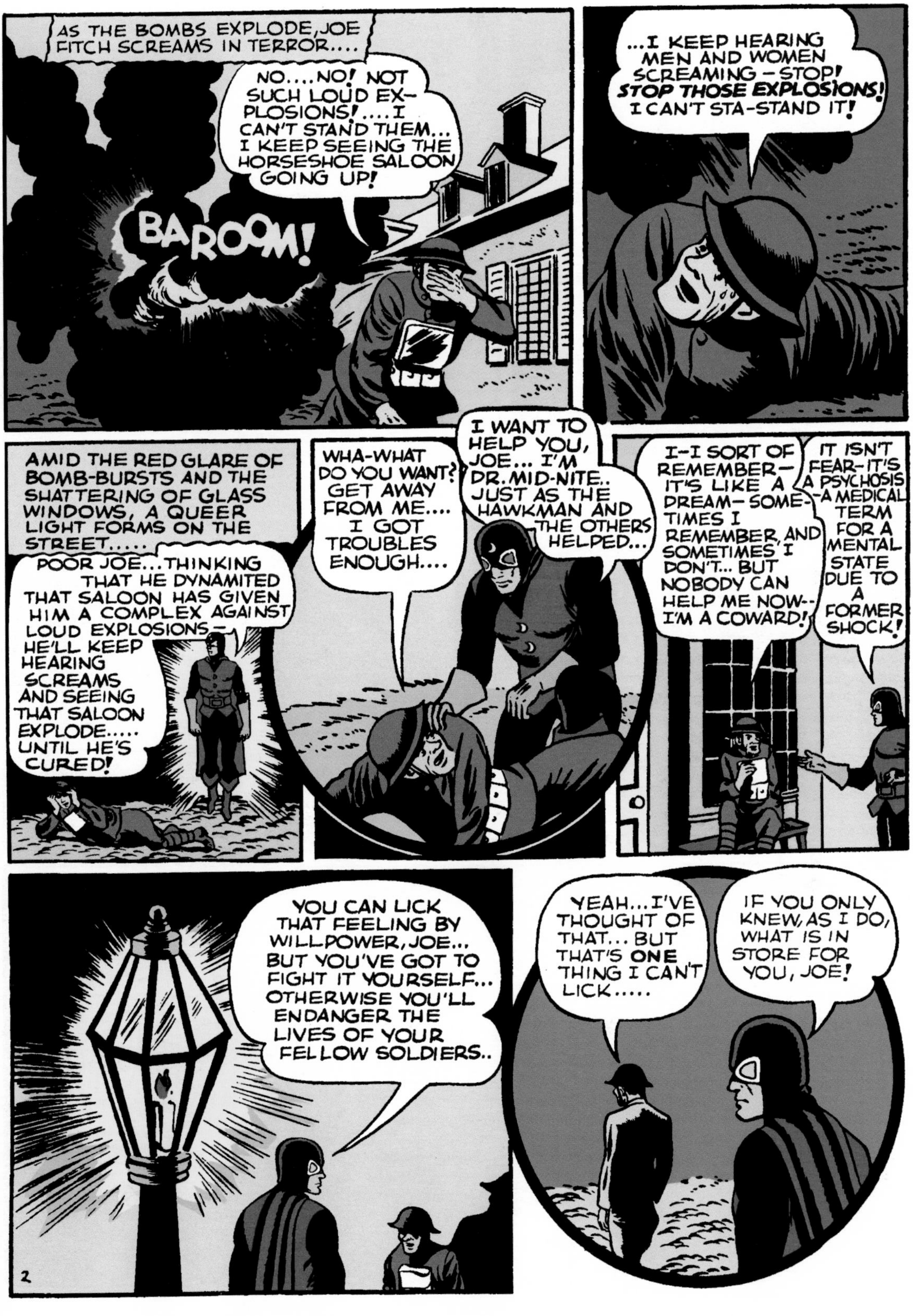
AS THE BOMBS EXPLODE, JOE FITCH SCREAMS IN TERROR....
NO....NO! NOT SUCH LOUD EXPLOSIONS!....I CAN'T STAND THEM... I KEEP SEEING THE HORSESHOE SALOON GOING UP!
BAROOM!
...I KEEP HEARING MEN AND WOMEN SCREAMING - STOP! STOP THOSE EXPLOSIONS! I CAN'T STA-STAND IT!
AMID THE RED GLARE OF BOMB-BURSTS AND THE SHATTERING OF GLASS WINDOWS, A QUEER LIGHT FORMS ON THE STREET.....
POOR JOE...THINKING THAT HE DYNAMITED THAT SALOON HAS GIVEN HIM A COMPLEX AGAINST LOUD EXPLOSIONS— HE'LL KEEP HEARING SCREAMS AND SEEING THAT SALOON EXPLODE..... UNTIL HE'S CURED!
WHA-WHAT DO YOU WANT? GET AWAY FROM ME.... I GOT TROUBLES ENOUGH....
I WANT TO HELP YOU, JOE... I'M DR. MID-NITE.. JUST AS THE HAWKMAN AND THE OTHERS HELPED...
I-I SORT OF REMEMBER— IT'S LIKE A DREAM— SOMETIMES I REMEMBER, AND SOMETIMES I DON'T... BUT NOBODY CAN HELP ME NOW-- I'M A COWARD!
IT ISN'T FEAR- IT'S A PSYCHOSIS -A MEDICAL TERM FOR A MENTAL STATE DUE TO A FORMER SHOCK!
YOU CAN LICK THAT FEELING BY WILLPOWER, JOE... BUT YOU'VE GOT TO FIGHT IT YOURSELF... OTHERWISE YOU'LL ENDANGER THE LIVES OF YOUR FELLOW SOLDIERS..
2
YEAH...I'VE THOUGHT OF THAT... BUT THAT'S ONE THING I CAN'T LICK.....
IF YOU ONLY KNEW, AS I DO, WHAT IS IN STORE FOR YOU, JOE!

Collect Old Paper, Turn It In—Help Your Uncle Sam to Win

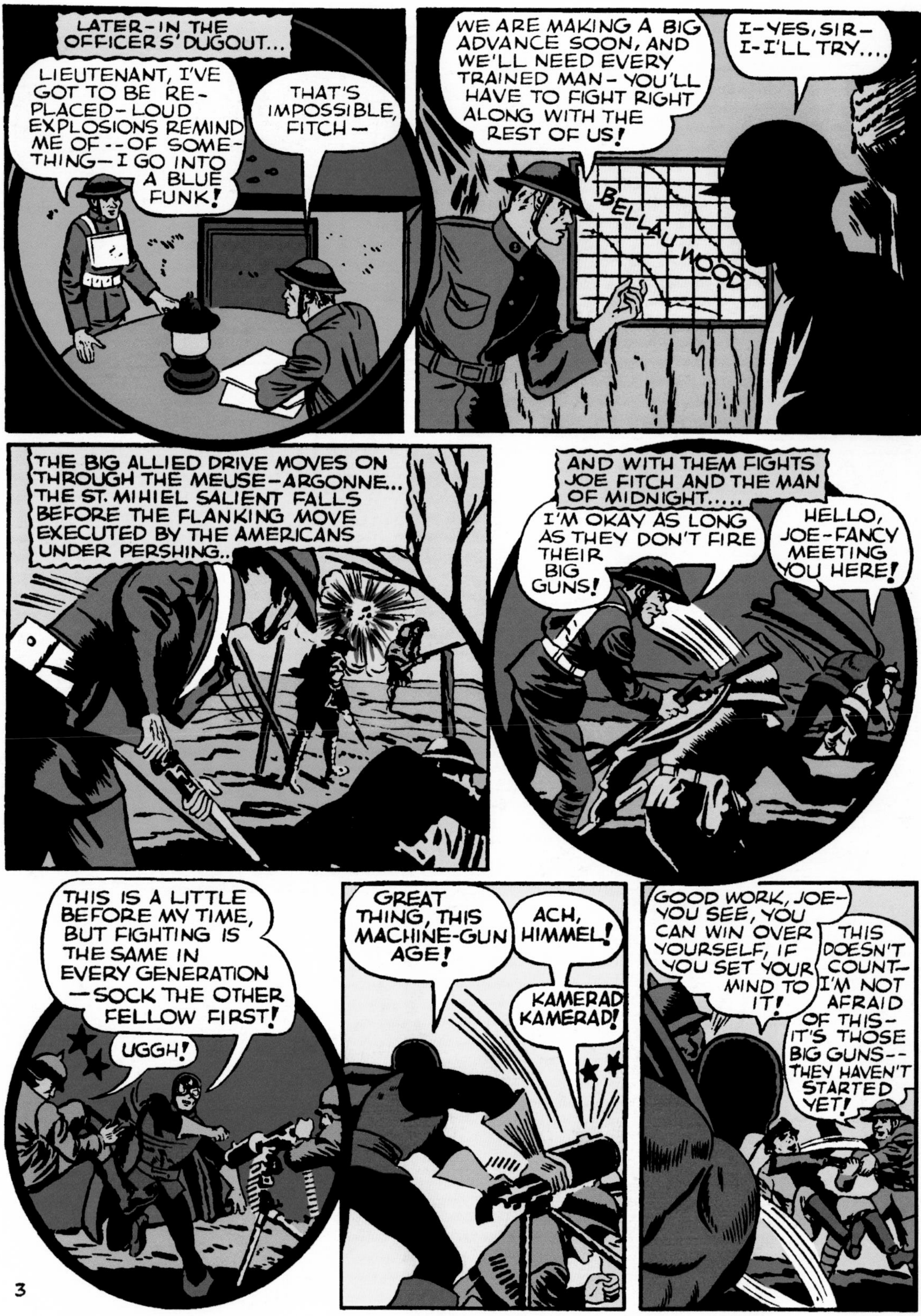
LATER–IN THE OFFICERS' DUGOUT...
LIEUTENANT, I'VE GOT TO BE RE-PLACED–LOUD EXPLOSIONS REMIND ME OF--OF SOME-THING–I GO INTO A BLUE FUNK!
THAT'S IMPOSSIBLE, FITCH–
WE ARE MAKING A BIG ADVANCE SOON, AND WE'LL NEED EVERY TRAINED MAN–YOU'LL HAVE TO FIGHT RIGHT ALONG WITH THE REST OF US!
BELLAU WOOD
I–YES, SIR–I–I'LL TRY....
THE BIG ALLIED DRIVE MOVES ON THROUGH THE MEUSE–ARGONNE... THE ST. MIHIEL SALIENT FALLS BEFORE THE FLANKING MOVE EXECUTED BY THE AMERICANS UNDER PERSHING..
AND WITH THEM FIGHTS JOE FITCH AND THE MAN OF MIDNIGHT.....
I'M OKAY AS LONG AS THEY DON'T FIRE THEIR BIG GUNS!
HELLO, JOE–FANCY MEETING YOU HERE!
THIS IS A LITTLE BEFORE MY TIME, BUT FIGHTING IS THE SAME IN EVERY GENERATION —SOCK THE OTHER FELLOW FIRST!
UGGH!
GREAT THING, THIS MACHINE-GUN AGE!
ACH, HIMMEL!
KAMERAD KAMERAD!
GOOD WORK, JOE–YOU SEE, YOU CAN WIN OVER YOURSELF, IF YOU SET YOUR MIND TO IT!
THIS DOESN'T COUNT–I'M NOT AFRAID OF THIS–IT'S THOSE BIG GUNS--THEY HAVEN'T STARTED YET!
3

You Can Walk to School and Store! Saving Gas Helps Win the War!

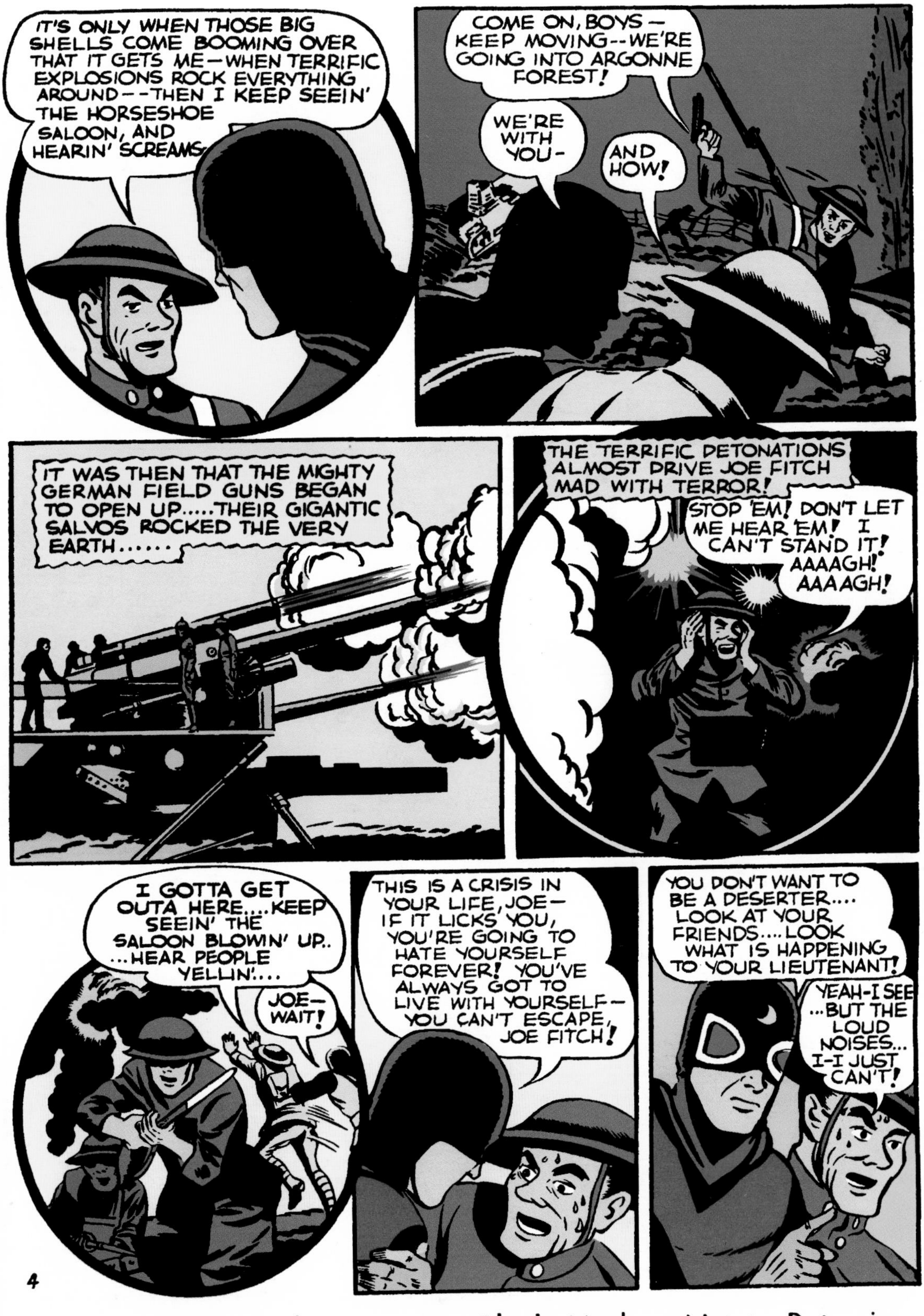
IT'S ONLY WHEN THOSE BIG SHELLS COME BOOMING OVER THAT IT GETS ME—WHEN TERRIFIC EXPLOSIONS ROCK EVERYTHING AROUND--THEN I KEEP SEEIN' THE HORSESHOE SALOON, AND HEARIN' SCREAMS.
COME ON, BOYS—KEEP MOVING--WE'RE GOING INTO ARGONNE FOREST!
WE'RE WITH YOU-
AND HOW!
IT WAS THEN THAT THE MIGHTY GERMAN FIELD GUNS BEGAN TO OPEN UP.....THEIR GIGANTIC SALVOS ROCKED THE VERY EARTH......
THE TERRIFIC DETONATIONS ALMOST DRIVE JOE FITCH MAD WITH TERROR!
STOP 'EM! DON'T LET ME HEAR 'EM! I CAN'T STAND IT! AAAAGH! AAAAGH!
I GOTTA GET OUTA HERE....KEEP SEEIN' THE SALOON BLOWIN' UP.. ...HEAR PEOPLE YELLIN'....
JOE— WAIT!
THIS IS A CRISIS IN YOUR LIFE, JOE— IF IT LICKS YOU, YOU'RE GOING TO HATE YOURSELF FOREVER! YOU'VE ALWAYS GOT TO LIVE WITH YOURSELF— YOU CAN'T ESCAPE, JOE FITCH!
YOU DON'T WANT TO BE A DESERTER.... LOOK AT YOUR FRIENDS.... LOOK WHAT IS HAPPENING TO YOUR LIEUTENANT!
YEAH-I SEE ...BUT THE LOUD NOISES... I-I JUST CAN'T!
4

Boys Are Smart, Girls Are Wise, Black Markets Not to Patronize

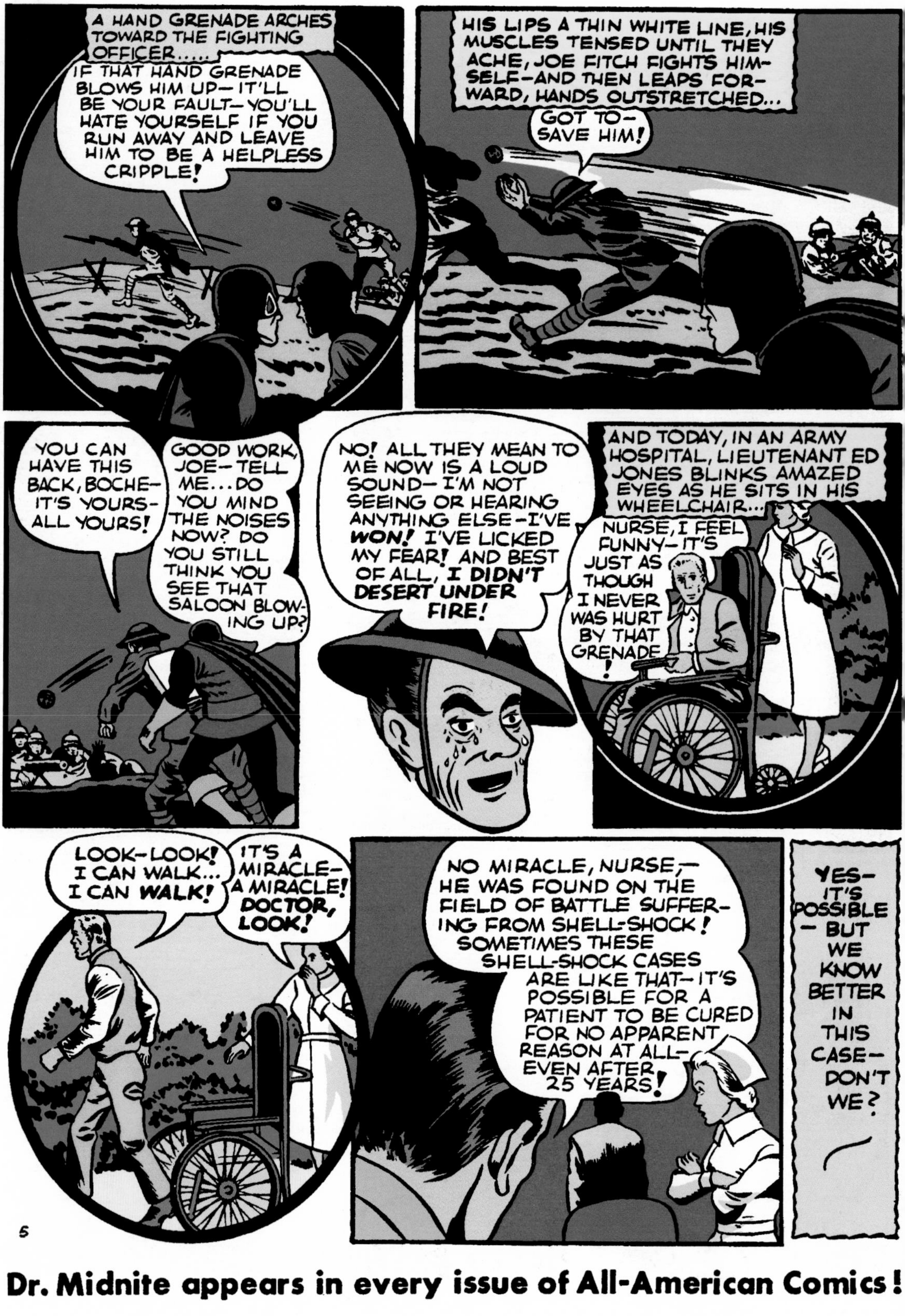
A HAND GRENADE ARCHES TOWARD THE FIGHTING OFFICER.....
IF THAT HAND GRENADE BLOWS HIM UP— IT'LL BE YOUR FAULT— YOU'LL HATE YOURSELF IF YOU RUN AWAY AND LEAVE HIM TO BE A HELPLESS CRIPPLE!
HIS LIPS A THIN WHITE LINE, HIS MUSCLES TENSED UNTIL THEY ACHE, JOE FITCH FIGHTS HIMSELF—AND THEN LEAPS FORWARD, HANDS OUTSTRETCHED...
GOT TO— SAVE HIM!
YOU CAN HAVE THIS BACK, BOCHE— IT'S YOURS— ALL YOURS!
GOOD WORK, JOE— TELL ME... DO YOU MIND THE NOISES NOW? DO YOU STILL THINK YOU SEE THAT SALOON BLOWING UP?
NO! ALL THEY MEAN TO ME NOW IS A LOUD SOUND— I'M NOT SEEING OR HEARING ANYTHING ELSE—I'VE WON! I'VE LICKED MY FEAR! AND BEST OF ALL, I DIDN'T DESERT UNDER FIRE!
AND TODAY, IN AN ARMY HOSPITAL, LIEUTENANT ED JONES BLINKS AMAZED EYES AS HE SITS IN HIS WHEELCHAIR...
NURSE, I FEEL FUNNY— IT'S JUST AS THOUGH I NEVER WAS HURT BY THAT GRENADE!
LOOK— LOOK! I CAN WALK... I CAN WALK!
IT'S A MIRACLE— A MIRACLE! DOCTOR, LOOK!
NO MIRACLE, NURSE,— HE WAS FOUND ON THE FIELD OF BATTLE SUFFERING FROM SHELL-SHOCK! SOMETIMES THESE SHELL-SHOCK CASES ARE LIKE THAT— IT'S POSSIBLE FOR A PATIENT TO BE CURED FOR NO APPARENT REASON AT ALL— EVEN AFTER 25 YEARS!
YES— IT'S POSSIBLE — BUT WE KNOW BETTER IN THIS CASE— DON'T WE?
5

Dr. Midnite appears in every issue of All-American Comics!

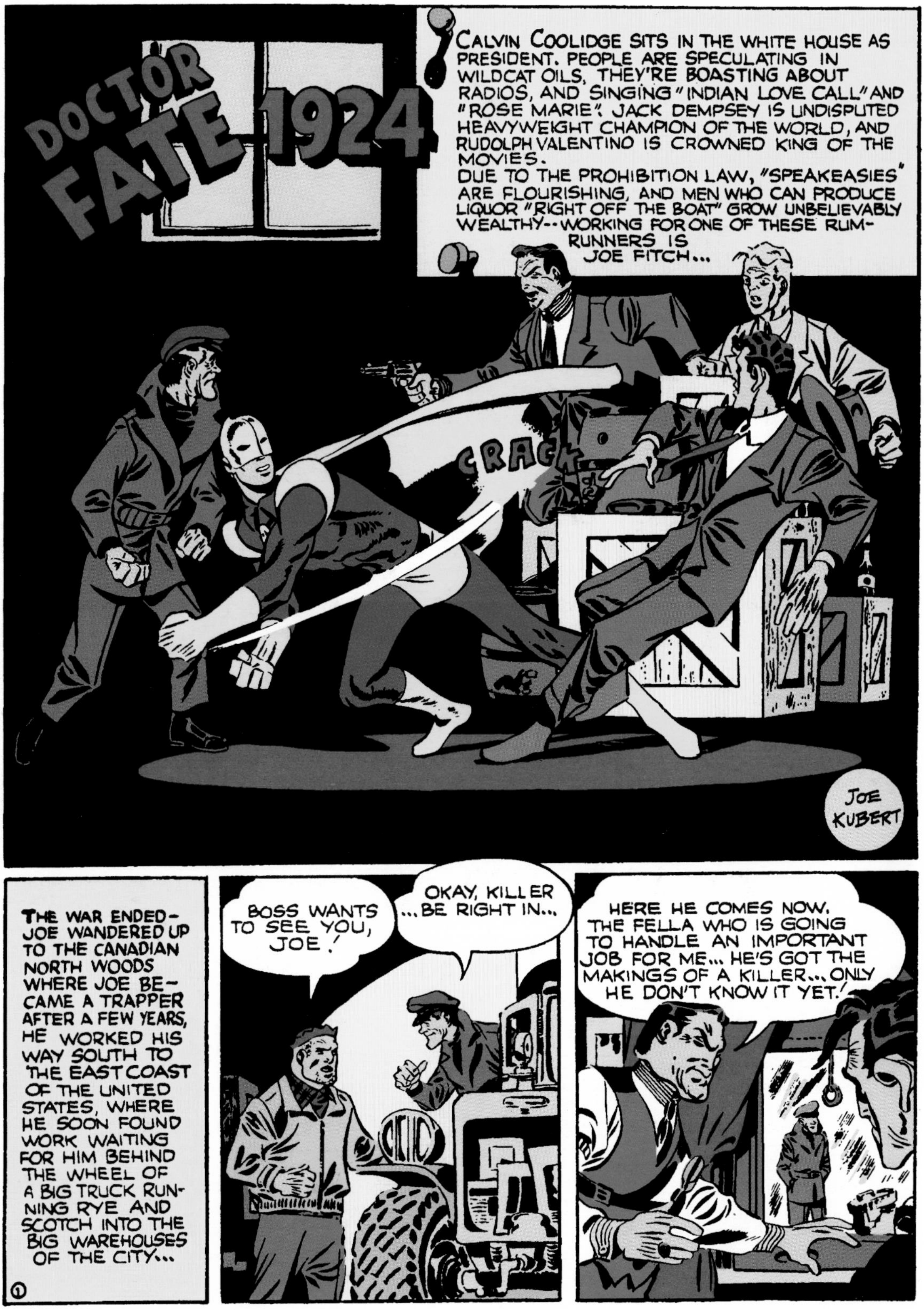
DOCTOR FATE 1924
CALVIN COOLIDGE SITS IN THE WHITE HOUSE AS PRESIDENT. PEOPLE ARE SPECULATING IN WILDCAT OILS, THEY'RE BOASTING ABOUT RADIOS, AND SINGING "INDIAN LOVE CALL" AND "ROSE MARIE". JACK DEMPSEY IS UNDISPUTED HEAVYWEIGHT CHAMPION OF THE WORLD, AND RUDOLPH VALENTINO IS CROWNED KING OF THE MOVIES.
DUE TO THE PROHIBITION LAW, "SPEAKEASIES" ARE FLOURISHING, AND MEN WHO CAN PRODUCE LIQUOR "RIGHT OFF THE BOAT" GROW UNBELIEVABLY WEALTHY--WORKING FOR ONE OF THESE RUM-RUNNERS IS JOE FITCH...
CRACK
JOE KUBERT
THE WAR ENDED-JOE WANDERED UP TO THE CANADIAN NORTH WOODS WHERE JOE BECAME A TRAPPER AFTER A FEW YEARS, HE WORKED HIS WAY SOUTH TO THE EAST COAST OF THE UNITED STATES, WHERE HE SOON FOUND WORK WAITING FOR HIM BEHIND THE WHEEL OF A BIG TRUCK RUNNING RYE AND SCOTCH INTO THE BIG WAREHOUSES OF THE CITY...
1
BOSS WANTS TO SEE YOU, JOE!
OKAY, KILLER ...BE RIGHT IN...
HERE HE COMES NOW. THE FELLA WHO IS GOING TO HANDLE AN IMPORTANT JOB FOR ME... HE'S GOT THE MAKINGS OF A KILLER... ONLY HE DON'T KNOW IT YET!

IF YOU STILL HAVE METAL SCRAP, TURN IT IN TO BEAT THE JAP

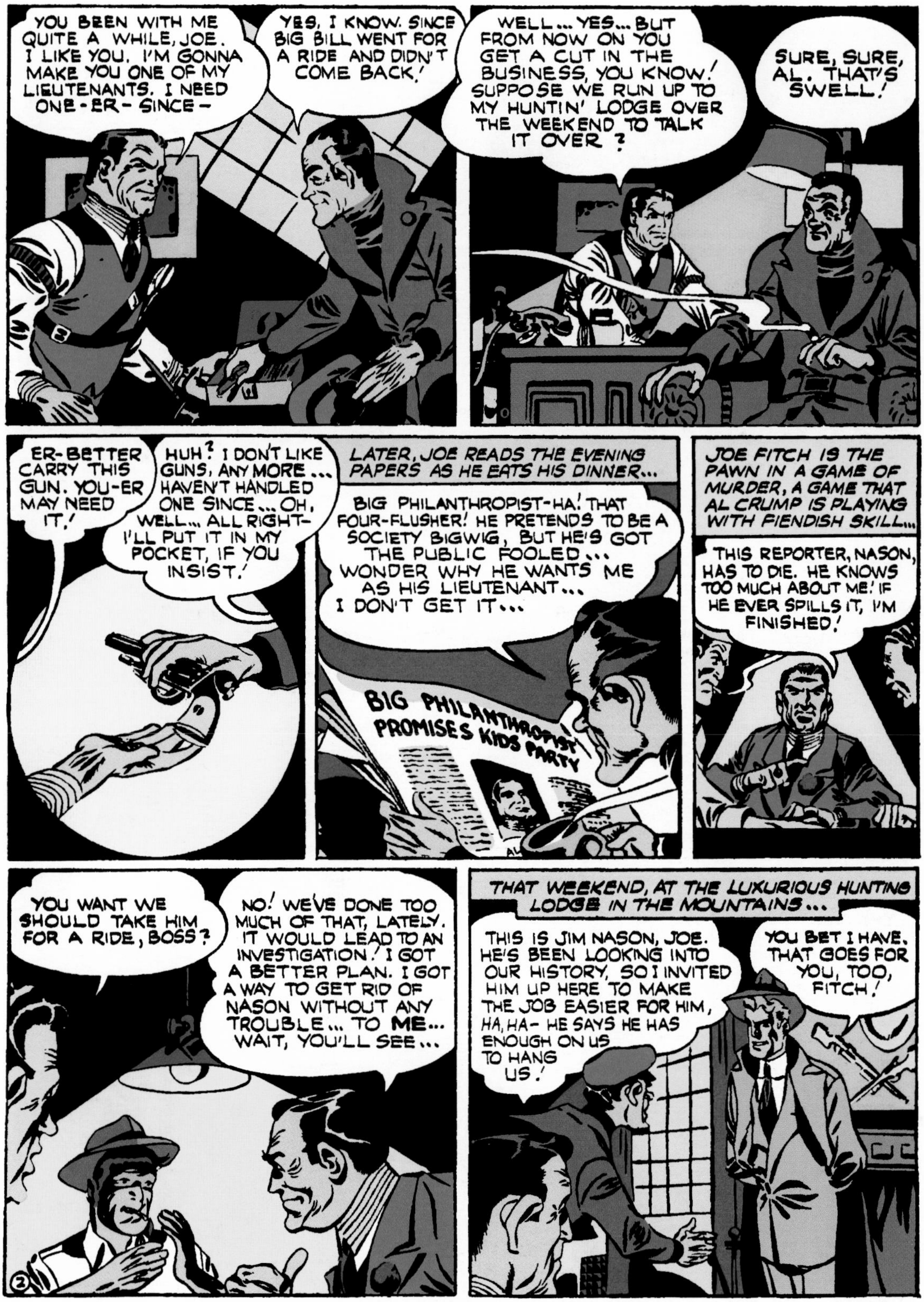
YOU BEEN WITH ME QUITE A WHILE, JOE. I LIKE YOU. I'M GONNA MAKE YOU ONE OF MY LIEUTENANTS. I NEED ONE-ER-SINCE-
YES, I KNOW. SINCE BIG BILL WENT FOR A RIDE AND DIDN'T COME BACK!
WELL... YES... BUT FROM NOW ON YOU GET A CUT IN THE BUSINESS, YOU KNOW! SUPPOSE WE RUN UP TO MY HUNTIN' LODGE OVER THE WEEKEND TO TALK IT OVER ?
SURE, SURE, AL. THAT'S SWELL!
ER-BETTER CARRY THIS GUN. YOU-ER MAY NEED IT!
HUH? I DON'T LIKE GUNS, ANY MORE... HAVEN'T HANDLED ONE SINCE... OH, WELL... ALL RIGHT-I'LL PUT IT IN MY POCKET, IF YOU INSIST!
LATER, JOE READS THE EVENING PAPERS AS HE EATS HIS DINNER...
BIG PHILANTHROPIST-HA! THAT FOUR-FLUSHER! HE PRETENDS TO BE A SOCIETY BIGWIG, BUT HE'S GOT THE PUBLIC FOOLED... WONDER WHY HE WANTS ME AS HIS LIEUTENANT... I DON'T GET IT...
BIG PHILANTHROPIST PROMISES KIDS PARTY
JOE FITCH IS THE PAWN IN A GAME OF MURDER, A GAME THAT AL CRUMP IS PLAYING WITH FIENDISH SKILL...
THIS REPORTER, NASON, HAS TO DIE. HE KNOWS TOO MUCH ABOUT ME! IF HE EVER SPILLS IT, I'M FINISHED!
YOU WANT WE SHOULD TAKE HIM FOR A RIDE, BOSS?
NO! WE'VE DONE TOO MUCH OF THAT, LATELY. IT WOULD LEAD TO AN INVESTIGATION! I GOT A BETTER PLAN. I GOT A WAY TO GET RID OF NASON WITHOUT ANY TROUBLE... TO ME... WAIT, YOU'LL SEE...
2
THAT WEEKEND, AT THE LUXURIOUS HUNTING LODGE IN THE MOUNTAINS...
THIS IS JIM NASON, JOE. HE'S BEEN LOOKING INTO OUR HISTORY, SO I INVITED HIM UP HERE TO MAKE THE JOB EASIER FOR HIM, HA, HA- HE SAYS HE HAS ENOUGH ON US TO HANG US!
YOU BET I HAVE. THAT GOES FOR YOU, TOO, FITCH!

Turn Out Lights Not in Use—War Production Needs the "Juice"

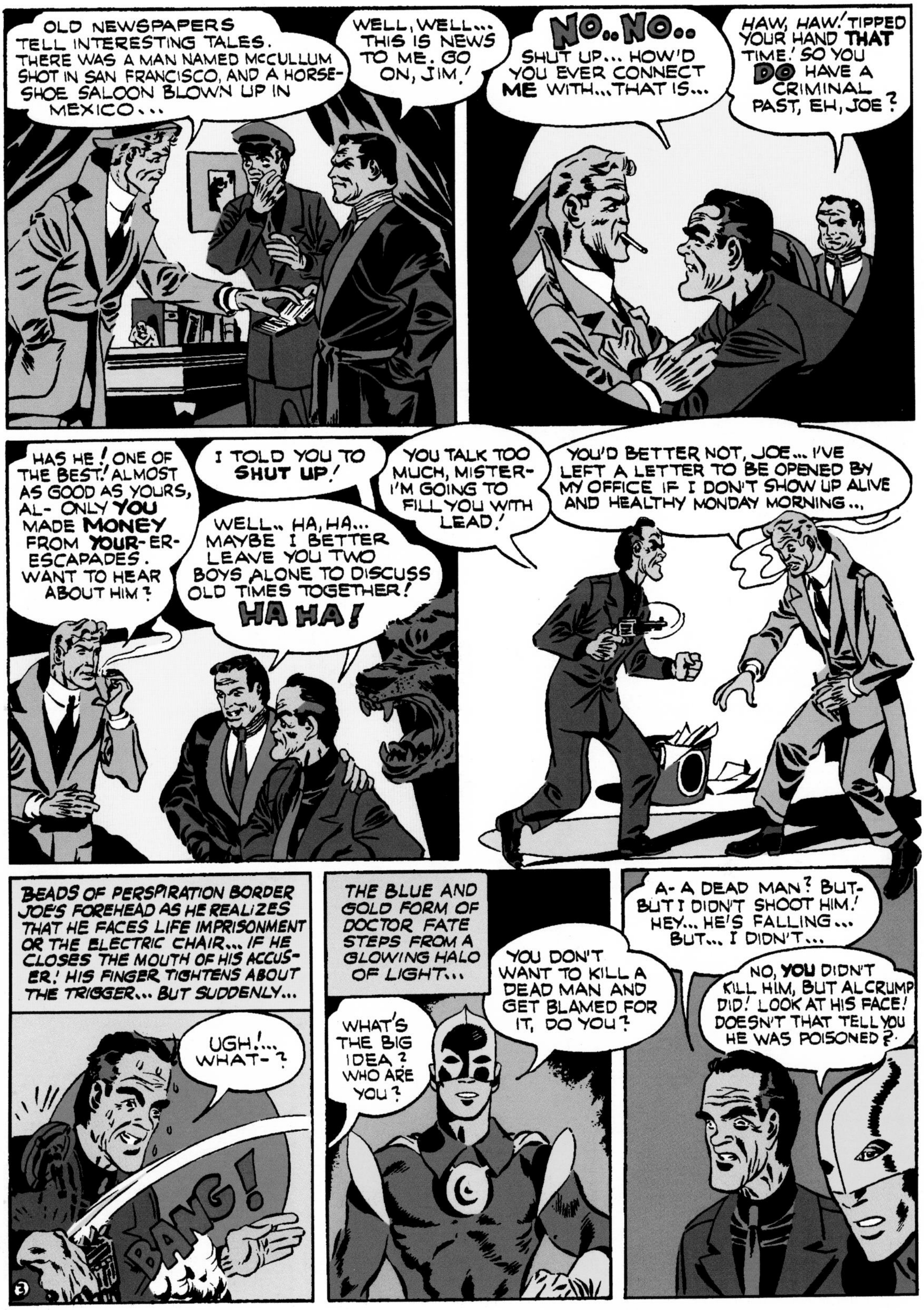
OLD NEWSPAPERS TELL INTERESTING TALES. THERE WAS A MAN NAMED McCULLUM SHOT IN SAN FRANCISCO, AND A HORSE-SHOE SALOON BLOWN UP IN MEXICO...
WELL, WELL... THIS IS NEWS TO ME. GO ON, JIM!
NO.. NO.. SHUT UP... HOW'D YOU EVER CONNECT ME WITH... THAT IS...
HAW, HAW! TIPPED YOUR HAND THAT TIME! SO YOU DO HAVE A CRIMINAL PAST, EH, JOE?
HAS HE! ONE OF THE BEST! ALMOST AS GOOD AS YOURS, AL- ONLY YOU MADE MONEY FROM YOUR-ER-ESCAPADES. WANT TO HEAR ABOUT HIM?
I TOLD YOU TO SHUT UP!
WELL.. HA, HA... MAYBE I BETTER LEAVE YOU TWO BOYS ALONE TO DISCUSS OLD TIMES TOGETHER! HA HA!
YOU TALK TOO MUCH, MISTER- I'M GOING TO FILL YOU WITH LEAD!
YOU'D BETTER NOT, JOE... I'VE LEFT A LETTER TO BE OPENED BY MY OFFICE IF I DON'T SHOW UP ALIVE AND HEALTHY MONDAY MORNING...
BEADS OF PERSPIRATION BORDER JOE'S FOREHEAD AS HE REALIZES THAT HE FACES LIFE IMPRISONMENT OR THE ELECTRIC CHAIR... IF HE CLOSES THE MOUTH OF HIS ACCUSER! HIS FINGER TIGHTENS ABOUT THE TRIGGER... BUT SUDDENLY...
UGH!... WHAT-?
BANG!
THE BLUE AND GOLD FORM OF DOCTOR FATE STEPS FROM A GLOWING HALO OF LIGHT...
WHAT'S THE BIG IDEA? WHO ARE YOU?
YOU DON'T WANT TO KILL A DEAD MAN AND GET BLAMED FOR IT, DO YOU?
A- A DEAD MAN? BUT- BUT I DIDN'T SHOOT HIM! HEY... HE'S FALLING... BUT... I DIDN'T...
NO, YOU DIDN'T KILL HIM, BUT AL CRUMP DID! LOOK AT HIS FACE! DOESN'T THAT TELL YOU HE WAS POISONED?

Tin Cans in the Garbage Pile Are Just a Way of Saying "Heil!"

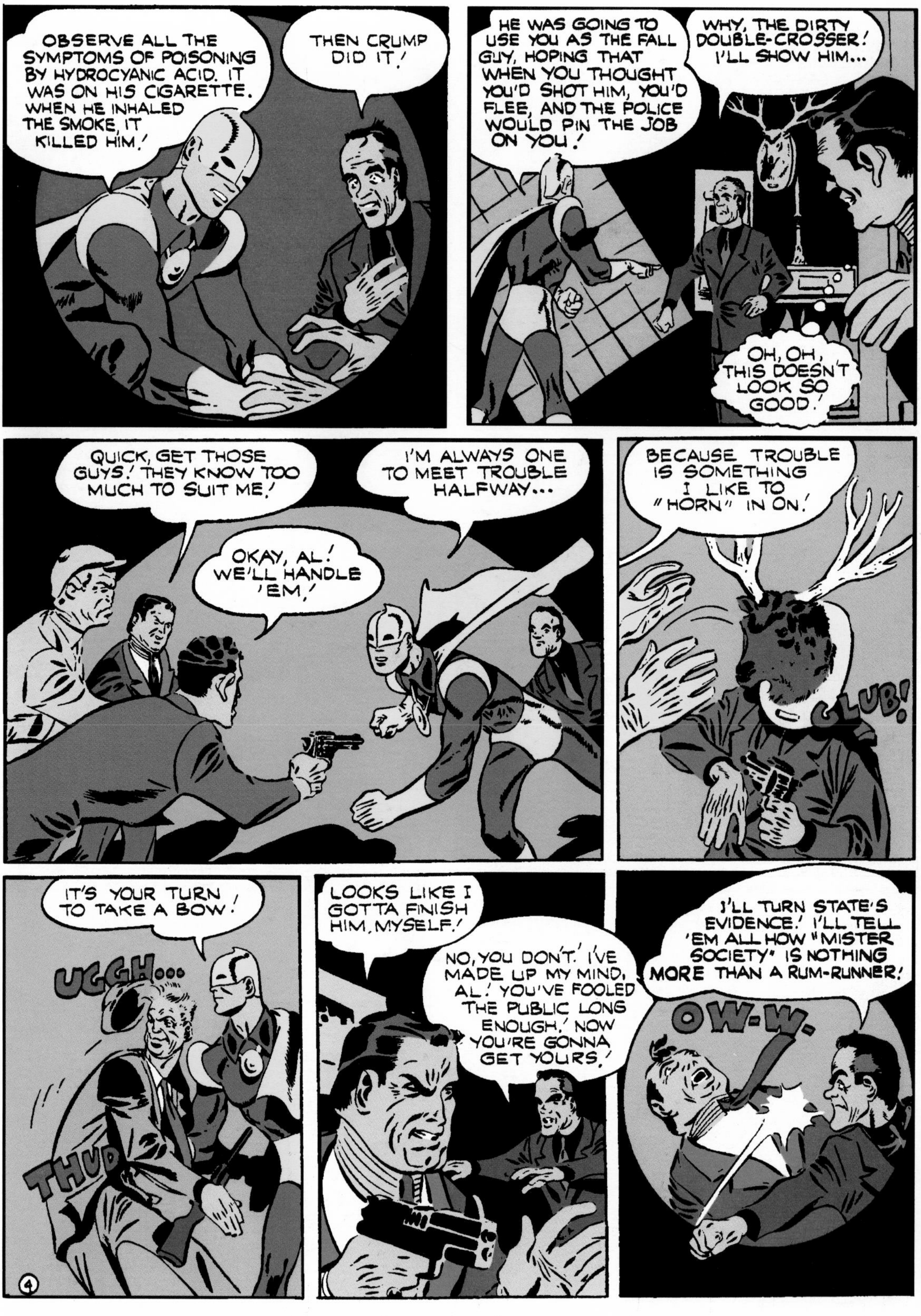
OBSERVE ALL THE SYMPTOMS OF POISONING BY HYDROCYANIC ACID. IT WAS ON HIS CIGARETTE. WHEN HE INHALED THE SMOKE, IT KILLED HIM!
THEN CRUMP DID IT!
HE WAS GOING TO USE YOU AS THE FALL GUY, HOPING THAT WHEN YOU THOUGHT YOU'D SHOT HIM, YOU'D FLEE, AND THE POLICE WOULD PIN THE JOB ON YOU!
WHY, THE DIRTY DOUBLE-CROSSER! I'LL SHOW HIM...
OH, OH, THIS DOESN'T LOOK SO GOOD!
QUICK, GET THOSE GUYS! THEY KNOW TOO MUCH TO SUIT ME!
I'M ALWAYS ONE TO MEET TROUBLE HALFWAY...
OKAY, AL! WE'LL HANDLE 'EM!
BECAUSE TROUBLE IS SOMETHING I LIKE TO "HORN" IN ON!
CLUB!
IT'S YOUR TURN TO TAKE A BOW!
UGGH...
THUD
4
LOOKS LIKE I GOTTA FINISH HIM, MYSELF!
NO, YOU DON'T! I'VE MADE UP MY MIND, AL! YOU'VE FOOLED THE PUBLIC LONG ENOUGH! NOW YOU'RE GONNA GET YOURS!
I'LL TURN STATE'S EVIDENCE! I'LL TELL 'EM ALL HOW "MISTER SOCIETY" IS NOTHING MORE THAN A RUM-RUNNER!
OW-W-

Waste Fats in Good Condition Help to Make Fine Ammunition

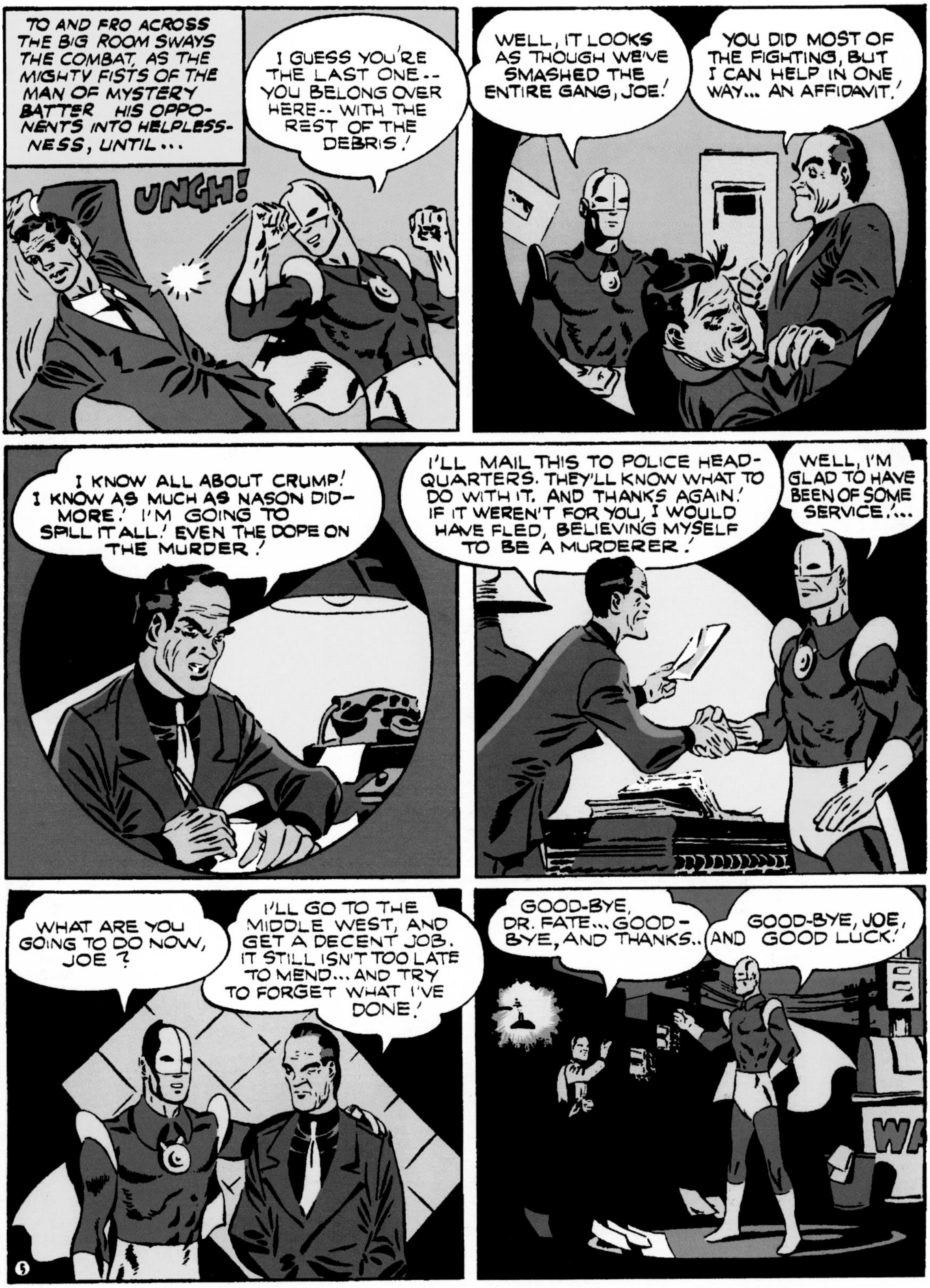
TO AND FRO ACROSS THE BIG ROOM SWAYS THE COMBAT, AS THE MIGHTY FISTS OF THE MAN OF MYSTERY BATTER HIS OPPONENTS INTO HELPLESSNESS, UNTIL...
I GUESS YOU'RE THE LAST ONE-- YOU BELONG OVER HERE-- WITH THE REST OF THE DEBRIS!
UNGH!
WELL, IT LOOKS AS THOUGH WE'VE SMASHED THE ENTIRE GANG, JOE!
YOU DID MOST OF THE FIGHTING, BUT I CAN HELP IN ONE WAY... AN AFFIDAVIT!
I KNOW ALL ABOUT CRUMP! I KNOW AS MUCH AS NASON DID-MORE! I'M GOING TO SPILL IT ALL! EVEN THE DOPE ON THE MURDER!
I'LL MAIL THIS TO POLICE HEADQUARTERS. THEY'LL KNOW WHAT TO DO WITH IT. AND THANKS AGAIN! IF IT WEREN'T FOR YOU, I WOULD HAVE FLED, BELIEVING MYSELF TO BE A MURDERER!
WELL, I'M GLAD TO HAVE BEEN OF SOME SERVICE!...
WHAT ARE YOU GOING TO DO NOW, JOE ?
I'LL GO TO THE MIDDLE WEST, AND GET A DECENT JOB. IT STILL ISN'T TOO LATE TO MEND... AND TRY TO FORGET WHAT I'VE DONE!
GOOD-BYE, DR. FATE... GOOD-BYE, AND THANKS..
GOOD-BYE, JOE, AND GOOD LUCK!

DR. FATE appears in every issue of More Fun Comics!

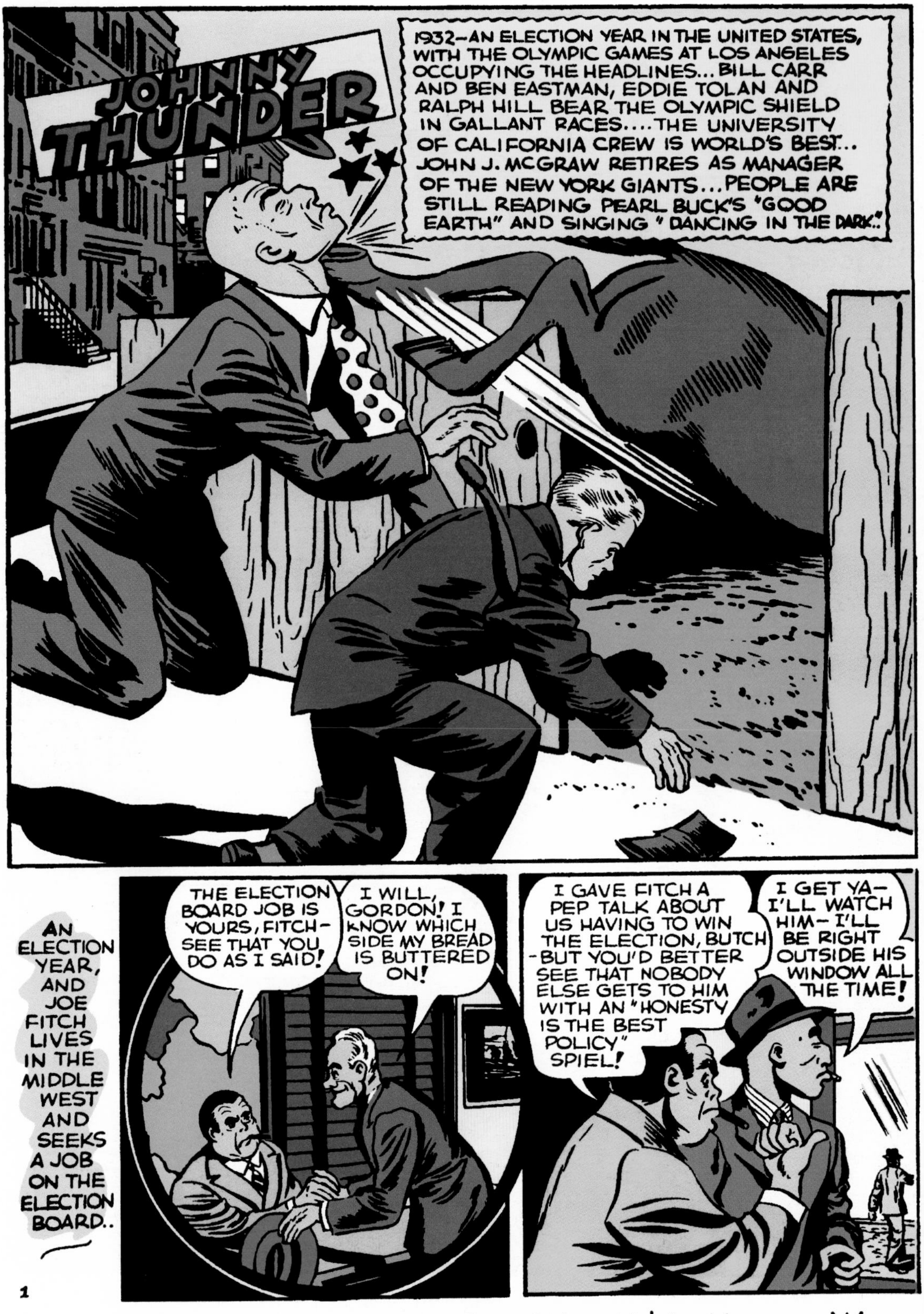
JOHNNY THUNDER
1932—AN ELECTION YEAR IN THE UNITED STATES, WITH THE OLYMPIC GAMES AT LOS ANGELES OCCUPYING THE HEADLINES... BILL CARR AND BEN EASTMAN, EDDIE TOLAN AND RALPH HILL BEAR THE OLYMPIC SHIELD IN GALLANT RACES.... THE UNIVERSITY OF CALIFORNIA CREW IS WORLD'S BEST.. JOHN J. McGRAW RETIRES AS MANAGER OF THE NEW YORK GIANTS... PEOPLE ARE STILL READING PEARL BUCK'S "GOOD EARTH" AND SINGING "DANCING IN THE DARK."
AN ELECTION YEAR, AND JOE FITCH LIVES IN THE MIDDLE WEST AND SEEKS A JOB ON THE ELECTION BOARD..
THE ELECTION BOARD JOB IS YOURS, FITCH—SEE THAT YOU DO AS I SAID!
I WILL, GORDON! I KNOW WHICH SIDE MY BREAD IS BUTTERED ON!
I GAVE FITCH A PEP TALK ABOUT US HAVING TO WIN THE ELECTION, BUTCH—BUT YOU'D BETTER SEE THAT NOBODY ELSE GETS TO HIM WITH AN "HONESTY IS THE BEST POLICY" SPIEL!
I GET YA—I'LL WATCH HIM—I'LL BE RIGHT OUTSIDE HIS WINDOW ALL THE TIME!
1

Boys and Girls, Every Day, Can Give War Aid in Many a Way—

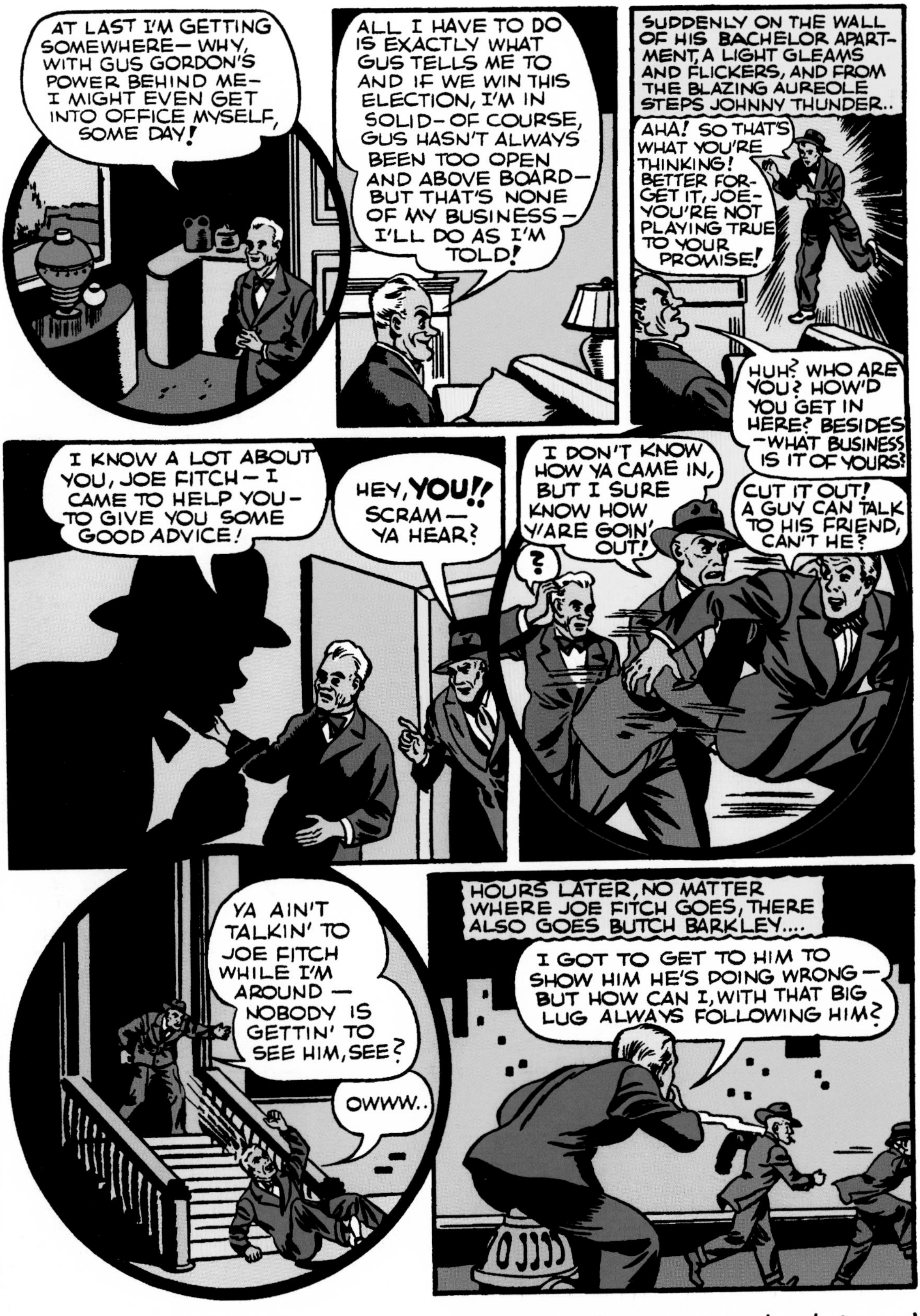
AT LAST I'M GETTING SOMEWHERE— WHY, WITH GUS GORDON'S POWER BEHIND ME— I MIGHT EVEN GET INTO OFFICE MYSELF, SOME DAY!
ALL I HAVE TO DO IS EXACTLY WHAT GUS TELLS ME TO AND IF WE WIN THIS ELECTION, I'M IN SOLID— OF COURSE, GUS HASN'T ALWAYS BEEN TOO OPEN AND ABOVE BOARD— BUT THAT'S NONE OF MY BUSINESS— I'LL DO AS I'M TOLD!
SUDDENLY ON THE WALL OF HIS BACHELOR APARTMENT, A LIGHT GLEAMS AND FLICKERS, AND FROM THE BLAZING AUREOLE STEPS JOHNNY THUNDER..
AHA! SO THAT'S WHAT YOU'RE THINKING! BETTER FORGET IT, JOE— YOU'RE NOT PLAYING TRUE TO YOUR PROMISE!
HUH? WHO ARE YOU? HOW'D YOU GET IN HERE? BESIDES —WHAT BUSINESS IS IT OF YOURS?
I KNOW A LOT ABOUT YOU, JOE FITCH— I CAME TO HELP YOU— TO GIVE YOU SOME GOOD ADVICE!
HEY, YOU!! SCRAM— YA HEAR?
I DON'T KNOW HOW YA CAME IN, BUT I SURE KNOW HOW Y'ARE GOIN' OUT!
CUT IT OUT! A GUY CAN TALK TO HIS FRIEND, CAN'T HE?
?
YA AIN'T TALKIN' TO JOE FITCH WHILE I'M AROUND— NOBODY IS GETTIN' TO SEE HIM, SEE?
OWWW..
HOURS LATER, NO MATTER WHERE JOE FITCH GOES, THERE ALSO GOES BUTCH BARKLEY....
I GOT TO GET TO HIM TO SHOW HIM HE'S DOING WRONG— BUT HOW CAN I, WITH THAT BIG LUG ALWAYS FOLLOWING HIM?

Every Time You Buy a Stamp, You Feed the Flame in Freedom's Lamp!

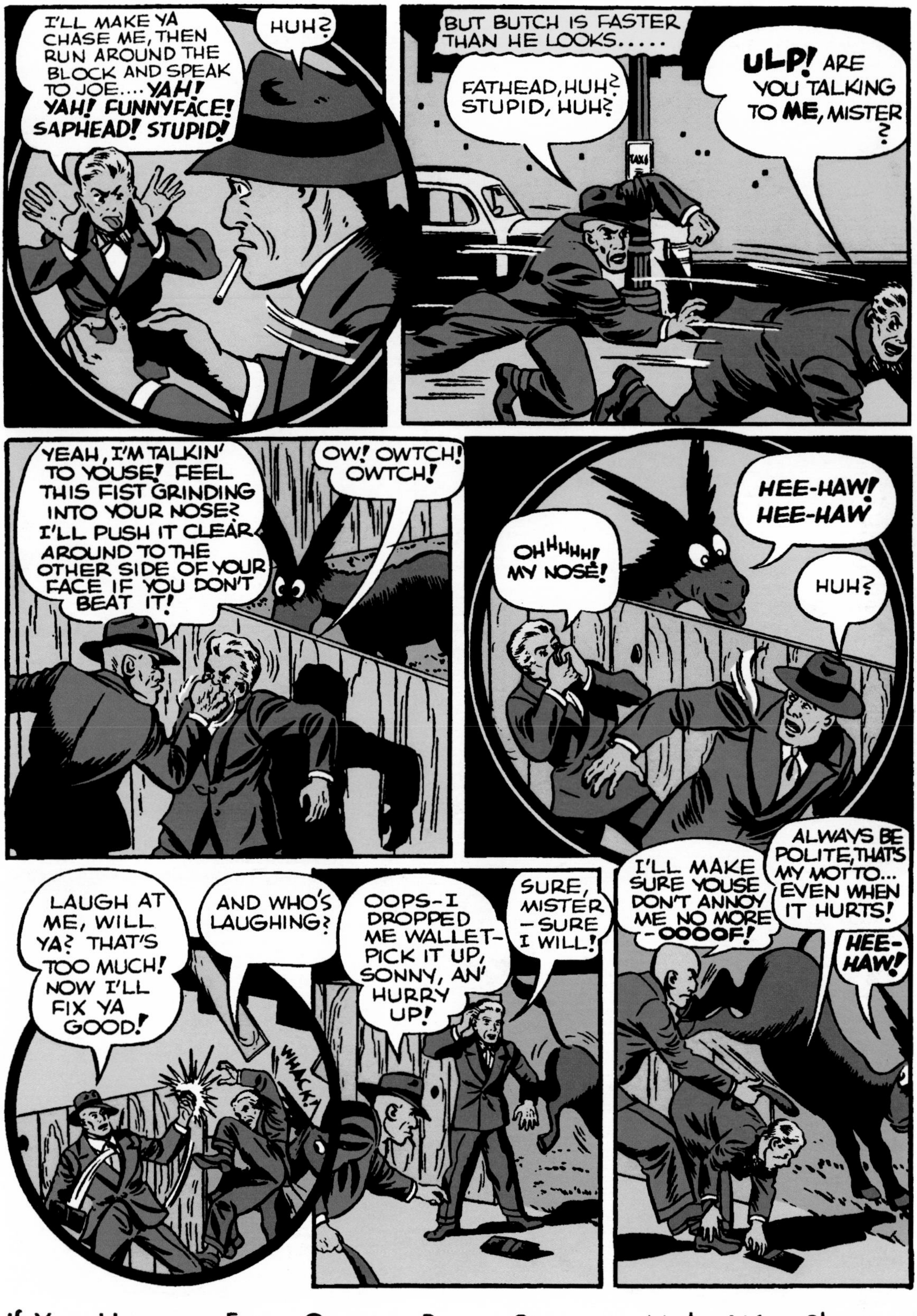
I'LL MAKE YA CHASE ME, THEN RUN AROUND THE BLOCK AND SPEAK TO JOE.... YAH! YAH! FUNNYFACE! SAPHEAD! STUPID!
HUH?
BUT BUTCH IS FASTER THAN HE LOOKS.....
FATHEAD, HUH? STUPID, HUH?
ULP! ARE YOU TALKING TO ME, MISTER?
YEAH, I'M TALKIN' TO YOUSE! FEEL THIS FIST GRINDING INTO YOUR NOSE? I'LL PUSH IT CLEAR AROUND TO THE OTHER SIDE OF YOUR FACE IF YOU DON'T BEAT IT!
OW! OWTCH! OWTCH!
HEE-HAW! HEE-HAW
OHHHHH! MY NOSE!
HUH?
LAUGH AT ME, WILL YA? THAT'S TOO MUCH! NOW I'LL FIX YA GOOD!
AND WHO'S LAUGHING?
WHACK!
OOPS-I DROPPED ME WALLET-PICK IT UP, SONNY, AN' HURRY UP!
SURE, MISTER -SURE I WILL!
I'LL MAKE SURE YOUSE DON'T ANNOY ME NO MORE -OOOOF!
ALWAYS BE POLITE, THAT'S MY MOTTO... EVEN WHEN IT HURTS!
HEE-HAW!

If You Have an Extra Quarter, Buy a Stamp to Make War Shorter

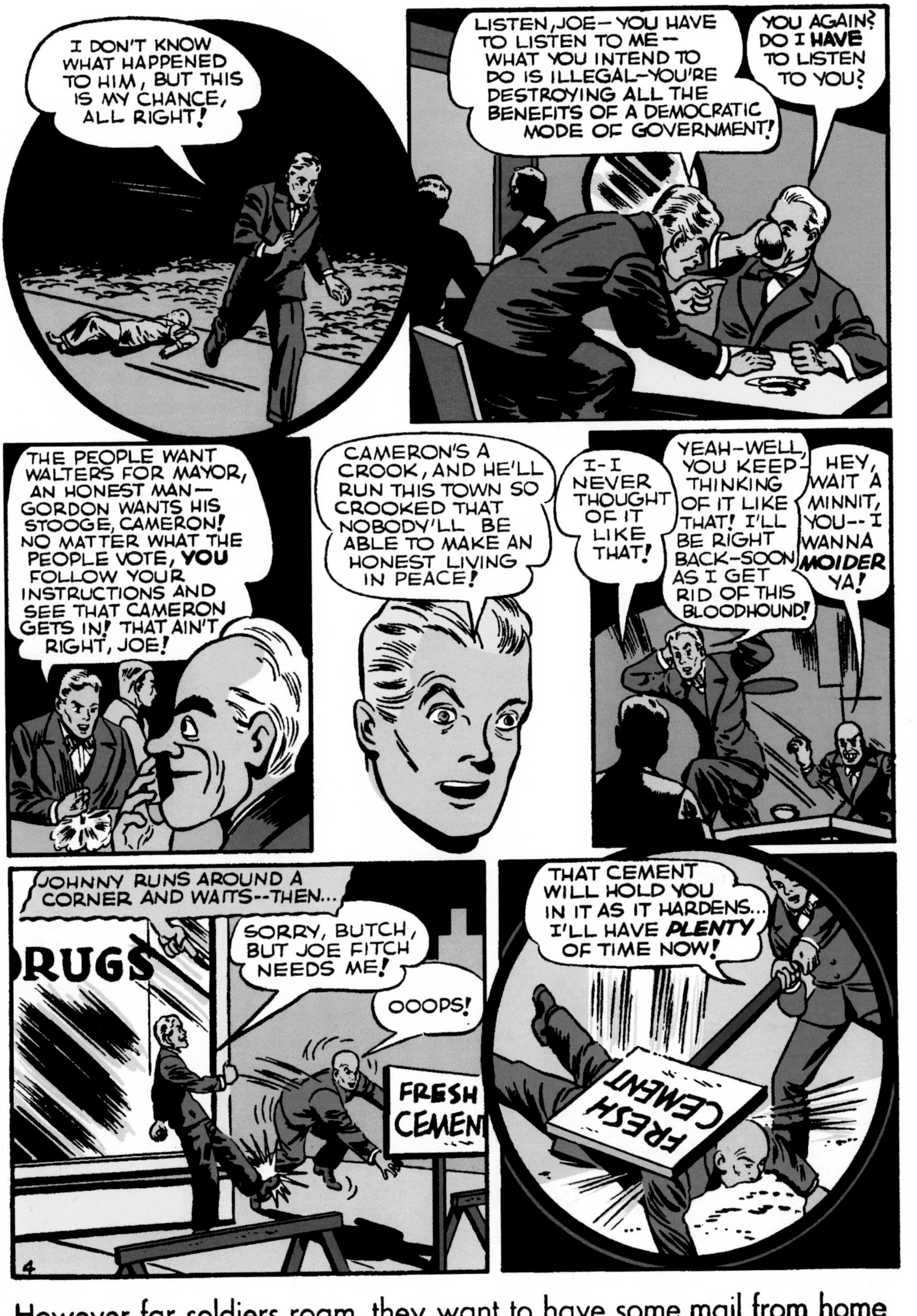
I DON'T KNOW WHAT HAPPENED TO HIM, BUT THIS IS MY CHANCE, ALL RIGHT!
LISTEN, JOE--YOU HAVE TO LISTEN TO ME--WHAT YOU INTEND TO DO IS ILLEGAL--YOU'RE DESTROYING ALL THE BENEFITS OF A DEMOCRATIC MODE OF GOVERNMENT!
YOU AGAIN? DO I HAVE TO LISTEN TO YOU?
THE PEOPLE WANT WALTERS FOR MAYOR, AN HONEST MAN--GORDON WANTS HIS STOOGE, CAMERON! NO MATTER WHAT THE PEOPLE VOTE, YOU FOLLOW YOUR INSTRUCTIONS AND SEE THAT CAMERON GETS IN! THAT AIN'T RIGHT, JOE!
CAMERON'S A CROOK, AND HE'LL RUN THIS TOWN SO CROOKED THAT NOBODY'LL BE ABLE TO MAKE AN HONEST LIVING IN PEACE!
I-I NEVER THOUGHT OF IT LIKE THAT!
YEAH-WELL, YOU KEEP THINKING OF IT LIKE THAT! I'LL BE RIGHT BACK-SOON AS I GET RID OF THIS BLOODHOUND!
HEY, WAIT A MINNIT, YOU--I WANNA MOIDER YA!
JOHNNY RUNS AROUND A CORNER AND WAITS--THEN...
DRUGS
SORRY, BUTCH, BUT JOE FITCH NEEDS ME!
OOOPS!
FRESH CEMEN
4
THAT CEMENT WILL HOLD YOU IN IT AS IT HARDENS... I'LL HAVE PLENTY OF TIME NOW!
FRESH CEMENT

However far soldiers roam, they want to have some mail from home

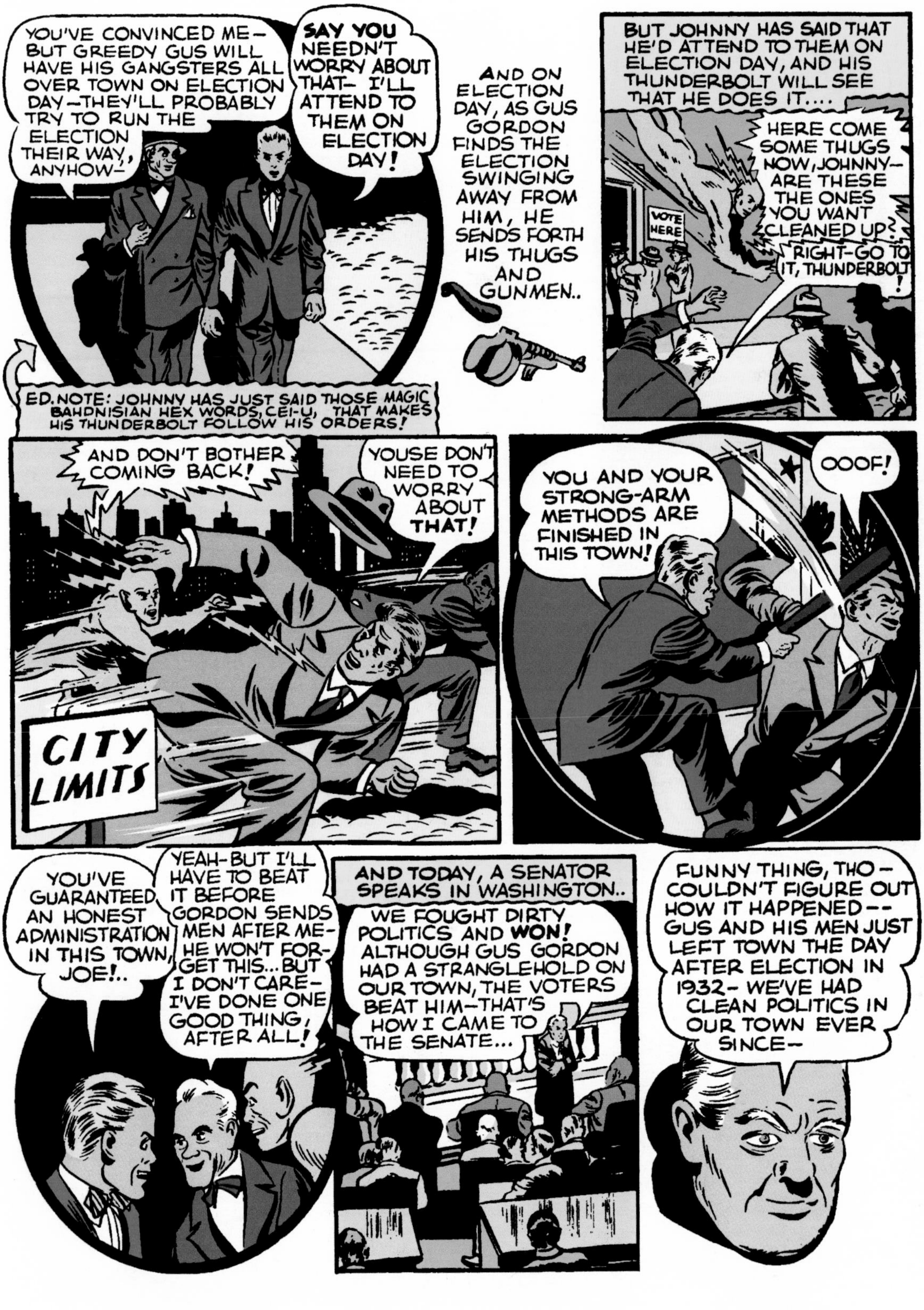
YOU'VE CONVINCED ME— BUT GREEDY GUS WILL HAVE HIS GANGSTERS ALL OVER TOWN ON ELECTION DAY—THEY'LL PROBABLY TRY TO RUN THE ELECTION THEIR WAY, ANYHOW—
SAY YOU NEEDN'T WORRY ABOUT THAT— I'LL ATTEND TO THEM ON ELECTION DAY!
ED. NOTE: JOHNNY HAS JUST SAID THOSE MAGIC BAHDNISIAN HEX WORDS, CEI-U, THAT MAKES HIS THUNDERBOLT FOLLOW HIS ORDERS!
AND ON ELECTION DAY, AS GUS GORDON FINDS THE ELECTION SWINGING AWAY FROM HIM, HE SENDS FORTH HIS THUGS AND GUNMEN..
BUT JOHNNY HAS SAID THAT HE'D ATTEND TO THEM ON ELECTION DAY, AND HIS THUNDERBOLT WILL SEE THAT HE DOES IT....
HERE COME SOME THUGS NOW, JOHNNY— ARE THESE THE ONES YOU WANT CLEANED UP?
VOTE HERE
RIGHT—GO TO IT, THUNDERBOLT!
AND DON'T BOTHER COMING BACK!
YOUSE DON'T NEED TO WORRY ABOUT THAT!
CITY LIMITS
YOU AND YOUR STRONG-ARM METHODS ARE FINISHED IN THIS TOWN!
OOOF!
YOU'VE GUARANTEED AN HONEST ADMINISTRATION IN THIS TOWN, JOE!..
YEAH—BUT I'LL HAVE TO BEAT IT BEFORE GORDON SENDS MEN AFTER ME— HE WON'T FORGET THIS... BUT I DON'T CARE— I'VE DONE ONE GOOD THING, AFTER ALL!
AND TODAY, A SENATOR SPEAKS IN WASHINGTON..
WE FOUGHT DIRTY POLITICS AND WON! ALTHOUGH GUS GORDON HAD A STRANGLEHOLD ON OUR TOWN, THE VOTERS BEAT HIM—THAT'S HOW I CAME TO THE SENATE...
FUNNY THING, THO— COULDN'T FIGURE OUT HOW IT HAPPENED—— GUS AND HIS MEN JUST LEFT TOWN THE DAY AFTER ELECTION IN 1932— WE'VE HAD CLEAN POLITICS IN OUR TOWN EVER SINCE—

JOHNNY THUNDER appears in every issue of FLASH Comics!

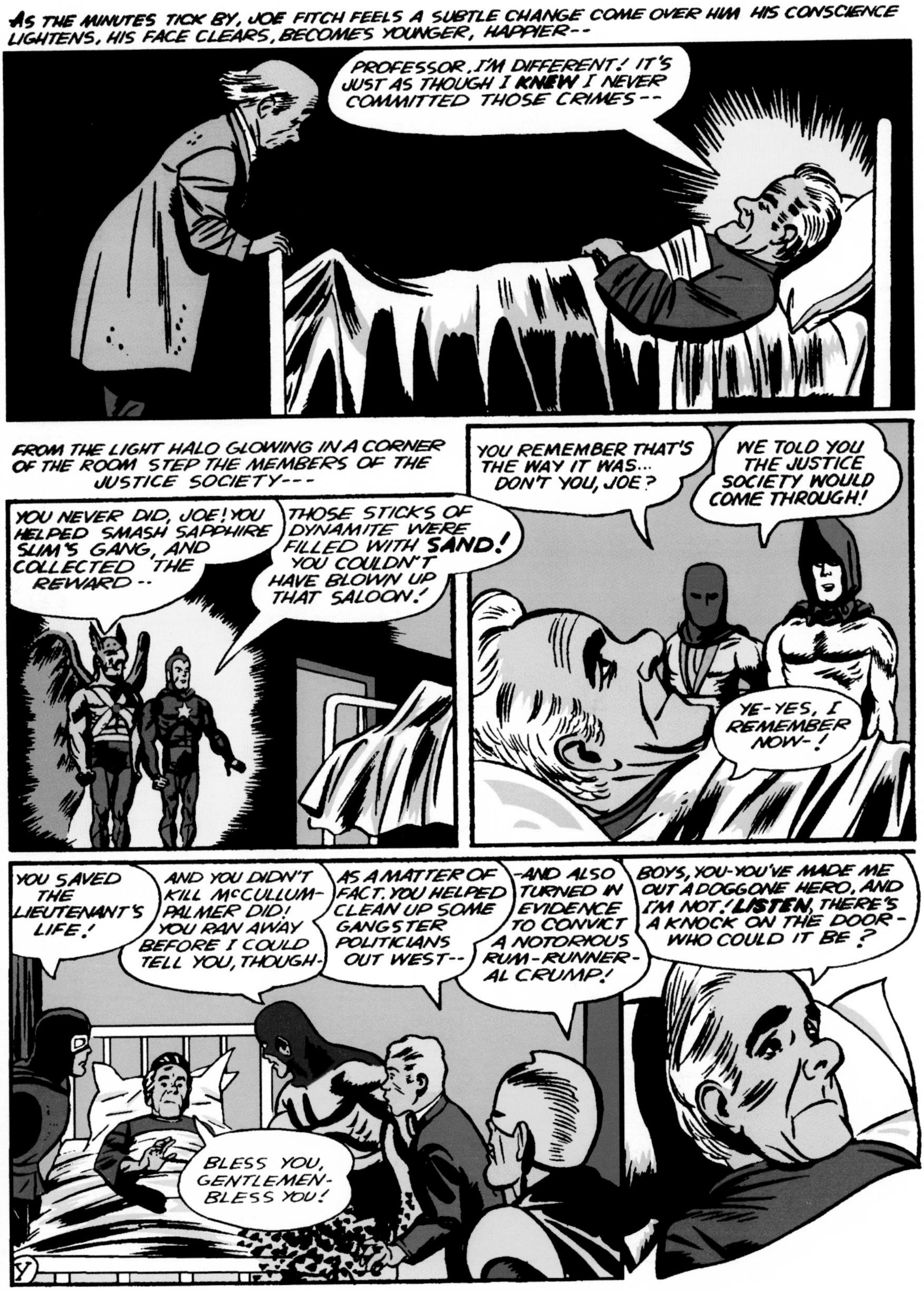
AS THE MINUTES TICK BY, JOE FITCH FEELS A SUBTLE CHANGE COME OVER HIM HIS CONSCIENCE LIGHTENS, HIS FACE CLEARS, BECOMES YOUNGER, HAPPIER--
PROFESSOR, I'M DIFFERENT! IT'S JUST AS THOUGH I KNEW I NEVER COMMITTED THOSE CRIMES--
FROM THE LIGHT HALO GLOWING IN A CORNER OF THE ROOM STEP THE MEMBERS OF THE JUSTICE SOCIETY---
YOU NEVER DID, JOE! YOU HELPED SMASH SAPPHIRE SLIM'S GANG, AND COLLECTED THE REWARD--
THOSE STICKS OF DYNAMITE WERE FILLED WITH SAND! YOU COULDN'T HAVE BLOWN UP THAT SALOON!
YOU REMEMBER THAT'S THE WAY IT WAS... DON'T YOU, JOE?
WE TOLD YOU THE JUSTICE SOCIETY WOULD COME THROUGH!
YE-YES, I REMEMBER NOW-!
YOU SAVED THE LIEUTENANT'S LIFE!
AND YOU DIDN'T KILL McCULLUM-PALMER DID! YOU RAN AWAY BEFORE I COULD TELL YOU, THOUGH-
AS A MATTER OF FACT, YOU HELPED CLEAN UP SOME GANGSTER POLITICIANS OUT WEST--
-AND ALSO TURNED IN EVIDENCE TO CONVICT A NOTORIOUS RUM-RUNNER-AL CRUMP!
BLESS YOU, GENTLEMEN-BLESS YOU!
BOYS, YOU-YOU'VE MADE ME OUT A DOGGONE HERO, AND I'M NOT! LISTEN, THERE'S A KNOCK ON THE DOOR-WHO COULD IT BE?

Collect Old Paper, Turn It In — Help Your Uncle Sam to Win

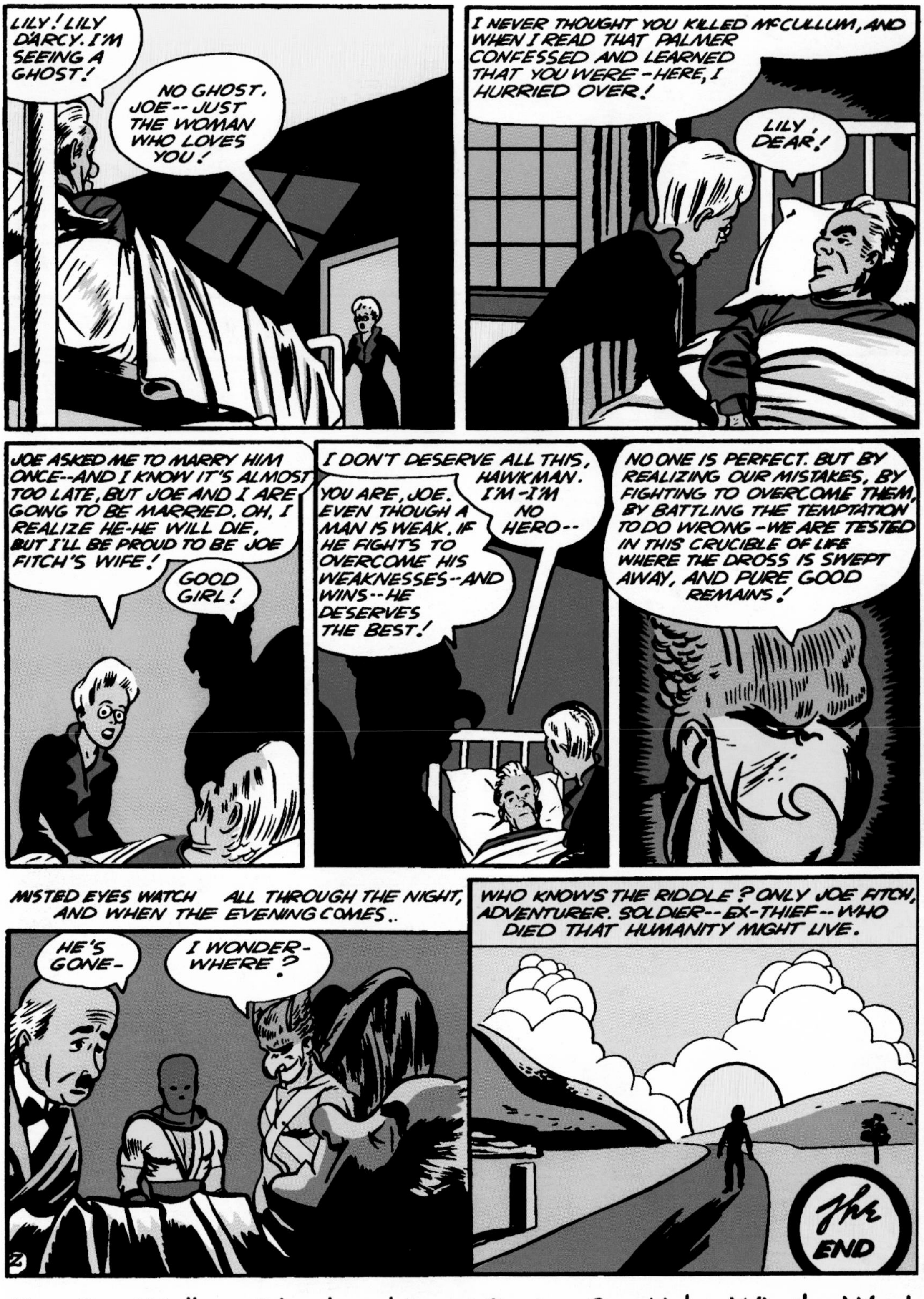
LILY! LILY D'ARCY. I'M SEEING A GHOST!
NO GHOST, JOE -- JUST THE WOMAN WHO LOVES YOU!
I NEVER THOUGHT YOU KILLED McCULLUM, AND WHEN I READ THAT PALMER CONFESSED AND LEARNED THAT YOU WERE - HERE, I HURRIED OVER!
LILY, DEAR!
JOE ASKED ME TO MARRY HIM ONCE -- AND I KNOW IT'S ALMOST TOO LATE, BUT JOE AND I ARE GOING TO BE MARRIED. OH, I REALIZE HE-HE WILL DIE, BUT I'LL BE PROUD TO BE JOE FITCH'S WIFE!
GOOD GIRL!
I DON'T DESERVE ALL THIS, HAWKMAN. I'M -I'M NO HERO--
YOU ARE, JOE. EVEN THOUGH A MAN IS WEAK, IF HE FIGHTS TO OVERCOME HIS WEAKNESSES -- AND WINS -- HE DESERVES THE BEST!
NO ONE IS PERFECT. BUT BY REALIZING OUR MISTAKES, BY FIGHTING TO OVERCOME THEM, BY BATTLING THE TEMPTATION TO DO WRONG - WE ARE TESTED IN THIS CRUCIBLE OF LIFE WHERE THE DROSS IS SWEPT AWAY, AND PURE GOOD REMAINS!
MISTED EYES WATCH ALL THROUGH THE NIGHT, AND WHEN THE EVENING COMES..
HE'S GONE-
I WONDER-WHERE?
WHO KNOWS THE RIDDLE? ONLY JOE FITCH, ADVENTURER. SOLDIER -- EX-THIEF -- WHO DIED THAT HUMANITY MIGHT LIVE.
The END

You Can Walk to School and Store! Saving Gas Helps Win the War!

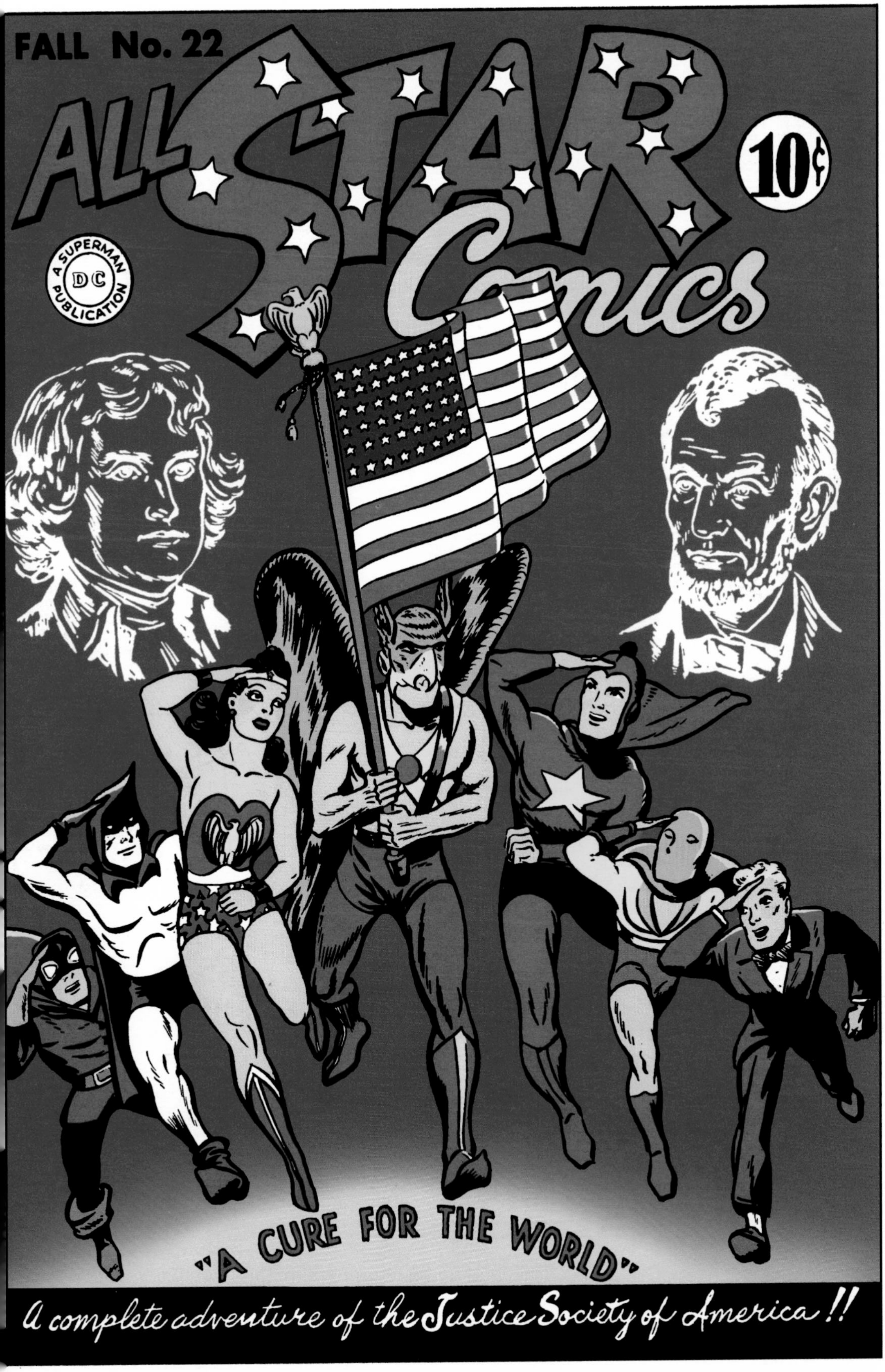
FALL No. 22
ALL STAR Comics
10¢
A SUPERMAN DC PUBLICATION
"A CURE FOR THE WORLD"
A complete adventure of the Justice Society of America!!

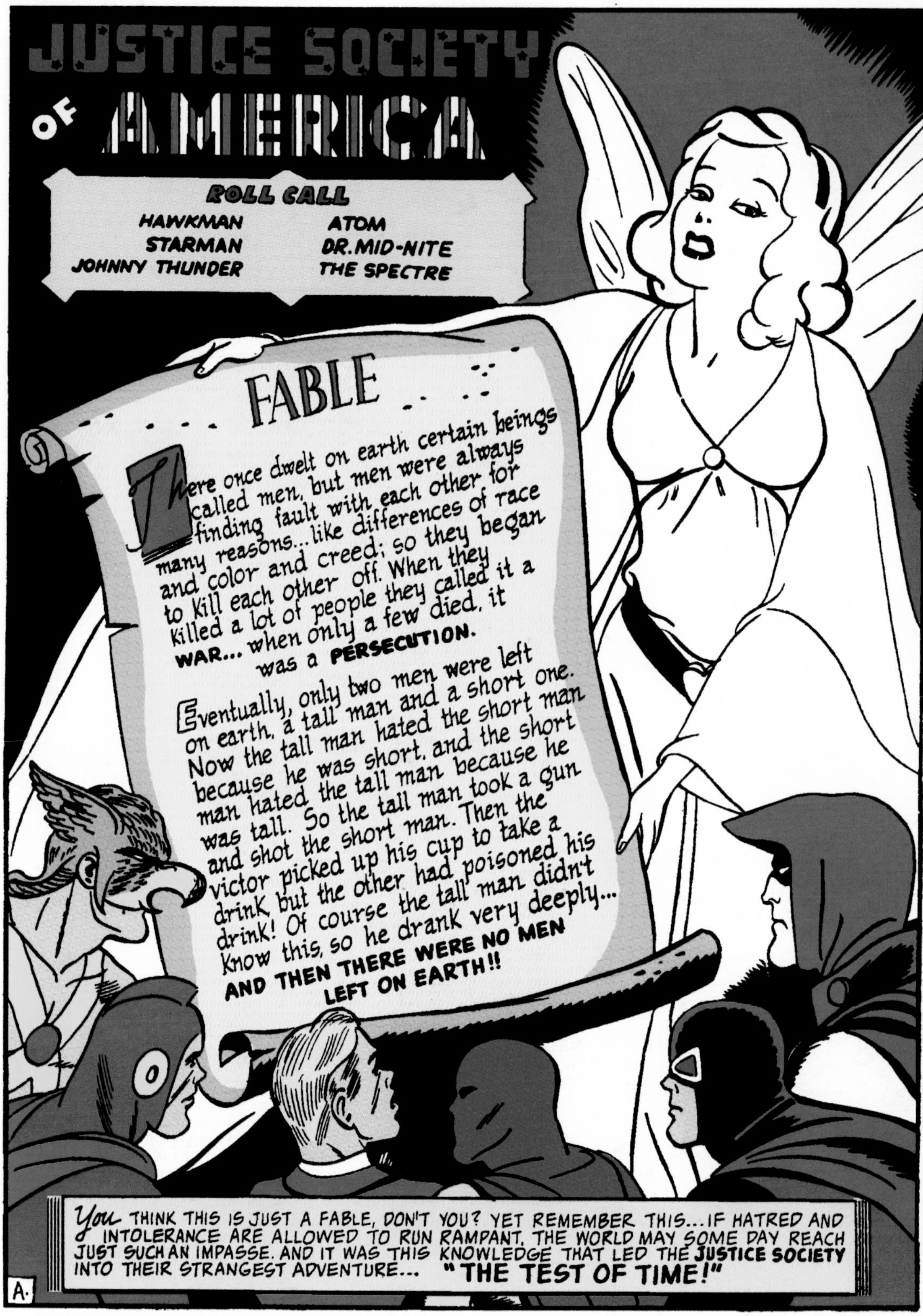
JUSTICE SOCIETY OF AMERICA
ROLL CALL
HAWKMAN
STARMAN
JOHNNY THUNDER
ATOM
DR. MID-NITE
THE SPECTRE
FABLE
There once dwelt on earth certain beings called men, but men were always finding fault with each other for many reasons... like differences of race and color and creed; so they began to kill each other off. When they killed a lot of people they called it a WAR... when only a few died, it was a PERSECUTION.
Eventually, only two men were left on earth, a tall man and a short one. Now the tall man hated the short man because he was short, and the short man hated the tall man because he was tall. So the tall man took a gun and shot the short man. Then the victor picked up his cup to take a drink, but the other had poisoned his drink! Of course the tall man didn't know this, so he drank very deeply... AND THEN THERE WERE NO MEN LEFT ON EARTH!!
YOU THINK THIS IS JUST A FABLE, DON'T YOU? YET REMEMBER THIS... IF HATRED AND INTOLERANCE ARE ALLOWED TO RUN RAMPANT, THE WORLD MAY SOME DAY REACH JUST SUCH AN IMPASSE. AND IT WAS THIS KNOWLEDGE THAT LED THE JUSTICE SOCIETY INTO THEIR STRANGEST ADVENTURE... "THE TEST OF TIME!"
A.

ON HIS WAY TO THE MONTHLY MEETING OF THE JUSTICE SOCIETY, DR. MIDNITE COMES TO A SUDDEN STOP...

OWTCH! CUT IT OUT! PLEASE, FELLAS...THAT HURT! OWW!

YEAH...WE JUST DON'T LIKE YOU, SEE? STAY AWAY FROM HERE...

OH-OH!

THIS'LL TEACH YA!

GOSH, IT-IT'S **DOCTOR MIDNITE!**

HOLY SMOKE! -IMAGINE SEEIN' YOU ON A CASE!

YOU OUT TO CATCH SOME CROOKS?

RIGHT NOW, YOU BOYS ARE MY "CASE"! WHY WERE YOU BEATING UP THIS YOUNGSTER?

AW, HIM! HE GOES TO A DIFFERENT CHURCH FROM US, WE-WE GO TO THAT RED ONE OVER THERE, BUT HE GOES TO THAT GREY ONE DOWN THE STREET!

YEAH, SO WE WANTED HIM TO KNOW WE WAS BETTER'N HIM, THAT'S ALL!

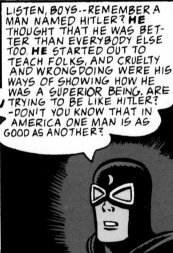

LISTEN, BOYS--REMEMBER A MAN NAMED HITLER? **HE** THOUGHT THAT HE WAS BETTER THAN EVERYBODY ELSE TOO. **HE** STARTED OUT TO TEACH FOLKS, AND CRUELTY AND WRONGDOING WERE HIS WAYS OF SHOWING HOW HE WAS A SUPERIOR BEING. ARE **YOU** TRYING TO BE LIKE HITLER? -DON'T YOU KNOW THAT IN AMERICA ONE MAN IS AS GOOD AS ANOTHER?

I'M DISAPPOINTED IN YOU. YOU'VE FORGOTTEN OUR COUNTRY'S GREAT DECLARATION OF INDEPENDENCE--"WE HOLD THESE TRUTHS TO BE SELF-EVIDENT-- **THAT ALL MEN ARE CREATED EQUAL...**"

AW, WE DIDN'T THINK, DR. MIDNITE!

YEAH, WE AIN'T NO HITLERITES, HONEST!

YOU'RE OKAY, FELLA!

YEAH, AN'IF ANYBODY PICKS ON YOU AFTER THIS, JUST TELL US!

TH-THANKS, GUYS!

COME WITH ME, YOUNGSTER -I WANT TO TELL YOUR STORY TO SOME FRIENDS OF MINE..

At JUSTICE SOCIETY HEADQUARTERS..

HMM---DR. MIDNITE IS A BIT LATE, BUT I'LL EXPLAIN THE BUSINESS AT HAND ANYWAY. CRIME IN THE UNDERWORLD HAS...

ONE MOMENT, PLEASE!.. -THERE'S SOMEONE I WANT YOU ALL TO MEET!

GULP!! THE-**THE JUSTICE SOCIETY!** HAWKMAN-STARMAN... **ALL** OF 'EM! **GOLLY!**

FELLOW MEMBERS, WE'VE GATHERED TO FIGHT CRIME. BUT NOW WE HAVE TO FIGHT SOMETHING **BIGGER! A CRIME AGAINST HUMANITY!** THIS BOY WAS JUST BEATEN UP BY A GANG... **WHY?**

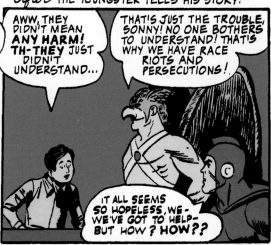

After THE YOUNGSTER TELLS HIS STORY!

AWW, THEY DIDN'T MEAN **ANY HARM!** TH-THEY JUST DIDN'T UNDERSTAND...

THAT'S JUST THE TROUBLE, SONNY! NO ONE BOTHERS TO UNDERSTAND! THAT'S WHY WE HAVE RACE RIOTS AND PERSECUTIONS!

IT ALL SEEMS SO HOPELESS, WE-WE'VE GOT TO HELP-BUT HOW? **HOW??**

AT THAT MOMENT, FAR OFF IN SPACE, AMIDST A SWIRLING CLOUD OF NEBULAE, A STRANGE FIGURE STIRS...

SOMEWHERE, THE SORROWING THOUGHTS OF MEN ARE BEATING THRU THE DIMENSIONS THAT SEPARATE US -- THEIR CONCENTRATED THOUGHTS ARE CALLING ME! **I MUST GO TO THEM AT ONCE!**

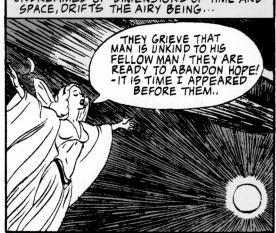

ACROSS A MILLION LIGHT-YEARS, THROUGH UNDREAMED-OF DIMENSIONS OF TIME AND SPACE, DRIFTS THE AIRY BEING...

THEY GRIEVE THAT MAN IS UNKIND TO HIS FELLOW MAN! THEY ARE READY TO ABANDON HOPE! -IT IS TIME I APPEARED BEFORE THEM..

WHO ARE-WHO ARE YOU?

YOU BROUGHT ME HERE. YOUR DEEP CONCENTRATION ON THE PROBLEM FACING YOU HAS MADE ME MATERIALIZE! YOU DESPAIR BECAUSE YOU WISH TO MAKE MEN UNDERSTAND THEIR FELLOWS? I HAVE A SOLUTION!

YOU MEAN FOLKS WOULD LEARN TO LIKE EACH OTHER? -THERE **IS** A WAY TO HELP THEM?

WHAT IS IT?

NOT SO FAST! THE KNOWLEDGE I BRING MUST BE EARNED BY YOU! ARE YOU ALL WILLING TO UNDERGO MY TEST?

REMEMBER--IT WILL NOT BE EASY! I WILL SEND YOU INTO THE PAST, WHERE YOU WILL LOSE ALL KNOWLEDGE THAT HISTORY AND SCIENCE HAS GATHERED THRU THE CENTURIES! AS MEN OF THE STONE AGE OR MEDIEVAL EUROPE, YOU WILL FACE AND PERHAPS SHARE THE PREJUDICE OF THOSE DAYS!

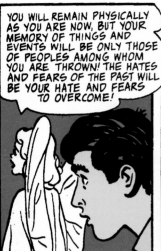

YOU WILL REMAIN PHYSICALLY AS YOU ARE NOW, BUT YOUR MEMORY OF THINGS AND EVENTS WILL BE ONLY THOSE OF PEOPLES AMONG WHOM YOU ARE THROWN! THE HATES AND FEARS OF THE PAST WILL BE YOUR HATE AND FEARS TO OVERCOME!

IN OTHER WORDS, YOUR PURPOSE IS TO TEST US BY SETTING UP AS OUR OPPONENTS THE VARIOUS PREJUDICES AND HATREDS OF THE PAST!

AND WE'LL FIGHT THEM AS A GREEK OR A ROMAN OR A STONE AGE MAN?

EXACTLY!

WE'LL TRY YOUR TEST!

SURE WE WILL!

IT WILL BE A PRIVILEGE!

GOLLY! IMAGINE SEEIN' ALL THIS HAPPENING --ALL ON ACCOUNTA ME GETTIN' BEAT UP!

REMEMBER, IF YOU LET THE DIFFICULTIES OF THE PAST OVERCOME YOU, YOU **FAIL!**

WE UNDERSTAND! WE'RE READY, WILLING AND, WE HOPE-ABLE!

AS THE STRANGE VISITOR GESTURES, A QUEER COLDNESS GATHERS IN THE ROOM...

I POSSESS POWER OVER THE WARDS OF TIME AND SPACE. I OPEN THE SECRET PASSAGES OF THE BEYOND SO THAT YOU MAY PASS THRU TO YOUR APPOINTED TASKS...

One BY ONE, THE MEMBERS DISAPPEAR INTO SWIRLING VACUUMS, TO BE TOSSED INSTANTLY BACKWARDS, CENTURIES INTO THE PAST

MAY YOU SUCCEED, EACH OF YOU-FOR THE FUTURE OF THE HUMAN RACE MAY WELL DEPEND ON WHAT YOU DO...

EXCUSE ME-BUT YOU DON'T KNOW THOSE GUYS VERY WELL, DO YOU?--SEE-THEY AIN'T NEVER FAILED YET-AN' I BET THEY DON'T FAIL NOW, EITHER!

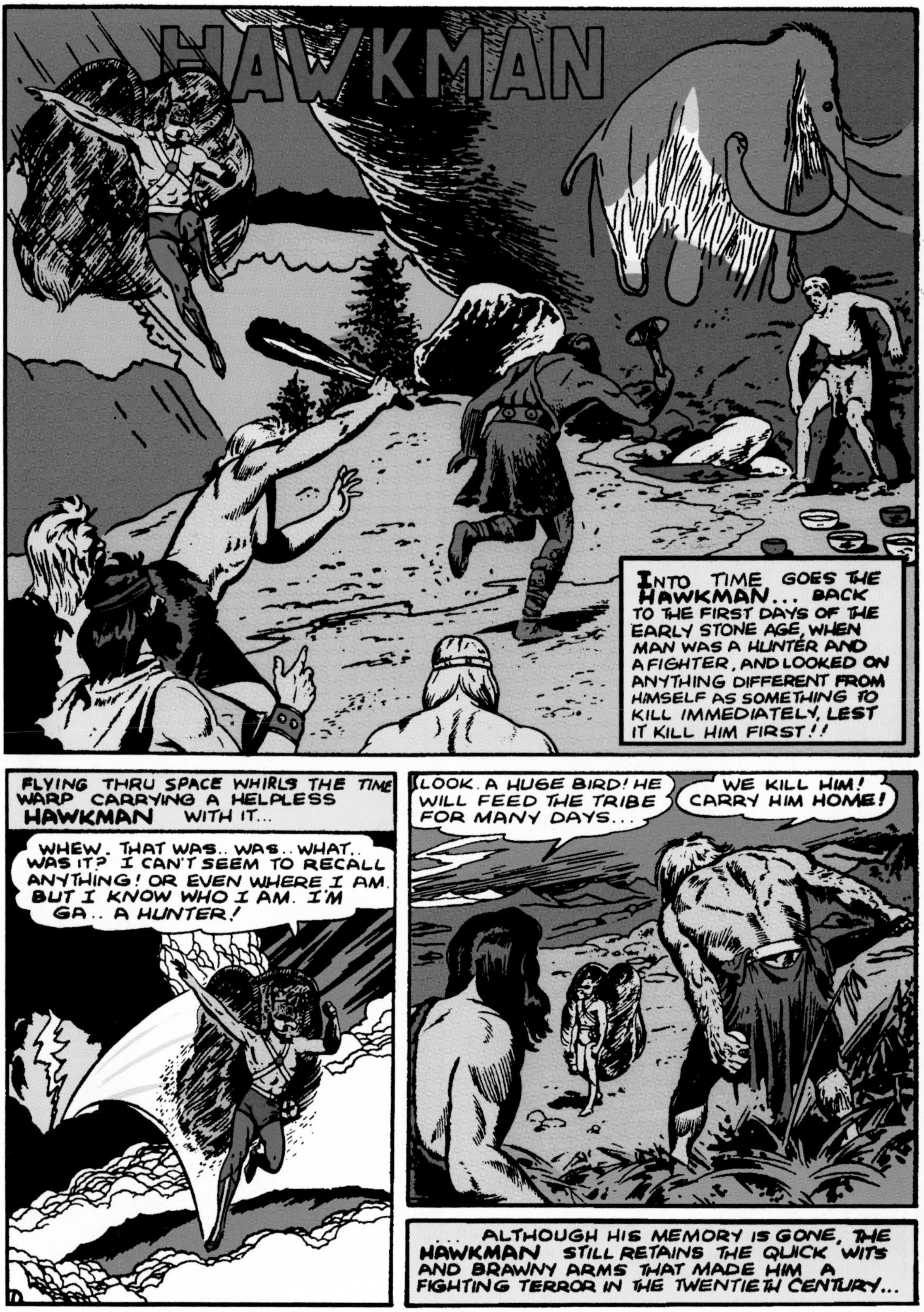
HAWKMAN
INTO TIME GOES THE HAWKMAN... BACK TO THE FIRST DAYS OF THE EARLY STONE AGE, WHEN MAN WAS A HUNTER AND A FIGHTER, AND LOOKED ON ANYTHING DIFFERENT FROM HIMSELF AS SOMETHING TO KILL IMMEDIATELY, LEST IT KILL HIM FIRST!!
FLYING THRU SPACE WHIRLS THE TIME WARP CARRYING A HELPLESS HAWKMAN WITH IT...
WHEW. THAT WAS.. WAS.. WHAT.. WAS IT? I CAN'T SEEM TO RECALL ANYTHING! OR EVEN WHERE I AM. BUT I KNOW WHO I AM. I'M GA.. A HUNTER!
LOOK. A HUGE BIRD! HE WILL FEED THE TRIBE FOR MANY DAYS...
WE KILL HIM! CARRY HIM HOME!
... ALTHOUGH HIS MEMORY IS GONE, THE HAWKMAN STILL RETAINS THE QUICK WITS AND BRAWNY ARMS THAT MADE HIM A FIGHTING TERROR IN THE TWENTIETH CENTURY...

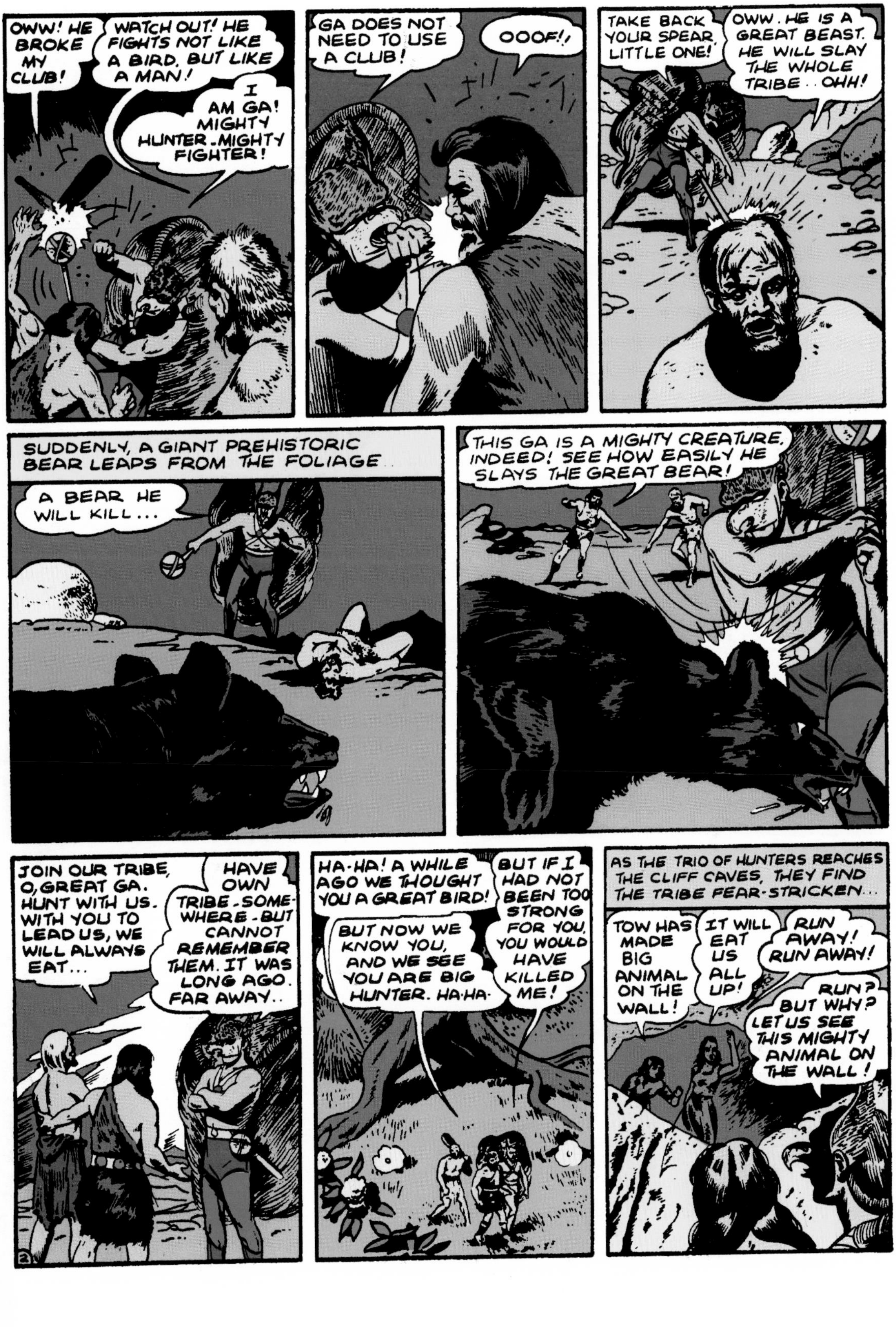
OWW! HE BROKE MY CLUB!
WATCH OUT! HE FIGHTS NOT LIKE A BIRD, BUT LIKE A MAN!
I AM GA! MIGHTY HUNTER - MIGHTY FIGHTER!
GA DOES NOT NEED TO USE A CLUB!
OOOF!,
TAKE BACK YOUR SPEAR, LITTLE ONE!
OWW. HE IS A GREAT BEAST. HE WILL SLAY THE WHOLE TRIBE .. OHH!
SUDDENLY, A GIANT PREHISTORIC BEAR LEAPS FROM THE FOLIAGE ..
A BEAR HE WILL KILL ...
THIS GA IS A MIGHTY CREATURE, INDEED! SEE HOW EASILY HE SLAYS THE GREAT BEAR!
JOIN OUR TRIBE, O, GREAT GA. HUNT WITH US. WITH YOU TO LEAD US, WE WILL ALWAYS EAT...
HAVE OWN TRIBE - SOMEWHERE - BUT CANNOT REMEMBER THEM. IT WAS LONG AGO. FAR AWAY..
HA-HA! A WHILE AGO WE THOUGHT YOU A GREAT BIRD!
BUT NOW WE KNOW YOU, AND WE SEE YOU ARE BIG HUNTER. HA-HA-
BUT IF I HAD NOT BEEN TOO STRONG FOR YOU, YOU WOULD HAVE KILLED ME!
AS THE TRIO OF HUNTERS REACHES THE CLIFF CAVES, THEY FIND THE TRIBE FEAR-STRICKEN...
TOW HAS MADE BIG ANIMAL ON THE WALL!
IT WILL EAT US ALL UP!
RUN AWAY! RUN AWAY!
RUN? BUT WHY? LET US SEE THIS MIGHTY ANIMAL ON THE WALL!

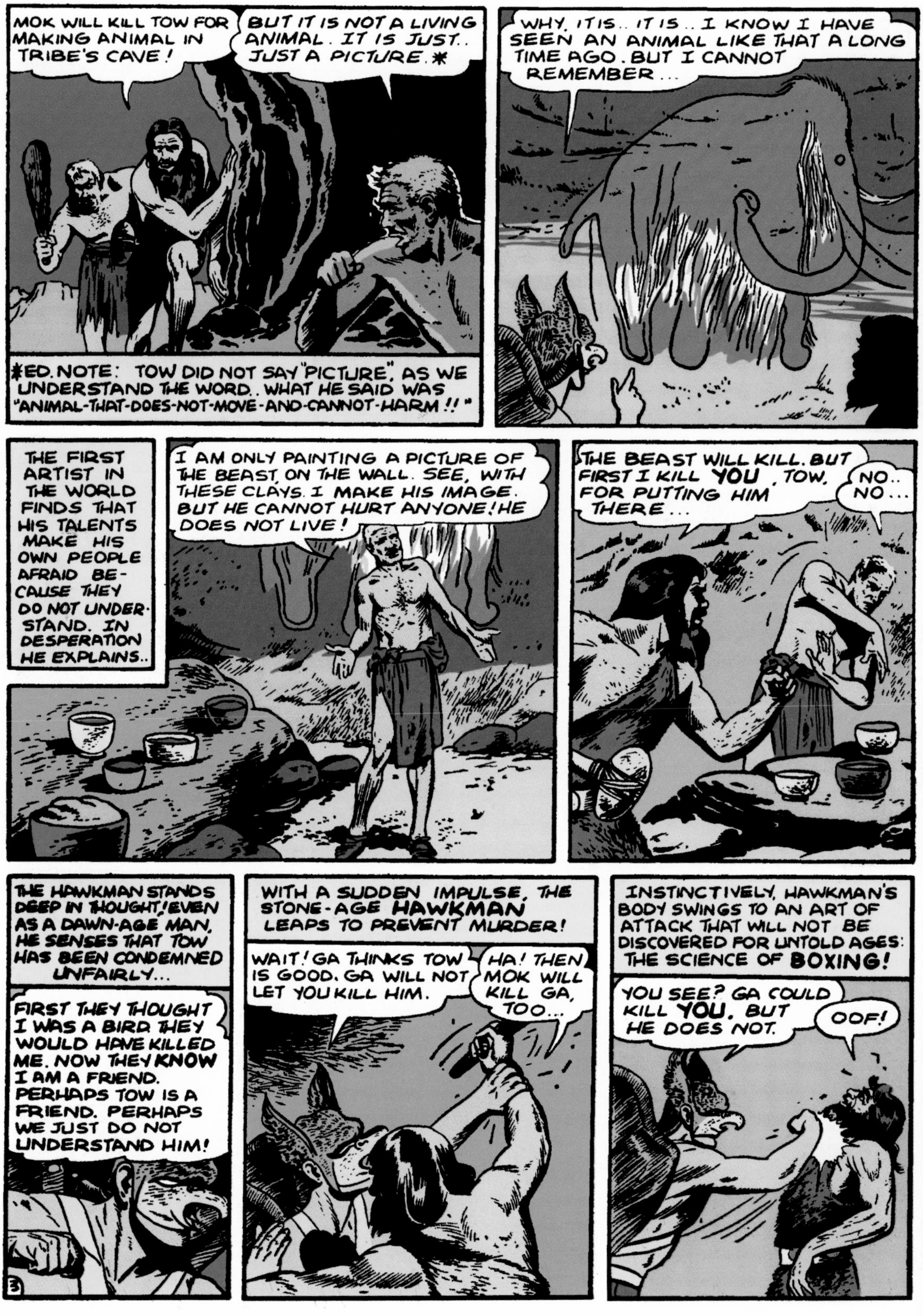
MOK WILL KILL TOW FOR MAKING ANIMAL IN TRIBE'S CAVE!
BUT IT IS NOT A LIVING ANIMAL. IT IS JUST.. JUST A PICTURE.*
*ED. NOTE: TOW DID NOT SAY "PICTURE", AS WE UNDERSTAND THE WORD.. WHAT HE SAID WAS "ANIMAL-THAT-DOES-NOT-MOVE-AND-CANNOT-HARM!!"
WHY, IT IS.. IT IS.. I KNOW I HAVE SEEN AN ANIMAL LIKE THAT A LONG TIME AGO. BUT I CANNOT REMEMBER...
THE FIRST ARTIST IN THE WORLD FINDS THAT HIS TALENTS MAKE HIS OWN PEOPLE AFRAID BECAUSE THEY DO NOT UNDERSTAND. IN DESPERATION HE EXPLAINS..
I AM ONLY PAINTING A PICTURE OF THE BEAST, ON THE WALL. SEE, WITH THESE CLAYS. I MAKE HIS IMAGE. BUT HE CANNOT HURT ANYONE! HE DOES NOT LIVE!
THE BEAST WILL KILL. BUT FIRST I KILL YOU, TOW, FOR PUTTING HIM THERE...
NO.. NO...
THE HAWKMAN STANDS DEEP IN THOUGHT! EVEN AS A DAWN-AGE MAN, HE SENSES THAT TOW HAS BEEN CONDEMNED UNFAIRLY...
FIRST THEY THOUGHT I WAS A BIRD THEY WOULD HAVE KILLED ME. NOW THEY KNOW I AM A FRIEND. PERHAPS TOW IS A FRIEND. PERHAPS WE JUST DO NOT UNDERSTAND HIM!
3
WITH A SUDDEN IMPULSE, THE STONE-AGE HAWKMAN LEAPS TO PREVENT MURDER!
WAIT! GA THINKS TOW IS GOOD. GA WILL NOT LET YOU KILL HIM.
HA! THEN MOK WILL KILL GA, TOO...
INSTINCTIVELY, HAWKMAN'S BODY SWINGS TO AN ART OF ATTACK THAT WILL NOT BE DISCOVERED FOR UNTOLD AGES: THE SCIENCE OF BOXING!
YOU SEE? GA COULD KILL YOU. BUT HE DOES NOT.
OOF!

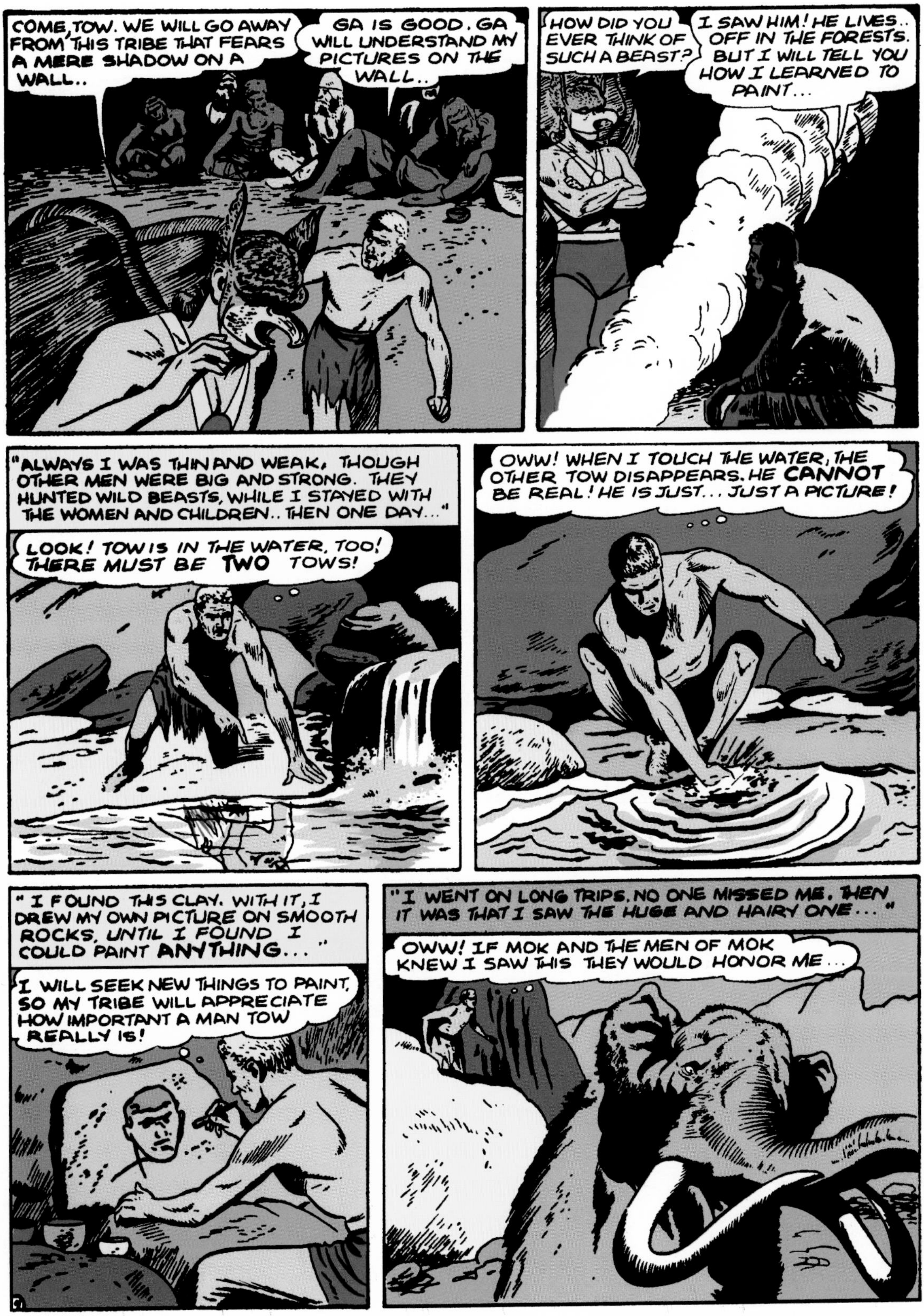
COME, TOW. WE WILL GO AWAY FROM THIS TRIBE THAT FEARS A MERE SHADOW ON A WALL..
GA IS GOOD. GA WILL UNDERSTAND MY PICTURES ON THE WALL..
HOW DID YOU EVER THINK OF SUCH A BEAST?
I SAW HIM! HE LIVES.. OFF IN THE FORESTS. BUT I WILL TELL YOU HOW I LEARNED TO PAINT...
"ALWAYS I WAS THIN AND WEAK, THOUGH OTHER MEN WERE BIG AND STRONG. THEY HUNTED WILD BEASTS, WHILE I STAYED WITH THE WOMEN AND CHILDREN.. THEN ONE DAY..."
LOOK! TOW IS IN THE WATER, TOO! THERE MUST BE TWO TOWS!
OWW! WHEN I TOUCH THE WATER, THE OTHER TOW DISAPPEARS. HE CANNOT BE REAL! HE IS JUST... JUST A PICTURE!
"I FOUND THIS CLAY. WITH IT, I DREW MY OWN PICTURE ON SMOOTH ROCKS, UNTIL I FOUND I COULD PAINT ANYTHING..."
I WILL SEEK NEW THINGS TO PAINT, SO MY TRIBE WILL APPRECIATE HOW IMPORTANT A MAN TOW REALLY IS!
"I WENT ON LONG TRIPS. NO ONE MISSED ME. THEN IT WAS THAT I SAW THE HUGE AND HAIRY ONE..."
OWW! IF MOK AND THE MEN OF MOK KNEW I SAW THIS THEY WOULD HONOR ME...

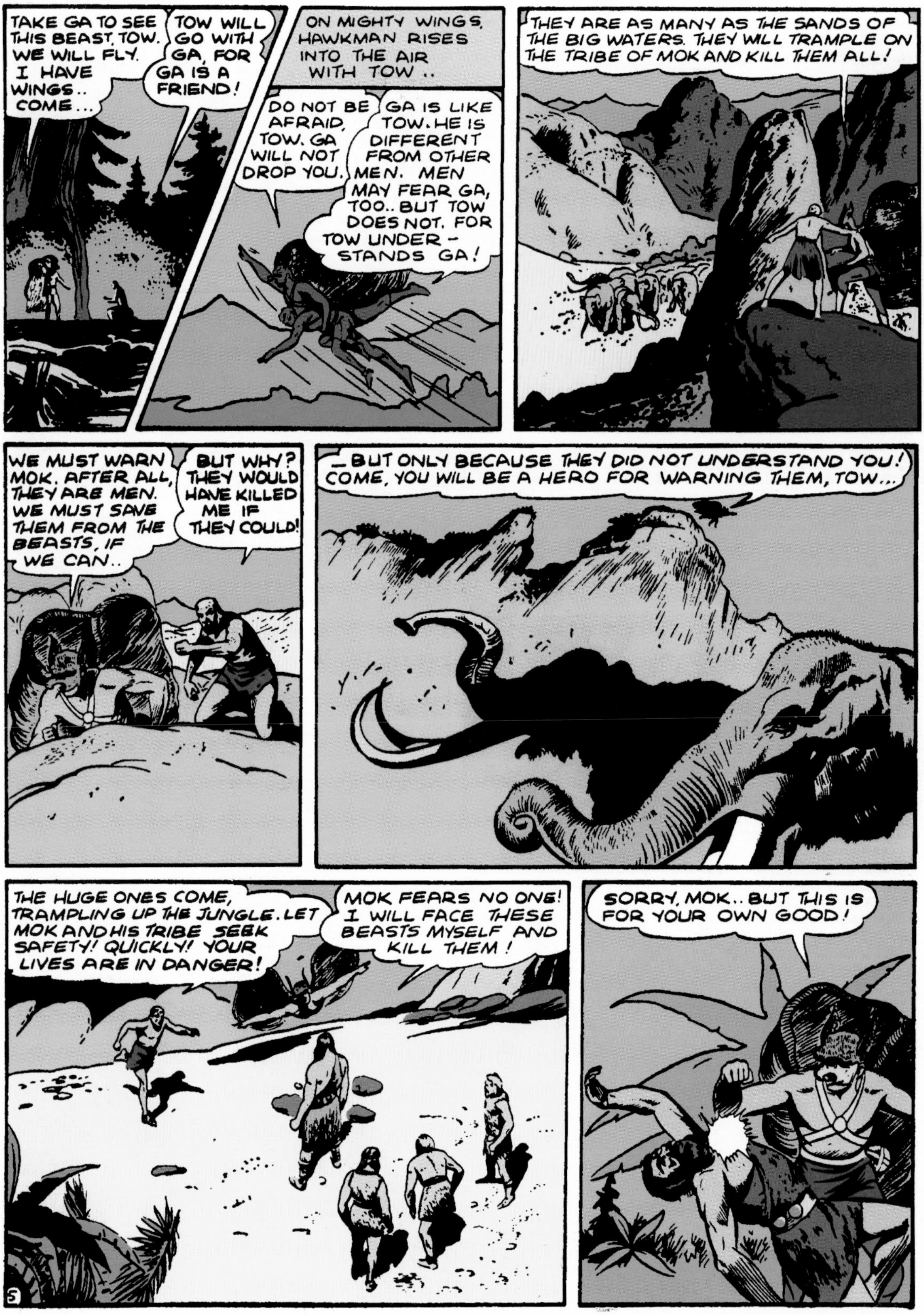

TAKE GA TO SEE THIS BEAST, TOW. WE WILL FLY. I HAVE WINGS.. COME...
TOW WILL GO WITH GA, FOR GA IS A FRIEND!
ON MIGHTY WINGS, HAWKMAN RISES INTO THE AIR WITH TOW ..
DO NOT BE AFRAID, TOW. GA WILL NOT DROP YOU.
GA IS LIKE TOW. HE IS DIFFERENT FROM OTHER MEN. MEN MAY FEAR GA, TOO.. BUT TOW DOES NOT. FOR TOW UNDER-STANDS GA!
THEY ARE AS MANY AS THE SANDS OF THE BIG WATERS. THEY WILL TRAMPLE ON THE TRIBE OF MOK AND KILL THEM ALL!
WE MUST WARN MOK. AFTER ALL, THEY ARE MEN. WE MUST SAVE THEM FROM THE BEASTS, IF WE CAN..
BUT WHY? THEY WOULD HAVE KILLED ME IF THEY COULD!
—BUT ONLY BECAUSE THEY DID NOT UNDERSTAND YOU! COME, YOU WILL BE A HERO FOR WARNING THEM, TOW...
THE HUGE ONES COME, TRAMPLING UP THE JUNGLE. LET MOK AND HIS TRIBE SEEK SAFETY! QUICKLY! YOUR LIVES ARE IN DANGER!
MOK FEARS NO ONE! I WILL FACE THESE BEASTS MYSELF AND KILL THEM!
5
SORRY, MOK.. BUT THIS IS FOR YOUR OWN GOOD!

CLIMB FOR YOUR LIVES. WHEN THE BEASTS COME, YOU WILL THANK TOW AND GA FOR WHAT THEY HAVE DONE.

WE WILL CLIMB!

HURRY HURRY!

FROM THE SAFETY OF STONE LEDGES, THE TRIBE OF MOK STARES DOWN AT WHAT WOULD HAVE BEEN THEIR DEATHBED..

THEN AS THE BEASTS THUNDER BY BELOW, THE FIRST PORTRAIT OF A MAN IS PAINTED!!

WHEN MOK SEES THAT, HE WILL BE MUCH PLEASED..

I-I HOPE SO.

LATER THAT SAME DAY..

OW! THIS IS GOOD. NOW THERE ARE TWO MOKS. TOW, YOU ARE A GOOD MAN. YOU WILL PAINT MANY OF THESE, AND I WILL GIVE YOU CHOICE BITS FROM MY OWN DINNER TABLE!

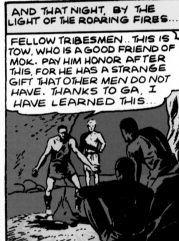

AND THAT NIGHT, BY THE LIGHT OF THE ROARING FIRES...

FELLOW TRIBESMEN.. THIS IS TOW, WHO IS A GOOD FRIEND OF MOK. PAY HIM HONOR AFTER THIS, FOR HE HAS A STRANGE GIFT THAT OTHER MEN DO NOT HAVE. THANKS TO GA, I HAVE LEARNED THIS...

SUDDENLY, A DAWN-AGE WOMAN SCREAMS! ALL ABOUT GA, THE HUNTER, THERE IS A STRANGE GLOW..

EEH! GA-GA IS DISAPPEARING!

HE CAME TO BRING US WISDOM. NOW HE GOES...

BUT WE SHALL NOT FORGET WHAT HE TAUGHT US. I, MOK, SWEAR TO THIS!!

BACK THROUGH THE AGES HURTLES THE HAWKMAN AT TERRIFIC SPEED, HIS TEST COMPLETED

HAWKMAN appears each month in Flash Comics- Don't miss it!

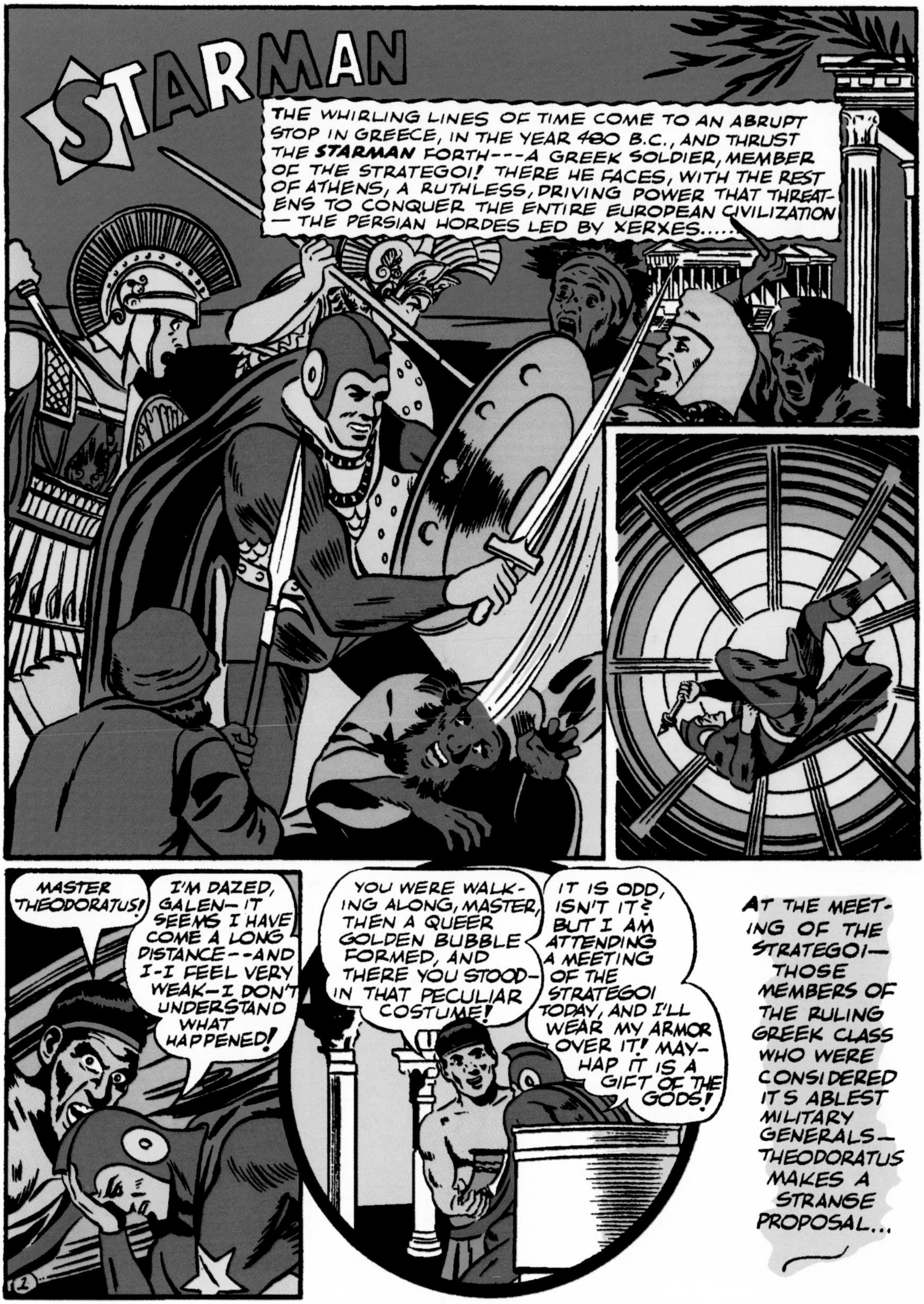
STARMAN
THE WHIRLING LINES OF TIME COME TO AN ABRUPT STOP IN GREECE, IN THE YEAR 480 B.C., AND THRUST THE STARMAN FORTH---A GREEK SOLDIER, MEMBER OF THE STRATEGOI! THERE HE FACES, WITH THE REST OF ATHENS, A RUTHLESS, DRIVING POWER THAT THREATENS TO CONQUER THE ENTIRE EUROPEAN CIVILIZATION — THE PERSIAN HORDES LED BY XERXES.....
MASTER THEODORATUS!
I'M DAZED, GALEN— IT SEEMS I HAVE COME A LONG DISTANCE--AND I-I FEEL VERY WEAK—I DON'T UNDERSTAND WHAT HAPPENED!
YOU WERE WALKING ALONG, MASTER, THEN A QUEER GOLDEN BUBBLE FORMED, AND THERE YOU STOOD—IN THAT PECULIAR COSTUME!
IT IS ODD, ISN'T IT? BUT I AM ATTENDING A MEETING OF THE STRATEGOI TODAY, AND I'LL WEAR MY ARMOR OVER IT! MAYHAP IT IS A GIFT OF THE GODS!
AT THE MEETING OF THE STRATEGOI— THOSE MEMBERS OF THE RULING GREEK CLASS WHO WERE CONSIDERED IT'S ABLEST MILITARY GENERALS— THEODORATUS MAKES A STRANGE PROPOSAL...

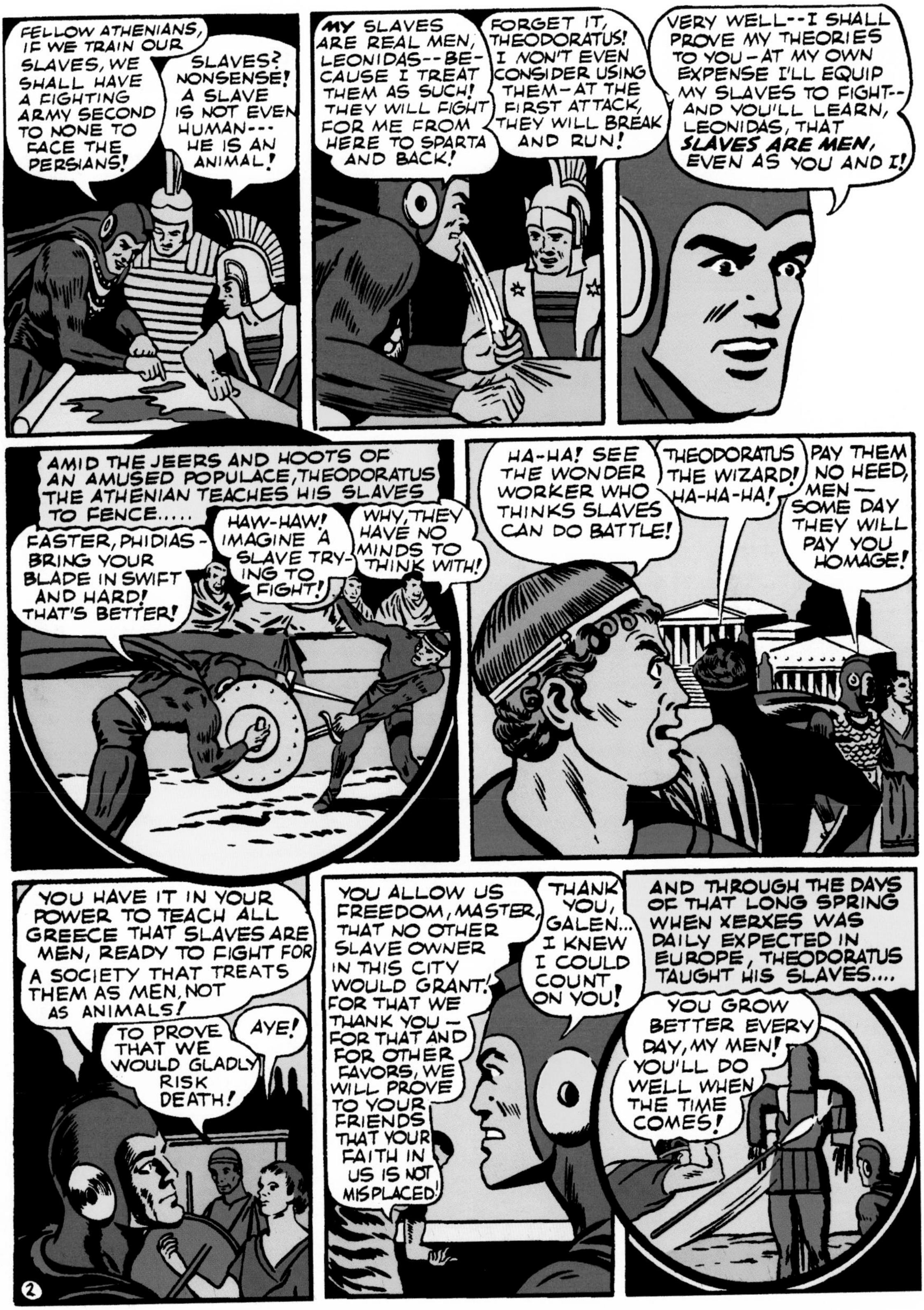
FELLOW ATHENIANS, IF WE TRAIN OUR SLAVES, WE SHALL HAVE A FIGHTING ARMY SECOND TO NONE TO FACE THE PERSIANS!
SLAVES? NONSENSE! A SLAVE IS NOT EVEN HUMAN--- HE IS AN ANIMAL!
MY SLAVES ARE REAL MEN, LEONIDAS--BECAUSE I TREAT THEM AS SUCH! THEY WILL FIGHT FOR ME FROM HERE TO SPARTA AND BACK!
FORGET IT, THEODORATUS! I WON'T EVEN CONSIDER USING THEM--AT THE FIRST ATTACK, THEY WILL BREAK AND RUN!
VERY WELL--I SHALL PROVE MY THEORIES TO YOU--AT MY OWN EXPENSE I'LL EQUIP MY SLAVES TO FIGHT--AND YOU'LL LEARN, LEONIDAS, THAT SLAVES ARE MEN, EVEN AS YOU AND I!
AMID THE JEERS AND HOOTS OF AN AMUSED POPULACE, THEODORATUS THE ATHENIAN TEACHES HIS SLAVES TO FENCE.....
FASTER, PHIDIAS--BRING YOUR BLADE IN SWIFT AND HARD! THAT'S BETTER!
HAW-HAW! IMAGINE A SLAVE TRYING TO FIGHT!
WHY, THEY HAVE NO MINDS TO THINK WITH!
HA-HA! SEE THE WONDER WORKER WHO THINKS SLAVES CAN DO BATTLE!
THEODORATUS THE WIZARD! HA-HA-HA!
PAY THEM NO HEED, MEN--SOME DAY THEY WILL PAY YOU HOMAGE!
YOU HAVE IT IN YOUR POWER TO TEACH ALL GREECE THAT SLAVES ARE MEN, READY TO FIGHT FOR A SOCIETY THAT TREATS THEM AS MEN, NOT AS ANIMALS!
TO PROVE THAT WE WOULD GLADLY RISK DEATH!
AYE!
2
YOU ALLOW US FREEDOM, MASTER, THAT NO OTHER SLAVE OWNER IN THIS CITY WOULD GRANT! FOR THAT WE THANK YOU--FOR THAT AND FOR OTHER FAVORS, WE WILL PROVE TO YOUR FRIENDS THAT YOUR FAITH IN US IS NOT MISPLACED!
THANK YOU, GALEN... I KNEW I COULD COUNT ON YOU!
AND THROUGH THE DAYS OF THAT LONG SPRING WHEN XERXES WAS DAILY EXPECTED IN EUROPE, THEODORATUS TAUGHT HIS SLAVES....
YOU GROW BETTER EVERY DAY, MY MEN! YOU'LL DO WELL WHEN THE TIME COMES!

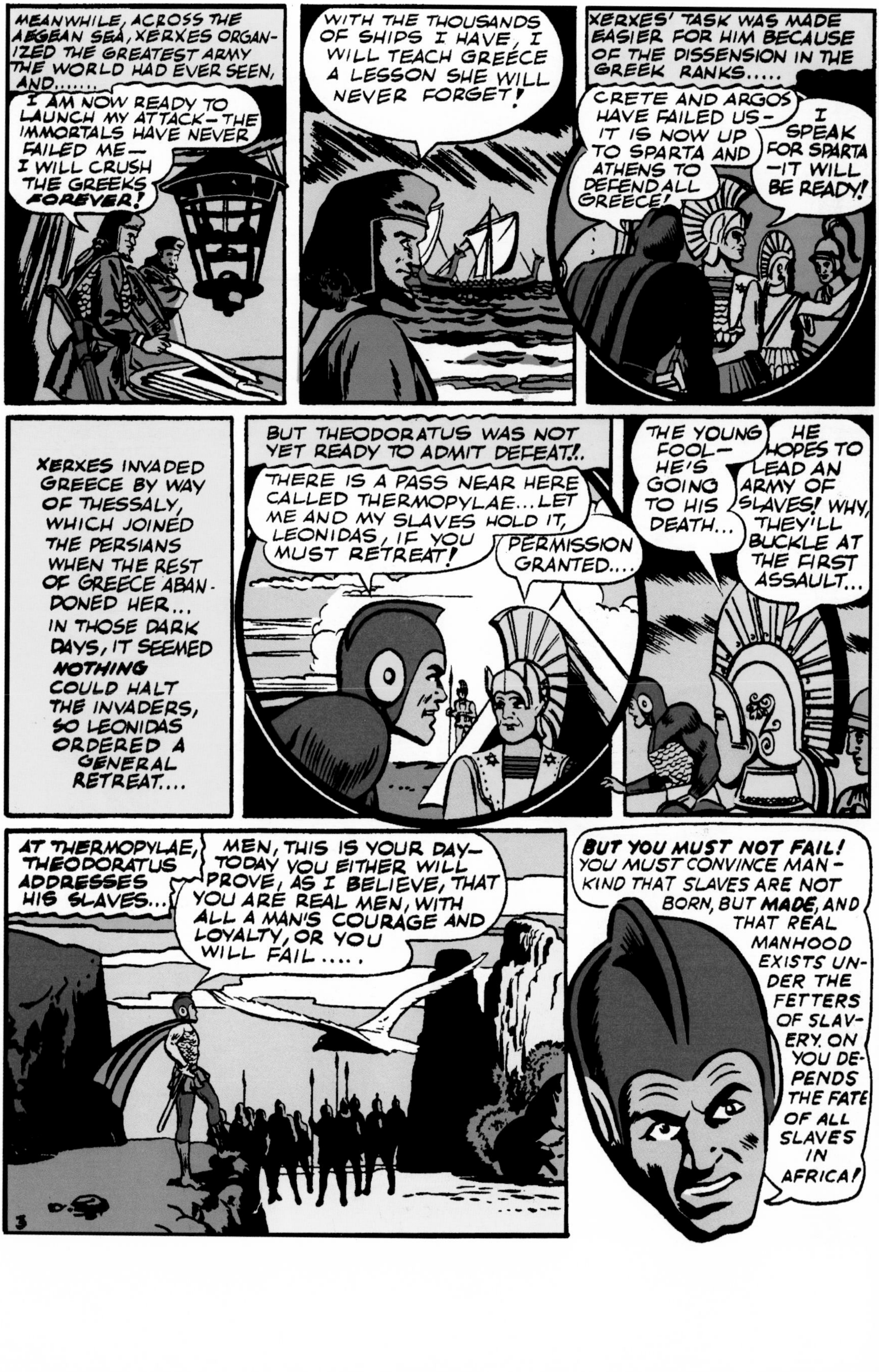
MEANWHILE, ACROSS THE AEGEAN SEA, XERXES ORGANIZED THE GREATEST ARMY THE WORLD HAD EVER SEEN, AND.......
I AM NOW READY TO LAUNCH MY ATTACK—THE IMMORTALS HAVE NEVER FAILED ME— I WILL CRUSH THE GREEKS FOREVER!
WITH THE THOUSANDS OF SHIPS I HAVE, I WILL TEACH GREECE A LESSON SHE WILL NEVER FORGET!
XERXES' TASK WAS MADE EASIER FOR HIM BECAUSE OF THE DISSENSION IN THE GREEK RANKS.....
CRETE AND ARGOS HAVE FAILED US—IT IS NOW UP TO SPARTA AND ATHENS TO DEFEND ALL GREECE!
I SPEAK FOR SPARTA —IT WILL BE READY!
XERXES INVADED GREECE BY WAY OF THESSALY, WHICH JOINED THE PERSIANS WHEN THE REST OF GREECE ABANDONED HER... IN THOSE DARK DAYS, IT SEEMED NOTHING COULD HALT THE INVADERS, SO LEONIDAS ORDERED A GENERAL RETREAT....
BUT THEODORATUS WAS NOT YET READY TO ADMIT DEFEAT!.
THERE IS A PASS NEAR HERE CALLED THERMOPYLAE...LET ME AND MY SLAVES HOLD IT, LEONIDAS, IF YOU MUST RETREAT!
PERMISSION GRANTED....
THE YOUNG FOOL—HE'S GOING TO HIS DEATH...
HE HOPES TO LEAD AN ARMY OF SLAVES! WHY, THEY'LL BUCKLE AT THE FIRST ASSAULT...
AT THERMOPYLAE, THEODORATUS ADDRESSES HIS SLAVES...
MEN, THIS IS YOUR DAY—TODAY YOU EITHER WILL PROVE, AS I BELIEVE, THAT YOU ARE REAL MEN, WITH ALL A MAN'S COURAGE AND LOYALTY, OR YOU WILL FAIL.....
BUT YOU MUST NOT FAIL! YOU MUST CONVINCE MANKIND THAT SLAVES ARE NOT BORN, BUT MADE, AND THAT REAL MANHOOD EXISTS UNDER THE FETTERS OF SLAVERY. ON YOU DEPENDS THE FATE OF ALL SLAVES IN AFRICA!
3

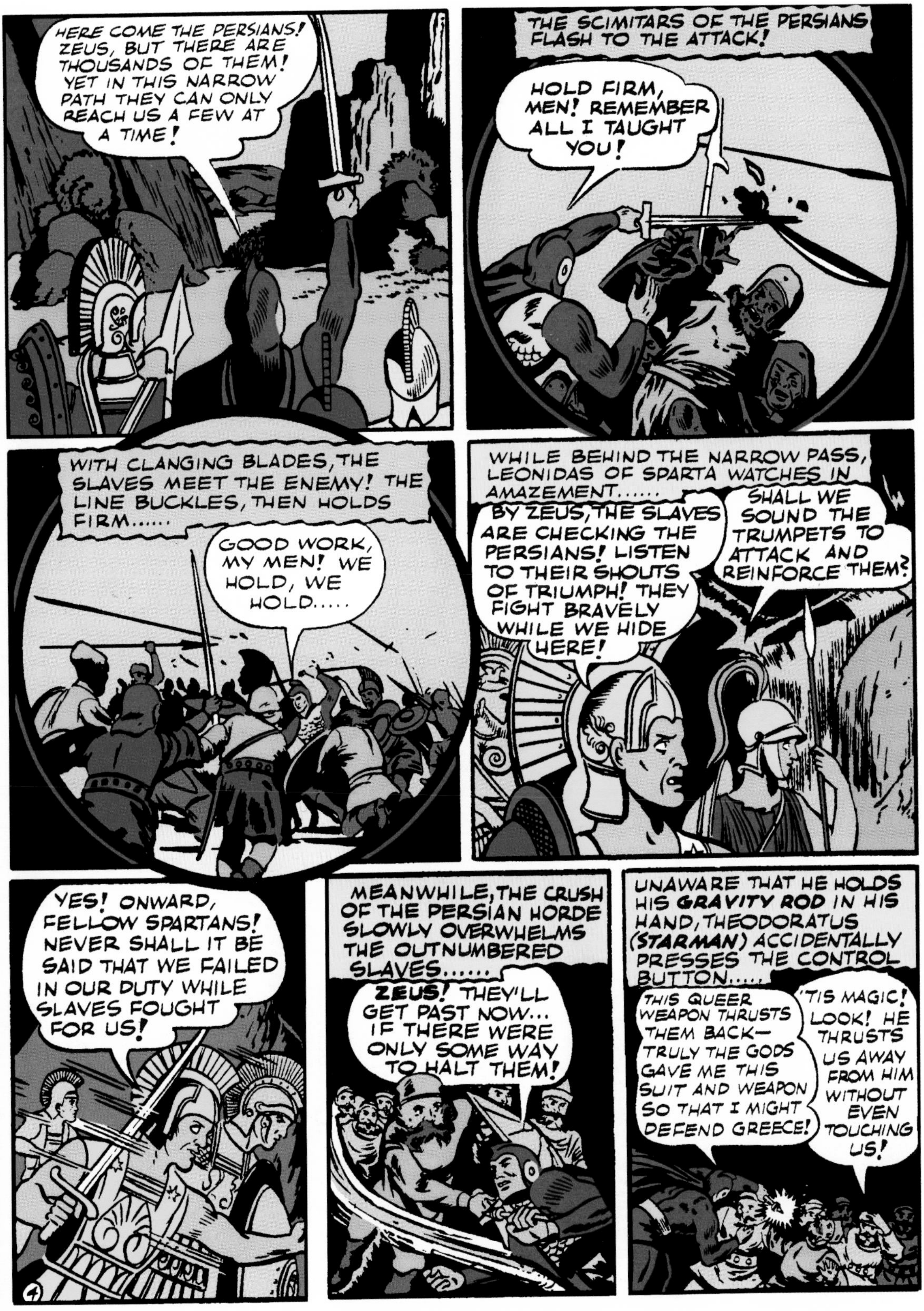
HERE COME THE PERSIANS! ZEUS, BUT THERE ARE THOUSANDS OF THEM! YET IN THIS NARROW PATH THEY CAN ONLY REACH US A FEW AT A TIME!
THE SCIMITARS OF THE PERSIANS FLASH TO THE ATTACK!
HOLD FIRM, MEN! REMEMBER ALL I TAUGHT YOU!
WITH CLANGING BLADES, THE SLAVES MEET THE ENEMY! THE LINE BUCKLES, THEN HOLDS FIRM......
GOOD WORK, MY MEN! WE HOLD, WE HOLD.....
WHILE BEHIND THE NARROW PASS, LEONIDAS OF SPARTA WATCHES IN AMAZEMENT.....
BY ZEUS, THE SLAVES ARE CHECKING THE PERSIANS! LISTEN TO THEIR SHOUTS OF TRIUMPH! THEY FIGHT BRAVELY WHILE WE HIDE HERE!
SHALL WE SOUND THE TRUMPETS TO ATTACK AND REINFORCE THEM?
YES! ONWARD, FELLOW SPARTANS! NEVER SHALL IT BE SAID THAT WE FAILED IN OUR DUTY WHILE SLAVES FOUGHT FOR US!
4
MEANWHILE, THE CRUSH OF THE PERSIAN HORDE SLOWLY OVERWHELMS THE OUTNUMBERED SLAVES......
ZEUS! THEY'LL GET PAST NOW... IF THERE WERE ONLY SOME WAY TO HALT THEM!
UNAWARE THAT HE HOLDS HIS GRAVITY ROD IN HIS HAND, THEODORATUS (STARMAN) ACCIDENTALLY PRESSES THE CONTROL BUTTON.....
THIS QUEER WEAPON THRUSTS THEM BACK— TRULY THE GODS GAVE ME THIS SUIT AND WEAPON SO THAT I MIGHT DEFEND GREECE!
'TIS MAGIC! LOOK! HE THRUSTS US AWAY FROM HIM WITHOUT EVEN TOUCHING US!

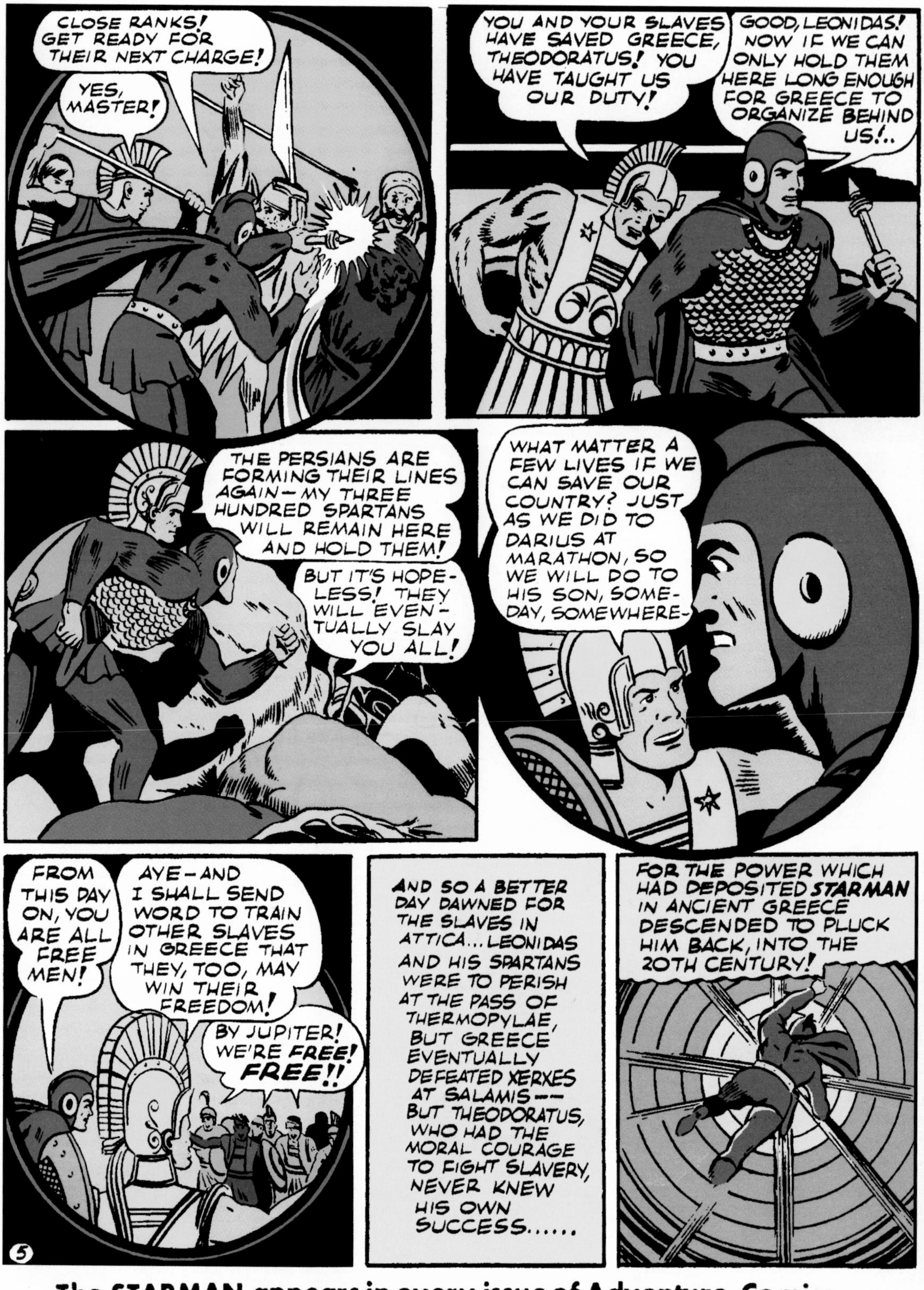
CLOSE RANKS! GET READY FOR THEIR NEXT CHARGE!
YES, MASTER!
YOU AND YOUR SLAVES HAVE SAVED GREECE, THEODORATUS! YOU HAVE TAUGHT US OUR DUTY!
GOOD, LEONIDAS! NOW IF WE CAN ONLY HOLD THEM HERE LONG ENOUGH FOR GREECE TO ORGANIZE BEHIND US!..
THE PERSIANS ARE FORMING THEIR LINES AGAIN—MY THREE HUNDRED SPARTANS WILL REMAIN HERE AND HOLD THEM!
BUT IT'S HOPELESS! THEY WILL EVENTUALLY SLAY YOU ALL!
WHAT MATTER A FEW LIVES IF WE CAN SAVE OUR COUNTRY? JUST AS WE DID TO DARIUS AT MARATHON, SO WE WILL DO TO HIS SON, SOMEDAY, SOMEWHERE-
FROM THIS DAY ON, YOU ARE ALL FREE MEN!
AYE—AND I SHALL SEND WORD TO TRAIN OTHER SLAVES IN GREECE THAT THEY, TOO, MAY WIN THEIR FREEDOM!
BY JUPITER! WE'RE FREE! FREE!!
5
AND SO A BETTER DAY DAWNED FOR THE SLAVES IN ATTICA... LEONIDAS AND HIS SPARTANS WERE TO PERISH AT THE PASS OF THERMOPYLAE, BUT GREECE EVENTUALLY DEFEATED XERXES AT SALAMIS-- BUT THEODORATUS, WHO HAD THE MORAL COURAGE TO FIGHT SLAVERY, NEVER KNEW HIS OWN SUCCESS......
FOR THE POWER WHICH HAD DEPOSITED STARMAN IN ANCIENT GREECE DESCENDED TO PLUCK HIM BACK, INTO THE 20TH CENTURY!

The STARMAN appears in every issue of Adventure Comics.

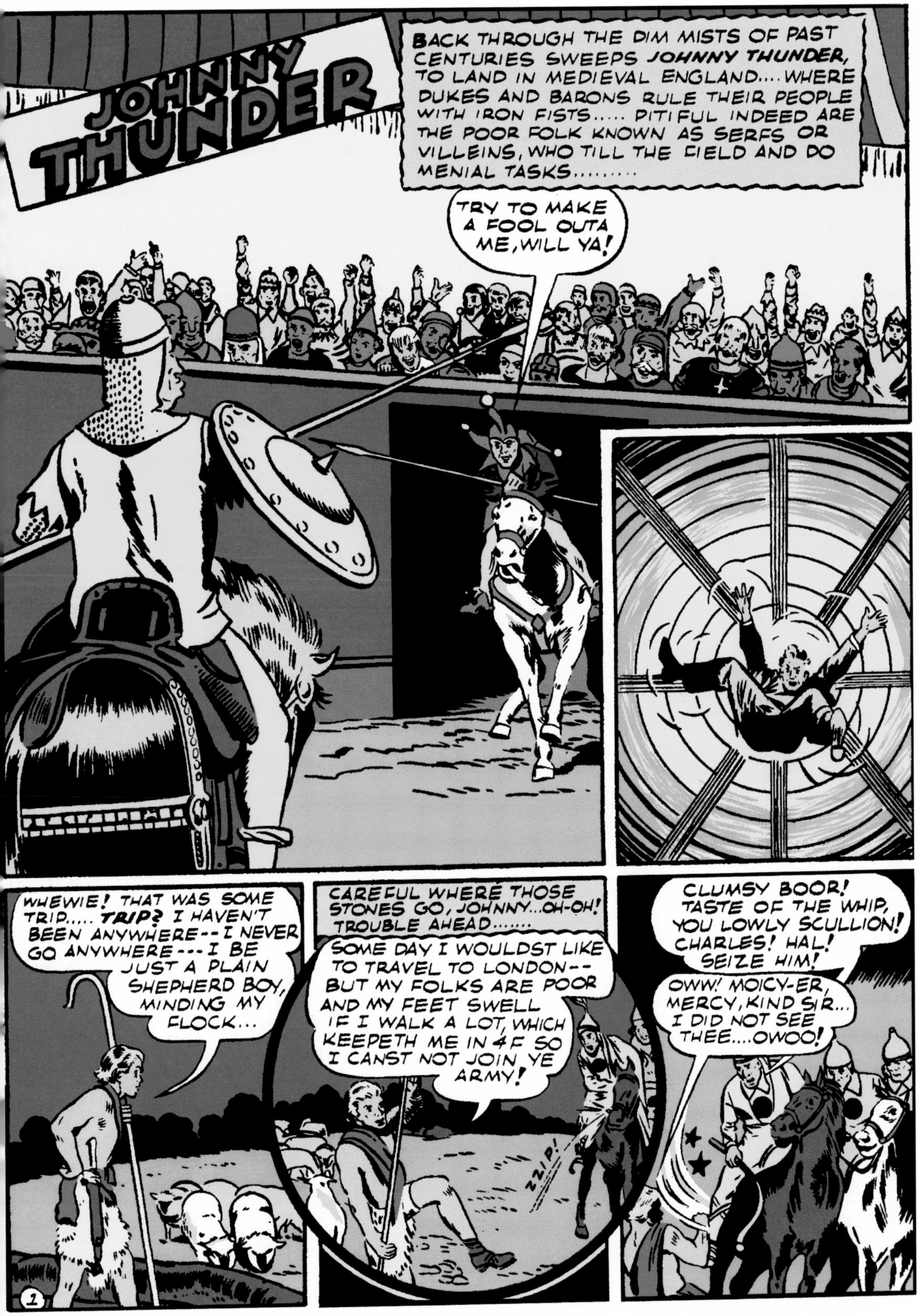
JOHNNY THUNDER
BACK THROUGH THE DIM MISTS OF PAST CENTURIES SWEEPS JOHNNY THUNDER, TO LAND IN MEDIEVAL ENGLAND.... WHERE DUKES AND BARONS RULE THEIR PEOPLE WITH IRON FISTS..... PITIFUL INDEED ARE THE POOR FOLK KNOWN AS SERFS OR VILLEINS, WHO TILL THE FIELD AND DO MENIAL TASKS.........
TRY TO MAKE A FOOL OUTA ME, WILL YA!
WHEWIE! THAT WAS SOME TRIP..... TRIP? I HAVEN'T BEEN ANYWHERE -- I NEVER GO ANYWHERE --- I BE JUST A PLAIN SHEPHERD BOY, MINDING MY FLOCK...
CAREFUL WHERE THOSE STONES GO, JOHNNY...OH-OH! TROUBLE AHEAD........
SOME DAY I WOULDST LIKE TO TRAVEL TO LONDON -- BUT MY FOLKS ARE POOR AND MY FEET SWELL IF I WALK A LOT, WHICH KEEPETH ME IN 4F SO I CANST NOT JOIN YE ARMY!
ZZIP!
CLUMSY BOOR! TASTE OF THE WHIP, YOU LOWLY SCULLION! CHARLES! HAL! SEIZE HIM!
OWW! MOICY-ER, MERCY, KIND SIR... I DID NOT SEE THEE....OWOO!
1

TAKE HIM ALONG—WE'LL FLOG THE MISCREANT BEFORE HIS FAMILY—AND TEACH THEM ALL A LESSON, METHINKS!

IF YOU LET GO OF ME, I'LL—

THEE WILL DO—*WHAT?*

COMMENCE SOMETHING — JUST COMMENCE, THAT'S ALL!

AW, DO YOU DO EVERYTHING A FELLOW ASKS OF THEE? GRAB HOLD OF ME AGAIN—

SOME TIME LATER, BEFORE THE WATTLE HUTS OF THE SERFS OF BARON LOTLANCE

BURN THEIR HOMES—HURRY, OUR LORD AWAITS US!

SIR, THOSE DO BE OUR ONLY SHELTERS—HAVE MERCY!

AYE, AND WITHOUT THEM WE WILL FREEZE!

QUIET, DOGS! KNOW YE NOT THE BARON NEEDS A NEW RUN FOR HIS DEER? AND SINCE THE DEER ARE MORE VALUABLE THAN YOU-- OUT YOU GO!

OHH!

THEN JOHNNY THE SHEPHERD BOY IS GIVEN A BRUTAL FLOGGING AS THE HUMBLE SERFS WATCH IN TERROR..... HOURS LATER, THE INJURED LAD LIES BEFORE A FIRE..

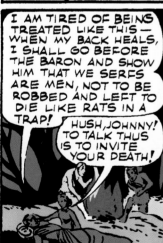

I AM TIRED OF BEING TREATED LIKE THIS — WHEN MY BACK HEALS, I SHALL GO BEFORE THE BARON AND SHOW HIM THAT WE SERFS ARE MEN, NOT TO BE ROBBED AND LEFT TO DIE LIKE RATS IN A TRAP!

HUSH, JOHNNY! TO TALK THUS IS TO INVITE YOUR DEATH!

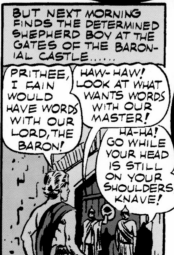

BUT NEXT MORNING FINDS THE DETERMINED SHEPHERD BOY AT THE GATES OF THE BARONIAL CASTLE.....

PRITHEE, I FAIN WOULD HAVE WORDS WITH OUR LORD, THE BARON!

HAW-HAW! LOOK AT WHAT WANTS WORDS WITH OUR MASTER!

HA-HA! GO WHILE YOUR HEAD IS STILL ON YOUR SHOULDERS, KNAVE!

NOW GET THEE GONE!

BE OFF, FOUL VARLET!

SAY YOU LET ME ALONE! I'M A HUMAN BEING!.. OWTCH! OWW!

OH-OH! JOHNNY HAS SAID THOSE BAHDNISIAN HEX WORDS CEI-U (SAY YOU)— WILL THEY STILL BRING HIS 20TH-CENTURY THUNDERBOLT?

②

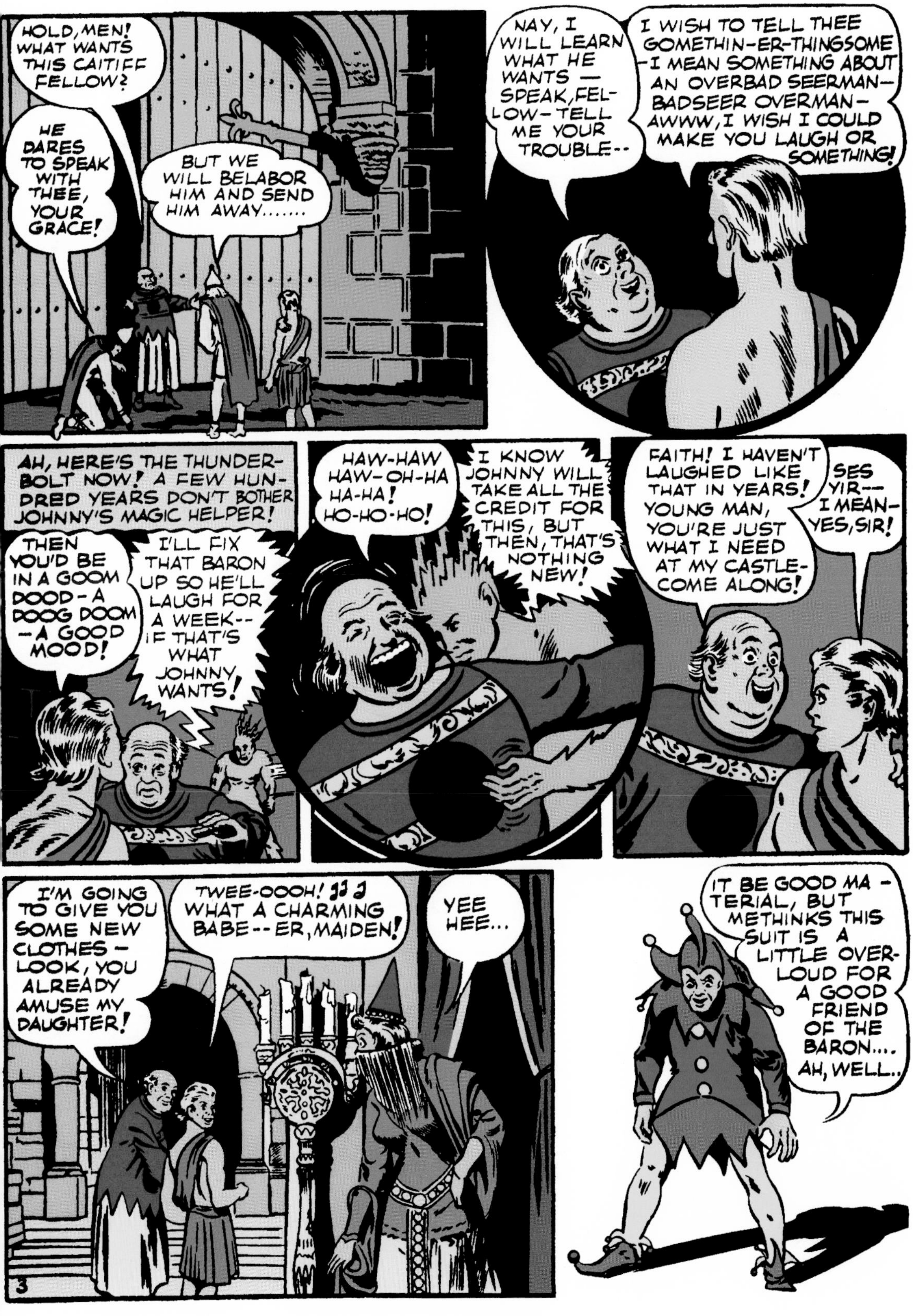
HOLD, MEN! WHAT WANTS THIS CAITIFF FELLOW?
HE DARES TO SPEAK WITH THEE, YOUR GRACE!
BUT WE WILL BELABOR HIM AND SEND HIM AWAY.......
NAY, I WILL LEARN WHAT HE WANTS — SPEAK, FELLOW— TELL ME YOUR TROUBLE--
I WISH TO TELL THEE GOMETHIN-ER-THINGSOME -I MEAN SOMETHING ABOUT AN OVERBAD SEERMAN- BADSEER OVERMAN- AWWW, I WISH I COULD MAKE YOU LAUGH OR SOMETHING!
AH, HERE'S THE THUNDERBOLT NOW! A FEW HUNDRED YEARS DON'T BOTHER JOHNNY'S MAGIC HELPER!
THEN YOU'D BE IN A GOOM DOOD-A DOOG DOOM --A GOOD MOOD!
I'LL FIX THAT BARON UP SO HE'LL LAUGH FOR A WEEK-- IF THAT'S WHAT JOHNNY WANTS!
HAW-HAW HAW-OH-HA HA-HA! HO-HO-HO!
I KNOW JOHNNY WILL TAKE ALL THE CREDIT FOR THIS, BUT THEN, THAT'S NOTHING NEW!
FAITH! I HAVEN'T LAUGHED LIKE THAT IN YEARS! YOUNG MAN, YOU'RE JUST WHAT I NEED AT MY CASTLE- COME ALONG!
SES YIR-- I MEAN- YES, SIR!
I'M GOING TO GIVE YOU SOME NEW CLOTHES - LOOK, YOU ALREADY AMUSE MY DAUGHTER!
TWEE-OOOH! ♫♪ WHAT A CHARMING BABE--ER, MAIDEN!
YEE HEE...
3
IT BE GOOD MATERIAL, BUT METHINKS THIS SUIT IS A LITTLE OVERLOUD FOR A GOOD FRIEND OF THE BARON.... AH, WELL..

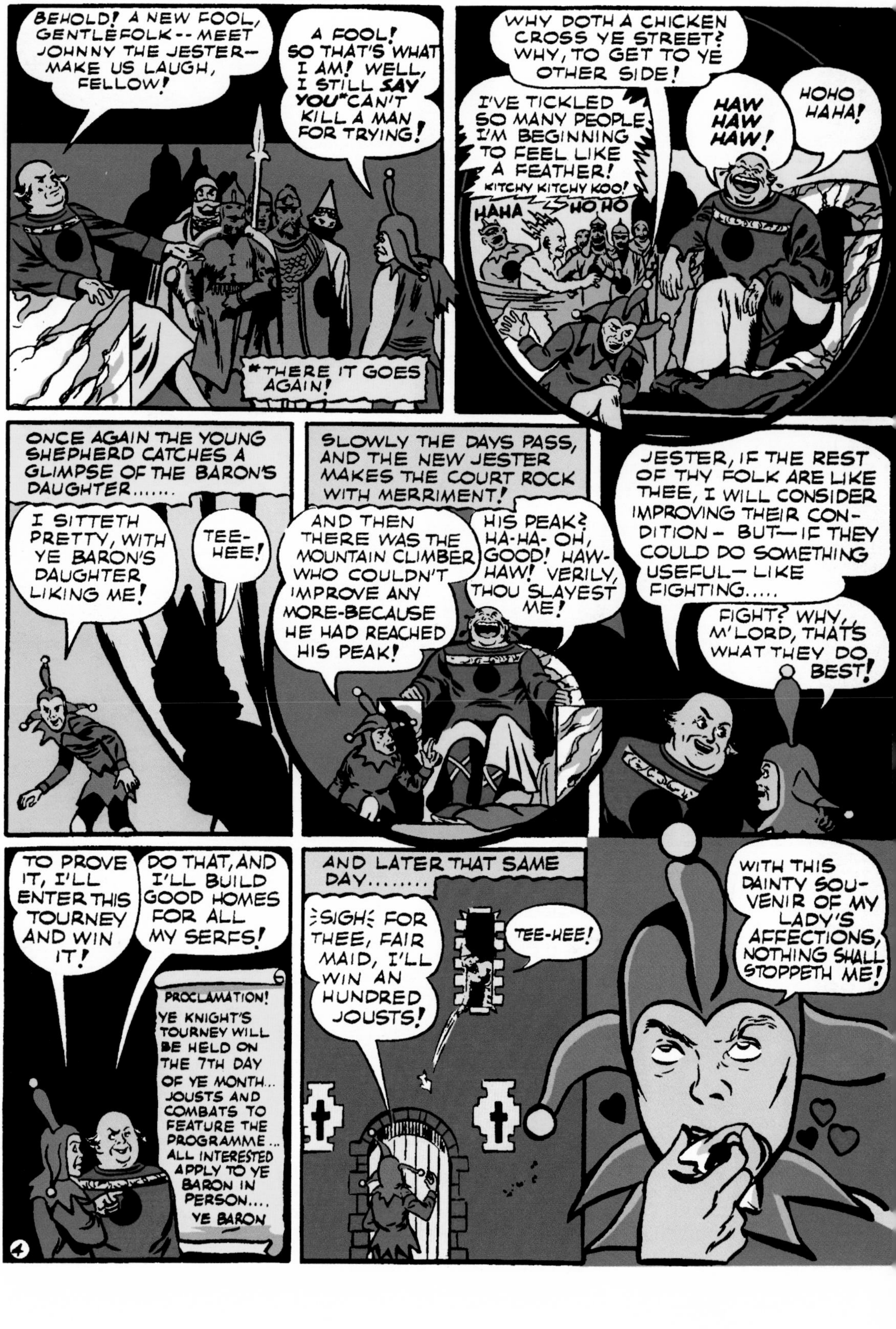
BEHOLD! A NEW FOOL, GENTLEFOLK--MEET JOHNNY THE JESTER-- MAKE US LAUGH, FELLOW!
A FOOL! SO THAT'S WHAT I AM! WELL, I STILL SAY YOU* CAN'T KILL A MAN FOR TRYING!
*THERE IT GOES AGAIN!
WHY DOTH A CHICKEN CROSS YE STREET? WHY, TO GET TO YE OTHER SIDE!
I'VE TICKLED SO MANY PEOPLE I'M BEGINNING TO FEEL LIKE A FEATHER!
KITCHY KITCHY KOO!
HAHA
HO HO
HAW HAW HAW!
HOHO HAHA!
ONCE AGAIN THE YOUNG SHEPHERD CATCHES A GLIMPSE OF THE BARON'S DAUGHTER.......
I SITTETH PRETTY, WITH YE BARON'S DAUGHTER LIKING ME!
TEE-HEE!
SLOWLY THE DAYS PASS, AND THE NEW JESTER MAKES THE COURT ROCK WITH MERRIMENT!
AND THEN THERE WAS THE MOUNTAIN CLIMBER WHO COULDN'T IMPROVE ANY MORE-BECAUSE HE HAD REACHED HIS PEAK!
HIS PEAK? HA-HA- OH, GOOD! HAW-HAW! VERILY, THOU SLAYEST ME!
JESTER, IF THE REST OF THY FOLK ARE LIKE THEE, I WILL CONSIDER IMPROVING THEIR CONDITION - BUT—IF THEY COULD DO SOMETHING USEFUL— LIKE FIGHTING.....
FIGHT? WHY, M'LORD, THAT'S WHAT THEY DO BEST!
TO PROVE IT, I'LL ENTER THIS TOURNEY AND WIN IT!
DO THAT, AND I'LL BUILD GOOD HOMES FOR ALL MY SERFS!
PROCLAMATION! YE KNIGHT'S TOURNEY WILL BE HELD ON THE 7TH DAY OF YE MONTH... JOUSTS AND COMBATS TO FEATURE THE PROGRAMME... ALL INTERESTED APPLY TO YE BARON IN PERSON.... YE BARON
4
AND LATER THAT SAME DAY........
SIGH FOR THEE, FAIR MAID, I'LL WIN AN HUNDRED JOUSTS!
TEE-HEE!
WITH THIS DAINTY SOUVENIR OF MY LADY'S AFFECTIONS, NOTHING SHALL STOPPETH ME!

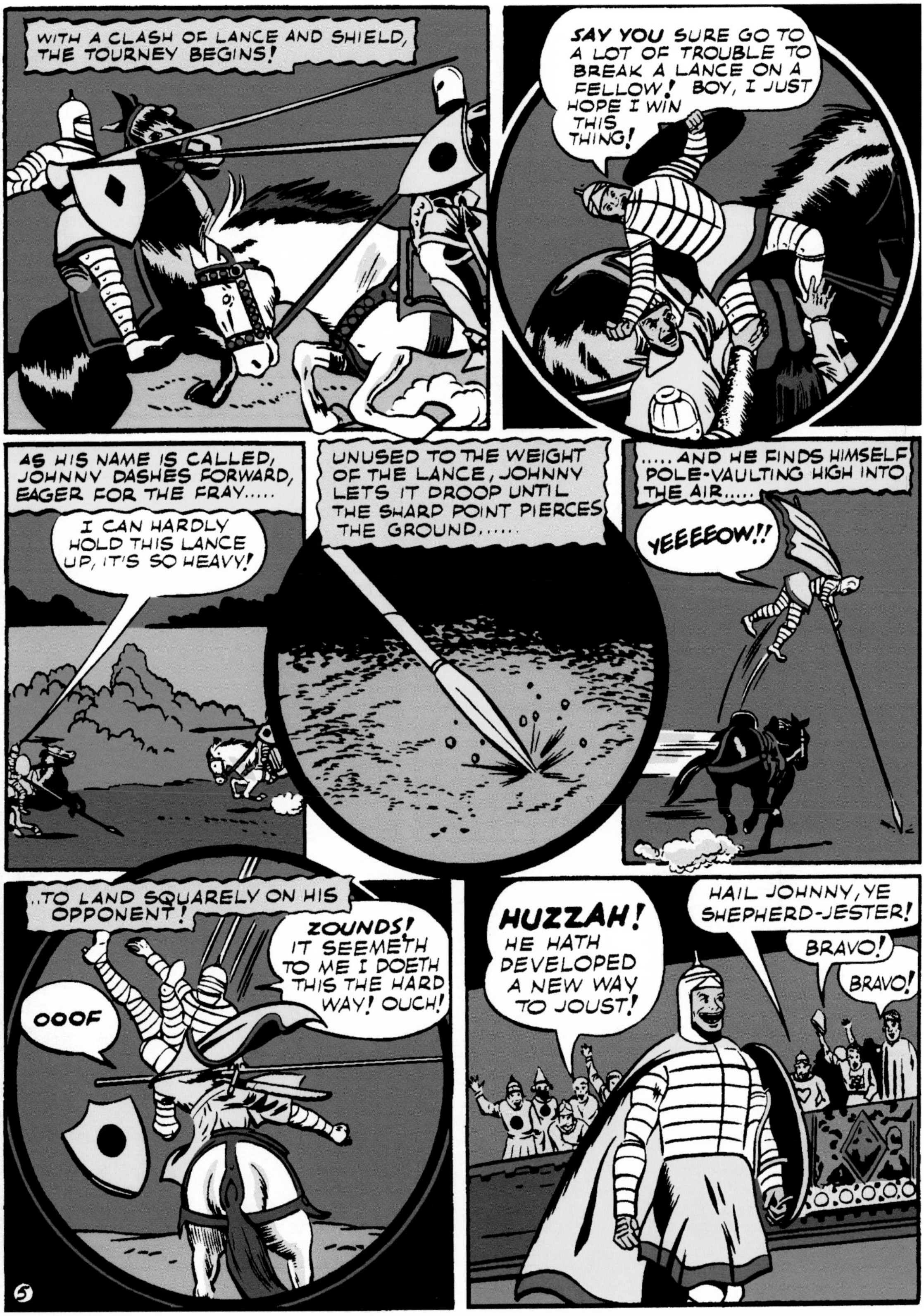
WITH A CLASH OF LANCE AND SHIELD, THE TOURNEY BEGINS!
SAY YOU SURE GO TO A LOT OF TROUBLE TO BREAK A LANCE ON A FELLOW! BOY, I JUST HOPE I WIN THIS THING!
AS HIS NAME IS CALLED, JOHNNY DASHES FORWARD, EAGER FOR THE FRAY.....
I CAN HARDLY HOLD THIS LANCE UP, IT'S SO HEAVY!
UNUSED TO THE WEIGHT OF THE LANCE, JOHNNY LETS IT DROOP UNTIL THE SHARP POINT PIERCES THE GROUND.....
.....AND HE FINDS HIMSELF POLE-VAULTING HIGH INTO THE AIR.....
YEEEEOW!!
..TO LAND SQUARELY ON HIS OPPONENT!
ZOUNDS! IT SEEMETH TO ME I DOETH THIS THE HARD WAY! OUCH!
OOOF
HUZZAH! HE HATH DEVELOPED A NEW WAY TO JOUST!
HAIL JOHNNY, YE SHEPHERD-JESTER!
BRAVO!
BRAVO!
5

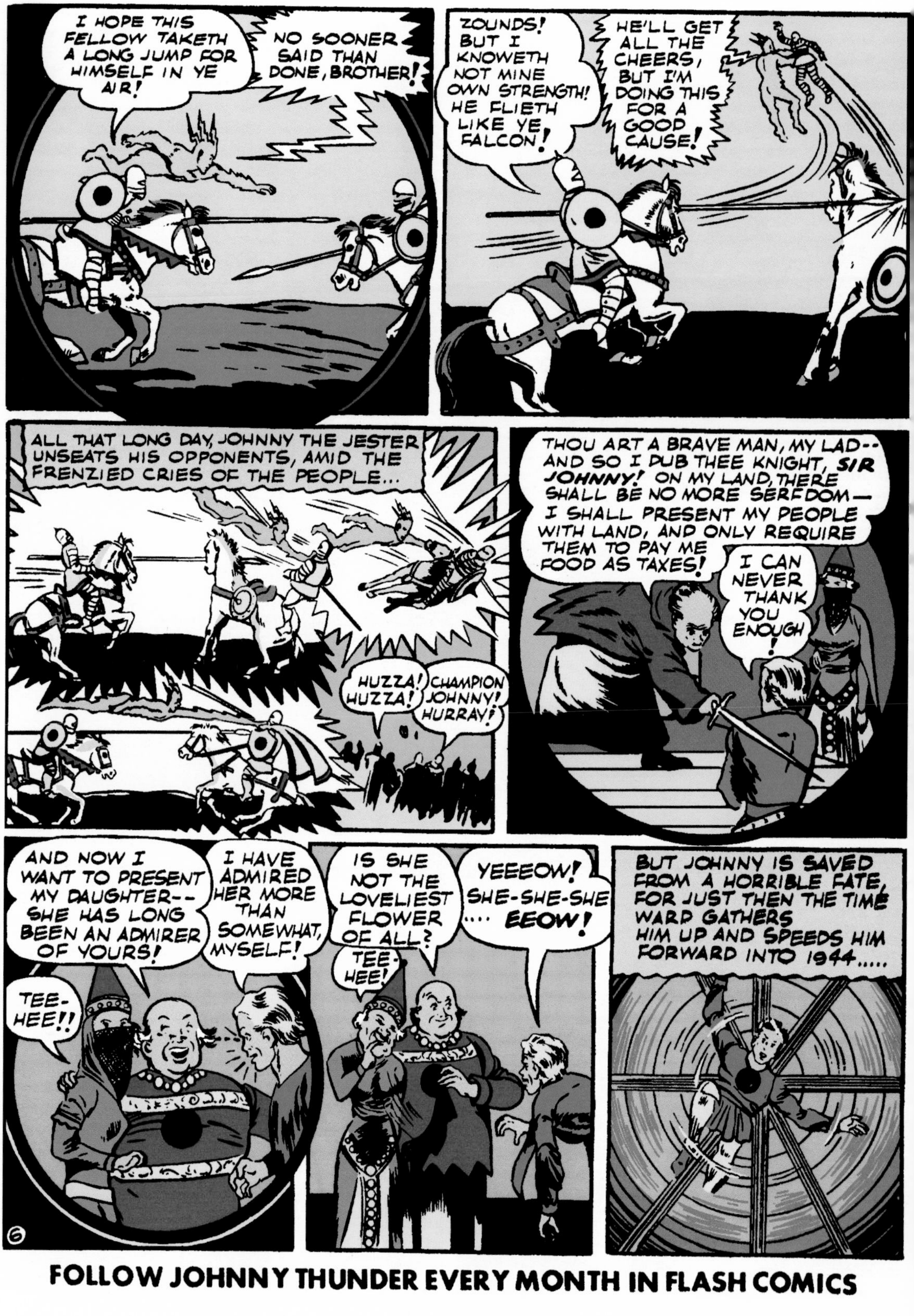
I HOPE THIS FELLOW TAKETH A LONG JUMP FOR HIMSELF IN YE AIR!
NO SOONER SAID THAN DONE, BROTHER!
ZOUNDS! BUT I KNOWETH NOT MINE OWN STRENGTH! HE FLIETH LIKE YE FALCON!
HE'LL GET ALL THE CHEERS, BUT I'M DOING THIS FOR A GOOD CAUSE!
ALL THAT LONG DAY, JOHNNY THE JESTER UNSEATS HIS OPPONENTS, AMID THE FRENZIED CRIES OF THE PEOPLE...
HUZZA! HUZZA!
CHAMPION JOHNNY! HURRAY!
THOU ART A BRAVE MAN, MY LAD-- AND SO I DUB THEE KNIGHT, SIR JOHNNY! ON MY LAND, THERE SHALL BE NO MORE SERFDOM— I SHALL PRESENT MY PEOPLE WITH LAND, AND ONLY REQUIRE THEM TO PAY ME FOOD AS TAXES!
I CAN NEVER THANK YOU ENOUGH!
AND NOW I WANT TO PRESENT MY DAUGHTER-- SHE HAS LONG BEEN AN ADMIRER OF YOURS!
I HAVE ADMIRED HER MORE THAN SOMEWHAT, MYSELF!
TEE-HEE!!
IS SHE NOT THE LOVELIEST FLOWER OF ALL?
TEE-HEE!
YEEEOW! SHE-SHE-SHE.... EEOW!
BUT JOHNNY IS SAVED FROM A HORRIBLE FATE, FOR JUST THEN THE TIME WARD GATHERS HIM UP AND SPEEDS HIM FORWARD INTO 1944.....
6

FOLLOW JOHNNY THUNDER EVERY MONTH IN FLASH COMICS

LEND-LEASE
FOR CHINA

*A Hop Harrigan adventure
based on the feature by
Jon L. Blummer
that appears in every issue of
ALL-AMERICAN COMICS*

MAJOR HILTON eyed Hop across the paper-strewn desk, from which issued the countless orders that kept things humming at the vast Calcutta airport.

Hop had just finished inspecting the specially-rigged bomber, riddled with Jap bullets, that he and Tank had flown to this base for repairs. The bomber had blown up a Jap supply dump in Burma and had been chased over the Bay of Bengal by six Jap pursuit planes. Remembering the surprise he'd given those pilots, Hop chuckled inwardly. He could still see their eyes bulging when the bomber's doors had opened and Hop's tiny fighter plane had dropped from the bigger plane's interior! Hop's small, maneuverable "stinger," aided by the bomber's guns, had made quick work of the Japs—but it was a badly damaged bomber that had limped into this Calcutta airport three days before.

"Harrigan,"—the Major's tone was solemn—"you saw that transport being loaded out there just now?"

"They were stowing a couple of engines in her," Hop nodded. "That's something the Chinese Air Force can sure use! Why—is something wrong, sir?" Harrigan asked, noting the Major's face.

"Plenty wrong!" the Major nodded, grimly. "Judging from what happened to the last three transports, I'm afraid this one won't get there either! Those other three vanished completely en route to Chungking!"

"Vanished!" Hop repeated. "You mean—they disappeared into thin air? No signs of any wreckage?"

"Exactly!" snapped the Major, his eyes sparking anger. "I have sent out recco pilots—all along the routes the ships were scheduled to take. Even cameras failed to pick up any sign of a wreck or any members of the crew. It—it's fantastic!" The Major shook his head. He got up and walked over to a wall map, ran a stubby finger along the highly secretive Calcutta-Chungking air route marked out with pins. "There"—his finger stabbed at a point over the mountainous region north of Burma—"is just about where it happens. The ship's radio goes out. Not completely—but there is a loud interference that prevents the operator from getting a message through. The Japs have some way of tuning in on our air waves and creating an interference."

Hop frowned as the grim import of the Major's words struck him. The air route from Calcutta to Chungking was the only way of getting supplies to China. The Burma Road was already in Jap hands. The new road from India to China, being bored through almost impossible mountain barriers, was not yet finished. The Allies' one method of getting supplies through to China *must* be protected! The *air route* must be kept open!

". . . and the Japs never attack until the transport is beyond range of fighter protection!" the Major went on, bit-terly. "They never attack anything but an unarmed transport. They won't take on a fighter, or a bomber—anything that can fight back. My opinion is that they have something highly secretive, and are taking no chances on an armed fighter getting away and telling us what it's all about. They're concentrating solely on cutting off supplies to China . . ."

Hop's mind had been racing as the Major talked. He grinned ruefully: "I never thought Mrs. Harrigan's little boy Hop would be asking for a *transport* job—but that's what I'm doing, sir! Give me and my partner, Tank, a couple of days to work on that transport in Hangar Y and . . ."

"Say no more!" the Major said, gripping Hop's hand with a look of relief on his craggy, sunburned face.

"*You* talked me into this!" Tank groaned aloud, to a Hop that was nowhere in sight. "Flying this crazy crate—smack into a Jap trap!" He sighed, at the sight of the desolate mountains that loomed, gray and forbidding, for miles in every direction. What had happened to those other transports? Had they crashed on the rocks below? Maybe it was just coincidence? Maybe it wasn't the Japs at all? And if it *was* a Jap trap—would their feverish preparations of the past two days get them out of it? Tinker's big frame shuddered.

Then the redhead saw the line of Jap planes curling up from below, like a huge snake climbing the sky! Five Zeros—coming right at the transport! Tank had no time to wonder where the Japs had come from. He was plugging in his radio headset and trying to get headquarters. Then he heard it—the loud static that had prevented the other pilots from getting their messages through! The Japs were jamming the air waves, though Tank, for the life of him, couldn't figure out how.

And seconds later, he couldn't figure what the Japs were up to! They weren't shooting! They made no attempt to knock the transport out of the sky. Instead, the five planes ringed the transport round and flew along with it! Then they waggled their wings, and pointed their noses slightly down, and Tank understood. The Nips were trying to tell him to *follow* them!

"This gets curiouser and curiouser!" gulped Tank. "What do those little brown devils want?"

Calmly, the Japs circled in a steep descent until they hovered a bare hundred feet over a massive mountain top. Then, before Tank's amazed eyes, the *entire cliff face slowly opened*—revealing a huge runway that jutted out from the cavernous depths of the mountain and was supported by solid rock below! The interior of that mountain was a miracle of engineering. It was divided into hangars, machine shops, supply rooms, everything conceivably necessary to an air base. A periscope ran through the mountain vertically and was disguised as a boulder at the top. Grimly, Tank took in the sight of *three American transports* in one of the mountain's hangars!

The Japs were descending to-ward the runway, Tinker in their dead center. His hand was on a lever specially wired to the door of the transport plane.

"This has just gotta work!" he breathed. "It's just *gotta!*"

Suddenly, he flipped the transport on her right side. Before the Japs could figure out what this move meant, the transport's huge door opened and Hop's tiny fighter plane fell clear! It was so small Hop had to fly it lying on his stomach!

Hop dove straight for the nearest Jap with a stream of lead that knocked the Zero apart in seconds!

"Oh, joy!" breathed Tank. "Keep the others busy like that, Hop—and I'll mash this cliff face's face in in no time at all!"

Before the surprised Japs below could send up a single burst of anti-aircraft fire, Tank had pressed another lever specially wired to what looked like two fuel tanks attached to the transport's wings. But released, the tanks fell apart—and *two five-hundred pound bombs went parachuting down!* Tank grinned, remembering the hours he and Hop had spent camouflaging those bombs inside specially-constructed fuel tanks. In his joy, he almost forgot to whip up the transport's nose—but the parachutes gave the heavy ship just enough time to clear the thunderous explosion that shook the Jap air base to a heap of useless rubble!

Tank leveled off just as Hop's fighter polished off the last of the Japs. Hop's tiny plane had buzzed among the startled Japs like an angry insect, getting in its sting before the Nips could successfully ward it off. Tank tried his radio and found that it worked. The radio apparatus in the mountain base was now where it would interfere with no more American planes! He contacted Hop.

"Great shooting, kid!" he roared. "Now climb that pee-wee back in here! And hurry ——" he grinned, flipping the transport onto its side and lowering a cable through the opened door to catch the hook on the fighter—"or I'll leave you out here by yourself, and the *birds* might pick on you!"

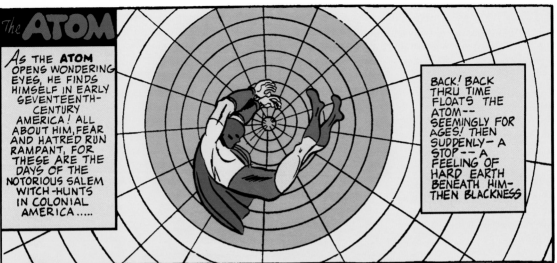

The ATOM

As THE **ATOM** OPENS WONDERING EYES, HE FINDS HIMSELF IN EARLY SEVENTEENTH-CENTURY AMERICA! ALL ABOUT HIM, FEAR AND HATRED RUN RAMPANT, FOR THESE ARE THE DAYS OF THE NOTORIOUS SALEM WITCH-HUNTS IN COLONIAL AMERICA.....

BACK! BACK THRU TIME FLOATS THE ATOM-- SEEMINGLY FOR AGES! THEN SUDDENLY- A STOP-- A FEELING OF HARD EARTH BENEATH HIM-- THEN BLACKNESS

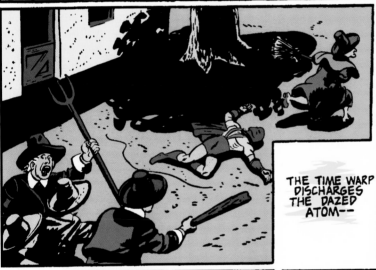

THE TIME WARP DISCHARGES THE DAZED ATOM--

I-I CAN'T SEEM TO REMEMBER A THING! -AND WHAT AM I DOING HERE? IT SEEMS MY NAME IS NATHANIEL PRATT... I SHOULD BE GOING HOME!

ALL MEMORY OF THE PRESENT HAS LEFT THE **ATOM'S** MIND! HE KNOWS HIMSELF ONLY AS A CITIZEN OF 17th CENTURY AMERICA !

THESE CLOTHES. HOW ODD! -BUT AT THE FAMILY HOME I CAN FIND NEW ONES!

WHY, IT'S NATHANIEL! I- WE THOUGHT YOU WERE IN ENGLAND!

HELLO, JULIE. I WAS, BUT-ER...I MUST HAVE RETURNED!

THAT NIGHT AT DINNER, "NATHANIEL PRATT" RECEIVES THE LATEST NEWS...

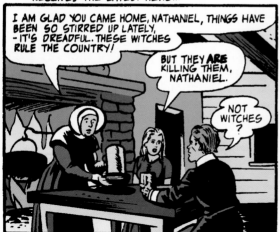

I AM GLAD YOU CAME HOME, NATHANIEL, THINGS HAVE BEEN SO STIRRED UP LATELY, -IT'S DREADFUL. THESE WITCHES RULE THE COUNTRY!

BUT THEY **ARE** KILLING THEM, NATHANIEL.

NOT WITCHES?

YES! WHY, ONLY YESTERDAY, YOUNG GILES MORRIS TOLD ME HE SAW MOTHER RATHLOW STUMBLE WALKING PAST HIS COW, AND LAST NIGHT THE COW DIED!

I-I GUESS WITCHES MUST BE PRETTY BAD, -OF COURSE, I DON'T KNOW MUCH ABOUT THEM...

IN THE DAYS THAT FOLLOW, THE **ATOM** SLIDES INTO THE ROLE OF NATHANIEL PRATT...

YOU'VE BEEN SO HELPFUL, NATHANIEL ≥SIGH≤ IF IT WEREN'T FOR THESE TERRIBLE WITCHES, I'D BE THE HAPPIEST WOMAN ALIVE!

WHAT IS IT, JULIE?

THE HOT WINE, SIR, AND A GENTLEMAN TO SEE YOU!

I KNOW IT'S A LOT TO ASK YOU, NAT, BUT THOSE PAPERS I SPOKE ABOUT HAVE TO BE SIGNED!

THAT MEANS A TRIP AT NIGHT THRU THE FOREST AND THEY SAY MOTHER RATHLOW, THE WITCH --LIVES THERE!

I COULD HAVE SOME SOLDIERS GO WITH YOU!

NO, THANKS... THEY'D BE NO USE AGAINST WITCHES' SPELLS. EITHER I ARRIVE SAFELY- OR NOT AT ALL. -I'LL BE GOING NOW...

IN THE 17th CENTURY, WITCHES WERE AS MUCH A CAUSE OF FEAR AS A TEN-TON BLOCKBUSTER TODAY. SO, IN THE OPINION OF HIS TOWNSFOLK, NATHANIEL PRATT WAS "A MIGHTY BRAVE BOY" TO CROSS THESE FORESTS ALONE THAT NIGHT...

2

SUDDENLY A CRY RINGS OUT IN THE DARK STILLNESS OF THE NIGHT...

EEEEEEH!

WHA-WHAT WAS THAT?

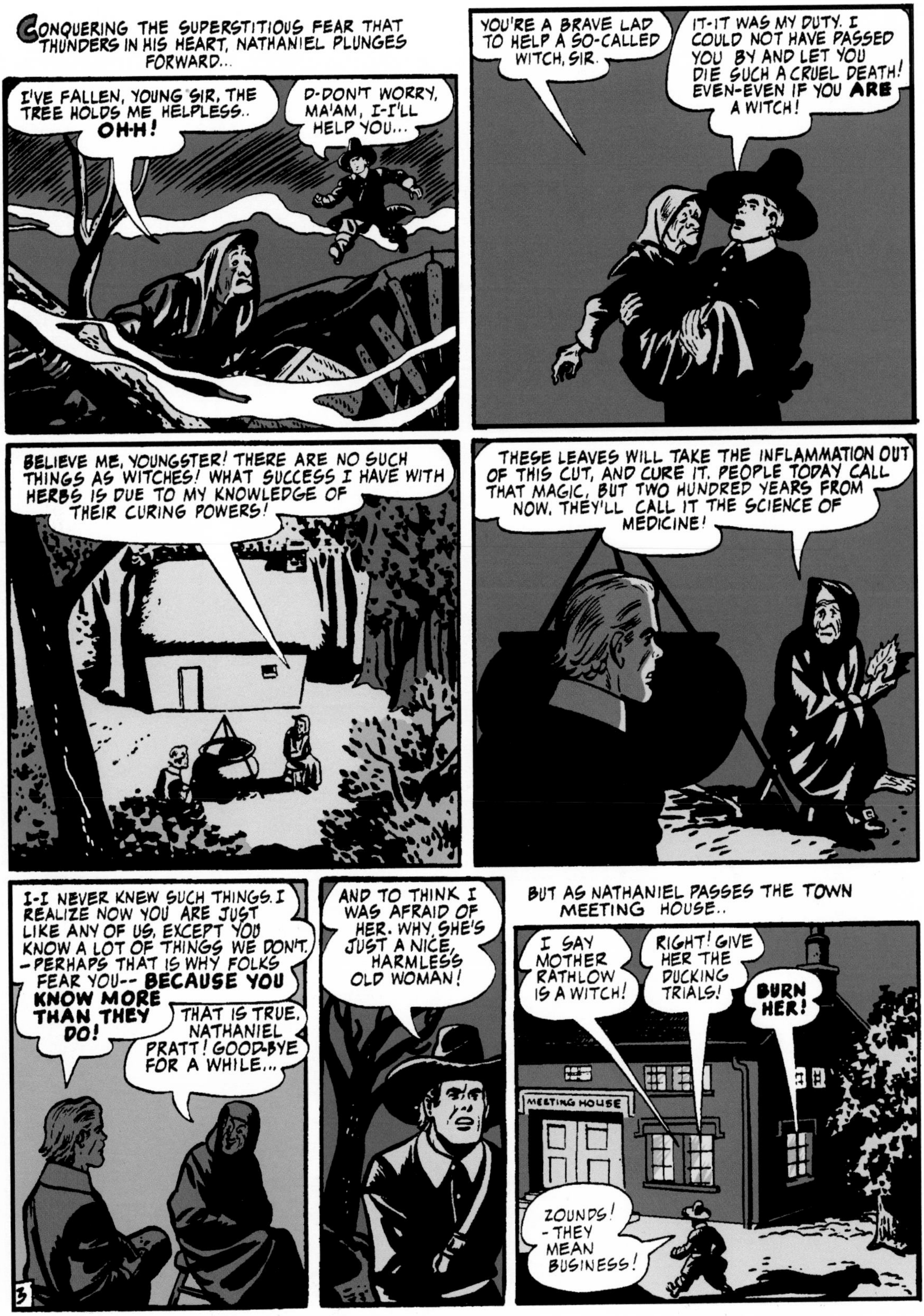
CONQUERING THE SUPERSTITIOUS FEAR THAT THUNDERS IN HIS HEART, NATHANIEL PLUNGES FORWARD...
I'VE FALLEN, YOUNG SIR, THE TREE HOLDS ME HELPLESS.. OH-H!
D-DON'T WORRY, MA'AM, I-I'LL HELP YOU...
YOU'RE A BRAVE LAD TO HELP A SO-CALLED WITCH, SIR.
IT-IT WAS MY DUTY. I COULD NOT HAVE PASSED YOU BY AND LET YOU DIE SUCH A CRUEL DEATH! EVEN-EVEN IF YOU ARE A WITCH!
BELIEVE ME, YOUNGSTER! THERE ARE NO SUCH THINGS AS WITCHES! WHAT SUCCESS I HAVE WITH HERBS IS DUE TO MY KNOWLEDGE OF THEIR CURING POWERS!
THESE LEAVES WILL TAKE THE INFLAMMATION OUT OF THIS CUT, AND CURE IT. PEOPLE TODAY CALL THAT MAGIC, BUT TWO HUNDRED YEARS FROM NOW, THEY'LL CALL IT THE SCIENCE OF MEDICINE!
I-I NEVER KNEW SUCH THINGS. I REALIZE NOW YOU ARE JUST LIKE ANY OF US, EXCEPT YOU KNOW A LOT OF THINGS WE DON'T. -PERHAPS THAT IS WHY FOLKS FEAR YOU-- BECAUSE YOU KNOW MORE THAN THEY DO!
THAT IS TRUE, NATHANIEL PRATT! GOOD-BYE FOR A WHILE...
3
AND TO THINK I WAS AFRAID OF HER. WHY, SHE'S JUST A NICE, HARMLESS OLD WOMAN!
BUT AS NATHANIEL PASSES THE TOWN MEETING HOUSE..
I SAY MOTHER RATHLOW IS A WITCH!
RIGHT! GIVE HER THE DUCKING TRIALS!
BURN HER!
MEETING HOUSE
ZOUNDS! -THEY MEAN BUSINESS!

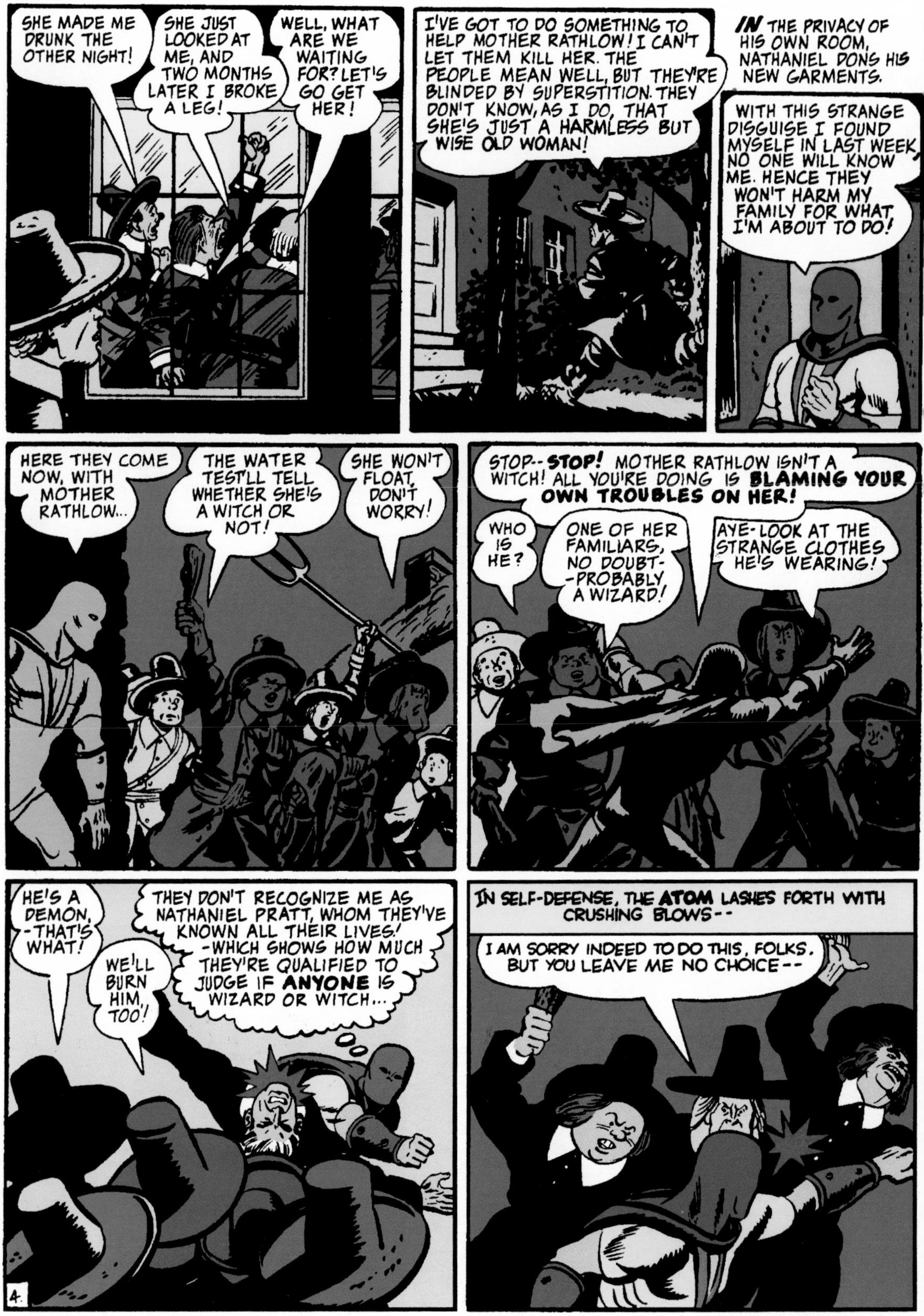
SHE MADE ME DRUNK THE OTHER NIGHT!
SHE JUST LOOKED AT ME, AND TWO MONTHS LATER I BROKE A LEG!
WELL, WHAT ARE WE WAITING FOR? LET'S GO GET HER!
I'VE GOT TO DO SOMETHING TO HELP MOTHER RATHLOW! I CAN'T LET THEM KILL HER. THE PEOPLE MEAN WELL, BUT THEY'RE BLINDED BY SUPERSTITION. THEY DON'T KNOW, AS I DO, THAT SHE'S JUST A HARMLESS BUT WISE OLD WOMAN!
IN THE PRIVACY OF HIS OWN ROOM, NATHANIEL DONS HIS NEW GARMENTS.
WITH THIS STRANGE DISGUISE I FOUND MYSELF IN LAST WEEK, NO ONE WILL KNOW ME. HENCE THEY WON'T HARM MY FAMILY FOR WHAT I'M ABOUT TO DO!
HERE THEY COME NOW, WITH MOTHER RATHLOW...
THE WATER TEST'LL TELL WHETHER SHE'S A WITCH OR NOT!
SHE WON'T FLOAT, DON'T WORRY!
STOP--STOP! MOTHER RATHLOW ISN'T A WITCH! ALL YOU'RE DOING IS BLAMING YOUR OWN TROUBLES ON HER!
WHO IS HE?
ONE OF HER FAMILIARS, NO DOUBT--PROBABLY A WIZARD!
AYE-LOOK AT THE STRANGE CLOTHES HE'S WEARING!
HE'S A DEMON, -THAT'S WHAT!
WE'LL BURN HIM, TOO!
THEY DON'T RECOGNIZE ME AS NATHANIEL PRATT, WHOM THEY'VE KNOWN ALL THEIR LIVES! -WHICH SHOWS HOW MUCH THEY'RE QUALIFIED TO JUDGE IF ANYONE IS WIZARD OR WITCH...
4.
IN SELF-DEFENSE, THE ATOM LASHES FORTH WITH CRUSHING BLOWS--
I AM SORRY INDEED TO DO THIS, FOLKS. BUT YOU LEAVE ME NO CHOICE--

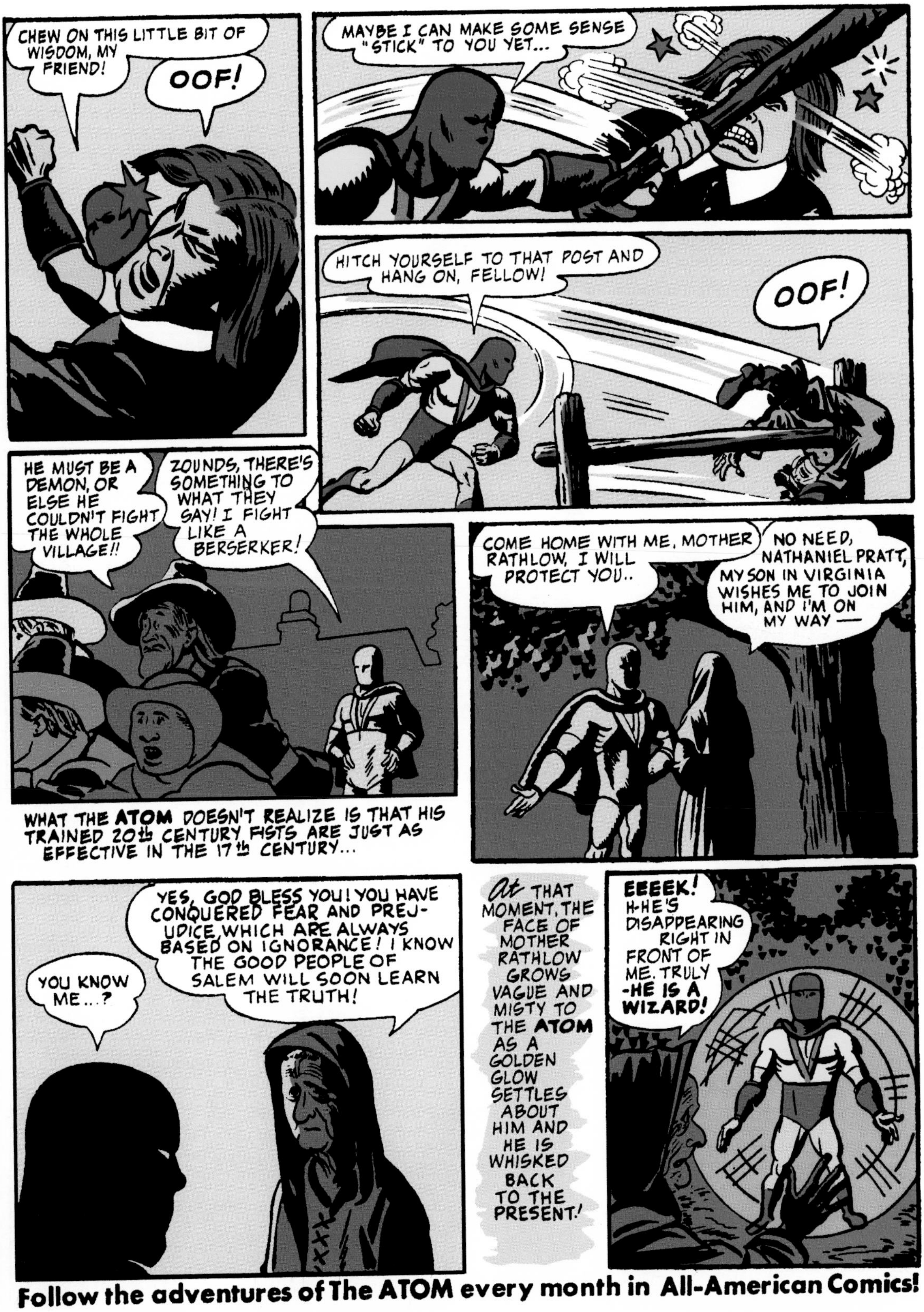
CHEW ON THIS LITTLE BIT OF WISDOM, MY FRIEND!
OOF!
MAYBE I CAN MAKE SOME SENSE "STICK" TO YOU YET...
HITCH YOURSELF TO THAT POST AND HANG ON, FELLOW!
OOF!
HE MUST BE A DEMON, OR ELSE HE COULDN'T FIGHT THE WHOLE VILLAGE!!
ZOUNDS, THERE'S SOMETHING TO WHAT THEY SAY! I FIGHT LIKE A BERSERKER!
WHAT THE ATOM DOESN'T REALIZE IS THAT HIS TRAINED 20th CENTURY FISTS ARE JUST AS EFFECTIVE IN THE 17th CENTURY...
COME HOME WITH ME, MOTHER RATHLOW, I WILL PROTECT YOU..
NO NEED, NATHANIEL PRATT, MY SON IN VIRGINIA WISHES ME TO JOIN HIM, AND I'M ON MY WAY —
YES, GOD BLESS YOU! YOU HAVE CONQUERED FEAR AND PREJUDICE WHICH ARE ALWAYS BASED ON IGNORANCE! I KNOW THE GOOD PEOPLE OF SALEM WILL SOON LEARN THE TRUTH!
YOU KNOW ME...?
At THAT MOMENT, THE FACE OF MOTHER RATHLOW GROWS VAGUE AND MISTY TO THE ATOM AS A GOLDEN GLOW SETTLES ABOUT HIM AND HE IS WHISKED BACK TO THE PRESENT!
EEEEK! H-HE'S DISAPPEARING RIGHT IN FRONT OF ME. TRULY -HE IS A WIZARD!

Follow the adventures of The ATOM every month in All-American Comics!

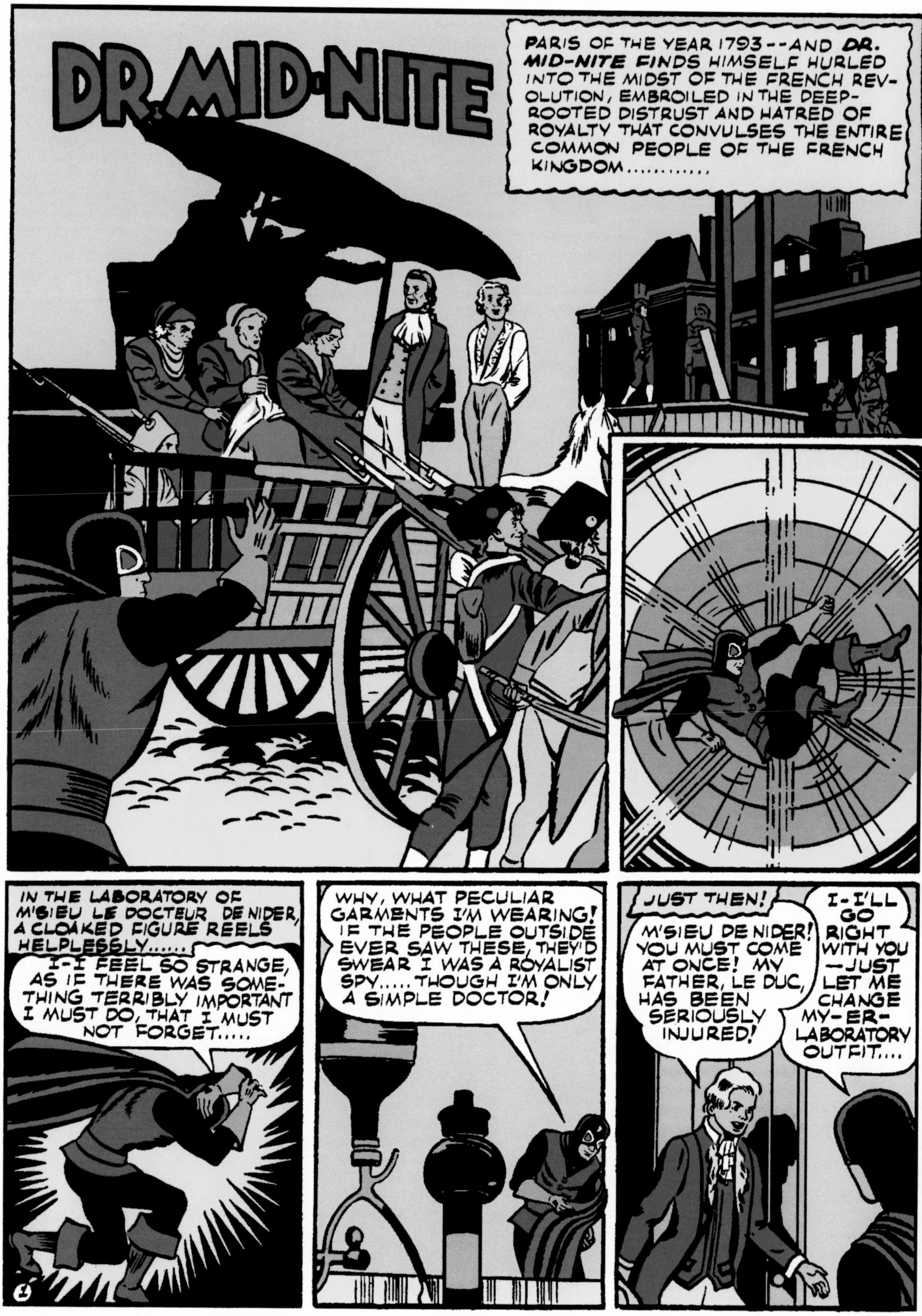
DR. MID-NITE
PARIS OF THE YEAR 1793--AND DR. MID-NITE FINDS HIMSELF HURLED INTO THE MIDST OF THE FRENCH REVOLUTION, EMBROILED IN THE DEEP-ROOTED DISTRUST AND HATRED OF ROYALTY THAT CONVULSES THE ENTIRE COMMON PEOPLE OF THE FRENCH KINGDOM...........
IN THE LABORATORY OF M'SIEU LE DOCTEUR DE NIDER, A CLOAKED FIGURE REELS HELPLESSLY......
I-I FEEL SO STRANGE, AS IF THERE WAS SOMETHING TERRIBLY IMPORTANT I MUST DO, THAT I MUST NOT FORGET.....
WHY, WHAT PECULIAR GARMENTS I'M WEARING! IF THE PEOPLE OUTSIDE EVER SAW THESE, THEY'D SWEAR I WAS A ROYALIST SPY.....THOUGH I'M ONLY A SIMPLE DOCTOR!
JUST THEN!
M'SIEU DE NIDER! YOU MUST COME AT ONCE! MY FATHER, LE DUC, HAS BEEN SERIOUSLY INJURED!
I-I'LL GO RIGHT WITH YOU --JUST LET ME CHANGE MY--ER--LABORATORY OUTFIT....

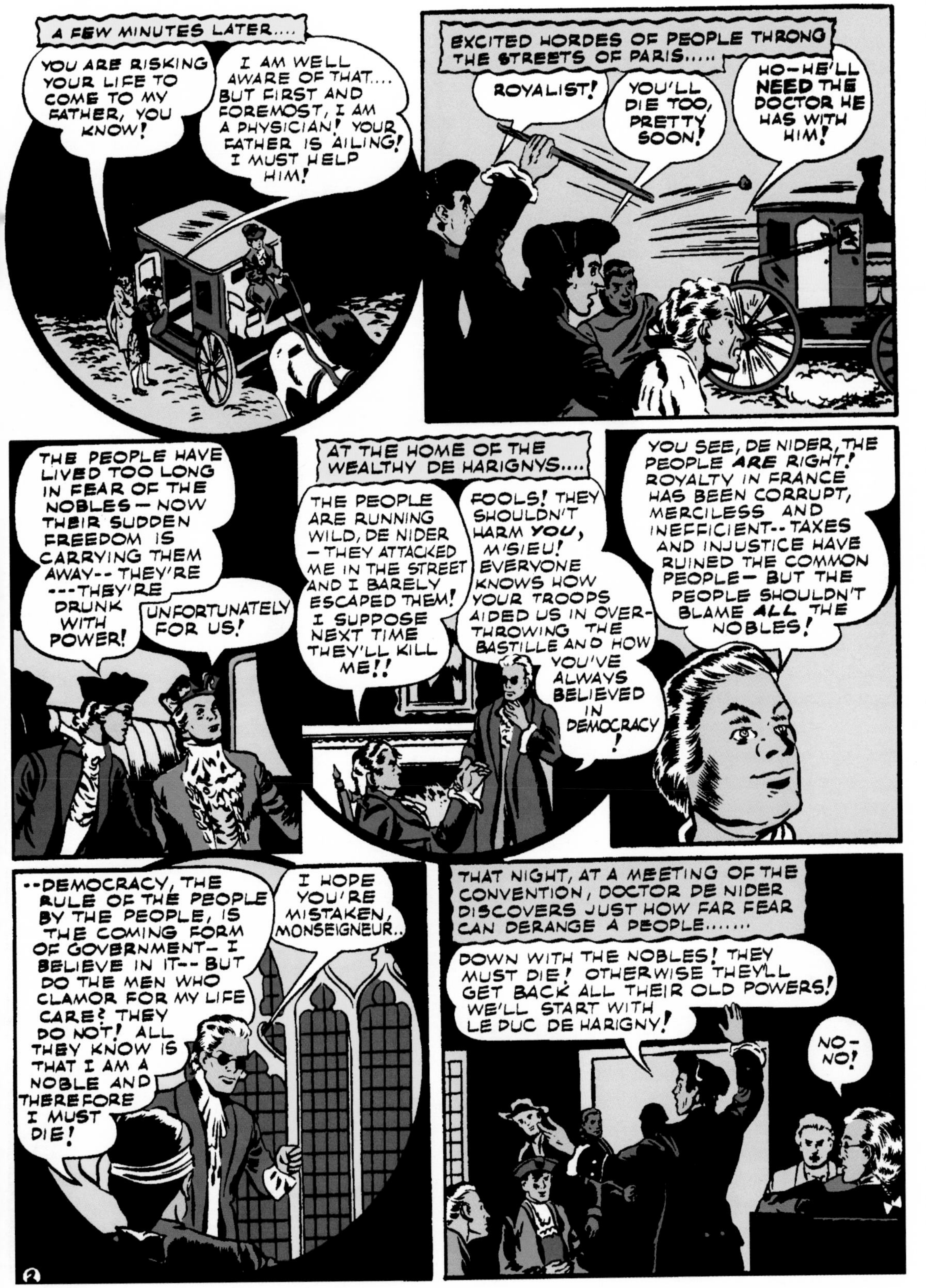
A FEW MINUTES LATER....
YOU ARE RISKING YOUR LIFE TO COME TO MY FATHER, YOU KNOW!
I AM WELL AWARE OF THAT.... BUT FIRST AND FOREMOST, I AM A PHYSICIAN! YOUR FATHER IS AILING! I MUST HELP HIM!
EXCITED HORDES OF PEOPLE THRONG THE STREETS OF PARIS.....
ROYALIST!
YOU'LL DIE TOO, PRETTY SOON!
HO-HE'LL NEED THE DOCTOR HE HAS WITH HIM!
THE PEOPLE HAVE LIVED TOO LONG IN FEAR OF THE NOBLES — NOW THEIR SUDDEN FREEDOM IS CARRYING THEM AWAY-- THEY'RE ---THEY'RE DRUNK WITH POWER!
UNFORTUNATELY FOR US!
AT THE HOME OF THE WEALTHY DE HARIGNYS....
THE PEOPLE ARE RUNNING WILD, DE NIDER — THEY ATTACKED ME IN THE STREET AND I BARELY ESCAPED THEM! I SUPPOSE NEXT TIME THEY'LL KILL ME!!
FOOLS! THEY SHOULDN'T HARM YOU, M'SIEU! EVERYONE KNOWS HOW YOUR TROOPS AIDED US IN OVER-THROWING THE BASTILLE AND HOW YOU'VE ALWAYS BELIEVED IN DEMOCRACY!
YOU SEE, DE NIDER, THE PEOPLE ARE RIGHT! ROYALTY IN FRANCE HAS BEEN CORRUPT, MERCILESS AND INEFFICIENT--TAXES AND INJUSTICE HAVE RUINED THE COMMON PEOPLE— BUT THE PEOPLE SHOULDN'T BLAME ALL THE NOBLES!
--DEMOCRACY, THE RULE OF THE PEOPLE BY THE PEOPLE, IS THE COMING FORM OF GOVERNMENT— I BELIEVE IN IT-- BUT DO THE MEN WHO CLAMOR FOR MY LIFE CARE? THEY DO NOT! ALL THEY KNOW IS THAT I AM A NOBLE AND THEREFORE I MUST DIE!
I HOPE YOU'RE MISTAKEN, MONSEIGNEUR..
2
THAT NIGHT, AT A MEETING OF THE CONVENTION, DOCTOR DE NIDER DISCOVERS JUST HOW FAR FEAR CAN DERANGE A PEOPLE.......
DOWN WITH THE NOBLES! THEY MUST DIE! OTHERWISE THEY'LL GET BACK ALL THEIR OLD POWERS! WE'LL START WITH LE DUC DE HARIGNY!
NO-NO!

MEN OF FRANCE! STOP AND THINK WHAT YOU'RE DOING! YOU WOULD CONDEMN A MAN JUST BECAUSE HE IS A NOBLE, FORGETTING ALL THE GOOD HE HAS DONE! THAT IS RANK TYRANNY!

NO NO!

TRAITOR! ROYALTY LOVER!

WE SHOULD KILL YOU TOO!

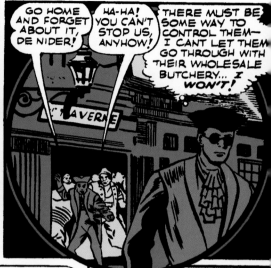

GO HOME AND FORGET ABOUT IT, DE NIDER!

HA-HA! YOU CAN'T STOP US, ANYHOW!

THERE MUST BE SOME WAY TO CONTROL THEM—I CANT LET THEM GO THROUGH WITH THEIR WHOLESALE BUTCHERY... I WON'T!

IF THEY KNOW I AM GOING TO TRY TO PREVENT THEIR SCHEMES, THEY'LL KILL ME, AND NOTHING WOULD BE GAINED! IF THERE WERE ONLY SOME WAY TO......WAIT A MOMENT!

WHY NOT USE THESE CLOTHES FOR A DISGUISE? NO ONE KNOWS WHERE THEY CAME FROM—NOT EVEN I! IN THIS COSTUME, NONE OF MY COLLEAGUES WOULD RECOGNIZE ME!

THE FOLLOWING NIGHT, A SURLY MOB MARCHES ON THE DE HARIGNY HOME...

VIVE LA REPUBLIQUE!

DOWN WITH THE NOBLES!!

I HAVE TO SAVE MY PEOPLE FROM THEIR OWN FOOLISHNESS—OTHERWISE, THEY WILL MURDER MANY OF THEIR FRIENDS —

CITIZENS OF FRANCE—HALT!

LOOK OUT!

WHA—!

3

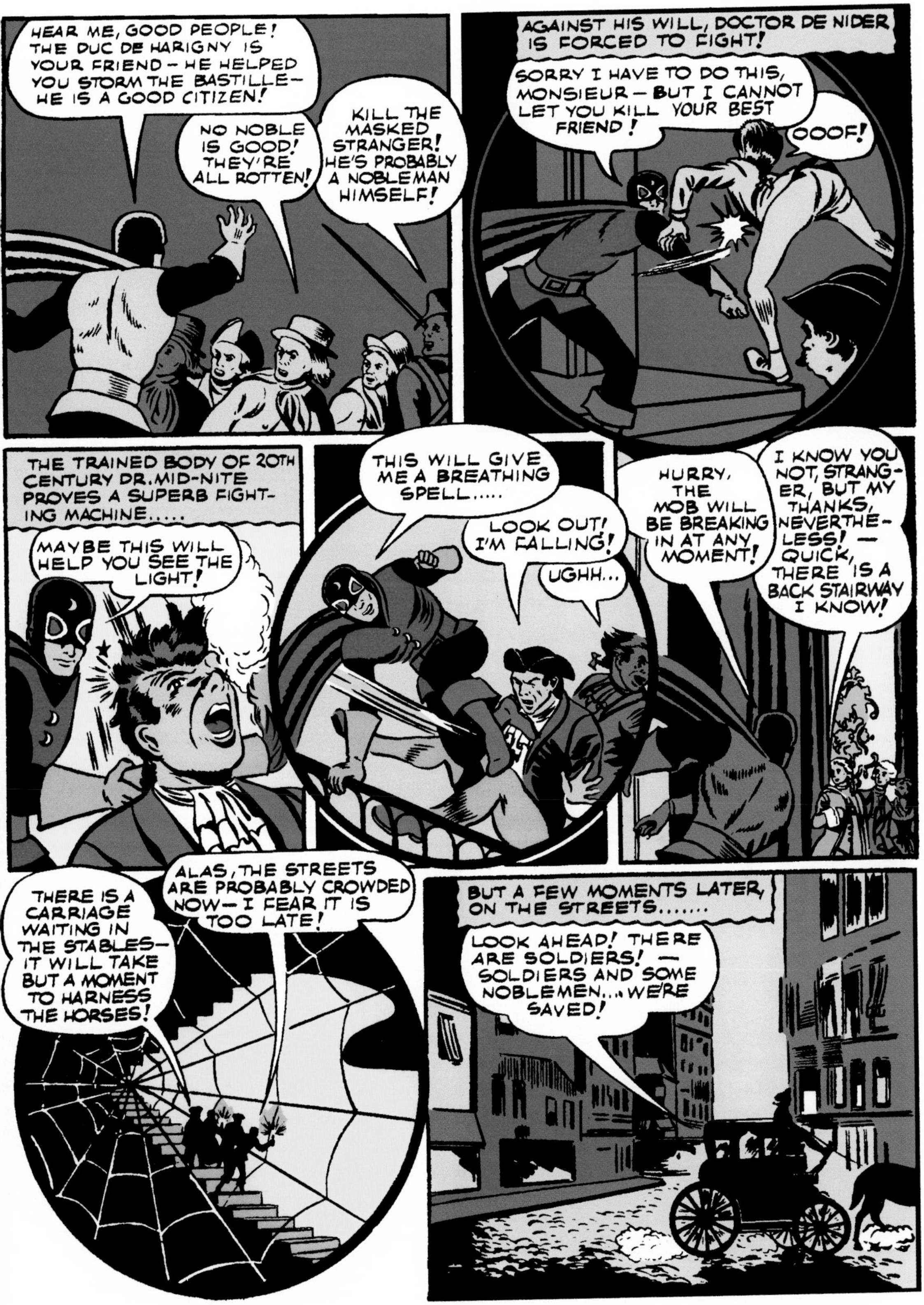
HEAR ME, GOOD PEOPLE! THE DUC DE HARIGNY IS YOUR FRIEND — HE HELPED YOU STORM THE BASTILLE — HE IS A GOOD CITIZEN!
NO NOBLE IS GOOD! THEY'RE ALL ROTTEN!
KILL THE MASKED STRANGER! HE'S PROBABLY A NOBLEMAN HIMSELF!
AGAINST HIS WILL, DOCTOR DE NIDER IS FORCED TO FIGHT!
SORRY I HAVE TO DO THIS, MONSIEUR — BUT I CANNOT LET YOU KILL YOUR BEST FRIEND!
OOOF!
THE TRAINED BODY OF 20TH CENTURY DR. MID-NITE PROVES A SUPERB FIGHTING MACHINE.....
MAYBE THIS WILL HELP YOU SEE THE LIGHT!
THIS WILL GIVE ME A BREATHING SPELL.....
LOOK OUT! I'M FALLING!
UGHH...
HURRY, THE MOB WILL BE BREAKING IN AT ANY MOMENT!
I KNOW YOU NOT, STRANGER, BUT MY THANKS, NEVERTHELESS! — QUICK, THERE IS A BACK STAIRWAY I KNOW!
THERE IS A CARRIAGE WAITING IN THE STABLES — IT WILL TAKE BUT A MOMENT TO HARNESS THE HORSES!
ALAS, THE STREETS ARE PROBABLY CROWDED NOW — I FEAR IT IS TOO LATE!
BUT A FEW MOMENTS LATER, ON THE STREETS.......
LOOK AHEAD! THERE ARE SOLDIERS! — SOLDIERS AND SOME NOBLEMEN... WE'RE SAVED!

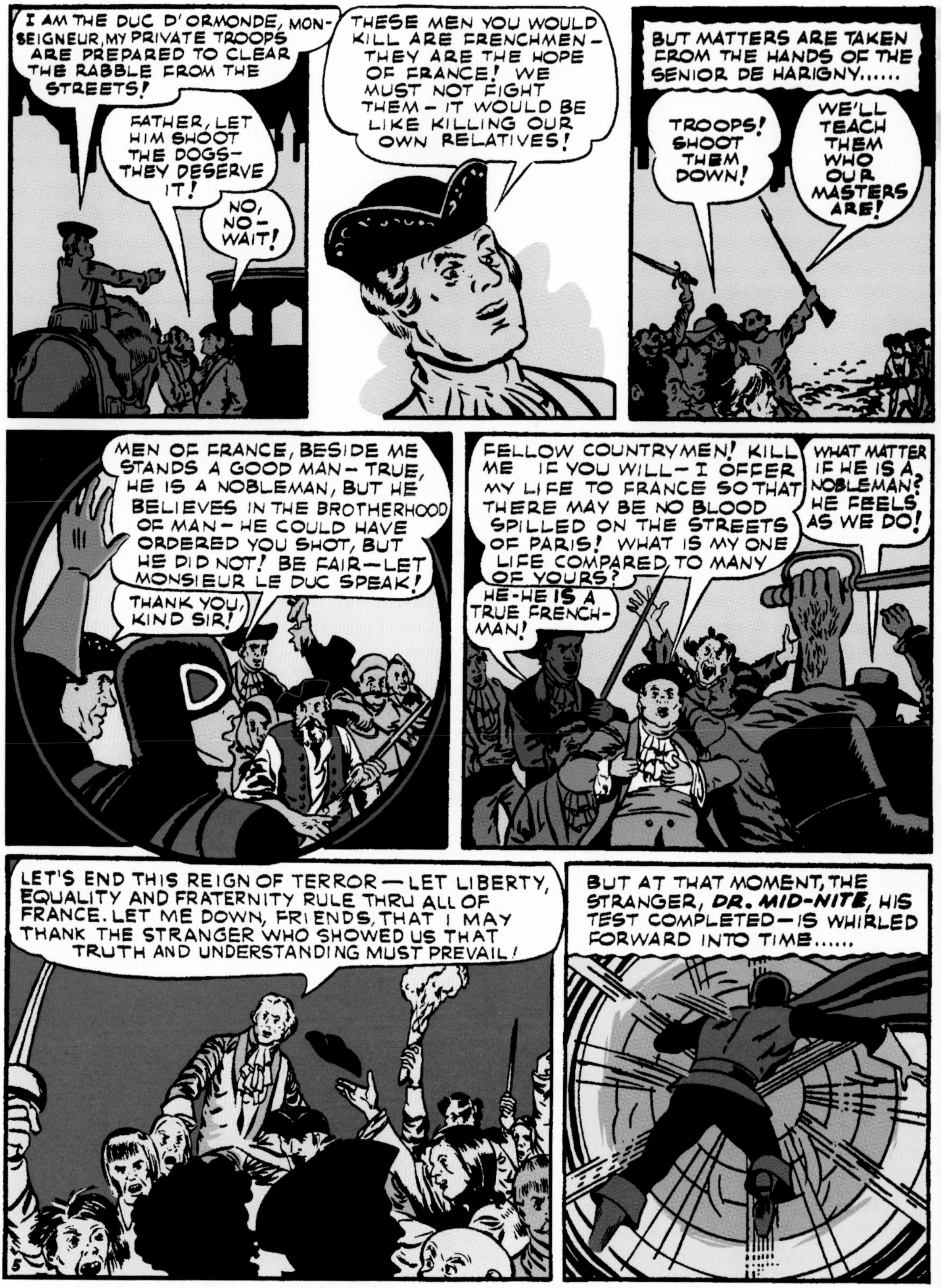
I AM THE DUC D'ORMONDE, MONSEIGNEUR, MY PRIVATE TROOPS ARE PREPARED TO CLEAR THE RABBLE FROM THE STREETS!
FATHER, LET HIM SHOOT THE DOGS-THEY DESERVE IT!
NO, NO-WAIT!
THESE MEN YOU WOULD KILL ARE FRENCHMEN-THEY ARE THE HOPE OF FRANCE! WE MUST NOT FIGHT THEM-IT WOULD BE LIKE KILLING OUR OWN RELATIVES!
BUT MATTERS ARE TAKEN FROM THE HANDS OF THE SENIOR DE HARIGNY......
TROOPS! SHOOT THEM DOWN!
WE'LL TEACH THEM WHO OUR MASTERS ARE!
MEN OF FRANCE, BESIDE ME STANDS A GOOD MAN-TRUE, HE IS A NOBLEMAN, BUT HE BELIEVES IN THE BROTHERHOOD OF MAN-HE COULD HAVE ORDERED YOU SHOT, BUT HE DID NOT! BE FAIR-LET MONSIEUR LE DUC SPEAK!
THANK YOU, KIND SIR!
FELLOW COUNTRYMEN! KILL ME IF YOU WILL-I OFFER MY LIFE TO FRANCE SO THAT THERE MAY BE NO BLOOD SPILLED ON THE STREETS OF PARIS! WHAT IS MY ONE LIFE COMPARED TO MANY OF YOURS?
WHAT MATTER IF HE IS A NOBLEMAN? HE FEELS AS WE DO!
HE-HE IS A TRUE FRENCHMAN!
LET'S END THIS REIGN OF TERROR—LET LIBERTY, EQUALITY AND FRATERNITY RULE THRU ALL OF FRANCE. LET ME DOWN, FRIENDS, THAT I MAY THANK THE STRANGER WHO SHOWED US THAT TRUTH AND UNDERSTANDING MUST PREVAIL!
BUT AT THAT MOMENT, THE STRANGER, DR. MID-NITE, HIS TEST COMPLETED—IS WHIRLED FORWARD INTO TIME......
5

Dr. Midnite appears in every issue of All-American Comics

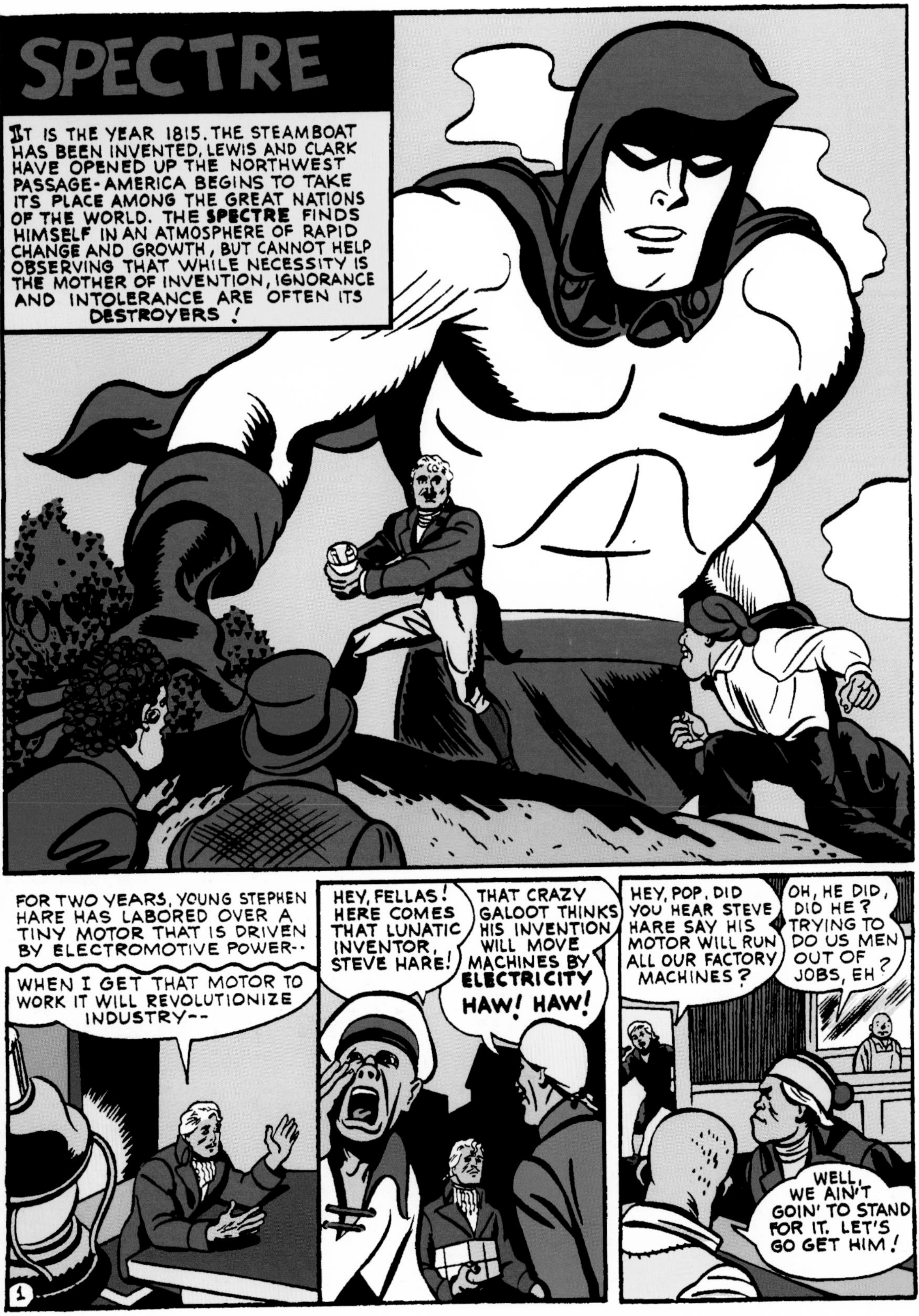
SPECTRE
IT IS THE YEAR 1815. THE STEAMBOAT HAS BEEN INVENTED, LEWIS AND CLARK HAVE OPENED UP THE NORTHWEST PASSAGE - AMERICA BEGINS TO TAKE ITS PLACE AMONG THE GREAT NATIONS OF THE WORLD. THE SPECTRE FINDS HIMSELF IN AN ATMOSPHERE OF RAPID CHANGE AND GROWTH, BUT CANNOT HELP OBSERVING THAT WHILE NECESSITY IS THE MOTHER OF INVENTION, IGNORANCE AND INTOLERANCE ARE OFTEN ITS DESTROYERS!
FOR TWO YEARS, YOUNG STEPHEN HARE HAS LABORED OVER A TINY MOTOR THAT IS DRIVEN BY ELECTROMOTIVE POWER--
WHEN I GET THAT MOTOR TO WORK IT WILL REVOLUTIONIZE INDUSTRY--
1
HEY, FELLAS! HERE COMES THAT LUNATIC INVENTOR, STEVE HARE!
THAT CRAZY GALOOT THINKS HIS INVENTION WILL MOVE MACHINES BY ELECTRICITY HAW! HAW!
HEY, POP, DID YOU HEAR STEVE HARE SAY HIS MOTOR WILL RUN ALL OUR FACTORY MACHINES?
OH, HE DID, DID HE? TRYING TO DO US MEN OUT OF JOBS, EH?
WELL, WE AIN'T GOIN' TO STAND FOR IT. LET'S GO GET HIM!

AS THE ANGRY WORKERS HEAD FOR HARE'S WORKSHOP, A STRANGE FIGURE STIRS IN THE SHADOWS--
WE'LL SMASH THAT GADGET OF HIS ONCE AN' FOR ALL.
AYE--AND MAYBE HIS HEAD, TOO!
I-I HEAR ANGRY VOICES BUT WHERE AM I? I CAN'T RECALL A THING!
I'M A SPIRIT--AND YET I HAVE POWER TO TOUCH THINGS, TO HEAR SOUNDS! I HEAR THOSE MEN CLEARLY THEY'RE GOING TO HARM SOMEONE-HARM? I-I CAN'T LET THEM DO THAT!
I'LL HAVE TO FIND OUT WHAT THIS IS ALL ABOUT, FIRST. THEN I CAN DECIDE WHAT TO DO!
THE ANGRY WORKERS OVERTAKE HARE IN HIS WORKSHOP--
YOU THINK THAT LITTLE THING COULD RUN A MACHINE?
WHETHER IT CAN OR NOT WE'LL KNOCK ANY IDEAS HARE HAS ON THE SUBJECT OUT OF HIS HEAD!
YOU'LL NOT BE DOING US OUT OF JOBS, STEVE HARE
GRAB HIS MOTOR - SMASH IT!
NO, NO, YOU IDIOTS! DON'T YOU UNDERSTAND? THIS INVENTION WILL MAKE EVEN MORE JOBS FOR YOU!
CAN'T YOU SEE THAT IF THOSE FACTORY MACHINES OF YOURS ARE DRIVEN BY MY MOTOR IT WILL MEAN A GREATER VOLUME OF PRODUCTION AT LESS COST TO THE BUYING PUBLIC? THIS IN TURN WILL LEAD TO A GREATER DEMAND FOR YOUR MANUFACTURED GOODS AND MORE JOBS AND MORE MONEY FOR YOU!
HE'S RIGHT!
2
A PACK OF LIES! HERE'S ONE INVENTION THAT AIN'T GONNA BE INVENTED!
YOUR MACHINE IS A "SMASHING" SUCCESS, HARE! HAW! HAW!
SMASH
STOP! STOP!

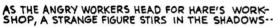

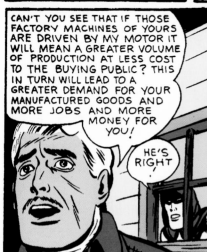

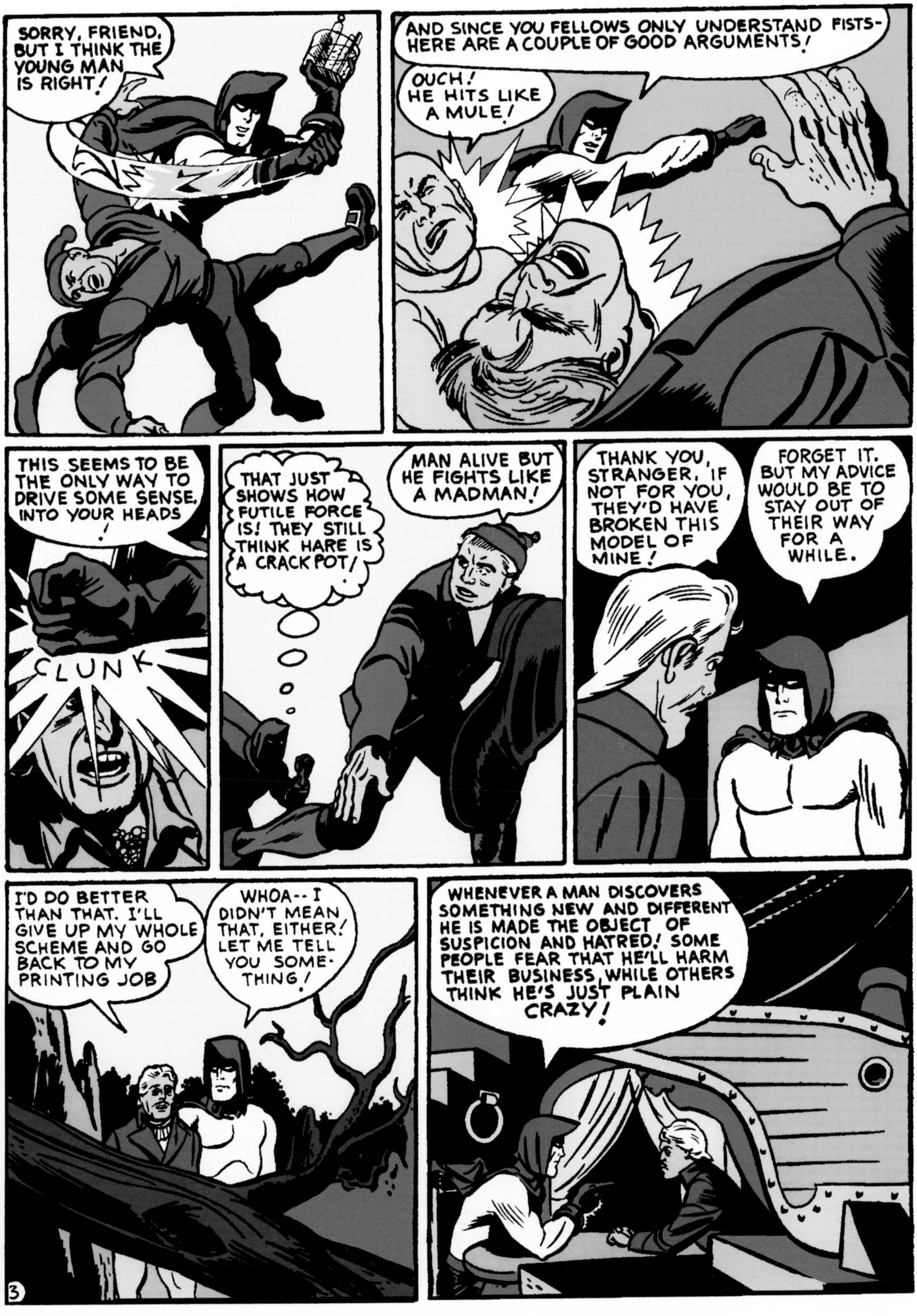
SORRY, FRIEND, BUT I THINK THE YOUNG MAN IS RIGHT!
AND SINCE YOU FELLOWS ONLY UNDERSTAND FISTS- HERE ARE A COUPLE OF GOOD ARGUMENTS!
OUCH! HE HITS LIKE A MULE!
THIS SEEMS TO BE THE ONLY WAY TO DRIVE SOME SENSE INTO YOUR HEADS!
CLUNK
THAT JUST SHOWS HOW FUTILE FORCE IS! THEY STILL THINK HARE IS A CRACKPOT!
MAN ALIVE BUT HE FIGHTS LIKE A MADMAN!
THANK YOU, STRANGER. IF NOT FOR YOU, THEY'D HAVE BROKEN THIS MODEL OF MINE!
FORGET IT. BUT MY ADVICE WOULD BE TO STAY OUT OF THEIR WAY FOR A WHILE.
I'D DO BETTER THAN THAT. I'LL GIVE UP MY WHOLE SCHEME AND GO BACK TO MY PRINTING JOB
WHOA-- I DIDN'T MEAN THAT, EITHER! LET ME TELL YOU SOMETHING!
3
WHENEVER A MAN DISCOVERS SOMETHING NEW AND DIFFERENT HE IS MADE THE OBJECT OF SUSPICION AND HATRED! SOME PEOPLE FEAR THAT HE'LL HARM THEIR BUSINESS, WHILE OTHERS THINK HE'S JUST PLAIN CRAZY!

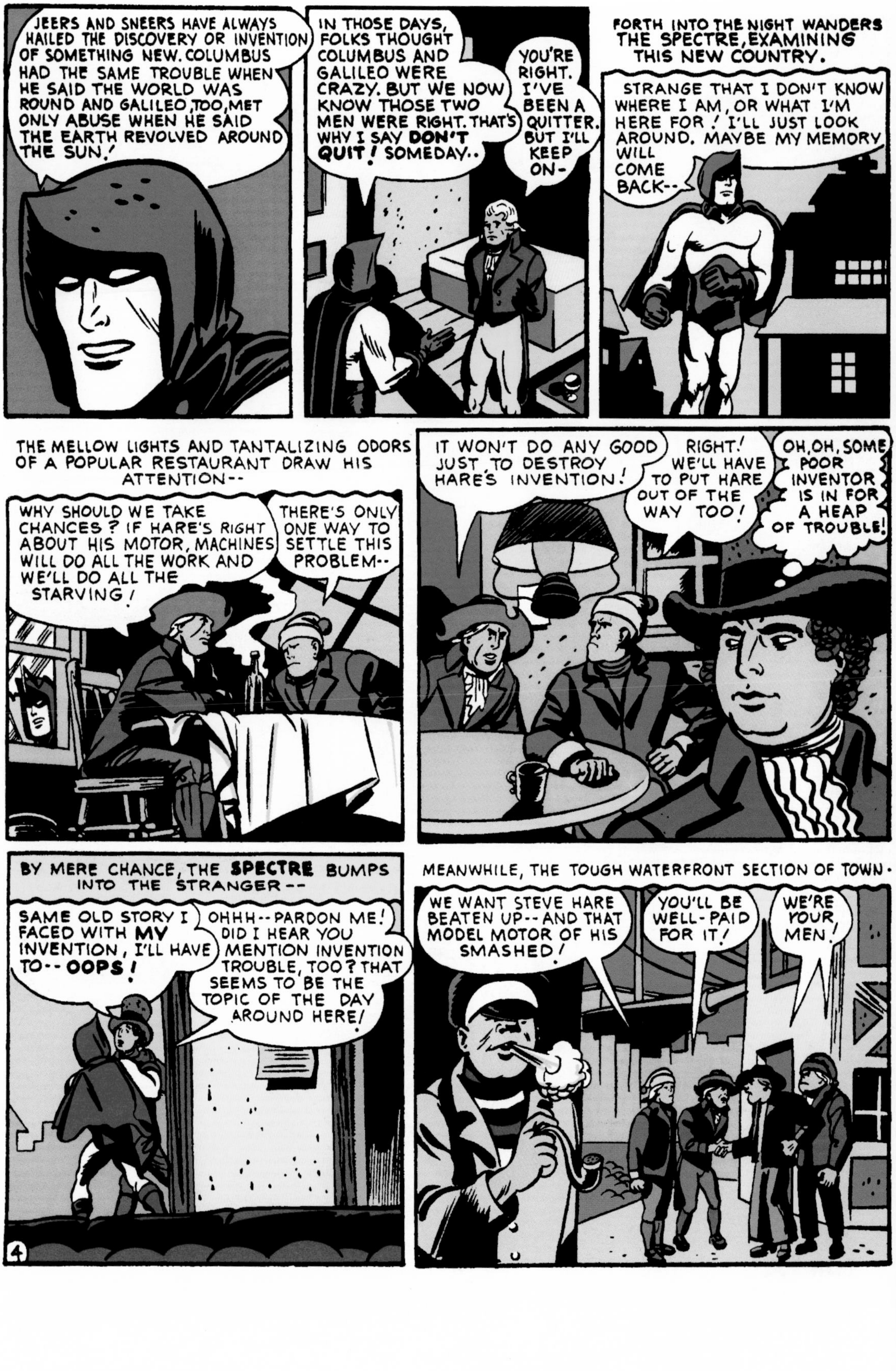
JEERS AND SNEERS HAVE ALWAYS HAILED THE DISCOVERY OR INVENTION OF SOMETHING NEW. COLUMBUS HAD THE SAME TROUBLE WHEN HE SAID THE WORLD WAS ROUND AND GALILEO, TOO, MET ONLY ABUSE WHEN HE SAID THE EARTH REVOLVED AROUND THE SUN!
IN THOSE DAYS, FOLKS THOUGHT COLUMBUS AND GALILEO WERE CRAZY. BUT WE NOW KNOW THOSE TWO MEN WERE RIGHT. THAT'S WHY I SAY DON'T QUIT! SOMEDAY..
YOU'RE RIGHT. I'VE BEEN A QUITTER. BUT I'LL KEEP ON-
FORTH INTO THE NIGHT WANDERS THE SPECTRE, EXAMINING THIS NEW COUNTRY.
STRANGE THAT I DON'T KNOW WHERE I AM, OR WHAT I'M HERE FOR! I'LL JUST LOOK AROUND. MAYBE MY MEMORY WILL COME BACK--
THE MELLOW LIGHTS AND TANTALIZING ODORS OF A POPULAR RESTAURANT DRAW HIS ATTENTION--
WHY SHOULD WE TAKE CHANCES? IF HARE'S RIGHT ABOUT HIS MOTOR, MACHINES WILL DO ALL THE WORK AND WE'LL DO ALL THE STARVING!
THERE'S ONLY ONE WAY TO SETTLE THIS PROBLEM--
IT WON'T DO ANY GOOD JUST TO DESTROY HARE'S INVENTION!
RIGHT! WE'LL HAVE TO PUT HARE OUT OF THE WAY TOO!
OH, OH, SOME POOR INVENTOR IS IN FOR A HEAP OF TROUBLE!
BY MERE CHANCE, THE SPECTRE BUMPS INTO THE STRANGER--
SAME OLD STORY I FACED WITH MY INVENTION, I'LL HAVE TO-- OOPS!
OHHH--PARDON ME! DID I HEAR YOU MENTION INVENTION TROUBLE, TOO? THAT SEEMS TO BE THE TOPIC OF THE DAY AROUND HERE!
4
MEANWHILE, THE TOUGH WATERFRONT SECTION OF TOWN.
WE WANT STEVE HARE BEATEN UP--AND THAT MODEL MOTOR OF HIS SMASHED!
YOU'LL BE WELL-PAID FOR IT!
WE'RE YOUR MEN!

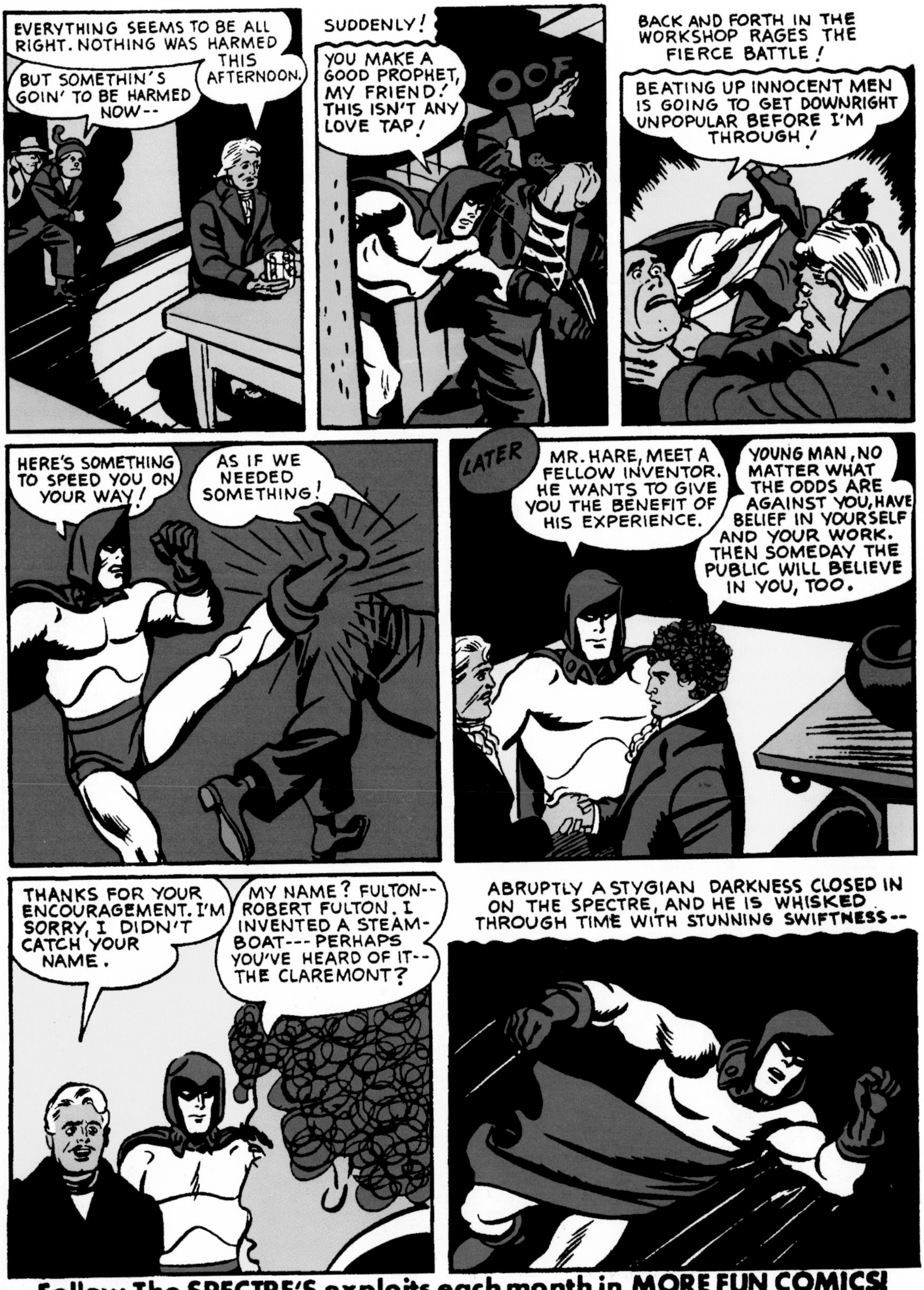
EVERYTHING SEEMS TO BE ALL RIGHT. NOTHING WAS HARMED THIS AFTERNOON.
BUT SOMETHIN'S GOIN' TO BE HARMED NOW--
SUDDENLY!
YOU MAKE A GOOD PROPHET, MY FRIEND! THIS ISN'T ANY LOVE TAP!
OOF
BACK AND FORTH IN THE WORKSHOP RAGES THE FIERCE BATTLE!
BEATING UP INNOCENT MEN IS GOING TO GET DOWNRIGHT UNPOPULAR BEFORE I'M THROUGH!
HERE'S SOMETHING TO SPEED YOU ON YOUR WAY!
AS IF WE NEEDED SOMETHING!
LATER
MR. HARE, MEET A FELLOW INVENTOR. HE WANTS TO GIVE YOU THE BENEFIT OF HIS EXPERIENCE.
YOUNG MAN, NO MATTER WHAT THE ODDS ARE AGAINST YOU, HAVE BELIEF IN YOURSELF AND YOUR WORK. THEN SOMEDAY THE PUBLIC WILL BELIEVE IN YOU, TOO.
THANKS FOR YOUR ENCOURAGEMENT. I'M SORRY, I DIDN'T CATCH YOUR NAME.
MY NAME? FULTON-- ROBERT FULTON. I INVENTED A STEAMBOAT--- PERHAPS YOU'VE HEARD OF IT-- THE CLAREMONT?
ABRUPTLY A STYGIAN DARKNESS CLOSED IN ON THE SPECTRE, AND HE IS WHISKED THROUGH TIME WITH STUNNING SWIFTNESS--

Follow The SPECTRE'S exploits each month in MORE FUN COMICS!

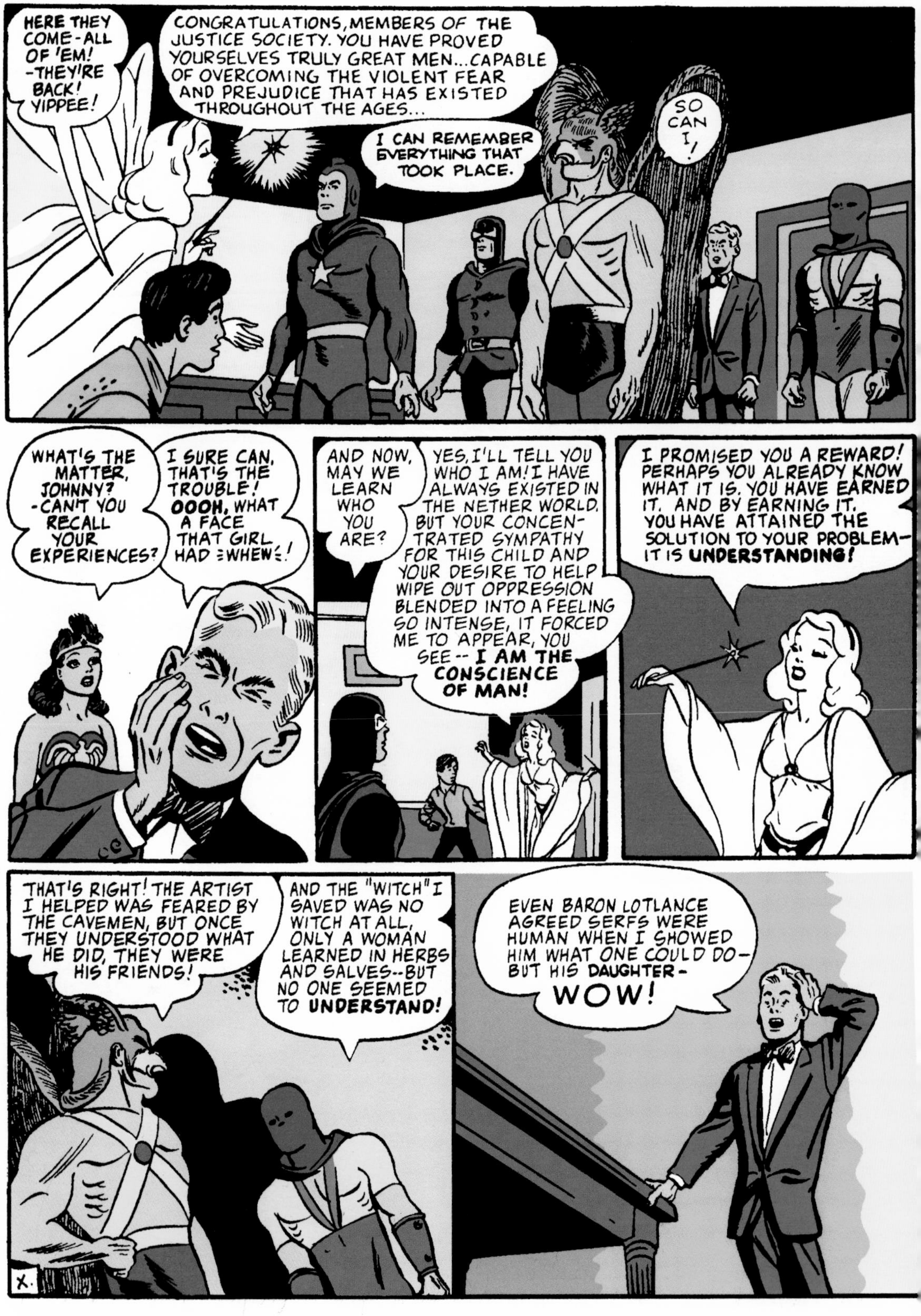
HERE THEY COME - ALL OF 'EM! - THEY'RE BACK! YIPPEE!
CONGRATULATIONS, MEMBERS OF THE JUSTICE SOCIETY. YOU HAVE PROVED YOURSELVES TRULY GREAT MEN... CAPABLE OF OVERCOMING THE VIOLENT FEAR AND PREJUDICE THAT HAS EXISTED THROUGHOUT THE AGES...
I CAN REMEMBER EVERYTHING THAT TOOK PLACE.
SO CAN I!
WHAT'S THE MATTER, JOHNNY? - CAN'T YOU RECALL YOUR EXPERIENCES?
I SURE CAN, THAT'S THE TROUBLE! OOOH, WHAT A FACE THAT GIRL HAD =WHEW=!
AND NOW, MAY WE LEARN WHO YOU ARE?
YES, I'LL TELL YOU WHO I AM! I HAVE ALWAYS EXISTED IN THE NETHER WORLD, BUT YOUR CONCENTRATED SYMPATHY FOR THIS CHILD AND YOUR DESIRE TO HELP WIPE OUT OPPRESSION BLENDED INTO A FEELING SO INTENSE, IT FORCED ME TO APPEAR, YOU SEE -- I AM THE CONSCIENCE OF MAN!
I PROMISED YOU A REWARD! PERHAPS YOU ALREADY KNOW WHAT IT IS. YOU HAVE EARNED IT. AND BY EARNING IT, YOU HAVE ATTAINED THE SOLUTION TO YOUR PROBLEM - IT IS UNDERSTANDING!
THAT'S RIGHT! THE ARTIST I HELPED WAS FEARED BY THE CAVEMEN, BUT ONCE THEY UNDERSTOOD WHAT HE DID, THEY WERE HIS FRIENDS!
AND THE "WITCH" I SAVED WAS NO WITCH AT ALL, ONLY A WOMAN LEARNED IN HERBS AND SALVES--BUT NO ONE SEEMED TO UNDERSTAND!
EVEN BARON LOTLANCE AGREED SERFS WERE HUMAN WHEN I SHOWED HIM WHAT ONE COULD DO - BUT HIS DAUGHTER - WOW!
X.

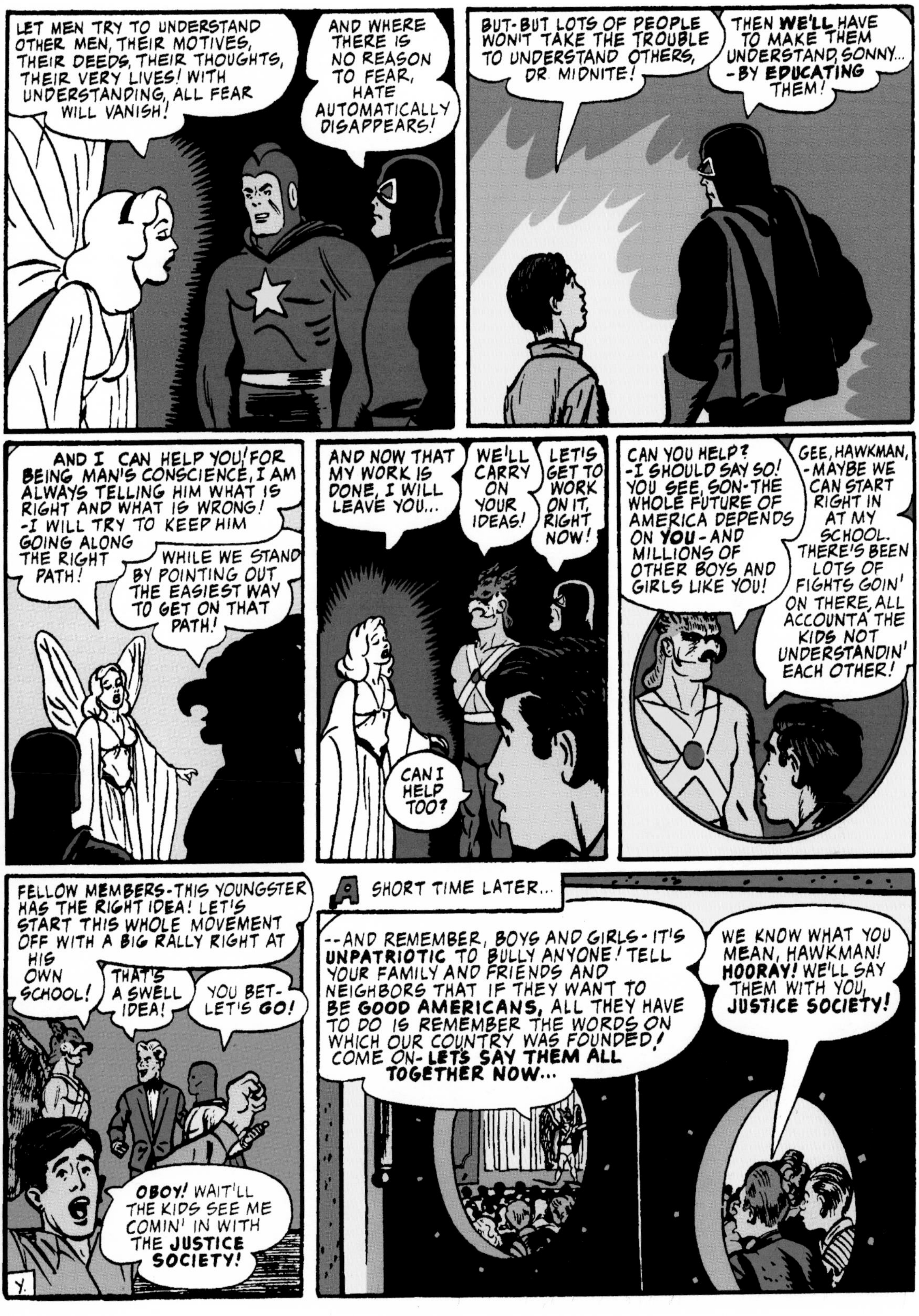
LET MEN TRY TO UNDERSTAND OTHER MEN, THEIR MOTIVES, THEIR DEEDS, THEIR THOUGHTS, THEIR VERY LIVES! WITH UNDERSTANDING, ALL FEAR WILL VANISH!
AND WHERE THERE IS NO REASON TO FEAR, HATE AUTOMATICALLY DISAPPEARS!
BUT-BUT LOTS OF PEOPLE WON'T TAKE THE TROUBLE TO UNDERSTAND OTHERS, DR. MIDNITE!
THEN WE'LL HAVE TO MAKE THEM UNDERSTAND, SONNY... -BY EDUCATING THEM!
AND I CAN HELP YOU! FOR BEING MAN'S CONSCIENCE, I AM ALWAYS TELLING HIM WHAT IS RIGHT AND WHAT IS WRONG! -I WILL TRY TO KEEP HIM GOING ALONG THE RIGHT PATH!
WHILE WE STAND BY POINTING OUT THE EASIEST WAY TO GET ON THAT PATH!
AND NOW THAT MY WORK IS DONE, I WILL LEAVE YOU...
WE'LL CARRY ON YOUR IDEAS!
LET'S GET TO WORK ON IT, RIGHT NOW!
CAN I HELP TOO?
CAN YOU HELP? -I SHOULD SAY SO! YOU SEE, SON-THE WHOLE FUTURE OF AMERICA DEPENDS ON YOU-AND MILLIONS OF OTHER BOYS AND GIRLS LIKE YOU!
GEE, HAWKMAN, -MAYBE WE CAN START RIGHT IN AT MY SCHOOL. THERE'S BEEN LOTS OF FIGHTS GOIN' ON THERE, ALL ACCOUNTA THE KIDS NOT UNDERSTANDIN' EACH OTHER!
FELLOW MEMBERS-THIS YOUNGSTER HAS THE RIGHT IDEA! LET'S START THIS WHOLE MOVEMENT OFF WITH A BIG RALLY RIGHT AT HIS OWN SCHOOL!
THAT'S A SWELL IDEA!
YOU BET- LET'S GO!
OBOY! WAIT'LL THE KIDS SEE ME COMIN' IN WITH THE JUSTICE SOCIETY!
A SHORT TIME LATER...
--AND REMEMBER, BOYS AND GIRLS-IT'S UNPATRIOTIC TO BULLY ANYONE! TELL YOUR FAMILY AND FRIENDS AND NEIGHBORS THAT IF THEY WANT TO BE GOOD AMERICANS, ALL THEY HAVE TO DO IS REMEMBER THE WORDS ON WHICH OUR COUNTRY WAS FOUNDED! COME ON-LETS SAY THEM ALL TOGETHER NOW...
WE KNOW WHAT YOU MEAN, HAWKMAN! HOORAY! WE'LL SAY THEM WITH YOU, JUSTICE SOCIETY!

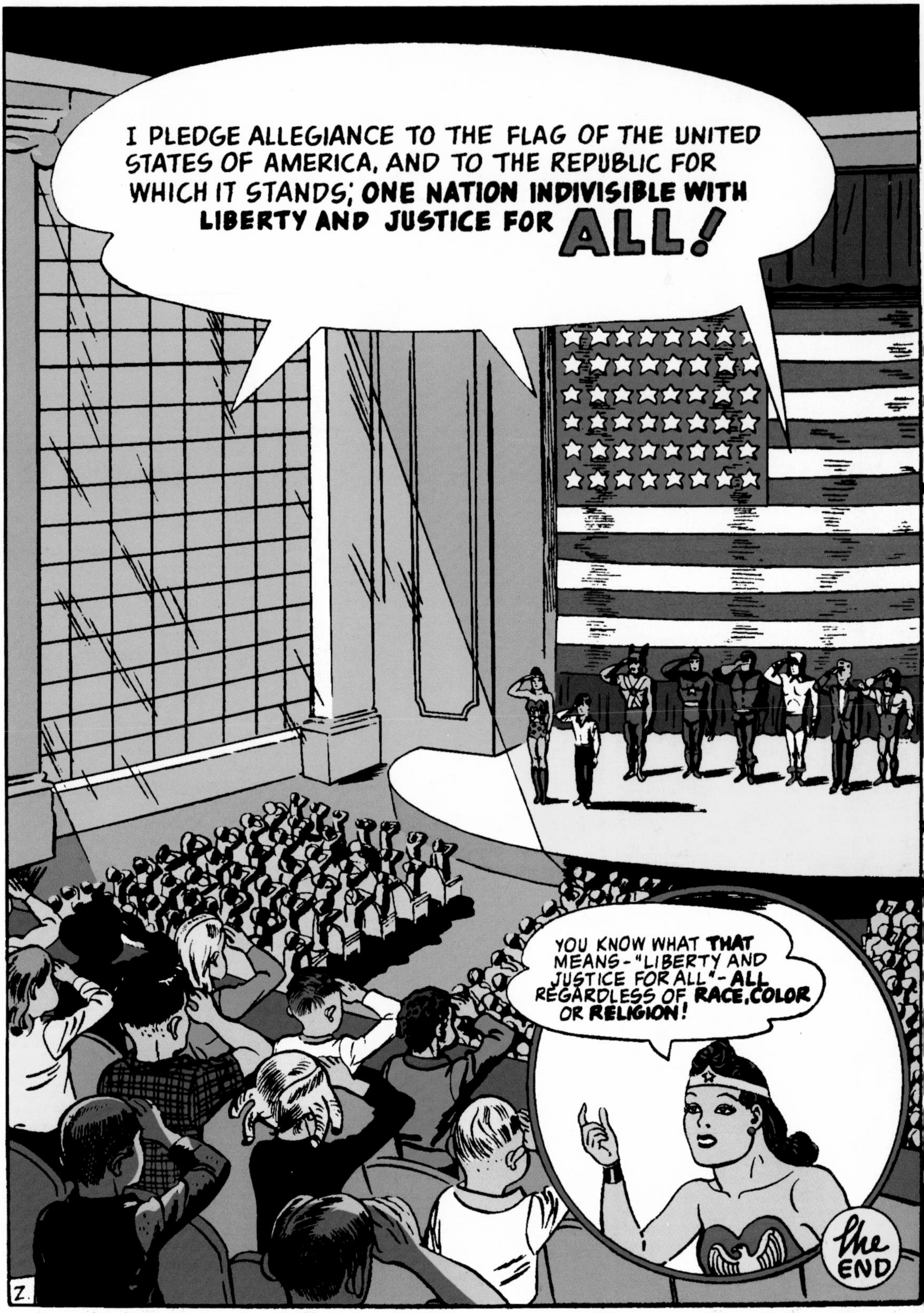
I PLEDGE ALLEGIANCE TO THE FLAG OF THE UNITED STATES OF AMERICA, AND TO THE REPUBLIC FOR WHICH IT STANDS; ONE NATION INDIVISIBLE WITH LIBERTY AND JUSTICE FOR ALL!
YOU KNOW WHAT THAT MEANS - "LIBERTY AND JUSTICE FOR ALL" - ALL REGARDLESS OF RACE, COLOR OR RELIGION!
the END
Z.

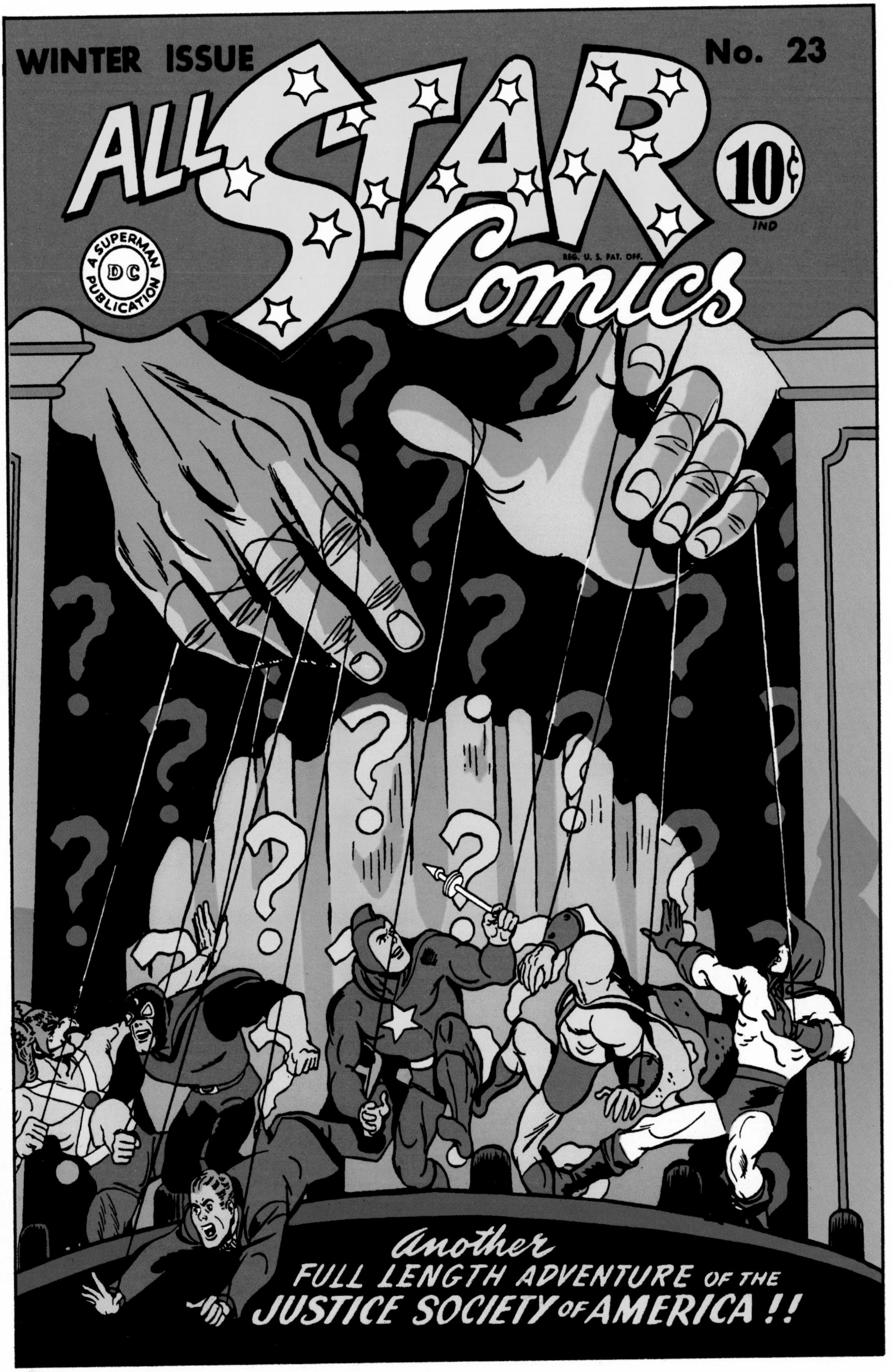
WINTER ISSUE
No. 23
ALL STAR Comics
10¢
IND
A SUPERMAN DC PUBLICATION
REG. U. S. PAT. OFF.
Another
FULL LENGTH ADVENTURE OF THE
JUSTICE SOCIETY OF AMERICA !!

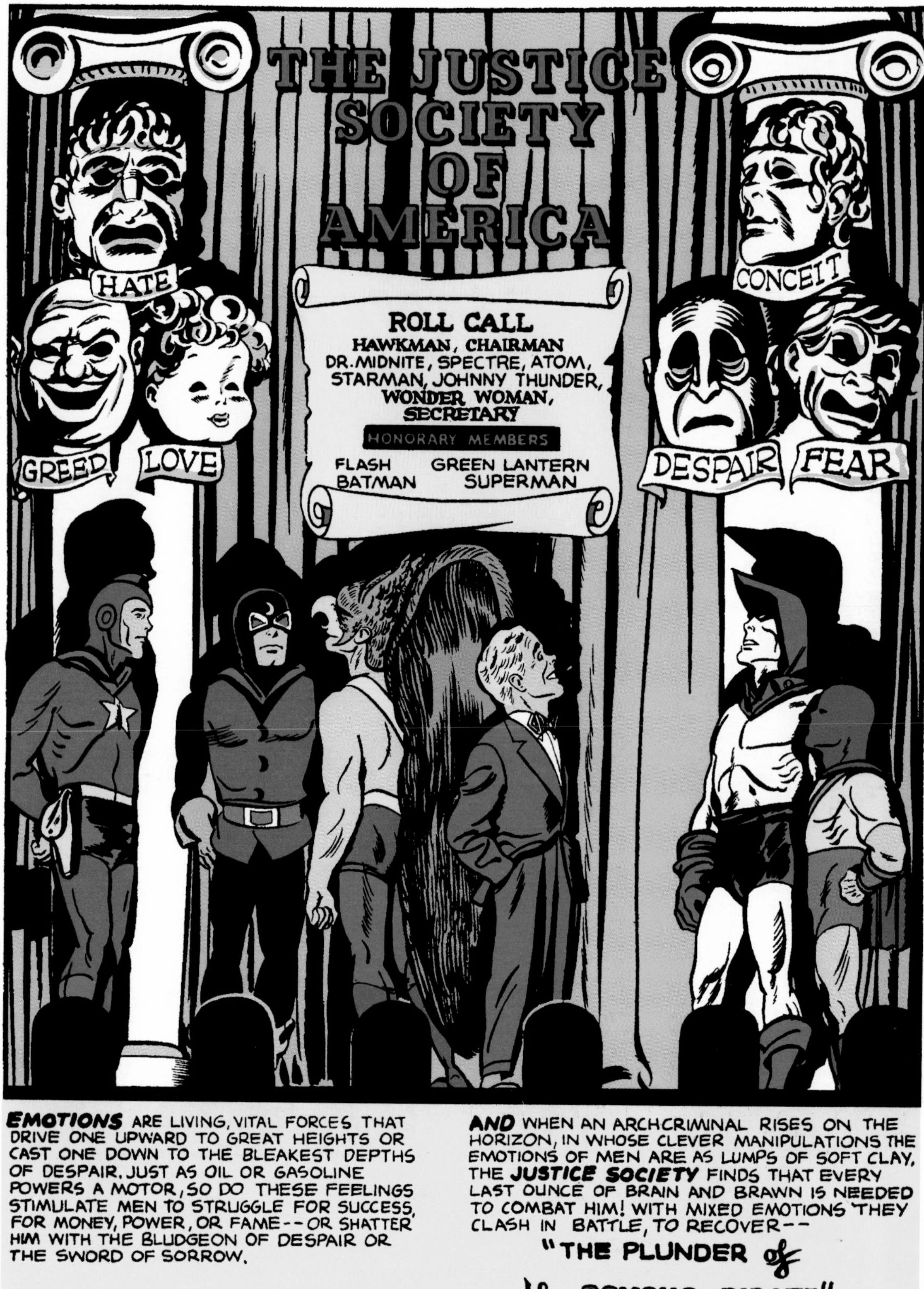
THE JUSTICE SOCIETY OF AMERICA
HATE
GREED
LOVE
CONCEIT
DESPAIR
FEAR
ROLL CALL
HAWKMAN, CHAIRMAN
DR. MIDNITE, SPECTRE, ATOM, STARMAN, JOHNNY THUNDER, WONDER WOMAN, SECRETARY
HONORARY MEMBERS
FLASH GREEN LANTERN
BATMAN SUPERMAN
EMOTIONS ARE LIVING, VITAL FORCES THAT DRIVE ONE UPWARD TO GREAT HEIGHTS OR CAST ONE DOWN TO THE BLEAKEST DEPTHS OF DESPAIR. JUST AS OIL OR GASOLINE POWERS A MOTOR, SO DO THESE FEELINGS STIMULATE MEN TO STRUGGLE FOR SUCCESS, FOR MONEY, POWER, OR FAME--OR SHATTER HIM WITH THE BLUDGEON OF DESPAIR OR THE SWORD OF SORROW.
AND WHEN AN ARCHCRIMINAL RISES ON THE HORIZON, IN WHOSE CLEVER MANIPULATIONS THE EMOTIONS OF MEN ARE AS LUMPS OF SOFT CLAY, THE JUSTICE SOCIETY FINDS THAT EVERY LAST OUNCE OF BRAIN AND BRAWN IS NEEDED TO COMBAT HIM! WITH MIXED EMOTIONS THEY CLASH IN BATTLE, TO RECOVER--
"THE PLUNDER of the PSYCHO-PIRATE"

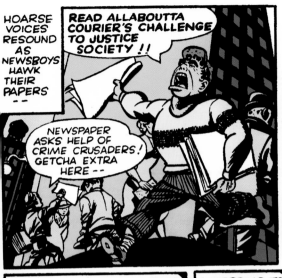

HOARSE VOICES RESOUND AS NEWSBOYS HAWK THEIR PAPERS --

READ ALLABOUTTA COURIER'S CHALLENGE TO JUSTICE SOCIETY!!

NEWSPAPER ASKS HELP OF CRIME CRUSADERS! GETCHA EXTRA HERE --

IN A ROOM ABOVE THE CROWDED CORNER SIT SIX MEN --

I CALLED YOU TOGETHER TO DISCUSS THE COURIER'S ADVERTISED CHALLENGE, FELLOW MEMBERS.

IT'S ABOUT THE MAN WHO CALLS HIMSELF THE PSYCHO-PIRATE, ISN'T IT?

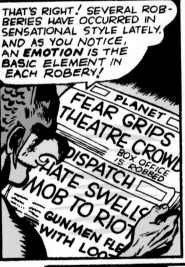

THAT'S RIGHT! SEVERAL ROBBERIES HAVE OCCURRED IN SENSATIONAL STYLE LATELY, AND AS YOU NOTICE, AN EMOTION IS THE BASIC ELEMENT IN EACH ROBERY!

PLANET — FEAR GRIPS THEATRE CROWD BOX OFFICE IS ROBBED — DISPATCH — HATE SWELLS MOB TO RIOT — GUNMEN FLE WITH LOO

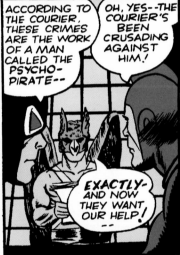

ACCORDING TO THE COURIER, THESE CRIMES ARE THE WORK OF A MAN CALLED THE PSYCHO-PIRATE--

OH, YES--THE COURIER'S BEEN CRUSADING AGAINST HIM!

EXACTLY-AND NOW THEY WANT OUR HELP! --

SUITS ME! I'M FOR IT.

PSYCHOLOGICAL CRIMES-- SAY,THAT'S SOMETHING I'D ENJOY SINKING MY TEETH INTO!

WELL, THEN - IT'S SETTLED. I'LL CONTACT THE COURIER RIGHT AWAY!

AN HOUR LATER, IN THE EDITORIAL OFFICES OF THE DAILY COURIER --

THE JUSTICE SOCIETY! WHEW! I CERTAINLY AM GLAD YOU TOOK UP MY OFFER!

WE'RE ALWAYS WILLING TO FIGHT CROOKED STUFF, MR. MORGAN!

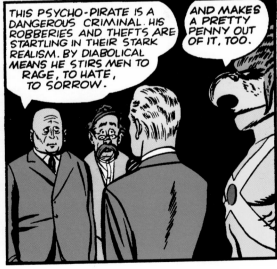

THIS PSYCHO-PIRATE IS A DANGEROUS CRIMINAL. HIS ROBBERIES AND THEFTS ARE STARTLING IN THEIR STARK REALISM. BY DIABOLICAL MEANS HE STIRS MEN TO RAGE, TO HATE, TO SORROW.

AND MAKES A PRETTY PENNY OUT OF IT, TOO.

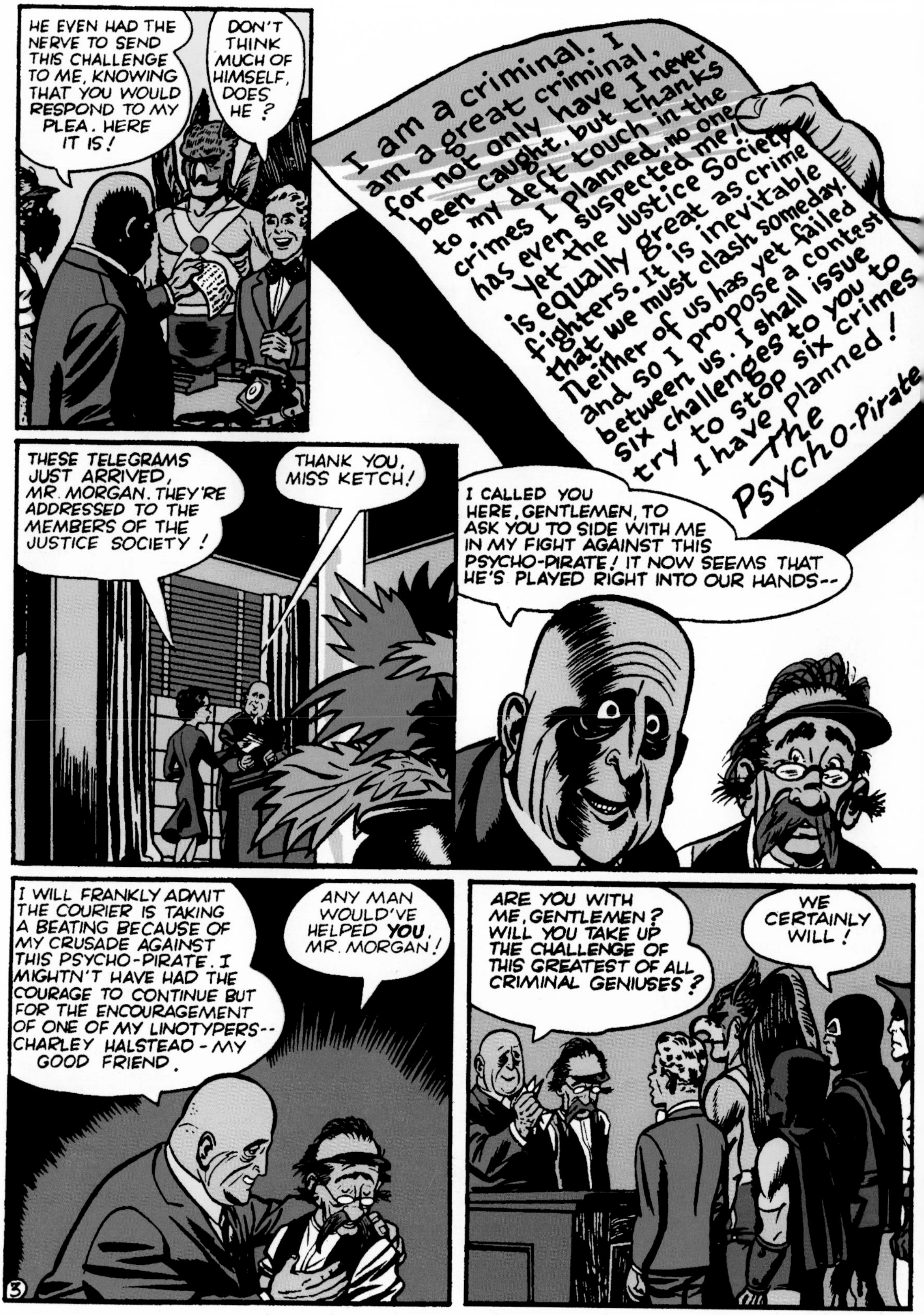
HE EVEN HAD THE NERVE TO SEND THIS CHALLENGE TO ME, KNOWING THAT YOU WOULD RESPOND TO MY PLEA. HERE IT IS!
DON'T THINK MUCH OF HIMSELF, DOES HE?
I am a criminal. I am a great criminal. for not only have I never been caught, but thanks to my deft touch in the crimes I planned, no one has even suspected me! Yet the Justice Society is equally great as crime fighters. It is inevitable that we must clash someday. Neither of us has yet failed and so I propose a contest between us. I shall issue six challenges to you to try to stop six crimes I have planned! The Psycho-Pirate
THESE TELEGRAMS JUST ARRIVED, MR. MORGAN. THEY'RE ADDRESSED TO THE MEMBERS OF THE JUSTICE SOCIETY!
THANK YOU, MISS KETCH!
I CALLED YOU HERE, GENTLEMEN, TO ASK YOU TO SIDE WITH ME IN MY FIGHT AGAINST THIS PSYCHO-PIRATE! IT NOW SEEMS THAT HE'S PLAYED RIGHT INTO OUR HANDS--
I WILL FRANKLY ADMIT THE COURIER IS TAKING A BEATING BECAUSE OF MY CRUSADE AGAINST THIS PSYCHO-PIRATE. I MIGHTN'T HAVE HAD THE COURAGE TO CONTINUE BUT FOR THE ENCOURAGEMENT OF ONE OF MY LINOTYPERS-- CHARLEY HALSTEAD - MY GOOD FRIEND.
ANY MAN WOULD'VE HELPED YOU, MR. MORGAN!
3
ARE YOU WITH ME, GENTLEMEN? WILL YOU TAKE UP THE CHALLENGE OF THIS GREATEST OF ALL CRIMINAL GENIUSES?
WE CERTAINLY WILL!

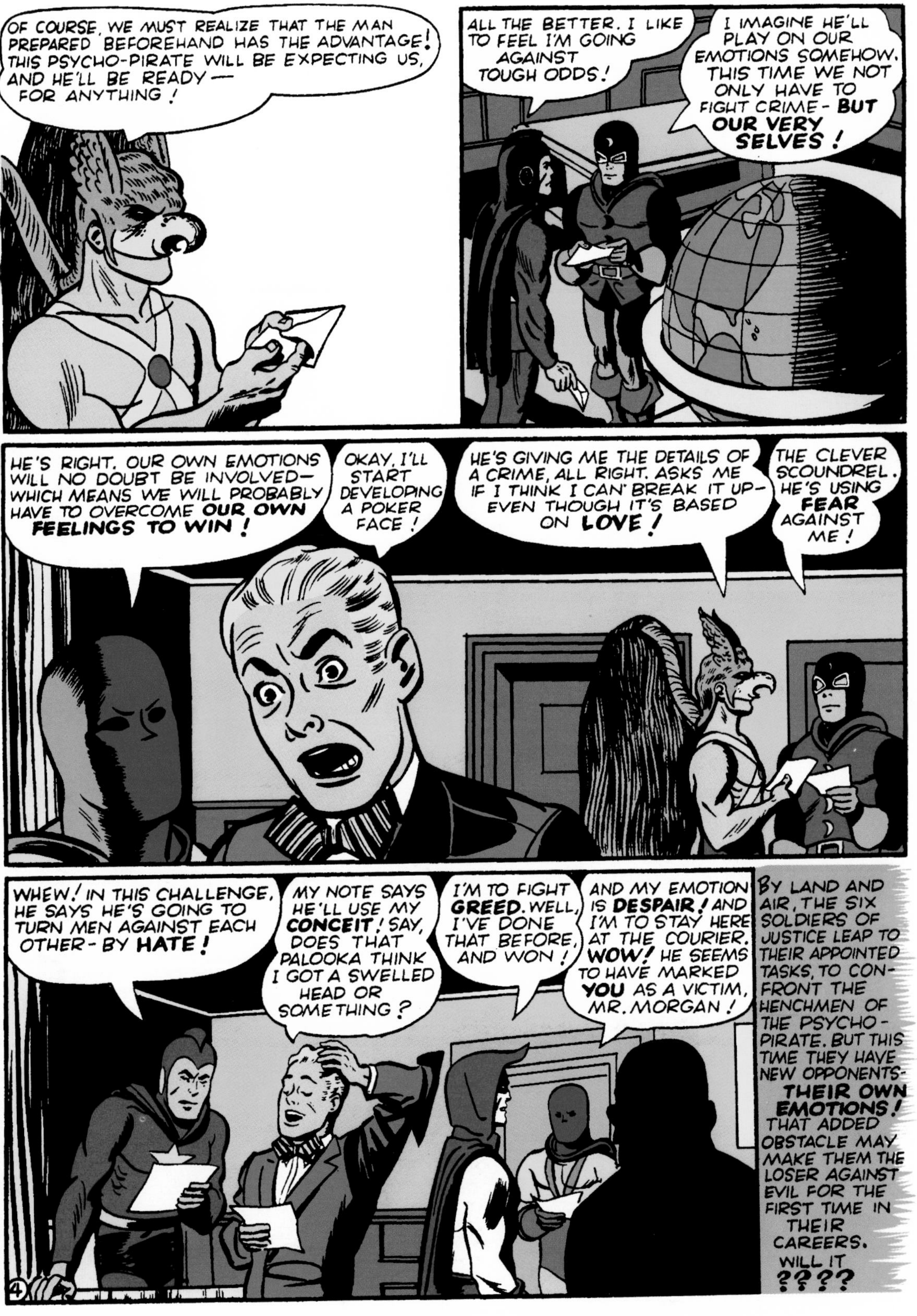
OF COURSE, WE MUST REALIZE THAT THE MAN PREPARED BEFOREHAND HAS THE ADVANTAGE! THIS PSYCHO-PIRATE WILL BE EXPECTING US, AND HE'LL BE READY— FOR ANYTHING!
ALL THE BETTER. I LIKE TO FEEL I'M GOING AGAINST TOUGH ODDS!
I IMAGINE HE'LL PLAY ON OUR EMOTIONS SOMEHOW. THIS TIME WE NOT ONLY HAVE TO FIGHT CRIME- BUT OUR VERY SELVES!
HE'S RIGHT. OUR OWN EMOTIONS WILL NO DOUBT BE INVOLVED— WHICH MEANS WE WILL PROBABLY HAVE TO OVERCOME OUR OWN FEELINGS TO WIN!
OKAY, I'LL START DEVELOPING A POKER FACE!
HE'S GIVING ME THE DETAILS OF A CRIME, ALL RIGHT. ASKS ME IF I THINK I CAN BREAK IT UP- EVEN THOUGH IT'S BASED ON LOVE!
THE CLEVER SCOUNDREL. HE'S USING FEAR AGAINST ME!
WHEW! IN THIS CHALLENGE, HE SAYS HE'S GOING TO TURN MEN AGAINST EACH OTHER- BY HATE!
MY NOTE SAYS HE'LL USE MY CONCEIT! SAY, DOES THAT PALOOKA THINK I GOT A SWELLED HEAD OR SOMETHING?
I'M TO FIGHT GREED. WELL, I'VE DONE THAT BEFORE, AND WON!
AND MY EMOTION IS DESPAIR! AND I'M TO STAY HERE AT THE COURIER. WOW! HE SEEMS TO HAVE MARKED YOU AS A VICTIM, MR. MORGAN!
BY LAND AND AIR, THE SIX SOLDIERS OF JUSTICE LEAP TO THEIR APPOINTED TASKS, TO CONFRONT THE HENCHMEN OF THE PSYCHO-PIRATE. BUT THIS TIME THEY HAVE NEW OPPONENTS- THEIR OWN EMOTIONS! THAT ADDED OBSTACLE MAY MAKE THEM THE LOSER AGAINST EVIL FOR THE FIRST TIME IN THEIR CAREERS. WILL IT ????
4

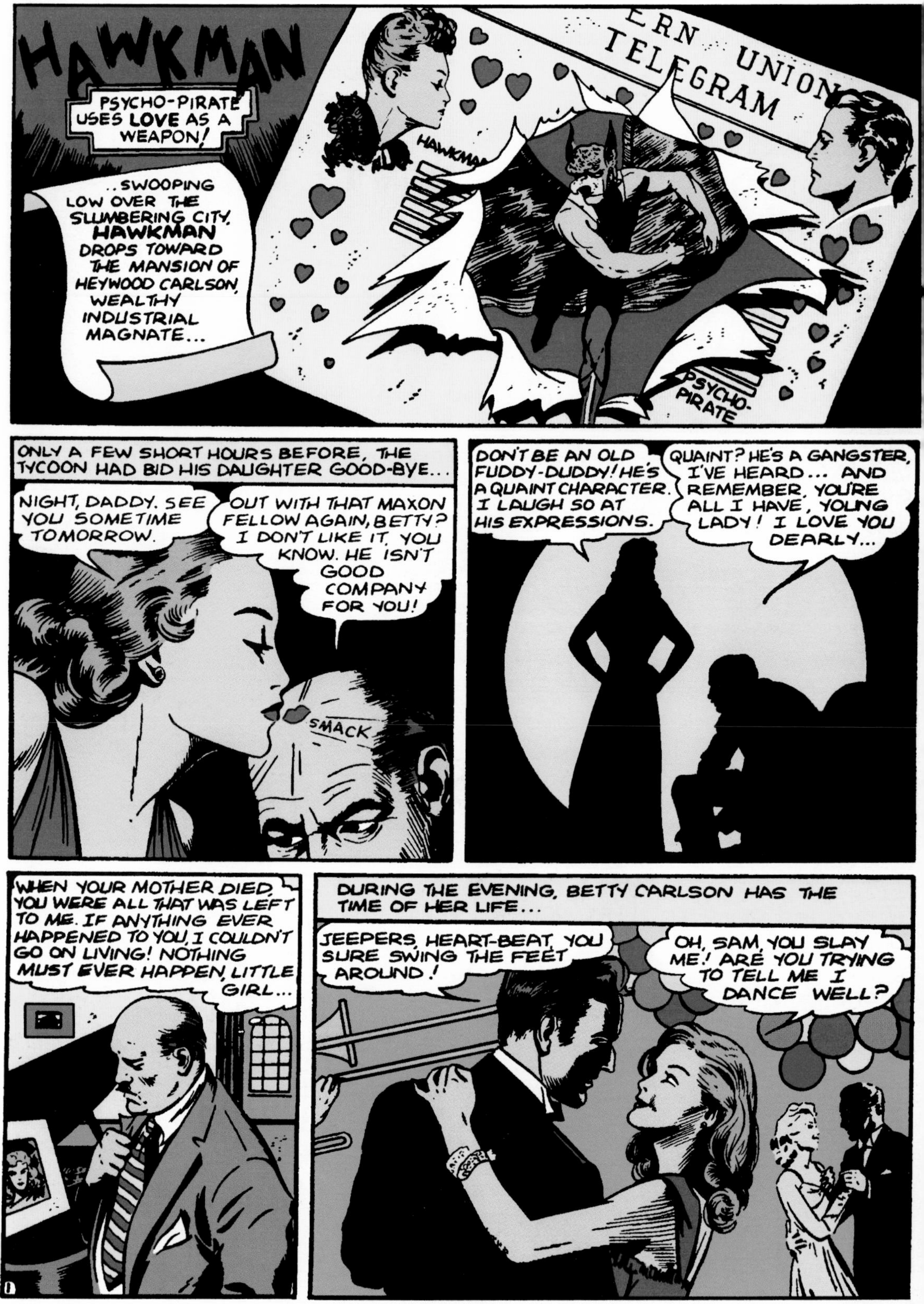
HAWKMAN
PSYCHO-PIRATE USES LOVE AS A WEAPON!
..SWOOPING LOW OVER THE SLUMBERING CITY, HAWKMAN DROPS TOWARD THE MANSION OF HEYWOOD CARLSON, WEALTHY INDUSTRIAL MAGNATE...
ERN UNION TELEGRAM
HAWKMAN
PSYCHO-PIRATE
ONLY A FEW SHORT HOURS BEFORE, THE TYCOON HAD BID HIS DAUGHTER GOOD-BYE...
NIGHT, DADDY. SEE YOU SOMETIME TOMORROW.
OUT WITH THAT MAXON FELLOW AGAIN, BETTY? I DON'T LIKE IT, YOU KNOW. HE ISN'T GOOD COMPANY FOR YOU!
SMACK
DON'T BE AN OLD FUDDY-DUDDY! HE'S A QUAINT CHARACTER. I LAUGH SO AT HIS EXPRESSIONS.
QUAINT? HE'S A GANGSTER, I'VE HEARD... AND REMEMBER, YOU'RE ALL I HAVE, YOUNG LADY! I LOVE YOU DEARLY...
WHEN YOUR MOTHER DIED, YOU WERE ALL THAT WAS LEFT TO ME. IF ANYTHING EVER HAPPENED TO YOU, I COULDN'T GO ON LIVING! NOTHING MUST EVER HAPPEN, LITTLE GIRL...
DURING THE EVENING, BETTY CARLSON HAS THE TIME OF HER LIFE...
JEEPERS, HEART-BEAT, YOU SURE SWING THE FEET AROUND!
OH, SAM, YOU SLAY ME! ARE YOU TRYING TO TELL ME I DANCE WELL?

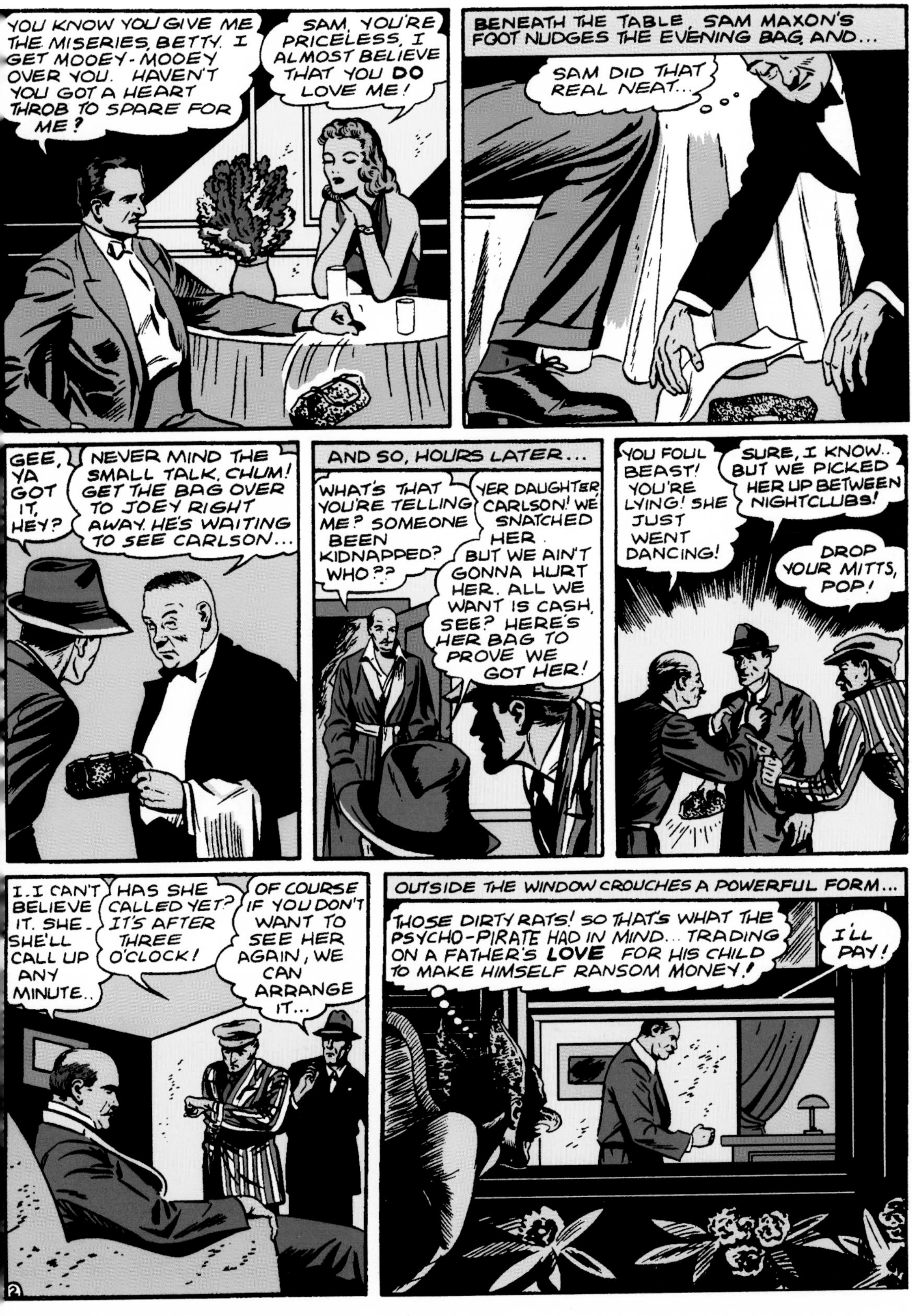
YOU KNOW YOU GIVE ME THE MISERIES, BETTY. I GET MOOEY-MOOEY OVER YOU. HAVEN'T YOU GOT A HEART THROB TO SPARE FOR ME?
SAM, YOU'RE PRICELESS, I ALMOST BELIEVE THAT YOU **DO** LOVE ME!
BENEATH THE TABLE, SAM MAXON'S FOOT NUDGES THE EVENING BAG, AND...
SAM DID THAT REAL NEAT...
GEE, YA GOT IT, HEY?
NEVER MIND THE SMALL TALK, CHUM! GET THE BAG OVER TO JOEY RIGHT AWAY. HE'S WAITING TO SEE CARLSON...
AND SO, HOURS LATER...
WHAT'S THAT YOU'RE TELLING ME? SOMEONE BEEN KIDNAPPED? WHO??
YER DAUGHTER, CARLSON! WE SNATCHED HER. BUT WE AIN'T GONNA HURT HER. ALL WE WANT IS CASH, SEE? HERE'S HER BAG TO PROVE WE GOT HER!
YOU FOUL BEAST! YOU'RE LYING! SHE JUST WENT DANCING!
SURE, I KNOW.. BUT WE PICKED HER UP BETWEEN NIGHTCLUBS!
DROP YOUR MITTS, POP!
I..I CAN'T BELIEVE IT. SHE..SHE'LL CALL UP ANY MINUTE..
HAS SHE CALLED YET? IT'S AFTER THREE O'CLOCK!
OF COURSE IF YOU DON'T WANT TO SEE HER AGAIN, WE CAN ARRANGE IT...
OUTSIDE THE WINDOW CROUCHES A POWERFUL FORM...
THOSE DIRTY RATS! SO THAT'S WHAT THE PSYCHO-PIRATE HAD IN MIND... TRADING ON A FATHER'S **LOVE** FOR HIS CHILD TO MAKE HIMSELF RANSOM MONEY!
I'LL PAY!
2

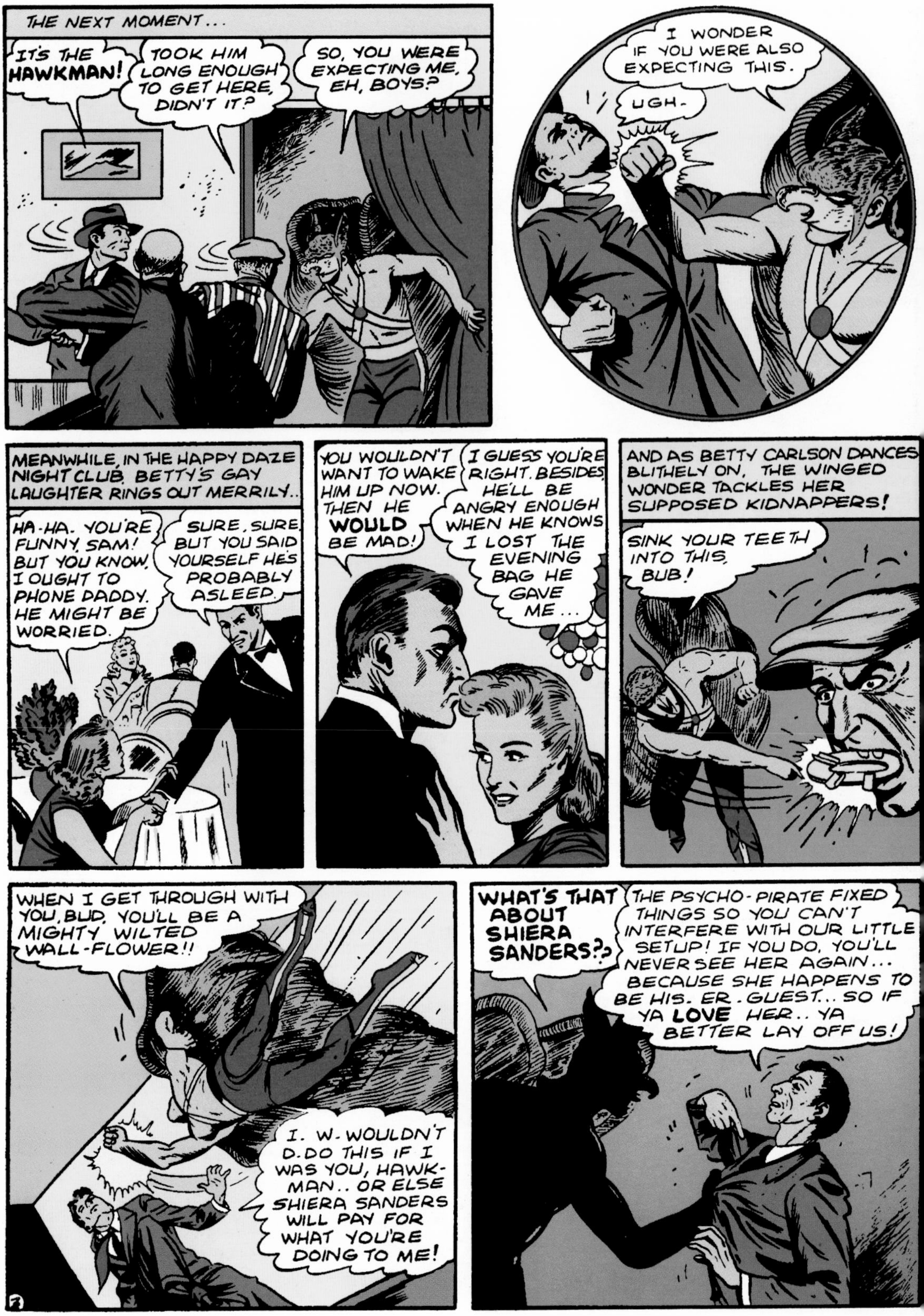
THE NEXT MOMENT...
IT'S THE HAWKMAN!
TOOK HIM LONG ENOUGH TO GET HERE, DIDN'T IT?
SO, YOU WERE EXPECTING ME, EH, BOYS?
I WONDER IF YOU WERE ALSO EXPECTING THIS.
UGH-
MEANWHILE, IN THE HAPPY DAZE NIGHT CLUB, BETTY'S GAY LAUGHTER RINGS OUT MERRILY..
HA-HA. YOU'RE FUNNY, SAM! BUT YOU KNOW, I OUGHT TO PHONE DADDY. HE MIGHT BE WORRIED.
SURE, SURE BUT YOU SAID YOURSELF HE'S PROBABLY ASLEEP.
YOU WOULDN'T WANT TO WAKE HIM UP NOW. THEN HE WOULD BE MAD!
I GUESS YOU'RE RIGHT. BESIDES HE'LL BE ANGRY ENOUGH WHEN HE KNOWS I LOST THE EVENING BAG HE GAVE ME...
AND AS BETTY CARLSON DANCES BLITHELY ON, THE WINGED WONDER TACKLES HER SUPPOSED KIDNAPPERS!
SINK YOUR TEETH INTO THIS, BUB!
WHEN I GET THROUGH WITH YOU, BUD, YOU'LL BE A MIGHTY WILTED WALL-FLOWER!!
I. W-WOULDN'T D-DO THIS IF I WAS YOU, HAWK-MAN.. OR ELSE SHIERA SANDERS WILL PAY FOR WHAT YOU'RE DOING TO ME!
WHAT'S THAT ABOUT SHIERA SANDERS?
THE PSYCHO-PIRATE FIXED THINGS SO YOU CAN'T INTERFERE WITH OUR LITTLE SETUP! IF YOU DO, YOU'LL NEVER SEE HER AGAIN... BECAUSE SHE HAPPENS TO BE HIS. ER. GUEST... SO IF YA LOVE HER.. YA BETTER LAY OFF US!
7

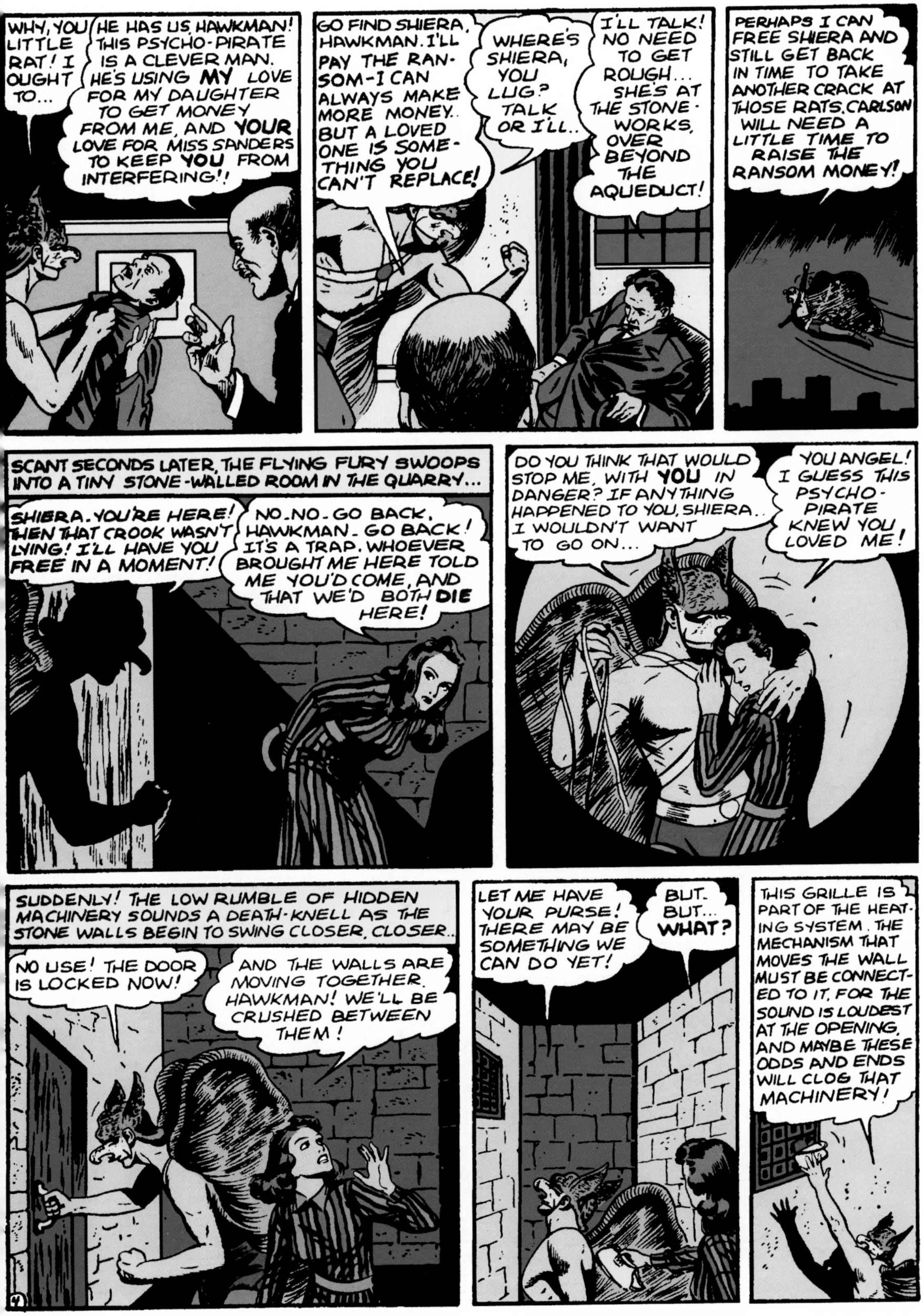
WHY, YOU LITTLE RAT! I OUGHT TO...
HE HAS US, HAWKMAN! THIS PSYCHO-PIRATE IS A CLEVER MAN. HE'S USING MY LOVE FOR MY DAUGHTER TO GET MONEY FROM ME, AND YOUR LOVE FOR MISS SANDERS TO KEEP YOU FROM INTERFERING!!
GO FIND SHIERA, HAWKMAN. I'LL PAY THE RANSOM-I CAN ALWAYS MAKE MORE MONEY.. BUT A LOVED ONE IS SOMETHING YOU CAN'T REPLACE!
WHERE'S SHIERA, YOU LUG? TALK OR I'LL..
I'LL TALK! NO NEED TO GET ROUGH... SHE'S AT THE STONE-WORKS, OVER BEYOND THE AQUEDUCT!
PERHAPS I CAN FREE SHIERA AND STILL GET BACK IN TIME TO TAKE ANOTHER CRACK AT THOSE RATS. CARLSON WILL NEED A LITTLE TIME TO RAISE THE RANSOM MONEY!
SCANT SECONDS LATER, THE FLYING FURY SWOOPS INTO A TINY STONE-WALLED ROOM IN THE QUARRY...
SHIERA. YOU'RE HERE! THEN THAT CROOK WASN'T LYING! I'LL HAVE YOU FREE IN A MOMENT!
NO..NO.. GO BACK, HAWKMAN.. GO BACK! IT'S A TRAP. WHOEVER BROUGHT ME HERE TOLD ME YOU'D COME, AND THAT WE'D BOTH DIE HERE!
DO YOU THINK THAT WOULD STOP ME, WITH YOU IN DANGER? IF ANYTHING HAPPENED TO YOU, SHIERA.. I WOULDN'T WANT TO GO ON...
YOU ANGEL! I GUESS THIS PSYCHO-PIRATE KNEW YOU LOVED ME!
SUDDENLY! THE LOW RUMBLE OF HIDDEN MACHINERY SOUNDS A DEATH-KNELL AS THE STONE WALLS BEGIN TO SWING CLOSER, CLOSER..
NO USE! THE DOOR IS LOCKED NOW!
AND THE WALLS ARE MOVING TOGETHER, HAWKMAN! WE'LL BE CRUSHED BETWEEN THEM!
LET ME HAVE YOUR PURSE! THERE MAY BE SOMETHING WE CAN DO YET!
BUT.. BUT... WHAT?
THIS GRILLE IS PART OF THE HEATING SYSTEM. THE MECHANISM THAT MOVES THE WALL MUST BE CONNECTED TO IT, FOR THE SOUND IS LOUDEST AT THE OPENING, AND MAYBE THESE ODDS AND ENDS WILL CLOG THAT MACHINERY!
4

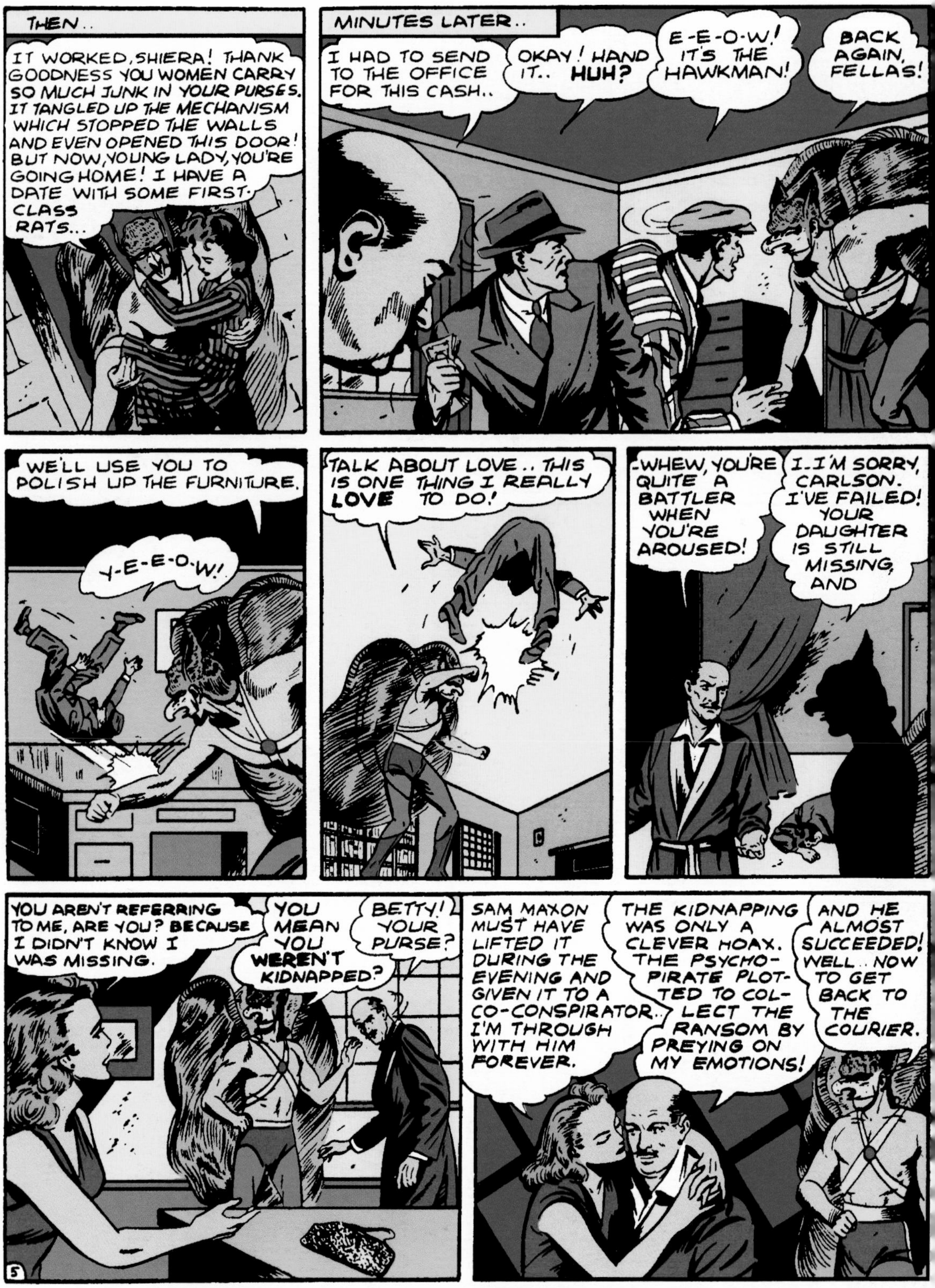
THEN..
IT WORKED, SHIERA! THANK GOODNESS YOU WOMEN CARRY SO MUCH JUNK IN YOUR PURSES. IT TANGLED UP THE MECHANISM WHICH STOPPED THE WALLS AND EVEN OPENED THIS DOOR! BUT NOW, YOUNG LADY, YOU'RE GOING HOME! I HAVE A DATE WITH SOME FIRST-CLASS RATS...
MINUTES LATER..
I HAD TO SEND TO THE OFFICE FOR THIS CASH..
OKAY! HAND IT.. HUH?
E-E-O-W! IT'S THE HAWKMAN!
BACK AGAIN, FELLAS!
WE'LL USE YOU TO POLISH UP THE FURNITURE.
Y-E-E-O-W!
TALK ABOUT LOVE.. THIS IS ONE THING I REALLY LOVE TO DO!
-WHEW, YOU'RE QUITE A BATTLER WHEN YOU'RE AROUSED!
I..I'M SORRY, CARLSON. I'VE FAILED! YOUR DAUGHTER IS STILL MISSING, AND
YOU AREN'T REFERRING TO ME, ARE YOU? BECAUSE I DIDN'T KNOW I WAS MISSING.
YOU MEAN YOU WEREN'T KIDNAPPED?
BETTY! YOUR PURSE?
5
SAM MAXON MUST HAVE LIFTED IT DURING THE EVENING AND GIVEN IT TO A CO-CONSPIRATOR.. I'M THROUGH WITH HIM FOREVER.
THE KIDNAPPING WAS ONLY A CLEVER HOAX. THE PSYCHO-PIRATE PLOTTED TO COLLECT THE RANSOM BY PREYING ON MY EMOTIONS!
AND HE ALMOST SUCCEEDED! WELL.. NOW TO GET BACK TO THE COURIER.

HAWKMAN appears each month in Flash Comics-Don't miss it!

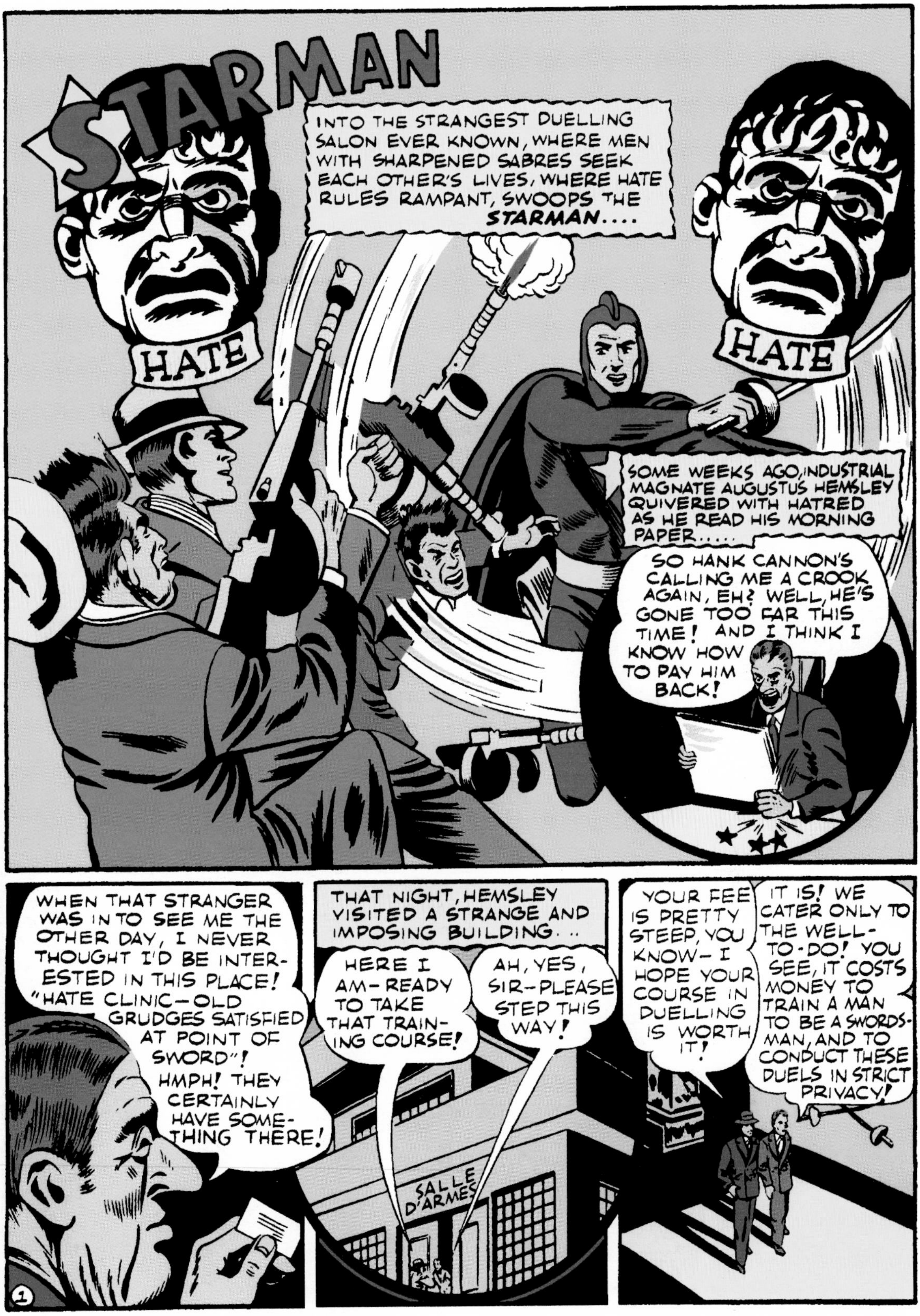
STARMAN
INTO THE STRANGEST DUELLING SALON EVER KNOWN, WHERE MEN WITH SHARPENED SABRES SEEK EACH OTHER'S LIVES, WHERE HATE RULES RAMPANT, SWOOPS THE STARMAN....
HATE
HATE
SOME WEEKS AGO, INDUSTRIAL MAGNATE AUGUSTUS HEMSLEY QUIVERED WITH HATRED AS HE READ HIS MORNING PAPER.....
SO HANK CANNON'S CALLING ME A CROOK AGAIN, EH? WELL, HE'S GONE TOO FAR THIS TIME! AND I THINK I KNOW HOW TO PAY HIM BACK!
WHEN THAT STRANGER WAS IN TO SEE ME THE OTHER DAY, I NEVER THOUGHT I'D BE INTERESTED IN THIS PLACE! "HATE CLINIC—OLD GRUDGES SATISFIED AT POINT OF SWORD"! HMPH! THEY CERTAINLY HAVE SOMETHING THERE!
1
THAT NIGHT, HEMSLEY VISITED A STRANGE AND IMPOSING BUILDING...
HERE I AM—READY TO TAKE THAT TRAINING COURSE!
AH, YES, SIR—PLEASE STEP THIS WAY!
SALLE D'ARMES
YOUR FEE IS PRETTY STEEP, YOU KNOW—I HOPE YOUR COURSE IN DUELLING IS WORTH IT!
IT IS! WE CATER ONLY TO THE WELL-TO-DO! YOU SEE, IT COSTS MONEY TO TRAIN A MAN TO BE A SWORDSMAN, AND TO CONDUCT THESE DUELS IN STRICT PRIVACY!

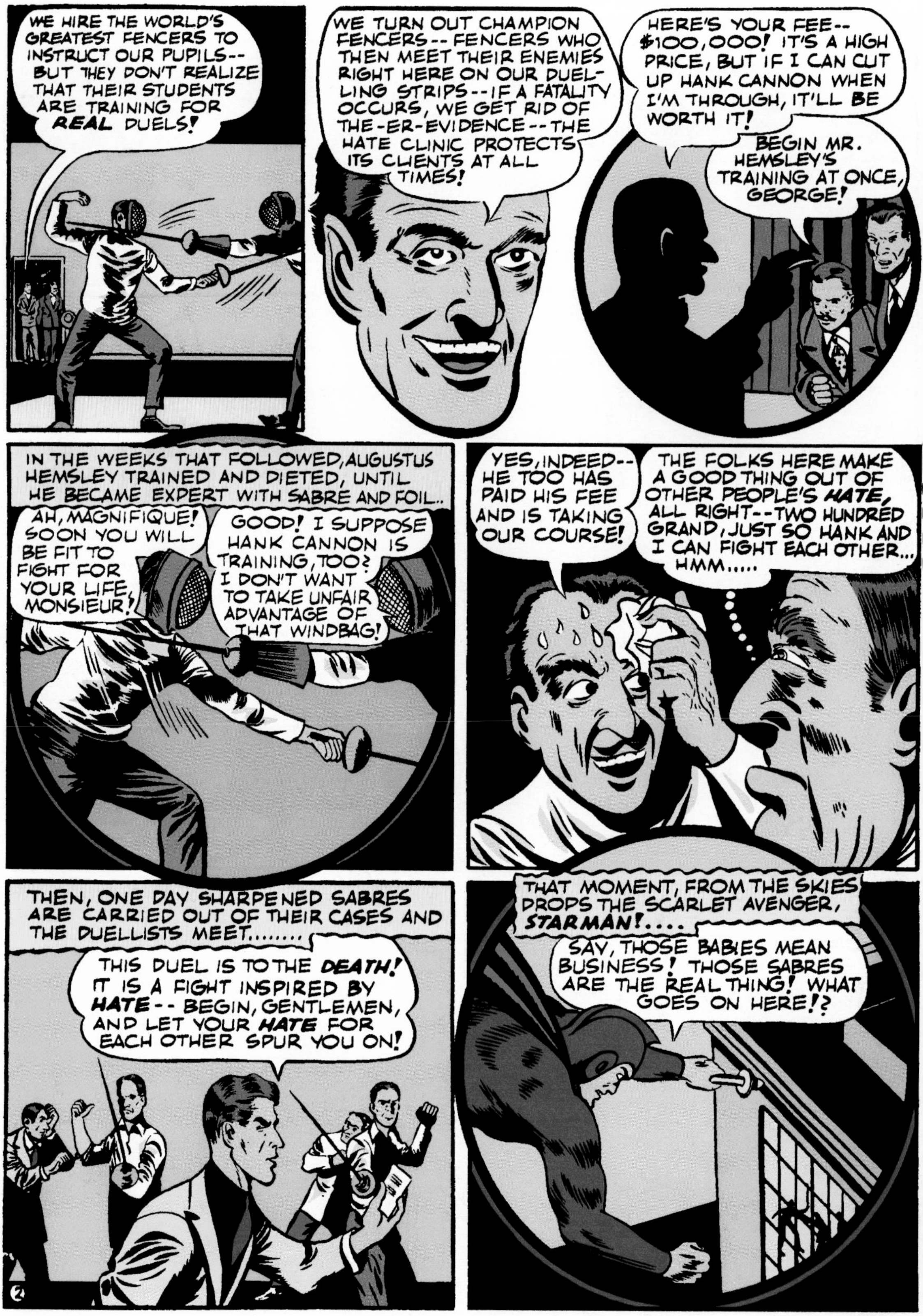

WE HIRE THE WORLD'S GREATEST FENCERS TO INSTRUCT OUR PUPILS--BUT THEY DON'T REALIZE THAT THEIR STUDENTS ARE TRAINING FOR REAL DUELS!
WE TURN OUT CHAMPION FENCERS--FENCERS WHO THEN MEET THEIR ENEMIES RIGHT HERE ON OUR DUELLING STRIPS--IF A FATALITY OCCURS, WE GET RID OF THE-ER-EVIDENCE--THE HATE CLINIC PROTECTS ITS CLIENTS AT ALL TIMES!
HERE'S YOUR FEE--$100,000! IT'S A HIGH PRICE, BUT IF I CAN CUT UP HANK CANNON WHEN I'M THROUGH, IT'LL BE WORTH IT!
BEGIN MR. HEMSLEY'S TRAINING AT ONCE, GEORGE!
IN THE WEEKS THAT FOLLOWED, AUGUSTUS HEMSLEY TRAINED AND DIETED, UNTIL HE BECAME EXPERT WITH SABRE AND FOIL..
AH, MAGNIFIQUE! SOON YOU WILL BE FIT TO FIGHT FOR YOUR LIFE, MONSIEUR!
GOOD! I SUPPOSE HANK CANNON IS TRAINING, TOO? I DON'T WANT TO TAKE UNFAIR ADVANTAGE OF THAT WINDBAG!
YES, INDEED--HE TOO HAS PAID HIS FEE AND IS TAKING OUR COURSE!
THE FOLKS HERE MAKE A GOOD THING OUT OF OTHER PEOPLE'S HATE, ALL RIGHT--TWO HUNDRED GRAND, JUST SO HANK AND I CAN FIGHT EACH OTHER... HMM.....
THEN, ONE DAY SHARPENED SABRES ARE CARRIED OUT OF THEIR CASES AND THE DUELLISTS MEET........
THIS DUEL IS TO THE DEATH! IT IS A FIGHT INSPIRED BY HATE-- BEGIN, GENTLEMEN, AND LET YOUR HATE FOR EACH OTHER SPUR YOU ON!
2
THAT MOMENT, FROM THE SKIES DROPS THE SCARLET AVENGER, STARMAN!....
SAY, THOSE BABIES MEAN BUSINESS! THOSE SABRES ARE THE REAL THING! WHAT GOES ON HERE!?

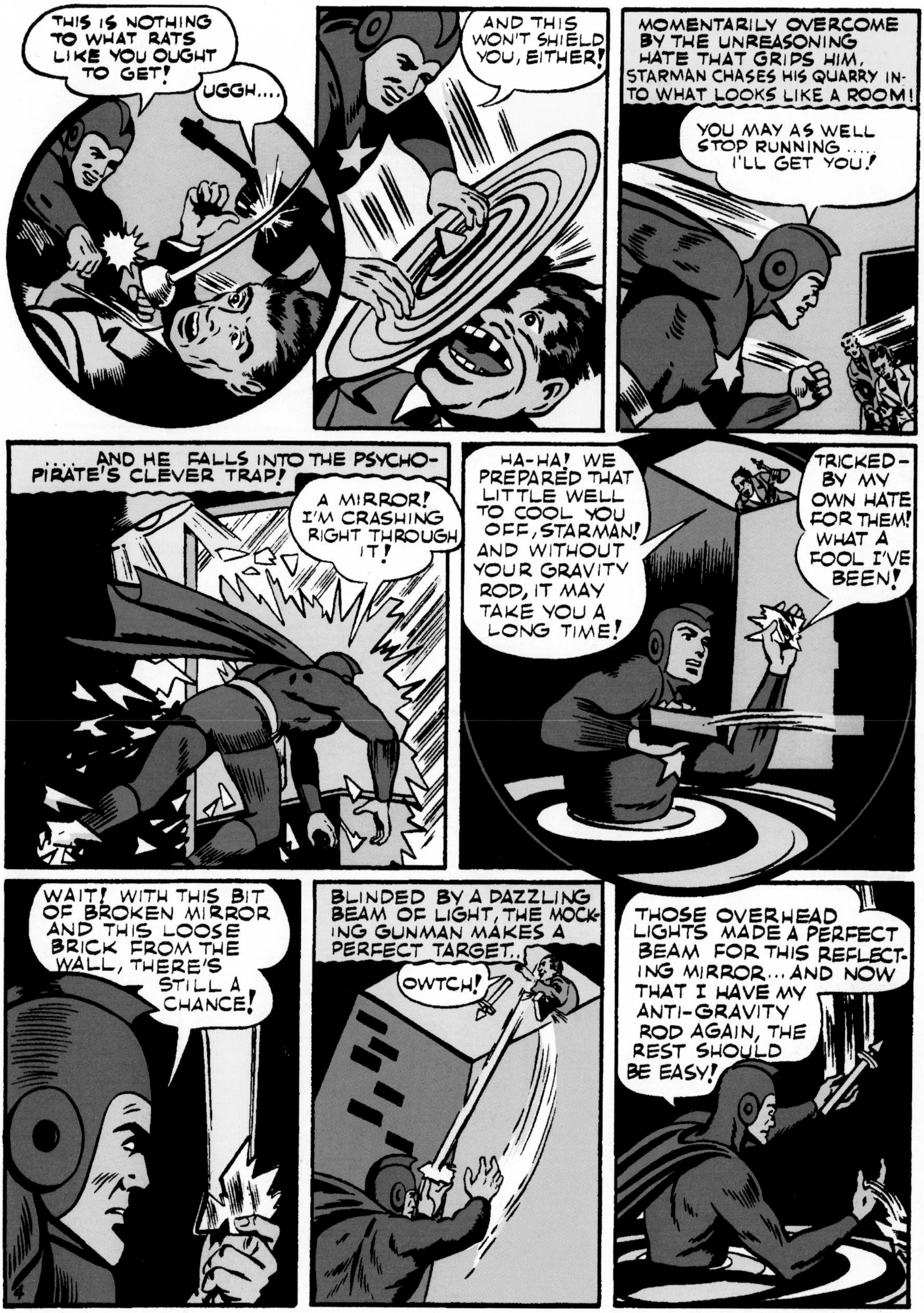
THIS IS NOTHING TO WHAT RATS LIKE YOU OUGHT TO GET!
UGGH....
AND THIS WON'T SHIELD YOU, EITHER!
MOMENTARILY OVERCOME BY THE UNREASONING HATE THAT GRIPS HIM, STARMAN CHASES HIS QUARRY INTO WHAT LOOKS LIKE A ROOM!
YOU MAY AS WELL STOP RUNNING ..... I'LL GET YOU!
.... AND HE FALLS INTO THE PSYCHO-PIRATE'S CLEVER TRAP!
A MIRROR! I'M CRASHING RIGHT THROUGH IT!
HA-HA! WE PREPARED THAT LITTLE WELL TO COOL YOU OFF, STARMAN! AND WITHOUT YOUR GRAVITY ROD, IT MAY TAKE YOU A LONG TIME!
TRICKED—BY MY OWN HATE FOR THEM! WHAT A FOOL I'VE BEEN!
WAIT! WITH THIS BIT OF BROKEN MIRROR AND THIS LOOSE BRICK FROM THE WALL, THERE'S STILL A CHANCE!
BLINDED BY A DAZZLING BEAM OF LIGHT, THE MOCKING GUNMAN MAKES A PERFECT TARGET..
OWTCH!
THOSE OVERHEAD LIGHTS MADE A PERFECT BEAM FOR THIS REFLECTING MIRROR... AND NOW THAT I HAVE MY ANTI-GRAVITY ROD AGAIN, THE REST SHOULD BE EASY!
4

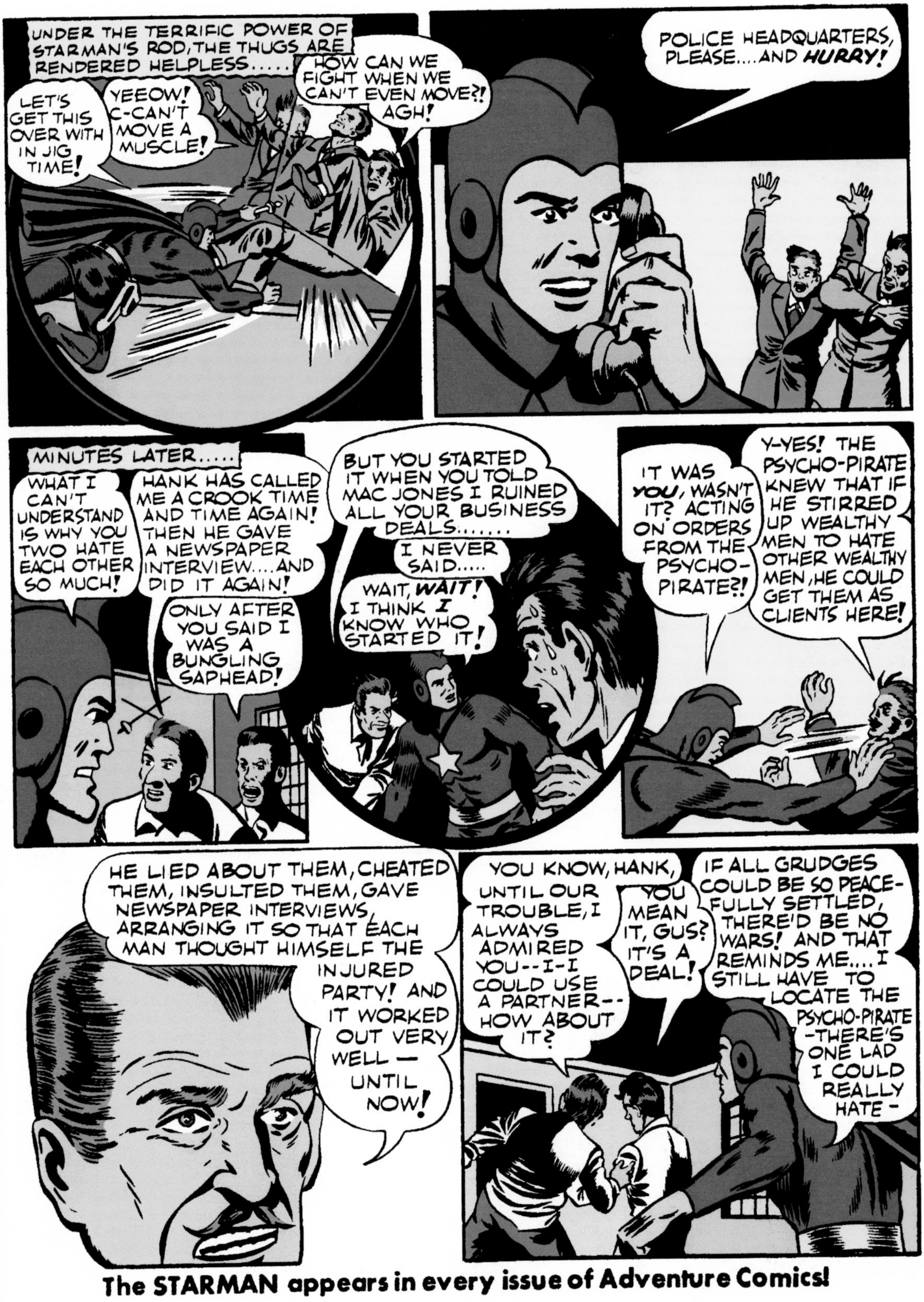
UNDER THE TERRIFIC POWER OF STARMAN'S ROD, THE THUGS ARE RENDERED HELPLESS.....
LET'S GET THIS OVER WITH IN JIG TIME!
YEEOW! C-CAN'T MOVE A MUSCLE!
HOW CAN WE FIGHT WHEN WE CAN'T EVEN MOVE?! AGH!
POLICE HEADQUARTERS, PLEASE....AND HURRY!
MINUTES LATER.....
WHAT I CAN'T UNDERSTAND IS WHY YOU TWO HATE EACH OTHER SO MUCH!
HANK HAS CALLED ME A CROOK TIME AND TIME AGAIN! THEN HE GAVE A NEWSPAPER INTERVIEW....AND DID IT AGAIN!
ONLY AFTER YOU SAID I WAS A BUNGLING SAPHEAD!
BUT YOU STARTED IT WHEN YOU TOLD MAC JONES I RUINED ALL YOUR BUSINESS DEALS.......
I NEVER SAID.....
WAIT, WAIT! I THINK I KNOW WHO STARTED IT!
IT WAS YOU, WASN'T IT? ACTING ON ORDERS FROM THE PSYCHO-PIRATE?!
Y-YES! THE PSYCHO-PIRATE KNEW THAT IF HE STIRRED UP WEALTHY MEN TO HATE OTHER WEALTHY MEN, HE COULD GET THEM AS CLIENTS HERE!
HE LIED ABOUT THEM, CHEATED THEM, INSULTED THEM, GAVE NEWSPAPER INTERVIEWS, ARRANGING IT SO THAT EACH MAN THOUGHT HIMSELF THE INJURED PARTY! AND IT WORKED OUT VERY WELL — UNTIL NOW!
YOU KNOW, HANK, UNTIL OUR TROUBLE, I ALWAYS ADMIRED YOU--I-I COULD USE A PARTNER--HOW ABOUT IT?
YOU MEAN IT, GUS? IT'S A DEAL!
IF ALL GRUDGES COULD BE SO PEACEFULLY SETTLED, THERE'D BE NO WARS! AND THAT REMINDS ME....I STILL HAVE TO LOCATE THE PSYCHO-PIRATE -THERE'S ONE LAD I COULD REALLY HATE -

The STARMAN appears in every issue of Adventure Comics!

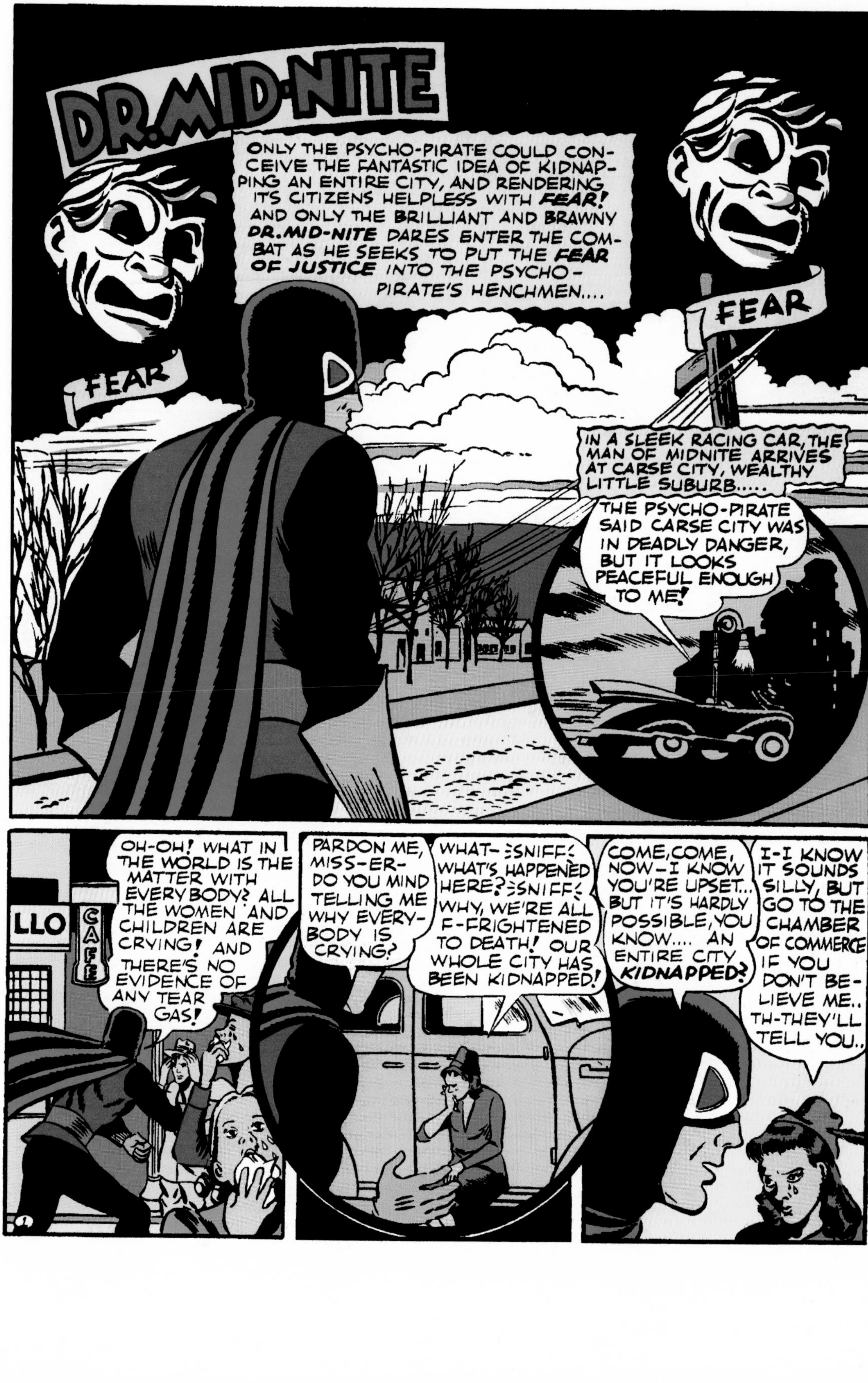
DR. MID-NITE
ONLY THE PSYCHO-PIRATE COULD CONCEIVE THE FANTASTIC IDEA OF KIDNAPPING AN ENTIRE CITY, AND RENDERING IT'S CITIZENS HELPLESS WITH FEAR! AND ONLY THE BRILLIANT AND BRAWNY DR. MID-NITE DARES ENTER THE COMBAT AS HE SEEKS TO PUT THE FEAR OF JUSTICE INTO THE PSYCHO-PIRATE'S HENCHMEN....
FEAR
FEAR
IN A SLEEK RACING CAR, THE MAN OF MIDNITE ARRIVES AT CARSE CITY, WEALTHY LITTLE SUBURB.....
THE PSYCHO-PIRATE SAID CARSE CITY WAS IN DEADLY DANGER, BUT IT LOOKS PEACEFUL ENOUGH TO ME!
OH-OH! WHAT IN THE WORLD IS THE MATTER WITH EVERYBODY? ALL THE WOMEN AND CHILDREN ARE CRYING! AND THERE'S NO EVIDENCE OF ANY TEAR GAS!
LLO
CAFE
PARDON ME, MISS-ER- DO YOU MIND TELLING ME WHY EVERYBODY IS CRYING?
WHAT- SNIFF! WHAT'S HAPPENED HERE? SNIFF! WHY, WE'RE ALL F-FRIGHTENED TO DEATH! OUR WHOLE CITY HAS BEEN KIDNAPPED!
COME, COME, NOW - I KNOW YOU'RE UPSET... BUT IT'S HARDLY POSSIBLE, YOU KNOW.... AN ENTIRE CITY KIDNAPPED?
I-I KNOW IT SOUNDS SILLY, BUT GO TO THE CHAMBER OF COMMERCE IF YOU DON'T BELIEVE ME.. TH-THEY'LL TELL YOU..

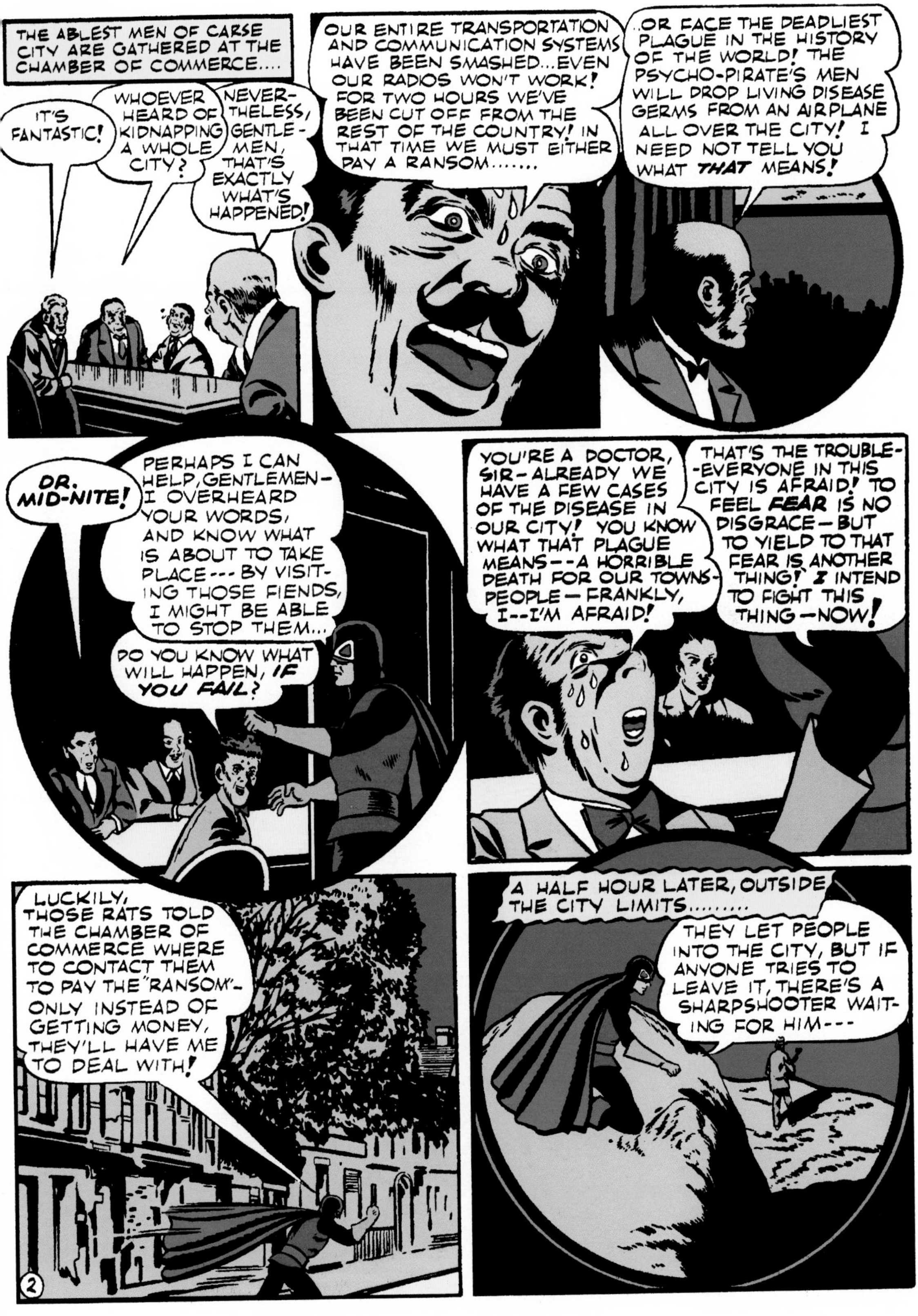
THE ABLEST MEN OF CARSE CITY ARE GATHERED AT THE CHAMBER OF COMMERCE....
IT'S FANTASTIC!
WHOEVER HEARD OF KIDNAPPING A WHOLE CITY?
NEVERTHELESS, GENTLEMEN, THAT'S EXACTLY WHAT'S HAPPENED!
OUR ENTIRE TRANSPORTATION AND COMMUNICATION SYSTEMS HAVE BEEN SMASHED...EVEN OUR RADIOS WON'T WORK! FOR TWO HOURS WE'VE BEEN CUT OFF FROM THE REST OF THE COUNTRY! IN THAT TIME WE MUST EITHER PAY A RANSOM.......
..OR FACE THE DEADLIEST PLAGUE IN THE HISTORY OF THE WORLD! THE PSYCHO-PIRATE'S MEN WILL DROP LIVING DISEASE GERMS FROM AN AIRPLANE ALL OVER THE CITY! I NEED NOT TELL YOU WHAT THAT MEANS!
DR. MID-NITE!
PERHAPS I CAN HELP, GENTLEMEN-I OVERHEARD YOUR WORDS, AND KNOW WHAT IS ABOUT TO TAKE PLACE--- BY VISITING THOSE FIENDS, I MIGHT BE ABLE TO STOP THEM...
DO YOU KNOW WHAT WILL HAPPEN, IF YOU FAIL?
YOU'RE A DOCTOR, SIR-ALREADY WE HAVE A FEW CASES OF THE DISEASE IN OUR CITY! YOU KNOW WHAT THAT PLAGUE MEANS--A HORRIBLE DEATH FOR OUR TOWNSPEOPLE-FRANKLY, I--I'M AFRAID!
THAT'S THE TROUBLE-EVERYONE IN THIS CITY IS AFRAID! TO FEEL FEAR IS NO DISGRACE-BUT TO YIELD TO THAT FEAR IS ANOTHER THING! I INTEND TO FIGHT THIS THING-NOW!
LUCKILY, THOSE RATS TOLD THE CHAMBER OF COMMERCE WHERE TO CONTACT THEM TO PAY THE "RANSOM"-ONLY INSTEAD OF GETTING MONEY, THEY'LL HAVE ME TO DEAL WITH!
2
A HALF HOUR LATER, OUTSIDE THE CITY LIMITS.........
THEY LET PEOPLE INTO THE CITY, BUT IF ANYONE TRIES TO LEAVE IT, THERE'S A SHARPSHOOTER WAITING FOR HIM---

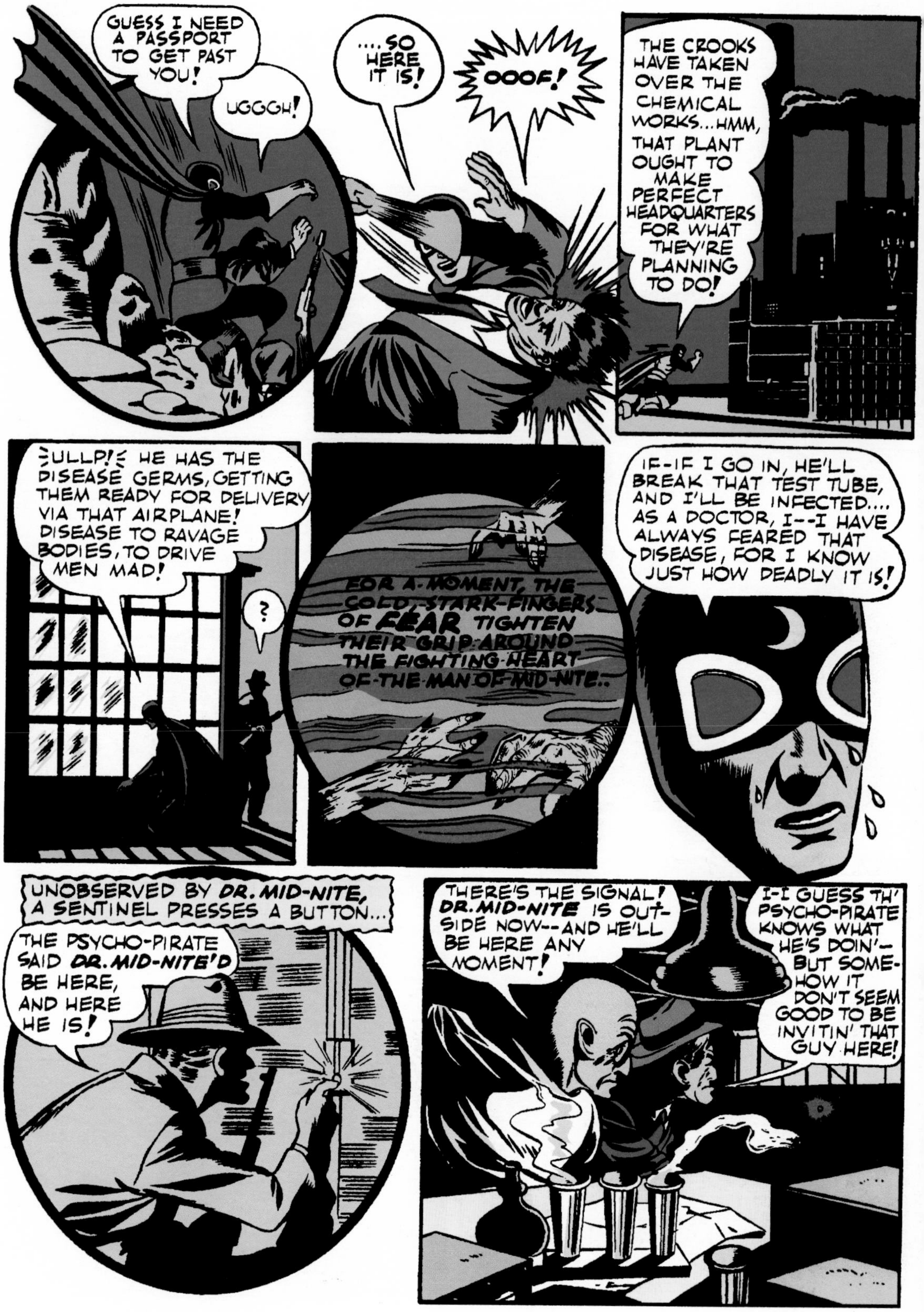
GUESS I NEED A PASSPORT TO GET PAST YOU!
UGGGH!
....SO HERE IT IS!
OOOF!
THE CROOKS HAVE TAKEN OVER THE CHEMICAL WORKS...HMM, THAT PLANT OUGHT TO MAKE PERFECT HEADQUARTERS FOR WHAT THEY'RE PLANNING TO DO!
ULLP! HE HAS THE DISEASE GERMS, GETTING THEM READY FOR DELIVERY VIA THAT AIRPLANE! DISEASE TO RAVAGE BODIES, TO DRIVE MEN MAD!
?
FOR A MOMENT, THE COLD, STARK FINGERS OF FEAR TIGHTEN THEIR GRIP AROUND THE FIGHTING HEART OF THE MAN OF MID-NITE..
IF-IF I GO IN, HE'LL BREAK THAT TEST TUBE, AND I'LL BE INFECTED.... AS A DOCTOR, I--I HAVE ALWAYS FEARED THAT DISEASE, FOR I KNOW JUST HOW DEADLY IT IS!
UNOBSERVED BY DR. MID-NITE, A SENTINEL PRESSES A BUTTON...
THE PSYCHO-PIRATE SAID DR. MID-NITE'D BE HERE, AND HERE HE IS!
THERE'S THE SIGNAL! DR. MID-NITE IS OUTSIDE NOW--AND HE'LL BE HERE ANY MOMENT!
I-I GUESS TH' PSYCHO-PIRATE KNOWS WHAT HE'S DOIN'-- BUT SOMEHOW IT DON'T SEEM GOOD TO BE INVITIN' THAT GUY HERE!

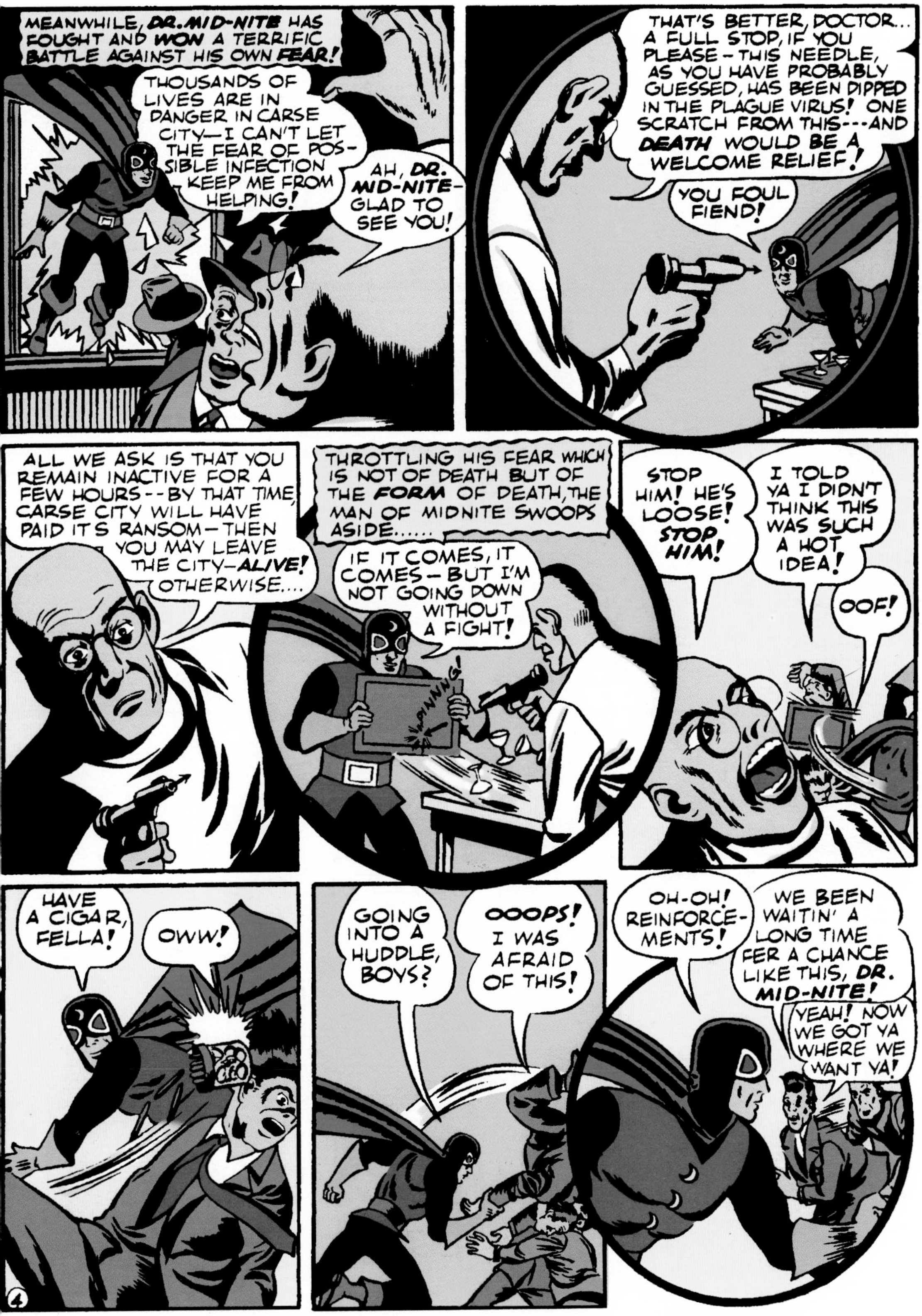
MEANWHILE, DR. MID-NITE HAS FOUGHT AND WON A TERRIFIC BATTLE AGAINST HIS OWN FEAR!
THOUSANDS OF LIVES ARE IN DANGER IN CARSE CITY—I CAN'T LET THE FEAR OF POSSIBLE INFECTION KEEP ME FROM HELPING!
AH, DR. MID-NITE—GLAD TO SEE YOU!
THAT'S BETTER, DOCTOR... A FULL STOP, IF YOU PLEASE—THIS NEEDLE, AS YOU HAVE PROBABLY GUESSED, HAS BEEN DIPPED IN THE PLAGUE VIRUS! ONE SCRATCH FROM THIS---AND DEATH WOULD BE A WELCOME RELIEF!
YOU FOUL FIEND!
ALL WE ASK IS THAT YOU REMAIN INACTIVE FOR A FEW HOURS--BY THAT TIME, CARSE CITY WILL HAVE PAID IT'S RANSOM—THEN YOU MAY LEAVE THE CITY—ALIVE! OTHERWISE....
THROTTLING HIS FEAR WHICH IS NOT OF DEATH BUT OF THE FORM OF DEATH, THE MAN OF MIDNITE SWOOPS ASIDE......
IF IT COMES, IT COMES—BUT I'M NOT GOING DOWN WITHOUT A FIGHT!
STOP HIM! HE'S LOOSE! STOP HIM!
I TOLD YA I DIDN'T THINK THIS WAS SUCH A HOT IDEA!
OOF!
HAVE A CIGAR, FELLA!
OWW!
GOING INTO A HUDDLE, BOYS?
OOOPS! I WAS AFRAID OF THIS!
OH-OH! REINFORCEMENTS!
WE BEEN WAITIN' A LONG TIME FER A CHANCE LIKE THIS, DR. MID-NITE!
YEAH! NOW WE GOT YA WHERE WE WANT YA!
4

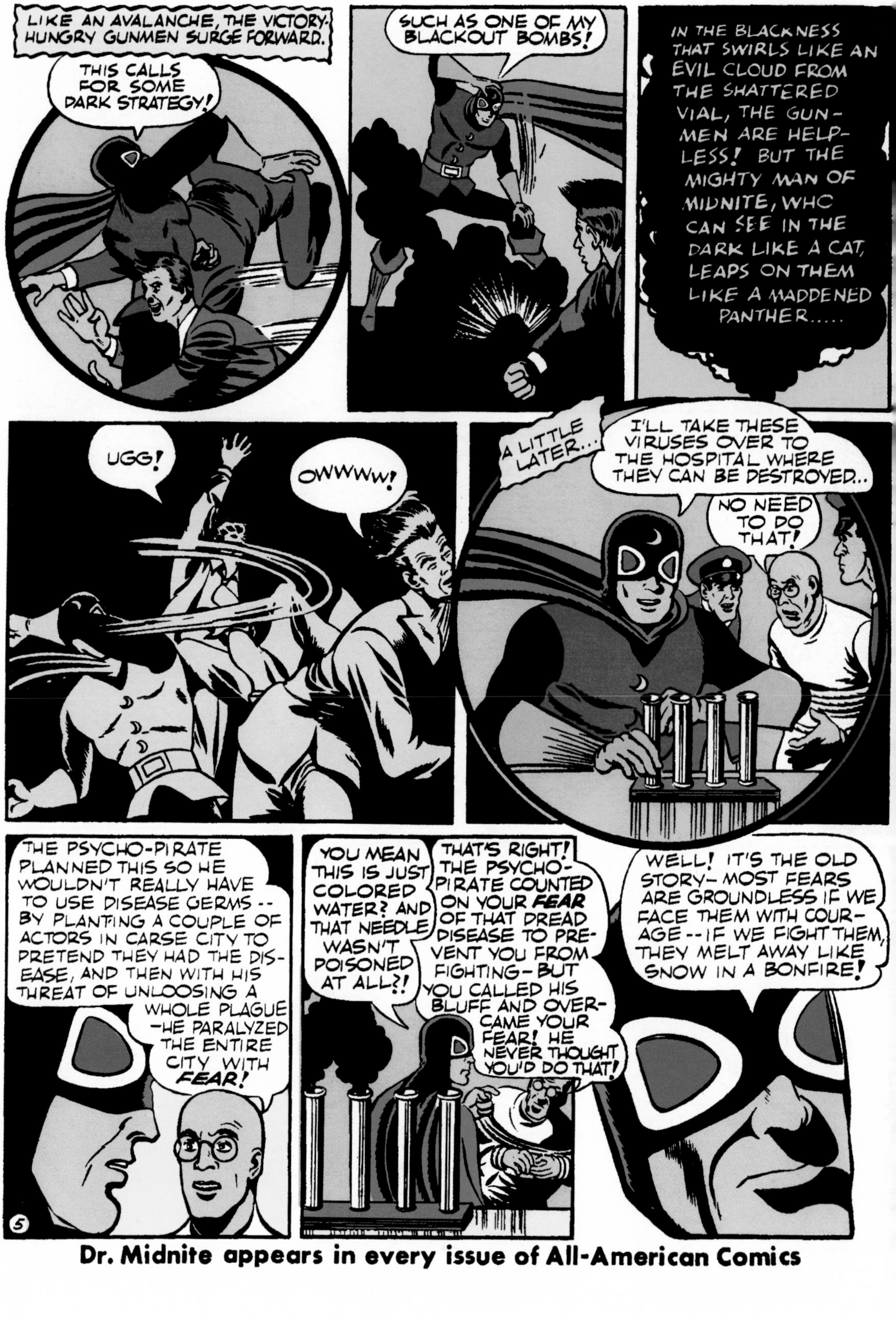
LIKE AN AVALANCHE, THE VICTORY-HUNGRY GUNMEN SURGE FORWARD.
THIS CALLS FOR SOME DARK STRATEGY!
SUCH AS ONE OF MY BLACKOUT BOMBS!
IN THE BLACKNESS THAT SWIRLS LIKE AN EVIL CLOUD FROM THE SHATTERED VIAL, THE GUN-MEN ARE HELP-LESS! BUT THE MIGHTY MAN OF MIDNITE, WHO CAN SEE IN THE DARK LIKE A CAT, LEAPS ON THEM LIKE A MADDENED PANTHER.....
UGG!
OWWWW!
A LITTLE LATER...
I'LL TAKE THESE VIRUSES OVER TO THE HOSPITAL WHERE THEY CAN BE DESTROYED..
NO NEED TO DO THAT!
THE PSYCHO-PIRATE PLANNED THIS SO HE WOULDN'T REALLY HAVE TO USE DISEASE GERMS -- BY PLANTING A COUPLE OF ACTORS IN CARSE CITY TO PRETEND THEY HAD THE DIS-EASE, AND THEN WITH HIS THREAT OF UNLOOSING A WHOLE PLAGUE -HE PARALYZED THE ENTIRE CITY WITH FEAR!
YOU MEAN THIS IS JUST COLORED WATER? AND THAT NEEDLE WASN'T POISONED AT ALL?!
THAT'S RIGHT! THE PSYCHO-PIRATE COUNTED ON YOUR FEAR OF THAT DREAD DISEASE TO PRE-VENT YOU FROM FIGHTING-BUT YOU CALLED HIS BLUFF AND OVER-CAME YOUR FEAR! HE NEVER THOUGHT YOU'D DO THAT!
WELL! IT'S THE OLD STORY- MOST FEARS ARE GROUNDLESS IF WE FACE THEM WITH COUR-AGE--IF WE FIGHT THEM, THEY MELT AWAY LIKE SNOW IN A BONFIRE!
5

Dr. Midnite appears in every issue of All-American Comics

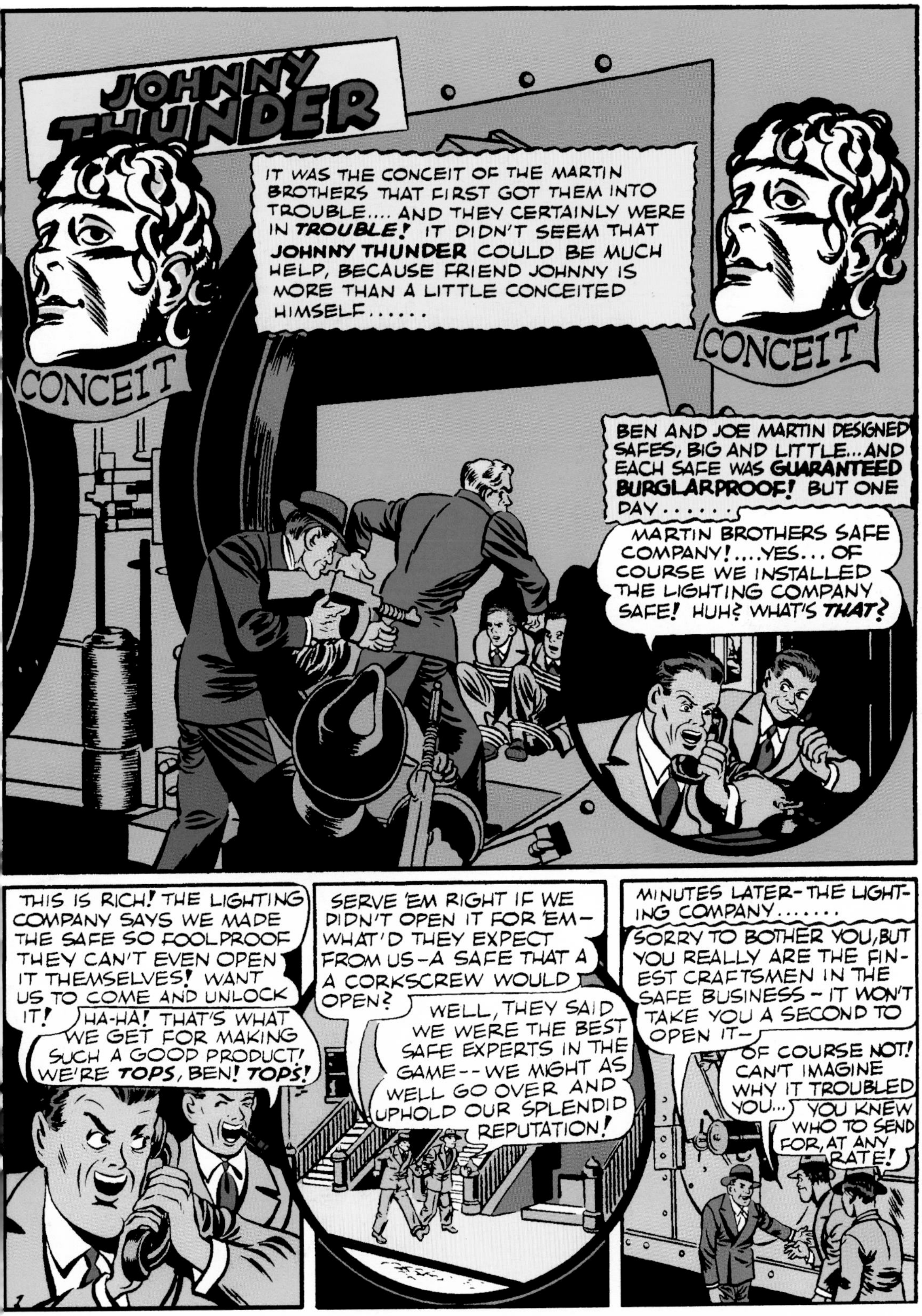
JOHNNY THUNDER
IT WAS THE CONCEIT OF THE MARTIN BROTHERS THAT FIRST GOT THEM INTO TROUBLE.... AND THEY CERTAINLY WERE IN TROUBLE! IT DIDN'T SEEM THAT JOHNNY THUNDER COULD BE MUCH HELP, BECAUSE FRIEND JOHNNY IS MORE THAN A LITTLE CONCEITED HIMSELF......
CONCEIT
CONCEIT
BEN AND JOE MARTIN DESIGNED SAFES, BIG AND LITTLE...AND EACH SAFE WAS GUARANTEED BURGLARPROOF! BUT ONE DAY......
MARTIN BROTHERS SAFE COMPANY!....YES... OF COURSE WE INSTALLED THE LIGHTING COMPANY SAFE! HUH? WHAT'S THAT?
THIS IS RICH! THE LIGHTING COMPANY SAYS WE MADE THE SAFE SO FOOLPROOF THEY CAN'T EVEN OPEN IT THEMSELVES! WANT US TO COME AND UNLOCK IT!
HA-HA! THAT'S WHAT WE GET FOR MAKING SUCH A GOOD PRODUCT! WE'RE TOPS, BEN! TOPS!
SERVE 'EM RIGHT IF WE DIDN'T OPEN IT FOR 'EM— WHAT'D THEY EXPECT FROM US—A SAFE THAT A A CORKSCREW WOULD OPEN?
WELL, THEY SAID WE WERE THE BEST SAFE EXPERTS IN THE GAME-- WE MIGHT AS WELL GO OVER AND UPHOLD OUR SPLENDID REPUTATION!
MINUTES LATER—THE LIGHTING COMPANY.......
SORRY TO BOTHER YOU, BUT YOU REALLY ARE THE FINEST CRAFTSMEN IN THE SAFE BUSINESS — IT WON'T TAKE YOU A SECOND TO OPEN IT—
OF COURSE NOT! CAN'T IMAGINE WHY IT TROUBLED YOU...
YOU KNEW WHO TO SEND FOR, AT ANY RATE!

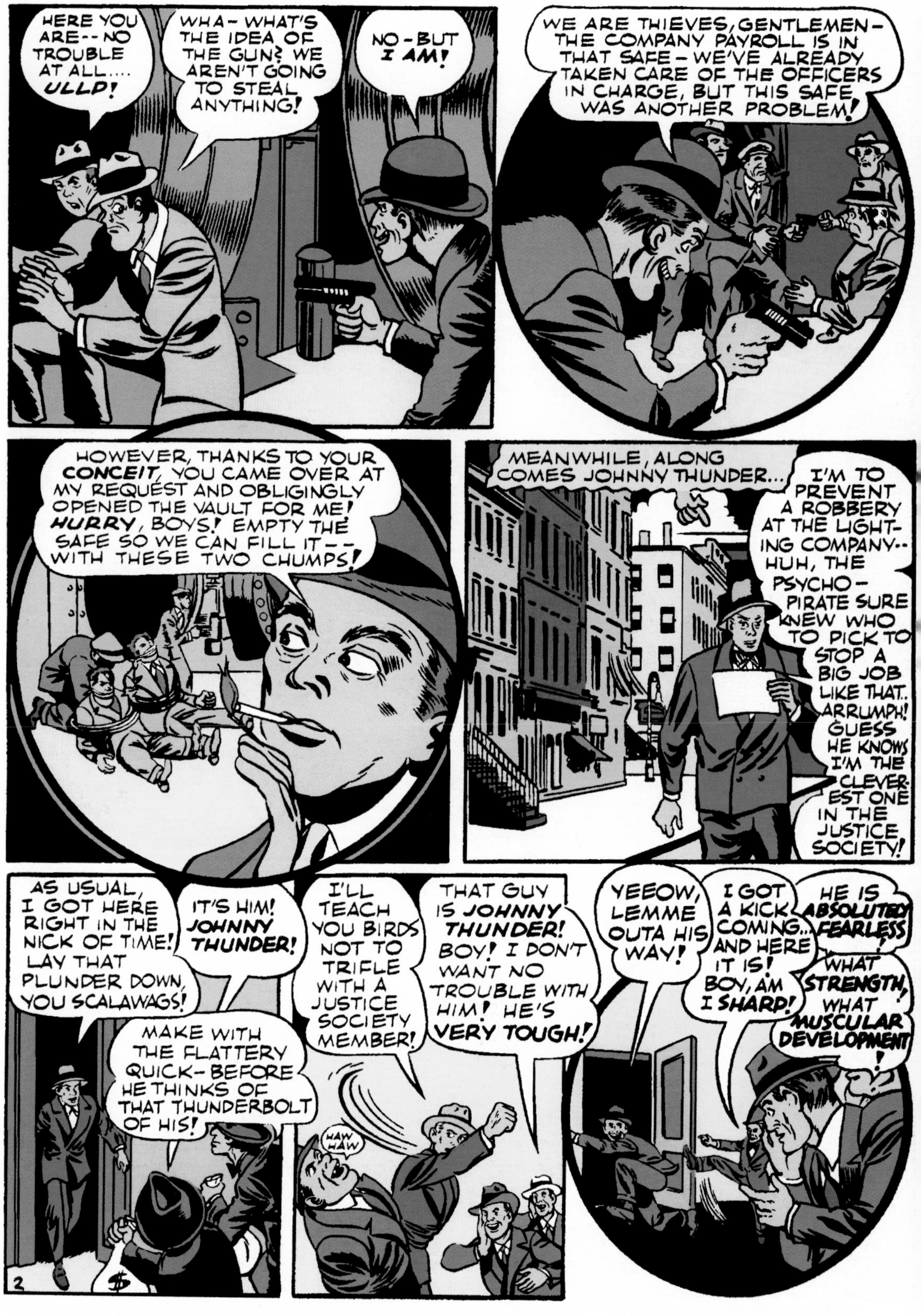
HERE YOU ARE--NO TROUBLE AT ALL.... ULLP!
WHA-WHAT'S THE IDEA OF THE GUN? WE AREN'T GOING TO STEAL ANYTHING!
NO-BUT I AM!
WE ARE THIEVES, GENTLEMEN-THE COMPANY PAYROLL IS IN THAT SAFE-WE'VE ALREADY TAKEN CARE OF THE OFFICERS IN CHARGE, BUT THIS SAFE WAS ANOTHER PROBLEM!
HOWEVER, THANKS TO YOUR CONCEIT, YOU CAME OVER AT MY REQUEST AND OBLIGINGLY OPENED THE VAULT FOR ME! HURRY, BOYS! EMPTY THE SAFE SO WE CAN FILL IT--WITH THESE TWO CHUMPS!
MEANWHILE, ALONG COMES JOHNNY THUNDER...
I'M TO PREVENT A ROBBERY AT THE LIGHTING COMPANY..HUH, THE PSYCHO-PIRATE SURE KNEW WHO TO PICK TO STOP A BIG JOB LIKE THAT.. ARRUMPH! GUESS HE KNOWS I'M THE CLEVEREST ONE IN THE JUSTICE SOCIETY!
AS USUAL, I GOT HERE RIGHT IN THE NICK OF TIME! LAY THAT PLUNDER DOWN, YOU SCALAWAGS!
IT'S HIM! JOHNNY THUNDER!
MAKE WITH THE FLATTERY QUICK-BEFORE HE THINKS OF THAT THUNDERBOLT OF HIS!
2
I'LL TEACH YOU BIRDS NOT TO TRIFLE WITH A JUSTICE SOCIETY MEMBER!
THAT GUY IS JOHNNY THUNDER! BOY! I DON'T WANT NO TROUBLE WITH HIM! HE'S VERY TOUGH!
HAW HAW
YEEOW, LEMME OUTA HIS WAY!
I GOT A KICK COMING... AND HERE IT IS! BOY, AM I SHARP!
HE IS ABSOLUTELY FEARLESS! WHAT STRENGTH, WHAT MUSCULAR DEVELOPMENT!

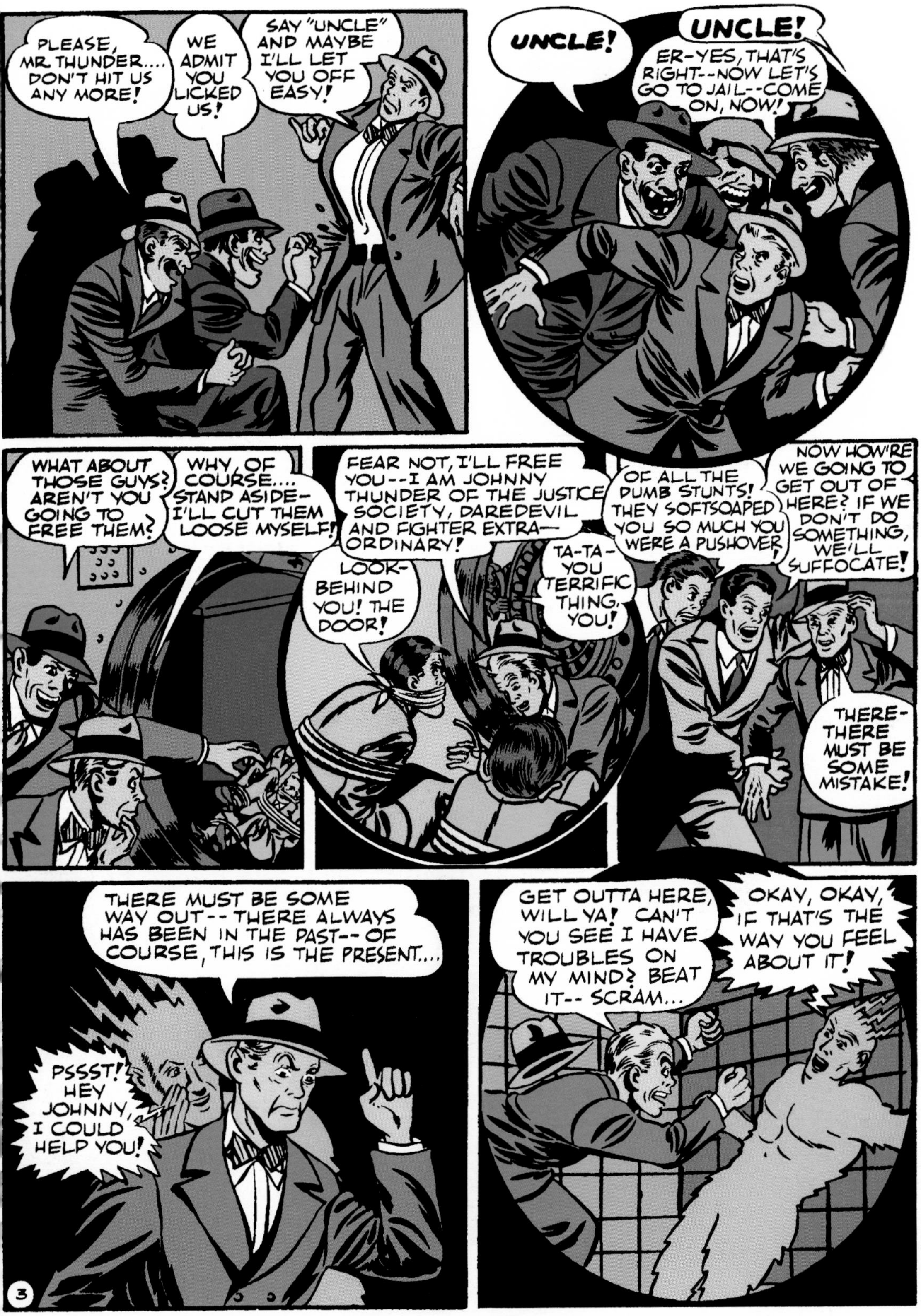
PLEASE, MR. THUNDER.... DON'T HIT US ANY MORE!
WE ADMIT YOU LICKED US!
SAY "UNCLE" AND MAYBE I'LL LET YOU OFF EASY!
UNCLE!
UNCLE!
ER-YES, THAT'S RIGHT--NOW LET'S GO TO JAIL--COME ON, NOW!
WHAT ABOUT THOSE GUYS? AREN'T YOU GOING TO FREE THEM?
WHY, OF COURSE.... STAND ASIDE-I'LL CUT THEM LOOSE MYSELF!
FEAR NOT, I'LL FREE YOU--I AM JOHNNY THUNDER OF THE JUSTICE SOCIETY, DAREDEVIL AND FIGHTER EXTRA-ORDINARY!
LOOK-BEHIND YOU! THE DOOR!
TA-TA-YOU TERRIFIC THING, YOU!
OF ALL THE DUMB STUNTS! THEY SOFTSOAPED YOU SO MUCH YOU WERE A PUSHOVER!
NOW HOW'RE WE GOING TO GET OUT OF HERE? IF WE DON'T DO SOMETHING, WE'LL SUFFOCATE!
THERE-THERE MUST BE SOME MISTAKE!
THERE MUST BE SOME WAY OUT-- THERE ALWAYS HAS BEEN IN THE PAST-- OF COURSE, THIS IS THE PRESENT....
PSSST! HEY JOHNNY, I COULD HELP YOU!
3
GET OUTTA HERE, WILL YA! CAN'T YOU SEE I HAVE TROUBLES ON MY MIND? BEAT IT-- SCRAM...
OKAY, OKAY, IF THAT'S THE WAY YOU FEEL ABOUT IT!

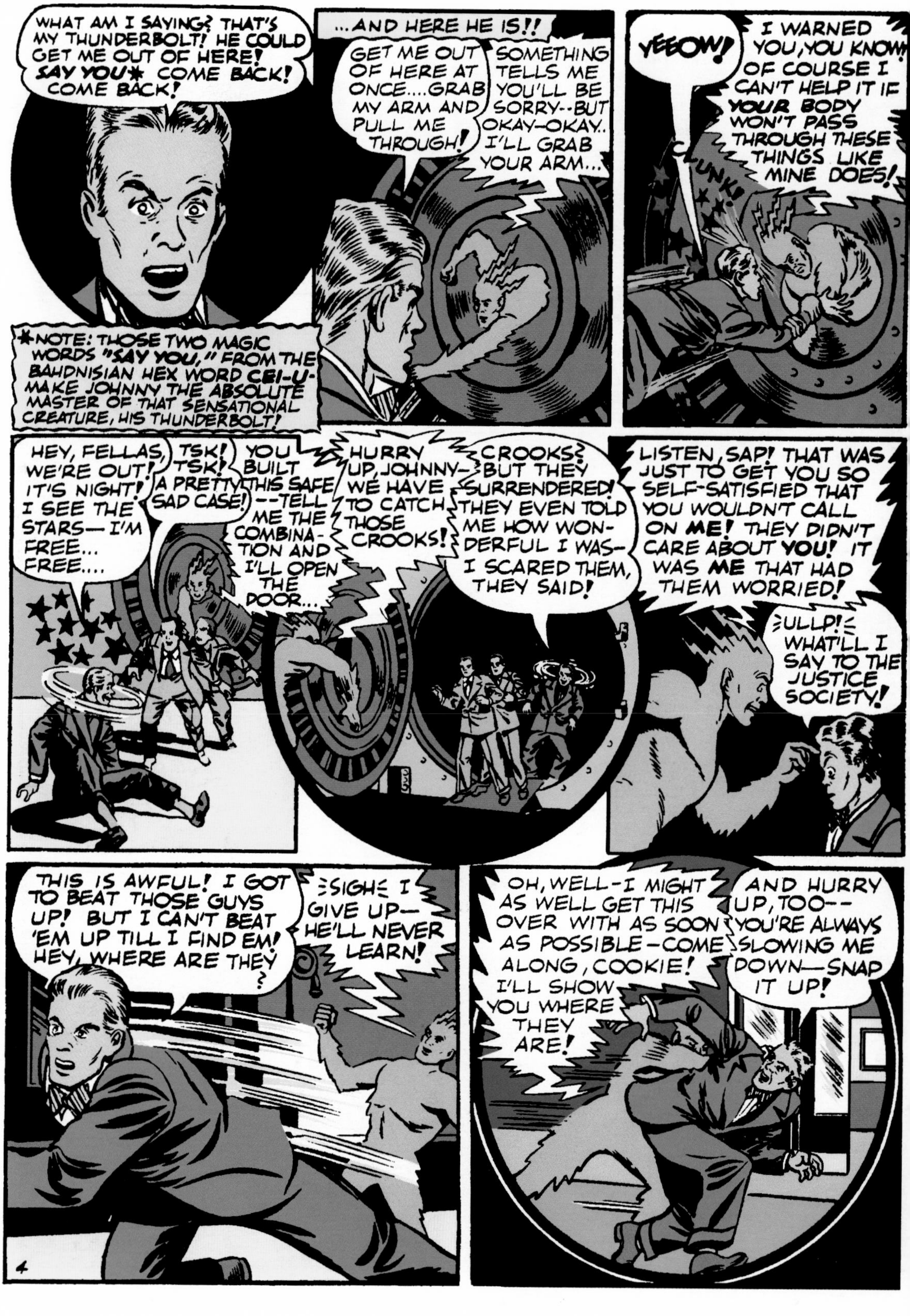

WHAT AM I SAYING? THAT'S MY THUNDERBOLT! HE COULD GET ME OUT OF HERE! SAY YOU✱ COME BACK! COME BACK!
✱NOTE: THOSE TWO MAGIC WORDS "SAY YOU," FROM THE BAHDNISIAN HEX WORD CEI-U MAKE JOHNNY THE ABSOLUTE MASTER OF THAT SENSATIONAL CREATURE, HIS THUNDERBOLT!
...AND HERE HE IS!!
GET ME OUT OF HERE AT ONCE....GRAB MY ARM AND PULL ME THROUGH!
SOMETHING TELLS ME YOU'LL BE SORRY--BUT OKAY-OKAY.. I'LL GRAB YOUR ARM...
YEEOW!
I WARNED YOU, YOU KNOW! OF COURSE I CAN'T HELP IT IF YOUR BODY WON'T PASS THROUGH THESE THINGS LIKE MINE DOES!
CLUNK!
HEY, FELLAS, WE'RE OUT! IT'S NIGHT! I SEE THE STARS— I'M FREE... FREE....
TSK! TSK! A PRETTY SAD CASE!
YOU BUILT THIS SAFE --TELL ME THE COMBINATION AND I'LL OPEN THE DOOR...
HURRY UP, JOHNNY- WE HAVE TO CATCH THOSE CROOKS!
CROOKS? BUT THEY SURRENDERED! THEY EVEN TOLD ME HOW WONDERFUL I WAS- I SCARED THEM, THEY SAID!
LISTEN, SAP! THAT WAS JUST TO GET YOU SO SELF-SATISFIED THAT YOU WOULDN'T CALL ON ME! THEY DIDN'T CARE ABOUT YOU! IT WAS ME THAT HAD THEM WORRIED!
ULLP! WHAT'LL I SAY TO THE JUSTICE SOCIETY!
THIS IS AWFUL! I GOT TO BEAT THOSE GUYS UP! BUT I CAN'T BEAT 'EM UP TILL I FIND EM! HEY, WHERE ARE THEY ?
SIGH I GIVE UP— HE'LL NEVER LEARN!
4
OH, WELL-I MIGHT AS WELL GET THIS OVER WITH AS SOON AS POSSIBLE-COME ALONG, COOKIE! I'LL SHOW YOU WHERE THEY ARE!
AND HURRY UP, TOO-- YOU'RE ALWAYS SLOWING ME DOWN—SNAP IT UP!

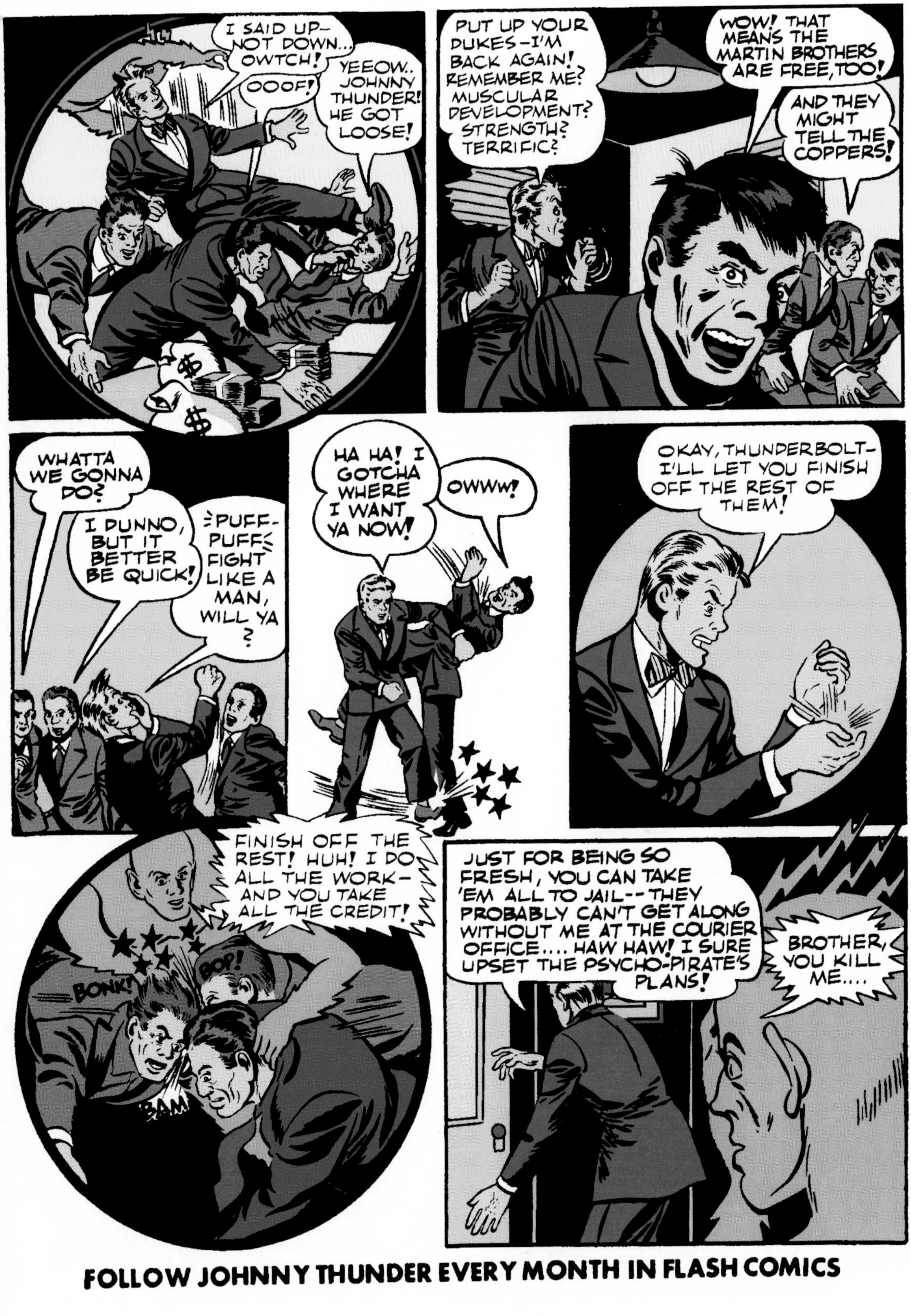
I SAID UP-NOT DOWN... OWTCH!
OOOF!
YEEOW.. JOHNNY THUNDER! HE GOT LOOSE!
PUT UP YOUR DUKES-I'M BACK AGAIN! REMEMBER ME? MUSCULAR DEVELOPMENT? STRENGTH? TERRIFIC?
WOW! THAT MEANS THE MARTIN BROTHERS ARE FREE, TOO!
AND THEY MIGHT TELL THE COPPERS!
WHATTA WE GONNA DO?
I DUNNO, BUT IT BETTER BE QUICK!
PUFF-PUFF FIGHT LIKE A MAN, WILL YA?
HA HA! I GOTCHA WHERE I WANT YA NOW!
OWWW!
OKAY, THUNDERBOLT-I'LL LET YOU FINISH OFF THE REST OF THEM!
FINISH OFF THE REST! HUH! I DO ALL THE WORK-AND YOU TAKE ALL THE CREDIT!
BONK!
BOP!
BAM
JUST FOR BEING SO FRESH, YOU CAN TAKE 'EM ALL TO JAIL--THEY PROBABLY CAN'T GET ALONG WITHOUT ME AT THE COURIER OFFICE.... HAW HAW! I SURE UPSET THE PSYCHO-PIRATE'S PLANS!
BROTHER, YOU KILL ME....

FOLLOW JOHNNY THUNDER EVERY MONTH IN FLASH COMICS

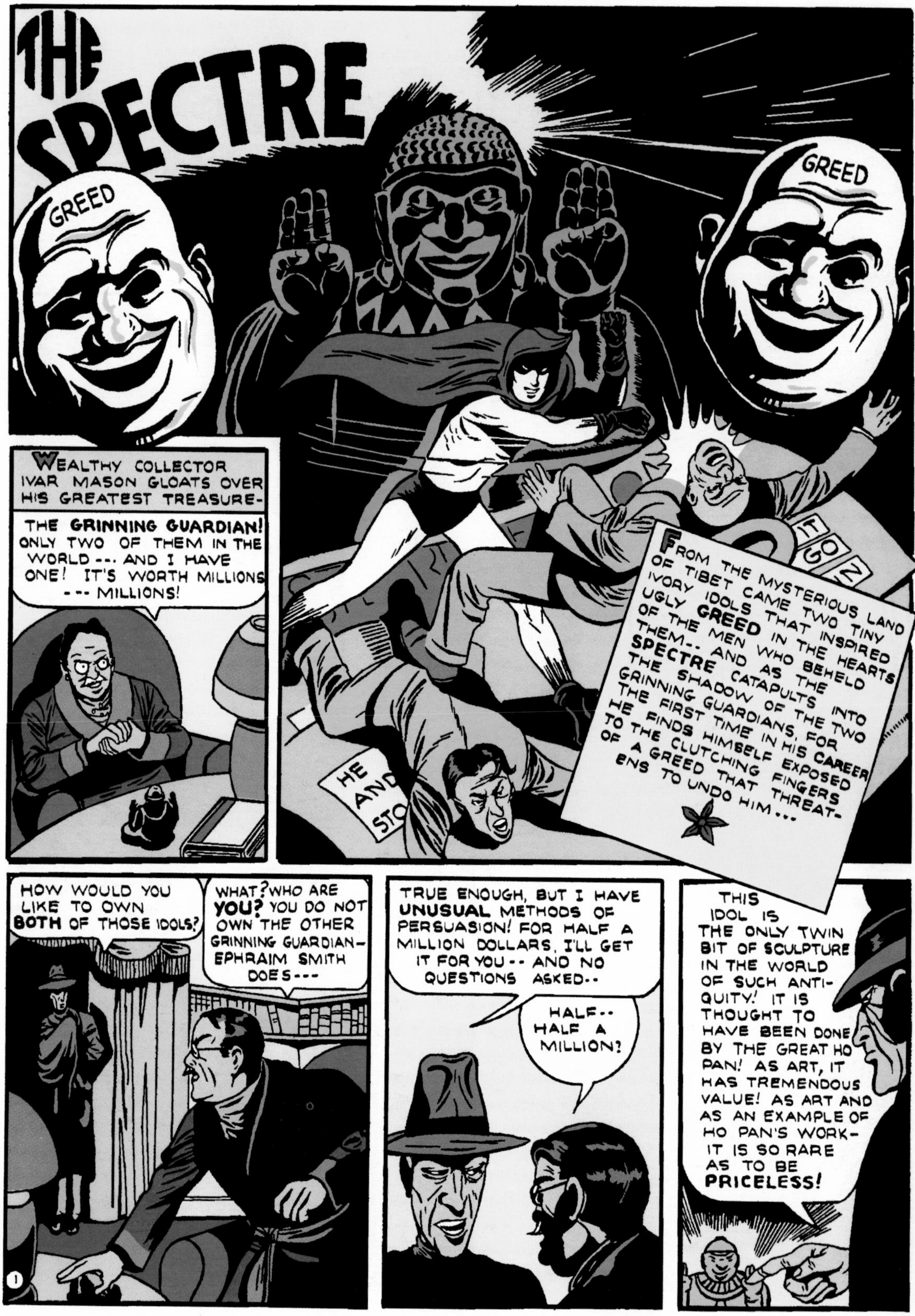
THE SPECTRE
GREED
GREED
WEALTHY COLLECTOR IVAR MASON GLOATS OVER HIS GREATEST TREASURE-
THE GRINNING GUARDIAN! ONLY TWO OF THEM IN THE WORLD --- AND I HAVE ONE! IT'S WORTH MILLIONS --- MILLIONS!
FROM THE MYSTERIOUS LAND OF TIBET CAME TWO TINY IVORY IDOLS THAT INSPIRED UGLY GREED IN THE HEARTS OF THE MEN WHO BEHELD THEM-- AND AS THE SPECTRE CATAPULTS INTO THE SHADOW OF THE TWO GRINNING GUARDIANS, FOR THE FIRST TIME IN HIS CAREER HE FINDS HIMSELF EXPOSED TO THE CLUTCHING FINGERS OF A GREED THAT THREATENS TO UNDO HIM...
HOW WOULD YOU LIKE TO OWN BOTH OF THOSE IDOLS?
WHAT? WHO ARE YOU? YOU DO NOT OWN THE OTHER GRINNING GUARDIAN- EPHRAIM SMITH DOES---
TRUE ENOUGH, BUT I HAVE UNUSUAL METHODS OF PERSUASION! FOR HALF A MILLION DOLLARS, I'LL GET IT FOR YOU -- AND NO QUESTIONS ASKED--
HALF-- HALF A MILLION?
THIS IDOL IS THE ONLY TWIN BIT OF SCULPTURE IN THE WORLD OF SUCH ANTIQUITY! IT IS THOUGHT TO HAVE BEEN DONE BY THE GREAT HO PAN! AS ART, IT HAS TREMENDOUS VALUE! AS ART AND AS AN EXAMPLE OF HO PAN'S WORK- IT IS SO RARE AS TO BE PRICELESS!

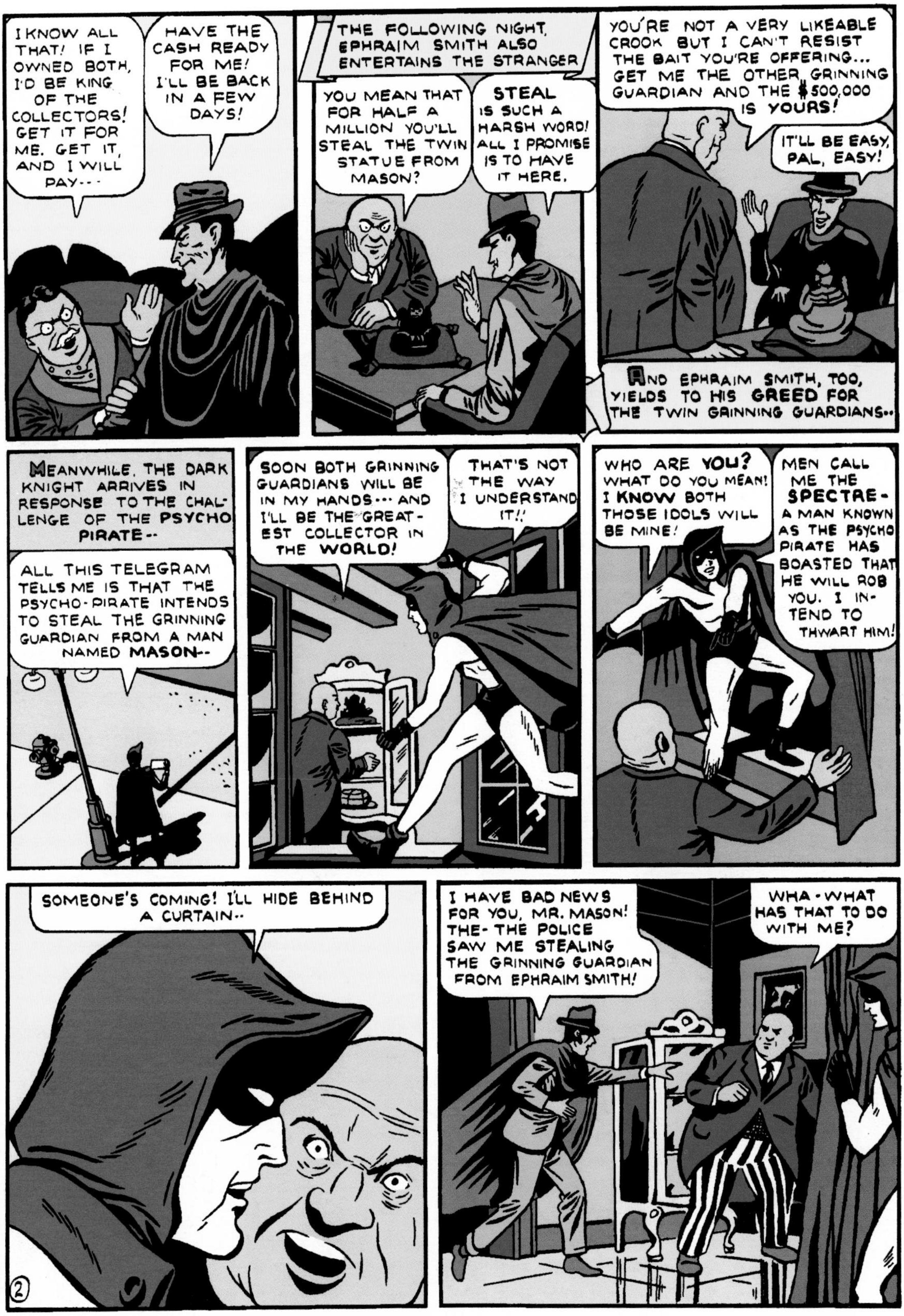
I KNOW ALL THAT! IF I OWNED BOTH, I'D BE KING OF THE COLLECTORS! GET IT FOR ME. GET IT, AND I WILL PAY---
HAVE THE CASH READY FOR ME! I'LL BE BACK IN A FEW DAYS!
THE FOLLOWING NIGHT, EPHRAIM SMITH ALSO ENTERTAINS THE STRANGER
YOU MEAN THAT FOR HALF A MILLION YOU'LL STEAL THE TWIN STATUE FROM MASON?
STEAL IS SUCH A HARSH WORD! ALL I PROMISE IS TO HAVE IT HERE.
YOU'RE NOT A VERY LIKEABLE CROOK BUT I CAN'T RESIST THE BAIT YOU'RE OFFERING... GET ME THE OTHER GRINNING GUARDIAN AND THE $500,000 IS YOURS!
IT'LL BE EASY, PAL, EASY!
AND EPHRAIM SMITH, TOO, YIELDS TO HIS GREED FOR THE TWIN GRINNING GUARDIANS..
MEANWHILE, THE DARK KNIGHT ARRIVES IN RESPONSE TO THE CHALLENGE OF THE PSYCHO PIRATE--
ALL THIS TELEGRAM TELLS ME IS THAT THE PSYCHO-PIRATE INTENDS TO STEAL THE GRINNING GUARDIAN FROM A MAN NAMED MASON--
SOON BOTH GRINNING GUARDIANS WILL BE IN MY HANDS--- AND I'LL BE THE GREATEST COLLECTOR IN THE WORLD!
THAT'S NOT THE WAY I UNDERSTAND IT!
WHO ARE YOU? WHAT DO YOU MEAN! I KNOW BOTH THOSE IDOLS WILL BE MINE!
MEN CALL ME THE SPECTRE - A MAN KNOWN AS THE PSYCHO PIRATE HAS BOASTED THAT HE WILL ROB YOU. I INTEND TO THWART HIM!
SOMEONE'S COMING! I'LL HIDE BEHIND A CURTAIN--
I HAVE BAD NEWS FOR YOU, MR. MASON! THE- THE POLICE SAW ME STEALING THE GRINNING GUARDIAN FROM EPHRAIM SMITH!
WHA - WHAT HAS THAT TO DO WITH ME?
2

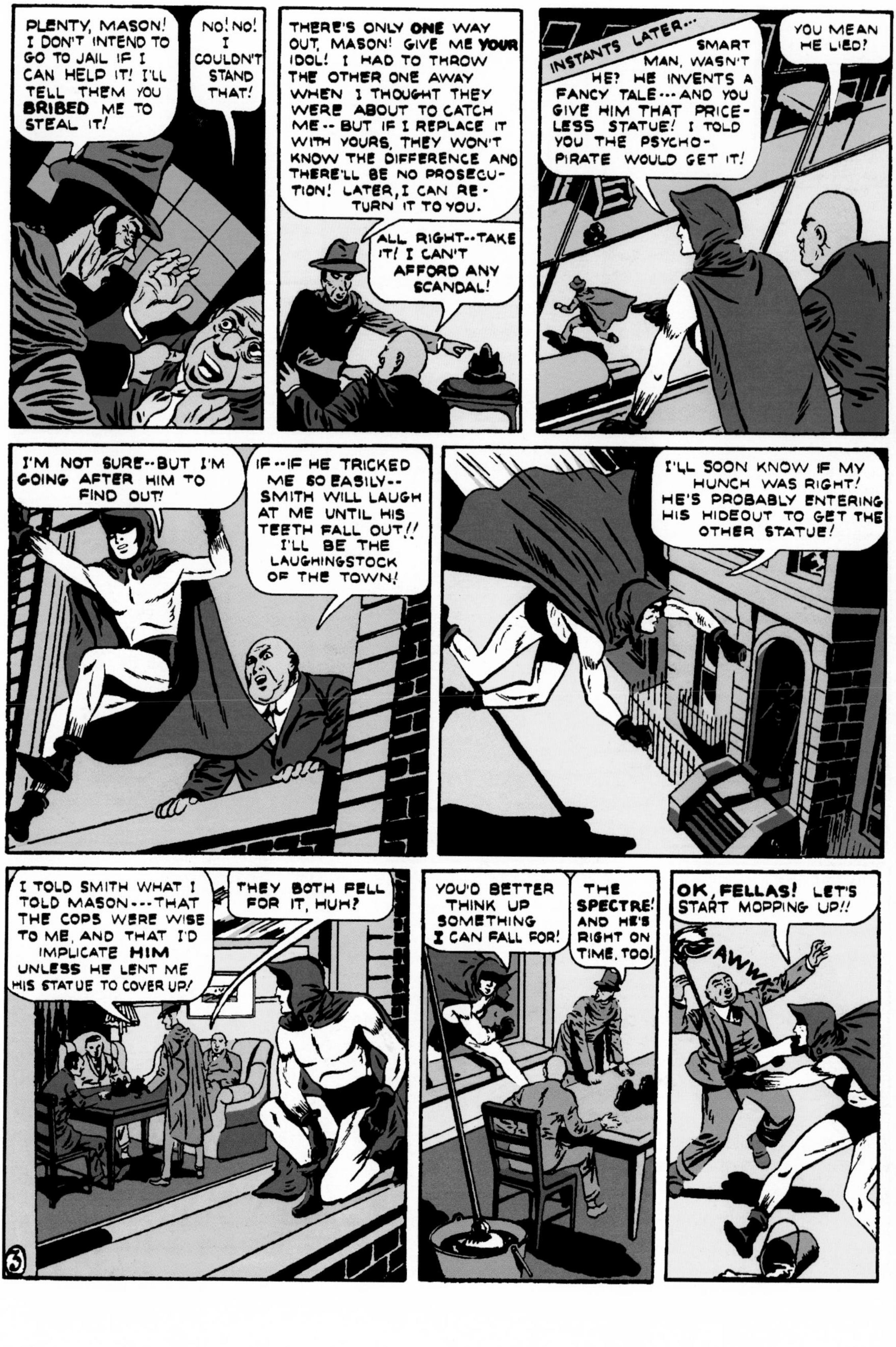
PLENTY, MASON! I DON'T INTEND TO GO TO JAIL IF I CAN HELP IT! I'LL TELL THEM YOU BRIBED ME TO STEAL IT!
NO! NO! I COULDN'T STAND THAT!
THERE'S ONLY ONE WAY OUT, MASON! GIVE ME YOUR IDOL! I HAD TO THROW THE OTHER ONE AWAY WHEN I THOUGHT THEY WERE ABOUT TO CATCH ME -- BUT IF I REPLACE IT WITH YOURS, THEY WON'T KNOW THE DIFFERENCE AND THERE'LL BE NO PROSECUTION! LATER, I CAN RETURN IT TO YOU.
ALL RIGHT--TAKE IT! I CAN'T AFFORD ANY SCANDAL!
INSTANTS LATER...
SMART MAN, WASN'T HE? HE INVENTS A FANCY TALE --- AND YOU GIVE HIM THAT PRICELESS STATUE! I TOLD YOU THE PSYCHO-PIRATE WOULD GET IT!
YOU MEAN HE LIED?
I'M NOT SURE--BUT I'M GOING AFTER HIM TO FIND OUT!
IF--IF HE TRICKED ME SO EASILY-- SMITH WILL LAUGH AT ME UNTIL HIS TEETH FALL OUT!! I'LL BE THE LAUGHINGSTOCK OF THE TOWN!
I'LL SOON KNOW IF MY HUNCH WAS RIGHT! HE'S PROBABLY ENTERING HIS HIDEOUT TO GET THE OTHER STATUE!
I TOLD SMITH WHAT I TOLD MASON---THAT THE COPS WERE WISE TO ME, AND THAT I'D IMPLICATE HIM UNLESS HE LENT ME HIS STATUE TO COVER UP!
THEY BOTH FELL FOR IT, HUH?
3
YOU'D BETTER THINK UP SOMETHING I CAN FALL FOR!
THE SPECTRE! AND HE'S RIGHT ON TIME, TOO!
OK, FELLAS! LET'S START MOPPING UP!!
AWW

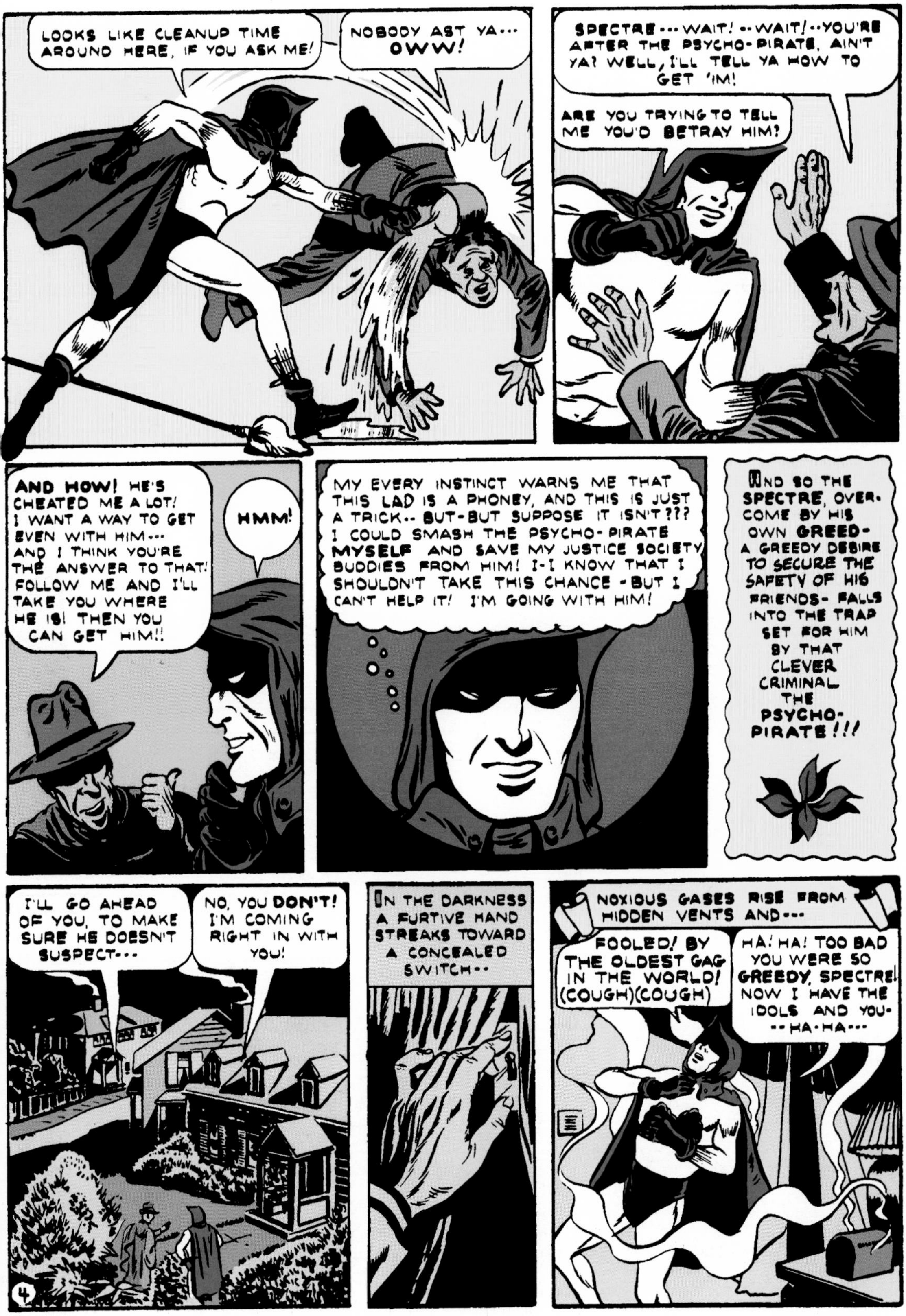
LOOKS LIKE CLEANUP TIME AROUND HERE, IF YOU ASK ME!
NOBODY AST YA... OWW!
SPECTRE...WAIT! --WAIT!--YOU'RE AFTER THE PSYCHO-PIRATE, AIN'T YA? WELL, I'LL TELL YA HOW TO GET 'IM!
ARE YOU TRYING TO TELL ME YOU'D BETRAY HIM?
AND HOW! HE'S CHEATED ME A LOT! I WANT A WAY TO GET EVEN WITH HIM--- AND I THINK YOU'RE THE ANSWER TO THAT! FOLLOW ME AND I'LL TAKE YOU WHERE HE IS! THEN YOU CAN GET HIM!!
HMM!
MY EVERY INSTINCT WARNS ME THAT THIS LAD IS A PHONEY, AND THIS IS JUST A TRICK-- BUT-BUT SUPPOSE IT ISN'T??? I COULD SMASH THE PSYCHO-PIRATE MYSELF AND SAVE MY JUSTICE SOCIETY BUDDIES FROM HIM! I-I KNOW THAT I SHOULDN'T TAKE THIS CHANCE - BUT I CAN'T HELP IT! I'M GOING WITH HIM!
AND SO THE SPECTRE, OVERCOME BY HIS OWN GREED- A GREEDY DESIRE TO SECURE THE SAFETY OF HIS FRIENDS- FALLS INTO THE TRAP SET FOR HIM BY THAT CLEVER CRIMINAL THE PSYCHO-PIRATE!!!
I'LL GO AHEAD OF YOU, TO MAKE SURE HE DOESN'T SUSPECT---
NO, YOU DON'T! I'M COMING RIGHT IN WITH YOU!
4
IN THE DARKNESS A FURTIVE HAND STREAKS TOWARD A CONCEALED SWITCH--
NOXIOUS GASES RISE FROM HIDDEN VENTS AND---
FOOLED! BY THE OLDEST GAG IN THE WORLD! (COUGH)(COUGH)
HA! HA! TOO BAD YOU WERE SO GREEDY, SPECTRE! NOW I HAVE THE IDOLS AND YOU- --HA-HA---

WITH A LAST DESPERATE EFFORT, THE **DARK KNIGHT** HURLS THE TWIN STATUES AT A CLOSED WINDOW!

THAT FRESH AIR MAY REVIVE ME--

LOOK--THE GRINNING GUARDIANS! HE'S THROWN THEM AWAY!

MAYBE IT'S NOT TOO LATE, AFTER ALL! I'VE GOT YOU NOW, YOU **RATS**!

HE'S COMING TO! WELL, HE WON'T GET THE PSYCHO-PIRATE!

AN ARM DARTS FORTH FROM THE PSYCHO-PIRATE AND SENDS THE GUNMAN ROCKETING INTO THE SPECTRE-

STOP HIM!!

OOF!

STAND ASIDE, YOU IDIOT!

BUT SPLIT SECONDS ARE ALL THE PSYCHO-PIRATE NEEDS, AND---

HE-HE'S GETTING AWAY!

UGHH

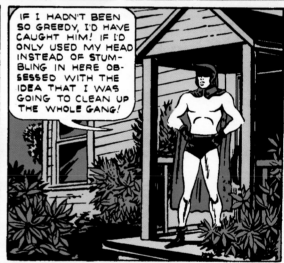

IF I HADN'T BEEN SO GREEDY, I'D HAVE CAUGHT HIM! IF I'D ONLY USED MY HEAD INSTEAD OF STUMBLING IN HERE OBSESSED WITH THE IDEA THAT I WAS GOING TO CLEAN UP THE WHOLE GANG!

WELL, AT LEAST I HAVE THE PSYCHO-PIRATE'S PLUNDER- HE DIDN'T GET THAT! AND I HAVE SOME OF HIS CROWD TO TAKE TO JAIL! I SHOULD BE SATISFIED WITH THAT.. AND I AM!

SOME MINUTES LATER

NOW FOR THE COURIER OFFICE TO SEE HOW THE REST OF THE BOYS ARE DOING!

5

Follow The SPECTRE'S exploits each month in MORE FUN COMICS!

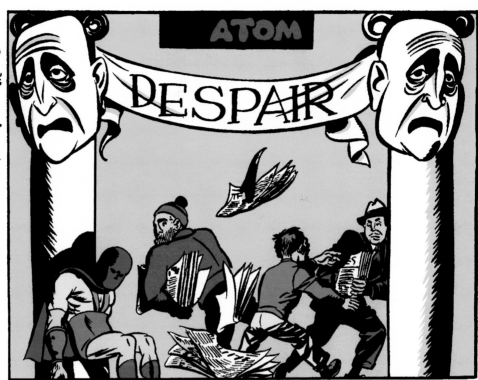

THERE IS NO EMOTION SO DEADENING, SO BENUMBING IN ITS SHOCKING PARALYSIS, AS DESPAIR. AND IT IS THIS STUPEFYING FEELING THAT THE ATOM MUST FIGHT IF HE IS TO SAVE STILL ANOTHER FROM THE PSYCHO-PIRATE'S GREEDY CLUTCHES!

AS THE OTHER MEMBERS OF THE JUSTICE SOCIETY START OFF ON THEIR VARIOUS MISSIONS, THE ATOM REMAINS AT THE COURIER OFFICES--

WE'LL TAKE CARE OF THIS PSYCHO-PIRATE IF HE TRIES ANY TRICKS, WON'T WE, MR. MORGAN?

I-I HOPE SO, ATOM!

-BUT I'VE FOUGHT SUCH A LOSING BATTLE THAT I'M NOT SURE--I'VE MORTGAGED MY HOME HEAVILY AND MADE LARGE LOANS, OFFERING THE COURIER AS SECURITY. FIGHTING THAT FIEND, THE PSYCHO-PIRATE, HAS BLED ME WHITE. IF HE ISN'T STOPPED SOMEHOW, I'M LICKED!

NO MAN IS LICKED UNTIL HE IS DEAD!

I KNOW, IT'S BEEN MIGHTY TOUGH-- BUT I'LL KEEP FIGHTING!

1

AND THEN-WHILE THE ATOM LOOKS HELPLESSLY ON- ONE BLOW AFTER ANOTHER HITS REX MORGAN-

IT'S THE BANK, SIR. THEY-THEY SAY THEY'RE GOING TO FORECLOSE ON YOUR HOME!

THEY CAN'T! LET ME TALK TO THEM.

OH- OH!

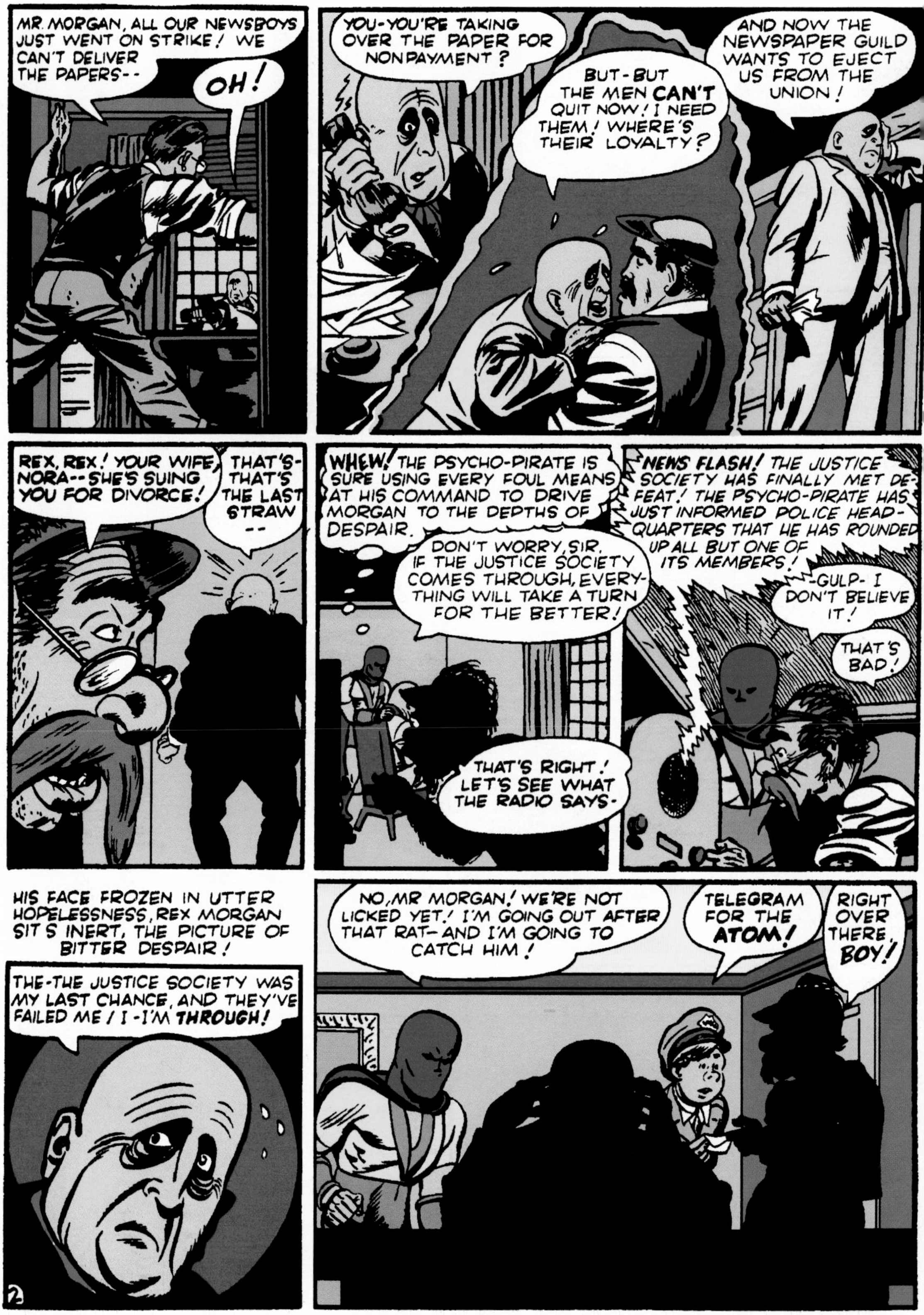
MR. MORGAN, ALL OUR NEWSBOYS JUST WENT ON STRIKE! WE CAN'T DELIVER THE PAPERS--
OH!
YOU-YOU'RE TAKING OVER THE PAPER FOR NONPAYMENT?
BUT-BUT THE MEN CAN'T QUIT NOW! I NEED THEM! WHERE'S THEIR LOYALTY?
AND NOW THE NEWSPAPER GUILD WANTS TO EJECT US FROM THE UNION!
REX, REX! YOUR WIFE, NORA--SHE'S SUING YOU FOR DIVORCE!
THAT'S-THAT'S THE LAST STRAW--
WHEW! THE PSYCHO-PIRATE IS SURE USING EVERY FOUL MEANS AT HIS COMMAND TO DRIVE MORGAN TO THE DEPTHS OF DESPAIR.
DON'T WORRY, SIR. IF THE JUSTICE SOCIETY COMES THROUGH, EVERYTHING WILL TAKE A TURN FOR THE BETTER!
THAT'S RIGHT! LET'S SEE WHAT THE RADIO SAYS-
NEWS FLASH! THE JUSTICE SOCIETY HAS FINALLY MET DEFEAT! THE PSYCHO-PIRATE HAS JUST INFORMED POLICE HEADQUARTERS THAT HE HAS ROUNDED UP ALL BUT ONE OF ITS MEMBERS!
-GULP- I DON'T BELIEVE IT!
THAT'S BAD!
HIS FACE FROZEN IN UTTER HOPELESSNESS, REX MORGAN SITS INERT, THE PICTURE OF BITTER DESPAIR!
THE-THE JUSTICE SOCIETY WAS MY LAST CHANCE, AND THEY'VE FAILED ME! I-I'M THROUGH!
2
NO, MR MORGAN! WE'RE NOT LICKED YET! I'M GOING OUT AFTER THAT RAT-AND I'M GOING TO CATCH HIM!
TELEGRAM FOR THE ATOM!
RIGHT OVER THERE, BOY!

It's an invitation from the Psycho-Pirate to visit him and see his seven-prisoners-my pals, the rest of the **Justice Society!**

All right! Mr. Morgan will organize biggest police hunt in history. We'll shoot those crooks down like dogs! We'll—

No, thanks, this is a personal matter with me, I'll settle for my friends **in my own way!**

We-ell whatever you say!

AN HOUR LATER, THE MIGHTY MITE APPROACHES THE WALLED ENTRANCE TO AN ABANDONED STONE QUARRY--

This is the place where the Psycho-Pirate claims the fellows are being held. Wonder where this tunnel leads to?

FIFTY PACES INSIDE—THE **ATOM** FINDS--

Hawkman! Starman! It's me--the **Atom!** I've come to free you!

Getaway, while you can, **Atom!**

It's useless to fight the Psycho-Pirate-- **useless!**

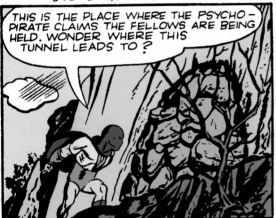

You, too? Do you men feel the same way?

Of course we do! Save yourself at all costs, keep up our work--

We never realized what we were up against, **Atom!**

No man can lick himself, Atom-and that's what we were trying to do! That clever fiend played on our emotions and beat us at our own game!

Y-yes! I-I-guess maybe you're right! I'd better get going-

LIKE A BATTERING BLUDGEON BEATING DOWN EVERYTHING BENEATH IT, THE ATOM'S DEEP DESPAIR CRUSHES HIM, FEET DRAGGING, HEAD HANGING, HE STUMBLES OUT--

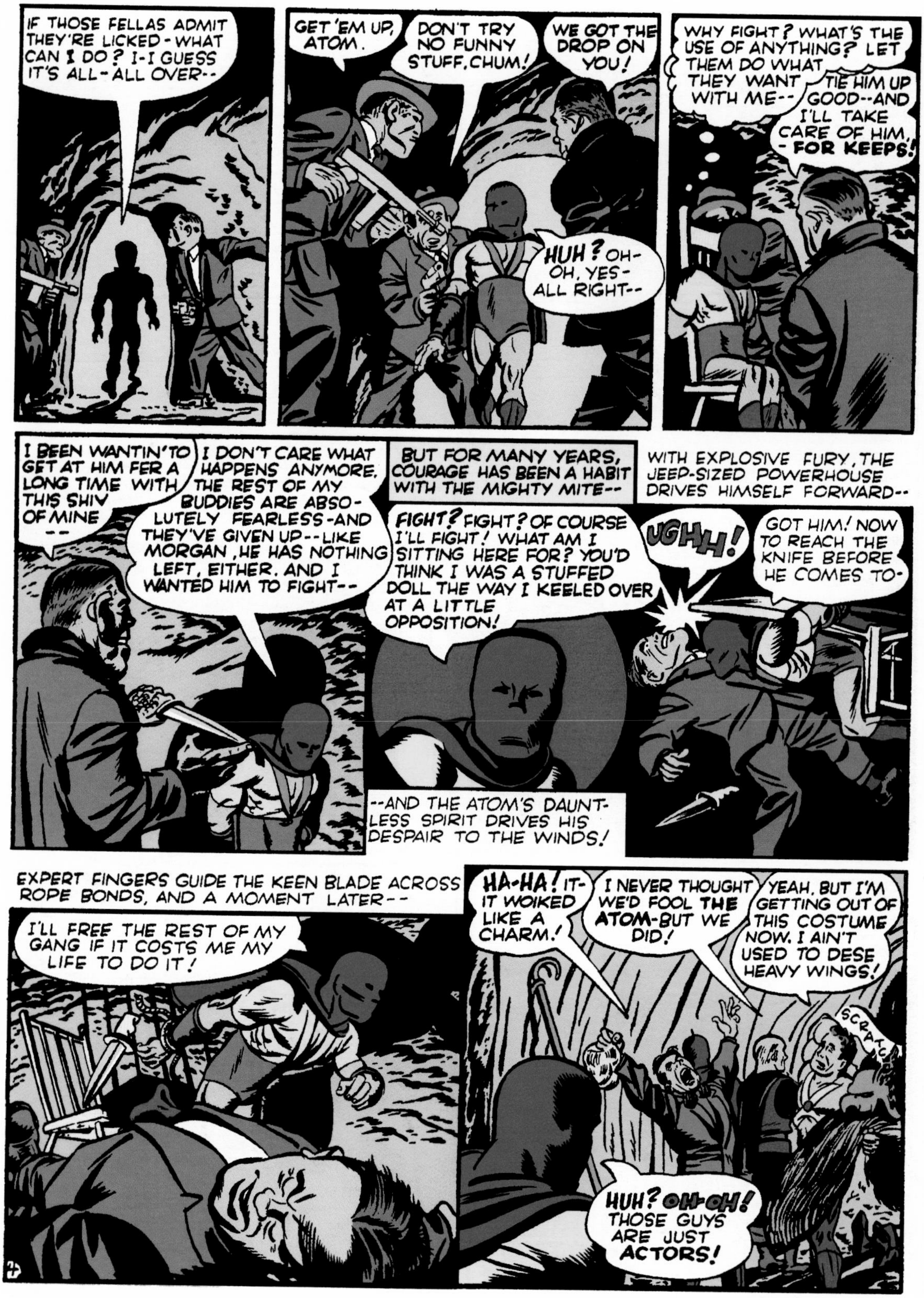
IF THOSE FELLAS ADMIT THEY'RE LICKED - WHAT CAN I DO? I-I GUESS IT'S ALL - ALL OVER--
GET 'EM UP, ATOM.
DON'T TRY NO FUNNY STUFF, CHUM!
WE GOT THE DROP ON YOU!
HUH? OH-OH, YES - ALL RIGHT--
WHY FIGHT? WHAT'S THE USE OF ANYTHING? LET THEM DO WHAT THEY WANT WITH ME--
TIE HIM UP GOOD--AND I'LL TAKE CARE OF HIM, - FOR KEEPS!
I BEEN WANTIN' TO GET AT HIM FER A LONG TIME WITH THIS SHIV OF MINE --
I DON'T CARE WHAT HAPPENS ANYMORE. THE REST OF MY BUDDIES ARE ABSOLUTELY FEARLESS - AND THEY'VE GIVEN UP -- LIKE MORGAN, HE HAS NOTHING LEFT, EITHER. AND I WANTED HIM TO FIGHT--
BUT FOR MANY YEARS, COURAGE HAS BEEN A HABIT WITH THE MIGHTY MITE--
FIGHT? FIGHT? OF COURSE I'LL FIGHT! WHAT AM I SITTING HERE FOR? YOU'D THINK I WAS A STUFFED DOLL THE WAY I KEELED OVER AT A LITTLE OPPOSITION!
--AND THE ATOM'S DAUNTLESS SPIRIT DRIVES HIS DESPAIR TO THE WINDS!
WITH EXPLOSIVE FURY, THE JEEP-SIZED POWERHOUSE DRIVES HIMSELF FORWARD--
UGHH!
GOT HIM! NOW TO REACH THE KNIFE BEFORE HE COMES TO-
EXPERT FINGERS GUIDE THE KEEN BLADE ACROSS ROPE BONDS, AND A MOMENT LATER--
I'LL FREE THE REST OF MY GANG IF IT COSTS ME MY LIFE TO DO IT!
HA-HA! IT-IT WOIKED LIKE A CHARM!
I NEVER THOUGHT WE'D FOOL THE ATOM - BUT WE DID!
YEAH, BUT I'M GETTING OUT OF THIS COSTUME NOW. I AIN'T USED TO DESE HEAVY WINGS!
SCRATC
HUH? OH-OH! THOSE GUYS ARE JUST ACTORS!
7

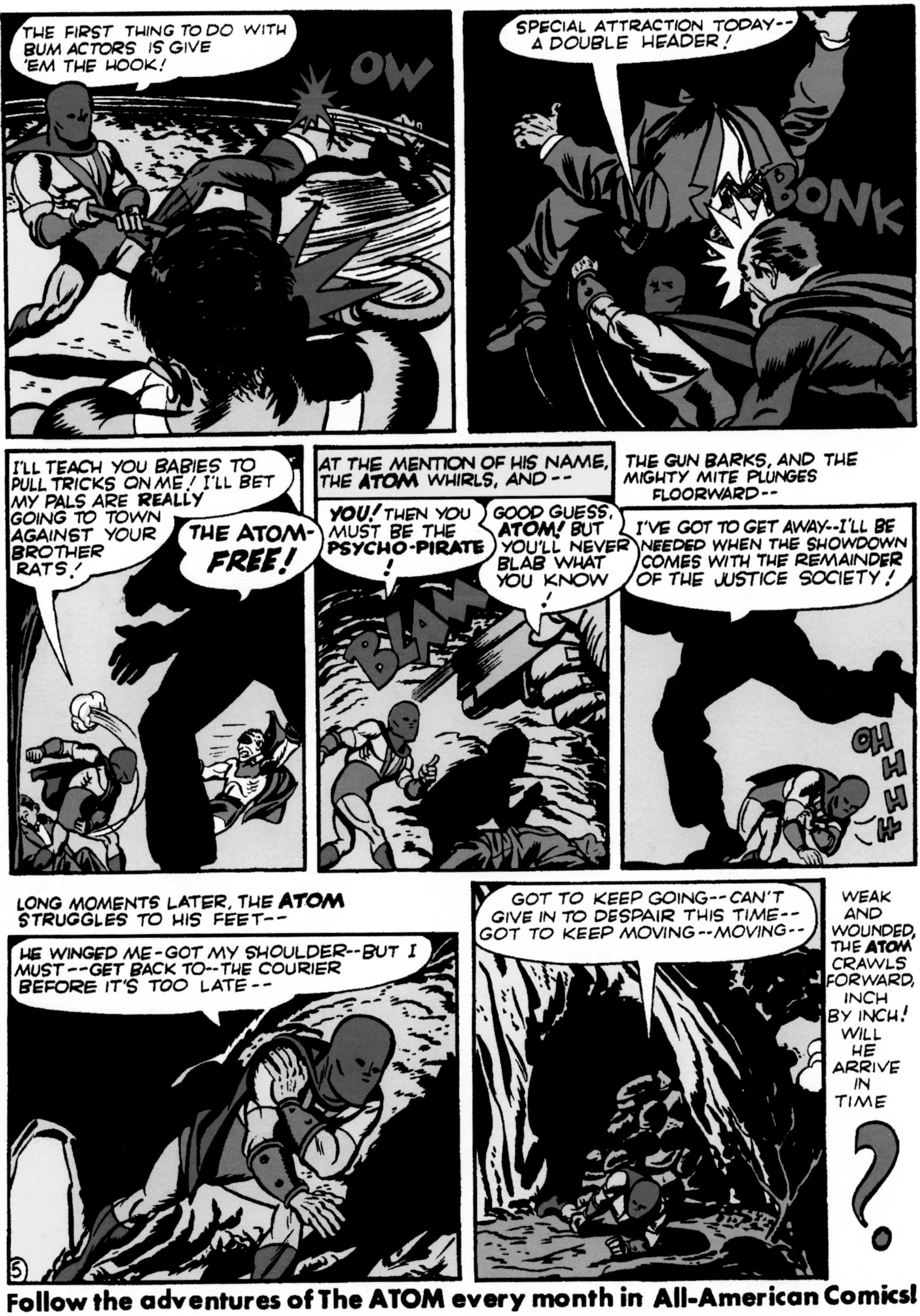
THE FIRST THING TO DO WITH BUM ACTORS IS GIVE 'EM THE HOOK!
OW
SPECIAL ATTRACTION TODAY-- A DOUBLE HEADER!
BONK
I'LL TEACH YOU BABIES TO PULL TRICKS ON ME! I'LL BET MY PALS ARE REALLY GOING TO TOWN AGAINST YOUR BROTHER RATS!
THE ATOM- FREE!
AT THE MENTION OF HIS NAME, THE ATOM WHIRLS, AND--
YOU! THEN YOU MUST BE THE PSYCHO-PIRATE!
GOOD GUESS, ATOM! BUT YOU'LL NEVER BLAB WHAT YOU KNOW!
BLAM
THE GUN BARKS, AND THE MIGHTY MITE PLUNGES FLOORWARD--
I'VE GOT TO GET AWAY--I'LL BE NEEDED WHEN THE SHOWDOWN COMES WITH THE REMAINDER OF THE JUSTICE SOCIETY!
OHHHH
LONG MOMENTS LATER, THE ATOM STRUGGLES TO HIS FEET--
HE WINGED ME-GOT MY SHOULDER--BUT I MUST--GET BACK TO--THE COURIER BEFORE IT'S TOO LATE--
5
GOT TO KEEP GOING--CAN'T GIVE IN TO DESPAIR THIS TIME-- GOT TO KEEP MOVING--MOVING--
WEAK AND WOUNDED, THE ATOM CRAWLS FORWARD, INCH BY INCH! WILL HE ARRIVE IN TIME
?

Follow the adventures of The ATOM every month in All-American Comics!

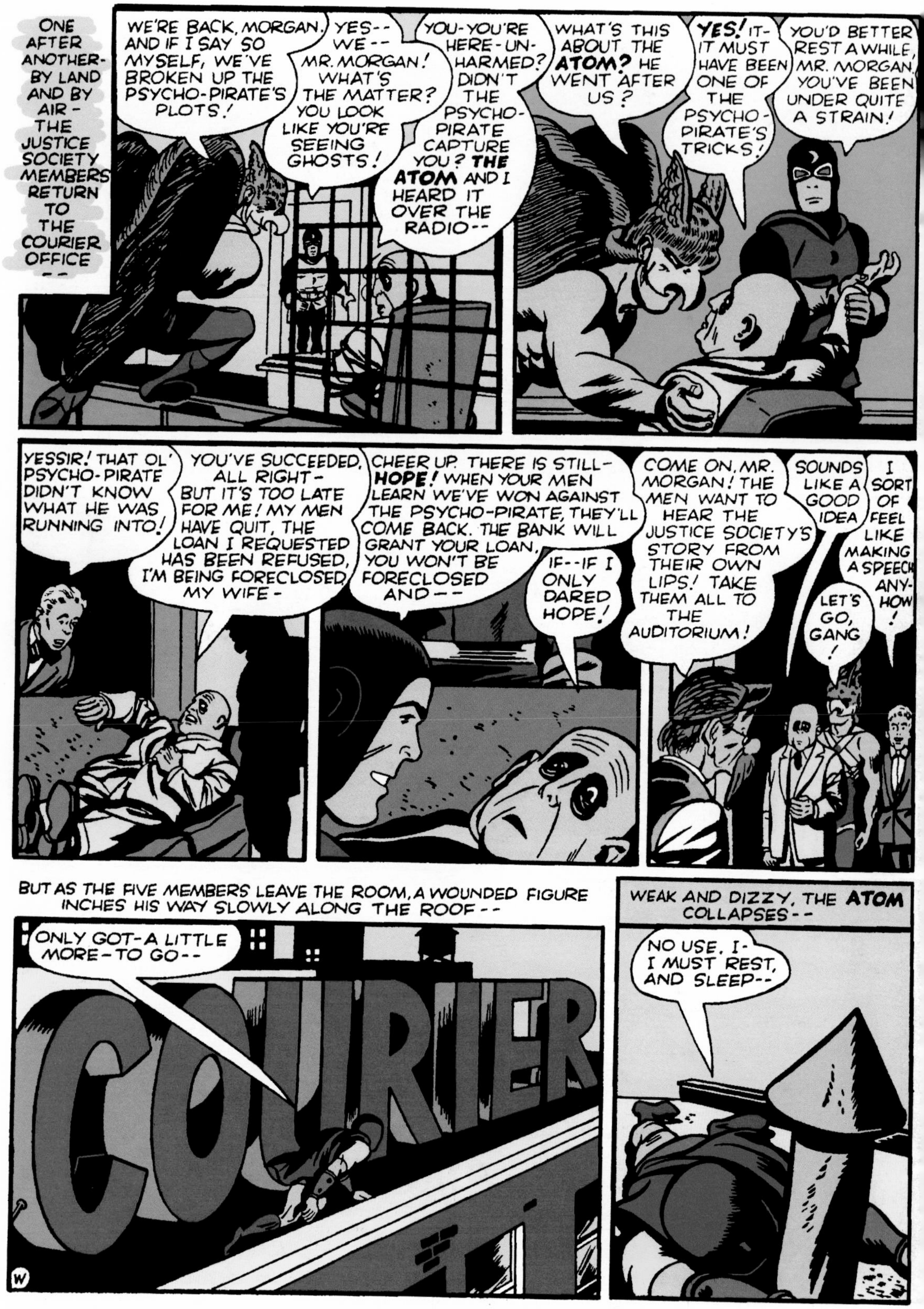
ONE AFTER ANOTHER- BY LAND AND BY AIR - THE JUSTICE SOCIETY MEMBERS RETURN TO THE COURIER OFFICE --
WE'RE BACK, MORGAN. AND IF I SAY SO MYSELF, WE'VE BROKEN UP THE PSYCHO-PIRATE'S PLOTS!
YES-- WE -- MR. MORGAN! WHAT'S THE MATTER? YOU LOOK LIKE YOU'RE SEEING GHOSTS!
YOU-YOU'RE HERE-UN-HARMED? DIDN'T THE PSYCHO-PIRATE CAPTURE YOU? THE ATOM AND I HEARD IT OVER THE RADIO--
WHAT'S THIS ABOUT THE ATOM? HE WENT AFTER US?
YES! IT-IT MUST HAVE BEEN ONE OF THE PSYCHO-PIRATE'S TRICKS!
YOU'D BETTER REST A WHILE, MR. MORGAN! YOU'VE BEEN UNDER QUITE A STRAIN!
YESSIR! THAT OL' PSYCHO-PIRATE DIDN'T KNOW WHAT HE WAS RUNNING INTO!
YOU'VE SUCCEEDED, ALL RIGHT- BUT IT'S TOO LATE FOR ME! MY MEN HAVE QUIT, THE LOAN I REQUESTED HAS BEEN REFUSED, I'M BEING FORECLOSED, MY WIFE-
CHEER UP. THERE IS STILL-HOPE! WHEN YOUR MEN LEARN WE'VE WON AGAINST THE PSYCHO-PIRATE, THEY'LL COME BACK. THE BANK WILL GRANT YOUR LOAN, YOU WON'T BE FORECLOSED AND--
IF--IF I ONLY DARED HOPE!
COME ON, MR. MORGAN! THE MEN WANT TO HEAR THE JUSTICE SOCIETY'S STORY FROM THEIR OWN LIPS! TAKE THEM ALL TO THE AUDITORIUM!
SOUNDS LIKE A GOOD IDEA
I SORT OF FEEL LIKE MAKING A SPEECH ANY-HOW!
LET'S GO, GANG!
BUT AS THE FIVE MEMBERS LEAVE THE ROOM, A WOUNDED FIGURE INCHES HIS WAY SLOWLY ALONG THE ROOF --
ONLY GOT-A LITTLE MORE-TO GO--
COURIER
WEAK AND DIZZY, THE ATOM COLLAPSES--
NO USE. I-I MUST REST, AND SLEEP--

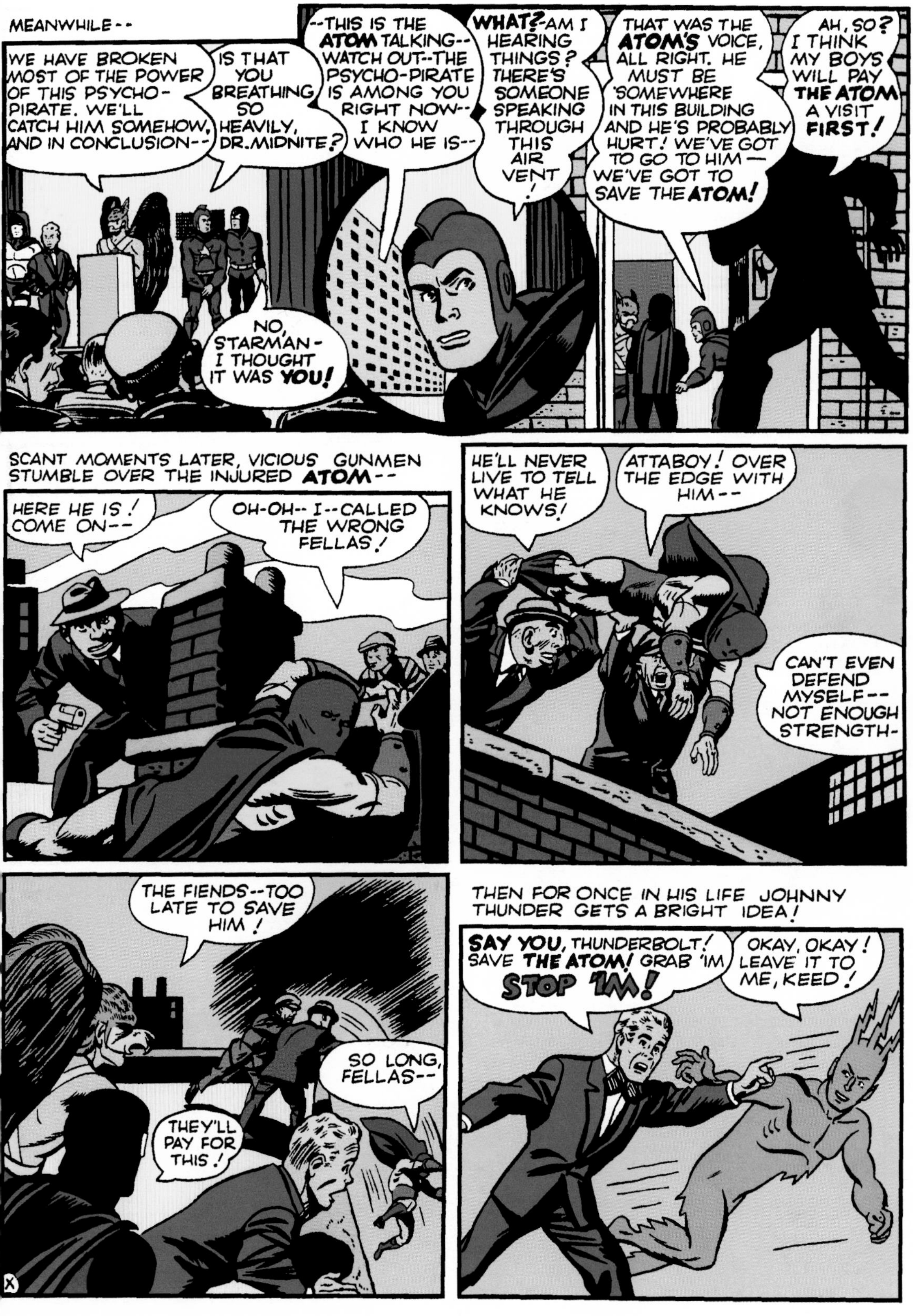
MEANWHILE--
WE HAVE BROKEN MOST OF THE POWER OF THIS PSYCHO-PIRATE. WE'LL CATCH HIM SOMEHOW, AND IN CONCLUSION--
IS THAT YOU BREATHING SO HEAVILY, DR. MIDNITE?
NO, STARMAN- I THOUGHT IT WAS YOU!
--THIS IS THE ATOM TALKING--WATCH OUT--THE PSYCHO-PIRATE IS AMONG YOU RIGHT NOW--I KNOW WHO HE IS--
WHAT?-AM I HEARING THINGS? THERE'S SOMEONE SPEAKING THROUGH THIS AIR VENT!
THAT WAS THE ATOM'S VOICE, ALL RIGHT. HE MUST BE SOMEWHERE IN THIS BUILDING AND HE'S PROBABLY HURT! WE'VE GOT TO GO TO HIM — WE'VE GOT TO SAVE THE ATOM!
AH, SO? I THINK MY BOYS WILL PAY THE ATOM A VISIT FIRST!
SCANT MOMENTS LATER, VICIOUS GUNMEN STUMBLE OVER THE INJURED ATOM--
HERE HE IS! COME ON--
OH-OH-- I--CALLED THE WRONG FELLAS!
HE'LL NEVER LIVE TO TELL WHAT HE KNOWS!
ATTABOY! OVER THE EDGE WITH HIM--
CAN'T EVEN DEFEND MYSELF--NOT ENOUGH STRENGTH-
THE FIENDS--TOO LATE TO SAVE HIM!
SO LONG, FELLAS--
THEY'LL PAY FOR THIS!
THEN FOR ONCE IN HIS LIFE JOHNNY THUNDER GETS A BRIGHT IDEA!
SAY YOU, THUNDERBOLT! SAVE THE ATOM! GRAB 'IM STOP 'IM!
OKAY, OKAY! LEAVE IT TO ME, KEED!

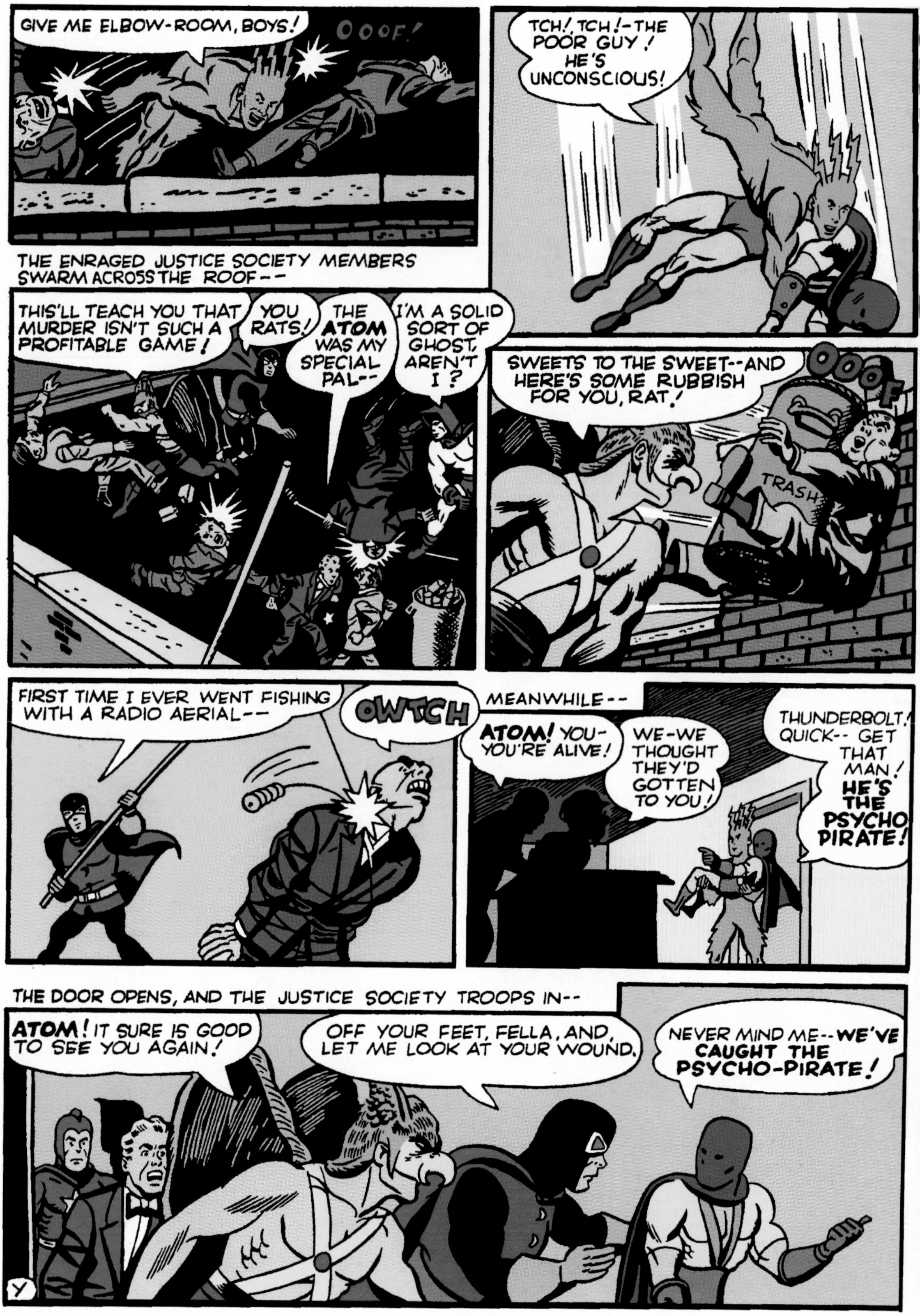
GIVE ME ELBOW-ROOM, BOYS!
OOOF!
THE ENRAGED JUSTICE SOCIETY MEMBERS SWARM ACROSS THE ROOF--
TCH!, TCH!-THE POOR GUY! HE'S UNCONSCIOUS!
THIS'LL TEACH YOU THAT MURDER ISN'T SUCH A PROFITABLE GAME!
YOU RATS!
THE ATOM WAS MY SPECIAL PAL--
I'M A SOLID SORT OF GHOST, AREN'T I?
SWEETS TO THE SWEET--AND HERE'S SOME RUBBISH FOR YOU, RAT!
OOOF
TRASH
FIRST TIME I EVER WENT FISHING WITH A RADIO AERIAL--
OWTCH
MEANWHILE--
ATOM! YOU-YOU'RE ALIVE!
WE-WE THOUGHT THEY'D GOTTEN TO YOU!
THUNDERBOLT! QUICK-- GET THAT MAN! HE'S THE PSYCHO PIRATE!
THE DOOR OPENS, AND THE JUSTICE SOCIETY TROOPS IN--
ATOM! IT SURE IS GOOD TO SEE YOU AGAIN!
OFF YOUR FEET, FELLA, AND, LET ME LOOK AT YOUR WOUND.
NEVER MIND ME--WE'VE CAUGHT THE PSYCHO-PIRATE!
Y

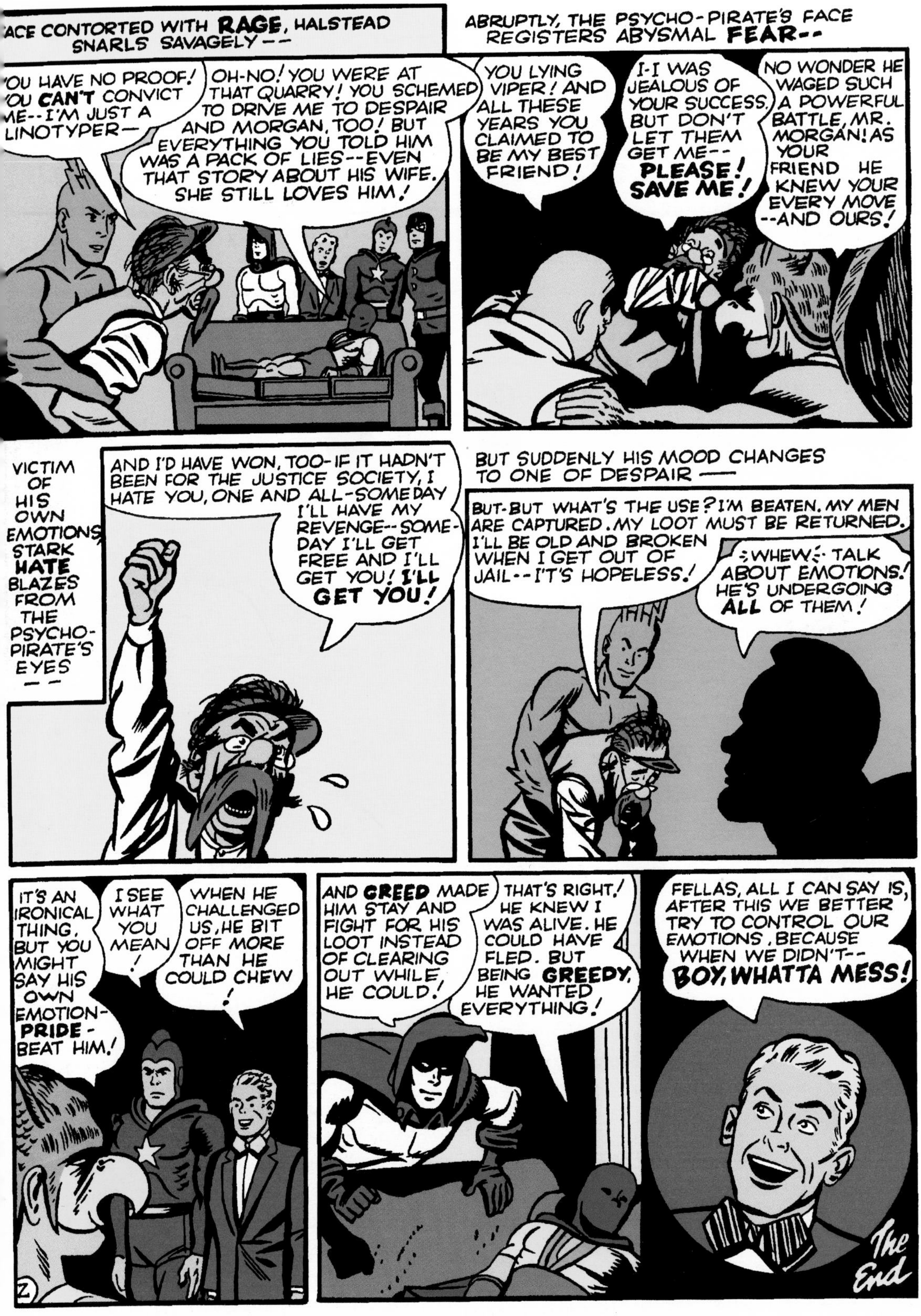
ACE CONTORTED WITH RAGE, HALSTEAD SNARLS SAVAGELY --
OU HAVE NO PROOF! OU CAN'T CONVICT ME--I'M JUST A LINOTYPER—
OH-NO! YOU WERE AT THAT QUARRY! YOU SCHEMED TO DRIVE ME TO DESPAIR AND MORGAN, TOO! BUT EVERYTHING YOU TOLD HIM WAS A PACK OF LIES--EVEN THAT STORY ABOUT HIS WIFE. SHE STILL LOVES HIM!
ABRUPTLY, THE PSYCHO-PIRATE'S FACE REGISTERS ABYSMAL FEAR--
YOU LYING VIPER! AND ALL THESE YEARS YOU CLAIMED TO BE MY BEST FRIEND!
I-I WAS JEALOUS OF YOUR SUCCESS, BUT DON'T LET THEM GET ME-- PLEASE! SAVE ME!
NO WONDER HE WAGED SUCH A POWERFUL BATTLE, MR. MORGAN! AS YOUR FRIEND HE KNEW YOUR EVERY MOVE --AND OURS!
VICTIM OF HIS OWN EMOTIONS, STARK HATE BLAZES FROM THE PSYCHO-PIRATE'S EYES --
AND I'D HAVE WON, TOO- IF IT HADN'T BEEN FOR THE JUSTICE SOCIETY, I HATE YOU, ONE AND ALL-SOME DAY I'LL HAVE MY REVENGE--SOME-DAY I'LL GET FREE AND I'LL GET YOU! I'LL GET YOU!
BUT SUDDENLY HIS MOOD CHANGES TO ONE OF DESPAIR ——
BUT-BUT WHAT'S THE USE? I'M BEATEN. MY MEN ARE CAPTURED. MY LOOT MUST BE RETURNED. I'LL BE OLD AND BROKEN WHEN I GET OUT OF JAIL--IT'S HOPELESS.!
WHEW! TALK ABOUT EMOTIONS! HE'S UNDERGOING ALL OF THEM!
IT'S AN IRONICAL THING, BUT YOU MIGHT SAY HIS OWN EMOTION- PRIDE - BEAT HIM!
I SEE WHAT YOU MEAN!
WHEN HE CHALLENGED US, HE BIT OFF MORE THAN HE COULD CHEW!
AND GREED MADE HIM STAY AND FIGHT FOR HIS LOOT INSTEAD OF CLEARING OUT WHILE HE COULD!
THAT'S RIGHT! HE KNEW I WAS ALIVE. HE COULD HAVE FLED. BUT BEING GREEDY, HE WANTED EVERYTHING!
FELLAS, ALL I CAN SAY IS, AFTER THIS WE BETTER TRY TO CONTROL OUR EMOTIONS, BECAUSE WHEN WE DIDN'T-- BOY, WHATTA MESS!
The End

STAN ASCHMEIER

Under separate pseudonyms, Stanley Aschmeier co-created two JSAers. As "Stan Asch," he and writer Charles Reisenstein produced Dr. Mid-Nite for ALL-AMERICAN COMICS; as "Stan Josephs," he illustrated John Wentworth's Johnny Thunder for FLASH COMICS.

BERNARD BAILY

From the Golden Age to the 1970s, artist Bernard Baily's expressive work was a mainstay in DC Comics, for whom he created Hourman and co-created, with Jerry Siegel, the macabre Spectre.

GARDNER FOX

Possibly the single most imaginative and productive writer in the Golden Age of comics, Gardner Fox created or co-created dozens of long-running features, among them Flash, Hawkman, Sandman, and Dr. Fate. Fox passed away in 1986.

JOE GALLAGHER

Joe Gallagher did comics work for Ace, Quality, and DC.

JACK KIRBY

Born in 1917, Jack Kirby has lent his distinctive art style to such Golden Age strips as the Sandman and Green Arrow, and co-created (with writer Joe Simon) the Boy Commandos, the Newsboy Legion, and Captain America. Often called "The King," Kirby was probably best known for helping usher in the "Marvel Age" of comics with Stan Lee. Kirby passed away in 1995.

JOE KUBERT

Joe Kubert's career in comics spans well over 50 years. While perhaps best known for his work on DC Comics' Sgt. Rock, he also worked on Hawkman, Enemy Ace, Tarzan and The Viking Prince, among others for the company. Joe was a pioneer in the field of 3-D comics in the 1950s, artist on the newspaper strip Tales of the Green Berets in the 1960s, and founded the Joe Kubert School of Cartoon and Graphic Art in the 1970s. More recently, he is also the writer/artist of the award-winning graphic novel Fax from Sarajevo.

SHELDON MAYER

The creative force behind DC's ALL-AMERICAN line of books in the 1940s, Sheldon Mayer was chief editor of ALL STAR COMICS through issue #41 (1948) and co-plotted the stories with Gardner Fox. Also well known as a prolific writer/artist, Mayer produced such well-loved strips as Scribbly in the 1940s, and the Three Mouseketeers and Sugar and Spike in the 1950s. He died in 1997.

SHELDON MOLDOFF

Closely associated with Hawkman, a 1940s strip in which he paid artistic homage to comic-strip greats Hal Foster and Alex Raymond, Sheldon Moldoff went on to become one of the foremost Batman artists of the 1940s and 1950s.

HOWARD SHERMAN

A pulp magazine cover illustrator, Howard Sherman drew the first Dr. Fate story for MORE FUN COMICS and continued with the strip for three years, his dark and moody style meshing perfectly with writer Gardner Fox's Lovecraftian tales.

JOE SIMON

Creator of patriotic heroes such as the Fighting American, the Boy Commandos and the Guardian, Simon came to work for DC with artist Jack Kirby shortly after the pair created Captain America. It was the Simon and Kirby team that gave the Sandman his purple and gold costume and introduced Sandy the Golden Boy to the strip.

Biographical material researched and written by Mark Waid, Jerry Bails, Steven Rowe, Jim Spivey and Bob Kahan.